IAIN MACLEOD

Iain Macleod

Robert Shepherd

HUTCHINSON
LONDON

This edition first published in 1994 by
Hutchinson

Random House (UK) Ltd
20 Vauxhall Bridge Road, London SWIV 2SA

Random House Australia (Pty) Ltd
20 Alfred Street, Milsons Point, Sydney, NSW 2061, Australia

Random House New Zealand Ltd
18 Poland Road, Glenfield, Auckland 10, New Zealand

Random House South Africa (Pty) Ltd
PO Box 337, Bergvlei, 2012, South Africa

A CiP catalogue record for this
book is available from the British Library

ISBN: 0 09 178567 7

Typeset in 10/12 pt Ehrhardt by
Pure Tech Corporation, Pondicherry, India.

Printed and bound in Great Britain by
Clays Ltd., St. Ives PLC

Contents

Illustrations

The author and publishers wish to thank the following for kind permission to reproduce photographs in this book.

Preface

From the day he first walked into the Conservative Parliamentary Secretariat in early 1946 until his death as Chancellor of the Exchequer at 11, Downing Street, in July 1970, Iain Macleod was at the hub of British politics. Yet this biography is the first study of this most intriguing of modern Tories which has been able to draw on the treasure trove of material covering his work behind the scenes at the highest levels of the Conservative Party and Government. I have had full access to the papers in the Conservative Party Archive for his entire career – including the Shadow Cabinet minutes and policy papers for the 1965–70 period that had previously been closed. In addition, the release of the classified Government documents of 1963, in January 1994, meant that the official papers relating to Macleod's ministerial and Cabinet career from May 1952 until he left the Government in October 1963 were available at the Public Record Office under the 30-year rule – we shall have to wait until January 2001 for the classified papers relating to his month as Chancellor in 1970.

Had Iain Macleod lived, he would have been 80 in November 1993. Sadly, it is becoming more difficult, year by year, to recapture something of his character and qualities from those who knew him well – as close friends or as political associates, or even as adversaries. Fortunately, I was able to talk with many people who had known him, but even while I wrote some of these died. I hope that I have been able to convey something of their impressions and recollections.

This book is not an 'authorized' or 'official' biography, but I owe a special debt of gratitude to Baroness Macleod of Borve and to other members of Iain Macleod's family, who have cooperated and given me every assistance and encouragement. Eve Macleod also granted permission for me to quote verbatim from the transcript of a tape-recorded interview that her husband gave on his period as Colonial Secretary to W.P. Kirkman in December 1967 for the Oxford Colonial Records Project, which has previously only been available to scholars on a background basis.

Among those who spoke or wrote to me about Iain Macleod, and to whom

I am deeply indebted, are: Lord Aberconway, Lord Aldington, Lord Alport, Lord Amery, Lt. Col. K.G. Anson, J.W. Anson, Dr W.D. Arthur, David Astor, Ethne Bannister, Michael Bannister, J.W.G. Barr, Joan Baylis, Nick Beacock, Sir Reginald Bennett, Humphry Berkeley, John Biffen, Sir Michael Blundell, Lord Boyd-Carpenter, Sir Harry Boyne, Sir Samuel Brittan, Ellis Butchart, David Butler, Lord Callaghan of Cardiff, R.W. Campbell, Lord Carr of Hadley, David Clarke, Lord Cockfield, Lord Colyton, R.G. Cooper, Ian Coulter, Lord Croham, Ian Dalziel, Sir Alan Dawtry, Lord Deedes, Ian Dewar, G.E. Dickson, Sir Nigel Fisher, Michael Foot, William Keegan, Lady Antonia Fraser, Lord Fraser of Kilmorack, Lord Gilmour, Geoffrey Goodman, Sir Anthony Grant, Dennis Grennan, Lord Hailsham, Colin Harding, Roy Hattersley, Lady Hayhoe, Lord Hayhoe, David Heimann, Diana Heimann (daughter), Sir Terence Higgins, Lord Home of the Hirsel, Anthony Howard, Lord Howe, David Howell, George Hudd, Lt. Col. F.A.R. Hunter, Lord Jenkin of Roding, Sir Glyn Jones, Colin Legum, John Lennox, Charles Longbottom, Sir Gilbert Longden, Rhoderick Macleod, Torquil Macleod (brother), Torquil Macleod (son), John Major, Rixi Markus, William Mathieson, J.P. Mewies, Sir Peter Middleton, Sir Leslie Monson, Sir Arthur Norman, Lord Orr-Ewing, the Earl of Perth, J. Enoch Powell, Sir Hilton Poynton, Lord Prior, Terence Reese, Lord Rees-Mogg, Lord Reigate, Dr Cedric Robinson, David Rogers, Malcolm Rutherford, Sir William Ryrie, Nicholas Scott, the Earl of Selkirk, Brendon Sewill, Sir Richard Sharp, William Shearman, William Shepherd, Dame Mary Smieton, Hilary Spurling, Elizabeth Sturges-Jones, Lord Swaythling (David Montagu), Sir Peter Tapsell, Lady Thatcher, Ambler R. Thomas, J.S. Thomas, J.W.M. Thompson, Lord Thorneycroft, Ronald B. Turnbull, Colin Turner, Dudley Turner, Sir William van Straubenzee, Peter Venters, Gerry Wade, Sir Alexander Waddell, Lord Walker, Alan Watkins, Sir Duncan Watson, F.D. (Max) Webber, Sir Roy Welensky, Eileen Weston, Viscount Whitelaw, Alan Whitaker.

Lord Jenkins of Hillhead generously sent me a copy of his chapter on Iain Macleod from his book, *Portraits and Miniatures*, prior to publication. Likewise, Vernon Bogdanor sent me a typescript of his chapter, 'The Conservative Leadership, 1902–90,' from a forthcoming collection of essays on the Conservative Party, edited by Stuart Ball and Anthony Seldon. Anthony Howard helpfully sent me the script of his *Reputations* profile of Macleod, broadcast by BBC Television in 1981, together with transcripts of the interviews that he recorded for the programme. Lady Antonia Fraser kindly gave me permission to quote from her diary. The surviving founder members of the 'One Nation' group also gave me access to their minutes for 1950–52, covering the period of Macleod's membership. David Butler thoughtfully offered to let me consult the interviews conducted for the Nuffield general election studies during Macleod's career, and to quote from them. Andrew Roth helpfully allowed me to consult his files on Macleod, now stored at the British Library of Political and Economic Science, LSE, London. Before her death, Joan Baylis kindly gave me permission to quote from the chapters in her unpublished memoirs on Macleod's editorship of the *Spectator*.

I am also grateful to the following for their assistance: the Reference Library, High Street, Skipton; the Craven Museum, Craven District Council, Skipton Town Hall, Skipton; Ewart Library, Dumfries; the Edinburgh Room, Reference Library, Edinburgh; the Principal and the Secretary, Mary Erskine School, Ravelston, Edinburgh; R.A. Cole Hamilton, Keeper of the Register, Fettes College, Edinburgh; Anne Neary, Archivist, Gonville and Caius College, Cambridge; David Gray, Crockford's Ltd, London; Mrs Marion Harding, Department of Archives, Photographs, Film and Sound, National Army Museum, London; Cockfosters Cricket Club; Saracens Rugby Union Football Club; Dr Sarah Street and Dr Martin Maw, Archivists, Conservative Party Archive, and the librarian and staff of the Bodleian Library, Oxford; James Hargrave, Archivist, The Welensky Papers, and the librarian and staff of Rhodes House Library, Oxford; Mr Kucia, Archivist, Lord Butler's Papers, Trinity College, Cambridge; Charles Seaton, Librarian, the *Spectator*; the London Library; the Chelsea Branch, Royal Borough of Kensington and Chelsea Libraries, Town Hall, King's Road, Chelsea.

Crown copyright material in the Public Record Office is reproduced by permission of the Controller of Her Majesty's Stationery Office. I am also grateful for permission to quote copyright material from the following sources: the Conservative Party Archive – the Chairman of the Conservative Party Organization and Mr Alistair B. Cooke, Director, Conservative Political Centre; from R.A. Butler's Papers, Trinity College, Cambridge – Lady Butler; from the *Spectator* – the editor.

I am particularly grateful to Richard Cohen, who first suggested the idea for this biography; to Neil Belton, who encouraged me during the research; and to Tony Whittome, whose enthusiasm and support facilitated the writing and completion of the book. Ian Gilmour read the chapters covering Macleod's career from the early 1960s, and made many helpful suggestions. Julian Durlacher gave valuable help with the final research. I should also like to thank Michael Shaw for his continuing advice and encouragement, and Gillian Shepherd, without whom the book would never have been finished.

ROBERT SHEPHERD
London, June 1994

1

Tir-an-Og

It is coming yet for a' that,
That man to man the whole world o'er,
Shall brothers be for a' that.
>   Extract from Robbie Burns, *For a' that and a' that.*

The Yorkshire hills are friendly hills
And sleepy to the sight.
Grey-washed with cottages and farms
And full of sudden light.
But the Harris hills are elfin hills
Blue-etched against the night.
>   Extract from Iain Macleod, *The Harris Hills.*

Islander Origins

Robbie Burns is an improbable inspiration for a Conservative politician. Yet the words of his that are quoted above were recited to the Conservative Party Conference at Brighton in October 1961 by Iain Macleod, when he was Colonial Secretary, during one of the most compelling political speeches of modern times. 'It is perhaps strange to an English and Welsh audience,' he acknowledged, 'to quote the greatest of our Scottish native poets.' But Macleod's speech that day, in which he declared his belief in 'the brotherhood of man', was his credo. The romanticism and the humanitarian ideal espoused by Burns in the final lines of his poem, *For a' that and a' that*, came naturally to Macleod.[1]

Iain Norman Macleod was born on 11 November 1913 in Skipton, the Yorkshire market town bordering the Dales, but his father and mother were Scots and he regarded himself as Scottish. 'My children regard themselves as Scots,' he commented in later life, 'I sign a register always as Scottish and I regard the English in a curious sort of way with tremendous affection and liking, as people not quite foreign but in some way rather different from me.' It was a perspective that he never lost. Although he was to spend almost a quarter of a century on the inside of the very English worlds of the Conservative Party, Westminster and Whitehall, there was a sense in which he always remained an outsider. His intense ambition for power was combined with a fierce independent-mindedness; an understanding of what it meant to be ruled by the English, and by a particular class of Englishman; and an analytical brain that enabled him to detach himself from the day-to-day, party political dogfight (in which he was a ruthlessly effective performer) and to assess the politics of any issue with clinical proficiency. Macleod possessed that mixture of realism and romanticism that characterizes the Scots. The romantic side often triumphed over his realism, but the latter strain was reinforced by his Airedale upbringing. This mingling of Scots and Yorkshire amused Macleod – he was an avowed Yorkshireman during the cricket season – and he loved to tell of an exchange that he overheard in a Skipton pub when he was paying a return visit to his home town after he had become a Minister:

'Isn't that Iain Macleod over there?'

'Ay.'

'A good Yorkshireman.'

'Nay, he's Scots.'

'Sire and dam were Scots, but he's Yorkshire born and bred.'[2]

Macleod's Scottishness was highly distinctive. Both parents were islanders, born and brought up on Lewis, the largest and most northerly island in the Atlantic chain of the Outer Hebrides, or Western Isles. Tales and images of the isles were ever-present during his childhood, and the family's long vacations on Lewis during his teens fuelled his poetic impulse. Where Housman's *A Shropshire Lad* laments 'those blue remembered hills' of lost youth, Macleod yearns for the Harris hills, 'Blue-etched against the night', and evokes 'an isle beyond the sunset in the Western main' – *Tir-an-og*, the mythical, Gaelic land of the ever-young. His roots on Lewis went deep, stretching back to the chieftains who ruled the Western Isles during the twilight of Norse power and the dawn of the Gaelic renaissance. As he proudly proclaimed, when proposing the toast to the Norwegian Ambassador, who was guest of honour in 1957 at the annual dinner for diplomats of the City firm, De La Rue, 'the clan to which I have the honour to belong were a Norwegian clan and came a thousand years ago from your shores to the Highlands and Islands of the North of Scotland, from where my forebears come.'[3]

The clan Macleod claims descent from Liotr, or Leod, who was born around the year 1200, a younger son of Olaf the Black, King of Man and the Isles. One of Liotr's sons, Torquil, was founder of the Macleods of Lewis. Iain Macleod's direct forebears – the Macleods of Pabbay and Uig, on the west of the island – are a branch of the main clan. The same male christian names – Iain, Norman, Rhoderick, Torquil – recur through more than twenty generations, underlining the continuity of the line from the thirteenth to the twentieth century. Iain Macleod's ancestry was important to him, and in September 1940 – shortly after his first experience of wartime active service – he compiled rudimentary genealogical charts from notes left by his maternal grandfather, Dr Rhoderick Ross. These showed that on many occasions the forebears of both sides of his family were related. His roots can be traced back through named individuals on both his father's and mother's sides for a dozen generations to the reign of James IV of Scotland. The founder of Iain Macleod's paternal line, Norman Macleod, was born about 1500, and became a tacksman (tenant-farmer) of the small west-coast island of Pabbay. Norman Macleod's wife was a MacDonald from the Isle of Skye, and is blamed for involving him in feuds with the MacAulays in nearby Uig. Coincidentally, Dugald MacAulay, Norman Macleod's rival, and like him a tacksman, also turns out to be Iain Macleod's oldest directly traceable ancestor on his maternal side. But the Macleod–MacAulay connection does have a more distinguished aspect, since Iain Macleod was also a distant kinsman of the Whig politician and Victorian historian, Thomas Babington (later Lord) Macaulay – as one of Macleod's 1940 charts demonstrates.[4]

Iain Macleod's mother, Annabella, or 'Lab' as she was known, was born in Stornoway, Lewis's main town, on 18 March 1880. It was a time of unrest and violence in the islands as crofters resisted fresh attempts to move them from the land. The Government in London feared another Ireland in the Hebrides – the Irish land problem had long bedevilled nineteenth-century politics. Lab was the first child of Rhoderick Ross, a local doctor, and Isabella MacDonald, who had been the inspiration for the heroine of a romantic novel about Lewis, *The Princess of Thule* by William Black. Lab's father, Rhoderick Ross, was a man of strong Calvinist convictions, who had distinguished himself as a medical student in Scotland in the 1860s and was urged by his contemporaries to pursue what promised to be a highly rewarding career on the mainland. But as a Gaelic-speaking islander, his duty lay on Lewis, and he returned to spend the rest of his professional life caring for what he called 'our people'.[5]

Lab was only ten years old when her mother, Isabella, died, but Dr Ross was determined that his daughter, who was a highly intelligent girl, should receive a good education. In the 1890s, she attended Edinburgh Ladies' College. Opportunities for girls, however bright, were then extremely limited. Duty summoned on Lewis. At the end of the summer term of 1896, aged sixteen, Lab returned to run her widowed father's household and medical practice at Borve on Lewis's Atlantic coastline, a few miles north of Barvas on the road to Port of Ness and the Butt of Lewis. It was to remain her home for more than a decade. The Ross family home has since been converted into an hotel, but the connection with Borve meant a great deal to Iain Macleod – so much so that in later life, when contemplating his eventual retirement from the Commons and possible membership of the House of Lords, he considered taking the title of Macleod of Borve. In the event, it was the title that his wife, Eve, chose when she was appointed a life peeress in 1971.[6]

Iain Macleod's father, Norman Alexander Macleod was, like his wife, a child of the hard years of the land troubles. Born on 8 August 1879, the youngest of six children, at Kershader, in eastern Lewis, he was the son of Iain Og Macleod, a fish-curer and general merchant. His father died when Norman was only six years old and his mother (also Annabella) struggled to make ends meet. Although Norman was a bright boy, he left Lochs parish school at the age of fourteen with no apparent alternative but to work on the family croft. Fortunately, the local schoolmaster lent him books and helped him to continue studying. The boy responded by winning a bursary to the Nicolson Institute at Stornoway, where he completed his secondary education. From there he won a scholarship to Glasgow University, but this had to be supplemented by his family from their modest income. Intending to read theology, a popular academic discipline at the time, particularly for a nineteen-year-old from staunchly Protestant Lewis, Norman Macleod left home in the autumn of 1898 and set out for Glasgow. As he sat on the train heading south through the Highlands he shared a carriage with some other theology students. They were dreary company. But he heard laughter and lively conversation from the adjoining carriage, and went to investigate. He discovered that its occupants were medical students and were much more to his liking. There and then, he decided that the moment he arrived in Glasgow he would switch to the medical faculty. Five years later, he graduated as a bachelor of medicine and chemistry.[7]

After qualifying, Norman Macleod initially followed the example of many of his kinsmen and emigrated to the Empire. He spent four years on the north-eastern fringes of the Raj as a medical officer on a tea estate in Assam, but the colonial life did not enthrall him and by his late twenties he was seeking to return and establish himself in practice. In 1907, he settled south of the border, in Skipton, but his Hebridean connections had helped determine his destination. On the recommendation of a fellow doctor from Lewis, Dr Bain, he took up a post as assistant to Dr Alec Waugh, who was also a Scot and had succeeded Bain as a partner in a medical practice in the town. Dr Waugh had his surgery and home in Clifford House, on the Keighley Road, near what was then a narrow bridge over the Leeds and Liverpool canal. When Dr Waugh left two years later, Norman Macleod bought into the practice as a partner – in the days long before the National Health Service medical practices were run as commercial concerns.[8]

Norman Macleod first met Lab Ross during a return visit to Lewis. Lab had been engaged to a local man, but he had died in 1908, probably of tuberculosis, which was then rife in the Western Isles. It is thought that he might have been a Macleod, and that Norman may have returned to Lewis to attend his funeral. Norman and Lab began seeing one another whenever his duties allowed him to leave Skipton. They were married on 29 December 1910, at the United Free Church, Renfield Street, Glasgow, the city where Norman had studied for five years and still had many friends. He was thirty-one, she was thirty.[9]

On their marriage, Dr Macleod, or 'Mac' as he was popularly known in Skipton, and his new wife moved into Clifford House. They were a striking looking couple. He was physically imposing, well built, with a dark complexion and black-brown hair, his countenance made all the more formidable by his bushy, thick eyebrows. Seventy to eighty years later, Skipton's older residents readily recalled that, as children, they had held 'Mac' in awe, while being confident that, deep down, he was 'a good man'. Lab was slim, with white-blonde hair and fine features, her Scottish accent adding to her charm. On Lewis, her long hair and eighteen-inch waist had earned her a reputation as the local beauty, and whenever she rode through Barvas in the dogcart, crofters' children would hurry down the road to see her go by. In some quarters, the Macleods were thought to fancy themselves, but this was an era when local doctors, like other professional people, were expected to set an example in their local community. Perhaps it was Lab's concern to live up to these high standards, or possibly her exceptionally intelligent mind, but some people found her rather starchy. However, Lab was widely liked, as well as being respected as the very model of a doctor's wife. Within a year of her marriage, she became a mother, with the birth of Rhoda Isabel (Rhodabel). The Macleods were fast putting down family roots in Skipton.[10]

Skipton childhood

When Iain Macleod was born, a little over two years after his sister, the family were firmly settled in the home and the busy routine that were to shape his childhood. It was a comfortable and secure existence. Clifford House was a square, stone-built, two-storey, early Victorian detached house. The upper floor was reached by a staircase that led from the main hall – at the age of seven, Iain Macleod squeezed between the banisters on the upstairs landing and fell through the central stairwell into the hall, crashing onto a card-table, which luckily broke his fall. None the less, he was ill for some weeks, and, in later life he quipped that his first experience with a card-table had been a very painful one.[11]

In addition to the Macleods' growing family – Iain's younger brothers were born in 1917 (Torquil) and 1920 (Rhoderick) – Clifford House accommodated the surgery, as it had during Dr Waugh's day, and gave a roof to Dr Macleod's medical assistant and two of the domestic staff, who were then an accepted part of a local doctor's household. The Macleods' cook and maid-servant lived in and were invariably Gaelic speakers from Lewis, recruited by

Lab from families whom she knew from her days at Borve. Two more staff lived locally – a nurse-cum-housekeeper and a chauffeur-cum-factotum, Harry Thurlow, whose brother had been coachman to Dr Waugh. Thurlow, whose name Lab pronounced with a Scottish burr on the 'r', was something of a confidant to Iain, his sister and younger brothers. His room in the out-buildings at the rear of the house was given an air of the macabre by Dr Macleod's jars of medical specimens. None the less, Thurlow's den sometimes served as a handy retreat for Iain and the other children, particularly when they were in trouble with their parents or with the long-serving cook, Kate Maclean, who 'raised hell' if they tried to steal food from the kitchen.[12]

Iain's early years coincided with the grim experience of the First World War – Armistice Day fell on his fifth birthday – but his immediate family was not seriously disrupted by the war. It was not until 1918 that Dr Macleod was appointed a Lieutenant in the Royal Army Medical Corps, and he served in hospitals on the home establishment. Iain was a happy little boy, and was closest to his sister Rhodabel, who was an attractive and bright girl. As the children of a doctor, they enjoyed the rare privilege of having a father who owned a car and on weekends and holidays they were taken for family picnics in the Dales. They would also join other children on the trips to the countryside organized by Mrs Robinson, the wife of another Skipton doctor and car-owner. Her son, Cedric, was the same age as Rhodabel and a schoolfriend of Iain's. Iain was something of a tearaway. His father observed that he spoke two different languages – one was the strong, local dialect that he used while playing in the town and on the canal bank; the other was spoken when the Macleods were entertaining guests.[13]

Home and the practice were inseparable. None of the Macleod offspring could avoid being immersed in their father's way of life. It was much more than simply being roped (usually willingly) into basic clerking, for example, having to check in those pre-NHS days that patients' bills were placed in the correct envelopes. However, there was never any likelihood that Iain would follow in his father's footsteps professionally. Dr Macleod would discuss medical problems over dinner with his assistant as a matter of course, and on at least one occasion, as they deliberated on the condition of a patient's duodenal ulcer while tucking into platefuls of tripe, the young Iain excused himself from the table.[14]

But the pastoral aspect of his father's work had a profound impact on Iain. Dr Macleod's practice comprised a mixture of middle- and working-class patients, including less well off people who paid only a nominal sum. As Skipton's so-called Poor Law doctor, he also cared for people who could not afford to pay anything. During school holidays, Iain would often accompany Dr Macleod on his house calls. Unlike many other children of professional or middle-class parents, he had contact with all sections of the local community, went into their homes and saw his father treat them the same.

Moreover, Dr Macleod was in the tradition of general practitioners who acted as philosopher-guides, and even as friends, to their patients – he would arrange his holidays according to his female patients' confinements. Eve Macleod is clear that her husband's having been a doctor's son had a crucial bearing on Iain's politics, giving him a social conscience and a sensitivity to people's problems.[15]

Neither Norman nor Lab were openly partisan and politics were never discussed in their home, but at elections they stuck doggedly to their conflicting party allegiances – he voting Liberal, she Conservative. 'It is not, I think, fanciful to see both strains – Radical and Conservative – in my political make-up,' Macleod, the mature politician, confided to James Margach, political editor of the *Sunday Times*. Yet his parents' party political difference was of less importance in shaping Iain's political outlook than their shared commitment to serving the community. Lab did an immense amount for the local hospital; helped set up one of the first clinics for the children of the poor; and, during the 1930s, undertook relief work for the unemployed. Her main efforts were devoted to the Women's Section of the British Legion, on whose behalf she travelled all over Yorkshire and became Area President. For an essentially non-political couple, the Macleods had a remarkable influence on their eldest son's politics. The seeds of his brand of Toryism – what was to become known as 'One Nation' – are unmistakably present in his parents' overriding sense of social duty.[16]

Iain Macleod's parents were not religious in any devout sense. Brought up as Presbyterians, they nonetheless had a pew in Skipton's Anglican church. This was more an act of public conformity than an expression of conviction. Whereas Dr Macleod seemed largely uninfluenced by the church, Lab was more inclined to defer to religious convention. While Norman would happily visit the home of Charles Butchart, his best man and fellow bridge player, on Sundays for pre-lunch cocktails, Lab observed the Sabbath and stayed at home. She had no objection to her husband and sons playing golf on Sundays in Skipton, but during family holidays on strongly Presbyterian Lewis she became infinitely more concerned that they should respect the Lord's Day, insisting they should not go fishing and arguing that they should refrain from their nightly card sessions on the grounds that the neighbours might find out – an eventuality that was highly unlikely, since the nearest house was some miles away. Yet Lab was not strait-laced. In her eighties, when the 1960s' sexual revolution was in full swing, she astonished her granddaughter by speaking to her approvingly of the good sense in a couple's sleeping together before they married.[17]

Sport was Dr Macleod's main relaxation. Despite his onerous medical duties, he sometimes managed a nine-hole round of golf after lunch on a weekday, had a gun in shoots at Hebden and Blackpotts, was a keen fisherman, especially during holidays on Lewis, and was a county standard bridge player. Iain inherited from his father both his passion for sport and what his younger brother Rhoderick has described as his 'analytical, bridge-playing temperament'. However, his son's precocious talent for the game was not entirely appreciated by Dr Macleod's close friends when, during school holidays, Iain began showing them how they should have played their hand. Dr Macleod also belonged to a highly competitive card-school, in which Bradford wool traders and professional men played bridge and gambled at poker. He followed the horses and sometimes did the football pools, but gambling was never as remotely as important to him as it was to become, for a time, to his son.[18]

It was probably by giving Iain a deep sense of Scottish identity that the Macleods made their strongest imprint on their eldest son. During his childhood, they would host evenings at Clifford House for other Lewis islanders who were living in the north of England – doctors, teachers, other friends and relatives (Lab's brother, John Ross, was a doctor in Darlington). On such occasions, they would reminisce about Lewis, often in Gaelic. The Macleod children were not taught Gaelic, but Norman and Lab would speak the language at home, usually when they were arguing and did not want them to hear what was being said. Iain and the others knew that the row had ended when their parents reverted to English. The Macleods would also attend Caledonian dinners in Skipton and Keighley with fellow Scots expatriates. It was only natural that Norman and Lab should look to Scotland to give Iain the best education they could afford.[19]

Schooldays

Macleod's education had an unconventional start. He first attended St Monica's Convent, a local Catholic girls' school. His parents' apparently eccentric choice reflected the expectation that a doctor's children should be educated privately and the lack of any other suitable fee-paying school in Skipton. Lab used to dress her sons in kilts for school, a practice which made them the butt of endless ribbing by other children in the town. Cries of 'Kiltie, kiltie, cold bum!' and other catcalls rained down on Iain, Torquil and Rhoderick in turn as they trailed to and fro each day between Clifford House and St Monica's.[20]

Macleod had a mischievous streak that the nuns who taught at St Monica's were never fully able to control and which sometimes they actively provoked. Not only were Iain and his friend, Cedric Robinson, in a minority in the Convent's kindergarten because of their sex, they were also set apart by being among the relatively few non-Catholics, or 'heathens' as they were insensitively designated by some of the nuns. On one occasion, as a fierce thunderstorm swept over Skipton, the 'heathens' were abandoned in a large room while the Catholic children were shepherded to a quieter area and comforted. Macleod was instrumental in wreaking a terrible revenge for this frightening experience by spitting surreptitiously in the bowls of holy water located around the school. A favourite trick of Iain's played on the nuns who sat on tree stumps supervising playtime, was to wait until they nodded off and then try to catch them with a skipping rope, causing them to fall from their perch. Another prank involved tying girls by their plaits to the school railings. This misbehaviour finally proved too great for the Reverend Mother, and Iain and Cedric's parents were required to remove the two boys from the school. Macleod used to quip many years later that he was the only old girl of St Monica's to have become a Cabinet minister.[21]

Macleod briefly attended Skipton's centuries-old grammar school, St Ermysted's, but in 1923, aged nine, he was sent to St Ninian's, a preparatory boarding school of 60 or 70 boys in the spa town of Moffat in the Dumfriesshire hills. His parents had high ambitions for Iain, since St Ninian's had been established in 1879 as a 'feeder' for Fettes College, the fee-paying school in Edinburgh that had been founded nine years earlier. St Ninian's headmaster, the Revd Frank Wingate Pearse, was a huge man, six and a half feet in height, who used to ride an immensely tall bicycle with a whole extra layer of frame and crossbar. Nicknamed 'The Bump' because of the protrusion on top of his bald head that reputedly became more prominent when he was angry, he was an absent-minded man utterly devoted to fishing, golf, his pupils and his school. None the less, he enforced a spartan regime. The boys' day began with a cold shower in winter and a length of the school swimming pool in the summer. Boys who showed any reluctance in learning to swim, but who were thought to be capable, were thrown in at the deep end – Macleod managed to complete his length of the pool, half-drowned and almost completely submerged, at the first attempt. Pearse readily wielded the cane, and a mischievous spirit like Macleod received his full share of thrashings. Pearse's wife – known as 'The Dame' – was, if anything, even stricter than her husband. In a notorious classroom incident, Macleod amused himself while 'The Dame' was marking a French exercise by surreptitiously placing red berries from a nearby pot plant in the parting between the top of her head and her bun. When she eventually inclined her head, the berries showered to the floor. 'The Dame' exacted a swift and severe punishment on Macleod, the rings on her fingers rendering her sharp blows across the back of his small hand all the more painful.[22]

During his four years at St Ninian's, Macleod appeared to be no more than slightly above average in ability. He was small for his age, but he was tough, as he showed in fights, often with bigger boys. Building branch huts in the local woods encouraged the formation of different gangs, and Macleod was involved in the ensuing scraps that erupted in the dormitories. Macleod also joined in the many official activities with equal enthusiasm – picnics in the nearby hills; fishing in river and loch, reached by bicycle, and 'guddling' for trout; golf between games of rugger and cricket; summer teas on the lawn with the Youngers at Auchen Castle; story-reading round the study fire on winter evenings; and the fierce rivalry, often manifested on the sports field, with other prep schools. Choir practice was probably his least favourite pastime, although even as a child he regarded his inability to sing in tune with good humour – as he wrote to his mother, 'Tonight is our carol performance. I have not been forbidden to sing . . . yet!' He was to remain tone deaf all his life. Rugger was already becoming a passion. During a match against St Mary's, a rival prep school at Melrose, the St Ninian's pack won the ball in a scrum near their opponents' line and heeled it back to Macleod at scrum half, who gathered it, made a dash through the opposing team's legs and scored a try. Even in later life, he would recall this boyhood incident as having been one of the moments of purest pleasure that he had ever experienced. It was to become the basis for a favourite Macleod maxim about life in general – if the ball rolls your way, pick it up and run with it.[23]

Two months before his fourteenth birthday, Macleod arrived at Fettes for the start of the 1927 autumn term. It was little surprise that he had not qualified as a 'scholar' with an award from the Fettes Foundation, but instead entered the school as a fee-payer. Fettes was a daunting experience for any newcomer, with its grandiose, grey-stoned, Gothic architecture and its view, from the first-floor library and classrooms looking down the main drive to the imposing Edinburgh skyline (later obscured by trees). But Macleod was not overawed by his new surroundings. 'We all thought of him as rather cheeky,' one of his contemporaries recalls, 'not being particular as to what he said to anybody, especially to those much senior – always giving us the appearance of plenty of self-confidence. He was a very independent character, very self-assured and self-sufficient.'[24]

Macleod was soon in the thick of schoolboy pranks. It was his mischievous reputation, rather than his small stature and scruffy appearance, that first earned him the nickname of 'Monkey Macleod', although it was not used by his closest companions. He was quite unconcerned about his appearance, and his untidiness was legendary. Friends recall the sight of him walking to church in Edinburgh on Sundays in the then obligatory morning-coat and silk hat – Macleod's 'topper' was 'always in need of a brush and his umbrella resembled the proverbial Mother Gamp's'. Seldom a 'goodie-goodie', he was popular with his peers, who recall his 'keen sense of humour which he frequently used' and his 'pleasant, friendly manner, with a very disarming quizzical smile – so often the jester and prone to tease at times but never with any malice – never boastful or ostentatious'.[25]

Time and again, acquaintances who knew him as a boy admit to having detected nothing outstanding and express their surprise at his adult achievement. Any enthusiasm that he exhibited was virtually always directed to sport. He was never quite good enough to play for either the first rugger XV or first cricket XI, but match reports on his appearances for the second teams and for Moredun in the school's cock-house competition indicate that he was a terrier-like scrum-half, who scored some valuable tries, and a keen wicket-keeper and sound batsman, who sometimes opened the innings. Notwithstanding his modest performances on the cricket field, he took an almost fanatical interest in the game, and was rarely seen without a copy of *Wisden*, the cricketer's almanac. Macleod found a kindred spirit in Ronnie Turnbull. While Turnbull supported Surrey, Macleod followed the cricketing fortunes of his native Yorkshire, who had won the County Championship four times in a row between 1922 and 1925 and were to win it seven times during the 1930s. Their respective heroes were England's opening batsmen of the period, Jack Hobbs of Surrey and Herbert Sutcliffe of Yorkshire. The two boys spent hours playing imaginary matches between teams of great cricketers, or sometimes historical characters – Julius Caesar (opening bat), Alexander the Great (forcing batsman), Machiavelli (spin bowler). Macleod was able to remember and cite the most obscure facts about the game. It was the one field where he most clearly displayed the prodigious memory for which he was later to become renowned.[26]

Macleod was at his happiest indulging in pastimes that engaged his quick wits and good memory. He organized a bridge 'school' in his study and would spend some of the precious time allocated for 'prep' playing the game, before completing his school work in about half the time available. Gambling sessions were often held in his study on Sunday afternoons, particularly during the winter, when Edinburgh was at its least inviting. Macleod invariably showed a profit, having relieved fellow members of Moredun of any pennies that had remained from their weekly shilling allowance.[27]

To the surprise of many of his contemporaries, Macleod became a keen member of the debating society. The attraction lay in the opportunity that its meetings provided for wit and verbal sparring, rather than any inclination on Macleod's part to play the budding statesman. His first recorded intervention came on 4 December 1929, when, in his third year at Fettes, he spoke from the floor to the motion that 'No member of this House shall give up his seat to a lady'. As the school magazine, *The Fettesian*, reported, 'I.N. Macleod, in a very good speech, which had the merit of being short and to the point, said that women had stolen all men's most treasured possessions, and that the best way to deal with them was to show their inferiority by offering them seats. But why not share the seat?' At the next meeting, he rebutted the proposition that civilization 'has not yet reached Scotland', arguing that Scotland had 'good schools, a fine church, Leith Docks, and Robert Burns', while adding sardonically that he 'also had used a telephone in Skye and had got a wrong number – a sure proof of an advanced civilization'. But there was a glimpse of Macleod's deeper convictions during a well-attended debate on hanging that was held a month before his seventeenth birthday. Expressing what was to be a lifelong sentiment against capital punishment, he quoted Galsworthy's *Escape* 'to show how narrow might be the strait dividing the murderer from the ordinary man'. In the event, the abolitionists were defeated by 65 votes to 20.[28]

Politics, during this period of Macleod's life, were a stage for his disputatious nature. In August 1931, shortly before he began his final year at Fettes, the great financial crisis split the Labour Government and led to the formation of a new National Government. With a general election imminent, Macleod and his colleagues quickly organized mock hustings 'to elect an MP for Fettes'. On 7 October, the day after the official announcement in Parliament of the general election, 'a bewildering variety of candidates were presented before the largest, and certainly noisiest, meeting' that the school's debating society had ever held'. Macleod stood for the New Party, recently founded by the former Labour Minister Sir Oswald Mosley, and his speech incited an already rowdy audience to become even more rumbustious. According to *The Fettesian*, he declared 'that when he was returned he proposed to abolish the dole, and to establish compulsory emigration'. He had joined Mosley's party, so he claimed, because 'youth was the only thing to save the country'. When the votes were counted, Macleod came third of the eight candidates, receiving 23 votes against 45 for the Conservative candidate and 25 for Ian Harvey, the would-be Scottish Nationalist, who was also to become a Tory MP and Minister.[29]

In the sixth form, Macleod had opted for the 'Modern Side' as opposed to the 'Classical Side', and in company with his friends, Ian Harvey and Ronnie Turnbull, frequently teased the history master, 'Ikey' Newman. Their sport involved asking awkward questions, or sometimes taking either the communist or fascist viewpoint, according to whim, and teasing their unfortunate victim. On other occasions, they would seize upon some comment of Newman's and distort it to prove that it was the opposite of what he had said the previous day, or that he was an atheist, or an anarchist – or that he was guilty on all counts.[30]

Yet Newman's efforts cannot have been entirely in vain, since Macleod, despite his longstanding lack of academic interest, was awarded the History prize in his final year. Indeed, Macleod appears to have experienced something of a late flowering of his scholastic talent. He was a keen member of the Shakespeare Society, whose meetings were hosted by the headmaster, Mr A.H. Ashcroft, on Saturday evenings in his study, and also in 1932 he shared with a fellow member, Ian Harvey, the Governors' annual prize for an essay competition on a Shakespearian subject. Macleod had developed the love of literature, and expecially of poetry, that was to stay with him all his life. His facility for composing verse had already been appreciated during his fourth year at Fettes by another friend, James Anson, who shared a study with him at the time, but who lacked his poetic skill. As Anson has recalled, when they were required to compose a poem or sonnet for their 'prep', Macleod 'was able with no trouble to write two such verses, one of which he handed to me'.[31]

Despite his mischievousness, Macleod achieved sufficient respectability by the latter part of his career at Fettes to be appointed as a House Prefect.

By the time he left, in the summer of 1932, he had formed a genuine affection for his school. A quarter of a century later, during his speech as guest of honour at the 1957 Founder's Day celebrations, he confessed to having been the author of an anonymous, sentimental three-verse poem that had been published in his final year in *The Fettesian*. 'Fettes, a sentinel of sculptured stone, / Stands, like an eagle stretched against the sky,' his opening lines had read, and his poem had concluded:

> And when in years still far ahead,
> When I grow weary of the cares of men,
> I may turn back to memories long dead
> And dream my carefree schooldays again.

Sentimental though these words were, they were genuinely felt. However, Macleod's feelings for Fettes could never compare with the passion that he felt for the real inspiration of his poetic being. This deeper, romantic source lay many miles away from either Edinburgh or his native Yorkshire, off the far north-west Scottish coast – it was, of course, his ancestral homeland, the Isle of Lewis. It, too, had woven its spell during Macleod's adolescent years.[32]

Hebridean Idyll

In the mid-1920s, while Macleod was at St Ninian's, his father bought Scaliscro Lodge, by Little Loch Roag, an inlet on the western Lewis coast, with 8,600 acres of rough moorland pitted with lochs and streams. The estate, which Dr Macleod had been surprised to secure for a bid of £1,000, had come on the market when Lord Leverhulme, the industrialist and philanthropist, who had bought tracts of Lewis and Harris after the First World War with a view to transforming the Hebridean economy, abandoned his venture in the face of local opposition. Resistance to his scheme had been especially fierce on Lewis, where the 'land wars' of the 1880s still smouldered and intense distrust was felt for the landed gentry, who, during the Victorian era, had used the land they had acquired from impoverished sheep farmers purely for sport. But the Macleods were Lewis people, and during Iain's teens they made Scaliscro their home, occasionally at Easter and invariably for the summer holidays. During the long vacations, they would often play host to family and friends, and sometimes visit old acquaintances on the island.[33]

The family's regular expeditions from Skipton to distant Scaliscro during the 1920s and 1930s became something of a ritual. They would leave Clifford House in the evening, travelling by car to York, where they would board an overnight sleeper to Inverness. The scene on the platform as they waited excitedly to catch first sight of the green steam engine, with its brass fittings and name-plate, hauling the express into the station, has remained vividly in Rhoderick Macleod's mind. Lab would be surrounded by the children, a pile of suitcases and a couple of red setter dogs, while Dr Macleod manoeuvred the family car onto one of the train's transporter trucks. Finally, they would all board and find their sleeping berths. On arrival at Inverness the following morning, Dr Macleod used to stock up with supplies of whisky for the stay at Scaliscro. From Inverness, the train took them to Kyle of Lochalsh, for the 70-mile boat journey across the Minches to Stornoway. The westbound road to Uig comprised the last 24-mile leg of their expedition, turning off to the right where Dr Macleod had placed a crimson chest for any mail, shortly before the descent to Little Loch Roag, and heading along the two-mile track to their lodge.[34]

A boy of Iain's age could spend all day wandering on the estate, fishing for trout in its lochs, shooting hares, and never see another soul, before returning dog-tired at night to Scaliscro. As Rhoderick, Iain's youngest brother, recalls, 'it was paradise'. A day's round-trip, with shooting on the way out during the morning and again on the way home, might take in four or five hours fishing on one or more of the forty or so lochs on the property and involve walking anything up to twenty miles. Iain would sometimes return after a long day with twenty or thirty trout and the odd hare. Again, he shared these enthusiasms with his father. According to Alasdair Alpin MacGregor, who wrote many books about his travels in the Western Isles at this time and often enjoyed the Macleods' hospitality, 'If you let Norman wander off in the early morning to a lochan he knows to abound in fins and gills, you may consider yourself flattered if he should turn up at Scaliscro before nightfall.' Sometimes, fishing was to be had on a nearby estate, where private rights were let out to visiting businessmen – the Macleods would often learn of a vacant lot for the day by a note sent with the morning post. Dr Macleod also kept sheep at Scaliscro, from which a local firm wove blankets and even the occasional suit. In addition, the estate offered shooting for grouse and snipe, and some stalking. As a result, the Macleods were largely self-sufficient during their stays on Lewis, with the option of having brown trout for breakfast, home-made scones for tea, grouse or their own mutton or venison for lunch and dinner, and mussels 'by the bucketful'. If they weren't too tired, most evenings were spent reading and playing cards.[35]

A vivid impression of life on holiday with the Macleods is conveyed by MacGregor, who associated Scaliscro with 'some of the happiest recollections of my wanderings in the Outer Hebrides'. Writing of the late summer of 1932, when Iain had left Fettes and was about to go up to Cambridge, MacGregor recalls that 'a succession of wet and blustrous days' and 'the encouragement lent by a couple of friends spending a fishing holiday with the Macleods' prompted them to play the card game, pontoon or *vingt-et-un*, that soon developed into an obsession. 'Night after night we played "vanty", and often during the day also, especially when, for one reason or another, Norman and his guests were prevented from trudging the moors in oilskins and gumboots to the more promising lochs on the Scaliscro property. Indeed, we now pursued our pontoon sessions with a fervour akin to fanaticism, I scarcely can believe to have been possible.' Iain, and his younger brothers, Torquil and Rhoderick, then aged fifteen and twelve, joined in the games, along with a boyfriend of Rhodabel, their elder sister. 'Torquil and Roderic [sic] usually dropped out early in the game, since the few pence at their disposal were soon in wilier pockets. But, somehow or other, Roderic would return in a nonchalant manner a few minutes later, ready to participate in the game once more. We suspected that a little cupboard love in the shape of a little loose change, surreptitiously slipped him by an adoring mother, enabled him to reinstate himself on these occasions.' The maximum stake permitted was twopence, and nobody was ever very much in pocket or very much out of pocket, usually nothing more than two or three shillings up or down in an evening. Nonetheless, the game was played with rare fervour. 'The only member of our school who, throughout, maintained an air of blasé indifference to our gains and losses was Iain, who, with his prodigious memory always knew after a few deals precisely the order in which the cards lay, upside down, in the banker's hand, except when a too recent "vanty" had necessitated their being reshuffled and cut.'[36]

After one such late-night pontoon session, MacGregor had slept in and was in danger of missing a lift to Stornoway for urgent repairs to the damaged wheel of his motor cycle. As he later recalled, having succumbed to the Macleods' advice that it was more important he should arrive in Stornoway with something in his stomach than with brushed hair and a washed face, he found himself being 'waited upon and harassed' by virtually the entire family. As MacGregor recounts, with some irritation, while he was cramming the food into his mouth, 'Close at hand stood Iain, generalizing most of the time about nothing, faithful in this respect to the highest traditions of the English public school (Don't take offence at this, Iain: it is not really meant for you so much as for what society is pleased to term education!).' The Scotsman's gibe at Fettes was well-chosen, since it had been modelled on the lines of an English public school. His pen-portrait of Iain Macleod rings true. On another occasion, the family had visited friends and were driving home when a heated discussion developed in the car. Iain was losing the argument, and, in a schoolboy huff, declared, 'If no one agrees with me, I will get out and walk.' Dr Macleod said nothing, but stopped the car and opened the door. Iain faced a thirteen-mile hike home and did not arrive till past midnight.[37]

Macleod's enduring love for his ancestral homeland is easier to understand from his experience of another long 'tramp across the Lewisian Wilderness' undertaken voluntarily and in the company of MacGregor during the latter's visit in 1932. MacGregor and Macleod 'were a little tired' by the time they finally returned to Scaliscro, late at night. 'A soft, soothing stillness crept over yon lamp-lit room, as we sat gazing into the glowing fire, speaking not a word.' Perhaps for the first time that day, MacGregor noted of his talkative, fellow adventurer, 'I wot not where Iain's thoughts were by this time.' For all his youthful garrulousness, Macleod's reverie in his innermost thoughts was to become a familiar experience for those who knew him in later life. On this occasion, it had been brought on by a day's walking on Lewis, and what remains today of his verse testifies to the enduring bond with his beloved isle. His inner sense of belonging to the Hebrides was expressed at the beginning of the Second World War, when, as a young man facing the prospect of battle, he wrote of the powerfully romantic lure of the mythical Gaelic land, Tir-an-Og:

There's an isle beyond the sunset in the Western main
Where the dead are done with dying and are young again
And the sun streams softly downwards like an endless rain
In Tir-an-Og.

There they live, the lovely women and the bravest of the men,
There the chiefs of Siol Torquil go out to war again,
And the pipes of the MacCrimmons are waiting in the glen
In Tir-an-Og.

There the sands go dancing downwards to meet the shining sea,
There the great hills rear triumphant heads disdainfully
    and free,
And all my dreams are haunted and are ever calling me
To Tir-an-Og.[38]

In later life, Macleod used to tell his son, Torquil, of the sheer beauty and romance of Lewis. The pressure on his time prevented Macleod returning to the island as often as he would have liked, but in the summer of 1968 he and his family went there on holiday. It became something of a pilgrimage, and was to be Macleod's last visit. He was totally in his element. At heart, he always remained an islander.[39]

2

'Tempered by War'

We had expected anything up to 40 per cent casualties in the landings, and somehow I had been convinced that I would be killed. Now, equally unreasonably, I became convinced that I would live through the war. I would see our second child, who was to be born in October. There would be a life after the war. D-Day was over.

Iain Macleod, 'One Man's D-Day', the *Spectator*, 5 June 1964.

Aimless Youth

The words, 'tempered by war', used by John F. Kennedy during his inaugural address as US President, to describe his own generation to whom the torch of political leadership had passed, might have been coined specifically to describe Iain Macleod. Before the Second World War, Macleod had drifted aimlessly, bereft of any idea as to what to do with his life and existing, in the menacing and uncertain days of the late 1930s, as a gambler and playboy. By the end of the War, he had developed an unshakeable conviction that his true vocation lay in politics.

Despite Macleod's relatively undistinguished academic achievement at school, his progression from Fettes to read modern history at Cambridge was unsurprising. Entrance requirements were minimal, amounting to little more than a formality for those whose parents were prepared to pay the fees. Macleod's headmaster, Mr A.H. Ashcroft, had been a respected scholar and rugger blue for the university, and Macleod became one of a steady stream of Fettesians who went up to Cambridge. Like a number of others, he was offered a place by their headmaster's old college, Gonville and Caius. However, Macleod mixed little with his fellow Old Fettesians, and although he had a room in college during his first year – number 3, staircase F, in St Michael's Court – his path and theirs rarely crossed. James Anson, who had shared a study with him at school, recalls being invited by Macleod to complete a foursome for tea in his room 'with two charming ladies from Newnham and Girton', but otherwise rarely having much to do with him.

Even Ronald Turnbull, Macleod's closest schoolfriend, seldom saw him. Macleod had always struck his contemporaries as being self-sufficient, and he and they had come to have less in common. Although Macleod tried his hand at acting, he did not share Turnbull's enthusiasm for amateur dramatics. Similarly, although he still loved sport and during the vacations used to play rugger for Skipton 'A' team, he played less rugby and cricket at Cambridge than at school.[1]

More surprisingly, in view of his enjoyment of debating at Fettes, he rarely attended the Cambridge Union. Indeed, he intervened only once, to speak against the 1932 Ottawa Agreements. Not too much should be read into his opposition, but it is at least an indication of liberal leanings and a lack of sentimental feeling for the Empire, since the Agreements instituted a system of Empire-wide protectionism against the rest of the world, and marked the high-water mark of 'tariff reform', or 'imperial preference', for which Joseph Chamberlain, the great romantic imperialist, and his sons, Austen and Neville, had long campaigned. Macleod was not called to speak in the Union debate until after 11.00 pm, almost three hours after the debate had begun. 'At last,' he wrote to his sister, Rhodabel, 'the President, an Indian called Dhavan, made a remarkable noise which sounded like Mr Maclooood.' Macleod concluded that this meant him,

> so I moved forward, glanced modestly at my feet and tried to remember what I was going to say. There were nearly 400 people there. I decided to risk a joke in doubtful taste, which got a laugh. After five minutes I launched in to a vicious and quite unpremeditated attack on Stanley Baldwin. It went down rather well. The *Granta* review said 'Mr I.N. Macleod (Caius) is promising' which, though short, was satisfactory; and the *Cambridge Review* made my speech sound better than it was.

But it was to be his sole contribution at the Union. Likewise, he developed no interest in organized politics, although his years as an undergraduate coincided with one of the most highly politicized periods at Cambridge. The great political ferment in the wider world appeared to pass Macleod by, although in time it was to catch up with him and transform his life.[2]

Poetry, racing and bridge comprised an unlikely trio of pursuits, but they received from Macleod the dedication and concentrated effort that his tutor vainly urged him to apply to his academic studies. He happily spent many hours in his room reading poetry and, years later, could still recite poems that he had read at Cambridge. His tastes were catholic, and included poets as diverse as T.S. Eliot, G.K. Chesterton, who was to remain a special favourite, and Richard Church. In 1933, he played Sweeney in a Cambridge production of *Sweeney Agonistes*. 'Throughout his life,' his friend, Michael Fraser, has recalled, 'he was immensely absorbed by poetry.' Fraser, who had first met him at Fettes when Macleod was fifteen and he was thirteen, and who also followed Macleod to Cambridge, later recalled that in London, during Macleod's

> bachelor days before the War he [Macleod] occasionally took pleasure in demonstrating his remarkable memory through poetry. He would ask one to pick a poem, 30 lines or so, not of course one that he obviously knew already. He would warn one off T.S. Eliot for this reason because he knew all that off by heart anyway. So you would pick something unusual and difficult and give it to him and he would bury himself in it with that immense concentration for a few minutes. Then he would close the book and recite it, indeed perform it, often word perfect and never with more than the odd word or two out of place.

Macleod's love of poetry was to communicate itself to a much wider audience than his friends who witnessed his party-piece recitals from memory: for, according to Fraser, Macleod's 'passion for words and the power of words' was later to infuse his political speeches and was to make him one of the most inspiring, as well as most effective, debaters of modern times.[3]

During his Cambridge days, nearby Newmarket was an irresistible lure. Macleod studied the form with the avid attention that he had applied to *Wisden* while at school. and developed an encyclopedic knowledge about horses. However, he seems to have been more successful at gambling on the Cottenham point-to-points, where he managed to glean inside information. During the vacations he sometimes went racing at Wetherby, the nearest course to Skipton, with his younger brother, Torquil. At one meeting at Wetherby, a Skipton man, Fred Chew, won £1,200, which was an enormous sum in the 1930s, and it took the Macleod brothers and the other celebrants three days to make their way home. Macleod never lost his passion for racing. His tips for the Derby and other major races became a regular feature of his *Spectator* notebook in the mid-1960s and he loved to escape to Sandown on a Saturday afternoon. Before the end of his life, he and his daughter, Diana, were planning to buy a racehorse and registered the Macleod colours with the Jockey Club. As with his poetry, his love of racing was to leave its mark on his approach to politics. He was not reckless, but was constantly weighing up the probabilities of different courses of action and always talked in terms of the odds, for or against, of a particular option being successful. But it was more than a matter of simply using the bookies' jargon: rather, he was acutely conscious that all political judgement is based on calculating probabilities and risks, and that absolute belief in political certainties is, at best, a mirage and, at worst, a dangerous delusion.[4]

At Cambridge, bridge became Macleod's abiding interest and was to exert the strongest influence on his life during the remainder of the 1930s. The first ever varsity match against Oxford was his brainchild. At the start of his final year, he and several others gathered in the room of a second year student at Magdalen, Colin Harding, to play cards. Harding and Macleod scarcely knew one another, but at the end of the game, Macleod stayed on and as they chatted, he suggested that they should challenge Oxford at bridge. Macleod nominated himself as captain and Harding as honorary secretary. It was the start of a close, lifelong friendship – even after Macleod had risen to Cabinet rank and his days were crammed with official business and political functions, he and his friend used to try and meet every week. As Harding later fondly recalled, they always spent their time together laughing.[5]

When Harding wrote to *Isis*, issuing the challenge, Macleod's flair for publicity was immediately apparent. 'A Contract bridge league has been formed in Cambridge,' *The Times* announced in their regular bridge column on 17 November 1934, 'with a view to promoting duplicate matches. The first Oxford and Cambridge bridge match has been arranged and will take place in London next month . . . Cambridge men who are interested should communicate with Mr Ian [sic] Macleod, Caius College, Cambridge.' The match was finally held three months later, on Saturday 16 February 1935 at the Albany Club, Savile Row, in London's West End. Macleod captained the Cambridge team which included Harding. Oxford, captained by Charles Maclaren (later Lord Aberconway) were the stronger team, and included Terence Reese, who was to become Britain's leading international player and bridge columnist, and Michael Noble, who, like Macleod, was to become a Tory Cabinet Minister. Organized under the auspices of the British Bridge League, this first varsity match consisted of 100 boards. 'Oxford led from the beginning and at one time were 5,900 points ahead,' *The Times* reported. 'Cambridge reduced the lead somewhat, but Oxford won by 3,800 points.'[6]

Macleod never allowed his enthusiasm for bridge to dim his desire for a good time. When Cambridge were due to play in Leicester, Macleod was the first to arrive in Harding's room, where the team had agreed to meet, to find that his friend was busily preparing pre-lunch cocktails. Harding had to leave to deal with a telephone call and during his absence Macleod took the opportunity to sample the 'white lady' cocktail that had been mixed for the whole team. By the time that Harding returned, Macleod had drunk the lot and 'was out for the count'. When the others appeared, Harding suggested that they should leave him behind, at which Macleod rallied, and declared, 'Macleod drunk is better than anybody else sober'. This reaction, Harding later recalled, was characteristic of Macleod's self-confidence. At lunch, Macleod was so drunk that he had trouble finding his mouth with his fork. Having finally made their way to Leicester, they discovered that the opposing captain was a vicar. Harding hurriedly ordered plenty of black coffee, but to little avail. When Macleod finally met his opposite number, he tried to light a cigarette but fumbled with his box of matches, before finally dropping it and spilling the contents everywhere.[7]

Yet Macleod's exploits at bridge were to secure him his first job after Cambridge. Among the members of a team from the English Bridge Union who visited the university for a match against Macleod and his colleagues was Bernard Westall, then chairman of the De La Rue, the City printing firm that specialized, appropriately, in producing bank notes and playing cards. Macleod's exceptional talent at bridge and his entertaining personality impressed Westall, who offered him a post with his company, there and then. Macleod had no idea what he wanted to do, but he had neglected his studies and was unlikely to earn a good degree that might bring some other opening. He was grateful for the offer, and readily accepted.[8]

In his final examinations, Macleod gained only a lower second class honours degree. When the news reached Clifford House, a deep gloom descended upon his father. Dr Macleod had worked his way up from a poor background and won his medical qualifications entirely by his own efforts. He had paid for Iain to have the best education, and was now deeply disappointed, since he knew that his son could have done better if only he had tried.[9]

Playboy

After going down from Cambridge in the summer of 1935, Macleod joined De La Rue and took cheap accommodation in Lancaster Gate. From the outset he led something of a double life. By day, he endured a humdrum existence in the firm's Dickensian premises in Bunhill Row, near the old Whitbread brewery, whose busy dray-horses littered the street with heaps of dung. In the evening, he exchanged these grim surroundings for the excitement of the bridge tables at Crockford's in Mayfair or Lederer's in Bayswater, and the pleasure-seeking nightlife of the late-1930s West End. There was never any doubt which of his two lives Macleod preferred.

Westall, who had taken him on at De La Rue, was a brilliant salesman, but Macleod was underused and no special effort was made to engage his interest. As with many other medium-sized companies at the time, there was no thought of career development. Work was done under the strict gaze of Leslie Newman, a military figure, who was over six feet tall and as straight as a ramrod, with a bristling moustache. Newman had served as a Major in the First World War, took a disciplinarian view of work and made no allowance for the unorthodox. Macleod always had a twinkle in his eye and was the archetypal nonconformist. Newman quickly became an ideal target for Macleod's wit, but it is unlikely that a more congenial regime would have persuaded Macleod to stay long at the company – even the word 'business' sometimes used to attract his mockery.[10]

The struggle to arrive for work at 8.00 am became an increasingly uphill one for Macleod, who had often stayed up till two or three o' clock the night before playing bridge and gambling at poker. When he put in an early appearance, he was often in no fit state to work and spent the morning trying to catch up on his sleep. He seldom joined his workmates at the local ABC or Lyons eating houses for lunch-time sausage and mash, but by the end of the day he had usually perked up and would sometimes urge them to go along with him that evening to his club for a drink or dinner and a night out. By their standards, he was a rich man. He was already making much more money by night from cards than any of them were paid for a day's work. He once told a colleague, in a matter of fact way without boasting, that the previous night he had won £100 at cards – average male *annual* earnings were then around £200 and Macleod's wages were £3 a week. Although he was generally in pocket from cards, he sometimes suffered heavy losses. On a few occasions, he had to turn to his father for £100 or so to meet his gambling debts. Whenever the morning post brought a begging letter from Iain, Harry Thurlow, Dr Macleod's long-serving factotum, used to warn Iain's brothers that it might be better if they kept out of their father's way for the day.[11]

There was no side to Macleod and he was popular with the workforce at De La Rue. He was generous to a fault, handing out free cigarettes and always offering to buy drinks or food for the drivers when he went out on deliveries. His appalling timekeeping and total inability to do anything about it was observed with wry amusement, and many of the staff wondered how long this wayward recruit would last. But when the company was at panic stations with a massive order for bank notes from China, Macleod seemed to relish the challenge. Although it played havoc with his beloved bridge, he readily mucked in, doing his full share of overtime at night and working at the weekend to meet an almost impossible Monday morning shipping deadline at Southampton.[12]

Accepting Macleod's invitation to a night out was, for most of his workmates, to enter an wholly foreign milieu. The evening usually began at Crockford's, then located in Hertford Street, Mayfair, and primarily a club for playing bridge and other card games, including poker. Over champagne, and perhaps dinner, Macleod would introduce them to his card-playing acquaintances, who were unlike anybody else they met – somewhat intense characters, with generally pallid complexions and smooth, unworked hands. Macleod attracted homosexuals, but did not reciprocate. He had an eye for good-looking women and was often accompanied by a beautiful girl – if he was not, he was usually chasing one.[13]

Had Macleod needed his wages from De La Rue, he might have tried to make a 'go' of his first job. It had been his skill at bridge that had landed him the post; when he was finally fired by Westall he was free, at last, to devote all his energies to the game. In an attempt to smoothe relations with his father, who was further disappointed at his having been sacked from a regular occupation, he declared his intention to read for the Bar. But they were empty words. He loved the good life too much and never pursued his legal studies seriously. From the age of 22, he was immersed in the world of bridge and lived as a playboy.[14]

In London, Macleod had quickly teamed up with the best bridge players of his generation. At a club in Acol Road, South Hampstead, he spent long hours with Maurice Harrison-Gray, Jack Marx and S. J. Simon devising a new system of bidding, which was based on the methods developed by the great American player, Ely Culbertson, but which also incorporated several features then in fashion in Europe. It took them many late nights, hurriedly writing hands on anything that was available – from cigarette packets to tablecloths – to perfect the technique. Their system, called 'Acol' after the road of its birth, was to bring them great success and become the basis of standard British bidding. Macleod and his Acol Road colleagues, together with his friend from Cambridge, Colin Harding, represented London in county matches. They were at their peak during 1937. In April, they pipped Middlesex to win the *Daily Telegraph* Cup, and the following month defeated Cheshire for the *Bridge Magazine* Gold Cup. Describing Macleod and his colleagues as 'worthy winners', *The Times* reported that they 'are now recognized as forming one of the strongest teams of match players this country has ever had'.[15]

Along with Terence Reese, who had been on the opposing side in the first Oxbridge varsity match, Macleod was regarded as a bridge prodigy. He became an international player the year after leaving Cambridge and always played for England, not Scotland, in the four-nation, home countries, Camrose Cup. In the opinion of Rixi Markus, the legendary bridge player and writer, who first met Macleod playing at Crockford's when she fled from Vienna to London in 1938, he was a player of the highest calibre. He was not reckless and, notwithstanding his love of a good time, was 'logical' and 'sober' in his play at the table. She was certain that had events not intervened, he would have become a leading international. Much though Macleod relished competitive bridge and took his game seriously, he also enjoyed the opportunities that it brought for having fun. Among the regular, annual highlights were the trips that he and Colin Harding made to the international tournaments at Cannes and Deauville. All expenses were paid by the French Bridge Federation and Macleod, who used to go with his girlfriend, only had to buy their drinks.[16]

When Markus first saw Macleod, he was working during the afternoons and evenings as a host at Crockford's in their 'ten shillings room' – ten shillings a hundred was then the highest stake allowed in the club. One of his tasks was to keep an eye on the membership – there was a certain amount of snobbery about belonging to Crockford's and it was somewhat ironic, in view of his own heavy gambling, that he was expected to ensure that the club was not infiltrated by too many semi-professional card-sharps. His principal duty was to ensure that the tables were occupied and that members who wanted to play were able to complete a foursome. This often involved making up the numbers himself and partnering one of the members. He was an attractive and popular host, and members were always keen that he should join their table. He had tidied up his appearance since his notoriously dishevelled school days and was a model bridge player with perfect etiquette. Although paid a modest sum, he did not have to pay the usual fee to play, received free food and drink and was able to make a very good living at the tables and from his out of hours gambling.[17]

Macleod was making up to £2,500 a year tax free, an extraordinarily high sum for a man in his early twenties and more than ten times the level of average annual male earnings. 'At that stage,' according to his friend, Michael Fraser,

> he was a gambler in the real sense of the word. He played and wagered for high stakes. I recall one occasion watching Iain in a high game of poker lose steadily throughout the evening so that eventually I could not watch any more and left, with a picture of him there, hunched, indrawn and apparently emotionless and then met him again six hours later, triumphant with a great victory under his belt.

Macleod had little trouble living up to his income. For many young people, the menacing international scene during the late 1930s encouraged them to pursue a hedonistic way of life with little regard to the future. This was the increasingly frantic milieu in which Macleod moved. A night's card-playing at Crockford's might be followed by the midnight cabaret at the *Café de Paris*, and then onto one of the West End's less reputable clubs. Around this period, he was living in an eighth-floor flat in Duncan House, one of the apartment blocks in the classy, private development at Dolphin Square, by the river between Westminster and Pimlico. At weekends, sometimes with his brother Torquil, he threw highly popular, all-night parties attended by friends from Fettes and Cambridge, who were also trying to make their way in London, and by his acquaintances from the card-tables and nightlife of the West End. Michael Fraser, who had also known Torquil at Fettes, was later to describe his friendship with Iain just before the War, 'as years when we laughed a lot'.[18]

Finally, on Sunday 3 September 1939, the declaration of War brought their easy living to a shuddering halt. The next day, Macleod, Harding and their friend Tommy Gay, went to Crockford's. The place was deserted. For all they knew, it might have been the last time they would play cards together and they therefore bet very high stakes. At the end of the evening, Macleod had 'won' £50,000; Harding £10,000; and Gay had 'lost' £60,000. None of them had taken it seriously and Gay never had to pay up. In a strange way, their fantastical game marked a fitting finale to a period in Macleod's life that had come to bear less and less relation to the real world.[19]

Soldier

Reality, in the shape of the outbreak of War, had intruded forcefully in Macleod's life. But it was not until later during the Second World War that his future was to be completely transformed. On 11 September 1939, only eight days after Chamberlain had announced that Britain and Germany were again at war, and two months short of his twenty-sixth birthday, Macleod enlisted as a private soldier in the Royal Fusiliers. While he waited for a posting, he enrolled as an ambulance driver in anticipation of the massive civilian casualties that the German bombers were expected to inflict at any time on a vulnerable capital from London's largely unprotected skies. He was interviewed for the job of driver by Eve Mason, an attractive woman of 24, who had joined the London County Council's (LCC) ambulance service almost a year earlier, after the ill-fated Munich agreement. Macleod was immediately struck by Eve's beauty, but at first had no idea that in addition to reality, romance was about to enter his life, since she was already married, having wed Mervyn Mason in 1937.[20]

Macleod's three months' service as a temporary ambulance driver coincided with the 'phoney war'. Macleod had little to do and spent his hours at Kingston House, the LCC's ambulance headquarters, keeping himself occupied working out bridge hands. One day, a mysterious message, apparently in code, was found on a slip of paper on the floor and prompted a full-scale spy scare. When the intelligence officers sent to investigate the matter questioned Macleod and showed him the 'message', that read 'A . . . A to K, xxx, Qxxx', he immediately recognized it as part of a bridge hand he had scribbled down and later thrown away.[21]

In December 1939, Macleod was posted to an Officer Cadets Training Unit at Colchester. His attitude was still wholly in keeping with his approach at Fettes, Cambridge and De La Rue. Petty regulations were resented and even flouted – cadets were only allowed to visit the local public house at weekends, but Macleod went there every night. Although patently bright, he made little effort, only ever doing the minimum required to pass. But his sense of humour and wit constantly entertained the other cadets and made him popular among his peers. While the 'phoney war' continued, there were still opportunities for Macleod and his friends in London to recapture something of their carefree, pre-war existence. In March 1940, he and a dozen acquaintances from Cambridge held a great party that lasted over three nights from Thursday until Saturday. None of them knew where, when, or indeed, whether, they might meet again. The following month, Macleod was commissioned as a Second Lieutenant in the Yorkshire-based Duke of Wellington's Regiment, whose 6th Battalion had comprised a territorial army based in Skipton before the War. In almost no time, he was in Europe.[22]

At the end of April, Lieutenant Macleod crossed to France with the 46th Division. He was with two battalions of the Duke of Wellington's Regiment that were stationed with other units near St Nazaire on the west coast, where they were employed road making, laying railway lines, erecting huts, unloading ships and working on ammunition and petrol dumps. On 10 May the Germans invaded Holland and Belgium and a week later 46th Division volunteered to assist the British Expeditionary Force, now in retreat, by taking a defensive role and helping stem the German advance. The Division set out by train across North West France on the evening of 18 May. Progress towards their secret destination – the town of Bethune in Pas-de-Calais – was slow because of the problems caused by refugees fleeing the German invasion of northern France. On the afternoon of 20 May, the last two trains carrying the Duke of Wellington's battalions were brought to a halt a mile short of Abbeville, on the river Somme, as the town had apparently fallen to the Germans. An air attack brought Macleod's first experience of enemy fire, forcing him and the rest of the 1,400-strong contingent to disembark hastily. Fifty miles from their planned destination, the Duke's battalions were out on their own without maps, with no knowledge of the locality and with the Germans bearing down on them. They withdrew towards the south-west, heading for Dieppe on the coast and Neufchatel, further inland. Macleod was among the detachments heading for the latter destination and, as a result, had to contend not only with large numbers of refugees on the roads but also with difficult terrain that made it hard to maintain contact, even within platoons. It was very hot; food was scarce, since the refugees who had already passed through had cleared the countryside like a plague of locusts; and the water was undrinkable. Most of the Duke's two battalions eventually reached Dieppe or Neufchatel during 22 and 23 May.[23]

It was near Neufchatel that Lieutenant Macleod and his men were ordered to put up a road block. As they dug a trench for shelter from air attack and shelling, they unearthed the skull of a First World War soldier. This macabre incident was to prompt Macleod, soon afterwards, to compose a sombre poem in which 'the ghosts of men' killed little more than 20 years earlier addressed their latter-day counterparts:

> And these dead things seemed to sneer
> 'ye are here, ye men of war,
> Digging trenches – digging graves
> Dying where we died before:
> We were here:
> Long ago – long ago.'
>
> Were they English. Were they Huns?
> Came no answer but the sobbing
> Of the breezes in the pines:
> And the low dull throbbing
> Of the guns:
> Coming near – coming near.

Macleod and his troops laid a pile of logs across the road, but before they could tie them together with wire, a German armoured vehicle came racing round the corner, crashed into the road block and sent the logs flying. One of the logs smashed into Macleod's leg, badly breaking his thigh. Using a bayonet as a splint, he somehow struggled to a dressing station. He was finally evacuated from St Nazaire in early June and taken to hospital at Exeter. Later in the month, the two battalions of the Duke of Wellington's Regiment left France, having suffered 163 casualties, of whom six officers and 80 other ranks were killed. In addition, 97 men were taken prisoner of war. Although Macleod's bone set, he was to be left with a limp for the rest of his life. But at this stage he was not yet affected by the debilitating and crippling spinal condition, ankylosing spondylitis, that was to afflict him in later life.[24]

The early months of 1940 had brought tragedy to Eve Mason. She was widowed when her husband was drowned after his convoy had been attacked off the coast of Ireland. As she began to recover from this terrible shock, she was again in touch with Macleod. After he was discharged from hospital, he returned to his regiment and was stationed at Halifax, in his native Yorkshire. By this time, their romance had blossomed and she followed him, transferring to the Bradford Ambulance Service. Eve had been born into the English landed gentry and minor aristocracy – the family of her father, the Revd Gervase Blois, had owned property in the east of England since the twelfth century and her mother, Hester, was a daughter of Lord Hampton. Her upbringing in Worcestershire had been typical of her class between the Wars – boarding school, tennis and lacrosse (at which she represented her county), plenty of riding and, as she grew older, attending hunt balls. She was presented at court, in keeping with the traditions of the time. Macleod was always rather proud, as the son of a local doctor, of Eve's origins.[25]

Macleod's parents were no longer living in Yorkshire. His father had sold the Clifford House practice at Skipton in 1938 and moved to Strathpeffer in the Highlands, on the railway route the family used to take from Inverness to Kyle of Lochalsh and thence to Lewis. Dr Macleod had bought the Spa practice but, on the outbreak of War, the area north and west of the Caledonian canal became a restricted area and so in 1940 he moved south to Blackpool, buying a practice on the Lytham Road. When Macleod took Eve to introduce her to his parents, he led her into the drawing room, where Dr Macleod was reading his paper. 'Can I introduce you to Eve?' Macleod asked. His father briefly lowered his paper and, by way of greeting, muttered a guttural 'eh' in a strong, Scottish accent and then raised the paper again and carried on reading. Despite this first gruff impression, Eve quickly discovered that Dr Macleod was a charming and generous man. Iain's mother, Lab, was an imposing figure for any girlfriend of her eldest son to meet. Highly intelligent and opinionated, she regarded Iain as her precious son and rather gave the impression that no woman was good enough for him. But in time, Eve and Lab were to get on well.[26]

Iain and Eve were married at Halifax on 25 January 1941, with fellow officers from his regiment forming a guard of honour. Their honeymoon was spent at the Devonshire Arms Hotel, close to one of the most picturesque spots in the Yorkshire Dales: Bolton Abbey, in Wharfedale. Friends had lent them a car and some petrol coupons – it was the era of strict rationing – and they decided they could make the long journey to Cheltenham for a day's racing. Macleod had no luck with his bets in the early races. By the final race of the day, he was down to his last pound and put it on a 25–1 outsider. The horse won and Macleod collected almost ten weeks pay – he earned eleven shillings a day as a Second Lieutenant. They returned to Yorkshire flush with funds and in some style.[27]

Not long after their marriage Macleod was seconded from the Duke of Wellington's Regiment to the staff of the 46th Division, whose headquarters were based at Wye in East Kent, between Ashford and Canterbury. His name had been suggested to Alan Dawtry, then Deputy Assistant Adjutant General of the 46th Division, who was looking for a Staff Captain to assist him in dealing with manpower and discipline. Macleod was reckoned, at twenty-seven, to be rather old as a platoon commander, but he was said to be bright and Dawtry decided that he was the man for the job. It was a fortunate move for Macleod. Dawtry was able to find him a room in Withersdane Hall, a beautiful house in Wye, which also accommodated the officers' mess. They were a happy group and, by the standards of wartime, were living high off the hog. The mess was equipped with an Aga stove and the cook had previously been a chef at the Aperitif restaurant in Edinburgh.

This relatively agreeable existence for Macleod lasted during most of 1941. He would play bridge in the mess, teaming up with another top-flight player, Donald Haslam, whom he had known before the War and who also happened to be stationed there. But Macleod and Haslam always gave Dawtry and the others a fair chance, never playing to their true potential. On Macleod's one day off duty each week he headed for London, where he sometimes met friends from pre-war days at one of their rendezvous – the dive bar at Scott's or the long bar of the old Carlton Hotel in Haymarket. Although the main part of the Hotel was destroyed during the May 1941 bombing raid that demolished the House of Commons, its bar and grill room continued to function for many years. Finally, he would always head for Crockford's, where he used to gamble for the rest of the night, before returning to Charing Cross for the early morning train back to Ashford. He usually covered his expenses and made a tidy profit. When Dawtry came on duty the following morning, he always found his Staff Captain looking smart and presentable and clearly capable of carrying out his duties without any difficulty for the rest of the day.[28]

Dawtry detected no inkling of Macleod's having any special interest in politics, but was enormously impressed by his intellectual grasp. They had to deal with a lot of complicated paper work, but Macleod had a very quick brain and would master any case, however detailed, very quickly. By comparison with anybody else with whom Dawtry served, he regards Macleod as having been outstanding. Dawtry could safely delegate any task with complete confidence, and knew that if he (Dawtry) was required to report back to his senior officers, Macleod would always brief him very well and ensure that he put up a good show. Not only was Macleod the brightest officer with whom Dawtry worked, he also had a good sense of humour and a very light-hearted approach to life. The two men got on famously. They shared the same office, working at the same desk and laughing a lot – often at the expense of senior officers.

Yet their comradeship might have ended in tragedy as a result of Macleod's foolhardiness. Late one evening, Dawtry, who had stayed in quarters and was sitting up reading, heard that Macleod had been seen mixing with bad company in the local public house and was drinking too much. Macleod eventually returned, drunk, past midnight, found Dawtry still reading in the officers' mess, and said, 'Alan, I want to play stud poker.' Stud poker is a form of the game that can be played by just two people and Dawtry, who was already angry at Macleod's behaviour, knew that he was no match for him and refused, ticking him off for being drunk. When Dawtry then stood up to go to bed, Macleod begged, 'Just for 30 minutes.' Dawtry again refused, but Macleod still pleaded, 'Just for 10 minutes, then?' Unmoved, Dawtry retired to his room for the night. Macleod was incensed. The next thing, Dawtry heard Macleod's voice at his door declaring, 'I'm going to shoot you!' Dawtry quickly took evasive action as Macleod fired three or four shots at the door with his service revolver to try and break the lock, but failed. Macleod realized, when he tried to fire again, that he had run out of bullets. 'I'm going for more ammunition,' he shouted, but soon returned and began battering at the door with a piece of furniture. The door bulged as Macleod charged at it several times, before he finally crashed in, collapsing in a heap on Dawtry's floor. He had passed out. Dawtry carried him to his room and laid him out on the bed.[29]

Remarkably, their relationship was wholly unaffected by this potentially disastrous incident. At breakfast next morning, their conversation was as follows:

MACLEOD: Good morning, sir.
DAWTRY: Good morning, Iain.

And after a pause . . .

MACLEOD: I think you owe me an apology.
DAWTRY: What for?

MACLEOD: For not playing stud poker with me last night.

As Fisher relates, many years later, after both men had established themselves in successful careers in public life, Macleod told the story to a mutual friend and added: 'If I had killed Alan Dawtry, he would never have become Town Clerk of Westminster and I should never have become a member of the Cabinet.' And when Dawtry wrote to congratulate Macleod on his appointment as Minister of Health, Macleod wrote back:

My dear Alan,

Bloody silly ain't it? I'm glad I missed you.

Yours ever,
Iain.

It was also a measure of Macleod's character that when, towards the end of 1941, he received another posting, he persuaded Dawtry to take on his brother, Torquil, as his replacement – a preferment that was outside normal army procedures. Macleod owed Dawtry a great debt of gratitude and after his departure from Wye wrote him a generous and warm letter of appreciation.[30]

Over the next two and a half years, Macleod remained in the country, but his many postings took him to an array of army stations, mostly in southern England. At Dungeness during Christmas 1941, he and his brother, Torquil, wrote and produced what was to be the first of several witty and well-received revues for their fellow officers. In February 1942, Eve gave birth to their first child, a son, who they named Torquil – the name recurs over many centuries since the origins of the clan Macleod. Eve sometimes took furnished rooms so that she and the baby could be near Iain and at other times stayed with either her parents or Iain's. Among his many postings, Macleod volunteered to go on a course at Newmarket, his old haunt from Cambridge days, in order to enjoy some racing. During a spell at Dover Castle, he had little work to do and passed the time playing himself at chess with a miniature chess set and teaching other officers to play poker. Trips to Crockford's financed his debts in the mess. He kept the clerks in the Brigade Major's office amused by his sung renditions (he was tone-deaf) of the more fatuous military instructions and his idiosyncratic filing system – he left most letters to answer themselves and 'filed' them in a huge old wastepaper basket, but sometimes he was proved wrong and then had to empty the lot on the floor and search desperately through the pile for the one that he needed.[31]

It was not until Macleod was 30 years old, during the autumn of 1943, that he first realized that he might do something worthwhile with his life. The catalyst for this realization was his selection for the twelfth War Course at the Staff College, Camberley. In peacetime, the course lasted two years, but during the War took only four months and attracted higher calibre officers. Others on the course with Macleod who by coincidence included his brother, Torquil, were impressed by his ability to grasp a problem and to suggest practical solutions. The Macleod brothers were recruited to write and produce another of their Christmas revues, but on this occasion their material had to comply to supposedly tight guidelines. The commanding officer ordered that the revue should not include anything that might shock his sixteen-year-old daughter – an instruction that revealed how completely out of touch he was and would, if carried out to the letter, have entailed practically no censorship. The Macleods wisely vetted their script according to the girl's presumed innocence.[32]

It was while writing *The Blues in the Night*, as they called their revue, that the two brothers began discussing their plans after Staff College and Iain first spoke of his sudden realization that they were as good as anybody on the course, and a cut above most. They were officer class, capable of becoming corps commanders. There was also an element of calculation in Macleod's thinking – they had every incentive to become 'lead men', because commanding officers told everybody else what to do and, as they were leadership calibre, they would find giving orders much less arduous than having to do the work themselves. Macleod was never in any doubt that Staff College had transformed his life. Many years later, when Torquil asked him what had first set him on the road to a career as a leading politician, Macleod replied, 'You have probably forgotten, but it was *The Blues in the Night*.' He was thinking back to their conversations in late 1943. As Macleod was to reflect on the importance of his months at Camberley, 'I'd never been pushed into competition with people of first class ability before, and it was there that I found, genuinely to my very great surprise, not only that I could keep up, but that I could beat them.'[33]

Macleod had no idea when he graduated from the Staff College in early February 1944, that within a matter of months he would be back in France, at the heart of the Allied invasion of Europe. Twenty years later, in 'One Man's D-Day', a first-rate piece of journalism that he wrote while editor of the *Spectator*, he was to recount his experiences. He had had exactly one day of the leave that was due to him after Camberley, when he received a telegram. 'I was to report with the rank of Major to an address in Ashley Gardens, near Victoria Station. There were no other details.' He arrived to discover that he had been appointed as an extra Deputy Assistant Quarter Master General (DAQMG) on the planning staff of the famous 50th (Northumbrian) Division. The Northumbrians had been the last to leave the beaches of Dunkirk and had fought for more than two years in the North African desert, but the significance of his posting was that '50 Div.', as everybody knew them, had been brought back from Sicily to East Anglia to begin planning and preparing for the Allied invasion.[34]

Major Macleod quickly got to grips with his new task, impressing other officers in 50 Div. by his application, hard work and grasp of detail. The logistics of such a massive exercise were extremely complicated. 'The attack was now planned on a five-division front with 50 Div. in the centre,' he later wrote. On their right were two American Divisions and on their left the 3rd British and 3rd Canadian Divisions. Moreover, as Macleod explained,

> 50 Div. was almost the size of a small Corps when it landed. A fourth infantry brigade and an armoured brigade came under command. So did a crowd of artillery units and a proportion of the 'comics' – special units often with Heath Robinson type equipment designed for a special task. In all, there were about 40,000 men.[35]

During most of the planning stage, Macleod did not expect to land with the Division. 'Probably when the planning was over I would either be given another appointment or, more likely, be held temporarily in Montgomery's pool of staff officers to wait for the inevitable vacancies that the assault would bring.' But under the strain of the planning the Acting Assistant and Quarter Master General fell ill, and Tom Black, 50 Div.'s DAQMG, was promoted to take his place. Macleod took Black's job. 'I studied the landing sheets again. H plus forty, I saw, was "my" time. In other words, I was due to land forty minutes after the first wave of assault troops went in.' Macleod still did not know when D-Day was due, but 'by an odd chance' discovered where the invasion was to take place. 'Thumbing through a file in the Headquarters of the 2nd Army I saw a receipt for a map marked TOP SECRET OVERLORD (the invasion code name).' By coincidence, the map sheet number, based on St Lo, had been the one he had used for an exercise at Staff College. 'I took the receipt away and burned it. So we were not to land in the Pas-de-Calais, but in Normandy' – Macleod's destination was to be about thirty miles to the west of Deauville, his old bridge-playing haunt.[36]

During the spring, the Division moved to the South Coast, where they teamed up with 'Naval Force G' at Weymouth and 'rehearsed endlessly' at Studland Bay, along the Dorset coast. 'And in due course in the last two days of May a tide of men and machines began to roll towards Southampton.' As he later revealed in his often irreverent weekly column in the *Spectator*, the combination of the Derby and the D-Day commemorations had again reminded him of a 'sad venture', born of his inventiveness and passion for racing. 'Partly to fill in the time of waiting for the assault,' he recalled,

> I made a book at 50 Division Headquarters on the 1944 Derby. Very few of my colleagues knew one end of a racehorse from the other. So – poor simple souls – they backed on the old woman's system of name association.

And all with one accord settled on the same two horses. Ocean Swell won at 18–1 and Happy Landing was third at 33–1.[37]

By 1 June, 50 Div. were afloat. 'No more telephones, and very little to do. If we hadn't thought of everything already, it was too late.' D-Day had been scheduled for 5 June, but bad weather caused a twenty-four-hour postponement. 'Even so, the weather was cold and the sea was rough.' Nonetheless, General Eisenhower 'took the greatest gamble in all military history', and the Allied armada was launched. 50 Div.'s HQ was split between two ships and Macleod found himself with men of the 1st Hampshires of 231 Brigade. 'Perhaps I was helped by my early voyages on the Minch, but I slept soundly enough through the rough night and came on deck somewhere around first light.' The waves were still choppy. The landing was clearly going to be 'a hazardous and in part a haphazard affair'. But the day was warming up, and the coast of Normandy emerged from the haze.

And then as full light began to come one saw the ships and the planes. It was a sight so paralysing that tears came to my eyes. It was as if every ship that had ever been launched was there, and even as if the sea had yielded up her wrecks. It was as if every plane that had ever been built was there, and, so it seemed in fantasy, as if the dead crews were there too. There has never been since time began such a rendezvous for fighting men: there never will be again. And I remember reciting, not in scorn, but out of sheer delight at being part of the great company in such a place, 'And gentlemen in England now abed . . .'[38]

The naval guns began to blaze out the German shore defences, while their return fire did little damage. Overhead, came the endless fire from the planes and the whine of their bombs. As the sound of war reached a crescendo, 'so came H-hour'. 50 Div.'s assault boats headed for the beaches. 'The infantry were magnificent,' Macleod wrote in a letter home. 'They went up the beaches under fire as if they were doing an exercise on Ilkley moor. Due to their speed and determination, the casualties were light.' The Hampshires' task of securing the key coastal villages, including Arromanches, which was earmarked as the site of the artificial port, known as Mulberry, ensured for them 'a day of heavy fighting and severe casualties'. As Macleod later recalled, while watching the landing assault craft (LCAs) carry the Hampshires ashore and waiting for his own turn,

I thought that as a martial gesture I would load my revolver. When I unbuttoned my ammunition pouch, I found that my batman, who knew more about war than I did, had filled it not with bullets but with boiled sweets. He was quite right. They proved much more useful.

Few things went exactly to plan, the biggest disappointment being the failure of the secret waterproofed tanks to negotiate the heavy seas. Instead of paddling the last few miles to the beach and providing covering fire for the assault troops, the craft had to be taken ashore before the tanks were disembarked. The neighbouring American assault force risked their tanks in the heavy swell, but all sixty-four that were launched were swamped, nearly all their crews drowned and the cover-fire was lost.

'H plus forty' soon came. Macleod and his colleague during the landing, Lieutenant Colonel 'Bertie' Gibb, then ADOS in charge of the Ordnance Supplies, 'climbed with elderly dignity down the scrambling nets that were slung over the ship's side and dropped down into our LCA'. As they began to cruise towards the beach, something went wrong. For some reason – possibly the congestion of craft near the beach, perhaps the obstruction of underwater mines – the naval officer in charge of the craft began circling about a hundred yards from shore for what seemed a long time. Macleod began to doze under the hot sun. Suddenly, they stopped turning and ran straight for the beach. The landing ramp 'smacked down', and Macleod and Bertie stepped into the thigh-deep water and waded carefully ashore.

The beach was alive with the shambles and disorder of war.

There were dead men and wounded men and men brewing tea. There were men reorganizing for a battle advance, and men doing absolutely nothing. There were even some German prisoners waiting patiently for heaven knows what. There was a whole graveyard of wrecked ships and craft and tanks of every size. It was like an absurdly magnificent film by Cecil B. De Mille. It was like war.

Macleod and Gibb wandered over the beaches and climbed the dunes behind them. They found that the German minefields 'were most carefully marked (*Achtung Minen*) and wired', and took a sandtrack between villages, without realizing that they were still German-held. They made their way to the orchard at Meuvaines, about a mile and a half inland, which was to be their D-Day headquarters. 'Only a motley collection of vehicles had arrived but one of them was the intelligence truck and in it a staff officer was busy marking up the reports of the progress of the leading battalions.' The rest of Macleod's day was 'a patchwork of memories'. He recalled 'a flurry of shots into the orchard from a small nest of Germans we had overlooked. There was a journey back to the beaches to see the build-up. There was a journey on the back of a policeman's motor cycle to find the forward brigades.' He could not remember when he ate, but remembered what he ate. Although he had been issued with twenty-four-hour packs of concentrated dried food, '50 Div. were used to looking after themselves. From somewhere my batman produced both the great delicacies of 1944 – tinned steak pudding and tinned Christmas pudding. These and whisky were my food.'

By nightfall, nearly all their objectives had been taken.

Patrols were moving into Bayeux, which was to fall next morning. The St Léger feature was in our grasp. The 47th Royal Marine Commando (under our command for the landing) had started its successful battle for Port-en-Bessin. Hideous close fighting in the Bocage lay ahead, but at least on the 50 Div. front the day had gone well.

Macleod was about to snatch some sleep in a barn, where his batman had secured him a corner, when Tom Black, whom he had succeeded as 50 Div. DAQMG, came looking for him. Together they went outside, and, standing under the trees, sipped whisky from Black's flask and looked back towards the sea:

A few fast German fighter planes were making a tip-and-run raid on the beach, and the red tracer bullets climbed lazily into the sky after them. I looked at my watch. It was exactly midnight. I had lived through D-Day. We had expected anything up to 40 per cent casualties in the landing, and somehow I had been convinced that I would be killed. Now, equally unreasonably, I became convinced that I would live through the war. I would see our second child, who was to be born in October. There would be a life after the war. D-Day was over.[39]

As an officer at divisional headquarters, Macleod's life was much more comfortable and incomparably safer than if he had been in the front line. As DAQMG, he had a jeep, a Humber car and a caravan fully equipped as an office. His clerks were accommodated in a neighbouring lorry and the officers' mess was housed in another lorry in the adjoining field. Even battle periods generally proved less arduous than he had been taught to expect at the Staff College. Between battles he had time to play poker dice and, like other Allied officers, was fêted whenever he visited nearby French towns. It was while he was still in Normandy that he first expressed his plan to go into politics after the War. He was in no doubt about his politics, and drafted a letter with Bertie Gibb applying to have his name added to the Conservative candidates' list. He mentioned the idea again during the autumn advance into Holland, when his companion was Major William Urton, who, unknown to Macleod, happened to be a Conservative Party agent – Urton was later to become General Director of Conservative Central Office and was to fail signally to impress Macleod when the latter served as Party Chairman. Their wartime conversation was interrupted by a German plane dropping anti-personnel bombs, forcing them to dive into a slit trench. When they re-emerged, Urton asked what would be Macleod's aim. 'To be Prime Minister,' was Macleod's candid reply.[40]

In November 1944, 50. Div. were withdrawn from the Continent and

Macleod returned to his native Yorkshire. The previous twelve months had seen him progress from the Staff College to D-Day and were to prove the pivotal period in his life. Eight years earlier, he had lived only for bridge and led a playboy's existence, without an idea in his head about the future. Eight years later, he was a Minister of the Crown in Churchill's Government, running an important department of state and with his sights set on the highest office.

3

Political Apprentice

We must have SOCIAL SECURITY for all on the lines of the Beveridge
Report.
Extract from the election address of Major Iain Macleod, National
Government parliamentary candidate for the Western Isles, June
1945.

Blooded

The War had given Macleod ambition and defined his purpose in life. His
new-found commitment to politics flowed from his having realized his true
ability for the first time at the age of thirty. 'Fame is the spur,' Macleod
used to tell his close friend Reggie Maudling, when they began working
together as Conservative backroom boys after the War. His ambition should
never be underestimated, but he was too much of a romantic to have entered
politics merely as a careerist. Despite his self-confidence, privately he
doubted whether he would make it to the very top. 'He was overtly a
Highlander,' Enoch Powell, another colleague from those postwar years,
recalls, 'and believed that he had the natural weakness of the Highlander.'
As Macleod once confessed to Powell, 'You know, in the end I should give
in. That's the Highlander's weakness.'[1]

Macleod's inspiration, like that of many of his contemporaries in the
Forces who were to enter politics and public service after the War, was the
sense of national unity and the powerful mood for radical reform that had
emerged during wartime Britain in reaction to the depression of the 1930s.
Churchill's wartime Coalition Government had given this mood official
endorsement in the 1942 Beveridge Report that presaged the new welfare
state; the 1944 White Paper that heralded the all-party commitment to full
employment; and Rab Butler's 1944 Education Act which ushered in greater
equality of opportunity. What made Macleod's commitment to this new
politics compelling was that they echoed and reinforced the values that he
had imbibed during his upbringing in Skipton.

The doctor's son knew at first hand of the plight of the poor between the wars. Macleod had seen his father caring for all sections of the community, his mother working tirelessly to help the unemployed and both parents playing an active part in establishing a new hospital in their home town in the early 1930s. He needed no convincing that, as William Beveridge had argued in his epoch–making report, five giants had to be slain on the road to recovery – disease, idleness, ignorance, squalor and want. But there was no question of Macleod's signing up for the Labour Party. His comfortable, country-town, middle-class background predisposed him towards the Tories and he was never an egalitarian nor an adherent of the view that, in the words of the Labour politician, Douglas Jay, 'the gentlemen in Whitehall really do know better what is good for the people than the people know themselves.' Instead, the public-spirited ethos and sense of national soli- darity generated during the War was to foster a new brand of reformist Toryism with which Macleod was to become closely identified. His oppor- tunity to enter politics came sooner than he expected, and he seized it with both hands.[2]

In October 1944, a month before Macleod returned from the Continent with 50 Div., Eve gave birth to their second child, Diana. The first Macleod heard of their daughter's birth was when he read about it ten days after the event in *The Times* in Nijmegen, but he was home in time for the christening in Worcestershire. Macleod was stationed in Britain for the remainder of the War in Europe. During late May 1945, a fortnight after VE Day, he was enjoying a spell of leave with Eve and their children at Scaliscro, when the general election was announced – the first for a decade. It was too good an opportunity for Macleod to miss, and he was in an ideal location to 'blood' himself in national politics. The Western Isles were a political graveyard for the Conservatives and there was no local Conservative organization, let alone a Tory candidate. Macleod and his father, who was a lifelong Liberal, but admired Churchill and thought that his fellow islanders should at least have a chance to express their support for the wartime leader, immediately set to work. Dr Macleod called an inaugural meeting of the Conservative Associ- ation in the Western Isles in order to nominate a candidate for the forth- coming election. Since only he and Iain attended the meeting, they elected Dr Macleod as chairman and Iain as candidate. They informed Conservative Central Office of their *fait accompli*, and Dr Macleod sent a telegram to Churchill telling him of Iain's selection. The Prime Minister's endorsement and good wishes arrived by return of post.[3]

'I offer myself to you as National Government candidate for the Western Isles,' Major Iain Macleod declared in an election address that was astutely pitched for his Hebridean audience. 'My home is in the Isles,' he continued, 'where my family on both sides have lived for many generations.' His address was given as 'Scaliscro, Uig, Isle of Lewis', with no mention that it was the family's holiday home. 'I am a man of the Isles,' he proclaimed and his profile attested to his parents' origins on Lewis, while making no reference to his Skipton birth or Airedale childhood. Although Macleod was presenting a selective picture to the electors, it was not misleading in essence. He was, at heart, 'a man of the Isles'.[4]

Playing the patriotic card and laying claim to the loyalty vote for Churchill were much safer bets than campaigning as a Conservative, or Unionist, in the Outer Hebrides. 'A Vote for MACLEOD is a Vote for CHURCHILL' was his campaign slogan. He was not afraid to emulate the great war-leader's scaremongering about Labour. 'The people of the islands are individuals not robots,' he protested. 'Most have their own croft, or loom, or boat; often all three. Under the Socialist threat of nationalization these things will go.' And in an echo of Churchill's notorious broadcast of 4 June, in which the Prime Minister had argued that no socialist system could be established without a political police and having 'to fall back on some form of Gestapo', Macleod stated, 'We must remain individuals and not submit to the dictation of the State. Socialism leads to FACISM [sic].'[5]

Even more striking than Macleod's presentational skill was his whole-hearted endorsement of the wartime plans for a new welfare state. In his ten point election programme, Macleod unequivocally declared, 'We must have SOCIAL SECURITY for all on the lines of the Beveridge Report.' Similarly, 'the problems of housing and re-construction' had to be solved 'urgently', and 'in resettlement the men of the Armed Forces and the Merchant Navy MUST have priority'. Macleod was sensitive to the islanders' special contribution, both in the services and the merchant marine. At the local level, he pledged to 'provide in the Islands homes and work and freedom from want for all', proposing an ambitious, interventionist programme including modernization of the fishing fleet and facilities and 'protection for the Harris Tweed, small businessmen and crofters'. He left unsaid the catch-phrase of the era, 'never again', but it permeated his programme at local and national level. 'This time', he declared, 'the pledges given to the fighting men, which includes, of course, the men of the Merchant Navy to whom the nation owes its life, must be redeemed in full.'[6]

Although Macleod was fighting a lost cause in a constituency of thinly populated islands stretching across 150 miles of stormy seas, it was still the age of the public meeting and his campaign was enlivened by a group of young hecklers who followed him from one venue to another. Such was the rapport that developed between the candidate and his vociferous companions, that when he discovered them stranded by their broken-down car on the way to his last country meeting, he stopped and gave them a lift. However, they were disarmed by his gesture and Macleod received an unusually quiet hearing. When the services' votes were finally counted and the result declared at the end of July, Macleod had, as expected, come bottom of the poll. Labour's Malcolm Macmillan had beaten the Liberal by 1,600 votes in a poll of only 13,000. Macleod at least had the satisfaction that his vote of 2,756 was the highest Conservative vote in a three-cornered contest in the constituency. As his friend Fisher recounts, Macleod used to say that only his cousins voted for him, 'but I've got a lot of cousins in the Western Isles'. Far more important than the result, Macleod had enjoyed his first experience of the hustings and when, the following year, he first met David Clarke, who was then running the Conservative Parliamentary Secretariat, he only 'lit up' when recounting his campaign.[7]

Yet by the time that he fought his next general election campaign, many hundreds of miles further south, the Macleods' home at Scaliscro and its surrounding estate had been sold, breaking the direct link with Lewis that the family had enjoyed since the mid-1920s. Dr Macleod and Lab had intended to retire to Scaliscro, but found that advancing age made that impractical. Only eighteen months after the 1945 election, Iain's father suffered a stroke following a prostate operation in a Bradford nursing home and died, aged 67, on 24 January 1947, the day that severe cold weather hit Britain and the great two-month freeze began. Dr Macleod was buried at Gargrave, the village in Airedale, several miles upstream from the former family home and his surgery at Clifford House, and where his eldest daughter, Rhodabel and her husband, Thomas Garnett, lived. After Dr Macleod's death, Scaliscro was sold for around £7,500 to provide for Lab, who moved to London, where Iain and his young family were living. Her youngest son, Rhoderick, now in his late twenties, had settled in Kenya after the War, and Torquil, her second son, was soon to emigrate to Canada. Lab bought a house in Putney, at Number 4, The Embankment, where she was to live until November 1968, and which Iain used to refer to as 'bush telegraph, main transmitter, Putney', since the family used to phone Lab on a Sunday and she, in turn, delighted in passing on all their gossip.[8]

After the excitement of the 1945 election campaign, Macleod had to return to his duties as DAQMG of 50 Div., but he now knew for certain that when he was demobilized no other career except politics would satisfy him. 50 Div. were stationed near York, but in August 1945, Divisional Headquarters were posted to Norway. 'So far I haven't been present, or even in the same country,' he wrote from Oslo to Diana, his daughter, on her first birthday, 'for either of the 8th Octobers that you have seen.' But at least the NAAFI 'On Active Service Letter Form' carried his promise to be there next year. In the meantime, he urged her, 'I should insist – and yell if you don't get it – on an extra ration of milk and orange juice and jam.'[9]

In Oslo, Macleod lived at the Royal Norwegian Automobile Club and was in charge of supplies, including Vinmonopolet, the organization that handled the country's wines and spirits. Most of Vinmonopolet's vast store, amounting to millions of bottles, had been looted by the Germans from France. 'All I did was to sign the chits and fix the prices,' he later recalled modestly. 'One shilling for red and white wines, three bob for a bottle of champagne, many of excellent vintage, five bob for the most admirable brandy and the top price of 7s 6d. for Cointreau and Benedictine, because I only had a few thousand bottles of them.' As he was to reflect, somewhat ruefully, 'Of course the news got round, but the prices held firm and the supplies lasted. Someone (I suppose it was NAAFI) made an awful lot of money. I didn't.' Only a fortnight before Macleod published this story in the *Spectator* in August 1965, Edward Heath, the newly elected Tory leader, had appointed him shadow chancellor. Few other future Chancellors have been able to point to such practical success at matching supply and demand, managing a market and showing a profit.[10]

Before leaving the army, Macleod also had an opportunity to demonstrate his skill of advocacy for a seemingly lost cause when he appeared, around Christmas 1945, 'for the last time as a defending officer in a court martial'. He had, he later recalled, 'something of a reputation as a barrack room lawyer', which would not have surprised 'Ikey' Newman, his old history teacher at Fettes, but which Macleod attributed to his having been 'the only person around who had read the Manual of Military Law'. His last case also happened to be the first occasion where he had to defend an officer who had been accused 'under the splendidly Kiplingesque section which relates to "conduct unbecoming an officer and a gentleman".' In this instance, his client, 'a colonel in a distinguished corps in the British army', whom Macleod referred to by the fictitious name of 'Colonel Jones', had kidnapped an infant. However, this bare statement concealed a farcical and incredible chain of events. 'Brooding over the case,' Macleod saw only one possible chance: 'Perhaps the powers that be had charged him under the wrong section.' Nonetheless, Macleod assumed that the Colonel would be found guilty. So certain was he of defeat that the announcement of Colonel Jones's acquittal failed to register, and he began to deliver a 'passionate plea for mercy', before being stopped after a few sentences. 'As they say in Parliament,' Macleod continued,

> I resumed my seat. And so my second and even better speech was never delivered. This is a calamity which I have become accustomed to in later years, but it was stark tragedy at the time – except, of course, for Colonel Jones.

The court congratulated Macleod warmly. The prosecuting barrister forecast a successful career for Macleod at the Bar and inquired whether he could buy champagne at reduced prices – he was asking the right man in Oslo. Colonel Jones kept wringing Macleod's hand and asking him if he would accept as a token of his esteem an engraved silver cigarette case. But having assured the Colonel that he would, Macleod later 'had some qualms as to whether this was or was not in order. I need not have worried. I never saw Colonel Jones again, and I am still waiting for the cigarette case.'[11]

At the centre of the Tory web

Divisional Headquarters returned to Britain in time for the New Year, and in January 1946 Macleod was demobilized after more than six years in the army. He lost no time in pursuing his political career. Rhodabel, his elder sister, intervened on his behalf asking her friend, Eleanor Yorke, to put in a word for Iain with her brother, Ralph Assheton (later Lord Clitheroe), who was at the time Chairman of the Conservative Party Organization. It was a timely move, since Assheton was the driving force behind the party's new Parliamentary Secretariat, that had been set up in the aftermath of the Conservatives' 1945 election rout and was designed to restore the effectiveness of a much-reduced parliamentary party and of the Tory front bench. Assheton had found the money to launch the Secretariat and persuaded David Clarke, who had been appointed Director of the Conservative Research Department, to set it up. The Secretariat was initially accommodated at 24 Wilton Street, a private house near Buckingham Palace, discovered by Mrs Assheton. The ground-floor drawing room was used for meetings and the smaller, upstairs rooms served as offices. By the end of 1945, three officers, including Reggie Maudling whom Assheton had recruited, were having to service twenty-three parliamentary party committees. In early 1946 Clarke interviewed Macleod following the latter's contact with Assheton. It was a fairly formal meeting, largely because the two men did not have many interests in common, although it was more conversational and relaxed than the interview of another recruit, Enoch Powell.[12]

Neither Macleod's academic record nor his brief, undistinguished career at De La Rue before the War indicated that he might be a high-flyer, but Clarke was definite in his own mind after meeting him that he wanted Macleod on the staff. A myth has since developed that Macleod faced very little competition and that virtually anybody who was at all suitable was appointed to the Secretariat. However, Clarke was highly selective. Indeed, he had to minute Assheton to seek the Chairman's approval for an increase in the Secretariat's establishment in order to offer Macleod a post. One of Macleod's strong attractions was his Scottishness, since Clarke felt under an obligation to find a Scot to service the Scottish Unionist Committee. The Secretariat, who were already overworked, sometimes had to try to master a Scottish subject and prepare a brief on it for a Commons debate with only forty-eight hours' notice. Clarke was therefore immensely relieved to recruit a suitable Scotsman. The Scottish Committee had been passed, among a rag-bag of subjects that included Defence, India and Housing and Local Government, to Enoch Powell, an Englishman of Welsh extraction who had joined the Secretariat only a matter of weeks before Macleod. Powell could not wait to pass it on. When Macleod arrived in the spring of 1946, Powell greeted him before reaching for the Scottish Committee papers to hand them over, only to discover that Macleod had already helped himself. It marked the beginning of a relationship between the two men that was to last for nearly a quarter of a century, mingling comradeship with rivalry. Almost 20 years later, Macleod was to reflect in a profile of Powell that, during their careers, their 'paths have run together, diverged and come together again'. But by the end of Macleod's life, he and Powell were almost totally estranged.[13]

Major Macleod and Brigadier Powell, as they were initially known in the Secretariat, along with Mr Maudling, the former RAF Intelligence officer and private secretary to the Air Minister, were intent on entering the Commons. Maudling, like Macleod, had stood unsuccessfully in the 1945 election (at Heston and Isleworth), whereas Powell had yet to contest a seat. Although the three men were colleagues and became friends, their contemporaries sensed always a competitive edge to their relations with one another: all three were conscious that they were gifted and that they were aiming for the top prizes. Macleod was much closer socially and politically with Maudling than with Powell. Maudling's easygoing nature and love of the good life – by the age of thirty he had already developed a Churchillian penchant for large cigars – disguised an acute intelligence, sharp political brain and pragmatic approach to economic policy. This combination of qualities appealed to Macleod. The two men often lunched together at Crockford's, sometimes not returning to the Secretariat until late in the afternoon. They also used to meet in the evenings, when they would sit up till all hours gossiping and talking over their ideas. 'We talked, and argued, and thought, and discussed about politics day after day,' Maudling remembered thirty years later, 'but we were never, I believe, solemn, because we realized that you do not have to be solemn in order to be serious.'[14]

However, Macleod was a shrewd judge of character, and their friendship did not blind him to Maudling's frailties. On one occasion, Maudling had been deputed by Macleod and others who were disgruntled at their low salaries and heavy workload, to put their case for a pay rise to Clarke. As they plotted the best tactics, Macleod sensed the risk of Maudling's being bought off by an increase for himself but not for anybody else, and concluded their discussion by remarking sharply to Maudling, 'So you won't just say "gimme".' The Macleods and Maudlings also lived relatively close in north London – Enfield and Barnet, respectively – and Macleod happily became godfather to one of the Maudlings' sons. He took a broad view of his duties. 'Here is a quid for you,' he once said to his godson over lunch, 'and here is another quid if you undertake to put it on the favourite in the 3.30 tomorrow at Newmarket.'[15]

Although there was never the same degree of closeness in Macleod's relations with Powell, they became friends in addition to being colleagues in the office. Powell had preceded Macleod at the Secretariat by only a few weeks, but as Macleod later recalled, he 'was already something of a legend. He used to travel from Earls Court on a workman's ticket at some unearthly hour of the morning and in full hunting pink, to revel in a day's hunting.' It is as difficult to imagine Macleod doing likewise as it is to imagine Powell gambling. Also, Macleod had no taste for Powell's asceticism, as evidenced by his seemingly lonely bachelor existence in his small Earls Court flat and the long hours he worked in the Secretariat until he had mastered the first principles and every detail of whatever subject came his way. Powell occasionally stayed overnight at the Macleods' Enfield home when the two men were attending a political engagement together, or Powell was speaking in the vicinity. Macleod later told Patrick Cosgrave, the journalist and biographer of Powell, of his astonishment when he first heard the news – after both he and Powell had become MPs – that Powell had become engaged to a former Research Department secretary. 'They tell me Enoch's getting married,' Macleod commented to Eve, 'I can hardly believe it.'[16]

Yet the two men had one interest in common other than politics – their love of poetry. Powell regards Macleod as having been 'a good judge of the genuineness of poetry', and was grateful to him for having read and given his critical opinion of his book of poems, *Dancer's End and the Wedding Gift*, that Powell published in 1951. Nonetheless, it was politics and the varying progress of their careers that determined the fluctuating state of their relationship down the years. From the outset, Powell was indebted to Macleod. Whereas Macleod was in the fortunate position of having been selected as a candidate within a few months of his joining the Secretariat, Powell had to embark upon what was to become a lengthy search for a seat. In all, Powell received nineteen rejections and fought a hopeless seat in a by-election before he was finally adopted in Wolverhampton at the end of 1948. During this frustrating period he was grateful for Macleod's encouragement. Macleod 'was very anxious' that Powell should use the same skills that he (Macleod) had used in obtaining selection as a candidate. 'When I was going to be interviewed for a constituency,' Powell recalls, 'he used to take me through the questions likely to be put to me and to brief me on the manner in which to handle them.' Powell remembers Macleod's assistance 'particularly kindly', but in a revealing insight into Macleod's approach, adds that he (Macleod) 'was always a gamesman'. In Powell's view, 'He was playing a game and playing it to win. He wished me to play the game and play it in order to win.'[17]

The political ambitions shared by Macleod, Maudling and Powell differentiated them from the staff being recruited to the newly revived Conservative Research Department, which initially sought to pursue its pre-war practice of appointing people who had no plans to become candidates. In May 1946, soon after recruiting Powell and Macleod to the Secretariat, Clarke returned to his work in the Research Department, now restored to its pre-war home, 24 Old Queen Street. During the War, Conservative Central Office had occupied the premises, but the party organization had now moved to Abbey House in nearby Victoria Street. Old Queen Street was a stone's throw from the Palace of Westminster and by the autumn of 1946 Macleod and his colleagues in the Secretariat had left Wilton Street, which was inconveniently distant from parliament, and moved in with the Research Department which also rented a substantial part of 34 Old Queen Street.[18]

Macleod was instantly in his element at the Secretariat, and always imagined that others were as keen as he was to enter politics. He never understood how Clarke could be sufficiently interested in politics to work for the party, yet have no ambition to enter the Commons. Their different outlook on life prompted good–natured banter between the two men in the office, with Macleod teasing Clarke and the latter retaliating by extolling the pleasures of having a life away from politics and being able to grow chrysanthemums and such like. As Clarke realized, Macleod hated the idea of gardening and would be provoked into an even greater show of incredulity. Macleod had no greater success with Michael Fraser whom he had known since Fettes. Shortly after joining the Secretariat, he wrote to Fraser telling him that he was now near the centre of the Conservative web and urging Fraser to become Unionist candidate for one of the seats in Aberdeen, a city that Fraser knew well. Although the two men had seen one another from time to time during the War in the bar of the old Carlton Hotel or in Scott's, Fraser failed to recognize the handwriting and had no idea that Macleod had embarked on a political career. The christian name signature on the note was indistinct and Fraser assumed that it must be from Ian Harvey, another Fettesian who wanted to become an MP. But Harvey told him that he had not written and that the note must have come from Macleod. Fraser had been enjoying a holiday with his wife in Scotland after his recent demobilization, but in May 1946, after his return to London, lunched with Macleod at the Carlton Grill. To Fraser's surprise, he found that Macleod had become intensely political and was enthusiastic about the fascination of being on the inside of Tory politics. Macleod gave much the same impression when he visited the Frasers' London flat: so persuasive was he that Fraser abandoned his planned career in corporate management in favour of the Tory backroom. But, like Clarke, he had no desire to become an MP, and instead joined the Research Department.[19]

Clarke's early departure from the Secretariat was a disappointment to Macleod and the other officers whom Clarke had recruited. Although the new head, Henry Hopkinson (later Lord Colyton), had served as Clarke's deputy and – unlike Clarke – had political aspirations in common with his new charges, there was little meeting of minds. Macleod, in particular, was unimpressed by his new boss. Hopkinson was from a different generation and background to the new breed of ambitious Conservatives. Whereas they were in their late twenties to early thirties and were from middle-class (in Powell's case, lower middle-class) families with little wealth, Hopkinson was already in his mid-forties, had served in the Foreign Office for 20 years and, as an old Etonian of great wealth (he had married into the American Eno's fruit salts family), was more in the mould of pre-war Tory politicians. Macleod was never to feel at one with the scions of the English Establishment. Hopkinson's greatest contribution to the Secretariat was probably to introduce a new filing system in the style of the Cabinet Office. He was later to become a minister, but failed utterly to master the House of Commons.[20]

However, Macleod was too engrossed in his new career in politics to let his lack of rapport with Hopkinson get him down. He was enthralled, learning the ropes of parliamentary business and delighting in a milieu where his closest colleagues, Maudling and Powell, shared his political ambitions. He was an avid reader of political biographies, not least the very substantial Victorian ones. The tasks of compiling briefs, advising Churchill and his shadow cabinet and helping them with their speeches, and attending the round of weekly backbench committee meetings, rarely troubled Macleod, although he was thrown in at the deep end. In addition to servicing the Scottish Committee and briefing on Scottish business in the Commons – a tricky business because of the separate party organization in Scotland – he was soon briefing the Tory Opposition on the National Health Service Bill, one of the most important postwar reforms which was being piloted through parliament during the summer and autumn of 1946.[21]

Macleod's enthusiasm is clear from the letter he wrote to his parents at the end of October 1946:

> The Health Bill in the Lords was a great triumph. Not so much the amendments we defeated them on – because the Commons will bounce two of those back again – but the points we got the Government to accept and bring forward as their own. I've had a nice 'bouquet' from the BMA on it. It's rather fun working with the Peers: there is much less politics and consequently much more consideration given to the interests of the patients and doctors.

The NHS was the proud creation of the then Minister for Health, Aneurin Bevan, and Macleod's early apprenticeship was to stand him in good stead when, almost six years later, he was no longer briefing Conservative spokesmen and MPs on their line on the NHS, but was able to confront Bevan directly in the House of Commons.[22]

By the summer of 1947, Macleod was handling, in addition to Scottish affairs and health, labour, the social services, Home Office issues, welfare and local government, while his assistant, Miss Rose, was helping with insurance and pensions. When the new system of social security and the NHS were set up, he had to cope with a flood of queries from Conservative MPs seeking guidance to the mass of new regulations as they struggled to deal with constituents' problems. Moreover, trying to keep abreast of

Scottish politics and liaise with the party in Scotland created special difficulties. This became apparent during the passage of the Scottish Legal Aid Bill in December 1948, when Macleod admitted to the Scottish Unionist MP, Lieutenant Commander Clark-Hutchison, that he had not known and had 'no means of knowing that there was any agitation in Scotland against this Bill'. His only source of information was the *Scotsman*, which he received a day late, and he was not able, as was the case with an English bill, 'to go and see the societies concerned'. But the prospect of a desk officer from London appearing to tread on the corns of the Scottish party led Clark-Hutchison to advise Macleod to drop his plans for an early visit to Edinburgh, with dark warnings of 'trouble brewing behind the scenes' and the need for the 'utmost care' to be taken in collecting information.[23]

There was never any question of Macleod suffering fools gladly: they were not to be suffered, period. It was a trait that was to deny him an equable life, especially in Conservative politics. In the Secretariat, he could be very short with anybody whom he found slow or who inadvertently disrupted his concentration as he ordered his thoughts before drafting a brief or memorandum. His method of working was idiosyncratic, but extremely efficient. He used to turn off his telephone and sit quietly, sometimes leaning back in his chair with his feet on his desk, looking into the distance as though he might be day-dreaming. In fact, he was focusing his mind completely on the subject in question until he was clear precisely what he wanted to say. Only then would he summon a secretary and dictate his entire composition in one sitting. He might subsequently make a few minor corrections, but never needed to change much of substance. His impatience with people was to become more pronounced in later years as the ankylosing spondylitis that afflicted his spine ran its course and the pain grew more intense and persistent. During his thirties, although he was already feeling some back pain, he appeared to have only a slight limp, caused by his war injury, and was marginally less supple than his contemporaries.[24]

Macleod's reputation as a young high-flyer began to spread beyond Old Queen Street. As early as October 1946, he was proudly telling his parents that 'My speaking engagements now get reported in *The Times*, which is progress.' And, he added, much to his amusement:

Three or four days ago the column 'today's arrangements' had:
    Mr Anthony Eden at Plymouth Town Hall, 8 pm
    Major Iain Macleod, Church Hall, Cockfosters, 8 pm
    Mr Harold Macmillan etc
    Mr Richard Law etc
    Etc.
I like the order!! Anyway I was not only the non MP mentioned but the only non ex-Cabinet Minister.

However, he had not yet developed his extraordinary talent as a speaker and could appear diffident when addressing an audience, although he had a certain presence about him. Robert Carr, who later was to become a close friend and political ally of Macleod's, first saw him when he addressed one of the regular candidates' meetings – in addition to hearing speeches by Churchill, Butler, Eden, Macmillan and other frontbenchers, the candidates' association sometimes used to invite officers from the Research Department and Secretariat to give talks. The curious feature about Macleod's speech is that although Carr was disappointed at his somewhat stilted performance, he recalls that Macleod nonetheless left a lasting impression – more than forty years later, Carr could still recall the occasion vividly in his mind's eye. 'There was something about Iain even when he didn't impress you,' Carr remembers, 'that nevertheless left a mark . . . You were aware that you had been listening to someone out of the ordinary.'[25]

The War had brought Macleod rank and responsibility and, like other desk officers of his time, he dealt with MPs in a way that later generations of desk officers, many of whom entered the Research Department almost straight from university, never dared. On one occasion, he delivered a crushing response to a request for advice from the backbencher, F.W. Harris, who had forwarded a constituent's bizarre list of suggested topics for questioning Ministers. The list included the alleged problems of employees taking their bosses' money to bet on horses, and 'the gangsters who for the most part occupy Soho'. Replying on 27 October 1948, Macleod told Harris that 'the questions you forwarded to me are all ridiculous ones and I am certain nothing can be based on them. I suspect that your constituent is a little touched.' Nonetheless, Macleod accepted his role as a servant of the parliamentary party. In a note of 22 April 1948 to Sir Anthony Eden, drafted after the Commons had backed Sydney Silverman's call for a trial five-year suspension of capital punishment, he not only put to one side his personal detestation of capital punishment but also argued against ministers being allowed a free vote on the issue. Yet during his own parliamentary career, Macleod was to be one of the first to defend the right to a free vote on the death penalty and to welcome the repetition of 'this sorry precedent'.[26]

Despite his onerous range of responsibilities in the Secretariat, Macleod was too quick a worker to have to put in long hours. He used to arrive late and leave early – a pattern that he was to impose on office work for the rest of his career. His extraordinarily speedy dispatch of paperwork and his ability to compartmentalize his life enabled him, until the early 1950s, when he became a minister, to continue indulging his passion for cards. How much Macleod made or lost on his gambling can never be known, but his exceptional memory put him at an advantage over most other players. Maudling used to be astonished at Macleod's ability in the bar at Crockford's before lunch to remember all four hands dealt during a game of bridge three weeks earlier and the sequence of play that followed. From all accounts he seems to have been in pocket more often than he was out, and on balance his pastime probably benefited the Macleods financially, especially when he developed a lucrative sideline writing about bridge. As a desk officer in the Secretariat, he received only around £700 – a small salary on which to raise a young family. But during his political apprenticeship he was also paid £500 a year by the *Sunday Times* for a weekly column on bridge that he reckoned took him half an hour to write at weekends – he also set and judged the paper's bridge competitions.[27]

Conservative Research Department

From November 1948, the merger of the Secretariat with the Research Department and the party's information service to form an enlarged Conservative Research Department made matters easier for Macleod. He was promoted joint head, with Powell, of the Home Affairs Section, sharing a first floor room in the Research Department annexe at 34 Old Queen Street. Maudling became head of the Economics Section. Macleod's salary had increased to £1,250, and from the middle of 1949, when Powell began working on a part-time basis following his selection as a candidate in Wolverhampton, Macleod was sole head of section.[28]

Yet probably the greatest boon from the merger was that, by being taken under the wing of the Conservative Research Department, he was brought into closer, more frequent contact with its chairman, Rab Butler. Macleod was soon to become Butler's protégé and would maintain much stronger links with the Research Department after he had become an MP than either Maudling or Powell, playing a key role in party policy-making during the 1950s. Despite his not having been involved initially in the postwar policy work of the Research Department, Macleod was a strong supporter of the new, enlightened economic and social Toryism for which Butler was fighting, against both Churchill's indifference and the diehard, *laissez-faire* opponents of Government intervention and the welfare state. The *Industrial Charter*, which was the product of the Industrial Policy Committee and was approved at the 1947 party conference 'thanks to an amendment skilfully moved by Maudling' was in line with Macleod's thinking and the direction in which he wanted to see the party develop. Its originator, Butler, neatly summed up their common approach, when he later wrote in his memoirs that, 'The Charter was first and foremost an assurance that, in the interests of efficiency, full employment and social security, modern Conservatism would maintain strong central guidance over the operation of the economy.' Macleod was never to deviate from his mentor's definition of modern Toryism.[29]

Macleod's commitment to the basic tenets of the new welfare state is evident from memoranda he wrote on the NHS and social security. His concern was always that the party should not launch an unqualified attack on every action by a Labour Minister and every aspect of the new welfare state, since this would give the impression that despite their statements of support for the Beveridge Report, they were, to all intents and purposes, still wedded to the attitudes of the 1930s. In a draft speaking note, although Macleod attacked Bevan's failure to appreciate doctors' fears over their pay and status in the new NHS, he was prepared to recognize that 'on the question of the sale of practices within the public scheme, the Minister's case is probably stronger than that of the BMA'. Similarly, in June 1948, the month before NHS vesting day, Macleod advised Conservative Central Office against being associated 'in any way' with a pamphlet that was 'clearly designed to encourage people to stay out of the Health Service and remain as private patients'.[30]

Advising Butler three months later that he should say little about the social services at the October 1948 party conference, Macleod nonetheless provided a speaking note that epitomized the moderate Tory line. 'The 5th July this year,' read his draft, 'was the appointed day for the four great measures of social legislation which, together with the Family Allowances Act, implement the schemes initiated by the Coalition Government for social security.' This reminder to the party faithful that their leaders had been responsible for the new schemes was an astute counter to those Conservatives who opposed the welfare state. 'Schemes as vast as these,' continued Macleod's note, 'must have their "teething" troubles and I do not propose this afternoon to make any petty criticisms either of the schemes or their administration.' And although he suggested focusing on the level of spending on the welfare state – equivalent, if education was included, 'to the total of a pre-war Budget' – the moral that Macleod suggested should be drawn was 'not that the social services are too expensive but that only a prosperous country can afford schemes of such magnitude'. Reiterating in his final paragraph that, 'We do not, of course, want any cheese-paring in the National Health Service or in any of the social measures', Macleod urged the need to 'keep a close watch on expenditure so that the full value may be obtained for the vast sums we are expending.' The aim of running the welfare state more efficiently than Labour, and not undermining it, was to be the basis of Conservative policy for more than three decades.[31]

As the next election approached, Macleod became one of the most outspoken proponents of the need for a more positive approach on policy. The Conservatives' failure to win the Edmonton by-election helped concentrate his mind – by this stage, he was himself a candidate in a north London seat. When the Conservatives also failed to win in Hammersmith in February 1949, the demands from the party for a clear statement of policy became irresistible. During the spring and summer, Macleod was heavily involved in drafting the party's first comprehensive, postwar policy document, *The Right Road for Britain*. This added the social policies on which he had been working to the previously published Charters on agriculture and industry. This great declaration of moderate, consensus-style Toryism was launched to the accompaniment of a concerted series of speeches by leading frontbenchers in July 1949. Over the following months, Macleod also had a key role in preparing drafts for the election manifesto.[32]

During the autumn of 1949, however, he still despaired that the Conservatives were failing to get across their moderate message on the NHS. Following criticism at a meeting of the backbench 1922 Committee of the party's failure to identify savings in the NHS, Macleod wrote Clarke a long memorandum that he described as 'an expression of a political paradox'. By this, he meant 'that there is no single subject on which we have been so consistently right as on health, but equally there is no subject on which it is more believed that we have been consistently wrong'. It was galling for Macleod since he believed the proposals on health contained in *The Right Road for Britain* commanded 'fairly general agreement', as evidenced by Bevan's failure to attack them. Macleod attributed the party's failure to several causes – the impossibility of finding large savings in the NHS, although a very considerable amount of £15–20 million might be saved by charges on dental, optical and other services; poor leadership; poor propaganda; and, apart from isolated successes, 'some most unfortunate debating experiences in the House on health matters'. It was too late to set up a policy committee and in any case he doubted whether it would achieve anything useful. Instead, he proposed that two things should be 'urgently done'. First, 'one of our leaders should devote a major broadcast speech, either now or at the Election time, to the problems of health'. And secondly, 'there should be an authoritative document produced as late as possible before the Election, which should point out and prove how our attitude towards Bevan's scheme has been abundantly justified, and how his own rigid methods are crippling essential parts of the Service.'[33]

Within three months of his *cri-de-coeur* to Clarke, Macleod had abandoned the frustrations of the backroom and was launched on his national political career, campaigning during the February 1950 election as a Conservative candidate in a winnable seat. He was about to join one of the most impressive Tory intakes to the House of Commons in modern times and to find that a number of other new young Conservative MPs also despaired of their party's inadequate performance across the whole field of social policy that had now become central to success or failure in British politics.

4

'One Nation' Tory

> It is a major object of Conservative policy to defend the value of the Social Services.
>
> Election Address of Iain Macleod, Conservative candidate for Enfield West, February 1950.

Enfield – rites of passage

Even before Macleod was elected to the House of Commons, he was being talked of as a possible future Conservative leader. Introducing Macleod to the voters of Enfield West at the general election in February 1950, the Conservative constituency association chairman, County Councillor S. Graham Rowlandson, proudly declared that they were 'most fortunate' in their candidate, who 'was recently described in a national newspaper as one of three young Conservatives from whom the future leader of the Conservative party may be chosen'. It was an auspicious start to his campaign for a man who had set his sights on the highest office.[1]

Enfield West was a far cry from the constituency where he had cut his teeth as a candidate – the Western Isles – not only geographically, but in almost every respect. The old Middlesex town of Enfield had long since become a commuter suburb of London. But in addition to addressing meetings in north London suburbia, Macleod's campaign took him to quaint-sounding, village communities – Botany Bay, Bull's Cross, Hadley Wood, Maiden's Bridge, South Mimms and White Webbs – and also to Potters Bar, already an urban district. There were still more than a dozen farms in the constituency, and Crews Hill boasted a substantial trade in market-gardening. After the War, Trent Park no longer played host to the great and the good who had graced Sir Philip Sassoon's weekend parties. But the Parker-Bowles family, who owned Forty Hall, provided a squirearchical touch. There was fox-hunting on Enfield Chace, and point-to-point. Enfield West had all the trappings of a safe Conservative seat. But Macleod had only become the party's candidate by chance and through a curious set of circumstances.

It is not surprising, perhaps, that Macleod's first contact with Enfield came via the bridge table. Among the regulars at Crockford's was Dr Fraser Allen, who – as one of his wartime patients, the international bridge player, Rixi Markus, realized – was ambitious to succeed at bridge and wanted to partner a top player like Macleod in competitions. The two men teamed up at Harrogate in early 1946, shortly after Macleod had been interviewed by David Clarke at the Conservative Parliamentary Secretariat. During the competition, Macleod received Clarke's telegram offering him a job and after cabling his acceptance, mentioned to Allen that he would need to find a home in London. Allen, who at the time had a practice in Enfield, immediately invited him to stay until he could find somewhere and also happened to mention that the local Conservatives were looking for a new parliamentary candidate. Moreover, the chairman of the local constituency association, Douglas Waite, was a patient of his and Allen had his telephone number. That evening Macleod called Waite, told him that he was coming to live in Enfield and that since the Conservatives were looking for a candidate, they might like to add his name to their list. When Waite replied that they already had 47 names, Macleod retorted that a forty-eighth would not matter. Waite invited Macleod to see him as soon as he arrived in Enfield.[2]

Macleod was the only applicant whose name was not on the list of approved candidates provided by Conservative Central Office, but at Waite's suggestion he was added to those who were in the running for Enfield. By early May, the field of runners had been whittled down to a shortlist of four, ready for what was expected to be the final run-off before a selection meeting of the constituency Executive Committee. The chairman of Enfield's Young Conservatives, Christopher Reeves, who had attended the selection committee meetings, and his YC secretary, Colin Turner, were agreed that the YCs had to support Macleod. As a result, a 'three-line whip' was issued on the thirty-two-strong YC contingent on the Executive to turn out and vote for Macleod. Among the YCs who attended and were to vote for Macleod were Anne Thornton, who lived on The Ridgeway, an upmarket road of detached houses, and who was to become a neighbour of Macleod's; and Norman Tebbit, a fifteen-year-old branch officer from working-class Ponder's End, where Enfield's YCs were derided as 'The Ridgeway Social Club'.[3]

Nobody who attended the run-off between the four candidates on Wednesday 8 May could ever have imagined that one of the four aspiring candidates would go on to become the greatest Tory debater of modern times. Macleod gave a dismal performance. He had a distracting habit of putting his hands together in front of him, almost as though he were praying – the fingertips pressed together – and, as he spoke, moving them from side to side. His speaking voice was high-pitched, and he kept hitching up his trousers. Already quite bald, he was short and unprepossessing. Despite his utterly uninspiring display, the YCs' vote held firm and 31 voted for

Macleod. Only one YC rebelled, a girl from Ponder's End who resolutely refused to toe the line.[4]

Despite the YCs' support, Macleod only came second. However, he had managed to come within ten per cent of the votes cast for the top applicant, Eric Bullus. This was crucial, since the selection committee had agreed that if the winning applicant failed to secure a lead of this margin, a second run-off would be held before a general meeting of the constituency party. However, Waite had forgotten to tell the Executive Committee of this additional requirement and when he informed them, there was a storm of protest. Amidst allegations that the procedure had been rigged and demands that Macleod's name should not be considered further, representatives from two wards – in all, about forty people – walked out in protest. But Waite stood firm. The final contest, billed in the *Enfield Gazette* as 'D-Day in Enfield's Battle Against Socialism', was held at a packed annual meeting of the constituency association on Monday 3 June 1946 at Southbury Road School. Macleod gave a better speech and won easily – the unlucky Bullus later became MP for Wembley North.[5]

A further factor working in Macleod's favour was that nobody at the selection meeting had raised the question of seeking a financial contribution from the candidate. Before the War, a Conservative candidate might be expected to make a substantial donation to the constituency party – to all intents and purposes, enabling a well-off applicant to buy a seat. This practice was to be curtailed later in the 1940s when a reasonable limit was put on the size of candidates' contributions by Lord Woolton during his chairmanship of the party organization. Woolton's action was to open the Conservative Party's doors to candidates who lacked any great wealth. But Macleod had been formally adopted before this rule change was made, and if Enfield Conservatives had sought a substantial contribution from their candidate, as they might well have done, Macleod would probably have been ruled out.[6]

On the face of it, Enfield was not much of a prize for an aspiring Conservative politician. Labour had won the seat the previous July with a majority of more than 12,000 votes, and there seemed little prospect of the Tories capturing Enfield next time. However, the postwar election was fought on the old pre-war parliamentary boundaries. These were to be redrawn. It did not need a political genius to calculate that extra seats would be created where the population had grown most and that this would entail a reduction in the number of MPs representing inner-city constituencies and an increase in MPs representing the suburbs. Having been selected for Enfield early in the 1945 parliament, Macleod was well placed to benefit from any changes. When, in due course, Enfield was divided into two constituencies – East and West – it was clear that in most elections Labour could expect to hold Enfield East, while the Tories should win Enfield West. In December 1948, the new Conservative association in Enfield West unanimously asked Macleod, as the prospective candidate for the old Enfield constituency, to fight the new seat. They were handing him, in effect, his key to the House of Commons.[7]

After first moving to Enfield at the time of his adoption, Macleod lived briefly in digs, but the Macleods soon set up home in the constituency. Rationing and shortages made life difficult in the years immediately after the War and, like other young couples fortunate enough to find a house, the Macleods took out a mortgage – they had to pay a deposit of 10 per cent, or £250, and his parents helped financially. In October 1946, Macleod was asking his parents if they could spare any rugs or floor coverings – 'They are hellishly expensive and anyway very difficult to get.' After a brief spell in Drapers Road, just off The Ridgeway, they moved to number 22, The Ridgeway. Ladykirk, as the house was called, was to be their home until the end of the 1950s. It was a three-storey detached house, set back from the road.[8]

It was Macleod's good fortune to become a candidate and serve as an MP in the days before they were weighed down by their constituency case-loads. Macleod did not enter politics to become a glorified county councillor or social worker – he had neither the aptitude nor the desire for either role. He had set his sights on the national stage. Nonetheless, it is remarkable that he never conducted constituency surgeries or employed a constituency secretary. Macleod used to maintain that he lived in Enfield, or later – after a short break – in Potters Bar, and people knew where to find him if he was needed. As Macleod's ministerial career developed this function was increasingly taken by Eve, who was to devote enormous energy both to looking after the constituency and undertaking voluntary work. Before Macleod was elected MP, she had taken a leaf from her mother-in-law's book and become President of the Women's Section of Enfield British Legion. She also did a great deal for local hospitals, their patients and relatives through the League of Friends; and she later became a member of the local magistrates' bench.[9]

In other respects, however, Macleod played an active part in the life of his constituency. During the winter, he used to enjoy watching the Saracens, the local rugby team, on Saturday afternoons. Until the end of the 1950 cricket season, he occasionally kept wicket for the second or third XI of Cockfosters, the Southgate-based club. The injury to his leg, suffered during the War, prevented him running much, if at all. He never claimed many victims or scored many runs. But he enjoyed the game immensely, remained a member of the club after he had stopped playing, and liked having a drink with the players in The Cock public house.

Every Sunday morning, he and Eve used to attend the church of St Mary Magdalene in Windmill Hill, where he was a sidesman for fifteen years. On Armistice Day he always used to attend services in several local churches, in addition to the special open air service on Enfield Common. His friends had the impression that he was a churchgoer not from any deep conviction, but more because it was the thing to do – 'he probably knew that he would be invited back somewhere for a drink afterwards' was one comment. His romantic side was attracted to Catholicism and he used to say that he wished he could become a Roman Catholic. However, he never showed any great inclination to take the step.[10]

Macleod regularly attended his local party's meetings, but he never found the social occasions easy. Conservative party activists were not his cup of tea and he was not naturally gregarious or outgoing. He would turn up and be seen at their fairs, fêtes and wine-and-cheese parties, but he had to try hard to put on an act. Although he was never rude, the mask tended to slip. He used to spend his time in conversation with one or two people on the edge of any gathering and avoid having to circulate. If there was a seat in a corner of the room, Macleod would make for it 'like greased lightning'. Once he had found a quiet corner and was involved with one or two people, all efforts to persuade him to move and meet other people were firmly rebuffed – 'No, Colin, I'm fine here,' or 'No, Douglas, I'm busy with Mr A or Mrs B.' Although he had the knack of making anybody with whom he talked feel that they were important, he also had a tendency to withdraw into his own thoughts. He normally managed to control this trait at party functions, but on other occasions in Enfield, local Tories were annoyed when he appeared to cut them.[11]

It was a tremendous asset to Macleod that from the outset he was able to develop a good relationship with the YCs. They had been delighted when the selection went their way, and Macleod always enjoyed a close rapport with them during his political career. They were a force to be reckoned with in the party during the 1950s and 1960s, and in Enfield they canvassed enthusiastically for him. Later, Macleod was too involved in the national campaign to do more than the bare minimum in his own constituency. Moreover, he could always rely on their support at local party meetings. His party was not the easiest to handle, since it contained fairly autonomous groups – Hadley Wood and Potters Bar Conservatives had their own associations and used to send representatives to meetings of the constituency association. Among Tories in Enfield, the Potters Bar members were regarded as being especially independent-minded, inclined to be right wing and giving the impression that they regarded themselves as being somewhat superior. There were also several strong Conservative Clubs in Enfield which attracted a working class membership and where Macleod would sometimes go at weekends or on a rare free evening for a drink and a chat. But it was only when the Macleods lived in London for a few years during the early 1960s that he began to experience any criticism or trouble in his local party.[12]

Local parties generally like having a high-flyer represent their constituency. His appointment to the parliamentary party's Secretariat had en-

abled him to make an all-important good first impression with the constituency chairman, Waite, and the selection committee, since it marked him
as a young high-flyer with the potential to achieve high office. It was to be
a further help in his constituency that, once he had arrived on the Tory
backbenches, Macleod rapidly began to enhance his reputation as the party's
'golden boy'.

An opportune debut

Overturning Labour's 1945 landslide majority of 146 seats in one fell swoop
at the next election had never seemed to be realistically on the cards for the
Conservatives, despite the widespread disillusion felt by the end of the 1940s
at the continuation of rationing, queues and the housing shortage. But
Attlee's decision to call the 1950 election as early as February worked to the
Tories' advantage. Behind the Prime Minister's action lay the highly
moralistic conscience of the Chancellor of the Exchequer, Sir Stafford
Cripps, whose concern to demonstrate that the thought of anything as
unseemly as a pre-election, spring budget had never entered his mind,
precipitated a pre-budget election. Labour were thrown into an election only
four months after having devalued the pound, and their majority was
reduced to a mere six seats. Among the 298 seats won by the Conservatives
on 23 February was Enfield West, where the 36-year-old Iain Macleod
secured a majority of 9,193 votes.[13]

Campaign propaganda can be notoriously unreliable guides to politicians'
subsequent actions, but the language and presentation can be revealing of a
party's, or a candidate's, approach and of the political mood of the times.
The Conservative's 1950 manifesto, *This is the Road*, promised fewer
controls and a greater emphasis on market economics, but was shrewdly
pitched to appeal to an electorate that was predominantly (around two-
thirds) working class. The Conservatives were careful to reflect the cross-
party consensus on maintaining full employment and supporting both the
mixed economy and the welfare state. 'We pledge ourselves to maintain and
improve the Health Service,' their manifesto declared, in one of the sections
that Macleod had worked on most closely. 'The Conservatives,' observed
the *Manchester Guardian*, 'have never in their history produced so enlightened a statement on social policy – from full employment to education and
the social services.'[14]

Nowhere was this moderate approach more strongly echoed than in
Macleod's own election address in Enfield West. 'All parties,' he emphasized, 'are pledged to maintain a high and stable level of employment.' Within
the party's overall rubric of the period – that they would manage the postwar
settlement better than Labour and not demolish it – Macleod highlighted
their immediate priorities: reducing direct taxation, reviewing PAYE 'so
as to encourage extra production', and cutting 'wasteful Government

expenditure'; building 'more houses more cheaply'; cutting 'the Socialist shackles from trade and industry'; and, on nationalization, promising only 'to repeal the Iron and Steel Act' and to 'hand back road transport to private enterprise'.[15]

By far the most significant and highly unusual aspect of Macleod's election address as a Conservative candidate, however, was the priority he accorded to 'Social Services'. 'It is in this field that my deepest political interests lie,' he declared, pledging to 'safeguard the value of the social service benefits which have been slashed by Socialist mismanagement.' Giving a ringing declaration of his aims in social policy, he pledged his own – and his party's – full-hearted commitment to the welfare state:

> It is a major object of Conservative policy to defend the value of the Social Services. We will maintain the existing benefits and treat more sympathetically the problems of the elderly. We would insist on administrative efficiency through the Health Service. We would put back the family doctor to his true position as the mainspring of the Service. In education we would implement the 1944 Butler Act, and I hope that the salaries of men and women teachers will become appropriate to the great responsibility that they carry.[16]

February 1950 was an opportune moment for an ambitious, young Conservative to be elected to parliament for the first time. As Enoch Powell, Macleod's former Research Department colleague and a fellow member of the 1950 Tory intake recalls: 'We had the God sent opportunity with a narrow majority in the House, when one's services were in demand.' The Tory frontbench and whips' office encouraged the newcomers to play a full part in harrying the Government at every turn and to speak in debates and vote in the lobbies. The 'class of 1950' were one of the most impressive Tory intakes and, in addition to Macleod and Powell, included Maudling, also from the Research Department, Julian Amery, Robert Carr, Edward Heath, Angus Maude and Christopher Soames. They were all ambitious, but none more so than Macleod. Even his choice of seat in the House of Commons chamber was deliberate. Ian Orr-Ewing recalls discussing with Macleod where they should sit and deciding that the best position was below the gangway, two or three benches back. They reasoned that by sitting below the gangway instead of directly behind the frontbench, they would more easily be able to catch the attention of their party leadership when they asked questions or took part in debates, since anybody sitting on the frontbench would be able to lean back, put his ear to the small amplifier in the bench, and look down the length of the chamber to see who was speaking. In Macleod's case, this ploy was to pay dividends.[17]

Macleod made his maiden speech within a fortnight of the opening of the new session, in the debate on the Supplementary Estimates held on 14

March. Apart from an early, passing reference to 'the traditional courtesy and kindliness' accorded by the House, and the fact that he spoke for thirteen minutes – the average for a maiden speech – he wisely avoided the customary confessions of nervousness and dispensed with non-partisan pleasantries. Many years later, in an amusing article in the *Spectator*, he wrote of the meaninglessness of the 'traditional rites', but appeared to have forgotten that he had discarded them. In a telling comment that explained his success as a parliamentary debater, he added, 'I have never felt awe of the House of Commons. Respect and affection, yes; exhilaration and depression, yes; fear, no.'[18]

Whereas Captain Harry Crookshank, the Opposition frontbench spokesman on health had made an aggressive speech, accusing the Government of having failed to honour its pledges to economize, other Conservative speakers conspicuously failed to bay for cuts and charges. Macleod and his fellow maiden speaker that day, Dr Charles Hill, adopted a more conciliatory tone. The Commons were being asked to sanction additional spending of £148 million on social services, of which something like two-thirds, or nearly £100 million, was attributable to the NHS. Macleod concentrated mainly on the subject of NHS spending, drawing on the expertise that he had developed in briefing the shadow cabinet and backbenches – often, it had seemed, to no avail. There was a sense about his speech that he could scarcely wait a moment longer to fire the ammunition that he had been regularly supplying, only to see it wasted by others less talented than himself.

As Macleod reminded MPs, since the NHS scheme had first been presented in 1946, the estimated cost had grown from '£152 million a year, or about £3 per head, until the proposed Estimate for next year [1950–51], which is about £400 million, or some £8 per head.' In an effort to halt this inexorable rise in spending, the Chancellor, Sir Stafford Cripps, had announced at the start of the debate that a ceiling was to be placed on NHS spending for the next year. However, as Macleod argued, NHS costs were bound to continue to rise, because 'we are an ageing population, and for the next generation, in the absence of dramatic scientific or medical discoveries, the demands of sickness will inevitably increase'. Although he appeared more prescient than the Government, he had not foreseen that medical advances would generate new demands on the NHS. But he had identified the central point about the NHS, even though his caricature of Cripps and Bevan as being in the position of 'Alice and the Red Queen' might be applied to every postwar Chancellor and Minister of Health. As Macleod explained:

> The inhabitants of Looking-glass Country had to do all the running they could do to stay in the same place, and if they wanted to get somewhere else they had to run twice as fast. If our resources . . . are inadequate – and they are and they will be for a long time to come – then it follows

that we must establish priorities as between social services and also within the social services.

Alert to the arguments being advanced by Labour Ministers from his days in the Research Department, where he had monitored their every word, Macleod noted that even Bevan, at the previous year's Labour Party conference, had argued that priorities were the religion of socialism.[19]

Addressing priorities in the NHS, Macleod focused on the fact that the bill for general dental services was exceeding the bill for general medical services. Moreover, one of the very few priorities that had been identified within the NHS – dental treatment for young children and infants – had failed, since in many parts of the country the schools' dental service had 'virtually broken down'. On the point about costs, he argued that 'some 10,750 dentists are being paid more in terms of gross income than some 21,000 doctors'. Even allowing for the heavier cost of practice expenses, 'the dentist at the moment is paid by the State far more in terms also of net income than is the doctor', an outcome that he described as 'an indefensible position'. Informing the House, he was 'both the son and grandson of a doctor', he argued that:

Relative to their training, their qualifications, their ability, the load of responsibility that they ceaselessly shoulder, and above all the hours during which doctors are at the patients' service – in my father's house as in every other general practitioner's that was 24 hours of the day and seven days of the week – doctors are by far the worst remunerated profession in the service.

Although he had 'not the slightest doubt' that there was no question of there ever being a doctors' strike, he nonetheless cautioned that: 'We should be wise not to presume too far on the infinite and most statesmanlike patience which the medical profession has shown in these last two years.'[20]

Most fascinating of all, Macleod took the opportunity of his first speech in the Commons to signal his longer term thinking on the welfare state and revealed himself as an early exponent of 'selectivity', as it has become known, or targeting, in the social services. Reflecting on the 'formidable figures' that were before the House and arguing that 'all thinking people' and everyone concerned with the future of the social services 'are also agreed that the priorities are in many cases unsound', he wondered, 'Is it possible for us to suggest what has gone wrong?' 'Very diffidently,' Macleod attempted to explain what he thought had happened. 'The traditional function of the social services,' he suggested, 'is to rescue the needy from destitution, the sick from ill-health and the unfortunate from the consequences of their misfortunes.' It was this principle that Churchill had supported in 1948 when he spoke of 'the establishment and maintenance of a basic minimum standard of life and labour below which a man or woman of good will, however old and weak, will not be allowed to fall.' Macleod recalled in addition that in October 1949, Eden had wondered whether the time had not come to 'recognize that the principle of the social services ought to be that the strong should help the weak and not try to aid everybody alike indiscriminately?' It was not altogether surprising for an aspiring back-bencher to quote his party leaders, but Macleod probably had particular reason to do so. Neither Churchill nor Eden were experts on the new welfare state and as a Research Department officer, Macleod had advised them on the social services and almost certainly had drafted, or at least had a hand in writing, the words that he now quoted in support of his argument.[21]

At long last, Macleod was in a position to develop the argument in his own words. They were to represent an important strand in Tory social policy:

> Today – and this is what I think has gone wrong – the conception of a minimum standard which held the field of political thought for so long, and in my view should hold it still, is disappearing in favour of an average standard. To an average standard, the old fashioned virtues of thrift, industry and ability become irrelevant. The social services today have become a weapon of financial and not of social policy. This may sound Irish, but it is both true and tragic that, in a scheme where everyone has priority, it follows that no one has priority. This principle goes deep in the difference between the two sides of the House.

However, the difference that Macleod had identified was to be less clear cut than he had supposed, since the Labour Government were soon to extend selectivity.[22]

Macleod later mistakenly recalled his own maiden speech as 'a pedestrian affair'. But it had earned him, in the words used in *The Times*'s parliamentary report: 'Loud Cheers'. As Macleod self-deprecatingly noted, 'They cheered more easily in those days.' However, he had struck a chord with other Conservative newcomers. As events were to turn out, Macleod had helped define the philosophy that was to unite an influential group of new Tory MPs who shared his anxiety that their party should urgently develop a distinctive and effective approach on the social services.[23]

One Nation

Dissatisfaction with the party's inept handling of social policy – despite the statement of support for the welfare state in *This is the Road* – was felt by a number of MPs among the 1950 Conservative intake. Having got to know one another as candidates, the new Tory MPs immediately began mixing easily in the tea and smoking rooms of the House of Commons. As one of their number, Ian Orr-Ewing recalls, Macleod was 'very much one of the gang'. Many of them had been through the War and had deferred their entry into politics, and now they were in buoyant mood because of a general feeling that Labour were on the way out. Macleod joined one of the dining clubs, to which around a dozen or so new Tory MPs, including Orr-Ewing, Julian Amery and Reggie Maudling, belonged. But these gatherings were to have less significance than those of an altogether more earnest ginger group created within weeks of the 1950 election. Accounts vary of the precise sequence of events that led to its birth, but what is clear is that the discontent felt by its founders with the party on social policy had built up over several years and, once the idea was sown, a number of the new Tory intake came together almost simultaneously.[24]

Cub Alport had already realized before he won Colchester from Labour in 1950 that one of the most effective ways for young MPs to make an impact is to form a group. He had identified Angus Maude, a Deputy Director of the independent research organization, Political and Economic Planning (PEP), as a likely ally in any such venture. But the particular catalyst for their coming together had been their despair at yet another dismal perform-ance on housing from the frontbench. The fact that Richard Law, Duncan Sandys and Walter Elliot are each identified as the culprit in different accounts suggests that lamentable efforts on social policy by Conservative spokesmen were by no means unusual. Powell believes that Macleod and Maude had first bemoaned together Tory frontbench inadequacy on housing some years earlier, but it seems that Alport and Maude may have finally been prompted to act by Bevan's savaging of Elliot on 13 March, the day before Macleod's maiden speech.[25]

Alport soon broached the idea of forming a ginger group with Gilbert Longden. After discussing their thoughts over lunch, Alport, Maude and Longden decided to press ahead. Events moved fast. Robert Carr, Richard Fort and John Rodgers were recruited almost straight away. Edward Heath believes that he was involved in the initial discussions, but according to Fisher, it was Rodgers who enrolled Heath and, shortly afterwards, Macleod. As Alport remembers, 'one of those that we immediately turned to was Iain Macleod because he was extremely able and well-informed on social policy, health and housing and all the rest of it.' Macleod made an immediate impact when the eight members met for lunch at PEP's office at 16 Old Queen Street, proposing the recruitment of an additional, ninth, member and giving the group its first project. 'We've got to have Enoch,' Macleod is reputed to have urged, when he recommended that they should recruit his former Research Department colleague, Powell. 'Presumably,' as Powell recalls, 'he regarded me as having a creative approach to party policy.' Macleod also told his new colleagues of the CPC pamphlet that he had been asked by the Conservative Political Centre to write on the social services, and suggested that it should become a joint production of the group. They agreed that each member should write a chapter and that Macleod and Maude should become joint editors.[26]

Macleod chaired the group's first meeting, but thereafter the author of whichever chapter was under discussion usually took the chair. The authorship of each chapter remained anonymous. The group's name did not come until later, during the summer of 1950, when they had to find a title for their book. It is unclear whether Macleod or Maude proposed that it should be entitled *One Nation* – inspired by Disraeli's novel, *Sybil, or the Two Nations*, in which the former Tory leader condemned the divisions in society brought about by unbridled, *laissez-faire* capitalism. According to Fisher, Maude proposed the title and Macleod approved it before it was sent to the printers, but Alport believes that Macleod had first suggested the title. Whatever its paternity, *One Nation* captured the underlying philosophy that united them. They were the new generation of Tories who strongly disapproved of the party's uncaring approach in the 1930s.[27]

With perfect timing, *One Nation* was published on the eve of the October 1950 Conservative conference at Blackpool. It was the party's first conference since their recovery at the polls in February and it was possibly to be their last before they returned to office. The press were hungry for any indication of new Tory thinking, while the party faithful were anxious for any sign of new ideas that showed the Conservatives were ready for government. Rab Butler's foreword gave *One Nation* added weight, despite his including the standard, nervous, CPC disclaimer that the views expressed were those of the authors and did not necessarily reflect party policy. But the book, subtitled 'A Tory Approach to Social Problems', attracted great interest and sold 8,500 copies within a couple of months, a figure that was impressive for a political publication. Macleod proved himself the most effective political salesman and, to the chagrin of some other members, rather stole the show at the launch, being widely – and wrongly – described in the press as the group's chairman. This was hard on Maude, who had taken the main burden of the editing, but Macleod had first proposed the project to the group and the introductory chapter closely reflected the emphasis on priorities and targeting that had informed his maiden speech in the Commons.[28]

As with Macleod's maiden speech, *One Nation* sought to define a constructive, Tory approach on social policy. In certain limited respects, its proposals were radical and went further than anything attempted by any Conservative Government before Mrs Thatcher's in 1979. But there is a world of difference between, on the one hand, the Tory acceptance of the welfare state that underpinned *One Nation* and its authors' wish to make it work more effectively; and, on the other hand, the *laissez-faire* rejection of state provision that increasingly influenced Conservative thinking on the welfare state during the 1980s. The essence of *One Nation* was captured by Butler, who recommended the book 'as a healthy piece of constructive work', which would help 'sustain the confidence of democracy in the programmes which have been undertaken'. This theme was fully developed by the authors, who reminded their readers that 'the (predominantly Conservative) Coalition Government . . . as early as June 1941 – even before the shadow of defeat was lifted,' had begun 'to plan nobly for the future.' Beveridge's appointment was described as having been 'not the least of the great decisions of the Second World War, his Report not the least of its victories.' And referring to the role of Beveridge and the Coalition Government in 'the conception of the Welfare State as we know it today,' *One Nation* observed:

> These were the leaders whose efforts prompted a foreign observer to say, 'The people of England in their long pilgrimage have come at last "to the top of the hill called clear", whence they can see opening before them the way to freedom and security.'

Macleod and his colleagues defined their view unequivocally: 'The wall of social security has been built at last. Here and there stones need shifting or strengthening, here and there we could build better and more economically.' *One Nation* sought 'to examine these possibilities'.[29]

Among the possibilities identified by *One Nation*, housing and education were given priority, both in terms of action and spending. Its call for a much higher rate of house-building gave further ammunition to the campaign for the Conservatives to pledge themselves to a target of 300,000 houses a year – a commitment that the leadership were forced to concede at the 1950 conference, only days after the publication of *One Nation*. The chapter on health bore the hallmark of Macleod's thinking and accepted the Government's position – as Macleod had during his maiden speech – that no extra spending was possible in the immediate future. On the principle that 'the greatest need must be met first', *One Nation*'s authors were ready 'to impose such charges as may be necessary to pay for the improvements we seek'. In total, £35 million was to be raised through prescription charges – Labour had passed the necessary legislation – and by charging hospital in- patients for their board, a controversial proposal that no British Government has ever seen fit to introduce. Hospital costs were to be held down by ending demand-led budgeting and instead imposing 'whatever sum the national finances allow for hospital expenditure'.[30]

For the longer term, the building of Health Centres was proposed, at a cost of £500 million, when resources were available. Macleod had spoken highly in his maiden speech of the preventive health care pioneered by the Peckham Health Centre, which had foundered through lack of funds. Now, *One Nation* argued that until more Health Centres were built, the NHS would 'remain a makeshift conception'. Moreover, the authors recognized that the state 'must take over the duties' for research and the application of discoveries 'that many private benefactors used to accept'. But the conclusion of the health chapter returned to the priority of housing. From the incontrovertible premise 'that ill-health springs mainly from bad living conditions', *One Nation* drew what has proved to be a false conclusion: 'Nothing would do more to slash the bills for the National Health Service than a vigorous housing drive and the progressive clearance of slums.' Wishful thinking it may have been, but it was certainly not the language of market forces.[31]

The maintenance of full employment – another lynchpin of the new welfare state – was endorsed by Macleod and his colleagues as 'a first responsibility of Government'. Although they added the incontestable rider that, in the long run, full employment could only be guaranteed by the competitiveness of British industry and its responsiveness to changing demand, they fully supported the Conservative *Industrial Charter*. The competitive, free enterprise system that they supported, 'must not be the old system of *laissez-faire*, but what Mr R.A. Butler has described as "private enterprise in the public interest".' Accordingly, *One Nation* urged new factory legislation and that service agreements, or contracts of employment, should be made compulsory. In keeping with the British tradition, improvements in industrial relations were to be sought mainly by voluntary means. Despite being 'fundamentally opposed' to the trade union practices of 'political' closed shops and the requirement on union members to contract out of paying the political levy, and warning that they 'should feel compelled to take some action', the authors ruled out re-enacting the old Trade Disputes Act and promised to 'confer with the Trade Unions in a sincere attempt to find an agreed solution to these problems'. *One Nation*'s 'only positive political pressure' was to recommend that a Code of Industrial Relations, approved by Parliament, 'should after a reasonable time be made a condition of all Government contracts', on the lines of the Fair Wages Clause. In their readiness to use the power of the state to improve working conditions and impose best practices on industry, Macleod and his colleagues marked themselves as progressive Tories, not Manchester liberals.[32]

Since the group had first started meeting and discussing their plans for the welfare state, the economic and political outlook had been transformed during the summer by the outbreak of the Korean War and Attlee's rapid commitment of British troops. Faced with the prospect of increased spending on defence, *One Nation* might have been expected to argue that spending on the social services had to be cut, especially since the authors argued that the level of Government expenditure was already too high 'for normal times' and the level of taxation, at 40 per cent of national resources, had to be reduced. However, these were not 'normal times'. Instead, they accepted both the extra needs of defence and their continued commitment to the welfare state. 'Our task is plain,' they enjoined. 'Our emphasis now must be on finding ways of maintaining the social services.' In an echo of Macleod's call for greater targeting, they urged the removal of the indiscriminate food subsidies, since the rich benefited as well as the poor – the savings could be used to compensate the poor for higher prices. But *One Nation*'s main message was that the extra resources needed to meet the defence bill and maintain the welfare state could only come from additional output. 'Whether this increase in production can be obtained or not,' *One Nation* recognized, 'will therefore depend to a large extent on all those engaged in industry.' And in a remarkable statement, Macleod and his colleagues added: 'We must call on them for a great effort to save the social services.' That Tory politicians could make this appeal was a reflection of the extraordinary degree of popular support for the new welfare state. It was something that Macleod was never to forget during his political career.[33]

When parliament reassembled following the publication of *One Nation* in the autumn of 1950, Macleod and his co-authors debated whether to continue meeting as a group. They agreed to carry on Powell, who had dissented, was rewarded with the task of writing the minutes. These minutes reveal that during Macleod's membership, the 'One Nation' group, as they were now known, were not merely a Tory debating club, but were operating as an organized ginger group on the Opposition backbenches. Week after week, they discussed tactics on the most detailed aspects of parliamentary business – adjournment debates, private members' motions, praying against statutory regulations, and which questions to table to Ministers. Similarly, the likely agendas at forthcoming Conservative backbench committees were discussed, with a view to the group's attending and influencing the party's line on an array of issues. In early 1951, with the Korean War dominating political debate, 'One Nation' took a line on issues ranging from the call-up to talk of coalition. Frontbench spokesmen were also invited to meet the group and before they met Rab Butler in February, they agreed that they should stress both that nothing they had written in *One Nation* was affected by the prospect of rearmament and the danger of certain elements in the party urging the necessity to slash housing and other social services. Although Macleod missed this planning session, there is no reason to doubt that he shared his colleagues' sentiments.[34]

Critics caricatured 'One Nation' as 'One Notion' – that notion being its members' political self-advancement. There was an element of truth in this, but only in so much as like virtually every other MP, its members had entered politics to make their mark and part of their purpose in founding a group had been to do just that. But the accusation was given greater credence by the group's practice of organizing for elections to party backbench committees. They were helped in their task, because it was easier for a small group to influence elections for the party's committees on social affairs than for the more popular committees like Imperial Affairs or Defence. The 'One Nation' group had the nous to realize that the election of their members, or of like-minded MPs, to backbench party committees was essential to their cause – by 1951, Macleod was secretary to the party's parliamentary health and housing committee. Backbench committee officers gained greater access to frontbench spokesmen who chaired the parliamentary party's committees in Oposition and were more likely to be called to speak in Commons debates. This latter convention would not only help 'One Nation' remedy the weakness in the postwar Conservative parliamentary party that had first caused the group to come together, but it would also, in due course, provide Macleod with his golden opportunity to catch the eye of Winston Churchill.[35]

Macleod and Powell were given an early opportunity to display their detailed expertise on social policy during 1951 when the Labour Government introduced legislation needed to achieve the savings announced by Gaitskell in his spring budget. The legislation was geared to fund large-scale rearmament – the National Health Service Bill imposed charges on NHS dentures and spectacles, and the National Insurance Bill reduced Exchequer funding of the national insurance scheme. In the climate of intensifying Cold War, the Opposition accepted that increased defence spending necessitated economies elsewhere – Labour's cuts scarcely amounted to slashing the welfare state, and notwithstanding the 'One Nation' group's earlier fears, Macleod readily acknowledged that 'there can be no social security unless there can be national security first'. But Macleod was active at the National Health Service Bill's committee stage and successfully pressed an amendment that limited the Government's capacity to revise the scales of NHS charges upwards without fresh legislation.[36]

Labour's legislation was to prompt a new, joint effort between Macleod and Powell on social policy. The Conservatives' principal criticism of the NHS Bill was its proposed use of the National Assistance Board to deal with cases of hardship. The focus of their attack was what Powell termed, 'the transformation of this social service into another by the application of charges linked with a means test.' This line of argument was further developed by Macleod and Powell, when – at Macleod's suggestion – they renewed their collaboration from Research Department days and examined, in a new pamphlet, the vexed question of the means test. Both Labour's bills had the effect of applying 'the means test to services hitherto without it', causing Macleod and Powell to ponder the underlying principles on which state aid is distributed. The two men discussed their ideas during the long hours they were spending at the Commons as they played their part in the Opposition tactic of forcing the Government to 'keep a House' by debating even the most routine statutory regulations and constantly threatening to divide the House (call a vote). On nights when the House sat into the small hours, Macleod would sometimes stay overnight at Powell's Earls Court bachelor flat, where their discussions used to continue.[37]

Macleod and Powell completed their work in December 1951, and *The Social Services: Needs and Means*, was published the following month. Their

35-page pamphlet prompted an editorial in *The Times* that supported their inquiry: '. . . they [the authors] conclude rightly that the question that should be asked is not "should a means test be applied to a social service" but "why should any social service be provided without a means test".' Raising this issue was a radical step in itself in early 1950s Britain, but Macleod and Powell had not written an ideological polemic: neither their tone nor their conclusions were dictated by right-wing doctrine. Although Powell tended to be the controversialist among the 'One Nation' group – seeing how far he could take others along the road to market economics – he was ready to compromise. Macleod was certainly never a dogmatist and Powell, as his biographer, Cosgrave, shows, has always supported a role for state provision in education, health and welfare, particularly for those elements that 'are believed to be desirable on other than economic grounds and which might otherwise not be maintained'. Indeed, in 1950, Powell fiercely criticized the increase in the price of school meals from 5d to 6d and argued that they should be provided free. What emerged from the collaboration between Macleod and Powell during 1951 was their concern that the social services should not revert to little more than 'poor relief'. In this respect, they were poles apart from Conservatives who seem to regard the welfare state as the problem rather than the cure.[38]

In the somewhat academic main body of their study, Macleod and Powell showed that the various social services could be classified according to whether they were rendered in kind or in cash or with or without a means test. In their more political conclusions, however, they detected that, by 1951, there was 'a crisis in the social services, a crisis all the more dangerous for being unrecognized'. 'Already,' they wrote, 'the plans laid down by the Coalition Government which sprang from the Beveridge Report are becoming a patchwork.' In their view, the most serious problem was the spread of the National Assistance Board's means test. This threatened to reverse the process that had been going on since the late nineteenth century – 'the application of different means tests, *well above the subsistence level*, to different social services through the agency of the authorities respectively administering them [author's emphasis].' Labour's charges on dentures and spectacles had further extended the National Assistance Board's means test into the NHS at the expense of the free service principle. Macleod and Powell did not approach the problem as latter-day Gradgrinds, nor as Treasury mandarins *manqués*, counting the candle ends. 'If the principle of charges based on means is to be extended farther,' they argued, 'it is imperative that the test of means should be applied upon a considered basis fixed well above subsistence and separated sharply from the administration of the subsistence minimum for the purposes of national assistance.'[39]

Macleod and Powell were particularly exercised at the replacement of national insurance as a guarantee of security by national assistance. The latter, as they argued, was only ever intended by the Coalition and Beveridge as protection for the small minority. However, when insurance benefits had first come into force in 1948, they had been set at a level that was already 8s (40p) a week below the subsistence minimum, and by 1951 this gap had widened to 22s (110p) in unemployment and 14s (70p) in retirement. Notwithstanding improvements in other aspects of the welfare state, over two million people were dependent on means-tested national assistance in 1950 – more than had been receiving 'poor relief', to use its old name, in 1900. Postwar inflation had been the principal culprit, but economic measures 'to give stability to the pound' were beyond the remit of their pamphlet. Instead, they were forced to conclude that the national insurance scheme could be restored only by further increases in national insurance contributions – whether by employers, employees or the Exchequer. It was scarcely the stuff of what is loosely termed, 'the radical right'.[40]

Most of the work drafting the pamphlet was completed by Powell, which is not perhaps surprising, especially since Macleod was busy writing a book of his own – about bridge. He had continued as bridge columnist of the *Sunday Times* after becoming an MP and, in April 1950, shortly after entering the Commons, had written to the Director of Programmes at BBC's Alexandra Palace proposing that he might present a television series about the game. His proposal was rejected, and instead he wrote a lucid guide to the 'ACOL' system, that he had helped devise and pioneer. Published in early 1952, his book was entitled *Bridge Is An Easy Game* – a witty title likely to entice aspiring bridge players to buy it. The copy in the library at Number 10 Downing Street bears Macleod's inscription on the fly leaf: 'This is the only book in this place that is certain to profit its reader.' Macleod earned about £80 a year in royalties from the book for the rest of his life, but he was still regularly making money at the bridge table while he was a backbencher, despite the demands of frequent late nights and the need to remain within earshot of the Commons division bell in order to troop through the voting lobbies. Such was Macleod's prowess that almost everybody in London's gentlemen's clubs wanted to play him. His opponents generally had more money than sense and Macleod would usually win. Bill Deedes, another member of the 1950 intake, used to rib Macleod when he appeared in the Commons smoking room in the evening, 'Have you been robbing them again?'[41]

An additional supplement to Macleod's salary of £1,000 a year as an MP (£250 less than he was earning as Head of Section in the Research Department), came from his work as a Director of the London Municipal Society, which can probably best be described as the Conservative Party's equivalent to the Research Department for the London County Council area. He was paid around £500 a year and was responsible for the party's organization in the LCC elections. His brilliantly convincing performance as a Labour councillor at one of the weekend conferences for LCC Conservative candidates caused some of the putative Tory councillors to turn red-faced with rage.[42]

While visiting Venice during September 1951, as non-playing captain of the England bridge team in the European championships, Macleod first heard the news that Attlee had called a second general election for 25 October. The effects of having served in office continuously since the formation of the wartime coalition in May 1940 had taken their toll on Labour's senior ministers. So too had the strain of trying to govern with a wafer-thin majority, in the face of the Opposition's guerilla-like parliamentary tactics. None had been more active than Macleod, despite his bridge-playing exploits. During the 1950–51 parliament, he voted in 187 out of 188 official divisions, only missing one that was called unexpectedly when he was taking part in a broadcast debate with a Labour MP. Macleod rushed back from Venice to organize his election campaign, in which the Conservatives majored on the threat to world peace and the promise of 'setting the people free' after years of rationing and regulations. Macleod slightly increased his majority in the general swing to the Conservatives which saw them returned to office with a working majority of seventeen seats.[43]

When Churchill's dispositions in his first peacetime administration were announced, Macleod had particular reason to rejoice. Although it had been widely expected that Oliver Lyttelton, who had been chairman of the parliamentary party's finance committee, would become Chancellor of the Exchequer, Churchill instead appointed Rab Butler. Whereas Lyttelton was a City figure, who, with 'his watch chain dangling aggressively from his waistcoat', seemed to many Labour MPs the embodiment of big business, Butler was both Macleod's mentor from Research Department days and the torch-bearer in the leadership of the ideals espoused by the 'One Nation' group. On the Sunday after polling, 28 October 1951, Macleod wrote to Butler:

> My very delighted congratulations. It was the one appointment I was desperately anxious about. There just couldn't be a happier choice with the storms there are ahead of the Government. I am certain the Party will be as thrilled as I am.

As one of the more impressive members of the 1950 intake, Macleod might reasonably have expected to become a junior minister, but Edward Heath, who had served as an Opposition whip, was the first of the 'One Nation' group to join the new administration, as a junior whip. Nobody, least of all Macleod himself, realized quite how soon Macleod was to become a Minister in charge of his own Department.[44]

5

The Doctor's Son

I am the son and grandson of general practitioners and if I had not been
something of a late developer would have been a GP myself. As it was, I
became Minister of Health instead, and it is not for me to speculate on
whether the country gained or not from the switch.

Iain Macleod, the *Spectator*, 26 February 1965.

A Sudden Appointment

Despite his pleasure at the Conservatives' return to office and his delight at
Butler's appointment to the Treasury, Macleod had grounds for concern
during the autumn of 1951. The health service had hardly been mentioned
in the 1951 manifesto, in contrast to 1950, and with defence and economic
problems again taking priority it remained to be seen whether the new
Conservative Government would act on the lessons of their shattering defeat
in 1945 and keep to the constructive approach on social policy that Macleod
had helped devise in opposition. Faced with an immediate balance of
payments crisis caused by the shortages and inflation resulting from world-
wide rearmament, Butler proposed an early package of tough economic
measures. There was a certain irony in the fact that, as almost his first act
in office, one of the principal architects of modern, postwar Toryism had to
look to the social services for a contribution to his economies.

The NHS appeared especially vulnerable. The Labour Government had
set a ceiling of £400 million a year on health service spending, and since
Attlee's removal of housing from the Ministry of Health's responsibilities in
early 1951 the department had lost much of its clout. Moreover, the new
Minister of Health, Captain Harry Crookshank, was 'poles apart' from the
thinking of the 'One Nation' group in his attitude to the social services and,
like many older Conservatives, was highly suspicious of the NHS because
of its Labour associations. To make matters worse, Crookshank had been
given the additional responsibility of Leader of the House, after Eden, who
had been restored to the Foreign Office, announced that he could not

manage the post. As a result, Crookshank was not a keen attender at his office in the Ministry of Health.[1]

The chain of events that was to lead to Macleod's rapid promotion to the frontbench and his replacing Crookshank as Minister of Health began almost as soon as the new parliament met. The election of officers to the parliamentary party's backbench committees had to be held as a matter of priority. It had been accepted among the 'One Nation' group that health was principally the preserve of the 'Doctor's son', and on Tuesday 20 November, Macleod, who had served as secretary to the party's health and housing committee in the previous parliament, was elected vice-chairman of the Conservative backbench health and social security committee. The chairmanship had gone to Sir Hugh Lucas-Tooth, but at the start of February 1952, only three months after his election, he was appointed as an additional junior minister at the Home Office. Thus Macleod took the chair and on Tuesday 26 February was formally elected chairman.[2]

Macleod's occupation of the chair of the parliamentary party's health and social security committee coincided perfectly with the return of the NHS to the centre of political debate and was to provide him with the launch pad for his ministerial career. On Tuesday 29 January, Butler announced his package of economic measures. In addition to restrictions on imports and hire purchase, the Chancellor imposed additional NHS charges for prescriptions, dental treatment and a few hospital appliances (e.g. wigs, hearing aids, surgical belts and trusses). The reception on the Conservative backbenches was hostile. According to the senior Tory MP, Robert Boothby, 'backbencher after backbencher got up, really understanding the subject and expressing consternation at the harm being done to the Health Service.' The 'One Nation' group were deeply concerned at the proposed NHS charges. Of the ten MPs who gathered for a planning session of the party's health and social services committee on Monday 4 February, on the eve of the Minister of Health's attendance, six were members of 'One Nation', including Macleod, who took the chair for the first time after Lucas-Tooth's promotion. The following evening, Crookshank was questioned for over an hour by more than twenty anxious backbenchers, but he was unable to reassure them. A fortnight later, on Tuesday 19 February, 115 MPs attended the committee to hear both Butler and Crookshank speak on the issue. The Chancellor bowed to backbench pressure and signalled his readiness to consider some concessions, on the grounds that the economies proposed initially were expected to reduce the cost of the health service to something below £400 million. Ministers subsequently abandoned dental charges for adolescents and for the preliminary inspection and also gave up their plan to charge for hearing aids.[3]

Crookshank's position as Minister of Health was now extremely weak. He was privately dismayed at ministerial and backbench reaction to the proposed NHS charges and the press were speculating about his future. Butler happened to dine with the 'One Nation' group a couple of days after his appearance with Crookshank at the party's health and social services committee and, after Butler had left at the end of the evening, his acolytes fell to considering a suitable nomination for Minister of Health. Had Crookshank been moved in a ministerial reshuffle as early as February, it is highly improbable that Macleod would have been plucked straight from the backbenches to replace him. But a month later, Macleod had staked his claim in the most dramatic fashion imaginable.[4]

Circumstances could scarcely have conspired to be more fortuitous for Macleod on the evening of 27 March 1952 when he rose to deliver his speech during the second reading of the National Health Service Bill. On the face of it, he had an unenviable task. Widespread antipathy persisted towards the new NHS charges among Conservative MPs. Moreover, three days before the second reading debate, the arbitration award in the dispute between the Government and the BMA over doctors' salaries was announced by Justice Danckwerts, who had virtually accepted the BMA's case. Although many Conservatives, including Macleod, thought the doctors should be paid more, the award would add £40 million to the NHS salary bill spread over four years and largely wipe out the annual savings of between £18 million and £20 million from the controversial new charges. Not only was it a further blow for Crookshank; it also threatened the Government's efforts to control public sector pay and, coinciding with the row over charges, exacerbated Conservative anxieties.

Conservative MPs desperately needed something to lift their hearts and give them cause to cheer. But the hapless Crookshank, who opened the second reading debate on the NHS Bill, was not up to the task. However, a fluke in parliamentary procedure handed Macleod a golden opportunity. It was one that he – more than any other Tory backbencher – had the expertise and, as he was to prove, the talent to seize. Possibly only Powell could have rivalled his ability to exploit the situation. But after the years that Macleod had spent in the Research Department briefing on the NHS – including the historic 1946 Act – his mastery of the subject was second to none.[5]

In his new capacity as chairman of the Conservative parliamentary party's committee on health and the social services, Macleod could expect to 'catch the Speaker's eye' and be called to speak early during the debate. By convention, the Speaker endeavours to call MPs from opposing sides of the House in turn, beginning – when the debate is on a Government motion – with the Government and Opposition frontbenches respectively, and thereafter alternating between Government and Opposition backbenches, giving precedence to former Ministers and privy councillors. On this occasion, Crookshank's speech was followed by Dr Summerskill's reply for the Opposition and, since no former minister or privy councillor on the Government benches planned to speak, Macleod would normally have followed

Dr Summerskill. Indeed, when the then Speaker, W.S. 'Shakes' Morrison, vacated the chair, he suggested to his deputy, Sir Charles MacAndrew, that he should call Macleod next on the Government's side of the House. However, MacAndrew realized that a new Conservative MP, Ingress Bell, was anxiously waiting to make his maiden speech and suggested that Bell should be called first. Morrison agreed and Macleod had lost his opportunity to launch an immediate assault on the Shadow Minister. Now he would have to wait his turn until after another speech had been made from the Opposition benches. But his disappointment was to be shortlived.

Aneurin Bevan, who had recently been absent from the Commons through ill-health, had decided to intervene in the debate. As a former Minister of Health and privy councillor, he was the first to be called from the Opposition backbenches. Macleod immediately realized that he would now follow Bevan, and that this presented him with a heaven-sent opportunity. Bevan was the architect of the NHS and had resigned over the Labour Govern-ment's introduction of charges only the previous year. Moreover, he was the best debater in the Commons and was held in something approaching awe on all sides of the House. Indeed, it was a measure of the respect for his powers as a debater that when Bevan was called, Churchill came into the chamber to hear his speech – the Prime Minister's presence on the front-bench was to be an additional, uncovenanted bonus for Macleod.

But it was one thing for Macleod to be presented with the opportunity, and quite another to take it. Macleod concentrated on what Bevan was saying and, as he listened, began recasting in his mind what he was going to say. He had spent years briefing his party on the NHS and knew Bevan's deeds and words on the subject better than anyone else on the Conservative benches. With his excellent memory, he was able to call on a great fund of facts and figures, giving him the confidence to take on Bevan on his own ground. Bevan spoke for just over 40 minutes and in his peroration accused the Conservatives of making the arms programme into an excuse 'to dismantle the welfare state'. In a last rhetorical flourish, he claimed that they were taking 'the first long step' towards 'the beginnings of the end of British parliamentary democracy'. It was a few minutes after 6.30pm when Bevan finally sat down. The Deputy Speaker called Macleod, and as he rose, the House was unaware of the drama that was to unfold. In Powell's analogy, Polyphemus was about to be attacked by Odysseus – the giant taken on by the unknown.[6]

'I want to deal closely and with relish with the vulgar, crude and intemperate speech to which the House of Commons has just listened,' Macleod began. It was an arresting start. Conservatives pricked up their ears: none of them had ever dared confront Bevan so directly, let alone on the NHS. Churchill, who had been about to leave the chamber, hesitated and sat poised on the edge of the frontbench, waiting to hear what might follow. After briefly taunting the Liberals for their contradictory statements on

NHS charges, Macleod turned his fire on the Opposition frontbench, reminding them that when they had been faced with the same dilemma – reconciling extra spending on health with an overall limit on the NHS budget – they, too, had raised charges. 'Governments can change in a year, but logic cannot,' he scathingly told Hilary Marquand, who had briefly followed Bevan as Minister of Health.[7]

But it was Macleod's clash with Bevan during the next fifteen to twenty minutes that was to become the stuff of parliamentary legend. Macleod began with a telling gibe that came to him on the spur of the moment. He had intended to observe that a debate on the NHS without Bevan would be like putting on Hamlet without the ghost, but a different punch-line suddenly came to him. Instead, he commented that 'a debate on the National Health Service without the Rt Hon Gentleman [Bevan] would be like putting on Hamlet with no one in the part of the First Gravedigger.' It was an audacious and witty improvisation which brought a roar of laughter from the Conservative benches. After their trials and tribulations on NHS charges over the previous few months, somebody had, at last, given them something to cheer.[8]

At this point, Churchill turned to the Government Chief Whip, Patrick Buchan-Hepburn who was sitting next to him on the frontbench. 'Who is this?' the Prime Minister asked. 'Macleod, sir.' Their exchange was overheard by Macleod's friend, Nigel Fisher, who was sitting on the bench immediately behind, occupied by parliamentary private secretaries. After a pause, Churchill suggested, 'Ministerial material?' Buchan-Hepburn replied warily, 'He's still quite young' – Macleod was 38 years old. 'What's that got to do with it?' snapped Churchill, who had become President of the Board of Trade at the age of 33 and Home Secretary at 35. Macleod's coming to Churchill's attention in dramatic circumstances was significant, since the Prime Minister was not always sure who some of his ministers were, let alone able to recognize backbenchers.[9]

By now, Macleod was developing his attack on Bevan over the charge on prescriptions. Reminding the House that Labour had introduced the necessary legislation in 1949, Macleod noted that the number of prescriptions and the cost of drugs had since risen. Urging MPs to read Bevan's previous speeches on the subject, Macleod referred in particular to Bevan's comments during the 1949 debate on the prescription charge: 'It is true that if we read now, we can find, like raisins in a bun, arguments put forward by the Rt Hon. Gentleman why this charge was impracticable; but he knew something that nobody else did. He knew that he was going to go behind the back of his Cabinet and his leader to defraud the House of Commons.' Bevan protested that it was 'a most unworthy statement'. Other Labour MPs insisted that Macleod should withdraw his comment, but Macleod refused: 'The Rt Hon Gentleman [Bevan] has been a long time in this House and I do not think that he objects to this form of debating at all.'[10]

Bevan was provoked by Macleod to intervene three more times. When the former Labour Minister sought to rebut the allegation that he had failed to keep the promises on the dental service made when setting up the NHS, Macleod retorted that Bevan's argument was 'inaccurate'. 'The Rt Hon Gentleman made a great reputation in the previous two Parliaments by always speaking at the end of the health debates and never answering any points,' Macleod declared. 'He is much less effective when he comes down into the arena.' It was a wounding charge, and when other Labour MPs sought to intervene, Macleod added, 'I appreciate that the Rt Hon Gentleman [Bevan] is in need of care and protection.' The wrangle between the two men over the school dental service ended when Macleod dismissively described what was to be Bevan's final intervention as 'utterly ineffective', adding that he [Bevan] 'does not know what he is talking about'.[11]

But Macleod had not quite finished with Bevan. As he pointed out, Bevan had recently explained his conduct in the House to his constituents – 'something which I gather is in the nature of an annual event' – and had been reported as saying that during the debates on the NHS charges, he would 'not be restrained by any previous commitments made by anyone'. Macleod claimed that it was now clear that Bevan 'was not going to be restrained even by the commitments he made himself'. For good measure, Macleod rubbed salt in Labour's wounds by recalling their divisions during the passage of their 1951 Bill that had first imposed NHS charges. As he recalled, the 'general tenor' of Labour MPs who spoke then was 'that they disliked the Bill a great deal but that they preferred the Bill to a Tory Government.' When this prompted a cry of 'Hear, hear' from a Labour MP, Macleod was ready with his response: 'I am glad the Hon. Gentleman agrees, because it has obviously escaped him that he has ended with both the Bill and with a Tory Government.'[12]

By now it was seven o'clock. Macleod had already spoken for twenty-six minutes, but his speech was interrupted for three hours while the House held an emergency debate, secured by Anthony Wedgwood Benn, on the Commonwealth Secretary's action in deposing Seretse Khama as chief of the Bamangwato tribe in Bechuanaland (later Botswana). With the debate on NHS charges due to resume at ten o'clock, Macleod left the chamber to consider whether he should continue his attack on Bevan or be more constructive in the last part of his speech. As he pondered his tactics, he was congratulated by a number of colleagues, among them John Vaughan-Morgan, who saw him in the 'Ayes' lobby at about 7.30pm and was surprised to discover that he was trembling with the tension – he had not shown any sign of nerves in the chamber. Macleod was inclined to be more positive in the later part of his speech, a judgment endorsed by Dr Charles Hill, a fellow member of the 1950 intake, whose advice he sought. Accordingly, when the debate resumed, he spoke for a further eighteen minutes in support of NHS charges, qualifying his support on two counts – by suggesting that Ministers might consider smaller charges for the less well-off; and by repeating the point that he and Powell had made about Labour's charges, that the National Assistance subsistence minimum was too low to serve as a means test for the health service.[13]

Like many legendary events, Macleod's speech has since tended to assume an aura that some of those who witnessed it did not detect at the time. Bevan and his cronies, who gathered in their usual corner of the smoking room for a drink after the first part of Macleod's speech, were unperturbed. To their mind, Macleod had not sustained his accusations against Bevan, and they agreed, fairly casually, that there was no need to return when the debate resumed – Bevan assumed that Macleod had finished his speech. Most Conservatives realized, like Powell, that Macleod had 'scooped' the day's debate, but although some, like Carr, were greatly impressed, others were surprised at the way his speech was subsequently written up. Paradoxically, Bevan was to help transform Macleod's performance into parliamentary legend. 'I was in the middle of a good tempered and hard-hitting duel with the Rt Hon. Member for Ebbw Vale [Bevan],' Macleod commented, when he rose to complete his speech at ten o'clock, 'but at the moment the Rt. Hon. Gentleman does not appear to be in the Chamber.' Macleod said nothing more. There was no need. Bevan's absence was taken by Conservatives as showing that a Tory David had slain Labour's Goliath. The truth was more prosaic, but the myth was to persist.[14]

Nonetheless, Macleod had undoubtedly lifted Conservative spirits and had secured a tactical victory at the second reading – by taunting Labour over their divisions on NHS charges, he had put up a smokescreen over the concern felt by many Conservatives. However at the committee stage the Opposition launched a major assault, tabling numerous amendments to a Bill that consisted of only six short clauses and forcing the Government to introduce their first 'guillotine'. Although few Conservative amendments were tabled, backbench unease at the charges was clear. Macleod was particularly troubled by the inconsistency between the 1951 and 1952 legislation regarding arrangements governing any increase in the level of NHS charges, since the requirements in the 1951 Act had resulted from amendments that he and other Conservatives had moved. But when Crookshank rejected his argument, Macleod agreed not to press his amendment.[15]

In early May, a reshuffle was occasioned by the resignation of the Transport Minister, John Maclay, through ill health. Churchill took the opportunity to move a relieved Crookshank from Health, appointing him Lord Privy Seal and keeping him in the Cabinet. Macleod had no inkling that he might be promoted to run a department so soon. He had recently irritated the Chief Whip by refusing to serve a second term as a party representative at the Council of Europe, having been bored there the previous year, but he was astonished to be summoned to 10 Downing Street the following morning. As he told Eve, he could not think why the Prime

Minister had sent for him – Churchill was not small-minded enough to waste time ticking him off about the Council of Europe. Eve drove her husband to Downing Street and waited in the car outside. When Macleod emerged fifteen minutes later, he looked grey and shaken, and immediately asked Eve to drive him to a telephone box. He had just been appointed Minister of Health, but had no idea of the whereabouts of the department. The quickest, and least embarrassing, way to find out was to look in the directory.[16]

Macleod had been an MP for a little over two years and was only 38 when his appointment as Minister of Health was announced on 7 May 1952. Now he was in charge of one of the most politically sensitive departments in the Government, as the previous few months had demonstrated. He was also accorded Privy Councillor status, and although he was not made a member of the Cabinet, he was the first of the new generation of Tories to achieve high ministerial rank. Churchill had appointed Macleod on the recommendation of James Stuart, the influential Scottish Secretary and former Chief Whip, whom the Prime Minister sometimes consulted. Macleod's Scottish background had helped, since Stuart had known him from his days in the Secretariat and Research Department when he assisted the Scottish Unionists' committee. It was a sudden but shrewd appointment. Describing Macleod as the 'hero of the Government backbenches', the *Manchester Guardian* noted that Macleod's promotion was 'popular in the Tory Party'. The previous autumn, Churchill had appeared to overlook the new generation of Tories when he formed his administration, but the choice of Macleod to run a major department removed any cause for complaint by the younger backbenchers and appeared to show that the Prime Minister was on the lookout for new blood. Noting that Churchill had 'poached' their bridge correspondent, the *Sunday Times* quipped – in the game's vernacular for an ambitious bid – that it had been a 'jump take-out' promotion.[17]

Press comment on Macleod's meteoric rise was highly favourable. 'It is good to see that Mr Churchill is rewarding ability,' the *Manchester Guardian* observed approvingly in its editorial, adding that Macleod 'showed in a recent brilliant speech that he understands the NHS as few men do and, even more to the point, has the ability to debate with (and to rout) Mr Aneurin Bevan on it.' The choice of Macleod at Health, opined *The Times*, 'could not be better'. 'Mr Macleod's progress as Minister of Health will be watched with particular interest,' noted the *Daily Telegraph*, suggesting, with a sense of anticipation, that he was one of a group of 'efficiency experts' who had entered the Commons in 1950. Macleod wanted the NHS to become more efficient and to reorder its priorities, but he had no plans to shake up a service that had been operating for less than four years.[18]

Macleod had been due to attend a meeting of 'One Nation' on the evening of 8 May, but under the group's rules he ceased to be a member on his appointment to the Government the previous day. Yet despite his having technically left the group, 'One Nation' Toryism was to remain his lodestar as a Minister. But he now saw his continuing commitment not in terms of a bounden duty to try and implement every detailed proposal outlined in either their first book or advocated by him and Powell in their subsequent pamphlet. 'Everything which is put forward theoretically has to be politically digested,' Powell observes, 'and I think that Iain was perhaps more than most conscious of the processes of political digestion.'[19]

Macleod concentrated on the overriding, political objective that his generation of progressive Tories shared with Rab Butler and other architects of postwar, enlightened Toryism – namely, ensuring that the Conservative Party continued to be committed to the postwar settlement. Despite the Conservatives' role in conceiving the new approach during the wartime coalition, their party's appalling pre-war image still lingered and remained a potentially lethal weapon in Labour's hands during the first half of the 1950s. The Conservatives' stewardship of the recent National Health Service during their first six months in office had done little to inspire confidence. The health service had come into effect as recently as July 1948 and, although it had barely had time to settle down when the Conservatives took charge, it had already transformed people's sense of security. The removal of both any financial barrier to visiting the doctor and of the widespread anxiety that a person might be denied treatment if they fell on hard times represented a great improvement in quality of life for the vast majority of people. Macleod well appreciated this from his days spent accompanying his father on his house visits in pre-war Skipton, but his party were now in danger of giving the impression of being, at best, incompetent and, at worst, uncaring. The handling of the additional medical charges in early 1952 shook many of their own backbenchers, particularly among the new intake. Morcover, Crookshank had had to abandon promised legislation on dental health intended to encourage preventive dentistry and improve standards by establishing a General Dental Council.[20]

After these early setbacks, Macleod's immediate priority was to steady the ship. In one sense, Macleod was helped in that much of the flak for the imposition of the new NHS charges had been taken by Crookshank, and he could make a fresh start. But before he could deal with the larger issues, he first had to despatch this awkward, unfinished business. Macleod's officials were quickly made aware of the sure political touch. On 1 May, following an unanimous decision of the Parliamentary Labour Party, Marquand, the Shadow Health Minister, had announced that a Labour Government would end all NHS charges from 1 April 1954. Macleod saw the opportunity to repeat his exercise in the Commons and distract attention from the Government's problems by exploiting Labour's divisions. Shortly after entering the Ministry, he wrote to Lord Woolton, Conservative leader in the Lords, suggesting that he should press Lord Jowitt to disassociate Labour peers from Marquand's statement. Nonetheless, the Government came under heavy pressure in the Lords from lobbies for the chronically sick and terminally ill. Although no significant amendments were made, Macleod offered sufficient minor concessions in implementing the regulations to contain the criticism. Moreover, his officials were relieved to discover that he shared their view that charges for conservative dentistry should be scrapped.[21]

Macleod faced formidable pressures as a young departmental Minister, especially since he had no seat at the Cabinet table – he was only summoned to attend Cabinet when an item on the agenda related directly to his department. He was also having to learn the ropes of running a ministry from scratch, lacking any previous experience in government. The Health Ministry represented an unique challenge. Bevan had, in effect, nationalized the health service. This vast, new organization still needed time to settle down. When Macleod took over, the Ministry had only about twenty officials who were Assistant Secretary grade or above, yet they were administering fourteen regional hospital boards, 377 hospital management committees, 138 executive councils, 145 local health and welfare authorities, and a complex consultative machinery. In addition, the department had to deal with the medical profession, who had shown themselves to be one of the most articulate and powerful lobby groups in British politics.[22]

Most of the Ministry's senior officials felt more comfortable with Macleod than they had with Crookshank, because he was a family man from a less elevated social rank. Others thought him cold and unfriendly, but a mixed reaction to Macleod was not uncommon, since he never bothered to try and be friends with everybody. He had already impressed the department with the technical knowledge on the health service that he had displayed in the Commons, but they were less happy about his strong ideas on policy, especially since his views were thought not to be widely shared in his party. Despite his strong public image, at least one senior official was surprised to detect a tendency to timidity in facing up to Cabinet colleagues, but this reflected Macleod's lack of Cabinet rank and his being concerned at this stage in his career not to ruffle too many feathers.[23]

Despite possessing little clout in Whitehall, Macleod nonetheless set about trying to consolidate the NHS – an important task both in itself and politically for his party – while establishing himself as a Minister who was capable of making sound progress in his department. Macleod's role-model as a departmental minister was the emollient Minister of Labour in Churchill's administration, Sir Walter Monckton – the Macleods were to become close friends of Monckton and his wife, Biddy. Macleod's caution was not what some officials had expected. 'God, we've got the whizz-kid,' Pat Hornsby-Smith, already a junior minister at Health, had overheard officials saying on the day of his appointment, 'do you think he'll turn us upside down?' However, there was no sign of the Young Turk when, only a month after his promotion, Macleod made his first visit as Minister to his old stamping ground, the Conservative backbench health and social security committee. His sound grasp of the tricky issues that he had inherited reassured MPs. A week later, on 17 June, he emerged publicly as a consolidator, declaring that the NHS needed 'a time of tranquillity in which the different parts of the service were properly integrated and all the resources available, however limited, were being used to the best advantage.' Three months later in Taunton, Macleod stated that he wanted to be the first Minister of Health not to pass any legislation: 'It is about time that we stopped issuing paper and made the instructions work.'[24]

Whether or not the NHS would enjoy a 'time of tranquillity' largely depended on how the Government responded to the massive pay award that Danckwerts had recommended for doctors – a problem that occasioned Macleod's first appearance at Cabinet, also during June 1952. Besides adding £40 million over a period of four years to the NHS pay bill, the award was likely to have knock-on effects. Lord Moran, Churchill's doctor, had already warned in the Lords that the consultants would demand parity. The staff side of the Medical Whitley Council – the negotiating machinery for NHS pay – duly called for the Danckwerts' principle to be extended to hospital staff. In the event, the Cabinet decided against holding up the large pay increase for doctors and instead decided to press ahead, while arguing that the doctors' hefty pay rise had no relevance to other levels of remuneration. The decision to go ahead with Danckwerts was a political bonus for Macleod. Although the settlement added to costs, the doctors were to remain quiescent during Macleod's tenure at Health, relieving him of a major headache and allowing him to consolidate the NHS.[25]

After his first six weeks as a Minister, Macleod had reason to be in good spirits when he and Edward Heath attended the 'One Nation' dinner on 26 June as 'old boys' of the group. However, two days later, his family suffered a devastating, personal tragedy. Eve Macleod collapsed with meningitis and polio. She was desperately ill for weeks, at first paralysed from the waist down. Besides being deeply anxious about his wife, Macleod had the worry of caring for their children, Torquil and Diana, who were aged ten and seven. At first, he arranged for them to spend a week at a children's guest house in Suffolk. When he went to collect them, he spent the day on the beach looking after his own and the other children, periodically disappearing with them to buy sweets and doughnuts. During the summer, Torquil and Diana stayed with various friends and relatives in the country. Macleod visited his wife every day at the National Hospital for Nervous Diseases in Queen's Square, despite having to deal with his ministerial work and attend the Commons to vote each evening. This last necessity was the result of the Government's small majority and the constant harrying of Labour MPs, in revenge for the tactics that Conservative MPs – including Macleod – had deployed against Attlee's Government.[26]

In the past when the House had sat late, Macleod sometimes stayed overnight at Powell's Earl's Court flat, but a *froideur* had developed between the two men since Macleod's appointment at Health. Powell attributes their changed relationship to the alteration in their roles: 'There is a distance between a minister in office and a backbencher which arrives quite suddenly upon the appointment of a minister.' However, as Powell's biographer Cosgrave notes, Powell resented Macleod's rapid promotion, since he felt that he had been the more industrious of the two men. Yet Macleod was later to reveal how Powell responded with practical generosity to his family crisis. As Macleod sat in his room at the Commons, 'wondering desperately how to cope' and trying 'to conjure up a hundred solutions for all our family worries, Powell strode into the room and threw a key on my desk. "There's a room ready in my flat," he said. "Come and go as you wish." And the door banged behind him.' [27]

Eve gradually began to recover. She regained the use of one leg and partial use of another, but when she returned to Enfield in October she still needed a wheelchair. By November, she was able to go on a six-week recuperative cruise to South America with her sister-in-law, Rhodabel. She displayed extraordinary will-power in overcoming her disability and was able to walk again, although she needed two sticks. Macleod also bought a special car for her to drive, with the accelerator and brake on the steering column. Remarkably, she was able to resume a full life, playing an active part in Macleod's work at Health, especially in promoting and supporting the voluntary sector. It had been a stressful time emotionally for Macleod, but he remained 'buttoned up' about it: friends found that he spurned any opportunities when he might have talked over his feelings. His own physical disability was also beginning to afflict him by this time – on his first day at Health, he had asked for a pillow to ease his arthritic shoulder. As a sufferer from ankylosing spondylitis, he was to suffer back pain for most of his remaining years, accompanied by an increasing stiffness in the neck that was eventually to prevent him being able to move his head to look either upwards or sideways. [28]

Yet there was a much happier side to the 1950s for Macleod. He had made a flying start to his ministerial career and was still fit enough to enjoy the good life. Although he no longer wrote his bridge column in the *Sunday Times* and had to give up international competitions and tournaments, he continued to play around the London clubs, notably at White's in St James's, for a while before his workload at Health finally became too much. Indeed, he caused something of a scandal among its members when he stayed up all night there playing cards – members were shocked at the Minister of Health, of all people, behaving in this way, while he was also having to endure many late nights at the Commons. White's had a special cachet, and Macleod was immensely proud when he was elected as a member in 1953. He saw no contradiction between his hatred of snobbery and desire for a less class-ridden society, and his joining such an exclusive club. His choice of proposer and seconder reflected the composition of White's – the Hon.

Richard Stanley, a member of the Derby family and a Tory backbencher, and Christopher Soames, another member of the 1950 intake and Winston Churchill's son-in-law and Parliamentary Private Secretary. White's appealed to the Tory romantic in Macleod and he delighted in having a drink and dining there, happily mixing with other Conservatives who were poles apart from him in their politics.[29]

At this time, Macleod befriended Randolph Churchill, also a member of White's, and was rather taken up by the Prime Minister's aggressive, contentious and rumbustious son. Macleod enjoyed baiting Randolph and engaging him in banter, but had to pay the penalty of being added to Churchill's list of people – Michael Foot was another – whom he would phone at any hour of the night with gossip or to pester them for their view on some point. A particularly titanic battle of wits between Macleod and Churchill was witnessed one evening by Sir Reginald Bennett, who was Macleod's Parliamentary Private Secretary from the mid-1950s. Their sparring had begun in the bar at White's and, after a brief interruption for the ten o'clock vote at the Commons, was resumed over supper at Pratt's. Macleod used to goad Churchill: 'Randolph, as you know I'm devoted to you, I'm very fond of you, in spite of the fact that you are such a frightful shit.' As he had intended, Churchill would flare up: 'You talk to me like this when you're eating my salt!' A tirade of abuse ensued, followed by a momentous row. Macleod relished every minute and Randolph became more boisterous and ferocious as the night wore on. Ian Gilmour, who was to become a close friend and political ally of Macleod's during the 1960s, first met Macleod in October 1957, while spending a weekend at East Bergholt, Randolph Churchill's Suffolk home. 'Having been under fire for 36 hours on every imaginable issue,' Gilmour later recalled:

> The arrival for drinks of the Macleods, together with their hosts, the John Hares, was to me something like the relief of Ladysmith must have been to its defenders. 'John won't argue about politics with me,' said Randolph, 'but Iain always will', and battle was joined. It ended with them rendering in part-song Kipling's diatribe 'Gehazi'.[30]

The romantic strain in Macleod attracted him to similar personalities. It may appear surprising that he should become good friends with Nye Bevan, but Macleod and Bevan respected each other and when Macleod was at Health, they used to 'pair' for parliamentary votes. One night, Macleod had to be away from the House because he was giving a party for his mother, but Labour had imposed a three-line whip: Bevan obeyed orders by remaining at the Commons, but rather than let Macleod down, did not vote. The two men had much in common. They were the best debaters on either side of the House and, with their Welsh and Scots roots, injected passion and poetry into the English language in a way that has not been rivalled by any modern British politician. They had devil and originality, the qualities that terrify party managers. Above all, they believed that life was to be enjoyed. They also loved rugby football. When the Saracens played Bevan's local team, Ebbw Vale, Macleod invited Bevan to the match – the Welsh team won. The sight of these two renowned political adversaries watching together in the stand and enjoying a drink in the clubhouse after the game is still recalled by older members at Saracens.[31]

Consensus on the NHS

Like Bevan before him at Health, Macleod realized that finance lay at the heart of the battle on the NHS. He had to contend with the seemingly inexorable rise in health service costs while attempting some reordering of priorities. It was an imposing challenge. There was no prospect of any increase in his budget, since the Conservatives were pledged to reduce Government spending and gave priority among the social services to the ambitious target of building 300,000 houses a year. In addition, after their attacks on Labour over alleged extravagance and waste in the NHS, any breach of the £400 million a year ceiling on the health service imposed by the Labour Chancellor, Sir Stafford Cripps, was politically unacceptable for the Conservatives. The Treasury, however, were anxious to make economies in the health service budget, as were some Cabinet ministers, who remained highly suspicious of Bevan's creation. And yet the Treasury's action was to backfire, enabling Macleod to achieve his 'time of tranquillity' and reinforce the political consensus on the NHS.

The Treasury launched their initiative to cut the NHS budget during the autumn of 1952, when they decided to set up a small, independent committee of inquiry. However, the risk of this approach backfiring was immediately foreseen by Macleod's officials, who were convinced that any such inquiry, instead of identifying savings, would reveal the extent of unmet need in the NHS, especially in the areas of tuberculosis, mental health, mental handicap, and elderly and chronic care. The Treasury were 'playing with fire', they warned, 'and are liable to get very badly burned'. Instead of rejecting the proposal outright, Macleod suggested that the inquiry should be extended to the social services as a whole. Both tactical and strategic considerations appear to have been in his mind – such a wide-ranging inquiry would bring other spending ministers into battle with the Treasury and spin out the process, while his 'One Nation' perspective indicated the need for a comprehensive approach on social policy. But whatever his motives, his suggestion was too far-reaching for Butler, the Chancellor, who rejected it.[32]

Everything would now depend on the inquiry's terms of reference and membership. The Treasury fondly hoped that these would be approved by ministers in such a way as to produce the right answer – economies in the

NHS. However, political considerations were bound to come into play. Moreover, nobody in the Cabinet, other than Macleod, was more sensitive to this political dimension than the Treasury's own boss, Butler. As a result, the Cabinet hawks on NHS spending, Lord Cherwell, one of Churchill's 'overlords', and Peter Thorneycroft, President of the Board of Trade, were closer to the Treasury line than was the Chancellor in urging that the proposed inquiry should be directed primarily towards reducing the cost of the NHS to the Exchequer. However, Butler finally persuaded Thorneycroft that less restrictive terms of reference were necessary in order to avoid the accusation that the Government were launching a savage assault on the welfare state. Instead, it was agreed that the committee should merely consider how the 'rising charge' of the NHS upon Exchequer might be avoided.[33]

The Treasury were similarly frustrated on the committee's membership. Their suggestion of Ernest Brown, the wartime Minister of Health, as chairman, was vetoed by Macleod, since his pre-war role in the National Government would have raised objections from Labour. Macleod opted instead for Claude Guillebaud, his former economics tutor at Cambridge, whose left-wing past and independent standing would help disarm the Opposition. Likewise, primacy was accorded to the background of committee members and the need for balance, as opposed to their economic skills. When Macleod finally announced the appointment of the Guillebaud Committee to the Commons on 1 April 1953, it comprised Miss B.A. Godwin from the TUC; Sir Geoffrey Vickers, an industrialist; J.W. Cook, a Glasgow chemist; and Sir John Maude, a former Permanent Secretary at the Ministry of Health. Only Maude had direct knowledge of the NHS – and he was an administrator, not an economist. Given its membership, the Minister had little trouble in deflecting Labour's predictable criticism with the assurance that the exercise was an 'independent and objective inquiry', and not an 'economy cuts committee'.[34]

The very existence of the Guillebaud Committee was to act as a brake on Treasury pressure for savings in the NHS. This constraint was exacerbated by the delay in publication of Guillebaud's Report. In the event, the committee took two and a half years. Their report was not published until January 1956, a month after Macleod had left the Ministry. But only six months after they had begun work, Macleod was arguing in a letter to the Chancellor that it would be improper to embark on policy changes while the Guillebaud committee was still sitting. The committee had become his shield of armour against any suggestion of radical reform to the NHS or cuts in its budget.[35]

In one respect at least, Guillebaud was a mixed blessing for Macleod, since it inhibited his own cost-cutting instincts on the specific problem of the escalating NHS drugs bill. In response to Treasury demands during the autumn of 1952 for economies, Macleod had been prepared to increase the prescription charge further, from one shilling per form to one shilling per item – as he had told Conservative backbenchers in the summer, the last increase (to one shilling per form) had created little protest. Macleod was deeply concerned at the unrelenting increase in the NHS drugs bill and told James Stuart, whose responsibilities at the Scottish Office included the NHS, that spending on pharmaceutical products caused him 'more concern than any other item, even including the hospitals'. He blamed 'wholly improper pressure put upon doctors by patients on the one hand and more seriously by manufacturers on the other'. Nonetheless, when Macleod's call for another hike in prescription charges came to Cabinet, Stuart objected. The sudden disaster of the East Coast floods in early 1953 dissuaded Ministers from adding to public woe by pushing up prescription charges still further, but Ministers were also considering setting up the Guillebaud Committee, and as Butler admitted, any notion of increasing prescription charges was dead until after it had reported. The Chancellor's prophecy was fulfilled the following year when Macleod resisted the scheme that he had originally proposed for increased prescription charges by pointing out that any such savings would be introduced before Ministers had received Guillebaud's recommendations.[36]

Macleod's officials were soon vindicated in their initial warning that an inquiry into NHS costs might prove counterproductive. The tone was set at the committee's first meeting. Addressing the central question of rising costs in the NHS, Guillebaud advised his colleagues that 'it might well be that, at least in times of inflation there could be no satisfactory answer'. The committee interpreted their remit as being to seek improvements to the NHS as it was currently operating and to inquire into all aspects of the service, instead of focusing narrowly on costs and identifying possible savings. Inevitably, the committee's bias shifted in favour of recommending measures that involved additional expenditure and increasingly Guillebaud was invoked in favour of extra spending.[37]

The final nail in the Treasury's coffin was Guillebaud's decision to devolve the detailed, technical work on social accounting to a separate study, under the auspices of the National Institute of Economic and Social Research. The authors, Brian Abel-Smith and Professor Richard Titmuss, were committed to the welfare state and provided evidence that countered the widely held assumptions that the NHS was extravagant and subject to escalating costs. Indeed, they demonstrated that, according to certain standard social accounting criteria, the NHS was seriously underfunded. Their memorandum was to set the tone of the Guillebaud Report and overshadow the main report itself. By January 1955, the Treasury had accepted that Guillebaud, 'like all other committees which set out to secure economy, is likely to recommend big increases in expenditure.'[38]

Macleod's troubles were eased in the summer of 1953 when, despite ministers' fears of the knock-on effects of Danckwerts and Lord Moran's persistent lobbying for consultants, the hospital medical staffs nonetheless accepted a modest offer costing £3.25 million a year, with a flat rate increase of £400 for consultants. Although the settlement was more favourable to part-time consultants than the Government had originally wished, Macleod warned against penalizing them, because this might be taken as a precedent by Labour for abolishing the privileged part-time arrangement that Bevan had granted in order to lure them into participating in the new NHS. As with Danckwerts and the doctors, this settlement with the consultants helped bring the time of 'tranquillity' that Macleod had sought for the NHS. Pressure among the medical professions over their pay only began to build up again during 1955, but matters were not brought to a head until Macleod had left the Ministry.[39]

Despite his early problems over pay, Macleod faced a much more severe crisis in the NHS as a result of the persistently low levels of capital investment. The hospital service had been worst affected by the ceiling imposed on NHS spending, as building, modernization, the purchase of new equipment, maintenance, repair, and renovation, had all been cut back. Macleod had urged the need for more capital spending only a month after his appointment, but to no effect. With the Conservatives committed to expanding house and school building, Macleod had to concentrate on ensuring that the limited sums allocated for capital expenditure on health were spent as efficiently as possible. But by the spring of 1954 he was impatient that hospitals remained the Cinderella of public sector investment and pressed the Chancellor for an increase in hospital capital spending, from £10 million in the financial year 1954–55, to £16 million for 1955–56. Macleod was now using Guillebaud to add to the pressure on Butler, warning the Chancellor that his Ministry had made representations to the committee on this point. However, even the relatively modest increase to £11.5 million agreed by Butler was scuppered by that summer's exercise, undertaken by Lord Swinton, to curb public spending.[40]

The hospital service was in a desperate plight. As Macleod indicated to Butler, NHS capital investment between the financial years 1948–49 and 1953–54 had averaged only around £7 million a year, compared with £35 million spent in 1938–39. He was especially disappointed that the Government's abandonment of investment control regulations and the relaxation of building controls was not bringing proportionate benefits to the hospital service, and told the Chancellor that it was:

> Quite tragic that the result of the introduction of a NHS should be to cripple the capital development of our hospitals and to put us in effect right back where we were before the much needed expansion that started in the 1930s when local authorities were given general hospital responsibilities.

The building boom of the mid-1950s had made the relative destitution of the hospital service strikingly obvious. As the *Daily Telegraph* reported, 'The fourteen new towns now rising in Britain have houses, churches, factories, schools, shops, cinemas, inns, but not a hospital between them.'[41]

That autumn, with Ministers' minds turning increasingly to the next election and the Treasury in a more expansionist mood, Macleod renewed his battle, again pressing for increased capital spending. On this occasion, he won warm support at the Cabinet's Economic Affairs Committee. In his memorandum for the Cabinet, he reminded Ministers that during a period when capital investment on education and housing had increased by 100 per cent and 43 per cent, investment in hospitals had been reduced by 2.3 per cent. Macleod's case was accepted. However, his victory was not yet complete, since no hard figures had been agreed and he still had to battle for every penny of extra funds with the Treasury. Despite efforts to curtail his proposed expansion, Macleod managed to fight off the Treasury and keep his plans for future years largely intact.[42]

On 9 February 1955, Macleod was finally able to announce his programme of additional investment in hospitals. Although the £13 million capital budget for 1956–57 and £18 million for 1957–58 fell short of his initial ambitious bids, they represented significant improvements. But his battle was not quite over. Even these gains were threatened during the autumn of 1955 when the Chancellor was forced to introduce his second budget of the year – the first serious 'stop' in what was to become the 'stop-go' cycle. The Cabinet agreed to tight controls on public sector capital investment, but Macleod and Stuart countered that their hospital building programme should be exempt. The Health Ministers won. As Macleod declared of the projected increase in hospital building when he spoke in the Commons on 31 October, following Butler's infamous 'pots and pans' budget:

> That programme stands; every hospital, every bed, every ward in it. I am deeply grateful to the Chancellor that he has been able to keep the green light fixed on that particular programme . . . We are now coming into a period of building twice as much as the Socialists undertook.

Macleod had won a famous victory over the Treasury that was to benefit the NHS and that also gave a significant boost to his own standing. He bequeathed his successor the funds for a substantial improvement, but it was not until after 1960, when Powell was Minister of Health, that capital spending on hospitals exceeded pre-war levels.[43]

Within the limited funds available to him, Macleod put great store on humanizing the NHS. Mental health had been lamentably neglected before Macleod became Minister. Although 43 per cent of NHS beds were occupied by mental patients, conditions were often appalling, with dilapidated buildings, overcrowding, staff shortages, and long waiting lists. In his first speech from the platform at a Conservative Conference, at Margate in

October 1953, Macleod reiterated that it was 'the most difficult problem' facing him, and that 'it must have first priority'. Waiting lists were reduced, and by the end of 1953, after some experimentation, five day hospitals were in operation, saving money as well as bringing some advantages in treatment. In February 1954, Macleod set up a Royal Commission under Lord Percy of Newcastle to investigate the problems of mental illness and mental deficiency in greater depth.[44]

As part of his submission to the Chancellor in April 1954, Macleod told Butler that he regarded the capital needs of mental hospital services 'as unquestionably taking priority over anything else'. Whereas mental institutions had received only 16 per cent of capital spending on NHS hospitals between 1948 and 1954, Macleod raised the proportion to 25 per cent during 1954–55 and to 28 per cent the following year. In May 1954, Macleod laid the foundation stone at the Greaves Hall mental deficiency institution at Southport, the first new in-patient facility of any kind to be built in England and Wales since the Second World War. The report of the Royal Commission set up by Macleod was finally published in 1957 and was to do much to enlighten mental health care.[45]

Macleod was the first Minister of Health in the postwar period to recognize the great value of voluntary work to the NHS. Labour Ministers had tended to discourage voluntary effort, perhaps because it was associated with the pre-war health service and was seen as an excuse for cutting Government funding. Macleod accepted tight constraints on NHS funding as a fact of life, and – perhaps more important – had seen his parents make a personal contribution to Skipton's hospital service that went far beyond his father's professional call of duty. Moreover, Eve was already active in the Hospitals League of Friends, and so he knew at first hand of their problems under the NHS. He could see no reason why the NHS should be barred from tapping the enormous fund of good will that existed in the community. In his first party political broadcast on 30 October 1952, he complained that there had been less pride in local hospitals since the NHS had been set up and urged people to do more to help, particularly in old people's homes and: 'Most important of all, mental hospitals – cheerless and bleak as many of them still are. It is here, where the patients can do so little for themselves, that voluntary work can bring its richest and most satisfying reward.'[46]

During the early years of the NHS, voluntary effort had been actively discouraged by hospital regulations. 'All those trifling, petty restrictions have now been swept away,' Macleod told the 1953 Conservative Conference, 'and as far as I am concerned there will be no bar at all, while I am Minister of Health, to voluntary effort in any field throughout the Health Service.' At the end of 1952, there were 261 Leagues of Friends serving 512 hospitals. As a result of his initiative, 55 new Leagues were set up serving 99 hospitals during the first nine months of 1953, with another 60 Leagues in the process of being formed. This great upsurge in voluntary activity would not have been possible without Macleod's intervention – as the National League of Hospital Friends were the first to acknowledge.[47]

Primary and preventive care

One of the few commitments on health made in the 1951 Conservative manifesto was the pledge to give priority in dental care to mothers and children, and to preventive work. Macleod had repeatedly attacked the failures of the dental service under the NHS, referring to its shortcomings in both his maiden speech and during his sensational onslaught against Bevan. But as Minister he was hobbled in his ability to make dramatic improvements by his predecessor's abandonment of the Dentists Bill, with its provisions to allow ancillary staff to carry out routine dental treatment. Nonetheless, the revision of dental charges in 1952 had helped to reorder priorities. Children were exempt from the charges, and the number receiving dental courses rose dramatically – by 1954 about half of the six million courses completed on dental patients were on people under twenty-one.

Although one in five people in their twenties were visiting the dentist by 1953, compared with only one in ten adults before the War, there were still too few dentists to provide a comprehensive service – the numbers dipped marginally between 1951 and 1955, and at slightly below 10,000 were only one quarter of the requisite strength. In December 1954, Macleod launched an inquiry into dental recruitment, and the following spring was able to announce a dental salary review. The inquiry paved the way for a new Dentists Bill, introduced by Macleod in the autumn of 1955, only weeks before he was moved from the Ministry – it was his only legislation at Health. This measure would, at long last, help relieve the chronic shortage of dentists by making more use of dental assistants and making it easier for dentists from abroad to work in Britain.[48]

Macleod's criticism before his appointment at Health that doctors were getting a worse deal than dentists was put right by the Danckwerts award. With the problem of their remuneration settled, Macleod concentrated on improving the efficiency and quality of the general practitioner service. A revised system of payment introduced in April 1953 encouraged GPs to go where they were most needed, discouraged too large lists of patients and encouraged the formation of partnerships. The number of doctors in England and Wales rose from 17,298 in 1951 to 18,817 in 1955, while the proportion of the urban population living in under-doctored areas fell from 60 per cent in 1950 to 46 per cent by 1954. The maximum number of patients permitted on a doctor's list was reduced from 4,000 to 3,600, and the average number of patients per doctor fell from 2,431 in 1951 to 2,283 in 1955. It was appropriate that Macleod promoted group practices, since they had been pioneered in Skipton, where his father's old practice was the nucleus of one of the town's two partnerships. During 1953 alone, over 1,000 additional doctors entered partnerships.[49]

As the son and grandson of GPs, Macleod had a good rapport with the medical profession and understood the importance of the GP-patient relationship. This partly explains his reluctance to expand the programme of health centres that had been envisaged when the NHS was first set up. They were intended to become the focal point to serve as the base for local GPs and Macleod had made encouraging comments about their role as a back-bencher, but the opposition of the medical profession, who feared becoming salaried employees of local authorities and the lack of funds for capital projects, proved powerful disincentives to his sanctioning any great increase in the number of health centres.[50]

Macleod's other main departure from the intentions of the original NHS was his failure to promote a hospital eye service. Again, costs were part of the problem, since the initial expense would have been high. A hospital eye service had been favoured because it was medically superior, more acceptable to the consultant lobby and, in the long run, was potentially cheaper. His officials were disappointed by this approach, reiterating to Guillebaud that the hospital service would be cheaper in the long run. However, Macleod had decided not to accelerate its development and, on what seems to have been a personal initiative, he ruled out closing down the supplementary scheme.[51]

In the early years of the NHS, the opportunity had been missed to give priority to a more positive idea of health care. Many issues were either simply neglected or not taken up for fear of causing public controversy. One of Macleod's most positive initiatives was the new drive he launched in March 1954 to eliminate tuberculosis. This campaign was the first to use techniques of mass radiography. As he argued in a broadcast, although the death rate was already falling, and more cases were being detected earlier and were treated more efficiently, there were still too many cases.[52]

During the early 1950s, it began to emerge that the single most effective step in realizing the preventive ideal of the NHS would be to combat the habit of cigarette smoking. However, this question raised a host of difficult issues – economic, ethical, political. Macleod responded cautiously and failed to launch any effective propaganda to discourage smoking. In September 1950 an article by Dr Doll and Professor Bradford Hill in the *British Medical Journal* had suggested a relationship between smoking and lung cancer and a further article a couple of years later confirmed their conclusions. After further reports of research in the USA and submissions arguing that the link was not proven, in 1953 a panel was appointed under the chairmanship of the Government Actuary to inquire and report to the Cancer and Radiotherapy Standing Advisory Committee (Cancer SAC). On the basis of the panel's findings and other research, the Cancer SAC concluded that a relationship had been established between smoking and lung cancer and urged that the young should be warned of the dangers of excessive smoking. While Sir John Hawton, the Permanent Secretary at Health, was anxious that the Ministry should not risk the charge of suppression, Macleod decided that before making any statement he should consult other Ministers since the problem required 'delicate public relations handling'.[53]

Ministers were highly sensitive to the wider issues involved, not least the large amount of revenue that the Government raised from taxation on tobacco. There was also the tricky question of the offer by the tobacco industry, who were alarmed at developments, to donate £250,000 to the Government for cancer research. A Cabinet sub-committee was set up to consider the text of the proposed announcement on the Cancer SAC by Macleod. In the event, the advice of the Cancer SAC on the link was sufficiently unalarmist to serve as the basis for Macleod's statement. Even so, and despite his cautious approach, he faced opposition from Monckton, Salisbury (as Lord President of the Council, responsible for the Medical Research Council) and Boyd-Carpenter (representing the Treasury), who favoured toning down and postponing the announcement. However, Macleod countered that an early statement would create less of a sensation, acknowledging that quiet handling of this subject was essential because 'we all know that the Welfare State and much else is based on tobacco smoking'. In any case, it was impossible to delay the statement – so he argued – because the 'prime mover in all this is a man of extremely advanced left-wing opinions and would not hesitate to embarrass the Government if nothing appears soon.' The statement was approved by the Cabinet, and it was also agreed, despite some reservations, to accept the tobacco industry's offer of funds for research.[54]

Macleod's statement was made on 12 February 1954 in the form of a written parliamentary answer, accompanied by a press conference at the Ministry. He reported that the committee warned young people of the risks apparently attendant on excessive cigarette smoking, but pointed out that there was so far no firm evidence of the way in which smoking might cause lung cancer. In his replies to questions he was more blunt, stating that it was much more likely that a smoker would get lung cancer than a non-smoker, and that cigarettes were considered to have considerably more effect than pipes or cigars. Nonetheless, as he later recalled, he 'earned the plaudits of the Treasury, a lot of news coverage, and a headache by chain-smoking my way through my press conference announcing the first "conclusive" findings of the causal link.' Virtually a chain smoker at the time, Macleod was often photographed smoking – his official portrait at the Ministry of Health, issued after the Cancer SAC report, shows him seated at his desk holding a lighted cigarette. Shortly after his statement on smoking and lung cancer, however, he gave up his sixty cigarettes a day, not because of the link – in which he 'firmly believed' – but because he 'got bored with a messy habit'. However, he continued to smoke two or three small cigars a day until shortly before his death.[55]

Having made his public statement on the link between smoking and lung cancer, Macleod would go no further and vetoed any official propaganda campaign. That this represented a missed opportunity, there can now be little doubt, particularly in view of public concern at the time about the growing incidence of cancer. Evidence of the extent of public anxiety came at that autumn's Conservative Conference at Blackpool, when the balloted motion – chosen by representatives from subjects not on the conference agenda – called for extra funds to be devoted to cancer research. Replying to the debate, Macleod acknowledged that 'some factor as yet unknown is at work' in causing the steep rise in deaths from lung cancer. 'Various accusing fingers,' he continued, 'have been pointed at cigarette smoking, at air pollution, particularly in our cities where the toll is high, at the internal combustion engine or diesel,' but he did not know what the answer was. Although he gave an undertaking 'that when information comes to us that seems final', the Government would let people know it at once, he emphasized 'that until these matters are resolved – and they are not yet resolved – I will, under no circumstances, speculate on what the cause may be in advance of proof'. In terms of medical knowledge at the time about the precise mechanism by which smoking might cause lung cancer, Macleod was technically correct. But in view of the Cancer SAC's report it is extraordinary that he failed to reiterate that a link had been established and to warn young people about the dangers of excessive smoking. Macleod had a hatred of what he termed the 'Nanny state', but in this instance his predisposition not to tell people how to lead their lives appears to have led him to fail in his duty.[56]

Yet in another controversial area of people's lives – family planning – Macleod's active intervention was to prove an historic breakthrough. It is virtually impossible now to recapture the extent to which contraception was a taboo subject during the early 1950s – these were 'the dark days of family planning'. It was no exaggeration to speak of 'a conspiracy of silence'. The Ministry of Health regarded family planning as having practically no role in the NHS, the press scarcely mentioned it, and the fear of a Catholic backlash made it a politically sensitive issue. Macleod's interest was sparked by Lady Monckton, who had become involved with the Family Planning Association (FPA) following a conversation with the wife of Sir Vincent Tewson, General Secretary of the TUC – Lady Tewson was East Midlands representative on the FPA national executive, and was anxious to recruit a senior Conservative sympathizer to the Association.[57]

Given the friendship between the Moncktons and the Macleods, Lady Tewson had made an inspired choice. Lady Monckton was soon convinced that the Government should take an active interest, and invited Macleod to lunch to meet Lady Tewson and Mrs Margaret Pyke, chairman of the FPA national executive. Macleod responded to hearing how 'birth control was kept under the table', by saying that he would like to visit the FPA. When Mrs Pyke assured him the visit would be kept quiet, he insisted that they 'made the most of the occasion' by full-scale publicity.[58]

Macleod's official visit to the North Kensington branch of the FPA on 29 November 1955, to mark the Association's twenty-fifth anniversary, was the first occasion on which a Minister of Health had given such public recognition to a voluntary body promoting birth control. He strongly endorsed the FPA's work, commenting in his message to them on their silver jubilee that: 'Even today any trained social worker or wise citizen will tell you that a heavy load of ignorance and fear still exists about married life. It is your work to lighten this and to bring happiness and fulfilment to many families.' He posed for photographs outside the FPA, and was also pictured at a microscope in the sub-fertility laboratory at 64 Sloane Street.[59]

It was an act of great political courage. The impact was immediate. Overnight, the virtual ban on reporting the activities of the FPA was lifted by leading articles in *The Times* and *British Medical Journal*, and friendly notices in practically all the national newspapers. Mrs Pyke appeared on BBC television and was able to speak of the FPA's work with complete freedom. The public flooded the FPA with enquiries. More press articles and television programmes followed and the BBC ran a talk on *Woman's Hour*. Protest was minimal – Macleod received only a few objections from Catholics. According to the FPA, 'Mr Macleod overnight dispelled in large measure the clouds of prejudice and hypocrisy which had obscured our work and made free and frank discussion the order of the day.' Macleod's visit proved the turning point in postwar attitudes to birth control. Ministerial visits became a matter of course, the press treated birth control with greater understanding, local councils began to cooperate with the FPA, and demand for family planning accelerated – the FPA were opening clinics at the rate of more than one a fortnight during the late 1950s. In this respect, Macleod had more than fulfilled his duties as Minister of Health.[60]

Macleod's final weeks at the Ministry were conducted in a blaze of publicity. At the time of his path-breaking visit to the FPA, a bitter controversy was coming to a head between the Minister and the medical profession over his stated intention to ban the manufacture of heroin in Britain. Although there were only about 50 registered addicts in this country, heroin addiction was a serious international problem. In July 1954, the Economic and Social Council of the United Nations had urged all governments to prohibit the production of the drug. Britain was by far the largest manufacturer, producing 70 per cent of the world's heroin. Macleod consulted the NHS advisory bodies, who backed the UN, and in February 1955, the Home Secretary announced a ban on production from the end of the year. However, the proposed ban provoked an outcry from the medical profession who mobilized an effective lobby. Letters from doctors and their patients deluged the Ministry, MPs' mailbags and the columns of *The Times*.[61]

Macleod was unmoved, and despite a hostile editorial in *The Times* on 1 December, he persuaded the Cabinet to stand firm and confirmed the ban in the Commons that afternoon. But the lobbying persisted. On 5 December, seventy Conservative backbenchers attended a joint meeting of their parliamentary home affairs and health and social security committees. Still Macleod stuck to his guns. However, during a debate in the Lords on 13 December, Lord Jowitt, the former Labour Lord Chancellor, argued successfully that the Government did not possess the powers to enforce the ban by an Order under the Dangerous Drugs Act, as they had intended. Instead, a new Bill would be required. But since Ministers realized that any such legislation would be defeated in the Lords, the attempt to outlaw heroin production had to be abandoned. It was a somewhat sour end to Macleod's days at Health.[62]

A Clean Bill of Health for the NHS

A week after the Lords debate on heroin, Macleod was moved from the Ministry of Health. Shortly before his departure, Macleod had received a pre-publication copy of the Guillebaud Report. In the main, the NHS received a clean bill of health. No widespread extravagance had been detected, and the fact that NHS spending had increased by only 18 per cent between 1951 and 1955 while national output had risen by 25 per cent over the same period attested to the increased efficiency of the service – as a corollary, according to Abel-Smith and Titmuss, the percentage of national output spent on the NHS had fallen from 3.75 per cent in 1949–50 to 3.24 per cent in 1953–54. In the light of these figures, it is not surprising that Guillebaud was unable to suggest major economies and did not favour additional charges, instead concluding that deficiencies in existing services and the effects of inflation pointed to the need for increased spending, especially on capital investment.[63]

'I'm afraid it has very few useful proposals,' Macleod wrote to the Prime Minister. However, any disappointment was outweighed by his satisfaction at Guillebaud's vindication of his Ministry's efficient management of the NHS. Admitting at the Cabinet's Home Affairs Committee that he found the report 'almost embarrassingly favourable', he subsequently told his officials that he felt other Ministers had come to share his view 'that any idea of major economies, whether in the form of so-called administrative economies, or in the form of cuts in the Service through new charges or other methods, can no longer hold the field'. In their statement on publication of the Guillebaud Report in January 1956, the Government – on the insistence of the new Chancellor, Harold Macmillan – ruled out any additional financial commitment to the NHS for the time being. But it was a far cry from the major economies that some Conservatives had expected to make in the NHS when they returned to office four years earlier.[64]

Macleod, however, had seen from the outset that the NHS needed a period of stability if it was to succeed. Denied the luxury of additional funds as a result of the priority given to housing and schools, he concentrated on seeing that the NHS was run as efficiently as possible. At the same time, he achieved significant improvements to both the hospital and primary services, but eschewed any overhaul of the management structure while the NHS was still struggling to find its feet – in the early 1960s, Enoch Powell ruled out any reorganization while Minister of Health. When Michael Foot and Macleod spoke at the Cambridge Union towards the end of Macleod's tenure at Health, Foot was struck that after the debate Macleod told him he believed that his job at Health was finished and spoke as though there was nothing more that any Minister could do to improve the NHS. Macleod might have done more to increase NHS funds by requiring those who could afford to pay to contribute more to the service. Indeed, by 1955 charges contributed only five per cent of the £550 million budget. However, imposing extra charges would have entailed administrative costs and was fraught with political risks. In the event, the Opposition were forced to switch their line of attack from charges to hospital building and pay beds – the latter represented only one per cent of those available and when Bevan declared that Labour would abolish them, Macleod easily dismissed the threat as being irrelevant to the NHS.[65]

The period of stability created by Macleod allowed the NHS to be strengthened by the bonds of consensus. According to a Gallup survey in 1956, 89 per cent of people took a favourable view of the health service. Moreover, the political importance to the Conservative Party of Macleod's achievement in demonstrating their trustworthiness on the NHS and confounding their political opponents should not be underestimated. Had they failed to show their commitment to the NHS, their claims to have put the 1930s behind them and to support the new welfare state would have rung hollow. Macleod consolidated the NHS, and left it a more efficient and more humane service.

6

Rising Star

I believe firmly that the British system of free voluntary negotiation in industry, with the minimum of Government interference, is the best, and I believe firmly in the trade union system. Those views are fundamental to my political beliefs and I have not altered them in any way. Nor will I.

Iain Macleod, Conservative Conference, Llandudno, 12 October 1956.

Groomed for the top

From the moment that he became the first of his generation to take charge of a Government department, Macleod had confirmed his status as a future high-flyer. His impressive handling of a difficult brief at Health, where he won plaudits for his confident displays whenever he appeared at the Commons despatch box, reinforced his reputation. By 1954 it was a commonplace among senior Conservatives that Macleod had the makings of a future Prime Minister. Although he was not yet in the Cabinet, he was playing a key political role for the party that stretched far beyond his ministerial portfolio and was being groomed for the top. Behind the scenes he became actively involved in preparations for the next general election, and beyond the narrow confines of parliamentary debate he emerged on the national stage as an effective communicator.

In December 1953, Macleod was appointed to the Research Study Group which Rab Butler, in his capacity as chairman of the Research Department, had set up a couple of months earlier to work on material for the next Conservative manifesto. The following autumn, Macleod devised and presented a televised party political broadcast entitled, 'Home Town', that was set – as its title suggests – in Skipton and was designed to show the benefit to ordinary people of Conservative policies on health, housing, pensions and schools. The programme, which was filmed on location and featured friends from his birthplace as his cast, was one of the first such broadcasts to break away from the formal, stilted style that characterized the genre in its early days.[1]

Macleod's appointment to Butler's Research Study Group heralded a role at the heart of Conservative policy making that was to last for almost a decade while the party leadership remained in the hands of the Tory left. Having got to know Butler at the Research Department, Macleod had remained close to him after entering the House and seemed to have become, to all intents and purposes, his unofficial parliamentary private secretary. When Butler widened the membership of the Research Study Group to include Henry Brooke (another old boy of the Research Department, from pre-war days) and Macleod, the latter took on the role of Butler's lieutenant. While Brooke became chairman, Macleod acted as the group's link with ministers, chivvying people along and gingering up their thinking. With the prospect of an election being called as early as the autumn of 1954, Macleod set about finding what was happening in ministers' departments – establishing what progress had been made with outstanding pledges and trying to identify half a dozen or so major proposals and as many desirable minor reforms as possible, that might be included in the manifesto.[2]

Macleod constantly focused the group's efforts on the election. Time and again, the minutes reveal him pointing up the electoral implications of the argument and when an outline manifesto was produced, Macleod submitted a paper questioning the 'E-value' of some of its ideas. At the outset, the group could do little other than wait on developments on the broad, strategic policies, but there was a whole gamut of subject areas – including Macleod's own, Health – where they could seek specific policy proposals. In April 1954, Macleod floated the idea of commissioning 'a professional sample survey to discover what women really wanted from an election statement' – his concern that the Conservatives should garner the women's vote was to remain a major concern of his for the rest of his career.

The group's minutes provide fascinating early indications of his thinking. During a discussion on defence, Macleod pointed out that the only matter that affected the electorate was National Service. This was still the era of conscription and Macleod argued that any reduction would be a welcome gesture – almost exactly three years later, Macleod was to signal the end of National Service. Also, he believed as early as 1954 that 'something was missing in our colonial policy', by which he seemed to mean an humanitarian dimension, since he wanted poverty and disease to be mentioned earlier in the group's paper on the subject, and reference to law and order to be postponed till nearer the end. And in response to criticism from the party's Advisory Committee on Policy that the group's draft on employment and industrial relations had been vague, Macleod retorted that where the party had been vague in the past they had succeeded – Sir Walter Monckton had been able to give much substance to shadow – while positive proposals had always been blocked by the Trades Union Congress (TUC).[3]

In the event, there was no early election, but Macleod's mind was attuned to winning the next one, and at the group's meeting on 8 November 1954 he announced that he had coined a campaign slogan – 'Don't let them spoil it'. As he explained, its purpose was to 'remind people of the recurring crises under socialism'. Although Macleod's slogan was not taken up at the 1955 election, a version of it was used by the Conservatives four years later, when the rallying cry, 'Don't let Labour ruin it', was used to devastating effect. During the autumn of 1954, Macleod also advocated a more distinctive approach by the party at the next election. His thinking had been stimulated by a paper on scientific research and development, that caused him to stress that, from an electoral point of view, the key was to put the emphasis on the expansion, rather than the division, of wealth. This theme was to be hammered home remorselessly at the next election – whereas Labour concentrated on fair shares, the Conservatives stressed that people were getting better off under them.[4]

More intriguing was the discussion on 'the middle classes'. Macleod argued that 'it was essential that we should become more selective in our policy and do more to help the middle classes'. By 'the middle classes', the Research Study Group appeared to have in mind people earning between £500 and £1,000 a year. As average male manual earnings were around £530 a year, they were including skilled manual employees (the 'C2s' in pollster jargon) as well as non-manual employees. Among various, specific proposals, Macleod thought it was logical to go ahead with his plan for concessions to private patients (notably by allowing them to receive their drugs on the same basis as NHS patients), and felt strongly that certain proposals of this kind should go into the manifesto – it was Peter Goldman who pointed out that the middle class had benefited most from the NHS, but the service had been starved of money. Macleod also revealed that he had been 'converted' to the idea of giving income tax relief to people who wanted to educate their children privately.[5]

However, Macleod's initial excitement at the prospect of doing more for the middle classes was soon tempered by his acute awareness of electoral sensitivities. When the group came to discuss detailed proposals, he warned that the idea should be kept implicit in any policy statement and not made explicit – it was the type of theme that might attract the attention of leader writers. Indeed, even if the objective remained implicit, some of the measures would be unacceptable. In his own area of the health service, Macleod was quick to point out the political risks of helping private patients with the cost of their prescriptions and also highlighted the administrative problems of making hospital amenity beds available at a reasonable cost. Likewise, on education he judged that it would be harder for a future Labour Government to reverse additional tax relief given via children's allowances in general, as opposed to relief specifically targeted on parents who were paying school fees.[6]

Yet Macleod relished the idea of making a radical appeal if he judged that it would be electorally popular. Towards the end of their deliberations, he won the group round to putting greater emphasis on the subject of liberty and freedom from state regulation, urging that they should say that the Conservatives had 'got rid of 70 per cent of state controls'. Goldman countered that it would be difficult to remove the remaining 30 per cent, but Macleod responded that he thought it would be popular to do so, and that it could be accomplished in about seven bills. Macleod's suggestion was finally incorporated in the manifesto, in the section on wartime powers and regulations: 'Seven out of every ten have been eliminated, and we shall take steps to deal with the rest.'[7]

In March 1955, after years of cajoling by Ministers and much prevarication on Churchill's part, the 80–year–old Prime Minister finally accepted that he should retire and make way for his longstanding heir apparent, Sir Anthony Eden. The change at Number Ten confirmed Conservative plans for a May election, after Butler's April budget and while Eden was still enjoying his honeymoon period as the new Prime Minister. Macleod assumed a significant, though not central, role in the preparations for the election. During the final drafting of the manifesto, he questioned ministers directly in order to ascertain their departments' future plans and fill the gaps that still remained in the party's programme. He worked with Fraser and Goldman of the Research Department in editing the manifesto, as the final decisions were cleared by a small committee of senior ministers, chaired by Eden. Macleod also stood in for Butler at meetings with the chairmen of the party's backbench committees and with ministers who, like himself, were not members of the Cabinet, outlining the manifesto for them before it was published.[8]

The work of Macleod and his colleagues on the Research Study Group was reflected in the length and detail of the 1955 manifesto, *United for Peace and Progress*, which ran to thirty-two pages of small print. The party's emphasis on increasing prosperity and Eden's declared aim of bringing about a 'property-owning democracy' chimed perfectly with Macleod's view that the party should make an implicit appeal to middle income groups. Moreover, in his personal statement, Eden reaffirmed the Government's commitment to the postwar settlement in language that any of the founding members of the 'One Nation' group could heartily endorse. 'We have seen both employment and earnings reach new high levels,' Eden declared. 'We have seen new houses and new schools and new factories built and building, and soon we shall see new hospitals, too. We have seen the social services extended and improved.' For the first time, Macleod played a part in the national campaign, appearing with Butler, Eden, Macmillan and Monckton in an half-hour television broadcast during which they were questioned by ten newspaper editors. 'One of the few attempts at a joke came from Mr Macleod,' reported *The Times*, 'but nobody seemed to recognize it as such until it was too late.' However, Macleod succeeded in making some forceful replies to Dr Summerskill's accusations about the Conservative record on the cost of living. He also spoke outside his constituency – including a speech in Bexley in support of the local candidate, Edward Heath. In the wake of Butler's sixpence cut in income tax, the campaign was comparatively quiet. The Conservatives increased their majority to a commanding 53 seats, the first time since the election of 1900 at which a Government had been returned to office with an increased majority. Macleod's majority in Enfield West, in a straight fight with Labour, rose to 11,518.[9]

Eden had made very few changes in the Government when he entered Number 10 in April and Macleod could now look forward to the widely expected early reshuffle in which he was likely to be promoted to the Cabinet. However, the Prime Minister delayed, and Macleod found himself having to fulfil a string of engagements as Minister of Health which he had gladly accepted in the expectation that they would fall to his successor. In August, Henry Fairlie in the *Spectator* tipped him for promotion as Minister of Labour, in succession to Sir Walter Monckton; but as the weeks and months ticked by with no reshuffle, ministers became increasingly impatient. In October, Macleod learned of the possible timing of the long overdue changes when he was in touch with Monckton, both to thank him and his wife for the flowers they had sent Eve who had undergone an operation, and to consult Sir Walter about the vacancy for a chairman of St George's Hospital. Replying on Tuesday 18th, Monckton, who had been exhausted by his four years at the Ministry of Labour, wrote that he would not be kept on after the first part of December. When he added that he would be glad of a chance to talk, Macleod needed no encouragement to take up the offer. He confided that he was rather unhappily in the dark about everything and suggested lunch at White's, where the two men dined on Wednesday 26 October.[10]

Macleod's hopes were eventually realized on 20 December when, as expected, he was promoted to the Cabinet and succeeded Monckton at Labour and National Service. A much bigger surprise, which stole the headlines, was the transfer of Macmillan from the Foreign Office after only seven months – he had been one of Eden's few April appointments – to replace Butler at the Treasury. Macmillan was annoyed at what he saw as demotion and Butler, who became Leader of the House and Lord Privy Seal, came to regret the loss of a power base in a major department of state. But there was no such disappointment for Macleod. He had been the first of his generation to run a Ministry and now, at 42 years of age, he was the first to gain Cabinet rank. Although he was joined at the Cabinet table by Edward Heath, who had become Chief Whip and attended in an *ex officio* capacity, Macleod's former 'One Nation' colleague had no department and played no part in substantive Cabinet discussion. Of Macleod's other close contemporaries, Maudling, Economic Secretary at the Treasury since November 1952, had become Minister of Supply in April. But he remained outside the Cabinet, as did Powell, who joined the Government for the first time as junior minister at Housing and Local Government. Macleod was clearly still the frontrunner among the younger Tories. According to Eden's biographer, Robert Rhodes James, the Prime Minister's 'eyes had been on the exceptional Iain Macleod for some time'. Eden was later to write that he regarded the Ministry of Labour as a useful training ground for a possible future Prime Minister.[11]

Affairs of the heart

It was through his Parliamentary Private Secretary, Sir Reginald Bennett, that Macleod began attending the Thursday Club as a guest, before eventually becoming a member. Macleod and Bennett first met in the late 1940s, when Bennett, who was practising as a psychiatrist in Hampshire, offered to help brief the party on health. After they became MPs, both men happened to join White's. Bennett had served as Parliamentary Private Secretary to both David Maxwell-Fyfe, until the latter's elevation to the peerage, and Geoffrey Lloyd, who left the Government in Eden's December 1955 reshuffle. Shortly afterwards, Bennett received a note saying: 'As someone who's had two Ministers shot from under you, I wonder if you would consider coming and looking after me.' It was signed by Macleod.

The Thursday Club had been founded with the avowed purpose of compelling the weekend to begin on Thursday lunch-time and comprised some of the most witty scriptwriters and show business personalities of the day, including Larry Adler, Patrick Campbell, Arthur Christiansen, Macdonald Hastings, James Robertson Justice and Peter Ustinov. They used to meet in the top-floor room of Bernard Walsh's Wheeler's restaurant in Old Compton Street, Soho, where they drank the Chablis, ate the seafood and regaled one another with amusing anecdotes and witty repartee. Macleod delighted in these lunches, sometimes crying with laughter at their hilarity. He was more than capable of holding his own among such a gathering of brilliant raconteurs, relished the verbal banter, and earned the respect of the other members. After he left the Ministry of Labour, he had to take parliamentary questions on a Thursday afternoon and could no longer continue this diverting, weekly entertainment, but when the Thursday Club later merged into the *soi–disant* Wessex Hunting Club, that existed merely to provide convivial evenings for its members, he occasionally used to attend and join in their various japes.[12]

After becoming a Minister, Macleod only had time to play or watch the occasional game, often at White's. His winnings from a session of bridge usually provided the family's spending money for their annual holidays. He made no secret of his love for rugger, cricket and horse racing. The annual rugby international between Scotland and England for the Calcutta Cup was an immovable fixture in his diary each year and he used to insist that his officials at the Ministry of Labour should arrange a departmental visit to

Scotland, enabling him to attend the game whenever it was played at Murrayfield. He became a favourite speaker at the dinners following the match, when he would indulge in the conventional ribald humour. 'What's the difference between an MP and a shop steward?' he quipped at one such occasion, 'Answer: an MP knows all the facts in the country.' The Minister's coarse joke was soon circulating round the Commons and was quickly embellished. On the next Monday, Reggie Bennett was greeted by a senior Conservative, who began telling him a joke: 'What's the difference between a Minister of Labour and a shop steward?'[13]

News of the latest Test Match score was always welcome, however heavy the pressure of official business and he would be annoyed if his private secretaries could not tell him the state of play when he phoned from the House. During the Oval Test each August, when the Commons was in recess, he spent as much time as possible at the ground instead of behind his desk. He enjoyed occasional visits to the races and he tried to make an annual event of Oaks Day at Epsom. He loved the theatre but had no interest in art and was tone deaf. Although he was generally in favour of closer cooperation in Europe, overseas visits bored him and he found attending the International Labour Organization's conference at Geneva especially tiresome. When he was asked whether he had enjoyed an official visit to Germany, he responded, 'all right, but the Germans are terribly provincial'. He always hated being at a loose end or away from the action. Landscape and scenery bored him, and he would rather stay in his hotel than visit the local sights. From the late 1950s, the Macleods regularly spent their holidays at S'Agaro on the Costa Brava. Like another regular visitor, Selwyn Lloyd, Macleod had learned of the resort from Gerald O'Brien, a public relations consultant. As the Macleods travelled through France and Spain *en route* for S'Agaro, Iain would protest whenever they stopped to admire some scenic view.[14]

Macleod and his wife, Eve, showed immense personal courage in battling against the physical disability that afflicted both of them for the greater part of their married life. In the face of this challenge it would have been understandable if they had eased up and led quieter, less demanding and less public lives. But neither of them considered making any concession and they drove themselves with a fortitude that reveals an awesome will-power. Perhaps in their determination to overcome their disabilities, they overcompensated. They were not always the easiest of couples to get to know socially, although once the ice had been broken they were relaxed and entertaining and thoroughly enjoyed a good gossip.

Macleod was self-centred and could change in an instant with no apparent reason, from being self-absorbed, introspective, seemingly morose even, to being great fun and making anybody feel that he or she was the only person in the world. Acquaintances were sometimes shocked at Iain's apparent disregard for Eve's handicap, but when a close friend remonstrated with him about it he countered that she did not want any special consideration to be shown. However, at speaking engagements and other public occasions, Iain quietly took great care to ensure that Eve was never put in a position where her disability might prove awkward or embarrassing to her.

Iain and Eve always spoke their minds. A marriage between straight–forward and strong-willed characters was unlikely to create an atmosphere of perpetual serenity. Their natural climate was one of sunshine and showers. But in human relationships the bonds that withstand stormy weather can become unbreakable. This was true of the Macleods. Iain's roller-coaster political career always came first, and, as was the case with other middle-class couples in an era when the husband's work took pre-cedence, it became, in effect, a joint career. Eve took care of the problems in the constituency virtually single-handed and stood by Iain through thick and thin.

Macleod had been a playboy during the latter half of the 1930s and, in the view of his daughter, Diana, would have continued this way of life had the war not intervened and led to his discovering, fortuitously, that he had a vocation for politics. Many women were attracted by his highly romantic personality and natural wit. From the early 1950s, his emergence as the rising Tory star and his later Cabinet status added the aphrodisiac of power. His charisma and romanticism spawned friendships and liaisons, accom-panied by letters and poems in which his romantic impulse was given free rein. His blandishments to women friends needed to be taken with a pinch of salt and at least one recipient doubted at the time that his words were intended only for her.

Among his close women friends were Lady Pamela Berry, the political hostess, and Anne Thornton, whom he first met in his Enfield constituency. Lady Pamela, whom Eve nicknamed 'the raving beauty', was the daughter of F.E. Smith, a great Tory trumpeter earlier in the century. She was also a power in her own right, as both Eden (whom she vilified) and Macmillan (who snubbed her) discovered during their premierships. However, she championed Macleod, saying that she liked him because he was not a 'public school Tory'. This observation was galling for his colleagues, who used to remind her that Macleod had, in fact, attended Scotland's most prestigious public school. Anne Thornton's mother had found Macleod digs when he first became the Tory candidate in Enfield (Anne had attended the adoption meeting), and the Macleods later became next door neighbours on The Ridgeway.

There were various romances, and Macleod appears throughout as an incurable romantic. 'It's very wearing being in love ain't it?' he admitted in one letter, and added poignantly, 'Maybe I'll grow up sometime.' He was also excited by the risk he was taking, although knowledge of ministerial peccadilloes rarely leaked beyond a small circle until the Profumo scandal in 1963. Macleod could usually find some explanation for lunching a female companion if a journalist or fellow politician saw him. These lunches à deux might be taken at raffish haunts like Scott's Bar – Macleod would expect any companion to drink alcohol at his own prodigious rate (double gins or American martinis). Sometimes it would be champagne at the Ritz, where, on one occasion, after drinking the first glass he suggested to the waiter that it had, perhaps, seemed a little flat – a ploy that resulted in two fresh glasses of best champagne being provided on the house.

With apparent insouciance, Macleod penned personal letters on departmental stationery. His irrepressible wit was committed to Ministry of Labour notepaper, in a letter that began:

Sh! Look at me. Know what I'm doing? I look as if I'm working but I'm not. I'm surrounded by boxes an' files an' pamphlets an' reports an' anyone looking at me would say, 'There's a very busy Cabinet Minister busy with his boxes an' files an' pamphlets' . . . an' they'd say 'what a credit he is to the Government an' what an example to us all.' Wouldn't they now? But I'm not really thinking of my . . . I'm thinking of you. And I'm not writing pompous minutes to all my civil servants, I'm writing to my love.

Similarly, he wrote from Bath, where he took the waters in an attempt to relieve his worsening spinal condition. The effect of the extra intake of minerals prompted a pastiche of the penny dreadful:

I'm so full of iron now that I'm sure I'm a different man. Not that stocky paunchy weakling once you knew. Not on your Nellie! I'm the reincarnation of the hero of the ADVENTURES OF LOTTIE. 'Lottie was terrified. His steely jaws fixed her with a metallic glance. The iron jaw snapped. "At last we are alone." The voice rasped like a file. Lottie stumbled backwards onto the iron bedstead. ***** SEE NEXT WEEK'S THRILLING INSTALMENT. WILL LOTTIE ESCAPE?' Not on your. . . .

His poems were conventional, but revealed the feeling for words that was the well-spring of his ability to hold and lift an audience. In this extract from an untitled poem composed in early August 1957, he incorporates references to his boyhood holiday idylls on the Isle of Lewis and his wartime experiences – both deeply formative influences:

Oh, I have loved so many things, my sweet,
So much to hold in my memory:
The slanting sheen of rain in sullen street;
The call of curlew from the evening sky.
The lonely comradeship of men who fight

and die – that smaller men may live and scheme:
And sea trout flashing in an island stream.
Greenwater, and the beat of summer seas
Singing a requiem on my happy days;
My love, for you I will remember these,
My love, it is through you the magic stays.

The passion and jealousy that are a burden of any romantic's heart never entirely quelled Macleod's puckish sense of humour. As one romance neared its end, Macleod lampooned his jealousy of younger suitors – 'the wolf cubs,' as he called them:

Since I saw you I have been having the most luvverly [sic] nightmare every night. I can't wait to get to bed to dream it again. I parade the wolf cubs and a few more senior vulpines on the poop-deck. I don't know where a poop-deck is but that's the place for 'em. Yes sir that's the place. Then I cut their lilywhite throats. Twice. Once for killing and again for pleasure. Then I put a posy of sweet wildflowers into their palsied hands, and drop them in weighted hammocks off the blunt end. Full bottom five they lie, and anyone who wants to can make coral of their bones. Or soup.[15]

There always remained something of the playboy in Macleod. His romantic and poetic traits made him an attractive personality, but there was a darker side of self-centredness. He was not a moral paragon, but he emerges as a genuine human being. As far as he was concerned, his personal life had no bearing on his abilities as an MP or minister. There was no hypocrisy about Macleod. As a politician he did not seek to moralize. On the moral and social questions of his day, he took a libertarian and matter of fact line, believing that individuals, not politicians, were the best judges of how they led their lives.

Watershed at Labour

It is difficult now to recall that the Ministry of Labour and National Service was once a major department of state, at its peak not far below the Foreign Office, the Home Office and the Treasury in Whitehall's pecking order. Its high standing dated from the War, when that colossus of the labour movement, Ernest Bevin, had ensured that the British people were mobilized industrially, as well as militarily. The postwar commitment to full employment and the Ministry's role as an honest broker in settling industrial disputes gave the Minister of Labour a special aura, but few of Bevin's successors had exploited their opportunity to achieve a special standing in Cabinet and a high profile in the country. Although Monckton, the first Conservative postwar Minister of Labour, was widely respected, he concentrated primarily on meeting Churchill's remit to keep industrial peace and reassure the unions that the Government had no intention of introducing penal sanctions against them.

In contrast to Monckton, Macleod was politically ambitious and intended to restore the Ministry's position as a major department of state, fully involved in economic policy. During his tenure at Labour, he was concerned with the conundrum that bedevilled postwar British governments – maintaining full employment, while achieving sustainable growth without inflation. But implicit in the responsibilities of a Minister of Labour was a potential conflict between, on the one hand, his role as a politician and member of the Cabinet with collective responsibility for economic policy and, on the other hand, his role as the country's chief industrial peacekeeper. Reconciling these roles was to prove a severe test for Macleod in the circumstances of the late 1950s and in one crucial instance was to be beyond him. However, it was not his role as a politician that he was to sacrifice and he finally emerged with his political reputation and standing in the Cabinet greatly enhanced.

Macleod made an immediate impact when, shortly before Christmas 1955, he first entered his St James's Square office – a location he liked because of its proximity to Jermyn Street with its good restaurants. Not only in ambition, but also in style, he was a complete contrast to his predecessor: where Monckton had been genial, Macleod was brusque and could appear cold and distant. On his first morning, he ordered his private secretaries, 'Have a word with Gedling [his private secretary at Health] to find out how I like things done.' As at Health, he tended to work at the Ministry in the morning, and from his office at the Commons in the afternoon. Unusually at the time, Macleod believed in involving his junior minister, Robert Carr, to the full, showing him Cabinet papers and delegating to him about half of the department's work.

Macleod had no direct experience of industry and knew little about the industrial relations scene. However, he immediately impressed his officials as having a good mind which he applied to the issues. Briefing Macleod could be a daunting experience, especially for younger officials. Dame Mary Smieton, who was a deputy secretary at the Ministry, has recalled that 'you would think twice before going to see him about something, you stopped and thought whether you were really in command of the facts'. Other officials recall his being 'very fierce' if he thought he had been wrongly briefed, but – unlike some Ministers in such circumstances – never hysterical. 'He would listen in a withdrawn manner to the arguments presented to him,' recalls one of his closest advisers. 'Then his mind was revealed in blunt and confident phrases. Acceptance or dismissal of one's case differed little in the manner of delivery.' Macleod's mood varied greatly, depending on how he felt each day. Although he often appeared to be in great discomfort, he never talked about his disability or the pain he was suffering as his back condition worsened. This appeared to influence his manner. Whereas Monckton had enjoyed emollient chats at the Ministry, there was 'a certain impatience' about Macleod. But he was not a confrontationist. Sometimes, he would describe his preferred course of action as having, for instance, a 5 to 4 on chance of success, compared with an alternative option at 6 to 4 against – some officials rapidly had to brush up their bookmaking.[16]

Macleod's arrival coincided with a watershed in Britain's postwar industrial relations. Inflation was again a worry. After only moderate increases during 1953 and 1954, prices were rising at 3.5 per cent a year and wages at 4.5 per cent. This time, inflation appeared to be wage-driven and was accelerating. Moreover, as Geoffrey Goodman, an astute observer of the industrial scene, has noted, economic and technological change, allied with deep changes in society, were creating more aggressive attitudes among managers and on the shopfloor. Conscious of the threat from increasingly efficient competitors overseas, management had begun to take a harder line towards the unions. At the same time, the unions were coming under pressure to take a tougher stand as their members became less deferential and less inclined to accept old pay relativities. A few months after Macleod moved into St James's Square, the election of Frank Cousins as General Secretary of the powerful Transport and General Workers Union marked the emergence of a new type of union leader – assertive, outspoken and disrespectful of his traditionalist predecessors and the old guard who still dominated the TUC.[17]

The employers' offensive had begun only two months before Macleod's appointment, when the British Employers' Confederation called for immediate action to keep costs and prices stable, including wage restraint. Their initiative had been well timed after the Chancellor's post-election credit squeeze in July 1955 and, in turn, their stance bolstered the Chancellor's resolve to impose even tougher economic measures in his October budget. However, the employers were still not satisfied, and in November, the Federation of British Industry added their voice to calls for a Government statement on prices and wages. The Government responded by trying to reach an understanding on pay with employers and unions. Their White Paper, 'The Economic Implications of Full Employment', published in March 1956, marked a major shift in policy. In essence, the approach was now no different from that pursued by Labour in the late 1940s. The Conservatives had placed their faith in removing controls and deregulation; but now they were implicitly acknowledging that their pursuit of economic freedom had not worked.[18]

Macleod was under no illusion about the difficulties involved in securing cooperation on pay restraint from the unions. The first opportunity formally to sound their opinions occurred on 5 March, when Eden, Macmillan and Macleod met the TUC economic committee to hear their protests about the tougher economic policies pursued since the election. In his brief for Eden,

Macleod noted that the TUC economic committee were 'on the whole moderate and reasonable men' – Cousins had become a member only five days before this was written. However, Macleod warned that:

> We should not expect too much, and may get nothing at all. This is partly because the TUC have very little real power, partly because it is difficult for them to co-operate openly with a Tory Government, and partly because, whatever the Right Wing may try to achieve, we have no chance of influencing the Left Wing who control a number of important unions.

Macleod realized that the best approach was 'not to try to push them much at the first meeting, which should be largely explanatory and exploratory'. But he hoped that at a second meeting, armed with 'satisfactory assurances of help in regard to profits and dividends' from employers, they might be able to persuade the TUC 'to take a few steps along the road of restraint'.[19]

Macleod also accepted that any hope of an understanding on pay required some action on prices. In his notes for a speech by Eden in January 1956, Macleod had written:

> There is no hope of moderation in wage claims until we get more stable prices. When Cousins said, a day or two ago, that as long as prices rise, wages must rise too, he was no doubt talking economic nonsense, but it remains one of the awkward facts of life that we have to cope with.

During the spring, the Government intervened in public sector industries to prevent prices increases in transport, electricity, coal and gas. However, their move was tantamount to a pay and prices policy by the back door. By curbing price rises and thereby weakening the financial position of nationalized industries, Ministers had limited their ability to negotiate freely with the unions.[20]

On 10 May, Macleod joined Eden, Macmillan and Butler, to put the Government's formal appeal for wage restraint to the TUC General Council. According to the minute of the meeting, Macleod argued that 'the Government were not asking for an absolute freeze of wages', and he 'did not think the cost of living increases would be a serious problem, especially if the policy of stability were successful. What the Government wanted was much more moderation in the next round of wage increases than there had been in the last two rounds.' However, the TUC's response was inconclusive. By the end of the month speeches by Eden and Macmillan demonstrated the Government's determination to take a stand on pay. Their pleas for wage moderation and the prospect held out by the Chancellor of 'a plateau of stability' for prices provoked a fierce denunciation from Cousins. On 2 June Macleod reiterated the Government's message that Ministers 'have asked not for a freeze but for restraint'. Already, in the first four months of 1956, pay increases had added as much again to industry's costs as the £250 million added during the whole of 1955. 'If runaway inflation continues,' he warned, 'full employment will wither away.'[21]

Macleod was clear that the Government should continue to hammer home their warnings on the economy. As he reported to Eden on 4 June, that year's chairman of the TUC, Wilfred Beard, a skilled engineer, had told him that the moderates could only restrain large, general wage claims if they knew exactly what the position was going to be – thus Beard had welcomed the engineering employers' announcement, in advance, that they could not meet a general wage claim. Macleod concluded that the Government's campaign 'is biting rather deeper than the newspapers think', and 'we should go on being as blunt as we possibly can in our speeches about the economic position and our determination to push our policies through'.[22]

Against the background of this simmering conflict on wage restraint, Macleod was suddenly confronted during the spring and summer of 1956 by a major industrial relations crisis that seemed to blow up from nowhere. In April, the Standard Motor Company in Coventry announced large-scale redundancies that summer because of the automation of their tractor factory – new German machines would enable six men to do the work previously done by 28. Negotiations with the unions had failed and at the end of the month 11,000 Standard car workers went on a seventeen-day unofficial strike. Faced with a worsening market for British cars and vehicles as a result of the credit squeeze at home and new import controls in Australia there was little the unions could do. Standard insisted on dismissng 2,600 men, offering each worker £15 compensation. Almost overnight, the spectre of automation appeared to pose a threat to job security throughout British industry.[23]

Publicly, the Government sought to distance themselves from the problem, while seeking to play down shopfloor anxieties. But behind the scenes, Ministers were alarmed. In early May, Macleod wrote a memorandum to the Cabinet, in which he proposed a series of measures to deal with the crisis. His message to the Cabinet was bullish on the need to 'welcome and encourage' automation, since it would increase productive efficiency, improve the standard of living, 'and will therefore in the long run be to the advantage of the workers'. Nonetheless, he was sensitive to the 'genuine fear among industrial workers' and at Cabinet on 8 May warned that this 'might well be exploited by Communists'. Two days later, he was suggesting that in view of the unforeseen financial losses that some workers would suffer, Government departments concerned should consider whether any adjustments were needed in national insurance or social security in order to afford compensation. In addition to the setting up of an interdepartmental inquiry, Macleod's response to the crisis entailed a plan of action: a public education campaign to ensure that the problem be placed in proper perspective; employers should be encouraged to avoid the discharge of workers and should consult the unions; employment exchanges should help people find fresh employment; and there should be promotion of the opportunities for training in new skills.[24]

By way of reassuring people on the shopfloor, Macleod sought to elaborate this enlightened and practical approach in a series of speeches. On 9 May, he told MPs that it was essential if automation was being considered, that from the beginning management should bring the unions into the closest consultation. On 4 June, speaking in his constituency, he pledged he would do 'everything within my power to ensure that the introduction of automation has no harmful effects on what is still our most valuable asset, the skill and diligence of our men and women'. Reporting that his officials had set up special offices at the Standard works, he added: 'We can always help if early notice is given to us of intending changes in the labour force.' And addressing the International Labour Organization conference in Geneva on 21 June, he spoke of 'the real fear which must be understood and overcome'. To this end, the Government had a duty to maintain full employment and to ensure that 'its social services are adequate and imaginative enough for modern and changing conditions'.[25]

However, a much bigger bombshell hit the Midlands car industry less than a week after his Geneva speech. On Wednesday 27 June, as the summer holidays approached, the British Motor Corporation (later to become British Leyland) summarily sacked 6,000 workers with only one week's basic wage in lieu of notice. The lack of any warning or prior consultation with the unions had gone against everything Macleod had been saying. He was angered and deeply shaken, as was evident during his Commons statement, when he was critical of the BMC's handling of the dismissals. Jack Jones, the newly appointed TGWU Midlands regional secretary was impressed that a Conservative Minister had reacted so strongly. Three months later, Macleod's displeasure at what had happened at BMC was still apparent when he addressed the Conservative Party conference. Though talking about management in general, his meaning was clear when he commented that 'it ought to be easy, because automation must be part of the long term planning of a firm', for there to be 'consultation from the very beginning at all stages and at all levels'.[26]

During the summer, despite divisions on the shopfloor and the weak position of the unions in the car industry at the time, BMC factories were disrupted by unofficial action. After talks between management and the unions broke down, an official strike was called from 23 July. But within a week, Macleod had intervened to bring the two sides together for renewed negotiations. A settlement was finally reached a fortnight later when the BMC agreed to pay modest compensation to the dismissed workers and pledged to consult the unions in the event of any further redundancies. In an effort to help the sacked workers, Macleod's officials combed the country for vacancies, and other Ministries speeded up their labour intake. Indeed, by October, Macleod was able to report to the Conservative conference that only 230 men were still signing on the unemployment register, and only 21 of those placed by the exchange were found jobs that meant them living away from home. As Macleod was to observe much later, the BMC episode 'led over the years to vast improvements in our statutory machinery dealing with redundancy'. At the time of the sackings, he saw the need for research into the problems caused by redundancy. The National Institute of Economic and Social Research agreed to sponsor a survey and Professor Charles Madge at Birmingham accepted responsibility for the project. *Repercussions of Redundancy*, by Dr Hilda Kahn, was finally published eight years later. Based on a sample of ten per cent of the sacked BMC workers, it was a seminal work on the subject.[27]

The BMC sackings were to embitter industrial relations in the car industry for years to come. They also made for an unhappy prelude to the conference season during the autumn of 1956. Even more depressing for the Government, their hopes of fostering an understanding on pay restraint with the unions were rudely rebuffed at September's Trade Union Congress at Brighton. In his first speech to Congress as General Secretary of the TGWU, Cousins rejected wage restraint in language that had not been heard from a major union since the General Strike, thirty years earlier. 'In a period of freedom for all,' he declared, 'we are part of the all.' As Richard Crossman, the Labour politician who witnessed the speech, later noted, it spelled the end of 'Butskellism' as far as the unions were concerned. It also spelled trouble for Macleod at the Conservative conference a month later.[28]

Macleod recognized that a further round of big pay awards was a nightmare for many Conservatives. The prospect of profits and dividends being further outstripped by wages, and of fixed incomes being further eroded by inflation, spread alarm and despondency among the middle and lower middle classes, especially when the people who appeared to be gaining most at their expense were the unionized, Labour-voting working class. In his speech on industrial relations at the 1956 Llandudno conference, Macleod nodded in the direction of those people who felt, in effect, dispossessed by the coming of the annual pay round and seemingly ever bigger wage rises. The problem had been that 'inflation suited or rather seemed to suit too many people'. Vast pay demands were made, 'and when granted by the employers they were added on to the cost of the product and so in turn added to the cost of living.' But, he added:

Inflation did not suit everybody. It did not suit the pensioners. It did not suit the 'middle classes', however you may like to define that term. It did not suit all those who had no great organization to defend them. Let me say that in my view the Tory Party is, and must always remain, the natural spokesman of those who are undefended.[29]

Macleod had skilfully woven this assertion into the passage of his speech that revived the idea of a contract of service, originally proposed in the *Industrial Charter*, ten years earlier. Implicit in the idea of contracts of service was the notion of longer-term agreements on terms and conditions and Macleod promised to take up the idea of how best the contract of service – including the principle that the period of notice should be related to length of service – could be introduced into British industry. But he was too realistic a politician to imagine that this reform offered an early solution to inflation.

At Llandudno, Macleod also had to answer demands for unions to hold a secret ballot before they could call a strike. In rejecting the proposal, he courageously spelled out the realities of shopfloor attitudes to the Conservative Party faithful. 'The idea, of course, is that the workers are less militant than their leaders,' but, he added, 'All I can tell you, speaking frankly, is that this is not my experience, nor is it the experience of any Minister of Labour.' Indeed, if secret ballots were introduced, he believed 'the number of strikes would in fact increase'. This view had also been taken by Churchill and Monckton – 'if I am wrong I am in good company'.

Declaring his 'One Nation' belief in the ideal of partnership – not conflict – as the basis for industrial relations, he took the opportunity to signal to the unions that the Conservative Government had no intention of legislating against them:

I believe firmly that the British system of free voluntary negotiation in industry, with the minimum of Government interference, is the best, and I believe firmly in the trade union system. Those views are fundamental to my political beliefs, and I have not altered them in any way. Nor will I.

They were brave words to say at the Conservative party conference at any time, let alone the month after Cousins's outburst. But the much greater controversy of Suez dominated the conference and was dwarfing all other issues in British politics.[30]

Suez – close to resigning

The nationalization of the Suez Canal Company by President Nasser of Egypt on 26 July 1956 triggered a crisis that was to eclipse every other issue in British politics during the rest of the summer and autumn. The controversy it stirred was to polarize society more deeply than any other event since Munich eighteen years earlier. Its ramifications for the country and – as Macleod was one of the first to recognize – for the Conservative Party were to be felt for a long time to come. Macleod did not oppose the overall policy on Suez. Even long after the event, when Suez had become synonymous with deceit and humiliation, he never sought to dissociate himself publicly from it. During the crisis, Macleod kept his cards even closer to his chest than usual, but he had serious migivings and contrary to what has commonly been thought, he came close to resigning.[31]

Although Macleod was a member of the Cabinet, he was not one of the half dozen Ministers assigned to the Egypt Committee, set up to manage the Suez crisis. Like most other Ministers, he did not know everything that was going on behind the scenes. Even the members of the Egypt Committee were sometimes in the dark – Eden, for instance, appears to have been unaware of Treasury warnings that Macmillan received about the risk to sterling in the event of military action. But an important additional factor was at work that made Suez different from almost any other crisis. Although Eden's premiership was already being heavily criticized in the press and colleagues sometimes found him meddlesome and irritable, he was regarded as being the supreme master of international diplomacy, having scored great triumphs during 1954 and 1955, and was acknowledged to be an expert on the Middle East to boot. Whatever else they may have thought, virtually every Minister felt that Eden was uniquely qualified to handle Suez. Their comparative ignorance and inexperience in foreign policy meant that they were disinclined to press him or his loyal Foreign Secretary, Selwyn Lloyd, for more information or question their approach. The prevailing state of mind in the Cabinet as a whole might best be described as being 'Anthony knows best', or 'leave it to Anthony'. This attitude suited Eden, who was less than frank with his Cabinet and tended to present them only with the stark, strategic choice of pressing ahead or failing.[32]

It is important to understand the overall policy to which Macleod was party as a member of the Cabinet. As Sir Norman Brook, the Cabinet Secretary minuted Eden during the crisis, all Ministers agreed that Nasser should not be allowed to get away with what he had done, and that if he succeeded, Britain risked losing its oil, its standard of living, its position in the Middle East – where Britain remained the pre-eminent power – and its influence as a world power. The two key Cabinet decisions in the run-up to the crisis occurred on 21 March and 27 July 1956. At the first, Ministers endorsed Selwyn Lloyd's dual strategy to counter Nasser, who was thought to be leaning to the Soviet Union and plotting Britain's downfall in the region, and to build a new pro-British alliance based on Iraq and Jordan. The withdrawal of American and British financial asistance from the Aswan High Dam project, announced on 19 July, was one element in this anti-Nasser policy.[33]

The day after Nasser's nationalization of the canal – his riposte to the United States and Britain – the Cabinet agreed to denounce his action. They could not condemn it as illegal, since the Company, after all, was Egyptian, and it 'amounted to no more than a decision to buy out the shareholders'. Instead, Britain would argue that the canal was 'not a piece of Egyptian property but an international asset of the highest importance and it should be managed as an international trust'. This was the position to which Ministers who later came to doubt Eden's approach always held.

However, in response to Eden's 'fundamental question', the Cabinet also agreed that they were prepared 'in the last resort to pursue their objective by the threat or even the use of force', and, in the absence of help from the United States and France, to take military action alone. No Conservative minister was prepared, the morning after nationalization, to demur from such a course of action, especially since the phrase 'in the last resort' gave the impression – misleading, as events were to prove – that Eden was bent on achieving a diplomatic settlement. But the Prime Minister had been astute in securing the Cabinet's sanctioning of force at the outset, since it became extremely difficult for Ministers not involved in handling the crisis on the Egypt Committee to object later to military action that was, in reality, designed to achieve Eden's objective – shared by other hawks, notably Macmillan – of invading Egypt and overthrowing Nasser.[34]

During the late summer, while the diplomatic negotiations continued, Macleod actively sought to rally support for the Government within the trade union movement. In mid-August, his concern at the likely course of events at the annual Trade Union Congress prompted him to invite Sir Vincent Tewson, TUC General Secretary, who lived near him in Enfield, to his home one evening to talk over the crisis. Minuting Eden on their talk, Macleod reported that Tewson took 'a very "weak-kneed" attitude to the whole affair' and was 'ill-informed'. With every prospect that the Trade Union Congress would debate an emergency resolution on the crisis, Macleod was anxious that the right-wing leadership should be 'properly briefed'. He also wanted to influence the General Council to have any emergency resolution 'drawn up so that it will be as innocuous as possible'. Tewson had already approached Eden, and was seeing the Prime Minister privately the following day. Five days later, on Monday 20th, Eden, accompanied by Macleod, had a further private meeting at Number Ten with Tewson, and two moderates, Beard of the engineers and Geddes of the postmen's union. At Brighton, Macleod's hopes were realized and the Congress unanimously backed an equivocal resolution, moved by Geddes.[35]

Nonetheless, reactions in the trade union movement in the event of armed intervention were causing concern in Whitehall among those closely involved in masterminding the Suez operation. Their anxiety surfaced in the Cabinet minutes of 11 September, where it was noted that the Prime Minister would arrange for the Minister of Labour 'to ascertain at the appropriate stage from responsible trade union leaders whether it was likely that serious difficulties would arise within industry if it became necessary to undertake military operations in the Eastern Mediterranean'. It is not clear if Macleod's suspicions were aroused that something more sinister lay behind the veneer of contingency planning, leading him to query this remit.

Or possibly, Sir Norman Brook realized the danger that consulting union leaders was bound to lead to rumours about military planning. In any event, Brook advised Macleod 'to hold his hand for the moment, as this was not the appropriate time'.[36]

Brook had good reason to treat Macleod with kid gloves. By late August doubts about using force had increased within the Cabinet and even within the Egypt Committee, where on Friday 24th, an 'outburst' by the Defence Secretary, Monckton, had shaken his more hawkish colleagues. Assessing the state of Cabinet opinion in a note for Eden written the following day, the Cabinet Secretary listed Macleod among the minority of Ministers who 'will want to postpone the use of force until *all* else has been tried, or until Nasser provides us with a good occasion, whichever happens earlier'. Significantly, the two most notable doubters were the men whom Macleod most respected among the senior members of the Cabinet and to whom he was closest, Butler and Monckton – the latter was to rehearse his doubts about the use of force at a Cabinet review of the crisis on 28 August. Brook identified the other doubters as being the Earl of Selkirk, Heath, who, strictly speaking, was not a member of the Cabinet, and possibly Kilmuir and Heathcoat Amory. According to Brook, the six 'waverers', plus three 'unknowns' were outnumbered by ten who were 'pretty solid', i.e. hawks.[37]

During September and October, the plans for military action were refined and updated. The mood of the Conservative conference in early October was, predictably, hostile to any idea of 'appeasement' of Nasser. This can only have served to increase Eden's inclination to use force. To all intents and purposes, as far as Eden was concerned, the intense diplomatic activity was a charade that helped carry his Cabinet doubters with him and mollify international opinion. The crisis finally came to a head when Eden, now desperate that the Israelis suddenly seemed about to upset his grand design by attacking Jordan, took up a ploy devised by the French. In this scheme, Israel would attack Egypt through Sinai, apparently threatening the Suez Canal, and Britain and France would then demand withdrawal by both sides from the Canal Zone, allowing Anglo-French forces to enter and protect the waterway. The plan was agreed and signed – at Israeli insistence – by the British, French and Israelis at Sèvres during 22–24 October.[38]

How much did Macleod know about the collusion with Israel? He was one of a number of Ministers who missed the thinly attended but vital Cabinet meeting of 18 October. However, he received the minute summarizing Eden's report that he had told the French that every effort had to be made to prevent the Israelis attacking Jordan; and that through the French, he had made it known to the Israelis that, in the event of hostilities between Egypt and Israel, Britain would not come to Egypt's assistance. On 23 October, referring to Lloyd's talks at Sèvres, Eden told the Cabinet that: 'From secret conversations which had been held in Paris with representatives of the Israeli Government, it now appeared that the Israelis would not attack Egypt alone'. Macleod therefore knew that there had been direct contact with the Israelis on the circumstances in which hostilities against Egypt might begin.[39]

On 24 October, the Cabinet further considered the balance of argument for negotiation or using force. The die was finally cast at the fateful Cabinet held on 25 October. Eden reported that whereas on the 23rd it had no longer seemed likely that Israel would move alone, 'it now appeared, however, that the Israelis were, after all, advancing their military preparations with a view to an attack on Egypt'. But crucially, he sought to mislead the Cabinet. He kept the Sèvres protocol secret and spoke as though the scheme that had in fact been agreed with the French and Israelis was merely a contingency plan. Macleod was among the main doubters on the use of force, along with Monckton and Heathcoat Amory. The nature of Cabinet minutes makes it impossible to identify which particular objections were Macleod's, but among the most powerful were the lasting damage that would be inflicted on Anglo-American relations, and, in seeking to separate the Egyptian and Israeli forces, 'we should be purporting to undertake an international function without the specific authority of the UN'. Nonetheless, neither Macleod nor the other two doubters finally dissented from the Cabinet's agreement in principle to the course of action to be followed 'in the event of an Israeli attack on Egypt'.[40]

Macleod and most of the Cabinet had been deceived about the extent of collusion with the Israelis. They knew that there had been 'secret conversations' – a development that was hardly surprising given the Israeli threat against Jordan – and that the question of an attack against Egypt had come up. But they were not told that the contingency put to them by the Prime Minister was, in reality, a carefully laid plan, set out in a signed protocol, to provide the pretext for military action. Eden now had to contrive to maintain the fiction that he had created, even with his own ministers. But in trying to keep up his pretence as a peacemaker, he ensured that the 'quick and successful' military operation that he had envisaged was unattainable.[41]

On Monday 29 October, the Israelis attacked the Egyptian army in Sinai. At Cabinet on the morning of the 30th, the Foreign Secretary reported that the United States were determined to ask the Security Council to condemn Israel as an aggressor and proposed a delay in Anglo-French intervention for twenty-four hours in the hope that the Americans might be persuaded to back British and French efforts to end the fighting. Macleod and Amory were anxious about totally misleading the Americans, but took some comfort from the proposed delay. However, Eden's scheme was already going awry even before the Anglo-French ultimatum was issued that afternoon. Macmillan gave the first indication of his impending transformation from arch hawk into arch dove, as he reported the haemorrhaging of the gold and dollar reserves and pointed to the need to avoid alienating the US Government. Macleod was also making plain his view that the Cabinet had not been kept fully informed. He was particularly infuriated at Eden's using the phrase 'in time of war' by way of an excuse for his reticence in Cabinet and either now or during the following week, snapped, 'I was not aware that we were at war, Prime Minister!'[42]

Macleod, in addition, voiced serious misgivings at the crucial Cabinet meetings leading up to the Anglo-French invasion. Although the Opposition, almost all the Commonwealth and the United States were now opposed to the Government's plans, the bombing of Egyptian airfields by British and French planes went ahead on 31 October. The US Government suspected collusion with the Israelis and in the Mediterranean, the Sixth Fleet harassed the Anglo-French armada. At the United Nations, Britain and France were isolated, and on 2 November the United States sidestepped their blocking vetoes on the Security Council by winning overwhelming support in the General Assembly for a resolution demanding a ceasefire. But the Anglo-French hawks were not to be denied. In London, the Cabinet responded by deciding that even after a ceasefire, Anglo-French troops would still be needed to play a policing role until the UN were in a position to take over. Again, Macleod and Amory voiced their qualms, reflecting the concern felt on the left of the Conservative Party and arguing that an apparent readiness to hand over peacekeeping responsibilities to the UN was hard to square with an immediate assault. The UN might even feel that Britain's offer was not made in good faith.[43]

By the weekend of 3–4 November, the fighting between Egypt and Israel had virtually ceased. Yet in London on Sunday 4th, to the accompaniment of the noise from the mass anti-Suez demonstration in nearby Trafalgar Square, the Cabinet discussed whether the Anglo-French landings should go ahead. Eden asked each minister for his view. According to an additional record seen by Eden's biographer, Robert Rhodes James, three ministers opted for postponement – Salisbury, Monckton and Buchan-Hepburn; while four opted for a twenty-four-hour suspension – Butler, Kilmuir, Amory and an unnamed minister. It has proved impossible to confirm the supposition that the fourth minister was Macleod, but all the evidence suggests that he is the most likely candidate. Nonetheless, only Monckton's dissent was formally minuted as the other doubters agreed to accept the majority decision.[44]

It was on Sunday 4th, according to Randolph Churchill, who saw him regularly at this time, that Macleod 'seriously considered resignation'. However, Nigel Fisher, who was also a friend of Macleod's, stated in his biography that this was not the case. Fisher may be right that Macleod was not on the point of quitting on the 4th, given his apparent support at Cabinet for only a day's delay in the landings and his failure to join Monckton in formally dissenting. Fisher suggests that Macleod might have resigned if Butler had done so, but 'would never have gone on his own'. Carr, who was working with Macleod at the Ministry of Labour and who had previously been Eden's parliamentary secretary, had no indication that Macleod was on the point of resignation. He had a feeling that Macleod had very considerable doubts, but felt no moral outrage. Although Churchill may have been wrong about the date, other evidence suggests that he was right that Macleod thought he might have to leave the Government. Rees-Mogg, who was close to Butler, recalls gaining the clear impression that Butler had to spend some time dissuading Macleod from going. But more definite corroboration that at one point Macleod thought he should resign comes from a friend, who recalls his arriving suddenly at her apartment during the crisis. As he rushed up the stairs to her flat and burst through the door, he shouted, 'Shut up! Get me a drink! I think I'm going to have to resign!' He had been appalled to discover that ministers had not been told the truth. This incident echoes his rebuke to the Prime Minister in Cabinet.[45]

In the event, only Anthony Nutting, a Foreign Office Minister, and Sir Edward Boyle, a young, liberal Treasury Minister, resigned over Suez. The Anglo-French landings went ahead, but on Tuesday 6th, a massive run on the pound and America's refusal to provide financial help left the Prime Minister with no alternative except to call a ceasefire. For the next few weeks, while Anglo-French troops still occupied part of the Canal Zone, charges of collusion were rife and the Conservative Party were in a state of collective panic. Among the younger, liberal elements in the party, and in some quarters of the press, the view developed that the older generation of Conservatives were utterly discredited and only the younger generation could save the party and clear up the mess. Some looked to Boyle. When Eden finally went, Rees-Mogg, who was a parliamentary candidate in the North-East, even made a speech urging that Macleod should be appointed leader.[46]

It was in this fraught atmosphere that, on 14 November, David Astor, editor of the *Observer*, whose editorial on Sunday 4th had savaged Eden for his 'crookedness', wrote to Macleod. Boyle, who had just resigned, had signalled privately to Astor that he was not the man to carry the torch and it was also clear that Monckton, despite his qualms, was not the man to take up the fight. So Astor decided to try Macleod, with whom he had had a good journalist–politician relationship. 'I believe that the "collusion" charge is going to be proved,' he wrote, arguing that if 'the proving of this charge' were to be left to the Opposition and the press – and he thought that the *Economist* and *The Times* were on to it – 'the damage to the Conservative Party will be very great and of long duration'. And since, as he believed, 'the collusion was arranged by two Ministers and was made known only to a minimum of others, it is in fact unfair that this fate should befall your Party'. Unless the uncovering of the facts and 'the necessary action to clean our national reputation is carried out by a substantial element in the Tory party,' he warned that 'the Party will be tarnished until it is led by people who are today too young to have been in responsible positions.' Astor had approached Macleod, because 'you have a reputation for honour and for courage. You are also of an age which makes the future of the Tory party even more particularly your concern than its present'.[48]

Astor never received a reply, nor heard anything more from Macleod. However, Macleod took his letter to Number Ten. He was unable to see Eden, but showed it to Freddie Bishop, one of the Prime Minister's private secretaries, and Sir Norman Brook. In his note to Eden, accompanying the letter, Bishop wrote that Macleod had no intention of replying 'but wanted you to see it as soon as possible'. The seriousness with which Astor's letter was viewed is clear from Bishop's next comment:

> That Astor is using these tactics makes us feel quite sick, but it shows that he, and others, are pressing this point very hard. We wonder whether this state of affairs affects your plans for a rest. Might it not be wise to ask 3 or 4 of your senior colleagues to meet you on Sat. afternoon, to discuss all this?

Eden would have none of it. The next day, Cairncross, another private secretary, noted: 'The PM has seen this and did not think any meeting of Ministers was necessary abt [sic] it.'[48]

However, the matter did not rest there. The following Tuesday, the 20th, the charge of collusion was raised in Cabinet. The minutes prevent us knowing for certain who raised the matter, but in the light of his reaction to Astor's letter and the Prime Minister's failure to consult his colleagues, Macleod is the most likely person to have done so. Neither the Prime Minister nor the Foreign Secretary were present – Eden was on the brink of a breakdown and Selwyn Lloyd was in New York. Ministers felt while there could be no question of acceding to requests for an independent inquiry, the Government might well be pressed to make some further statement. For the time being, the Cabinet agreed that 'the best course' would be to repeat the Foreign Secretary's earlier assurance in the Commons.[49]

Despite Macleod's closeness to Butler since the late 1940s, and their common cause as doubters during Suez, he backed Macmillan for the leadership when Eden resigned in January 1957. Macmillan was every bit as committed to the postwar settlement and the ideals of 'One Nation' Toryism as Butler and had cut a more impressive figure than the downbeat Leader of the House in the weeks before Eden's resignation – a contrast that was starkly apparent when they both addressed the 1922 Committee on 22 November. Macmillan had realized during November that no financial assistance would be forthcoming from the Americans unless the Government abandoned its Middle East policy. Either the troops would have to be withdrawn unconditionally, or the Government would have to face the consequences and devalue. The former would humiliate Eden: the latter was unacceptable to Macmillan as Chancellor. Eden's retreat to Jamaica enabled

Macmillan to win the argument. The U-turn was made on foreign policy, not economic policy, and it was Butler who had to carry the responsibility – during Eden's absence – for the humiliating withdrawal from Egypt. Macmillan's adventurism when he, as Chancellor, knew of Britain's financial vulnerability, had helped create the dilemma in the first place. But in resolving it, he had constructed his springboard to the leadership. 'First in, first out', was the charge laid against him, but at least he seemed decisive and his sang-froid reassured Conservative MPs and Ministers.

The succession to Eden was settled by a headcount of the Cabinet after their meeting of 9 January, at which Eden had announced his decision to resign. Salisbury and Kilmuir acted as self-styled tellers – technically, they were helping prepare the advice on which the Queen could draw in deciding whom she should appoint as her next first minister. Each member of the Cabinet was seen individually in Salisbury's office in the Privy Council Offices. 'Well, which is it to be, Wab or Hawold?' asked 'Bobbety' Salisbury. Macleod was among the overwhelming majority who preferred Macmillan. Kilmuir later told Robert Rhodes James that only Buchan-Hepburn had said Butler, although Butler believed that Monckton, the Paymaster-General, and Stuart, the Scottish Secretary, had backed him. Perfunctory consultations with the Party Chairman, Oliver Poole, the Chief Whip, Heath, and John Morrison, Chairman of the 1922 Committee generally echoed the Cabinet's choice. Butler had been widely tipped in the press and was bitterly disappointed at his rejection. Even those, like Macleod, who had shared his doubts over Suez now judged that he was not the man to rally the party and save the Government.[50]

Those who had thought that only Macleod or someone of his generation could save the Conservative Party had reckoned without Macmillan's ruthlessness in winning the leadership and his brilliance in reviving the party and putting Suez behind them. Nonetheless, the party was to pay a heavy price for Suez in the longer term. During the 1950s, it had enjoyed quite substantial support among the 'opinion formers' – academics, commentators, journalists – but by the 1960s this group, who are few in number but influential, were alienated from the Conservatives. As Macleod later told Robert Blake, historian of the Conservative Party, Suez had been the biggest factor in the Conservatives' losing this 'intellectual vote'. A great many other factors were also at work, but Suez stands out as the single, most powerful, radicalizing event of its time.[51]

7

'Political Genius'

I never fight battles I can't win.
    Iain Macleod to his officials at the Ministry of Labour.

In the Aftermath of Suez

Harold Macmillan is rightly credited with saving the Conservative Government after Suez. This extraordinary political achievement has, however, been sullied in the eyes of many by the economic price that was allegedly paid – higher inflation and continued appeasement of the unions. Whether Macmillan is viewed, according to political taste, as the saviour of the party, or is cast as the villain who merely stored up trouble for the future, there can be no doubt that Iain Macleod was his willing lieutenant.

In the immediate aftermath of Suez, the economic and political landscape in which Macleod had to operate as Minister of Labour had been transformed. Before the crisis, the threat of rising inflation and the increasingly insistent demands by employers that the Government should act had led Macleod and his fellow ministers to take a tough stand against large pay claims. Cousins's fighting speech at the start of September had shattered any hopes that the Government's warnings might encourage the unions to reach an understanding on wage restraint, but nonetheless ministers were unshaken in their resolve. But now the Government were extremely vulnerable. They could not afford another crisis. The collapse of confidence in sterling and the prospect of a politically disastrous devaluation had precipitated Macmillan's *volte face* over Suez and led to British withdrawal. Now, as Prime Minister, he and his successor at the Treasury, Peter Thorneycroft, who during his first six months as Chancellor was firmly wedded to the postwar commitment to full employment, were only too aware that the pound was highly susceptible to any new shock. During the early months of 1957, there was a serious risk that a major industrial strike would be the trigger that would bring about a collapse in sterling, leading to the devaluation that had only been staved off during November at the cost of military humiliation. It was extremely doubtful that the Government would be able to survive such a crisis so soon after the catastrophe of Suez.

Yet the chances of avoiding major industrial unrest looked slim. Petrol rationing imposed during Suez had brought higher bus fares and road transport charges and in turn threatened the promise held out by Macmillan of a 'plateau' in prices. During November and December, the railwaymen and the municipal busmen won pay rises of 3 per cent. In the New Year, only two days before Eden resigned, Macleod briefed him on the worrying outlook. Referring to the pattern that had emerged of an increase of around 3 per cent based on the rise in the cost of living over the past year, Macleod warned that 'the cost of living index has risen one point and will rise a further point in ten days' time', because of the knock-on effects of petrol rationing.[1]

Even more worrying was the news from the Minister of Transport, who had alerted Macleod to developments in the wage bargaining for London busmen. Cousins had refused to accept an offer of 3 per cent. The employers, the British Transport Commission, responded by offering just over 4 per cent, an increase that, as Macleod noted, 'can be justified in view of the recent rise in the index'. However, as he continued, 'There can be no doubt now that the other unions in the wage queue will pitch their demands to this new figure.' Moreover, 'this new offer will be very irritating to private employers', who would claim, 'as they have done before, that although they were ready to resist wage claims, the pass has been sold by a nationalized industry and their position thereby hopelessly compromised.' The transport employers may have been right to argue that there would have been a London bus strike, that the tubes would have joined in, and that in any case at arbitration, in view of the rise in the index, an amount of not less than this would have been awarded. Nonetheless, Macleod thought it: 'very strange that decisions of such vast importance should be taken without the Government being informed in advance.' In what was to be one of Eden's final comments as Prime Minister, he noted in his own hand that he agreed with Macleod, adding balefully, 'But not for the first time – we get the pricks & do not even know.' A few weeks later, the executive of the national railwaymen repudiated their leader's acceptance of an offer of 3.5 per cent.[2]

Against this background of escalating prices and growing wage claims, negotiations were resumed in February 1957 for 3,000,000 engineering workers and a further 200,000 men in shipbuilding. The previous summer, the employers had sought, and had been given, a reassurance from the then Chancellor. 'So long as I have anything to do with the Government,' Macmillan had told them, 'we will stand behind you.' At the end of 1956, the unions' general claim for 10 per cent was rejected by both the engineering and the shipbuilding employers. By February, there was no sign that the unions would accept 3 per cent, nor any readiness on the part of the employers to accept arbitration, especially as they perceived – correctly, as it turned out – that Ministers were already backing away from any show-down.[3]

In early March, the unions stepped up their pressure by calling a strike in the shipbuilding yards. 'The dispute is full of politics,' Macleod wrote to Macmillan, clearly anxious that the Government were in danger of being drawn into a confrontation with the unions when they could least afford to do so. 'The employers, by rejecting the claim even before it was tabled, believe that they can carry out the policy of wage restraint that we urged so strongly last year.' Equally, as Macleod added: 'The union leaders believe that the employers are acting under our instructions and have said that "the real fight is against the Government".' In addition, the communist *Daily Worker* wanted to see the strike spread 'to something approaching a general strike', while the Labour Party, 'will see in this an opportunity to attack the Government when they believe it to be weak'.[4]

Macleod judged that whereas some union leaders would welcome his involvement, the employers 'would regard it as a betrayal if I appointed a Court of Inquiry'. Indeed, the ship owners wanted the strike faced, since they believed that they could afford it – a sanguine view that Macleod doubted. But even if the ship owners could afford a strike, there was, as Macleod put it:

> the other question – whether the government, both politically and eco-nomically, can do so? In particular, might it not lead to a renewal of confidence attacks upon sterling if the strike were prolonged and it spread, as I think it will, to other parts of our economy?

Macleod concluded that 'the only possibility is some form of arbitration'. He thought the employers would accept it, reluctantly, and even if it was rejected by some of the militant union leaders, 'something would probably be gained if I offered it'.[5]

Arbitration was offered, but the unions rejected it. On 16 March, an all-out strike began in the shipyards. Two days later, in his first major speech as Prime Minister, Macmillan signalled the shift in the Government's position since Suez. In the long run, he commented, 'the umpire is better than the duel'. On 19 March, the unions decided to introduce a phased call-out of their engineering members, starting on 23 March. The same day, Macmillan and Macleod met representatives of the employers at Number Ten – Eric Braby of the engineering employers, Sir John Hunter of the shipbuilders, Sir Colin Anderson, president of the British Employers' Confederation and Sir Brian Robertson of the British Transport Com-mission, who was facing a claim from the railwaymen. Macleod drafted the speaking note that formed the basis of the Prime Minister's dramatic appeal to the employers on the eve of his departure for Bermuda, where he was to have crucial talks with President Eisenhower aimed at repairing Anglo-American relations after the Suez débâcle.[6]

Macleod's note was designed to bring maximum pressure to bear on the employers and he couched the Prime Minister's appeal in appropriately spine-chilling terms. At the same time, it does reveal how desperately anxious Ministers were to avert industrial conflict on a scale that was likely to jeopardize the fragile confidence in sterling. Opening with a somewhat melodramatic reference to Macmillan's anxiety before he left 'to see if there was an honourable way out of perhaps the worst industrial trouble that has ever threatened us', Macleod spelled out the problem. They faced a battle on three fronts – shipyards, engineering and railways – and trouble was looming in the mines and other industries. 'It is impossible,' Macleod suggested arguing, 'to fight on all fronts at once in a modern society and, in particular, it is almost impossible to run the country if the railways are at a standstill.' He urged that they should separate the issues, 'and avoid battle at least on some of them'.[7]

But it was in the next two paragraphs that Macleod distilled the Conservatives' nightmare. 'Behind this there is a greater danger still,' he proposed warning the employers:

> The Chancellor of the Exchequer has emphasized in the gravest terms the threat to sterling, and we have seen that yesterday [18 March] sterling came under its heaviest pressure this year. It is very doubtful if we can stand a renewal of 'confidence' attacks on the pound. We mobilized our resources to meet the attacks made on it after Suez. We cannot do this again.
>
> Suez is the new factor in the position. It is perfectly true – and the Government accept their share of responsibility – that we urged wage restraint on the country and that some of the actions of the employers have flowed from this. Nevertheless, the point now is to decide what can be done.

In Macleod's view, it was 'impossible to "fight it out"', and equally impossible to keep the dispute strictly limited. The Government were grateful to the shipbuilding employers for having agreed to arbitration, but it was 'clear that unless some figure can come into the discussions no end can be seen'. Since it was 'important that this figure should emerge without surrender either by the Government or by the employers', Macleod proposed suggesting that they make use of the award to the railwaymen that was due the next day and was likely to be slightly higher than 3 per cent.[8]

Macleod's script largely formed the basis for his and Macmillan's appeals to the employers. Robertson was sure that he could achieve a railway settlement if left alone, but wanted to know whether he would then be accused by private industry of selling the pass as the Transport Commission had been in the past. He was reassured on that score, while Braby and Hunter could only agree to consult their members. However, the railwaymen's negotiations were to lead to a disagreement between Macmillan in Bermuda and Macleod in London. Robertson offered 4.5 per cent, but this did not please Macmillan. It gives some idea of the Prime Minister's deep anxiety that, during his crucial talks with President Eisenhower, he should take the trouble to wire Butler, who was deputizing for him at home, urging that the offer be increased to 5 per cent: 'The ordinary person would think it crazy to impose upon our very wobbly economy all the trouble of a railway strike for one-half per cent.' At Cabinet on 22 March, Macleod disagreed, arguing that 5 per cent should only be offered after the unions had issued strike notices. It also shows the general nervousness among Conservatives of risking any confrontation with the unions that Macleod's tougher stand won the support of only four other Ministers – Butler, Brooke (Housing), Lord Mills (Power) and Charles Hill (Chancellor of the Duchy of Lancaster). Macleod was overruled and Robertson settled with the railwaymen for 5 per cent, in return for a promise of continued cooperation in increasing efficiency. 'It looks likely that there will be a 5 per cent railway settlement this evening,' Macleod wired to Macmillan later on the 22nd. 'You know my views, and I will not press them further.'[9]

When the shipbuilding employers then followed with an offer of 5 per cent with conditions, the unions demanded 7.5 per cent. After talks at the Ministry between the two sides had broken down, Macleod again wired to Macmillan in Bermuda. 'It seems impossible to push the employers to concede more than this amount,' he reported, 'and the only course open is to appoint a Court of Inquiry.' The inquiry was duly established under the chairmanship of Professor Daniel Jack. The greater stumbling block remained the Engineering Employers' Federation (EEF), who had been mandated by their members to stand firm. Macleod spent three days cajoling and pleading with the employers' representatives, reiterating the dangers to the Government and the country of a lengthy, major strike. Finally, the engineering employers offered 3.5 per cent, with conditions. When this was rejected by the unions, he set up another Court of Inquiry, again under Professor Jack's chairmanship.[10]

Having incurred the wrath of the employers for putting so much pressure on them, it was not immediately clear that the unions would call off the strike. But while Cousins and the left pressed to fight on and the moderates argued there was no longer any point, Macleod received a welcome boost to his reputation as Minister of Labour. On 30 March, another of his Courts of Inquiry – this one headed by Lord Cameron – reported on a dispute that had occurred at Briggs Motors, part of the Ford Company, during February, when the management had suspended a shop steward and refused to reinstate him. Macleod had pressed the union leaders to agree to a Court of Inquiry, and the announcement of its setting up on 25 February had been a personal victory. The strike was called off the following day and the firm paid the shop steward's wages until the Court reported. The inquiry upheld the company's right to dismiss the shop steward and the unions were pressed to give urgent consideration to the amount of power wielded by the shop stewards at the factory. The outcome was seen as a success for Macleod, showing him to be even-handed and ready to be tough with the unions if they abused their power.[11]

In early April, with 780,000 men idle and more than six million working days already lost in the strike, the engineering and shipbuilding unions called off their strikes amidst much inter-union bickering and bitterness. On the basis of the Jack inquiry, the engineering workers finally won an increase of 6.5 per cent – with strings. After further protracted negotiations, the shipbuilding men fared even better. The employers had lost, although as Macleod pointed out the conditions of the deal precluded the unions from submitting any fresh pay claim for twelve months, which in effect, 'would probably mean no further increase for about 18 months', thereby moving away from the annual wage round. Macleod was also convinced that if the engineering employers 'had not been so determined to concede nothing, the employers could in fact have got agreement on 3.5 per cent without a strike'.[12]

Nonetheless, the engineering employers were furious with the Government for having abandoned their earlier promise to back them in taking a firm stand. They were especially livid with Macleod over his denial in a television interview that the Government had put any pressure on them to settle. In a booklet published by the EEF the following year, Macleod was to get his come-uppance for having given Suez as the reason for reneging on Macmillan's pledge, as that other symbol of British shame – Munich – was hung round the Government's neck. 'Like the Czechs in 1938,' the EEF said of the position in which they had found themselves, 'their complaint was that they were not allowed to resist in 1954 and 1957 after they had received every encouragement to have a firm purpose and to dare to make it known to the unions.' The spring and summer brought a rash of strikes – the provincial busmen, dockers, and the porters in London's Covent Garden all involving the aggressive Cousins. The total number of days lost during 1957 – 8,412,000 – was to be the highest since 1926. The Government had reaped the whirlwind of Suez and rising inflation, but it had survived. And in due course, Macleod was to find his opportunity to cut Cousins down to size.[13]

Looking for a way forward

Almost as soon as the engineering and shipbuilding strikes had been called off, and before the Courts of Inquiry had reported, the Prime Minister was consulting Macleod on the industrial situation. Major strikes still threatened and an undestandably anxious Macmillan wanted to establish whether a strike on the railways, in the mines, or at the docks, would paralyse the country. Macleod suspected that 'assuming reasonable stocks and a fairly steady pound', strikes by either the railwaymen or the miners would not be crippling, but that a protracted dock strike would probably be the most damaging, and he proposed having this examined. But Macmillan had more positive thoughts for the longer term. He had in mind putting much greater emphasis on productivity in pay deals and floated the possibility of meetings with the TUC on the matter. He also suggested renewing the Tories' campaign for a new Industrial Charter, including the right of workers to be given a month's notice before their employment could be terminated, and wondered whether this might help win the TUC's agreement to a system of compulsory arbitration.[14]

Macleod remained sceptical of talks with the TUC. 'We must always remember,' he counselled Macmillan, 'that the TUC have no power at all to negotiate agreements with us, nor to commit or even to speak for their constituent unions.' In his view, the Government had done well in restraining wages over the previous year, since the level of settlements had fallen from between 8 to 9 per cent twelve months earlier, to 3.5 per cent: it was only after Suez that they had begun to rise again. As a result, he believed that 'the best contribution the Government can make this year is to ensure that no deliberate action of theirs puts prices up'.[15]

As to the longer term, the Ministry of Labour were already doing 'a great deal' on productivity and the TUC were involved in the British Productivity Council. Macleod had presented his ideas for a contract of service to the employers and the TUC and hoped to incorporate them in a Code of Practice on workers' rights that would be affirmed by a resolution of the House of Commons – as opposed to legislation, since he was mindful of the Fair Wages Resolutions and the continuing effect they had had on the payment of fair wages and observance of fair conditions by Government contractors. However, he saw no prospect of the TUC agreeing to national negotiations, and no prospect that either side of industry was ready to abandon the opposition they had shown to compulsory arbitration procedures when the idea was proposed after the last round of big strikes in 1955. Conscious that he sounded 'rather negative', Macleod encapsulated his belief that there was no magic wand for improving industrial relations:

> There is no short cut to the problem of making men get on better with each other and there is little we can do, either by Government exhortation or by legislation, but there is a great deal that the work of this Ministry can do and that we are trying to do.[16]

Macleod was not being disingenuous, nor finding excuses for knocking down possible initiatives. He was an insightful, inventive Minister, but genuinely could not see any magic solution. The journalist and comment-ator, Geoffrey Goodman, who first met Macleod when he was a guest at a *News Chronicle* lunch, soon realized his anxiety to move from Monckton's passive approach – not by taking on the unions, but by giving industrial relations a new image. Macleod felt that many of the problems were caused by bad management – too often, British managers were appointed because of their family ties – and saw the urgent need for a new high-class corps of professional managers, such as existed in the United States and Germany. In the days when very few people ever thought about the need to train people to manage, Macleod was a passionate campaigner for management training. He reserved his scorn for the backwoodsmen on both sides of industry. 'Those coelacanths,' he used to say, 'who have somehow survived to the twentieth century but do not know how to respond to its needs.'[17]

Equally, he was anxious to establish a new dialogue with the unions. He worried about how greater order could be introduced into trade union affairs, but eschewed legislative measures. He was interested to explore the scope for more union mergers and developed close links with key figures at the TUC. George Woodcock and Victor Feather, who were both to become General Secretaries of the TUC, came from time to time to brief him – usually by the back door and unbeknown to each other or to their boss, Sir Vincent Tewson. Woodcock, regarded as the TUC's intellectual, held Macleod in high regard and privately often praised his ability. Macleod particularly respected Tom Williamson, the moderate leader of the General and Municipal Workers Union, and Tom Yates of the National Union of Seamen.[18]

Despite his reservations about some of Macmillan's grander ideas, when Macleod received the report of the engineering Court of Inquiry at the end of April 1957, he was attracted by a more modest proposal that had first been put forward in 1954 following the last such dispute. As Macleod informed Macmillan, the Jack report saw 'little hope of linking wage movements to productivity', and instead recommended setting up an 'au-thoritative and impartial body to consider the wider problems of wages policy in all branches of industry'. Macleod believed that having 'such a body of some independent authority considering the general economic position of the country as affected by wages, profits and prices' would have 'a useful effect on public opinion'. He therefore suggested to the Chancellor that officials should 'work out a definite scheme for the constitution and working of such a body'.[19]

During the summer of 1957, Thorneycroft was still in his Keynesian mode and wanted the new body to issue a 'guiding light' figure for pay increases. This figure would be compatible with stable prices and the Council would identify some of the grounds for exceptions. However, the Cabinet vetoed this idea, Macleod being among those who saw the danger of the guiding light becoming the minimum benchmark for the unions. Despite this setback for Thorneycroft, and notwithstanding the disdain shown towards his proposal by the TUC, the Chancellor nonetheless appointed the new Council on Productivity, Prices and Incomes in August. Chaired by Lord Cohen, with Sir Harold Howitt and Sir Dennis Robertson, an economist, as the other members, the 'Three Wise Men' were to be the first of a series of bodies appointed by governments to help in their attempts to restrain wages. It was not a success. Robertson was an advocate of 'tough money' policies, and the Council's first report in February 1958 defended Thorneycroft's September 1957 credit squeeze. Cousins and the left had boycotted the TUC's first meeting with the Council and now any vestigial hope that the TUC might cooperate more fully in its work disappeared.[20]

By the autumn of 1957, Macleod's plans for incorporating a Code of Practice on workers' rights in a Commons resolution had received a cool reception from both sides of industry. Instead, he decided that he should publish a booklet bringing to the notice of industry the best and latest practice. As he told the 1957 Conservative Conference at Brighton, he and Robert Carr had been compiling examples from large and small firms of good employment practice. These covered such matters as redundancy and employee security, length of notice, joint consultation between employers and workers' representatives, training and promotion and ways of presenting financial information to employees. In his foreword to *Positive Employment Policies*, published in March 1958, Macleod commended these examples to other firms and stressed that industrial efficiency depended as much upon human factors as upon mechanical and technical resources. The booklet flourished and was in demand for many years.[21]

During his final year at Labour, Macleod's Terms and Conditions of Employment and the Wages Councils Acts paved the way for more ambitious measures – the Contracts of Employment Act 1963 and the Redundancy Payments Act 1965. Should Macleod have been less satisfied with his modest achievements in regard to improving workers' rights? The time was not ripe for far-reaching legislation. In the late 1950s, both sides of industry still held passionately to the conviction that, with only limited exceptions such as safety at work, matters affecting the employment of workers were best handled by industry. Macleod felt strongly that what counted most in human relations was a mutual respect and confidence between the parties and that this would grow through voluntary agreements.[22]

At war with the monetarists

After the 1955 election, the Conservatives had become alarmed by a Treasury paper suggesting that while spending on the welfare state had risen by 35 per cent since their return to office in 1951, national output had increased by only 25 per cent over the same period. In addition, various commitments would increase spending still further – the ten-year qualification period for the full state pension fell in 1957. Macleod was appointed to the ministerial committee, chaired by Butler, that met during the first half of 1956 to review the welfare state and, so the Treasury hoped, identify major policy changes that would bring the increase back into line with economic growth. However, rather like the Guillebaud inquiry into the NHS, the Treasury's approach backfired. Not only did the committee reject a whole host of specific proposals, but even the Treasury's basic assumptions were contradicted. Macleod led the charge. Indeed, the committee was to provide ammunition for Macleod and other Ministers when they later fought to resist the Chancellor's cuts. The Cabinet crisis that followed was to become a defining moment of the Macmillan era.[23]

Macleod challenged the assumption on which the whole review exercise had been based and won a notable victory. In October 1956, the Cabinet not only rejected the stock argument – advanced by Macmillan, the then Chancellor – that the welfare state was becoming too great a strain on the economy, but went further. Noting that spending on the social services, despite tending to increase each year in absolute terms, 'was in fact taking a decreasing proportion of national income which was rising more rapidly', ministers agreed to 'give further publicity to this fact in order to meet criticism against the cost of the social services'. The Treasury's argument that high social spending contributed to inflation through its impact on the money supply, was turned on its head: cutting welfare provision – the social wage – was seen as inflationary, since it was likely to lead to higher wage claims. As to the Treasury argument that economies in social spending were needed to avert sterling crises, ministers also strongly resisted any notion that international speculators should, in effect, determine the future of the welfare state. And in January 1957 Macleod demanded that the Government should make a clear statement of the advantages, as opposed to the disadvantages, to be derived from public spending.[24]

One aspect of public spending that Macleod was happy to see cut was the defence budget. The consensus among Ministers held that defence spending was a far more serious cause of inflation than social spending, because it consumed scarce resources and, in a tight labour market, added to the demand for skilled manpower. The call-up was a prime target. National Service was already becoming unpopular, as Macleod had argued before the 1955 election. When the Government subsequently decided to base Britain's defence on the nuclear deterrent, any remnant of military logic for conscription disappeared. Macleod also had personal reasons for ending the call-up. He hated conscription – as he always scathingly called it – but as Minister of Labour and National Service had the unenviable task of considering the pleas for deferment that poured in to MPs. He was deeply troubled by the domestic hardship that the call-up sometimes brought. When he thought an appeal was genuine, he left his officials in no doubt how they should interpret the regulations. He was greatly relieved, on all counts, that he was able to herald the end of conscription. In February 1957, he announced the extension of the period of postponement of the call-up from six months to two years, and two months later, on 17 April, he declared that there would be no call-up of the 1940 class.[25]

During the summer of 1957, a sterling crisis prompted the Chancellor to impose a credit squeeze. As part of his September measures, Thorneycroft promised to curb public spending and persuaded Macmillan to urge all ministers that their departmental estimates for the next financial year, 1958–59, should not exceed those of the current year, 1957–58. Nonetheless, by December 1957, ministers' bids for the coming year added £273 million to the 1957–58 estimates. Some compromise might have been found, but Thorneycroft had undergone a conversion, becoming a believer in 'tough money' policies. In fact, the pace of wage inflation was already beginning to decline when Thorneycroft administered his deflation, but in common with his junior ministers, Nigel Birch and Enoch Powell, he had come to regard high public spending as inflationary. Their insistence on spending cuts took on the character of a crusade.[26]

Macleod used to refer dismissively at this time to Powell's espousal of free market economics as 'Enochery'. Macleod was prepared to take a tough line on public sector pay during the autumn, but, as Powell recalls: 'Iain Macleod was not one of those ministers who sympathized with the exploration of monetarism which was going on amongst the Treasury ministers.' Neither did the Cabinet. The Cabinet crisis came to a head in the New Year, 1958. On 2 January, Thorneycroft had warned Macmillan that he would resign if he could not reduce the estimates by £153 million. The Cabinet met three times on Friday 3 January, but were unable to agree economies that would meet the Chancellor's target. By the end of the day, there still remained a gap of around £50 million.[27]

Among Thorneycroft's proposals had been the withdrawal of family allowance from the second child – a saving of £68 million a year. However, this idea had been rejected before and the Cabinet endorsed ministers' earlier reasoning that withdrawal would lead directly to demands for compensatory wage increases, thus defeating the purpose of the painful exercise. Boyd-Carpenter, the Minister of National Insurance, would have resigned if the Treasury had won. Macleod was infuriated at Thorneycroft's rudeness and intransigence. At that day's final evening meeting of the Cabinet, Macmillan suggested £30 million should be sought from the civil estimates as a whole, but the Chancellor demanded that £30 million had to come from welfare. 'Iain Macleod said this was like Hitler tactics,' noted Boyd-Carpenter. Macmillan adjourned the Cabinet, warning that he would have to consider the Government's resignation if, after further talks over the weekend, there was still no agreement.[28]

At Macmillan's request, Macleod consulted other social service ministers, but found it impossible to meet the Treasury's demands. At Cabinet on

Monday 5th, Macleod reiterated the difficulties associated with the options that had been identified for possible cuts. It would be unwise to abolish the family allowance for the second child and increasing the charge for school milk would encounter serious opposition from school teachers. The introduction of a hospital boarding scheme would involve employing 1,000 additional clerical staff, whom it would be difficult to recruit when the Government had recently refused a pay rise for the grades concerned. The abolition of the ophthalmic service would break Government pledges and yield little more than £4.5 million a year. An increase in the charge for welfare milk to 6d a pint might deserve consideration, but it would be seen as a measure directed against the family. If all these measures were rejected, there remained only the possibility of increasing that element of the national insurance contribution that was attributable to the NHS, but this risked coinciding with the date on which the latest increase in national insurance contributions would come into effect. With no compromise in sight, Macmillan later invited Butler, Macleod, Sandys and Heath to discuss the crisis over dinner. It was Macleod who commented that Thorneycroft 'was obsessed and dominated by Powell'. The next morning, Thorneycroft, Birch and Powell resigned. Macmillan, who was about to depart on a Commonwealth tour, famously dismissed the loss of his entire Treasury team as 'little local difficulties', although privately he worried at the impact.[29]

Powell denies having exerted undue influence over the Chancellor. For his part, Thorneycroft later conceded that he and his team probably made their stand too soon. In Powell's view, Macmillan's 'love of the winning trick' predisposed him to an economic theory that enabled him to buy votes for the next election: 'He saw politics as essentially a game, just as Macleod saw it as a game of bridge . . . pure Whiggery.' Yet the Treasury team appeared to have gone to the other extreme and, in their crass performance, to have eschewed politics completely. Neither should they have expected to persuade the Cabinet to abandon the postwar economic settlement on the basis of the Chancellor's confused presentation of an unproven theory.[30]

What was not beyond dispute was that Thorneycroft intended to increase unemployment – he reckoned to between 2 and 3 per cent. But when unemployment approached 2 per cent the following autumn, the Cabinet were reduced to something approaching panic. The political imperative of this period, when folk memories of the 1920s and 1930s were potent and the great majority of voters were working class, was to keep the numbers registered as unemployed below half a million. Moreover, Macleod – like Macmillan – shared a genuine abhorrence of unemployment. Those who talked with Macleod during his tenure of St James's Square recall that he was obsessed with the problem of how to achieve economic growth without inflation, while maintaining full employment – this latter requirement was, for him, the *sine qua non* of economic policy.[31]

The battle that had to be won

Within three weeks of the resignations of Thorneycroft, Powell and Birch, Macleod was also considering leaving the Government. Whereas the Treasury team had quit in protest at Macmillan's economic policy, Macleod had to decide whether or not he should resign because of his support for that same policy, and in particular, one specific aspect of it – wage restraint. Ever since the Government had first moved decisively towards a pay policy in the spring of 1956, there had been a potential conflict between Macleod's two roles: one as a Cabinet Minister at the forefront of the campaign to curb pay increases; the other as the Minister of Labour, who traditionally sought to maintain a neutral position between the two sides of industry in order to provide industrial conciliation. This conflict was finally brought to a head by the London busmen's strike. By the end of it, Macleod had turned a near-disaster for his career into a personal triumph.

In October 1957, the Transport and General Workers' Union (TGWU) submitted a claim for an increase of 25s a week for 50,000 bus workers employed by the London Transport Executive (LTE). The London busmen had a militant tradition, and when the LTE rejected the claim, the bus workers rejected the TGWU's recommendation to accept arbitration. By the end of the year, further efforts by Harry Nicholas, the union's Assistant General Secretary who was handling the claim, and Frank Cousins, to break the deadlock between the LTE and the busmen had failed. Both sides turned to the Ministry of Labour, and specifically to Sir William Neden, the senior official handling industrial relations. His status as the Minister's Chief Industrial Commissioner reflected his key role in industrial conciliation.

On the morning of 10 January 1958 – shortly before he was due to meet Nicholas and Anthony Bull of the LTE – Neden received a telephone call from Harold Watkinson, the Minister of Transport. Neden had been minded to offer some form of court of inquiry in an effort to resolve the dispute, but Watkinson told him bluntly that he was not to give the union the slightest impression that they could get a penny from their wage demands. Claiming that this was a Cabinet instruction, he warned that no concession was to be made to the busmen. Neden immediately consulted Macleod, who had known nothing of Watkinson's intervention and was shocked at this flagrant interference in the work of his Ministry. As Neden later told Geoffrey Goodman, he informed Macleod that he intended to meet Nicholas and Bull and offer them a court of inquiry in everything but name – either a board of conciliation or a committee of investigation. Neden recalled Macleod's hesitating at this, apparently uncertain of his next step, but he did not reject the plan. Neden made his offer, and the LTE and the busmen reluctantly agreed to cooperate in a committee of inquiry. It seemed that a compromise might be found.[32]

However, Macleod was acutely aware of the dilemma that now confronted him. Neden's plan had taken formal shape as a request from the TGWU to Macleod to set up a committee to examine the claim and make recommendations to the parties. On 20 January, Macleod spelled out the problem to Butler, who was chairing the Cabinet while Macmillan toured the Commonwealth:

In normal circumstances, no Minister of Labour would have had any hesitation in acceding to such a request as part of his normal work of conciliation in industry. In present circumstances, however, I am very liable to be criticised . . . for assisting towards a settlement which might be a major breach in the wages front. On the other hand, to refuse the request would be a very marked departure from normal practice and would be construed as a definite Government move to have a showdown with the unions.

Macleod concluded that he should set up the committee – it would still be open to either side to reject its recommendations and he would appoint as chairman someone who understood 'the seriousness of the issues involved'. When the issue came to Cabinet on 22 January, ministers were split. Two days later, Macleod was overruled. As Butler explained in his cable to Macmillan, informing him of the decision, ministers had felt 'that it would be interpreted by public opinion as the beginning of a surrender to the unions'. Had Macmillan been presiding, Macleod's chances would have been improved – the Prime Minister was always anxious to avert any strike that might spread to the railways or docks.[33]

Macleod was in an almost impossible position. Having allowed Neden, his Chief Industrial Commissioner, to propose a committee of inquiry into the London bus strike, he now had to repudiate him. It was the first occasion on which the traditional assumption of an impartial government holding the ring in industrial negotiations had come into such direct and open coflict with a Government's pay policy. Macleod considered resigning, not because he opposed wage restraint – which he did not – but because of his predicament over the committee of inquiry. He consulted Alf (later Lord) Robens, his opposite number on the Opposition frontbench, who had served as Minister of Labour before 1951 and whom he greatly respected. Robens advised him not to resign. This did not prevent Robens publicly accusing Macleod of having been the first Minister of Labour to repudiate his conciliation officer – not that Macleod ever expected to be given any quarter. Macleod's decision to continue had also been facilitated by Butler, whose skilful summing up in Cabinet had prevented forcing the issue and postponed the final decision until agreement had been reached on the wording of Macleod's letter to the TGWU.[34]

Neden was in an even more difficult position than Macleod, and also came close to resigning. Courageously, he insisted on signing the letter rejecting the committee of inquiry, instead of hiding behind his Minister. News of the volte-face came as a shattering blow to Cousins, Nicholas and the busmen's leaders and even shocked the LTE chairman, Sir John Elliott, who felt some sympathy for the busmen's case. On 28 January, Cousins and Nicholas confronted Macleod in his office at St James's Square. Neden also attended. When Cousins demanded to know who had countermanded Neden's instructions, Macleod snapped that he had. During the course of their emotionally charged exchanges, Macleod suggested that no firm offer had been made by Neden, but Neden defended Nicholas's action in putting such an offer to the busmen. 'That is what I had proposed,' he added. Neden had accused his Minister of being a liar, but he was bitterly angry and was never to forgive Macleod for the incident.[35]

Now that the Government had allowed themselves to be drawn into the London busmen's dispute, Macleod was determined to ensure that they did not lose. He was in a position that had not been of his own choosing, but Cousins was in an even less enviable position – forced to represent a group over whom he had great difficulty exerting any authority and yet who wielded little industrial power. The key as far as Macleod was concerned – as he had argued from the outset – lay in keeping Cousins and the London busmen isolated.

Cousins realized that his best interests lay in resolving rather than prolonging the dispute, but that he faced a formidable challenge in persuading the busmen to settle. Nonetheless he made a heroic start. On 4 February, Macleod cabled to Macmillan the surprising news that the TGWU had: 'Decided to refer their wage claim to arbitration by the Industrial Court. Cousins just succeeded in pushing through this reversal of Union policy against strong, militant opposition.' On 13 March, the Court recommended an increase of only 8s 6d a week for the 36,000 central bus crews, and nothing for the remaining 14,000. The Transport Minister, Watkinson, again made a dramatic intervention, immediately insisting that every penny of any pay award had to come from London Transport finances. Cousins was willing to spread the sum across all London busmen – an increase of just 6s/6d, but the busmen rejected the Court's award and demanded a 10s/6d rise across the board. At the start of April, the TGWU notified LTE that they would call out their London bus members from 4 May.[36]

Within a week of the TGWU strike call, Macleod's tactic of keeping the London busmen isolated faced its most severe threat. The Railway Staff National Tribunal rejected the three railway unions' claim, and a national rail strike suddenly became a serious possibility. Macmillan, back from his Commonwealth tour, shared his Minister of Labour's assessment of the perils of being drawn into a large-scale confrontation with the unions. 'Of course some Ministers and a lot of the party want a showdown,' Macmillan noted privately at the time, 'but I don't think they realize how it may end.

Even if we win (which is doubtful) it will be a very heavy cost.' Macmillan invited the leaders of both sides to meet him at Number Ten, impressing upon them the need to avert a strike. Macmillan and Macleod saw their opportunity for a compromise in the minority report by a member of the Railway Tribunal, Edwin Hall, a miners' leader, in which he had proposed an increase of 3 per cent. This figure became the basis for the eventual settlement that was thrashed out between the employer, the British Transport Commission, and their paymaster, the Government, on the eve of the London bus strike.[37]

Nonetheless, there remained a serious threat of a nationwide strike from Whitsun by the largest union, the National Union of Railwaymen. With the London bus strike under way, Macleod was determined to remove the prospect of any escalation of industrial conflict, while at the same time achieving a rail settlement that could be presented as consistent with the Government's policy of wage restraint. The final stages of the talks were so delicate that at one point Macleod suggested to Cabinet that he could see no way of preventing a strike, when he had already won the Chancellor's informal support for a possible deal and had spelled out privately to Macmillan what would be involved. In mid-May, the unions finally accepted 3 per cent, with the further promise of a review of the pay structure – later conducted by Claude Guillebaud, who had reviewed the NHS – in return for cooperation with increased efficiency. Within another week, London Underground and its unions agreed to a 3 per cent pay rise. The railway settlement was criticized in some quarters of the party and the press but, as Macmillan appreciated, a national strike would have brought greater criticism. And crucially, it had isolated the London busmen.[38]

Macleod was now engaged in a straight fight with Cousins. Ever since his aggressive outburst against the Government at the 1956 Trade Union Congress, Cousins had become the focus of opposition to wage restraint. Macleod thought that Cousins was arrogant and silly, while Cousins, for his part, believed that Macleod was trapped by Macmillan's desire to make an example of a section of the union movement. The gladiatorial aspect of the London busmen's dispute appealed to the political press and brought Macleod to the centre of the political stage. On 26 April 1958, the *New Statesman*, in a profile of Macleod, wondered: 'Who indeed would have thought that the 1934 captain of the Cambridge University bridge team would one day have the task of negotiating with some of the tough snooker players of Transport House?' But the anonymous author detected something in common between the bridge room and the pool-room: 'Those who survive their fug learn lessons in singleminded concentration which serve them admirably in other spheres.' As to the prospects for the strike, the *New Statesman* advised that Cousins could do much worse than study the Minister of Labour's 'first principles': 'Always scheme and play to give the defenders as many chances of guessing wrong as you can contrive.' And in responding to a bid: 'Crawl along in the bidding if you want to, be as subtle and delicate in your inferences as you like, but force first.' Macleod was ready to play a tough hand, but had doubts about the resolve of his partner – Macmillan.[39]

By the time London's bus service had ground to a halt on Sunday 4 May, the busmen's strike was as much a political issue as it was an industrial dispute. Macleod therefore had to fight on two fronts. While preventing Cousins from gaining any ground, he also had to ensure that the Government dominated the political battle. During the first week of the strike, he delivered one of the finest parliamentary performances of his life. The occasion was unwittingly provided by Hugh Gaitskell, the Leader of the Opposition, who had intervened with a strongly worded attack on the Government in a speech in Glasgow. During the Commons debate on the strike on Monday the 5th, Gaitskell was involved in angry clashes, culminating in his announcement that he was tabling a motion of censure against the Minister of Labour – the debate was to be held that Thursday, the 8th. However, the Labour leader's intervention was singularly ill-judged, since his actions immediately united the Conservatives. On the eve of the debate, Macleod received full support at a packed meeting of the Conservative backbench labour committee.

As with Macleod's legendary attack on Nye Bevan in March 1952, being presented with the opportunity is one thing; having the nerve and skill to seize it, is quite another. Opening the censure debate for Labour, Robens was far shrewder than his leader and instead of launching an entirely personal attack – despite his moving a motion of censure against Macleod – devoted most of his speech to criticizing the Government. Nonetheless, it was a powerful performance and demanded an exceptional speech in reply. Macleod was not going to let slip the golden opportunity that Gaitskell had supplied. Having given a measured defence of his actions in the busmen's dispute, he expressed his agreement with Robens that 'the industrial situation is very grave indeed', and then stated:

> I have deliberately not launched an attack on the Rt Hon. Gentleman, or on the Labour Party; nor have I commented, as I thought at first I would, on the TUC statement that was issued yesterday.
>
> The House may, however, remember a saying of Mr Marx, of whom I am a devoted follower – Groucho, not Karl – who said, 'Sir, I never forget a face, but I will make an exception of yours.' So the House may perhaps allow me quite briefly one exception to this.

At this, Macleod paused. He had the attention of a packed House, except for one person – Gaitskell, who was sitting on the Opposition frontbench, head bowed, doodling. Eventually, the silence penetrated to Gaitskell's consciousness. As the Leader of the Opposition looked up, his eyes met

Macleod's, staring angrily back at him. 'However carefully I try to frame my words about the criticism which has been made against me by the Rt Honourable Gentleman,' Macleod declared, 'I am bound to say that I cannot conceal my scorn and contempt for the part that the Leader of the Opposition has played in this.'[40]

The effect of this sudden, ferocious assault on Gaitskell was as electrifying as had been the opening words of his onslaught against Bevan. His performance was made more dramatic by giving every appearance of having been delivered *ex tempore*, and by the absence of any gestures, apart from his constant patting of the despatch box. Macleod castigated Gaitskell for having forced a debate that was bound to make industrial relations more difficult. 'We are having this debate,' Macleod declared, 'because the Leader of the Opposition, in a Parliamentary scene on Monday, just could not control himself.' By the time he had finished savaging the Labour leader, the Conservative benches were ecstatic. Macleod stayed in the chamber out of courtesy for the speech that followed, but after it had finished he and his Parliamentary Private Secretary, Reggie Bennett, left to relax and have a drink. They were heading along the narrow passageway alongside what has become known as Annie's bar, when Robens suddenly appeared at the opposite end, heading straight towards them. Robens stopped, greeted Macleod, and told him, 'Iain, that was the best speech you've ever made in your life.' Robens's generous praise was mirrored in the notices that Macleod received in the press. The *Daily Telegraph* lauded Macleod's 'sudden and sharp counter-attack against Mr Gaitskell', while the *Manchester Guardian* judged that his speech had 'not been matched in power for some years' in parliament: 'Mr Macleod held the House throughout. Even when he was savaging Mr Gaitskell the Opposition was too much under his spell to make a demonstration against him.'[41]

This *tour de force*, followed a week later by the settlement of the rail dispute, convinced Macleod that he had Cousins on the run, and was insistent that the Government should keep to their tough line. His hawkish stance was undoubtedly influenced by his contacts with TUC leaders. Years later, he told Geoffrey Goodman that they had come to see him privately during the bus strike, urging that the Government should stand firm. 'They wanted Cousins taken down a peg,' Macleod recalled. 'They didn't like him. They wanted to ensure that the Government didn't cave in to him, because it would have made their job that much more difficult.' On 22 May, he was advising Macmillan that it was likely, 'indeed almost certain, that the strike will go on at least for a time but this is much better than a weak settlement'. Accordingly, they had to 'be prepared for attempts, even if not officially encouraged by Cousins, for the strike to deepen and spread'. But on 27 May, when Cousins informed Macleod that he and TGWU officials were ready for talks with the Minister and were willing to resume negotiations, Macleod bluntly refused. Two days later, Macleod was approached again – this time by a committee of five from the TUC who had become concerned that the dispute might escalate. Again, he took a tough line and refused to intervene, prompting the TUC to seek a meeting with Macmillan.[42]

However, Macleod had already mapped out the shape of a deal, and this formed the basis of the plan that Macmillan put to the TUC's committee when they saw the Prime Minister at Number Ten the day following Macleod's rebuff. In broad terms, the formula required the busmen to accept the award of 8s/6d for Central London busmen (or less, depending on the differential between them and the rest), that they had rejected in March; that the Green Line busmen, who were due to settle in July, should be included in any settlement; and that negotiations should resume to fix a date for a pay review for the remaining workers not covered by the Court's award. After further toings and froings, and another meeting between the Prime Minister and the TUC's committee, it was finally made clear to Cousins by his fellow union leaders that they were not prepared to back him. He had no alternative but to reach a settlement.[43]

Macleod relished Cousins's predicament. On the morning of Wednesday 11 June, Reggie Bennett called on him in his office, overlooking the corner of St James's Square and Duke of York Street. The blinds were drawn on the side facing the street. Bennett asked why, and was told that Cousins was due to arrive in a few minutes, 'and just in case the *Daily Express* or anyone are in the rooms opposite I thought I'd draw the blinds so that they won't see Cousins on his knees'. Reporting to Macmillan on his face-to-face meeting with his main union adversary, Macleod noted that: 'Cousins was in one of his best moods,' adding that he (Cousins) 'knows, of course, that this is a bad strike and that he can't win it.' The TGWU were still demanding 10s/6d a week all round, but it was clear from Cousins's comments that the difference between the two sides now hinged on the position of those workers excluded from the Court's award. As Macleod told the Prime Minister, the LTE had already privately told Tom Yates, the moderate union leader, that some extra money would be paid from 2 July. On 13 June, Cousins persuaded the busmen's delegates to recommend that their men return to work, hinting that the country busmen would receive some increase.[44]

Macleod had arrived in Geneva on Friday 13th, where he was to attend the annual conference of the International Labour Organization. He never enjoyed these occasions at the best of times, but to be away from London during a crucial, dramatic stage in the final throes of the busmen's dispute was purgatory. On Tuesday 17th, to everybody's amazement, the bus garages voted to reject their delegates' recommendation to resume negotiations. Two days later, London Transport gave a pledge of an increase for country busmen and a review for other excluded grades – although it soon became apparent to Ministers that the LTE chairman, Sir John Elliott, in his talks with Cousins, had gone beyond the conditions set down by the

Government. Macleod later recalled that they almost sacked Sir John 'there and then'. Meanwhile, the busmen had accepted and buses were back on the streets on 21 June. But then came a fresh dispute over the exact figure due to most of the country busmen – 6s/6d, as Cousins always insisted he had been offered, or a lower figure, as Ministers wanted. Towards the end of June, Macleod was still being hawkish, pointing out that 5s/6d, or a 3 per cent rise, would be in line with the rail and tube settlements, but that with the next round of negotiations for 177,000 provincial busmen already under way, it was 'of the first importance' that the award 'should be the lowest which we feel will hold'. He recommended pushing 'as hard as we can for a settlement under 5s between Elliott and Cousins' – ideally, 4s/9d. In the event, on 17 July, the TGWU finally accepted 5s. At long last, the London busmen's dispute was over.[45]

The dispute is often recalled as an unalloyed success for Macleod and an humiliating defeat for Cousins. In crude terms, Macleod had won and Cousins lost. But the reality is not so clear cut, and certainly Macleod was less than happy that the ending had been messy and – so he believed – had resulted in Cousins eventually gaining a better deal for the busmen than should have happened. Macleod never forgot that negotiations had gone awry during his absence in Geneva, and let Number 10 know as much on his return to London. Indeed, so annoyed did Macmillan become with Macleod's carping criticism of the busmen's settlement that the Prime Minister's private office suggested that St James's Square officials should drop a hint to their Minister to desist. One brave member of Macleod's staff who sought to carry out Downing Street's request was snapped at for his pains.[46]

The London bus strike marked a turning point in postwar industrial relations. The Ministry of Labour's role as an umpire on the industrial scene was bound to come under increasing strain as the Government's economic policy became more closely involved in wage bargaining. The London bus strike was the first occasion on which an industrial dispute had become a trial of strength between a union and the Government of the day. Such conflicts were to become more common as successive Governments resorted to incomes policies during the 1960s and 1970s, but the Macmillan Government at least had the sense to choose their opponents with more care than some of their successors.

Politically, the London bus strike *was* an unalloyed success for the Government in general and Macleod in particular. During the first half of 1958, the Conservatives had suffered a bad defeat in the Rochdale by-election and trailed Labour in the Gallup opinion poll, but in June they rallied and during the autumn established a consistent lead. Victory over the London busmen was seen by the Tories as the moment when their fortunes turned. After the long, dark days since the Suez fiasco eighteen months earlier, they had a triumph to cheer at last. The starring role in this Tory revival belonged to Macleod. He had demolished Gaitskell in the Commons and had defeated Cousins on the London streets. In October, at the Conservative Conference, he was hailed as the conquering hero and received lengthy praise from the Party Chairman, Lord Hailsham. Macleod's political star burned brighter than ever.

The Modern Tory

Within days of Macmillan becoming Prime Minister in January 1957, and before parliament had returned from the winter recess, a triumvirate of Tories began work behind the scenes planning Conservative strategy over the next three years or so up to the next election. Butler, shocked at his failure to become Prime Minister, was determined to retain his hold on party policy-making from his base in the chairman's room, on the third floor of the Conservative Research Department at 24 Old Queen Street. As a first almost automatic step, Butler turned to Macleod, asking him to repeat the invaluable role that he had played before the 1955 election of pushing forward and coordinating thoughts on future policy. On Friday 18 January, Macleod had a preliminary meeting with Michael Fraser, Director of the Research Department and his longstanding friend and colleague. Some indication of the state of the Tory mind in the immediate aftermath of Suez and Eden's tragic demise is Fraser's note of Macleod's view – 'he thinks there is hope'.

By the first week of February, Macleod was able to tell Butler that he had 'had some preliminary discussions with Michael Fraser about the work that you have given me to do, and I intend to form a small group of Ministers at this stage'. Macleod's new 'Policy Study Group' was to comprise David Ormsby-Gore (later Lord Harlech), Enoch Powell, Reggie Maudling and Jocelyn Simon (later Lord Simon), and, in addition, Peter Goldman and Michael Fraser from the Research Department. He had chosen his group 'entirely on personal grounds', but the Ministries in which they held office – the Home Office (Simon), Foreign Office (Ormsby-Gore), Treasury (Powell), Labour (Macleod) and Power (Maudling) – formed 'an excellent cross section of the most important departments'. However, when writing at the same time to Edward Heath, the Chief Whip, to inform him of this new initiative on policy-making, Macleod acknowledged his Policy Study Group's distinctive pedigree:

> For heaven's sake don't point out that all these people have been at one time linked with 'One Nation'. I know they have, but I did not realize it when I asked them. In any case, they are the people that I want to have, and I am not starting a cell on the Front Bench.

Macleod promised to send Heath the minutes of the Policy Study Group, inviting him to join them at a meeting 'or perhaps an occasional dinner'. In any event, Butler was well satisfied, telling Macleod on 6 February, 'I think your arrangements are excellent.'[47]

At the group's first meeting, held in Butler's room at the Research Department on the afternoon of Friday 15 February 1957, Macleod made the prescient suggestion that they should work on the assumption that the next general election would come in October 1959 – or at any rate between the spring of 1959 and the spring of 1960. Macleod's direction of his group's work was clear, efficient and highly professional. They began by identifying which subjects to tackle, deciding whether or not to delegate some of these to the Research Department, bring in another Minister, or refer a matter to the relevant backbench committee or another body, such as the Bow Group. In their discussions they always sought to distinguish between subjects by timing – those on which a decision was imminent; those on which it would be desirable to take a decision before the election; those which might form part of the manifesto; and matters involving 'longterm re-education of the party'. A dozen meetings were held during the year, including a number of dinner meetings at the Commons at which a Minister would be invited to discuss his thoughts. Often, aspects of their work related to various reviews being undertaken in Whitehall – for instance, on the idea of an 'opportunity' state as opposed to a welfare state, on the cost of the social services, and on the future of national insurance.[48]

By the time that the Prime Minister dined with the group on 15 July, Macleod was able to report that they hoped to begin the first drafts of a manifesto after the 1957 summer recess. In a personal note to Macmillan, briefing him before the dinner, Macleod addressed the question of the party's approach and appeal at the next election. Although he thought they had been doing much better lately:

> It is very difficult for a Government to overcome the inevitable boredom with their men and measures after eight years of one party rule. Probably, therefore, we should seek to develop our theme particularly in the fields where we have been notably successful and where we can present progress as a development of achievement. We ought to be able to do this, for example in the fields of housing, taxation and education, and to some extent of health.

Other matters that seemed to Macleod to be of political importance at the time included the question of what to do about pensions; his own idea of declaring a moratorium on the 'political football' of the ownership of road transport and steel, thereby putting the onus on Labour to upset the nationalize/denationalize apple-cart; and the re-organization of government departments and reduction of the civil service. Despite the problems facing the Tories, he said: 'We must, however, play to win, or at worst, to deprive the Labour Party of a working majority.'[49]

By the end of 1957, every area of policy had been examined and the next, more strategic, stage of policy-making was about to begin. Macleod noted to Macmillan on 11 November:

> It is true that in the great events of foreign affairs and in the struggle against inflation the Manifesto will probably write itself, and we cannot yet tell whether we will succeed or fail. But even so, we need a number of currants in the bread. How many, depends to some extent on the temper of events at the time. In May 1955, for example, we expected to win the Election, and the positive proposals in our Manifesto were few and unexciting. We may not be so fortunately placed next time.

Macleod's proposed timescale envisaged his group being ready with an outline of policy from Whitsun 1958. In the meantime, Macmillan had consulted Heath and Fraser about the need to bring strategic coherence to policy work – in addition to Macleod's group, there was a plethora of backbench committees, party bodies, ad hoc groups and unofficial organizations, all developing policy ideas. The solution was the setting up of a small, highly secret, Steering Committee, to oversee all policy work, bringing the many disparate threads together and providing some unifying theme.[50]

This new Steering Committee met for the first time at Number Ten on Monday 23 December 1957 and was, in effect, an inner Cabinet, comprising Macmillan, Butler, Hailsham, Heath and Macleod and serviced by Fraser at the Research Department – the Earl of Home was recruited three months later. The Steering Committee were an exceptionally gifted team of politicians, by any standards. Not only did they possess, individually and collectively, immense political acumen, they were widely read in the classics, literature and history. With Macmillan in the chair, their discussions ranged easily across the minutiae of bread and butter issues to take in grand allusions and the loftier themes of western civilization. Macleod shone in their company. Indeed, Macmillan was to confide that, in his judgement, two members of his Cabinet had 'political genius' – one was Hailsham, then his Party Chairman, and the other was Macleod.[51]

Macleod's Policy Study Group resumed its work with an enlarged membership in February 1958 and this group and the Steering Committee worked in tandem until the summer of 1959, when the group's work was complete. In early 1959, as the drafting of the manifesto was about to begin, Macleod took a personal decision to approach one of its original members, Powell, who had left the group the previous year following his resignation from the Treasury. Extending his invitation on 19 February, Macleod wrote that Powell's renewed membership 'would give me a great deal of personal pleasure, quite apart from the fact that I would be happy to have your mind with us when we study our programme for the next election'. 'I have been guilty of almost

Muscovite discourtesy,' Powell quipped, when it took him over a week to forward his acceptance. The old team were working together again. Macleod's initiative marked the start of Powell's rehabilitation in the party hierarchy – the following year, he was to be appointed Minister of Health.[52]

Macleod had indicated to Macmillan in late 1957 that the next election would largely be determined by the Government's performance on the big subjects, notably the economy. The loss of the Rochdale by-election to the Liberals in February 1958 confirmed him in this view and he was therefore appalled to read a Central Office paper, based on a privately commissioned post-election opinion poll in the town, which played down the impact of the Government's tough credit squeeze. Macleod responded with his own analysis of the Rochdale result, in which his strongest concern was rising unemployment. Dismissing the Central Office analysis as 'unreal', Macleod argued in his note of 10 March that:

> The significance of the figures is the class from which we lost our votes. The Conservative Central Office find this the most surprising feature. I think it is the most obvious. Of course we lost our votes from the lower middle and skilled working class. This is the result of the policies of restriction on which, rightly no doubt in the short term, we have embarked. It is these people above all others who fear the uncertainty of possible unemployment that policies of restriction must bring with them. It is these people we have lost steadily since the autumn 1955 budget. It is these people ('the three million trade unionists and their families who must vote Conservative if there is to be a Conservative Government') whom we lost at Rochdale and whom we will go on losing until we can find policies of expansion again. This is the main lesson of this, and all recent by–elections, and over this we have some control.

Unfortunately, Macleod's message did not penetrate the Treasury walls. Despite the departure of Thorneycroft and his team two months earlier, Heathcoat Amory's first budget unnecessarily prolonged the depressed state of the economy.[53]

Unemployment continued to rise inexorably during 1958 and by the autumn had reached its highest level since the War. Indeed, by the time of the Conscrvative conference at Blackpool, Ministers feared that the jobless total would reach 750,000 by the spring. Macleod acknowledged during his conference speech that the total was bound to rise still further during the winter, but nonetheless reaffirmed 'our belief in full employment'. Meanwhile, the Chancellor was coming under enormous pressure from anxious ministers and had to remind them that he had already taken eight separate expansionary moves to revive the economy. Nonetheless, Macmillan was fearful of a slump and demanded immediate action. Hire purchase restrictions were completely withdrawn, and in November and the following February further increases in public investment were announced.[54]

By January 1959, the unemployment total had risen to 621,000, or 2.8 per cent of the workforce – its worst during the 1950s. In expectation of more bad figures in March, Labour organized a Commons debate about unemployment on the day that the monthly figures were due to be published. It was a wretched mistake. Instead of rising, or even remaining steady around the 600,000 mark, the total showed an unexpected and dramatic fall of 58,000, from 2.8 per cent to 2.5 per cent – the largest drop in unemployment since the War, except for the 1947 fuel crisis year. Macleod had a field day. When he announced the figures, in a deadpan, matter of fact manner, during the course of his speech, *The Times* reported that:

> The effect on the Government ranks was electric. Their jubilation knew no bounds, 'Cheer up', they shouted at the silent Opposition, who had tabled a censure motion deploring the Government's failure to 'prevent the recent substantial and widespread rise in unemployment'.
>
> With gentle but deadly playfulness the Minister [Macleod] was later to express grave doubts how the Opposition could now call upon the House to vote on their motion which, he declared, 'is simply 100 per cent away from the truth'.

'I have no doubt the Opposition will improve,' Macleod teased. 'The first seven years in Opposition are always the most difficult.' In further mockery of their choice of debate, he added: 'I cannot help it if every time the Opposition are asked to name their weapons they pick boomerangs.'[55]

Despite the signs that a marked economic recovery was at long last under way, Heathcoat Amory's budget on 7 April gave a bigger stimulus to the economy than any since the War. The record budget deficit of £720 million was the net result of taking ninepence off income tax, cutting purchase tax, returning postwar credits and restoring investment allowances. If only Macmillan had heeded Macleod's words after Rochdale, instead of over-reacting twelve months later, the economy would have been able to pursue a more steady path to recovery.[56]

The shock of losing Rochdale caused a deep division on the Steering Committee on the question of how the Conservatives should respond to the Liberal revival – should they strike hard against the Liberals, or should they negotiate some form of anti-Socialist deal before the next election? The rough, near-verbatim note taken during the Steering Committee's meeting on 20 March 1958 reveals Macleod as a calculating hawk:

> Personally have never had any doubt. Not make speeches, not be dramatic. Think we must beat the Liberal Party out of politics in this country. Don't

think the possibility of a major deal exists, because don't think Liberal Party Headquarters are capable of making such a deal . . .

By contrast, Home emerged as the main supporter of a deal:

The floating voters are getting fed up with rigid Party attitudes. If they could see two anti-Socialist Parties trying to get together it would create very good impression. Perhaps handle this constituency by constituency. Hand over a few seats . . .

In the heat of debate came an intriguing exchange:

Macleod: Whole point of the Liberal Party is to climb back into office and if possible into Government by destroying the Conservative Party. Cold fact of the case is that you can't make a deal.
Heath: Conservative Party has largely existed through absorbing other Parties. Why should not it be possible to do this with Liberals?
Macleod: But the other Parties weren't out to destroy the Conservative Party.

Heath's comment was a precursor of events almost sixteen years later – after Macleod's death – when he sought a deal with the Liberals in order to try and remain in office after the inconclusive election of February 1974. The Steering Committee's debate raged for some time, as ministers puzzled on the implications of the Liberal revival. Then Home blithely put a figure to the number of seats the Tories might offer as the basis for a deal:

Home: Perhaps let twelve of them in and arrange with them about the rest of the country.
Macleod and Hailsham: NO.

Macleod never respected Home's political judgment. By the second half of 1958, the Conservatives had regained their lead in the opinion polls and the Liberal revival subsided. Talk of a deal evaporated.[57]

As Macleod acknowledged in July 1958, shortly after the end of the London bus strike, trade union legislation would be extremely popular with Conservatives and would attract the Liberal vote more than anything else. However, this presented a dilemma, since it was an extremely difficult subject to tackle, politically and in terms of the practical effects on industrial relations. The question of trade union reform had first been raised at the second meeting of the Policy Study Group in March 1957, in a discussion on 'private rights', when Goldman referred to a forthcoming pamphlet by the Inns of Court Conservative and Unionist Society. Macleod explained to the group the following month that he was not prepared to restrict the unions' protection under the law, but he was more attracted to consider the position of union members and cited as examples the problems of victimization and the closed shop. He was considering whether to make unions more responsible to their members, on the lines of the Company Act. However, he also thought that in the Conservative manifesto, they should consider proposing a royal commission into the system of collective bargaining and arbitration.[58]

By November 1958, Macleod's thinking on legislation had begun to crystallize. In the paper he submitted to the Steering Committee, following a report prepared for him by Richard Wood, his new junior minister, he was 'convinced that there is no case at all for legislation aimed at strikes or restrictive labour practices'. Indeed, such was his opposition to this form of legislation that when the Conservative barristers finally published their call for union reform, *A Giant's Strength*, and included a proposal to make unofficial strikes illegal, Macleod sent a senior Ministry of Labour official to warn the Inns of Court authors that the political damage caused by their pamphlet would be proportionate to the amount of publicity it received. In his own paper, Macleod thought that although there was 'certainly a case for an inquiry' into arbitration and collective bargaining, especially in the nationalized industries, such an inquiry 'would present great difficulties', since evidence would be given of 'constant communications between ministers and Chairmen of nationalized Boards'. Macleod specifically mentioned the contacts during 1958 between Ministers 'and indeed the whole Cabinet', on the one hand, and Sir Brian Robertson and Sir John Elliot on the other: 'It might be very undesirable for this to come out, as it would, in evidence.' But he did not rule out an inquiry completely and thought the TUC were likely to suggest the setting up of some inquiry into nationalized industry collective bargaining.[59]

However, Macleod was in 'no doubt that the greatest public disquiet is felt on the issue of the liberty of the individual'. Steps to afford the individual greater protection would be 'warmly welcomed by our supporters, and also by an important sector of middle-of-the-road opinion'. Nonetheless, Macleod was against legislating, 'briefly because it could not easily correct most of the forms of persecution to which individuals may be subjected'. He thought there might be a strong case for an inquiry, possibly headed by a judge, and suggested that such an approach would fit with the way that the Government had examined administrative tribunals through the inquiry chaired by Oliver Franks. Macleod's tentative conclusion was 'to recommend a high level judicial inquiry into the liberty of the individual and to set it moving before the election'. When the Steering Committee discussed the idea, Macmillan was concerned that many people had a double loyalty – years ago as trade unionists they voted Labour, but the Conservatives had convinced many of them that it was no longer necessary to do so. But 'if we start something like this and they think we are attacking the trade unions, they might get all very muddled and confuse their loyalties. And in an election things get so very hot.' In the event, the Committee decided to await publication of the inquiries that Macleod had set up into recent alleged cases of the abuse of union power, since action might then be taken with a measure of trade union support.[60]

It was not until the Steering Committee were involved in the detailed drafting of a manifesto during July 1959 that the subject was discussed again at any length. A strike by the printing unions was reviving concern about the abuse of union power, and Macleod now urged that the Conservatives should propose an inquiry in their manifesto. Macmillan and Home were doubtful, fearing that any such move would immediately be seen as an attack on the unions. Hailsham had doubts but could see the mood was changing. Butler and Macleod, with Heath's support, were arguing that it had become impossible not to say something because of the mood amongst Conservative supporters. 'I have found people demanding something to be done about the trade unions,' Macleod is reported to have said in the verbatim note, 'and something moderate like this would stop the real extremists.'[61]

At the start of September, final decisions had to be made. Macmillan remained reluctant about the idea. In his paper to the Steering Committee on 1 September, Macleod noted that the main argument against any such inquiry was that 'it looks as if we are now sailing quietly into harbour and we should not start out to tack round a new and uncharted reef'. He also acknowledged that the trade unions would criticize the plan. However, he urged keeping the proposal for three reasons. In the first place, it would be very popular, 'especially with our Party and with the Liberals'. Secondly, it could be presented as a natural development from the Franks Inquiry. And, thirdly, Macleod believed that 'it would have a steadying effect in our Party'. And, if the Conservatives were to win a large majority: 'It will be very useful to have this proposal as a bulwark against the ideas for abolishing strikes and restrictive practices by law that may be put forward as Private Members' Bills.' Despite a final plea that 'We must not take out everything that is striking or new out of our Manifesto,' Macmillan was taking no risks. The proposal was axed.[62]

However, the 1959 manifesto, *The Next Five Years*, reflected both Macleod's philosophy and his detailed work behind the scenes. Although he would have favoured complementing its tone of 'you've never had it so good', with a touch more radical spice, the manifesto represented the high-water mark of postwar, modern Toryism. 'Conservative policy is to double the standard of living in this generation,' the manifesto declared, 'and ensure that all sections of society share in the expansion of wealth.' Moreover, the manifesto's first major legislative commitment reflected Macleod's concern about dealing with high unemployment in specific localities – a problem that had alarmed him during the scare over automation in the Midlands in 1956 and that persisted in the depressed regions. The

Government now promised that their first major Bill in the new parliament would be one to 'remodel and strengthen' their powers for coping with local unemployment.[63]

Since 1955, Macleod had become an established member of the party leadership and he again featured in the national campaign. Macmillan eclipsed all other Conservatives during the campaign, especially in his final televised election broadcast, but Macleod made a notable impact. On 20 September, appearing with Macmillan, Butler, Hailsham and Heathcoat Amory, Macleod 'bustled his way into nearly every topic, sometimes ahead of cue' and was evidently determined that the broadcast 'should well impress on the popular mind the image of a forward-looking party'. But it was on 29 September, nine days before polling, that Macleod made his most telling contribution in a performance that led *The Times* to describe him as an 'actor-manager' – the description usually associated with Macmillan. Dubbing the Labour leader, 'Mr Rising Price himself', Macleod flung back at Gaitskell the accusation that Conservative estimates of the cost of the Labour programme were too high, and asked, 'Why not give us your own estimate?' This charge hit home. Labour's spending and tax plans simply did not seem to add up. The election rapidly began to slip away from Gaitskell as Macmillan and other senior Tories pressed home their advantage. [64]

On 8 October, the Conservatives won a landslide, gaining a 100-seat majority in the Commons and achieving an unprecedented, third successive election victory. Macleod chalked up a majority of 13,803 in Enfield West – it was to remain his largest margin of victory. The 1959 election triumph represented an extraordinary revival for the Conservatives after the débâcle of Suez and a vindication of the kind of Toryism in which Macleod passionately believed. 'Macleod dislikes the term Conservative and always prefers to be called a Tory,' the *New Statesman* had commented in its profile of him the previous year. 'He is, in fact, the Essential Post-War Tory, the Welfare State Tory, the Tory New Dealer who combines high hopes both for himself and for One Nation.' This very modern Tory was about to be given the greatest challenge of his political career.[65]

8

Statesman

It may be that I startled Macmillan, to some extent, indeed I am sure I did, by the speed with which I moved . . .

> Iain Macleod interviewed about his approach as Colonial Secretary, 29 December 1967.

Not such a surprise after all

The week after the Conservatives' resounding victory in the October 1959 general election, Harold Macmillan summoned Iain Macleod to the Cabinet Room at 10 Downing Street. The two men were alone and chatted briefly about the election. Then the Prime Minister said: 'Iain, I've got the worst job of all for you.' Macleod realized immediately that he was being offered the Colonial Office. Despite the doomladen tone of Macmillan's offer, it was the job that Macleod most wanted. A month short of his forty-sixth birthday, Macleod was about to embark on the greatest political challenge of his life.[1]

By 1959, Macleod urgently wanted promotion and to broaden his experience. Although he had been the first of the 1950 intake of MPs to be given charge of a ministry and, in 1955, the first to enter the Cabinet, he had remained its junior and youngest member for almost four years and was at risk of being caught up by contemporaries such as Ted Heath and Reggie Maudling, whom he expected to join him at the Cabinet table in the not too distant future. Macleod had 'been conscious of rumours for some time' before the election that the Prime Minister intended to move him from the Ministry of Labour in a post-election reshuffle. But to which department?[2]

Macleod's specialization in social policy in a party in which knowledge of the welfare state was rare had been the key to his rapid rise, but it now imperilled his progress. He was in danger of becoming marooned in the lower to middle reaches of the Cabinet. Likewise, his Scottishness in a party in which Scots were underrepresented (although they were not yet as scarce as they were later to become) raised another anxiety, since it was suggested in the Whips' Office that he might make a popular Scottish Secretary. Other

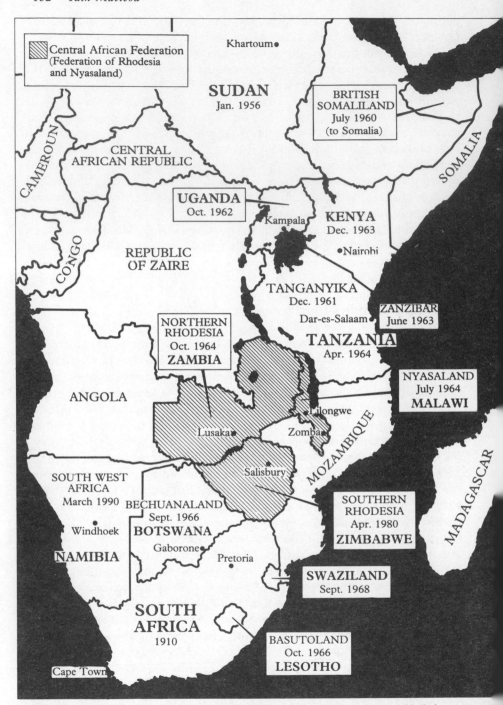

Central and Southern Africa, showing dates of independence of British colonies with their new name printed in **bold** type.

politicians might have bided their time and been grateful to remain in the Cabinet, but Macleod was too ambitious ever to have done so.[3]

Macleod's imagination was fired by the drama that was unfolding in Africa. This was the raw politics that excited him: the realities were stark, the differences of interest were deep, and the conflicting ideals were passionately held. Britain, like other democratic European powers, had neither the will nor the resources to maintain colonial rule by force. But progress towards majority rule, unless skilfully managed, brought a serious risk of becoming embroiled in civil and racial war. Macleod's liberal convictions left him in little doubt as to how a Conservative Government should discharge their duty. Here was a great historic challenge and he had the confidence to seek the responsibility for meeting it. Africa had become the focus of his ambition and had won his heart.

Sixty-four years earlier, in 1895, Joseph Chamberlain had been in such a powerful position that the Prime Minister, Lord Salisbury, had made it clear that any office was open to him, even the Chancellorship of the Exchequer. His choice of the Colonial Office surprised the political world. Macleod was in nothing like the same position in Macmillan's Cabinet and his appointment appeared, at first sight, to be equally surprising. In 1959, the Colonial Office seemed to be one of the least likely destinations for Macleod. He was among the first of a new breed of Conservative politicians who lacked the personal wealth required to follow the example of Rab Butler and his two predecessors at the Colonial Office, Oliver Lyttelton and Alan Lennox-Boyd, who had financed their own travels and acquainted themselves with 'the outer Empire' consciously to equip themselves as politicians of a great, colonial power.[4]

Even so, Macleod's lack of any specialization in overseas affairs was exceptional for a young Conservative politician, even by the standards of the 'One Nation' group – after all, Heath made his maiden speech on Britain's relations with Europe and Powell retained his interest in defence and overseas affairs. Indeed, there was a powerful incentive to develop a reputation on matters of external policy. The Foreign Office, Colonial Office, Commonwealth Relations Office, the Admiralty, the Air Office, the War Office and the Ministry of Defence, provided opportunities to put a foot on the first rung of the ministerial ladder, whereas there were fewer domestic departments than was to be the case from the 1960s. Moreover, Britain's colonies frequently captured the headlines and dominated political debate. Britain still ruled great tracts of Africa, stretching from Bechuanaland (modern Botswana) in the south to Kenya and Uganda in the north and an array of territories in the Caribbean, the Mediterranean, the Pacific and the Persian Gulf. By 1959, only the Gold Coast and Sudan among Britain's African territories had become independent. A commitment had been made that Nigeria would soon follow. But there was no sign of similar progress in East and Central Africa, where large numbers of Europeans had settled. By the end of the 1950s, Kenya had around 68,000 settlers (one in 93 of Kenya's total population); Northern Rhodesia, 72,000 (one in 31); and Southern Rhodesia, 207,000 (one in 13); whereas Nyasaland had only 8,300 (one in 328) and Tanganyika 22,330 (one in 408). The settlers had often worked hard to build up farms and businesses, and – particularly in Kenya and Southern Rhodesia – tended to look on the country as their own. Many of them were opposed to majority African rule in the foreseeable future. Their intransigence put them on a collision course with the increasingly impatient demands of nationalist politicians.[5]

During the 1950s, the names of nationalist leaders – Kwame Nkrumah in the Gold Coast (Ghana), Jomo Kenyatta in Kenya, Dr Hastings Banda in Nyasaland (Malawi), Archbishop Makarios in Cyprus – became as familiar as those of the leading British politicians. Violence flared in many colonies, notably Malaya, before its independence in 1957, and Cyprus. In Kenya, the Mau Mau movement, which was characterized by ritualistic practices and a highly secretive organization, had initially directed its violence against other Africans. After the arrest of Kenyatta, the nationalist leader, for his alleged involvement in the movement, the Mau Mau fighters also attacked and murdered white settlers. These outrages received sensational coverage in the British press. Many British people had a direct, personal interest in what was happening in the colonies as a result of family links and because thousands of young men were completing national service in various corners of the globe.

Yet Macleod had never set foot inside a British colony when he became Colonial Secretary. When Julian Amery, who was already a junior minister at the Colonial Office at the time of Macleod's appointment and a long-standing specialist in overseas subjects, heard of Macleod's plan to visit Kenya within a month or so of becoming Colonial Secretary, he decided to pass on his own knowledge. Amery happened to ask Macleod whether he would be flying direct to Nairobi. Macleod replied that he would be stopping overnight at Malta and added, 'It's odd isn't it, but that will be the first time that I've ever been in a British colony.' Amery was surprised and rather shocked.[6]

Yet the impression that Macleod had neither interest in, nor knowledge of, the colonies before he entered the Colonial Office is seriously misleading. It was virtually impossible by the late 1950s for any thinking politician not to have formed some views about Britain's remaining colonies, particularly those in Africa. Macleod was no exception, and brought to the subject his rare ability for political analysis, as David Astor, editor of the *Observer*, the liberal, Sunday newspaper which specialized in reporting Africa, discovered long before Macleod became Colonial Secretary. Unlike most of Astor's Conservative contacts, Macleod had impressed Astor in their conversations about Africa as being knowledgeable, following events and being prepared to think through the issues.[7]

Macleod also had a close, personal link with Africa. His youngest brother, Rhoderick, had served in Africa during the War and afterwards became a farmer in Kenya's so-called 'white highlands'. 'I think he had started with a fairly orthodox rightish-view attitude towards politics when he came out of the army,' Macleod said of Rhoderick, 'but he had come to see that the African must be given – and quickly – much more responsibility.' In Rhoderick's view, the Second World War had been the critical watershed for African aspirations. Having fought in the British army and experienced some of the most bitter action against the Japanese, the African ex-soldier, 'didn't take kindly to removing his hat in his own country in the District Commissioner's Office in order to ask for a pass to visit a cousin in the next village'. However, this decisive change in attitude seemed to pass largely unnoticed at the time. Rhoderick developed a more liberal view than many other white settlers. Having attended part of Kenyatta's trial, he was unconvinced by the prosecution evidence, and later as an inspector in the intelligence branch of the police was surprised at the large number of detainees who had been held for several years before their innocence could be established. In the spring of 1959, Rhoderick became a founder-member of the New Kenya Group, whose leader, Michael Blundell, had resigned as Agriculture Minister in the Kenyan Government in order to campaign for a multi-racial Kenya.[8]

Iain Macleod's passionately-held liberalism was to be a crucial deter-minant of his attitude and subsequent policy as Colonial Secretary. During the early months of 1959, tragic events in two of Britain's African territories deeply troubled his liberal conscience. In Kenya, eleven African detainees died in suspicious circumstances in Hola Camp. In Nyasaland, the Governor declared a state of emergency. Police and troops arrested 1,322 people, including Banda and other leading nationalists, who were imprisoned in Southern Rhodesia, which formed, together with Nyasaland and Northern Rhodesia, the Federation of Nyasaland and Rhodesia, sometimes referred to as the Central African Federation. In the ensuing Nyasaland disturbances, a further 48 Africans were shot by police.

In the late spring of 1959, Macleod had first learned that the Prime Minister was considering a new approach in Africa. Only two years earlier, in the wake of the Suez débâcle, Macmillan had commissioned a balance sheet of Empire that showed Britain's colonies as being neither a great boon nor a heavy burden. But these latest crises in Kenya and Nyasaland prompted a political reassessment by Macmillan. Failure in Eastern and Central Africa would pose a grave threat to Western interests. Moreover, for the sake of its relations with the United States – to which Macmillan attached such importance – and also with the Commonwealth and the rest of Europe, Britain could ill afford to adopt the role of an illiberal, colonial power. At a pre-election policy discussion just before the 1959 Whitsun recess, Macmillan suggested that Conservative policy for Africa should be a form of 'Blundellism' – a reference to the liberal politics advocated by the New Kenya Group. This comment gave Macleod his cue.[9]

On Monday 25 May 1959, very soon after Macmillan's suggestion that Michael Blundell's views should be applied to Africa, Macleod wrote a personal letter to the Prime Minister. The pretext was an approach that he had received from David Stirling, the wartime founder of the Special Armed Services (SAS), who was contacting British politicians in order to rally support for an all-party, pre-election declaration on colonial policy in Africa. Stirling had lived in Africa since 1950, and was founding chairman of the Capricorn Society, who were committed to reforms that would speed British withdrawal from East and Central Africa and enable Africans and Europeans to share power instead of seeking to perpetuate white minority rule after independence. Stirling's approach was a conscious rejection of the racialist policy of separate development, or *apartheid*, that was being practised by the white minority Government in South Africa.[10]

Also towards the end of May, Macleod happened to meet Michael Blundell late one night at the Carlton Club. Blundell was visiting London to put across the New Kenya Group's views to the British public and had addressed the Bow Group, which then acted as the Conservative Party's liberal conscience. In fact, Blundell was trying to persuade his hosts to moderate their line and not to demand rapid progress to 'one man, one vote' in Africa. Their discussion had continued at the Carlton Club, and, as Blundell recalled, 'some of the Bow Groupers went over to fetch reinforcements in the person of Iain Macleod'. It was the first time that the two men had met. As Blundell later recalled, Macleod questioned him closely on the Hola Camp incident, 'and I think it probably re-emphasised in his mind his feeling that the time for substantial changes in Kenya was overdue'.[11]

Macleod's letter to Macmillan was couched, as befitted his policy making role and the purpose of Stirling's mission, in terms of domestic, electoral considerations. He noted:

> Black Africa remains perhaps our most difficult problem as far as relationships with the vital middle voters is [sic] concerned. It is the only one in which our policies are under severe criticism and for example the only one on which we are regularly defeated at the universities. Indeed the universities feel more strongly on this issue than on any other single matter.

Macleod went on to refer to the report of the inquiry, headed by the judge, Sir Patrick Devlin, into the Nyasaland emergency. The Devlin Report was expected in July and was awaited with trepidation by the Government. Although Macleod dismissed as 'rather special pleading' the argument advanced in the *Spectator* that, 'this issue is the only one on which the

Socialists can reasonably still hope to turn the tide', he warned the Prime Minister that 'unquestionably we are in a difficult position'.

Macleod's own liberal thinking on Africa shone through. What attracted him to Stirling's initiative was its liberal premise. He wrote:

There is only one sentence that matters, and that is the suggestion that the rights of the individual should be secured to him by virtue of his position as a citizen rather than because of the colour of his skin or his membership of a particular community. This goes perhaps a little further than Blundell would like to go, but is really no different from Cecil Rhodes's old idea of 'equal rights for all civilised men'.

This reform would entail 'the end of separate electoral rolls' for different races and 'no doubt it would mean in many territories African majorities on the unofficial side' (i.e. elected members as distinct from officials nominated by the Governor). Macleod acknowledged that during the period of 'tutelage' (the patronizing term then used for the transitional period to majority rule), 'it would be necessary . . . perhaps to have a fairly stiff qualification for the right to vote. But whatever it is it would be the same for everyone.'

Stirling's immediate aim was to persuade all parties to 'join hands now in a declaration along these lines before the General Election'. He had seen the Labour MPs, Gordon Walker and Callaghan, 'in what he fondly claims to be confidence', as Macleod commented. A press conference was provisionally planned for 3 June to launch the declaration, followed by a debate in the Lords, and backed by a public campaign. 'Such a programme', Macleod warned, 'could not fail to be extremely embarrassing and dangerous for us.' In an effort to spare the Government's embarrassment, Macleod had told Stirling that: 'as we were going to win the next Election by far the most effective thing to do was to have some paragraphs in the Conservative Manifesto which would point the way to a liberal solution in Africa.'

Macleod encouraged the Prime Minister's evident interest in a more liberal policy:

You may remember that when we discussed future policy just before the Whitsun Recess you said that our policy for Africa should be a form of 'Blundellism'

And he added:

I am sure this is true and we may be able to secure the right formula although no doubt the Colonial Office would have many reservations and it may be that the particular idea of Sterling's [sic] goes too far at the present time.

Macleod recommended that Macmillan should see Stirling himself and try to persuade him to drop the idea of an all-party declaration 'because this subject is potentially so explosive . . . and we then see how far we can go in the phrasing of some paragraphs to meet him.' It is remarkable that Macleod had held out to Stirling the possibility that the Conservatives might announce in their manifesto a dramatic change in colonial policy. Macmillan's response was guarded. He scrawled a note in red ink at the top of the letter, telling his private secretary to send Macleod a reply without any definite comment – he wanted time to consider how to handle the matter, particularly since the Colonial and Commonwealth Secretaries were away from London.[12]

A fortnight later, in the afternoon of Thursday 11 June, Macmillan, accompanied by the Commonwealth Secretary, the Earl of Home, met Stirling in the Prime Minister's room at the House of Commons. Their response makes a fascinating comparison with Macleod's. Macmillan was willing to consider, albeit cautiously, how political progress might be advanced in Africa and acknowledged that 'white people in Africa would have to recognize that one day the black majority would have to make itself effective, although not necessarily right away'. He feared that a civil war might be caused by two forces that were at work:

> If we pressed on too fast with the extension of the franchise, the more reactionary white people [in the Federation] might try and join the Union [of South Africa]. If we did not move fast enough, the Africans would lead the disturbances.

Home actively discouraged Stirling, and afterwards circulated his own draft declaration, headed 'British Colonial Policy in Africa', to members of the Africa Committee and the party leader's pre-election Steering Committee. Home restated the deliberately vague principle that 'The goal of Colonial policy is self-government', but this was unclear as to the pace of reform and in which territories full independence was envisaged. Although he incorporated the notion of a non-racial, electoral 'common roll', Home appears to have revealed his real attitude by his comment that: 'In the United Kingdom it took 600 years to graduate from the qualified franchise to that of "one man one vote".' Although he added that, 'today no one suggests such a lengthy apprenticeship', his heavy emphasis on the demanding pre-conditions for self-government or independence and his lack of any recognition of nationalist pressures, demonstrate a serious lack of understanding of the force and speed of change in Africa. Although Stirling had been dissuaded from launching his declaration, when the manifesto drafts were finally completed a couple of months later there was no sign of a sharp policy change on Africa.[13]

Only hours before Macmillan and Home met Stirling, they had been made fully aware of Macleod's unhappiness at the Government's handling of the African crisis. That morning's Cabinet had discussed the Hola Camp incident and the eventual disclosure that the African detainees had been killed 'by a combination of ignorance and brutality amongst the guards'. Recalling the Cabinet's difficult and tense meeting, Macleod later explained its full significance for his thinking:

> Everyone, of course, was shocked and horrified by what had happened, but two people's feelings, Quintin Hailsham and myself, went beyond that. I think we both felt outraged that such a thing could happen and for me this was the decisive moment when it became clear to me that we could no longer continue with the old methods of government in Africa and that meant inexorably a move towards African independence.

In the ensuing censure debate, Opposition MPs demanded the resignation of the Colonial Secretary, Lennox-Boyd, but the most damaging attack came from the Government's own backbenches, in a coruscating speech by Enoch Powell. As Macleod recalled, it was 'a very fine speech . . . which made a very deep impression on the House, and indeed upon me'.[14]

Cub Alport, by then a minister of state at the Commonwealth Relations Office, noticed that Macleod, whom he could not recall previously ever having taken any interest in colonial or Commonwealth affairs, suddenly began to appear on the Government front bench, whenever these subjects were being debated. Initially, Alport was puzzled, but he had, 'a pretty shrewd idea that he [Macleod] was given a hint that that was the thing he should apply his mind to'. The Cabinet knew during the summer of Lennox-Boyd's intention to retire at the election and take up the chairman-ship of Guinness, the Dublin-based brewers into whose family he had married. It was, in Macleod's words, 'at least possible' that he (Macleod) was in the running for the Colonial Office.[15]

Much to Macmillan's relief, Africa was not a major issue at the 1959 election. In the Prime Minister's view, the Conservatives had 'just succeeded . . . in "getting by" on this'. But he was far from sanguine: 'Africa . . . seems to be the biggest problem looming for us here at home.' East and Central Africa appeared to be teetering on the brink of bloody, racial catastrophe, in which Africans would be pitted against the European settlers, and into which British troops would be drawn. The civil war in Algeria provided a terrible warning for any colonial power. The French army were unable to restore control and the crisis had precipitated the collapse of the Fourth Republic. Britain had only recently experienced bitter division over Suez. What might be the consequences of a bloodbath in its African territories?[16]

Macmillan seized the moment of his election triumph, which had created a commanding Commons majority of 100 seats, to launch a new initiative in Africa. He was in no doubt that British withdrawal had to be speeded up.

But somehow, he needed simultaneously to reassure the African nationalists and the European settlers that their demands were being met and their interests upheld. Squaring this circle required political genius. Both sides had vociferous support in Britain, but the white settlers' lobby exerted great influence in the upper echelons of British finance and society, and many people were susceptible to calls to stand by their 'kith and kin' in Africa. The Conservative right wing were bound to oppose a more liberal colonial policy.

So daunting was the challenge facing the new Colonial Secretary, that among Macleod's closest friends such as Robert Carr, the suspicion developed that, 'Iain was being pushed out on a limb to have the branch cut off'. They feared that Macleod was being set up as 'the main scapegoat' for whatever troubles arose from the new approach in Africa. Was the Prime Minister, who was personally committed to decolonization, nonetheless not too unhappy at the prospect of Macleod's having to face the flak within the party? After all, if Macmillan's leadership was threatened over Africa, he might not want Macleod, probably the strongest front runner among the next generation of potential leaders, to be too strong a rival. However, Macmillan's motivation, in this instance at least, owed less to Machiavelli and more to the pressing need for a new approach.[17]

Macleod fitted the Prime Minister's job specification. Macmillan knew from his personal letter in May that he was probably more strongly committed to the cause of African independence than any other senior Conservative. Macleod would speed change in Africa, thereby reassuring the African nationalists and international opinion (Britain was under constant pressure at the United Nations to decolonize). Macleod's political genius meant that that he was more likely than anybody else in the Government to square the circle of conflicting interests in Africa – Hailsham was the other, but he was out of favour because of a misunderstanding by the Prime Minister about his personal life. At the same time, by retaining the conservative-minded Home at the Commonwealth Relations Office, Macmillan offered some reassurance to Conservative right-wingers and to the white settlers, particularly in Central Africa, since the Commonwealth Secretary was ministerially responsible for the Federation and Southern Rhodesia. Macleod would also bring to the task his rare gift of inspirational oratory. Macmillan was concerned to lift the debate on Africa on to a higher plane and to counter the romantic yearning for empire with an idealistic motif for the end of empire.[18]

There was also an affinity between the two men that was particularly strong around this period. Alport 'always thought that the nexus between Macmillan and Iain was the fact they were both Highlanders', a judgement echoed by Michael Fraser, then head of the Conservative Research Department, who shared their Highland descent. Indeed, Macmillan went as far as to claim 'that the problems of Africa, based as they were on tribal affinities, were very much like those of the clans in Scotland'. Alport believed that this view 'probably led him to a good many misjudgements', but it nonetheless helps explain why Macmillan appointed Macleod. Both Macmillan and Macleod had a sense of the outsider about them. They had at least some understanding from their family's collective memory of what it was like to be under the yoke of English rule. This set them apart from most other senior Conservatives. And for Macleod, his crofter, Gaelic, Islander origins were central to his identity.[19]

Despite their affinity, Macmillan did not find Macleod 'an easy colleague' and attributed this to the Highland traits that he recognized in Macleod: 'very high-minded, very excitable, often depressed'. But as it transpired – and as Macmillan might have realized from Macleod's earlier interventions, notably on the Hola Camp incident – Africa brought out Macleod's 'high-mindedness' more than anything else, with the possible exception of unemployment.[20]

The Last Colonial Secretary

'It may be that I startled Macmillan,' Macleod was later to admit, 'indeed, I am sure that I did, by the speed with which I moved but that he expected me to move faster than Lennox-Boyd was certainly implicit in my appointment.' Macleod was determined from the outset to be more than merely Macmillan's henchman in Africa. On his appointment, he reportedly told Peter Goldman that he was going to take a thoroughly radical line in winding up the residue of the imperial system and that it was his intention to be the last Colonial Secretary.[21]

Only nine months before the election, in January 1959, the then Colonial Secretary, Lennox-Boyd, had chaired a conference at Chequers attended by his junior ministers, his officials and the three Governors of the East African territories, Kenya, Tanganyika and Uganda. It was tentatively agreed that Tanganyika might achieve independence by 1970, with Uganda the next and Kenya following by 1975. The story was to be much the same in central and southern Africa. The Federation of Rhodesia and Nyasaland had been created in 1953, and was regarded by Conservatives as the great hope for a multi-racial society. At the time of Macleod's appointment, the Prime Minister was hoping that the Federation might lead the way towards political agreement between Africans and Europeans throughout Africa and provide an example for Kenya to follow. Shortly after the Chequers meeting one of its participants, the Earl of Perth, Minister of State at the Colonial Office, went so far as to declare during a speech in Rhodesia that a halt was being called to the rapid advance of colonial territories to independence.[22]

The starting point for understanding the extent of Macleod's radicalism is to grasp 'how very sombre' the position was when he first entered the Colonial Office in their offices in Church House, Great Smith Street:

There was the aftermath in Kenya of the Mau Mau revolt, there was something like 90,000 people living in detention without trial. Nyasaland was under the Governor's orders and in a state of emergency and had been described as a 'police state'. There were people in Northern Rhodesia, including some of the political leaders, who were restricted by the Governor. There was Governor's rule in Malta and there were such eternal problems as Cyprus. It was a pretty dismal inheritance . . .

Macleod felt 'overwhelmingly' that his 'first problems were . . . concentrated in Africa, and that's where from the moment I went to my desk I started work'.

But, as Macleod was later to reflect:

The thing that seems to me odd was that this country generally – I don't just mean the cabinet – or the Conservative Party or even parliament – had not grasped what seemed so blindingly simple a few years later, and that is that if you give independence in West Africa you cannot deny it in East Africa just because there is a white settler community there.

He claimed that his lack of experience of the colonies was 'a very considerable advantage', because he was able to approach his task 'at what happened to be a decisive time . . . without any preconceived ideas'. But as he admitted, he possessed one overriding preconception – his 'own conviction . . . that although it was extremely dangerous to move quickly it would have been far more dangerous to try and hold back the tide of African nationalism.' Because of the build-up of nationalism, 'it was idle dreaming to think that Britain, by force, could hold her position. If General de Gaulle with a million men couldn't hold Algeria, then we couldn't hold about a third of the continent.' The leisurely progress towards independence envisaged by British ministers until 1959 depended on being prepared to use force to apply a brake on African nationalism. But Britain was no longer prepared to pick up the butcher's bill. As Macleod later wrote in the *Spectator*:

It has been said that after I became Colonial Secretary there was a deliberate speeding-up of the movement towards independence. I agree. There was. And in my view any other policy would have led to terrible bloodshed in Africa. This is the heart of the argument.[23]

This stark conclusion explains why Macleod accelerated the pace of political advance, although British territories were ill-prepared for majority rule. 'The political decisions were taken so quickly,' he later admitted, 'and their consequences snowballed to such an extent, to such a degree, that they did to some extent overwhelm the administrative preparations.' This lack of preparedness was another aspect of Macleod's dismal inheritance. Educational opportunities for Africans were at best extremely limited and at worst non-existent. The British colonial administration was one of the best in Africa, but the maintenance of high standards had taken precedence over recruiting and training African officials. Even by the late 1950s scarcely any Africans had been brought forward and entrusted with administrative responsibility. In fact, Macleod tried to speed measures that would support his political reforms:

> One went ahead all the time with things like planning the Africanization of the civil service, getting agreement from the Treasury and from the Cabinet, land schemes for Africans in the White Highlands [of Kenya] and elsewhere, but these matters were less in one's own control than the question of constitutional advance and the calling of a constitutional conference. And therefore to some extent they lagged behind.

There was a genuine dilemma, as Macleod recognized: 'It would have been nice and tidy if the two had kept step but if one waited until the administrative consequences were fully worked out, the momentum of the political advance would, in my view, unquestionably have been lost.' Since, in his judgement, the certain and almost immediate result would have been 'terrible bloodshed', he was bound to press on with political advance.

The dramatic change of policy launched by Macleod immediately after his appointment was not the result of an earlier, strategic review by the Cabinet. Indeed, Macleod could not recall 'having a single discussion . . . anyway in depth, on colonial matters' with either Macmillan or Rab Butler, 'the two most important men in the cabinet', before he became Colonial Secretary. But Macleod was wholly confident, because Macmillan and Butler, 'had a radical approach which would be on the whole – not necessarily in detail, but anyway in general – in instinctive sympathy with what I wanted to do'. In taking his early, critical decisions as Colonial Secretary, he 'started at least with the goodwill of not just the Prime Minister, but also the chief of staff, chief policy-maker [Butler]'. However, as he implied, he was not able to rely on their goodwill indefinitely.

In one sense, Macleod's radicalism was all about timing. As he later claimed:

> There never has been a change of colonial policy, if you look at the words alone, if you look at a speech about bringing any of the territories that once were colonies towards independence, you find it impossible, apart from peculiarities of language, to decide whether the speech was made by Joseph Chamberlain or Alan Lennox-Boyd or Arthur Creech Jones or Iain Macleod. The objective was always the same and always had been, to bring

that country at the right time towards its independence. But of course, everything depends on how you define the words 'at the right time'.

As he went on to argue: 'The change of policy that I introduced in October 1959 was, on the surface, merely a change of timing. In reality, of course, it was a true change of policy, but I telescoped events rather than created new ones.'[24]

Macleod's unusual combination of stark realism and deep idealism on Africa made an immediate impact at the Colonial Office. He was totally different from his urbane predecessors, Lyttelton and Lennox-Boyd, who typified old-style Conservatism and oiled the wheels of colonial diplomacy through extensive contacts and lavish entertainment. The most fundamental change was in Macleod's treatment of Africa's white settlers. Previous colonial secretaries had tended to regard the white settlers as the experts to whom they should listen before deciding what should be done. Macleod shattered this cosy relationship. He had a clear idea of what had to be done and had no intention of giving preference to the views of the minority over the majority. This abrupt ending of their previously privileged position came as a rude shock to the European leaders, and lay behind their subsequent allegations of having been betrayed or double-crossed by Macleod.

The force of Macleod's personal intensity and political radicalism made its strongest impression in the Colonial Office's African department. Its officials, who were to work with Macleod almost non-stop for the next two years, soon came to hold him in the highest respect. Sir Leslie Monson, then its head, regards Macleod as 'the best Secretary of State for whom I ever worked', and straightaway found him 'approachable and ready to dscuss problems and hear what his officials had to say'. 'Max' Webber, head of the East Africa section, was struck that unlike Labour's Colonial Secretary, Creech Jones, who would happily chat for hours, Macleod's meetings 'had a beginning, a middle and an end. He knew what he wanted out of a meeting and didn't waste time on anything else at all'. Sir Duncan Watson, head of the Central Africa section, recalls that Macleod, 'had to be sure of you, you could sense him in your early contacts summing you up, but if he accepted you, he listened to argument.'[25]

However, Macleod 'didn't really click' with Sir Hilton Poynton, who was then Permanent Secretary at the Colonial Office. Macleod never disguised a lack of personal rapport. As a result, Poynton felt that, in contrast to Lyttelton or Lennox-Boyd, Macleod had no sense of humour: 'It was as if every subject was almost sacred and you mustn't laugh about it.' Macleod expected to consult his Permanent Secretary as events unfolded, whereas Poynton felt that he could not be an expert on every colony and delegated policy work, concentrating instead on the massive task of colonial administration.[26]

The African department's officials were uniquely placed to observe

Macleod at close quarters when he was having to make some of the most difficult decisions of his career. He was 'a civil servant's ideal Minister', in Watson's view, 'because he was clear-minded, decisive, forceful once he'd decided on where he was going, but yet he was open to argument'. His speed of decision-making and the efficiency with which he dispatched his work were second to none. Max Webber reckons that Macleod 'could get through the equivalent of 20 hours' work in a normal working day through sheer economy of effort'. As a result, the new Colonial Secretary would often end his working day at his office at around six o'clock.[27]

Although Macleod might escape the office, he could never escape his work at night or at weekends. Often, he would need to meet leading figures from the constant flow of colonial representatives who visited London, either for conferences and formal meetings, or for informal discussions. Until his appointment, the Macleods had continued living in the constituency, but because of the round-the-clock demands that came with his new job, they moved to a temporary flat in Hans Crescent, behind Harrods in Knightsbridge, and then to a larger one at 36 Sloane Court West in Chelsea, a stone's throw from the Royal Hospital. He and Eve frequently entertained the leaders and representatives of different colonial groups. 'I used to see people from breakfast-time till the small hours of the morning, day after day,' Macleod recalled. At one point in the summer of 1961, five constitutional conferences were being held simultaneously in London, and in addition to chairing all five, Macleod was attending Cabinet meetings, dealing with his frontbench duties in the House of Commons and coping with his constituency work. From this period, although the Macleods returned to live in the constituency several years later, he could never quite command the same degree of personal loyalty from his local party.[28]

The informal, private discussions at the Macleods' flat were 'at least as significant for the future of Africa' as the formal constitutional conferences at Lancaster House. Eve took care of the hospitality, even preparing the food. As Macleod commented: 'It must have driven my wife slightly crazy to provide endless supplies of meals and coffee and things.' Her only help from government hospitality was the provision of a waiter for the more formal occasions and a *per capita* reimbursement for the guests, that covered only about a third of the actual costs.[29]

Moreover, Macleod 'felt very much the fact that my two predecessors, Lyttelton and Lennox-Boyd, had been men of considerable wealth, [and] that I had virtually no money at all and no proper place of my own to entertain. It cost me a lot of money as a matter of fact, being Colonial Secretary'. According to his close friend, Nigel Fisher, Macleod 'was obliged to cash in his £1,500 life insurance policy to defray the expenses'. It now seems extraordinary that Colonial Secretaries were expected to finance such an important part of their work from their own pockets and to make their own homes available for official business at all hours.[30]

Crises continually flared up that demanded Macleod's urgent attention. The first sign of trouble generally came in a telegram from a Governor, that might arrive at any time of the day or night. If a reply could wait until normal hours, Macleod's officials would be summoned to his office. 'Everyone round the table would have their say,' Monson recalls, 'he wouldn't merely seek the views of the senior officials.' Often, Macleod began by asking one of the junior officials, 'What do you think?' When Macleod had weighed up the problem, he would state the line of action that he wanted taken and the reply that should be sent.[31]

During the many tense periods, or when the Prime Minister, or the Commonwealth Secretary, or Macleod, was visiting Africa, the exchange of telegrams at all hours of the day and night sometimes became frenetic. The potential for confusion was immense – messages crossed and contradictory advice flowed between Governors (and sometimes ministers or officials) in colonial capitals such as Salisbury, Lusaka, Nairobi or Zomba, and the Colonial and Commonwealth Offices in London. Even so, Macleod never returned to the office or summoned officials from their homes at the weekend. Instead, he was content for the head of section to consult other officials and then phone him, often at his London flat, with a draft. He listened to the proposed reply and suggested changes. Whether the line of his reply was agreed on the phone, or perhaps the next day in his office, he never insisted on having the final wording read to him or seeing the final draft. If asked, he replied, 'No, you write it, I trust you.'[32]

Macleod's minister of state, the Earl of Perth, whom he inherited from Lennox-Boyd, found the new Colonial Secretary more of 'a loner' than his predecessor. In Perth's view, Macleod was very much somebody who worked things out on his own intellectually, rather than fashioning his judgement by discussion with others. Having decided to give independence, he approached it with complete conviction. Yet on specific problems, Macleod would invite help and discussion. Despite Perth's earlier public avowal of the need to slow down progress towards independence, the two men worked easily together. Perth responded to his ability to generate a great respect and affection, and was to defend Macleod against fierce attacks in the House of Lords from Conservative traditionalists, notably the Marquess of Salisbury, who were the mouthpiece for the white minorities in Africa.[33]

The Colonial Office exacted a punishing schedule of conferences, meetings, overseas visits, paperwork and parliamentary business. At the same time, Macleod's back trouble was becoming progressively worse. Some evenings he could be seen emerging from his official car outside Sloane Court West almost doubled up. His overseas visits, which invariably involved a demanding itinerary, were made even more onerous by the pain and discomfort. He never complained, but at times his disability became obvious. During one stopover between flights in Rome, Macleod and Sir Leslie Monson, then head of the Africa department of the Colonial Office, took the opportunity for some sightseeing. Inside St Peter's, Monson happened to point up to the interior of the dome, but Macleod said it was no use his even trying, as he simply could not move his head back.[34]

In those days, the Colonial Secretary had to answer oral questions on two afternoons each week, with the result that he and his junior minister (Perth was in the Lords) might answer up to 90 questions in a single week. In addition, Macleod found time, often on a Friday afternoon, to continue the weekly, 'off the record' press briefings, that Lyttelton had initiated, for the inner circle of Commonwealth correspondents of the *Economist*, the BBC, Reuters and the quality papers. In Macleod's day, Colin Legum of the *Observer* and Oliver Woods of *The Times* were among the most regular attenders. He trusted them not to break his confidentiality and spoke very freely about the way that he saw things and what he was trying to do. From the outset, he made clear his commitment to independence in Africa and although he was under no illusion that this would be unhelpful to him in the party, he was not deterred.[35]

The only other minister in the Commons when Macleod arrived was Julian Amery, who had served as Parliamentary Under-Secretary for almost a year. Amery quite often went to see his new boss at Sloane Court West, but their relationship remained distant as Amery spent much time from January 1960 negotiating with Makarios in Cyprus, and reported not to Macleod but to the Foreign Secretary, Selwyn Lloyd. They might have got to know one another better during the 1960 summer recess. The Amerys planned to visit Venice, where they were to be joined by Ted Heath, Macleod's successor as Minister of Labour, and asked Macleod and his wife to join them. However, Macleod preferred to visit Rome with his son, Torquil, for the 1960 Olympics. The prospect of Heath in Venice was not Macleod's idea of a good holiday, especially when set against an opportunity to indulge his passion for watching sport.[36]

When Macmillan promoted Amery by appointing him Minister for Air in October 1960, he gave Macleod the pick of the field to choose a replacement. Macleod's selection of Hugh Fraser was partly romantic and partly political. As a scion of the Scottish aristocracy, Fraser appealed strongly to Macleod's Tory romanticism. His background also gave him strong links with the party's traditionalists and yet he shared Macleod's radical thinking on Africa. He was therefore ideally suited to help Macleod in his battles with the right-wing – he was exactly the kind of Conservative to whom tradition-alists would at least listen.

Macleod and Fraser had a good rapport. Many nights, after the Commons ten o'clock vote, they would return to the Frasers' home in Campden Hill Square, where Macleod enjoyed exchanging ideas over whisky. It is a testimony to the intimacy of their friendship that Sir Hugh and Lady Antonia, who were Catholics, asked Macleod to be godfather to their eldest son. It is remarkable, but perhaps not a coincidence, that for almost twelve months during the Department's most radical period, the Colonial Office was in the hands of three Scots – an Islander (and Old Fettesian), Macleod, supported by two aristocrats, Perth and Fraser.[37]

History in the Making

From the moment that Macleod first entered his office, he orchestrated the politics of decolonization, both in Whitehall and in Africa with a determined, ruthless skill. During his early, critical months as Colonial Secretary, his tactics and timing were almost faultless as he created the momentum for rapid constitutional advance and majority rule. He was prepared to tack or trim – 'going to Birmingham by way of Beachy Head' as he later recalled, quoting Chesterton – usually because of the need to reassure the sizeable European minorities in East and Central Africa about their future. But he would not be deflected from his main objective.[38]

His predecessor, Alan Lennox-Boyd had responded to pressures from African and Asian political leaders for changes in Kenya's system of government by promising to hold a constitutional conference early in 1960, but he had done so without any clear ideas as to what should be done. Before Macleod had properly got his feet under his new desk, he met the Governor of Kenya, Sir Patrick Renison, who had been due to see Lennox-Boyd for a preliminary talk about the conference. Macleod realized that the constitutional conference had to be his main instrument if he was to achieve relatively peaceful decolonization. During a succession of such conferences, almost all held at Lancaster House, Macleod brokered and fixed the balance of power between African nationalists and European settlers during the extremely delicate, transitional phase to majority rule and eventual independence. As he later candidly said of this process, 'you really decide the election at the conference table, not at the polling booths'.[39]

The precise moment at which Macleod's officials realized that his appointment heralded an about-turn in policy was never forgotten by those who witnessed it. No sooner had Macleod settled in, than he summoned his senior advisers, including Sir Hilton Poynton, the permanent secretary, Sir Leslie Monson, and 'Max' Webber, the recently appointed head of the East Africa section, and asked them, 'What are we hoping to get out of this conference on Kenya?' His question was met by a long silence. It was finally broken by Webber, who had been anxious about the lack of discussion on strategy and who now suggested that the time had come for a breakthrough to African majority rule. Macleod simply nodded his assent, uttering not a single word. It was an historic moment. Macleod had signalled his radical intent and with it the end of Britain's African empire.[40]

Before Macleod could achieve any political progress in Kenya, he would first have to remove a major stumbling block. Since October 1952, the territory had been ruled under a state of emergency that had been imposed in response to the Mau Mau uprising. Macleod's priority was to end the seven-year emergency. In his first paper to the Cabinet's Colonial Policy Committee on 5 November and his first presentation as Colonial Secretary to the Cabinet five days later, he proposed lifting the emergency, while introducing specific legislation in Kenya in order to ensure that the Governor could maintain law and order. As part of the plan, 2,500 prisoners, who had committed offences connected with the emergency, were to be released and the remaining 120 serious offenders would become eligible for rehabilitation and subsequent release. Macleod had thus foreshadowed the highly symbolic act of eventually freeing Kenyatta who had long been the acknowledged political leader of the majority, Kikuyu tribe and was the founding-father of Kenyan nationalism. The lifting of the emergency was approved on 10 November and announced later that day. Coming within only four weeks of his appointment, Macleod's dramatic initiative represented the clearest possible statement of radical intent. Kenya's state of emergency formally ended on 12 January 1960, less than a week before the scheduled start of its constitutional conference.[41]

Macleod expected that Kenya's progress to majority rule and independence would be slower than in Tanganyika, Uganda and Zanzibar. Just ten days after the proposed ending of the Kenyan emergency had been announced, Macleod presented plans to the Colonial Policy Committee for speeding majority rule in Tanganyika. He later attributed much of the credit for this initiative to the recently appointed Governor of Tanganyika, Sir Richard Turnbull, whom he found an imaginative and 'interesting character', who 'saw at once that the future of Tanganyika, for good or ill, lay largely with Julius Nyerere and his supporters'. Macleod had already received a commendation of Nyerere from a source whom he respected. Jim Callaghan, then Labour's colonial affairs spokesman, had written a friendly, personal note welcoming Macleod to his new post, and had added his hope that Macleod 'would push Tanganyika on quickly, because he had the highest regard for Julius Nyerere'. With Nyerere and Turnbull, Macleod 'became the third member of a triumvirate that brought independence very quickly indeed to Tanganyika'.[42]

Macleod's role was to persuade the Cabinet that it was time to take the decisive step and extend majority rule beyond West Africa. As he told his ministerial colleagues, all communities in Tanganyika were agreed on the desirability of making an early move towards 'responsible' government, and there was general support for the Tanganyikan African National Union (TANU), led by Julius Nyerere. He therefore proposed that the Governor should make a statement in December, to the effect that after the 1960 elections the majority of both the executive (the Council of Ministers) and the legislature (the Legislative Council) should consist of elected members instead of non-elected officials. Moreover, the elections would be conducted on the basis of a widened franchise. The precise arrangements were to be settled at a conference in London during February 1960.

Macleod argued that his initiative in Tanganyika would not create 'any serious difficulties in Kenya, where it would obviously not be possible to make such a rapid advance', but he proposed to minimize any repercussions on January's Kenyan constitutional conference by deferring any more detailed announcement until negotiations had been held with Tanganyikan representatives. Significantly, other ministers were concerned less at the impact in Kenya and more at the ramifications for the Central African Federation. Widening the franchise in Tanganyika would lead – so it was argued – to demands for similar moves in Northern Rhodesia and Nyasaland. Moreover, this reform would not be acceptable to the Southern Rhodesian government. Macleod should therefore wait until the review of the Federation, being conducted under the chairmanship of Viscount Monckton, had reported and should limit the extension of the Tanganyikan franchise as narrowly as possible.

Macleod countered that Tanganyika's status as a trust territory – after the First World War, the League of Nations had entrusted Britain with this former German colony – meant that Britain was continually being asked in the United Nations about its plans for constitutional reform. Failing to take an opportunity for a peaceful advance to self-government would be difficult to justify. Moreover, the option of retarding progress in Tanganyika carried the risk that TANU would adopt a policy of non-cooperation and violence, leading to a breakdown in administration. The inadequacy of the police and the general lack of sympathy that the Government would encounter in Tanganyika and at the UN, would make it hard to contain any violent opposition.[43]

After a further meeting of ministers, Macleod agreed to a modest limitation on the extension of the franchise by introducing an income requirement in addition to the literacy, office-holder and property qualifications. He also accepted a slight postponement of the proposed Tanganyika conference from February until April or May 1960. But he had won his overriding objectives. The Cabinet accepted the inevitability of some repercussions on the Federation, but backed a dramatic acceleration of the timetable for majority rule in East Africa. Turnbull was able to make his announcement of a new constitution for Tanganyika, as planned, in December. The way was clear for a majority of African elected members in the legislature and on the Council of Ministers and even to Nyerere's emergence as Chief Minister.[44]

Having already launched two decisive policy initiatives in East Africa within less than two months of his appointment, Macleod set out during December on his first visit to the region. After stopping at Malta *en route*, his itinerary took him to Kenya, Tanganyika, Uganda and Zanzibar. Macleod's subsequent personal report to the Prime Minister, demonstrates that despite his lack of firsthand experience of the colonies, the new Colonial Secretary nonetheless brought fresh political insight into their problems.

Macleod's reflections written between Christmas 1959 and the New Year, were especially welcome to Macmillan as he turned his mind increasingly to his own forthcoming visit to Africa in January 1960. 'Colonial Secretary,' the Prime Minister scrawled on Macleod's report in red ink, 'I am grateful for a most interesting and imaginative report.' Also in December, during Macmillan's visit to France, the other great colonial power in Africa, the Prime Minister was told by President de Gaulle that all African states would become independent and the West would be faced with 20 to 30 African members at the United Nations: this might be tiresome, but would have to be accepted. It was clear from Macleod's report and de Gaulle's comment that 'the wind of change', of which Macmillan was to speak during his 1960 African tour, was a statement of fact.[45]

'The one common factor in the four East African territories,' Macleod concluded from his visit, 'is that in each of them something is happening on constitutional advance, but this is almost the only point they have in common and our approach to them will have to differ very widely.' In Tanganyika, Macleod discovered that the Governor's announcement had gone down very well, although there was some criticism of the Government for having rejected a wider franchise. 'There were very large demonstrations when I arrived at the airport, but in a sense these demonstrations (urging earlier and faster independence) were against Nyerere rather than me.' But he thought that Nyerere could 'ride the storm'.

Macleod was extremely optimistic following his talks with Nyerere, for whom, as he later recalled, he 'formed an immediate liking . . . He had, I think perhaps more than any other African leader, a peculiarly not just Western, but British, sense of humour, which is an odd sort of quirky thing.' Such was Macleod's rapport with Nyerere that he was able to tell Macmillan that he did not, 'even think now that it will be necessary to hold the Tanganyika Conference in London in the spring because the ideas Nyerere put forward to me on the Council of Ministers were almost exactly those that in any case we intended to offer'. Although there were a couple of matters still to clear up, Macleod believed that they might be able to do so without a conference. 'This would be very satisfactory.' Indeed, Macleod and Nyerere were able to finalize the shape of Tanganyika's independence constitution when Nyerere visited London in 1960 during two or three long talks in Macleod's flat. As a result, Macleod was happy to agree to Nyerere's suggestion that Tanganyika's independence conference should be held not at Lancaster House in London, as had become the tradition, but in Dar-es-Salaam in early 1961.[46]

As in Tanganyika, the relatively small number of European settlers in Uganda did not present a serious problem to majority rule. However, the politics of Uganda were infinitely more complicated because of the conflict between the politicians and the four African kings, who ruled parts of the country, including Buganda, in which Uganda's capital, Kampala, was situated. 'When I arrived in Uganda,' Macleod reported to Macmillan, 'it became clear to me that there was an utterly confused political situation, complicated by the position of the Kabaka and his central Kingdom of Buganda and by the splintering of the weak political parties that existed.' Macleod decided that the report of an advisory committee on constitutional reform – the Wild Committee – should be published at once, 'partly to try and bring some certainty into a confused situation and partly because I was sure (as in fact did happen) that it would soon leak to the press, who were following me'. The report was to be debated in Uganda's Legislative Council in February 1960, 'and we ought by then to be ready with our decisions'. However, Macleod counselled that some of the committee's recommendations, which included universal adult suffrage, 'go far beyond anything that we can accept'.

Nonetheless, Macleod judged that 'we can and should' give Uganda 'a major measure of constitutional advance'. Indeed, he told the Prime Minister that he 'would be reasonably confident about the future of this country, were it not for the Kabaka. The combination of being weak and obstinate and a king is a difficult one to deal with.' Macleod had two interviews with the Kabaka. 'At the first he was unpleasantly difficult and indeed uncivil,' but Macleod thought it worth seeing him again at the end of his visit and on this occasion he came to Government House. Somehow, they 'established more amicable relations'. However, 'the fundamental difficulty of his position and that of Buganda still remains and if there is a rock on which we will be shipwrecked in Uganda this is it'. Yet Macleod reassured Macmillan that he had 'some ideas for steering round the rock', which he would put to ministers in his proposals for reform in Uganda.[47]

As Macleod had hoped, the Cabinet approved his plans for Uganda in time for the Governor, Sir Frederick Crawford, to announce them during the final week of February. Uganda's pace of constitutional advance was to be slower than Tanganyika's. Its Legislative Council was to be predominantly directly elected on a common electoral roll, although the Governor would have the power to nominate members so as to retain a Government majority. The existing Executive Council was to be replaced by a Council of Ministers, with a majority of 'unofficial' members (i.e. people who were not also members of the administration). But Macleod did not accept the recommendation of the advisory committee that there should be a Chief Minister. As regards 'steering round the rock' of the likely hostile reaction from the Kabaka and the other kings, Macleod suggested that, in the last resort, the Kabaka might have to be replaced. But his main ploy was that the Governor should renew the pledge to maintain the position of the kings and should also announce that it was intended to set up an inquiry into the future pattern of government in Uganda.

The Cabinet's main worry over Macleod's proposals for Uganda centred, as had happened over Tanganyika, on his proposal to extend the franchise.

Again, the root of the anxiety was likely impact elsewhere of such an extension. Macleod suggested that, for the time being, the Governor should say that the Ugandan Government were sympathetic to the principle of a wide extension of the franchise and that the detailed implications were to be studied. There was some 'misgiving' about going this far, but ministers were finally persuaded that 'it was desirable that the Government should show a sympathetic attitude to the principle of universal adult suffrage'.[48]

'Kenya, of course,' Macleod emphasized, 'is the real problem for us.' Although his plans were radical by comparison with previous thinking in the Government and with the views of many of his ministerial and party colleagues, Macleod was scathing about the 'weak thinking going on here at home' about Kenya. He singled out for particular criticism the *Economist*, for having, as he put it, 'cheerfully' asserted that 'the settlers in Kenya must accept the same position as in Tanganyika.' But Macleod's view was that:

They forget – i) that Kenya's only just emerging from a seven-year-long reign of terror and emergency; ii) that the political parties in Kenya are not united at all in the way they are in Tanganyika; iii) that the problem of the settler and the European and Asian businessman is far greater and more formidable in Kenya than in any other of the Colonial territories.

Macleod was a radical, but he was also a realist. 'When I arrived in Kenya I made two simple points which I kept plugging to the end,' he told Macmillan. 'The first was that Kenya's problems were peculiar to Kenya and the pace at which she moved must be one that suited her.' His second point was directed to the following month's constitutional talks: 'I asked people to come to the London conference not completely committed in advance to their own particular solutions.' Macleod believed that 'in the end I had some success over this.' Although the Africans were planning to present a joint front at the conference, their unity was far from secure and there were 'many personal antagonisms clearly to be seen within it'. When he had first arrived, he had found that 'everybody was certain that the Kenya conference was doomed to failure', but opinion had changed. Tom Mboya, the young, elected member of the Legislative Council from the minority Luo tribe, who had emerged as the new leader of Kenyan nationalism in the vacuum created by Kenyatta's detention, had stated that he now accepted the principle of reserved seats in the Legislative Council for appointees of the Governor. To Macleod, this suggested some grounds for hope. There was a feeling that the conference 'has a true chance of success'. Macleod did not 'rank the prospects higher than this, but even so this improvement alone would have made my trip well worthwhile'. [49]

Settling Kenya's Future

'My objective in the first Kenya Conference was quite a simple one,' Macleod later recalled, 'although I don't think I ever put it into a sentence. It was to get Michael Blundell's group and the Africans to agree.' Macleod never thought that he could carry the right-wing Europeans with him, and 'always thought there was a possibility that one or two splinter groups might hive off from the Africans'. But his 'overwhelming desire' was to bring delegates 'who could reasonably be described as "moderate" people together, to see if from that one could fuse something that could lead, in time, to a Government in Kenya'.

Macleod was encouraged that in Kenya there were 'a large number of liberal-minded Europeans who saw that the African was bound to rule in Kenya in the comparatively near future, and who not only didn't despair of this prospect but who actually welcomed it'. This was why, he explained some years later, he had thought that it might be 'possible to move in Kenya with some success'. But Macleod's recollection understates the scale of the challenge that he clearly recognized at the time. Although there were more liberals among Kenya's 60,000 Europeans than there were in Northern and Southern Rhodesia, the Kenyan settlers' representatives in the Legislative Council had, by 1959, become more liberal than many people in the white minority community. In part this was a tribute to the persuasive powers of Michael Blundell and the support that he had won for his New Kenya Group. But the anxiety felt by the settlers concerning their prospects after majority rule – especially that felt by the farmers for the security of their property – rendered them susceptible to the reactionary ideas of Group Captain Briggs, leader of the United Party, who favoured policies that were, in Macleod's view, 'very close to apartheid'. There was always a strong temptation for many settlers to imagine that they could behave much as they always had, as if Kenya were their country, and that neither the British Government nor the Africans had any right to interfere.[50]

During the Kenyan talks, Blundell's delegates – now formally organized as the New Kenya Party (NKP) – were continually looking over their shoulders for fear that their support would desert them. Macleod, who was desperately keen to achieve a settlement in Kenya for fear of the alternative, realized the risk that if he pushed them too hard, he might be driving many more settlers into the hands of the die-hards. At the same time, he wanted to keep the pressure on the NKP to make some concessions in order to prevent the African delegates losing their support to extreme, militant nationalists.

Three days before the talks at Lancaster House were due to begin, Macleod set out his thinking in a secret note to Butler, who was standing in for Macmillan during January and early February while the Prime Minister toured Africa. Macleod hoped that 'the emergence of Blundell's multi-racial party, and other signs of a move away from sectional racial thinking, have given us a chance to make improvements in the system, which I hope will emerge from the Conference.' But he left Butler in no doubt about the difficulties that lay ahead: 'the individual participants have very different ideas and prejudices and it will not be at all easy.'

Kenya's system of government prior to the constitutional talks had been imposed by Lennox-Boyd in 1957. It included a mixed Government of which about half were civil servants, a quarter were elected by Europeans and a quarter by Africans and Asians. In the 91-seat legislature, the power of the Ministers to govern was secured by the 43 members nominated by the Governor; 'the driving power' came from 36 elected members chosen by their own race; and the remaining 12 members of all races chosen on a very limited common roll principle. About a quarter of the legislature were Africans. 'If things go well,' Macleod told Butler, he would try to secure a significant shift in favour of the Africans, notably by the 'development of one and probably two common rolls (one with a very low, one with a very high franchise); one would probably elect Africans only, and the other moderate Africans and non-Africans.' And with an eye to reassuring Europeans, Macleod would seek agreement: 'in principle upon certain safeguards (to be examined further) for incorporation later in the Constitution.'[51]

The Kenya conference was the first such gathering over which Macleod was to preside, and it was to set a precedent. His strategy, as he later revealed, emerged 'primarily in my own mind, and then I tested it out in a long series of talks every day for weeks and weeks with the principal officers of my Department, with my two Ministers, particularly David Perth, the Minister of State, [and] with my colleagues in the Cabinet'. In fact, he took care to limit the Cabinet's involvement:

What I used to do in the Cabinet was not, of course, to work out in detail in advance how the constitution would go, and put it to the Cabinet for approval, because that would leave me no room for negotiation at the conference and it would have been a hopeless way of negotiating, particularly in the circumstances of an African negotiation. But, of course, what I did was to put a paper to the Cabinet saying in outline what I proposed and giving the broad limits of discretion within which I intended to achieve a settlement. And these were always approved by the Cabinet and so with very wide limits of discretion – and the Cabinet were very generous to me on this – I had the Cabinet's authority for the sort of line that I was going to take.[52]

Before the Kenyan conference began, Macleod assured Butler that he would, 'of course, keep you [Butler] *and if it seems desirable the Cabinet*, closely informed as the Conference goes forward. If we come close to decisions we should perhaps send advance information to the Prime Minister [author's emphasis]'. Butler, who shared Macleod's and Macmillan's general attitude on Africa, got the hint: 'Please exercise your discretion on what you tell Cabinet on Monday,' he told Macleod. While Macleod retained the Prime Minister's backing – and, in Macmillan's absence, Butler's backing – he was able to enjoy substantial freedom of manoeuvre.[53]

Macleod's caution over the prospects for success seemed fully justified even before the talks had formally opened. First of all, there was a call from the African delegation, consisting of the fourteen elected members of Kenya's Legislative Council, for the immediate release of Kenyatta and his participation in the conference. This demand had been made by Oginga Odinga, Mboya's older and more hard-line rival. Macleod refused even to discuss the idea, since it 'would have been a breaking point, it would have been quite impossible at this stage to have released Kenyatta, and all one would have released would have been a flood of violence, and of murder in Kenya'. The second demand, in Macleod's words, 'came straight out of the blue'. It emerged that Thurgood Marshall, the American civil rights laywer who was to serve as the Africans' special adviser, had been appointed by only one faction of the African delegation. However, Odinga wanted to appoint Peter Koinange, a close associate of Kenyatta's who had been implicated in Mau Mau activities and was living in exile because of a detention order issued against him in Kenya. Macleod refused Koinange admission to the conference, since this would have placed the Government in an impossible position, and many European members would walk out. The African delegation immediately announced a boycott.[54]

The procedural wrangle over Koinange took up the first three scheduled days of the conference. Many meetings were held at Macleod's flat in an effort to resolve the deadlock. Macleod cabled Macmillan on 21 January, explaining that he had delayed his opening 'keynote' speech, but when no immediate agreement could be reached over Koinange he had decided to press ahead. During the afternoon of Wednesday 20th, he addressed the conference in private, as previously planned. The Africans were absent from their places, but he later gave his speech to them separately. 'There is some hope,' Macleod reassured the Prime Minister, 'that we can now get down to matters of substance, even though the Africans may not technically attend the conference at all.' Meanwhile, Downing Street officials were worrying that Macleod's refusal to admit Koinange, although it may have been correct, would be difficult to explain publicly since the evidence against him had not been thought sufficiently strong to justify his extradition to Kenya. Butler even wondered whether Koinange's 'curriculum vitae' could be made 'to look more vicious?'[55]

In fact, Macleod's opening speech went a long way to resolve the problem over Koinange. 'I said quite clearly,' Macleod later recalled, 'that the time had come to recognize that majority rule would come in Kenya and that the Africans were the majority race.' He found it 'curious that this, at the time, created less impression amongst the Europeans than it did amongst the

Africans'. Some years later, members of the African delegation still remembered his comment, and told Macleod that they 'knew that from that moment everything was going to be all right'. For whatever reason, 'the Europeans didn't take this as quite such a definitive statement of policy as it was meant to be'.[56]

By the end of that first week, the dispute over Koinange had been settled. The solution, Macleod later admitted, 'was a rather wet one'. The Africans were issued with a blank card allowing one person's admission to Lancaster House. They could write Koinange's name on it, but although he would be admitted to the room set aside for the African delegation, he would not be admitted to the conference chamber. It was the 'sort of compromise' that Macleod observed he 'had spent years at the Ministry of Labour devising. It was in one sense absolutely meaningless and in another sense all-important, because at least the conference got under way.' Macleod was able to write to Macmillan on 27 January that they had 'found a suitable compromise for the Kenya Conference and that the atmosphere, as sometimes happens, is infinitely better because of last week's wrangle than it would have been without it.'[57]

Once the opening formalities were concluded, Macleod introduced the procedure that he was to follow at every constitutional conference. He held what he called, in House of Commons parlance, a 'second reading debate'. This allowed every delegate who wished to make a speech. Macleod was quite cynical about its purpose:

Every delegate comes to London with at least one speech boiling inside him and if you can get all these over in a stream of speeches, which I may say begin to bore the conference after the first day or two, then it is possible to get down to hard conference negotiation when that is over.

Because the full conference was unwieldy, Macleod invariably conducted 'the committee stage' in negotiations with small groups outside the main conference chamber, often in other rooms at Lancaster House or at the Macleods' flat.[58]

On Monday 1 February, the day on which 'the committee stage' began at Lancaster House, Macleod spelled out his thinking on the kind of agreement that he was seeking with the Africans and Blundell's New Kenya Party in a personal telegram to Macmillan in Cape Town. 'It is of course from today that the real difficulties are going to show themselves,' he wrote. But he was encouraged by a leading article in *The Times*, that closely reflected his own thinking. *The Times*'s leader, that he paraphrased for the Prime Minister, had argued that one of Macleod's main concerns would be to lift Kenyan politics out of the communal rut and to simplify the constitution. Only the introduction of some form of common electoral roll could meet these two requirements. Some Europeans already accepted that African numerical superiority in Kenya would ultimately have to be reflected in the constitution, which would mean African majorities in the Legislative Council and the Council of Ministers. In return for compromise by the settlers on the direction of constitutional advance, African nationalism must make concessions on the pace of change. 'Time was,' the article concluded, 'when the British Government's role was to persuade the Europeans to make concessions to incipient African nationalism. Today the boot is on the other foot . . . Macleod's most difficult task is likely to be persuading the Africans to make concessions to the legitimate anxieties of the immigrants.'[59]

'I think *The Times* put it very well,' Macleod observed. 'A common roll must come', he added, 'and on a very wide franchise for it is neither possible nor wise to try and rig the common roll as, for example, in some other states in Africa so that we may exclude large numbers of people.' Under the existing system, Kenyan representatives were elected on a racial system 'and everyone agrees that this must go'. Mboya and the Africans wanted a Chief Minister system (as in Tanganyika), with all the Ministers appointed on his advice. They also wanted a complete common roll with universal adult suffrage and no reservation of seats for particular communities, or, if there was to be reservation, election of candidates in these seats by the whole of the electorate. 'This of course would mean that those people elected [for reserved seats] would in effect be elected by African votes and not by their own communities.' In Macleod's view: 'None of these things can be given and so there is a clear danger of a break here.'

Nonetheless, Macleod was 'certain that there must be a major move for a large number of seats (in my view around half) to be on a common roll and with a franchise that should be at least as wide as the Tanganyika system' – and conceivably with universal adult suffrage, since it would make no practical difference in these seats. 'But here I am afraid the Europeans are being very unimaginative.' This failure pointed to Macleod's dilemma:

> I am deeply anxious to protect the position of the New Kenya Party but this cannot be done by standing still and I must try and chart some way to achieve this and at the same time for the move forward in Kenya without which a major explosion is certain.

At this stage, Macleod and his advisers were thinking in terms of a scheme in which there would be about four Africans instead of the existing two in the Council of Ministers. Also, if the Africans' demand for a Chief Minister was not to be conceded, there would need to be a majority of unofficial members on the Council of State. As regards the Legislative Council, about 24 seats would be on a common roll with an extremely low franchise, if there was any franchise limit at all. About another twelve seats on the common roll would be elected on the basis of a high qualification, perhaps based on education, and would be overwhelmingly European. There might also be a further twelve reserved seats that would be allocated on a racial basis.[60]

Butler, who had been sent a copy of Macleod's telegram, confirmed that as far as he was concerned, the detailed negotiations had to be a matter for the Colonial Secretary and not the rest of the Cabinet. 'It is not because I am uninterested that I have not yet got in touch,' he noted, 'but because we all feel you are "on the Bridge".' Macmillan's response was revealing. 'This is very interesting. What would be the effect in Southern Rhodesia?' The Prime Minister, who was in South Africa at the end of his tour of Africa, was concerned, as he had been over the franchise in Tanganyika, at the effects further south.[61]

Macleod's forthright reply on 8 February was despatched to the Prime Minister aboard the *Cape Town Castle*, as he returned from his historic African tour. 'I am afraid there is naught for their comfort wherever Southern Rhodesians look in Africa today.' The pace of events in East Africa (the Cabinet Colonial Policy Committee were considering Macleod's plans for Uganda on the day he wrote) and in the Congo – where the Belgians had announced their intention to quit in six months' time – were 'bound to have serious effects on the future of the Central African Federation, and the territories within it'. Moreover, Macmillan had himself caused a sensation with his declaration that, 'The wind of change is blowing through Africa', when he spoke in the South African parliament on 3 February. Macleod was quick to point out to him that:

All the papers here applauding your speech comment with one voice that 'things in Africa can never be the same again'. Somehow we must try and get this into the heads of the men in Salisbury, but I do not underestimate for a moment the magnitude of the crisis that is now very close to us in the affairs of the Federation.

Macleod's message hit home with the Prime Minister. As Macmillan noted to Norman Brook, this 'passage . . . is rather formidable, but probably true.'[62]

Going for broke

By the start of February, the Lancaster House talks were again on the point of breakdown. Both Blundell's New Kenya Party and the African delegation rejected Macleod's initial proposals. On Tuesday 2nd, Blundell threatened not to participate in the committee stage, because Macleod's plan went much further than the NKP wanted. Part of the problem was that there was little rapport between Macleod and Blundell. Macleod respected Blundell's commitment to multi-racialism, but found that he was not a man for detail and preferred his deputy, Wilfred Havelock, whom he regarded as 'a less volatile and steadier person'. Blundell, for his part, has commented on the problems he encountered in his discussions with Macleod:

There was another part of his mind ticking away; examining the problem; speculating on various courses of action which was quite remote from anything immediately before us . . . On the many occasions when I left him, I always felt a curtain had fallen, severing our human relationship, and that he had returned to a world of his own.[63]

Blundell never adjusted to the fact that Macleod, unlike earlier colonial secretaries, had not automatically dealt with the leading spokesman of the white settlers as a natural friend or as the man on the spot, whose views should be given special weight above all others. Macleod's approach was quite different and he was not one for doing things by halves. 'In carrying out his task,' Blundell later wrote of Macleod, 'he was quite impervious to unpopularity and prepared to change the details of his approach overnight to achieve his objective.'[64]

As Macleod realized, Blundell was anxious to return home with an agreement on constitutional advance having formed the NKP in order to negotiate political reform in Kenya. Likewise, Macleod knew that the African delegates, having been assured of his commitment to majority rule at the outset, were equally anxious to reach a settlement that they could acclaim to their supporters. He was therefore bound to exert immense pressure on both sets of delegates. The Africans had never experienced anything else at constitutional talks, but now they were being treated as equals. 'Macleod was a master in the tactics of running a conference,' Mboya later commented, 'and it was a pleasure to watch his skill.'[65]

In contrast, Blundell later levelled a series of charges against Macleod for his treatment of the NKP delegation. But Blundell's strictures smack of a man trying to justify to his fellow settlers after the event his part in Kenya's rapid transition to majority rule. In an alleged incident at the Macleods' flat, Macleod supposedly handed Blundell a Colonial Office note reporting the Belgians' intention of leaving the Congo as early as June that year. According to Blundell, Macleod's only concern was that Britain would be the last colonial power to leave Africa rather than the first. Macleod later stated that he had no recollection of this incident. Yet the anecdote is significant because of the moral drawn by Blundell: 'A little flicker went through the back of my mind warning me that perhaps after all our future was to be decided not so much for our own good, as I had imagined, but for that of Great Britain.' It is extraordinary that Blundell had not previously thought that British ministers were acting on British interests. In any case, as Blundell later acknowledged, the 1960 talks marked a significant step forward for Kenya.[66]

Fearful of the consequences of a breakdown in the talks after the 'second reading' debate, the NKP and the African delegation began informal discussions. As Blundell candidly acknowledged: 'We began to see the sincerity of the African members and to appreciate the emotional forces behind them, while they on their side began to see us as individuals . . .' That Blundell, a liberal-minded settler, found he was only able to develop a real under-standing with African politicians after they had begun talking at Lancaster House, reveals the size of the gulf that existed between Europeans and Africans in Britain's remaining colonies.[67]

By 8 February, Macleod felt able to tell Macmillan that the talks looked more promising than had seemed possible at the beginning, or even the previous week. The most encouraging development was that 'Blundell's New Kenya Party and the African elected members have at last begun to talk among themselves and Blundell is showing real leadership and new understanding of how swiftly things are moving in Africa.' Even so, Macleod was cautions. 'This does not mean that agreement will be reached, although it is not impossible, but there is now a good chance of the main groups agreeing to work whatever constitution we finally lay down.'[68]

'You come to a point after weeks and weeks and weeks of negotiation,' Macleod later commented, 'when either you go on for more weeks until you exhaust everybody, or you judge that with a slightly brutal if you like, display of firmness you can bring things successfully to a head.' By the second week of February, Macleod judged that the moment had come:

> When, with great reluctance, I could get all those that I wanted to sign if I produced a document and said, 'This is virtually what we have agreed and we should now put our hands to it or acknowledge that we have wasted our work.'

The decision to go for broke was 'very much' Macleod's own, although 'it certainly wasn't against the advice of my Colonial Office people . . . What I would have done if they had disagreed, well happily it didn't arise, it might have halted me in my tracks.'[69]

Macleod informed Macmillan that he intended to put his final paper unofficially to the Kenya conference around Wednesday 10 February. It was 'something of a compromise' between the views of the New Kenya Party and the Africans, whose 'own plans are now surprisingly close'. His political assessment was clear:

> Nothing of course, could bring Group Captain Briggs into this, because he opposes all forms of advance for all races except Europeans but he has no sympathy whatever here. The Asians and the Arabs are on the sidelines and would accept whatever is finally agreed. I had a very large meeting with our Party [the Conservative backbench Commonwealth Affairs Com-mittee] a few days ago, and although some of them are understandably anxious about the pace of events in Africa, it turned out to be a very good meeting. All this, of course, may go wrong, particularly if Mboya decides to play the situation for a break, which he may well do. But at present we have a reasonable chance.[70]

Although Macleod had taken care to prepare his final, revised proposals in consultation with Blundell, the NKP leader had to be handled carefully as the final hurdle was approached. At Macleod's suggestion, Macmillan sent Blundell a message of support (drafted by Macleod). Butler, also at Macleod's prompting, had entertained Blundell at Number Ten at the outset of the conference, and at this critical moment in the talks sent him an encouraging, if somewhat awesome, hand-written note: 'Even if you drop a few hesitants now, the future for white civilization depends to a considerable extent on what you decide.'[71]

Macleod's formula reduced the Legislative Council from 91 to 65 members, 53 of whom would be elected on a common roll. Thirty-three of the seats would be 'open' (there were none in the existing legislature) and 20 would be reserved for Europeans and Asians. The remaining 12 seats would be elected on some restricted franchise, perhaps by the 53 other members, and each of the three main racial groups would have four seats. The franchise would be as for Tanganyika (a literacy, office-holder, or income of £75 per annum qualification). There would be no Chief Minister, but the Council of Ministers would be enlarged to comprise twelve members, with four 'officials' (civil servants) and eight 'unofficials,' who would comprise four Africans, three Europeans and one Asian. Ministers would continue to be appointed by the Governor, not by the majority party – otherwise, the African majority in the legislature would have led to African domination of the executive.[72]

Although the proposals represented a major leap forward on any previous Kenyan constitution, Macleod had stopped far short of African demands for full adult suffrage on a common roll, an African Chief Minister and the abolition of reserved seats in the legislature. Macleod was prepared for the expected objections from the Africans. As Mboya recalled, when they expressed their reservations, he 'looked firmly at them' and said that he had not asked for their views on the details, only whether they accepted or rejected them. But Macleod gathered from their comments that they rejected the proposals. He therefore intended to withdraw them, and instead, in about six months' time would send a commission to Kenya. 'It will report to me maybe in a year's time, if that's what you would like . . . Thank you very much.' The ploy worked brilliantly. 'No, sir, you misunderstand us!' cried almost everyone in delegation. 'He used these tactics to shock us,' Mboya commented, 'and certainly succeeded. This was the one reason why he got a "Yes" from us.' Macleod later suspected that he might have been able to negotiate a constitution that was slightly less favourable to the Africans even than the one that he proposed. This would have 'made it a little easier to sell to the Europeans', but he was 'determined that there should be no doubt in people's minds where the ultimate authority was going to rest and that is why I came down for a rather more definitive African majority than might have been saleable'.[73]

Contrary to all expectations at the time, the NKP rejected his plan. As Macleod reported to the Cabinet on 12 February, the sticking point had been the need for some safeguards of minority rights, particularly on the question of land. This cause was taken up by Humphrey Slade, a lawyer and NKP delegate, whom Macleod thought was 'something of a fanatic'. Nonetheless, Macleod was determined to press on, and formally presented his proposals to the conference on Monday 15 February. The NKP were now prepared to accept the plan, with the proviso that agreement could be reached on safeguards for the rights of minorities. Accordingly, a committee was established to consider such guarantees, although the Africans were unhappy that the issue had been raised when they had already agreed to a Bill of Rights. On Tuesday 16th, Macleod reassured the Cabinet that his plan 'provided for a slower constitutional advance in Kenya than in either Tanganyika or Uganda and contained no features unacceptable to Her Majesty's Government'. There was no discussion on this point.[74]

As the final lobbying on minority safeguards was fought out, Macleod again concentrated his efforts on Blundell's delegation. He advised Macmillan to turn down Briggs's request for a meeting – Briggs was so right wing that he had no backing from Conservative MPs ('not even the Suez Group would support him'). While he acknowledged that Briggs had attracted considerable support among the settlers in Kenya as a result of his outright opposition to Macleod's proposals, Macleod was confident that Blundell could 'certainly beat him in the end and we must do everything we can to ensure that he does'. He therefore urged the Prime Minister to see Blundell and several of his delegation. 'The importance of this is that they are going to have a very tough time when they go home, for they are taking a much more courageous line than any Europeans have dared to take in the complex problems of Africa, and much hangs on their success.' As Macleod counselled Macmillan, 'In short, the message is "*courage, mes braves*".' Macmillan duly put the onus on Blundell and his colleagues to reach agreement by impressing upon them that they could set the pattern for the whole of Africa. If their multi-racial approach failed, the likelihood was that the whites would be driven out of Africa.[75]

The climax was reached over the weekend of 20–21 February. Macleod had had a two-page formula drafted on property rights, for inclusion in a Bill of Rights. The Africans, who were anxious for an agreement, had told Blundell that they were prepared to accept the first page of the formula, but not the second. However, the NKP could not reach unanimity on this suggestion and the deadlock continued during Saturday. Macleod again called on Macmillan to use his influence and the Prime Minister duly invited all NKP delegates to Number Ten on Saturday evening.

Macmillan, according to the delphic note of his meeting with Blundell and his colleagues, 'delivered an oration on the general theme that change is inevitable in human affairs and is often less disagreeable than it seems in anticipation. This seemed to have a considerable effect on the delegates'. Nonetheless, the talks remained in deadlock until midday on Sunday 21st. But four hours later, and with 'unforeseen suddenness', Macleod made the breakthrough. He had made no attempt to produce a compromise formula on land safeguards; neither did he seek to end the stalemate by producing firm proposals, as he had done earlier when breakdown had threatened over the franchise and the legislature. Having weighed up the parties' positions on property safeguards, Macleod judged that there was no chance of agreement. He therefore set out the Government's views on the fundamental rights of individuals in Kenya in relation to the proposed constitutional changes, only asking the conference to 'take note' of them. In addition, he indicated the Government's readiness to take over the costs of the land forces in Kenya – which would release £1,500,000 of the colony's recurrent spending for agricultural and educational development – and to underwrite £5 million for resettlement purposes.[76]

Macleod's surprise tactics put the NKP delegates on the spot. They had made it a condition of agreement to Macleod's constitutional plan that there should be reasonable progress on the issue of land safeguards. In the end, they declared that this condition had been fulfilled, although nothing had been agreed. Macleod's pressure and the NKP's fear of the consequences of a breakdown had finally forced them to agree. Similarly the Africans, although they had not achieved their main demands, had decided that it was better to work the new constitution than risk making no progress.

At last, on Sunday afternoon, 21 February 1960, all parties to the conference, except the United Party, took note of Macleod's statement on individual rights and accepted that the changes to the franchise, the legislature and the executive should be implemented as the next stage in Kenya's advance. *The Times* reported that:

> There was an impressive atmosphere of geniality when the delegates gathered round the Long Gallery table in Lancaster House for the formal winding-up ceremony yesterday afternoon. Five weeks ago the talks opened with 14 seats left vacant by the African elected members, boycotting the proceedings over the Koinange issue. Yesterday the Africans sat smiling, smoking and waving their cow-tail switches (symbols of seniority among their leaders) under the glare of television lights.[77]

The strain on Macleod had been enormous and on Sunday evening he and Macmillan – who were both heavily preoccupied by the problem of Nyasaland and the Federation – were too exhausted to savour the moment. 'This is just a line to send you my warmest congratulations on the success of the Kenya Conference,' Macmillan wrote later that night. 'I am afraid when I saw you tonight we were both so tired that I did not really make you feel how deeply grateful I am. It is a great triumph of patience, imagination and perseverance.'[78]

'It came off,' was Macleod's reaction, but he recognized that 'it mightn't have come off and if it hadn't come off I would, of course, have set the cause of African advancement back by quite a time, and the course of events in Africa might have been very different.' But Macleod had no doubt that such a calculated gamble was the stuff of ministerial responsibility:

These are the decisions that if you hold high office in the State, you sometimes have to make, and make for yourself, and this isn't the sort of moment that you can get a Cabinet to decide for you, it is natural instinct which you acquire, is this the moment in which I can break through and secure what everybody really wants, except the fringe parties, or is it not.

Macleod was acutely aware that he had set all parties to the agreement, particularly Blundell's team, a difficult task on their return home. As he acknowledged, the 'highest praise' was due to 'the Blundell Europeans, who knew perfectly well when the crunch came that if they were going to side with the Africans and with me, that they would be abused in their own country when they went back'. At Nairobi, Blundell was greeted by a mob of die-hard demonstrators, one of whom abused him as a 'Judas' and hurled East African simunis, or sixpences – 'pieces of silver' – at his feet. Macleod had family experience of the hatred. His mother, who was then in her eightieth year, was asked what it felt like to be the mother of a traitor in Nairobi (her youngest son, Rhoderick, was a member of the NKP). As Macleod later reflected, 'this was hard enough for somebody like me to bear some thousands of miles away', but, he added:

To sign the future of your country away from the race that has governed it since it first started, knowing that you are going back to the same club, neighbours, who will take it out of you and in many cases I am afraid, out of your children. And I have always thought that Michael Blundell and Wilfred Havelock and the rest didn't get sufficient acknowledgement of an act of very real courage indeed in agreeing finally to sign the communiqué.[79]

A year later, Blundell wrote to Macleod that although, 'our agreement at Lancaster House practically killed me politically, nevertheless we were right . . . the alternative to Lancaster House was an explosion. The result of it is a real chance of success here.' Despite his subsequent sourness towards Macleod in his 1967 account of the Kenya talks, Blundell acknowledged before his death that Macleod's hastening of majority rule had meant that the Africans needed the Europeans in the new Kenya and therefore they had to reach some form of accommodation. Paradoxically, a slower period of transition would not have put the Africans under as much pressure and might have made life even more difficult for the Europeans.[80]

Macleod had achieved a famous success after a remarkable display of bargaining skill. Although he was cautious about the outcome of the talks until the details were worked out in Kenya, his handling of the conference had established the basis for solving what had long been Britain's most intractable problem in East Africa. Yet within forty-eight hours of his great triumph on Kenya, Macleod threatened to resign from the Cabinet.

9

African Omelette

I took the brutal, but I think practical view, that this was an omelette that you couldn't make without breaking eggs and you couldn't be friends with everybody.

Iain Macleod, interviewed about his policy on Africa, 29 December 1967.

Tackling the Nyasaland Crisis, 1959–60

When Macleod entered the Colonial Office, top of his agenda along with Kenya was Nyasaland. The Hola Camp murders in Kenya and the shooting of Africans and mass detentions without trial that followed the March emergency in Nyasaland had shocked British political opinion and provoked angry debate during the summer of 1959. Macleod could not afford to delay dealing with Nyasaland, since it posed a threatening crisis in Central Africa. He had to tackle both the Kenyan and Nyasaland crises in tandem.

Almost at once, Macleod began evolving his policy for Nyasaland. One of his first steps was to invite Sir Patrick Devlin, the judge who had chaired the Commission of Inquiry into the emergency, to meet him privately at White's, where they could talk freely. The Devlin Report, published in the summer of 1959, had strongly criticized the Government and found that there had been no plot by the followers of the nationalist leader, Dr Hastings Banda, in the Nyasaland Congress to murder Europeans, as Macleod's predecessor, Lennox-Boyd, had alleged. In addition, the inquiry found that Nyasaland had been 'a police state' – it was no consolation that this state of affairs in a British territory was said to have been 'only temporary'. The Government had been wrong to assume that Banda's offers to compromise were insincere; in imposing the emergency, Government officials had repeatedly broken the law; and, even among Africans loyal to the Government, there was no support for Nyasaland's membership of the Central African Federation. So great was Macmillan's embarrassment that he orchestrated a rapid, and highly tendentious, rebuttal. Macleod thought the Devlin Report was 'somewhat over-written', but accepted that its findings were 'technically true' and that the Government had been unwise to talk of a murder plot.[1]

From the outset, Macleod's 'mind was more or less made up' that the key to Nyasaland 'lay in the person of Banda, and although it was bound to take me a month or two to achieve it, I was really determined to release him from the moment I became Colonial Secretary.' Banda had lived away from Nyasaland for more than 40 years before his return in 1958, but he had come to be regarded by the Nyasas not only as their first university graduate, but also as a national hero. He had long been their most effective campaigner with the Colonial Office, and after his homecoming acquired the aura of a messiah for his people. As Macleod later revealed, his decision to release Banda was very much a decision of his own. At the start of December 1959, Macleod set out his thinking on Nyasaland in a secret minute to Macmillan, copied only to Home, the Commonwealth Secretary. 'I do not believe,' he wrote, 'that we can possibly justify for long the continuance of the Emergency. We would have no chance of defending our action if we could be brought before the [United Nations] Human Rights Commission.'[2]

About 470 men were still in detention – 380 in Nyasaland, and 90 in the custody of the Federal authorities in Southern Rhodesia, where the leaders were held at Gwelo. There was no question of the detainees 'being of the Mau Mau type', and the vast majority 'could only be convicted of minor violence, if that'. Macleod therefore proposed reducing the number of detainees as swiftly as possible to 'the true hard core' of around 50. But as Macleod stressed: 'the hard core does NOT include Banda. The Devlin Report draws a clear distinction, and in my view a correct one, between Banda and his young extremist lieutenants.' He was 'in no doubt at all that some time we will have to deal with Banda.' Drawing the moral of previous British blunders, Macleod told the Prime Minister that: 'We have proved so often that more moderate men do not arise and in any case there are no more moderate leaders likely to emerge than Banda himself.'[3]

The Nyasaland crisis and dealing with Banda were made infinitely more complicated by the question of the future of the Federation of Rhodesia and Nyasaland. Although British Conservatives looked to the Federation, which was strategically placed to the north of the apartheid regime in South Africa, as providing an example of the multi-racial approach in Africa, the Federal Government in Salisbury had signally failed to win African support for the Federation – a point made by Burke Trend of the Cabinet Office, who visited the Federation in the early autumn of 1959 and whose highly critical report was sent to the Prime Minister ('a *most* interesting paper,' thought Macmillan). In keeping with the terms on which the Federation had been established, the British Government announced in early September 1959, the appointment of Viscount Monckton, the former Conservative minister, to chair a Commission on the development of the Federation. Yet even before the Monckton Commission began work, it was difficult to see how they would be able to square the circle of conflicting demands: the insistence of Sir Roy Welensky, the Federal Prime Minister, and his United Federal Party that the Federation must continue; the growing pressure from Africans for rapid advance to majority rule and independence, particularly in Northern Rhodesia and Nyasaland; and the strong opposition of many European settlers, particularly in Southern Rhodesia, to anything other than the most gradual transition to majority rule.[4]

There was no doubt in Macleod's mind which of the demands should receive priority. Monckton had been appointed before Macleod became Colonial Secretary and thus before 'the effective decision to increase the speed of independence for African countries'. As a result, the Federal review was, in Macleod's words, 'an exercise that we had to go through' and 'the Monckton Report was out of date before it appeared'. Macleod already 'knew quite clearly as far as the two countries [in the Federation] for which I had responsibility – i.e. Malawi [Nyasaland] and Northern Rhodesia – what my policy was going to be'.[5]

In his comments to the Prime Minister and in Cabinet, however, Macleod stated his continuing commitment to the Federation, while warning of the opposition to it in the two northern territories of Northern Rhodesia and Nyasaland for which he was ministerially responsible. 'I believe the Federation is the best, indeed the only real solution for these territories,' he told Macmillan in his minute of 3 December:

> But I am sure we must not underestimate the strength of the forces that are at the moment speaking against it. It is not right as far as the Africans are concerned to think that this merely represents vocal African political opinion in Nyasaland. It is a conviction very deeply and widely held.

In part Macleod was paying lip service to an ideal that had become a Conservative article of faith. He was in close contact with Monckton and since he 'was content' with the way the Federal Review was developing, there was no point in raising the whole question of the Federation's future before Monckton had reported – particularly as the Federation was the responsibility of the Commonwealth Relations Office and not of his own department.[6]

Macleod told Macmillan that he was 'convinced, although this may sound paradoxical, [that] Banda is the most likely African Nyasa leader to keep Nyasaland within the Federation'. This was not entirely fanciful. As Macleod reported:

> When I asked Orton Chirwa, the leader of the Malawi Party, if he contemplated forms of association with the Rhodesias his answer to me was: 'If you ask me that question the answer must be No. The only man

who would compromise and give a favourable answer on this is Dr Banda himself ' .

The timing of Banda's release was to become a major bone of contention between the Federal and Southern Rhodesian Governments in Salisbury on the one hand and Macleod on the other. It was also to bring Macleod into conflict with Home, who, as Commonwealth Secretary, held ministerial responsibility for the Federation and Southern Rhodesia. And, in addition, it was eventually to cause Macleod's first major row with Macmillan.[7]

Following his visit to East Africa in December 1959, Macleod reported to the Prime Minister how 'very dissatisfied' he remained with the position in Nyasaland. He feared that the Governor, Sir Robert Armitage, whom he had asked to see at Dar-es-Salaam, was 'giving no real lead', and 'that Southern Rhodesia and the Federation are themselves too stubborn to appreciate the resentment that is building up in the Northern Territories against them. This will be our most difficult single problem to solve'. The ending of the emergency and Banda's release were the necessary first steps towards reform in Nyasaland. 'I am myself absolutely convinced,' Macleod told Macmillan, 'that whether the Federation like it or not an imaginative offer on constitutional advance at a fairly early date is certainly the best, and perhaps the only, hope of holding the position.'[8]

Before the turn of the year, Macleod envisaged a slower timetable for Banda's release than he was to urge later, while the Prime Minister, who now suggested accelerating the process, was later to urge delay. This turn-round was ironic in view of the row that they were to have. Macleod proposed in his first Cabinet papers on Nyasaland that Banda should be released after the Monckton Commission, who were due to visit Nyasaland during the spring, had left the territory. This would probably mean a date during April or May, and Macleod would be able to talk with Banda during his planned visit to the territory in June. However, before the Cabinet discussion, Tim Bligh drew Macmillan's attention to Macleod's taking it 'as accepted policy that Dr Banda should be freed only *after* the Monckton Commission leaves Nyasaland. This may be right but you may think the point worth exploring.' The announcement of rapid advance in Tanganyika had been 'very favourably' received in the press and Bligh added that: 'There may be something to be said for going too fast rather than too slow in Nyasaland.' 'I agree,' Macmillan scribbled in reply, adding: 'Can I see the Colonial Secretary *before* Cabinet?'[9]

An accelerated timetable was agreed at 'a little discussion' between Macmillan, Macleod and Home at 10 Downing Street on New Year's Day, 1960. In accordance with a revised schedule prepared by Macleod, the rate of release of detainees was to be speeded up, reducing their number to only a dozen by April; the Monckton Commission were to visit Nyasaland from the latter part of February until mid-May; the end of the emergency was to be announced at about the time of Monckton's arrival; and Banda was to be released during March, probably early in the month. This acceleration meant that Banda and other former detainees would be able to give evidence to the Monckton Commission – a move that was bound to anger the Federal and Southern Rhodesian Governments.[10]

The proposed date for Banda's release was brought forward even earlier – subject, as always, to the security situation – when the Cabinet approved Macleod's revised proposals. This further acceleration was not formally minuted and is only apparent from Macleod's subsequent, secret note to Macmillan, in which he referred to the Cabinet's provisional decision 'that Dr Banda should be released about the time you left the Federation (say, February 1st)'. In his telegram to the Governor, Macleod thought that Macmillan might leave the Federation sooner and identified the release date as 'the last few days of January, although you [the Governor] might see advantage in deferring for a few days'.[11]

In a major speech in Leeds on 7 January, Macleod signalled the Government's intentions by declaring that: 'the time must soon come when the question of constitutional advance in Nyasaland must be tackled again.' He also presaged the ending of the emergency and, in the meantime, speeding up the release of detainees. But before he had been able to deliver his statement, Macleod had a foretaste of the difficulties that he was soon to face from Welensky and Whitehead. Home had sent them an advance copy of Macleod's text and they immediately fired an angry warning shot by objecting to the proposed comments on the legal protection of witnesses who gave evidence to the Monckton Commission. Such protection, in their view, would allow outrageous allegations to be made against their Governments and transform the hearings into a public platform. Welensky and Whitehead wanted the hearings held in private, on the same lines as the Devlin Commission. But this was to ignore the difference between a security inquiry (Devlin) and a constitutional review (Monckton), and also overlooked the Government's commitment, made in parliament, to publish the evidence. Nonetheless, Macleod toned down his text.[12]

At this stage resistance from Armitage, the Governor of Nyasaland, was Macleod's main worry in achieving Banda's early release. Armitage advised, because of the security risk involved, that Banda should not be freed until 25 February. More helpfully, he suggested that Macleod's visit to Nyasaland should be brought forward to early March, enabling Banda and the Colonial Secretary to have talks on constitutional advance. Even so, Macleod's concern at the repercussions of any delay in Banda's release prompted him to cable Macmillan, who had begun his African tour, and suggest that when the Prime Minister saw Armitage he might put forward the 15th as the preferred date. But Armitage's continued insistence on the 25th and his view that military reinforcements would be needed in Nyasaland when Banda was released, began seriously to perturb Macleod – an increased military presence when Banda was freed would risk jeopardizing 'any political and security gain which we hope to obtain from announcement of early talks'. Again, he asked Macmillan to raise these points with Armitage.[13]

But Armitage delivered a much more serious blow to the plan only a few days before he was due to see Macmillan. In a top secret and personal telegram to Macleod, the Governor suggested that the emergency might have to continue for six to eight months and Banda be kept in detention for the same length of time. However, if Banda were to be released before the Monckton Commission had left Nyasaland, Armitage proposed that he should be released to the United Kingdom and not be allowed to return to Nyasaland. Macleod warned Macmillan of the Governor's sudden change of mind and reiterated the political advantages in releasing Banda by 15 February.[14]

Worse was to follow for Macleod when the Prime Minister failed to resolve the timing of Banda's release with Armitage. As Macmillan confessed to Macleod, he had been 'rather staggered to find, on arrival [in Nyasaland], the turn of events which had taken place and the entirely new proposal to remove Banda to London under restraint'. He suspected that the Governor had only agreed to Macleod's plans in Dar-es-Salaam against his better judgement and had been reproached by his advisers on his return. Nonetheless, Macmillan added that: 'We must take it as a fact that the Governor and his Council [of Ministers] now consider it an unacceptable security risk to have Banda at large in Nyasaland when the Monckton Commission is there.' The anxieties of the Governor of Northern Rhodesia, Sir Evelyn Hone, also had to be taken into account. 'If both Northern Rhodesia and Nyasaland exploded together, we should be in trouble. It looks as though we should then have to bring United Kingdom troops from Kenya.' On the other hand, Macmillan saw the great risks 'in hanging on without any positive policy'. He was therefore trying 'to find a middle course by which we should appear to be taking some positive step towards constitutional advance'. The idea of Banda's coming to London as a free man would, he thought, be seen as 'making an advance in that direction while at the same time meeting the Governor's fears about the security position in Nyasaland'.[15]

Macleod and Home, in a joint reply to the Prime Minister, rejected as unrealistic the notion that Banda would stay in London while the Monckton Commission were taking evidence in Nyasaland. Instead, they proposed an alternative 'firm plan', in which Macleod's intention to visit Nyasaland would be announced in mid-February; Banda would be released on 25/26 February; Macleod would arrive in Salisbury on the 27th and Nyasaland on the 29th; and, in the meantime, arrangements for reinforcements would be made by consultation between Armitage and Welensky. Macmillan agreed to these proposals, but the Governor in Nyasaland and the Federal Prime Minister still presented problems.[16]

On his return to Salisbury, after visiting Nyasaland, Macmillan had intended to discuss the Government's plans with Welensky. But instead of a working dinner, Welensky had arranged a social occasion and Macmillan managed only to tell him that Banda could not be held much longer. The Federal Prime Minister appeared to understand this, but Macmillan was unable fully to inform him of the Government's thinking before leaving for South Africa. The suspicion must be that although Macmillan had found his host not at all keen to 'discuss business', the Prime Minister had not pushed the matter – as he was to admit later, he felt in a difficult position because of the ambivalent advice that he had just received from Armitage and, to a lesser degree, Hone.[17]

By the time he reached Pretoria the Prime Minister was showing clear signs of cold feet. He cabled his agreement with Macleod's view that Banda's 'unconditional release soon' was preferable to indefinite detention, but warned: 'I think I ought to make it plain to you that in taking this course we shall be acting contrary to the view of the security position which is taken by the Governor and his advisers and shared by Welensky and Hone.' In addition, Macmillan was deeply concerned at the likely over-reaction of Nyasaland's Governor and his officials to any disturbances that followed Banda's release, since he had found them 'very quick to take repressive measures against demonstrators'. As he added: 'To be frank, I was not favourably impressed with the Administration there,' and, in a chilling warning, told Macleod that, 'we must be prepared for a repetition of what Devlin thought they did last time.' Not surprisingly, therefore, the Prime Minister would 'feel very much happier' if the Nyasaland Administration were strengthened immediately. Macleod had already taken steps by appointing Glyn Jones, then a Minister in Northern Rhodesia, to become Nyasaland's Chief Minister in the spring on the retirement of the existing incumbent, Footman. Jones was also a frontrunner for a Governorship. Such was the Prime Minister's concern, that he assured Macleod: 'If you would prefer to find a new Governor you could count on my full support. In other words I think that the course you recommend is right, but I doubt very much whether you have got in Nyasaland the men to carry it through.'[18]

Macleod's Africa policy at risk

Macmillan was soon to doubt Macleod's recommended course on Nyasaland. His second thoughts were caused at the beginning of February by the fierce reaction of Welensky and Sir Edgar Whitehead to the proposed plan. As members of the United Federal Party, neither man was as extreme as some European spokesmen (particularly in Southern Rhodesia), but both were intensely obdurate. Welensky, a former Rhodesian heavyweight boxing champion, engine driver and union leader, was always ready to issue dramatic threats – to fly to London immediately, to call up his troops, to call an election, and so on – in an effort to force the British Government to bow to his view; while Whitehead, who was virtually blind and almost deaf, was no less reluctant in pressing his demands, possessing an unending capacity for drinking beer and doggedly arguing his corner.

When Welensky learned from Home of the plan for Banda's early release, he threatened the resignation of his Government if the release occurred before the Monckton Commission had reported. This would be tantamount to keeping Banda in detention for most of 1960. Whitehead claimed that Banda's early release would probably result in the defeat of his Government, a swing to the extreme right-wing Dominion Party (precursors of the Rhodesian Front) and Southern Rhodesia's secession from the Federation. But Whitehead's real motivation was his belief that the plan gave him a chance to drive a hard bargain with London and he promptly drew up tough terms that would help entrench white minority rule in Salisbury and bar nationalists from power in Northern Rhodesia and Nyasaland.[19]

The rejection of Banda's early release was totally unacceptable to Macleod. While Welensky continued to rage against the intended release as 'an unfriendly act' by the British Government and as an act of appeasement of African nationalism, Macleod and Home jointly cabled Macmillan in Cape Town:

> Iain's view is that there is little give in the present plan that we can offer except perhaps postponement of Banda's release for a week or so. He cannot contemplate keeping Banda in detention until after Monckton Commission has left Nyasaland, i.e. mid-April.

The need for Banda to have the opportunity to see the Monckton Commission as a free man was to remain Macleod's sticking point during all the toing and froing between London and Salisbury over the next three weeks. Macleod also recognized, with Home, that there was little hope of bringing Welensky round by long-range correspondence, and they proposed that the Federal Prime Minister should be invited to London on 18 February, shortly after Macmillan's return from Africa.[20]

As Home reported to the Cabinet on 9 February, however, the suggestion of talks in London had failed to dispel Welensky's apprehensions. The Federal Prime Minister preferred that Home should visit Salisbury and now threatened to demand that the start of the Monckton Commission's visit to the Federation should be delayed until after his meeting with Macmillan. Any such action by Welensky would deeply embarrass the British Government, since it would reveal that they were at loggerheads with the Federal Government. Just how difficult Macleod's situation in holding to his plans for Banda's early release was likely to become was brought home to him when he heard the views of his Cabinet colleagues:

> Recent developments in Africa, particularly those in the Belgian Congo, had given rise to widespread anxiety among the white settlers. They felt

that the United Kingdom Government were always led by circumstances into negotiating with the extreme African nationalists, which made it impossible for the position of the settlers to be adequately safeguarded.[21]

That same day, Home gathered from Welensky that his real problem was Whitehead and if some concession could be made to the Southern Rhodesian Prime Minister, the dispute might be settled. Home cabled this news to Macmillan and reported that he and Macleod had been working on 'a fall-back position' that included a similar idea. However, as Home recognized, any concession to Whitehead on the Southern Rhodesian Constitution would militate against African interests. Home also reported that he, Butler and Macleod had agreed that it would be easier to prevent news of any conflict with the Federal Government emerging, if he were to see Welensky in Salisbury instead of Welensky suddenly coming to London so soon after the Prime Minister's visit.[22]

Unlike some earlier telegrams to the Prime Minister, this one had been sent by Home and not jointly with Macleod. Indeed, Home's minute prompted an unusually blunt note to Macmillan from Sir Norman Brook, the Cabinet Secretary, who felt impelled to stress that the: 'real point at issue is whether Banda's release would seriously endanger security in Nyasaland . . . Responsibility for that rests with the Governor and the *Colonial* Secretary. Decisions about it ought not to be settled through talks in Salisbury between the Commonwealth Secretary and the Federal Government.' Had Brook's advice been heeded, a potentially disastrous conflict in the Cabinet would have been avoided.[23]

On 15 February, the Colonial Secretary informed Armitage of the latest change of plan and of his thinking on constitutional advance for the territory. As Macleod explained, Home would seek to persuade Welensky to acquiesce in the launch of constitutional talks on Nyasaland and the release of Banda on 10 March. Macleod would arrive in Nyasaland five days earlier, having first visited Salisbury and Lusaka. In an effort to win acceptance from the Governments in Salisbury, two concessions were to be made – for Welensky, no constitutional advance was to be implemented in Nyasaland before the Federal Review Conference, which was to follow publication of the Monckton Report; and for Whitehead, the removal of the existing constitutional constraints on the Southern Rhodesian Government could be considered, provided that alternative safeguards were agreed and guaranteed. On this approach, the Government were contemplating constitutional conferences on both Nyasaland and Southern Rhodesia during the summer of 1960.[24]

These details provided the bare bones of the memorandum that Macleod presented to the Cabinet on Thursday 18th. Macleod's memorandum added that Welensky could be assured that Macleod would not commit the Government to any detailed constitutional changes during his preliminary talks with Banda following the latter's release, although Macleod would have to give a broad indication of the kind of constitutional progress that might now be made, if there were to be any chance of securing Banda's cooperation. 'My purpose,' Macleod noted, 'is to open up sufficient prospect of constitutional advance in his mind to keep him out of mischief until further constitutional talks could be held in London, in May or June.'

Regarding the extent of constitutional change that would be needed 'to have any appreciable effect on African opinion', Macleod argued that there would have to be 'considerably increased African representation in both the Legislative and Executive Councils', although abandoning an official majority in both Councils might not be appropriate at this stage.

> Thus far our ideas might be acceptable to Sir Roy Welensky; but what is most likely to meet with his objections are the franchise arrangements which are contemplated. In the light of decisions in Tanganyika, Uganda and Kenya, Dr Banda will be able to press for something a good deal wider than Sir Roy Welensky is likely to contemplate with equanimity.

Macleod acknowledged that his proposals for constitutional reform in Nyasaland might well lead to demands for further constitutional advance in Northern Rhodesia, but these pressures could be resisted for some time since any changes in Nyasaland would not come into effect until after the Federal Review was completed.[25]

Macleod had couched his memorandum in cautious terms, reflecting the evident concern of his colleagues at the pace of change in Africa. He recognized the fears of Europeans and sought to accommodate their concerns within the terms of any constitutional advance. But he was not prepared to deny his conviction that African demands for change had to be accepted and a faster transition to majority rule negotiated. His Cabinet memorandum reveals how, only four months after his appointment, he had already built up a momentum that would make change more difficult to resist in the Central African territories for which he was responsible. Nyasaland could not be totally isolated from the rapid advances already being made in East Africa; and Northern Rhodesia could not be treated entirely separately from Nyasaland.

Yet there were signs that Macleod's approach was about to bring him into conflict with the Prime Minister. Although the main impact of Macmillan's visit to Africa had been his 'wind of change' speech, in which he urged Africa's Europeans to face the reality of African nationalism, it was clear when he reported to Cabinet that one of the main impressions he had gained from his visit had been the strength of European settler feeling in Central Africa. At the Cabinet meeting on Nyasaland two days after his report, the Prime Minister suspected that Home's talks with Welensky and Whitehead might be unsuccessful, since they knew that Armitage and, to a lesser extent,

Hone, believed that Banda's release would entail an unjustifiable security risk. In that event, the Government might be faced with a serious situation:

> They might be forced to choose between abandoning their plans for the release of Dr Banda and the opening of talks on constitutional development in Nyasaland and being seen to do so under pressure from the Governments of the Federation and Southern Rhodesia, or taking the risk that Southern Rhodesia might secede from the Federation or that the Federal Government might make a unilateral declaration of independence.

This was the stark choice that soon faced ministers.[26]

During the weekend of 20–21 February, while the Kenyan conference in London was reaching its climax, in Salisbury Home encountered the most vehement reaction from Welensky and Whitehead to the Government's plan for Banda's release. Both the Federal and Southern Rhodesian premiers painted a lurid picture of the consequences. Welensky argued that Banda was utterly opposed to the Federation and would do his utmost to ruin the Federal Review. Whitehead was explicit: 'I tell you straight that if you release Banda in Nyasaland, Southern Rhodesia will blow up and leave the Federation and I shan't be able to stop them!'[27]

Faced with this impasse, Home proposed trying another tack that might go some way to meet their apprehensions. As Macmillan reported to Cabinet on Monday 22nd, the Commonwealth Secretary thought that the security risk would be reduced if there was a greater gap between Banda's release and the arrival of the Monckton Commission in Nyasaland. If the Commission's schedule were to be rearranged and they first visited Southern Rhodesia, they would not arrive in Nyasaland until the end of the first week in April. This would provide a month after Macleod's visit and the release of Banda, during which the situation could be observed.[28]

Home still failed to make any headway in Salisbury. Late on Monday night, he cabled Macmillan that 'we are now at the crunch'. In a further telegram in the early hours of Tuesday morning, the 23rd, he reported that Welensky had formally stated the Federal Cabinet's view that: 'Banda should not be released; but that if the United Kingdom Government decided that he had to be this should not be done until the Monckton Commission have finished in the Federation or at least in Nyasaland.' They were particularly influenced by the 'danger that if Banda is released before the Monckton Commission have left, African witnesses who would otherwise give evidence will not do so for fear of intimidation'. The Federal Government would not move from this position. Home judged that: 'there is no element of bluff though question [sic] how far they would in fact go if we persist in our plan is impossible to assess.'[29]

The prospect of the resignations of both the Federal and the Southern Rhodesian Governments and stormy election campaigns in which independence from Britain was the issue, persuaded Home and Macmillan to climb down. At Cabinet on the morning of Tuesday 23rd, the Prime Minister concluded that it would not be justifiable to risk the disruption of the Federation on the question of delaying the release of Banda by three or four weeks. Ministers generally supported this view, although they opposed any concessions being made to the Southern Rhodesian Government on constitutional safe-guards. Macmillan made much play of Home's supposed success in having persuaded Welensky and Whitehead to accept Banda's release after the Monckton Commission had left Nyasaland, but this was a poor fig leaf for Salisbury's veto on British policy in Africa. Indeed, Macmillan acknowledged in Cabinet that the delay would be interpreted as the Government's having yielded to pressure from Europeans in the Federation. In turn, he conceded, this would cause great political difficulty in Britain and prejudice the Govern-ment's policy in the Federation and elsewhere in Africa.[30]

But this was not to be the end of the argument. For Macleod, deferring Banda's release raised the dilemma of deciding between yielding to the Federal Government in matters that were his responsibility or overriding the Federal Government with the possible result of breaking up the Feder-ation. Macleod's conviction remained that Banda should be able to give evidence to the Monckton Commission as a free man. As to security, it could equally be argued that the risk of trouble in Nyasaland during March–April could be greatly increased if Banda were *not* released before Monckton's arrival in the territory.[31]

Macleod had accepted the need to consult Welensky and Whitehead, but he now decided that the time had come to be as intransigent as they had been. He knew that his resignation would be disastrous for Macmillan only four months after his appointment and especially in the wake of his triumphs in Tanzania and Kenya. Immediately the Prime Minister completed his summing up of the Cabinet discussion, Macleod intervened to say (in the words of the Cabinet minute):

> That while it might be necessary for the Government to follow the course recommended by the Commonwealth Secretary, this would greatly in-crease his difficulties in the discharge of his responsibilities as Colonial Secretary, and he would have to consider the implications of such a decision on the conduct of the Colonial policy in Africa.

Macleod's threat of resignation prevented the Cabinet from approving any delay in Banda's release.[32]

Macleod later recalled of his discussions with the Prime Minister that followed the fateful Cabinet meeting:

> [Macmillan] felt that I should give way to him on this and I felt that I simply couldn't because unless I had my own way in this field, that is the

release of Banda, I could not begin to solve the problems that he had given me as Secretary of State for the Colonies.

The news of Macleod's threat was cabled to Home in a secret and personal message from Macmillan – it also had its comic aspect as the Prime Minister contrived not to name Macleod or mention the word 'resignation', while making clear whom and what he meant. Macmillan wrote:

> For your private, repeat private, information we are having serious difficulties here and although the Cabinet including the Minister most responsible agreed that course B [delaying Banda's release] was inescapable, we are going to have great trouble in persuading our friend that he personally can honourably continue in view of his known attitude and public statements.

While urging Home that it was 'vital' that he should keep this point entirely to himself, nonetheless Macmillan suggested that it would be no bad thing for the Federation and Southern Rhodesia 'to realize how difficult we are finding this situation'.[33]

Macleod reckoned that the disagreement over Banda's release was the worst that he ever had with Macmillan. He was later understandably sharp in his assessment of his former boss – and perhaps more revealing as a result:

> I think the difficulty with Harold Macmillan in relation to Africa was that he had all the right instincts, as his 'Winds of Change' speech showed quite clearly. He was more than prepared for a rapid move to independence – as his appointment of myself showed. But from time to time he wanted, as I daresay we all do, the best of both worlds, he didn't want to fall out with his good friends either at home or in Central or East Africa as the case may be. Whereas, I took the brutal, but I think practical view that this was an omelette that you couldn't make without breaking eggs and one couldn't be friends with everybody however much one wanted to do it, while one was pursuing such a policy.

Although the relationship between Macleod and Macmillan was quickly repaired, the fault line in it that Macleod had identified was to have a profound impact the following year when controversy raged over the future of Northern Rhodesia.[34]

A lonely responsibility

Macleod's threat of resignation and the pressure that was belatedly brought to bear on the Federal Government finally yielded a breakthrough. After a flurry of telegrams and telephone calls between London and Salisbury,

Home proposed a new plan to Welensky on Thursday 25th, in which Banda would be released on 1 April – three weeks later than Macleod had previously agreed to as the latest date, but three or four days before the Monckton Commission were due to leave Nyasaland. Home insisted that he must have this concession and Welensky and his Cabinet agreed. The plan preserved Macleod's overriding condition – that Banda must be able to give evidence to the Commission as a free man. It also recognized the Federal Government's concern, by allowing plenty of time for Africans who favoured Federation, but who feared intimidation, to give their evidence before Banda's release.[35]

The British Cabinet approved the Prime Minister's outline of the new agreement on Thursday 25th. 'Many congratulations on your success,' Macleod cabled Home that evening, 'I am sure you understand how much it means to me personally and to us all as a Government.' The following day, Macleod wrote a personal, hand-written note to Macmillan, partly in gratitude and partly in self-justification of his threatened resignation:

My dear Harold,

I am content and deeply happy with the arrangement Alec has secured, But it is more important that the flag of African policy still rides high. Nothing could have concealed the fact that under Plan 'B' [delaying Banda's release] we were hauling it down.

I will always remember the understanding and the quick sympathy you gave to me in these last few difficult days. Thank you.

Yours ever,
Iain.[36]

Yet Macleod still had to face the ultimate test of his judgement. Only when Banda was finally released would it be shown whether Macleod was right. But he had some encouraging news of Banda's likely attitude. Macleod had been in touch with George Loft, an American Quaker, who had spent two years in the Federation and was well acquainted with African nationalists. Loft had visited the detainees as a religious adviser and towards the end of February spent an hour with Banda at Gwelo. Banda assured Loft that Macleod could rely on him to hold absolute peace and that he could control his people. When the new Chief Secretary in Nyasaland, Sir Glyn Jones, followed up Loft's meeting by seeing Banda for an hour and a half on 10 March, Banda was 'supremely confident that his influence would result in there being no disorders or breaches of the peace on his release'.[37]

Nonetheless, Macleod had a lonely responsibility to bear. As he reflected several years later, his decision went:

Against the advice of the Governor, Sir Robert Armitage, against the advice of all the various Governors and the Governor-General in Salisbury, against the advice of Welensky and his Cabinet, and indeed against the feeling of a considerable number of my colleagues in the Cabinet, including in the end the Prime Minister himself. But I was prepared to put my judgment against theirs . . .

The dire warnings continued up to the last minute. Macleod spent the last week of March in the Federation, arriving in Nyasaland two days before Banda's scheduled release. During his visit to Salisbury, Macleod found his talks with Whitehead, the Southern Rhodesian Prime Minister, 'rather baffling'. Macleod 'got the firm impression' that Whitehead 'didn't care at all about Dr Banda, although he intended to use the issue to press his own demands'. Macleod also met Welensky for the first time and the two men initially got on well. Even so, Welensky and his Cabinet warned Macleod 'in the most dramatic terms against what I proposed to do'.[38]

Macleod had particular reason to remember the terrible prediction of Sir Malcolm Barrow, the experienced and much respected Federal Cabinet Minister from Nyasaland, who reckoned that '10,000 Africans would be killed in the riots that would follow Banda's release'. As Macleod noted: 'this is a sobering reflection to have put to you by a man of Sir Malcolm's standing, to somebody who had never been in that part of the world before and who didn't really know what the consequences of the release were going to be.' But his own, overriding, political judgment was unshaken:

I simply didn't see how this country could go on as anything but an African country, there were only about 7,000 or 8,000 Europeans there, and whether one liked it or not Banda in jail or out of jail was the unquestioned leader. I remember saying at the time that in jail Banda was a myth, out of jail he would be a man, and I thought that I could deal with men.

As Macleod later wrote to Macmillan a couple of days after Banda's release:

Until the last moment warnings of disaster continued to be poured upon me. Blantyre was going to be in flames within a few hours time and hundreds of people would be killed. I am afraid that very many people here and in Salisbury were waiting to say, 'I told you so.'[39]

The press had followed Macleod closely while he was in Salisbury, in case he took the opportunity of visiting Banda at Gwelo jail. At times this game of cat and mouse descended into farce. On one occasion, Macleod left his hotel and was driven in the vague direction of Gwelo, pursued by a journalist from the *Daily Express*. The journalist's car broke down, but he found another and continued the chase. When he finally caught up with Macleod, he found the Colonial Secretary leaning over a hedge discussing artificial insemination on an African farm. Curiously, when Macleod left Salisbury, the press became convinced that he was not going to release Banda and lost interest.[40]

Banda was released from Gwelo jail, unobserved, in the early hours of Friday 1 April. He was flown to Nyasaland, and then driven to Government House at Zomba, again unobserved, where he met Macleod. The first indication that people had of Banda's release occurred a couple of hours later, when they heard Banda 'making an admirable short appeal on the radio to say that he had returned and that everyone was to maintain peace and a non-violent attitude'. Banda had given his broadcast at Macleod's request. As Macleod commented, it 'worked like a charm'. However, 'typically enough', as an exasperated Macleod told Macmillan: 'the local members of the United Federal Party objected to this on the grounds that this was a public meeting and that he should not have been allowed to speak, but there is really no measuring the bottomless stupidity of their members here and in all three territories.'[41]

Forty-eight hours later, Macleod was able to report to Macmillan:

Since Banda's release, nothing whatever has happened and everything has been very quiet. It would make salutary reading one day if those who warned us so often about what would happen immediately on Banda's release were to re-read the letters and telegrams that came to us over the past few months.

After all that Macleod had been through, his gibe was understandable. In the event, even nature had intervened on his side. On the day of Banda's release, a sunspot broke communications between Britain and Nyasaland, preventing journalists in the territory from sending their copy. 'I didn't organize that!' was Macleod's comment.[42]

Macleod had however, organized his first, crucial discussion with Banda 'in order to weigh up the man for myself':

I met him in the Governor's House in the small study absolutely alone. The Governor wasn't with me, nor did I have any private secretary, nor any recording device or anything else. There were just the two of us. Dr Banda came in his rather shapeless raincoat that he used to wear and I simply shook hands with him and we sat down and we talked for about an hour. We got on very well indeed.

'It is hard to explain the moment at which you know when you can deal with a man,' Macleod observed. As Colonial Secretary, he added: 'you meet so many different people from so many different countries, and you have got to make up your mind fairly quickly – "Can I do business with this man?" And within half an hour, perhaps less, I was sure I could with Dr Banda.' Neither the idea of a radio broadcast, nor a constitutional conference were suggested by Macleod until he was sure about Banda. As it was he 'bore no resentment whatever for his time in prison' and they had a general, preliminary conversation.[43]

But Macleod was not starry-eyed about Banda. Referring to Banda's almost immediate departure for London, where he was to make speeches and give television interviews, Macleod advised Macmillan that Banda, 'will exhaust his appeal pretty quickly for he is a vain and ignorant man'. Macleod was hoping to call a constitutional conference on Nyasaland in London during the latter half of July, but Banda's 'ideas about constitutions are hopelessly inadequate and naive and it is hard indeed to see anything but an imposed constitution [by the British Government] emerging from the talks'. Nonetheless, he told the Prime Minister: 'it is a great relief now to have the little man out of gaol because unless he proves himself in the end to be an effective leader, I am sure his authority will diminish rather than increase.' In one respect, at least, Macleod had seriously underestimated his man – Banda was to demonstrate a strong instinct for sheer political survival, ruling his country with an iron rod for 30 years.[44]

Although Macleod had thought the fears of a security breach had been 'exaggerated', he later admitted that 'even I was surprised and delighted by the results of Banda's release. It was just as if one had lanced a boil':

Everywhere one went in the country one saw clearly a relief of tension, one saw very great happiness amongst the people . . . There were formidable hurdles to overcome but the biggest hurdle of all was the release of Banda and the successful breaking of the tension in that country.[45]

It was not only the tension in Nyasaland that had, at long last, been broken. After months of seemingly interminable argument, during which Macleod had threatened to resign, and had overruled the security assessments of almost every senior British adviser and the Federal Government, his relief was palpable. With none of the predicted demonstrations or riots having materialized, perhaps the loudest noise in Zomba on the night of Banda's release was that made by a jubilant Colonial Secretary at the Governor's residence, as he celebrated by hurling cushions across the room, in the style of a rugby scrum-half, while the hapless Governor retrieved them.[46]

Feeling uneasy about Northern Rhodesia

During the spring and summer of 1960, Macleod was at pains to keep Welensky closely informed of his thinking on Nyasaland and Northern

Rhodesia, yet the two men never developed any rapport. A seemingly trivial incident during Welensky's visit to London, for the Commonwealth Prime Ministers' conference in May, vividly reveals the gulf between them. Macleod returned the hospitality shown him in Salisbury by Sir Roy and Lady Welensky by inviting Welensky to Sloane Court West to meet Eve and have dinner. 'I'm told that you're fond of music,' Macleod commented during the evening to Welensky, who replied that he was and particularly liked light opera. Macleod said that he had some records that he would like to play for him. This was odd – although Welensky was not to know it – since Macleod was tone deaf and seldom listened to music.

Macleod's choice was as different from light opera as it is possible to imagine. He greatly enjoyed the black-hearted songs of Tom Lehrer, the American satirist, whose compositions included, 'The Old Dope Pedlar' and 'Poisoning Pigeons in the Park'. Lehrer's wicked humour was the vogue among intellectuals and Macleod was so taken with the lyrics that he and Diana, his daughter, would recite the words off by heart. Lehrer's satire on the Cold War and the atom bomb,' 'We Will All Go Together When We Go', was a particular favourite, and it was one of the songs that Macleod put on the record player for Welensky's entertainment. But when Welensky heard it, he thought it was 'absolutely awful', and privately was appalled that anybody could laugh about the bomb. After Welensky left the Macleods' flat, he turned to his colleague, Julian Greenfield, the Federal Minister of Home Affairs and Law, who had accompanied him, and commented of Macleod: 'This fellow's a puzzle to me, how he could be amused by that kind of thing is beyond me.'[47]

Possibly Macleod was being mischievous and played the Lehrer recording for his own amusement and to see Welensky's reaction, since he might have suspected that a white Rhodesian former boxer and engine driver, who had a liking for light opera was unlikely to find the songs of an American satirist his cup of tea, but probably Macleod simply assumed that anybody who had not heard Lehrer's songs would find them enjoyable. Be that as it may, Macleod and Welensky were never able to see eye-to-eye.

The timing of any new constitutional talks on Northern Rhodesia would have to take into account the likely publication date of the Monckton Report (probably during the late summer or early autumn of 1960) and the subsequent Federal Review conference. The Government had held to the line that no further changes were being considered in Northern Rhodesia – at least not until the Federal Review had been completed – but Macleod's first visit to the territory at the end of March 1960 led him to conclude that this position was no longer tenable. 'I found Northern Rhodesia puzzling and worrying,' Macleod wrote to Macmillan after stopping off in Lusaka for a couple of days, *en route* from Salisbury to Nyasaland for Banda's release. Macleod had found that, 'almost everybody I met drew entirely different conclusions from the same set of facts'.

Many people believed that the coming of independence to the Congo – the Katanga copper belt straddled its 1,000-mile border with Northern Rhodesia – would be 'a major disruptive element', and that it was 'essential', particularly if there were constitutional progress in Nyasaland, 'to promise some form of constitutional advance' in Northern Rhodesia at the same time. The more liberal figures in the Federation, including the industrialist, Sir Ronald Prain, chairman of the Rhodesian Selection Trust group of companies, and the Reverend J.L. Pretorius, chairman of the Federal African Affairs Board, told Macleod that if some such promise of talks in Northern Rhodesia was not given, Kenneth Kaunda, the leader of the United National Independence Party (UNIP) 'could not hold his place' and 'worse men like Sipalo, the Secretary of UNIP who is a trained Communist, would take over'. Others, including Welensky and Winston Field, leader of the right-wing Dominion Party, believed that no more was needed than to indicate that they might look at Northern Rhodesia in the light of the Monckton Review.

Kaunda had replaced Harry Nkumbula, the leader of the Northern Rhodesian Congress, as the most powerful nationalist figure in the territory when the latter's moderation enabled his younger rival to attract popular support to his more extreme, breakaway party. Macleod was immediately able to test Kaunda's power over his party when he was greeted by a demonstration at Lusaka airport. Kaunda and Sipalo referred to this demonstration when they met Macleod and spoke of the great uneasiness and dissatisfaction in the country. They argued that 'something must be done before June.' However, Kaunda was told by Macleod 'in forcible terms' that he was not impressed by demonstrations and 'that if he wanted to show himself a true leader he must first show that he could control his own followers'. Macleod then 'invited him to go out to the very large crowd that was gathering at the gates of Government House to tell them to go away and to make a speech advocating non-violence and finally to call off demonstrations'. To Macleod's 'considerable surprise', Kaunda did this. 'The crowd dispersed without a murmur, he later made a speech advocating non-violence and there was not a single banner or placard when I left next day.' Macleod found it 'rather impressive' – Kaunda had 'some control, if he wishes to exercise it, over the Party'.

Yet the most important message in Macleod's letter to the Prime Minister was his doubt about the Government's position on constitutional advance in Northern Rhodesia. 'I left Northern Rhodesia with a very uneasy feeling indeed and I am by no means sure that we can hold the position of refusing to have constitutional talks until after the Federal Review.' Having heard the arguments in the Federation, he found himself – perhaps not surprisingly – more inclined to agree with the view taken by people like Prain and Pretorius than that of the Federal Government.[48]

Macleod's inclination to favour faster progress than had been envisaged in Northern Rhodesia was reinforced when he met Monckton in Nyasaland on the eve of Banda's release. At the root of African opposition to the Federation in the northern territories lay the fear that Welensky and his party favoured amalgamation rather than federation. However, Macleod gained the impression from Monckton that his Report would attempt to allay African fears by recommending a looser federation:

> Most of the Commission are beginning to look towards a solution which would retain Federation but put a number of powers from the Federal authority to the Territorial authority and have a system in which Nyasaland and Northern Rhodesia could look forward to becoming more or less independent so that they could ensure that the Southern Rhodesian policies to which they object so much could not be followed in their own Territory.

'I think if we were left to ourselves,' Macleod wrote to Macmillan:

> We could make a success of the Federation as I am sure it will be re-defined by Walter Monckton . . . But I am very much afraid that the United Federal Party think of the Federation and their own Party as one and the same thing and will be too stubborn in the end for all our efforts.[49]

The one, slim hope of preserving the Federation lay in winning over African opinion. As Macleod realized, Africans needed to be able to identify with, and be involved in, the government of their own territories. Constitutional talks on Nyasaland were scheduled for late July, but nothing was planned for Northern Rhodesia.[50]

At the end of May, Macleod sounded Welensky out on the possibility of announcing that constitutional talks on Northern Rhodesia would be held during 1961. In his letter, Macleod reiterated his commitment to the Federation, but was 'realist enough to know that the odds at the moment are against its full success and that we must work very hard to turn the scale'. The Colonial Secretary remained convinced, as he thought Welensky did, 'that the true problem is not really Nyasaland but Northern Rhodesia'. He sent Welensky a copy of a note of his recent interview with Kaunda, drawing the Federal Prime minister's attention to Kaunda's comment that: 'He [Kaunda] would do everything he could to hold to the position on a non-violent basis . . . but he added that if some clear indication could be given that there would be a Northern Rhodesian conference some time after the Federal review, that would make things much easier.'[51]

In Macleod's view, although Kaunda 'is no doubt a difficult person and not wholly reliable', he was much to be preferred to Sipalo or any other UNIP leaders. Macleod told Welensky that he was therefore inclined to try to give Kaunda some sort of encouraging indication. However, he thought that John Roberts, leader of Welensky's United Federal Party (UFP) in Northern Rhodesia, was bound to oppose any such initiative and asked Welensky to think it over. He bluntly told Welensky that the attitudes of both Roberts and Blackwood, the UFP leader in Nyasaland, were going to be 'the largest single obstacle to the success of the Federation'. His warning to Welensky was clear: 'I do not think we can hold the position by a Canute-like process of ordering the tides to return.' Although he suggested that, 'this does not mean that we cannot if we are wise move at our own pace and in our own time', he left Welensky in no doubt of his conviction: 'But move we must.'[52]

Macleod's overture fell on deaf ears. Welensky wrote to him on 17 June expressing his opposition to a Northern Rhodesian constitutional conference. In London, Macleod found that Home also disagreed with him, arguing that 1962 was quite soon enough. Accordingly, Macleod stuck to the Government's declared policy and avoided making any promise of early constitutional advance in Northern Rhodesia. But by the autumn, despite others' continued misgivings, the weight of the argument was to shift in Macleod's favour.[53]

Macleod's resolve to speed up the pace of change in Northern Rhodesia was greatly strengthened by two decisive developments during August and September 1960. On Thursday 4 August, a new constitution for Nyasaland was agreed after a two-week conference at Lancaster House. Macleod later suspected that he had only achieved unanimous agreement on the Nyasaland constitution because there was a strong body of opinion among Rhodesian Europeans who wanted to be shot of it from the Federation. The inclusion in the Federation of a territory with such a massive African majority had long rankled among settlers in Rhodesia. Some 'hoped that a European-dominated country consisting of Southern Rhodesia and a large part of Northern Rhodesia could be formed'.[54]

So great had been the differences between Nyasaland's African and European delegations at the outset of the talks, that Macleod had expected the conference to break down at any moment. But this wide divergence of view enabled him to present proposals that he had prepared in the Colonial Office and, as Macleod had hoped, Banda exerted a moderating influence. When Macleod's proposals failed to meet the demands of the nationalist Malawi Congress Party for self-government and universal suffrage, two of their delegates threatened to walk out and 'return to gaol'. But they were dissuaded after Banda, who had a private talk with Macleod, appealed to them at least to examine what was on offer.[55]

After detailed discussions, all sides agreed to a plan that was less favourable to Banda and his nationalist supporters than the relatively small European community in Nyasaland had initially dared hope. Even so, the new constitution launched the transition to African majority rule and had profound implications for Northern Rhodesia and the Federation. Executive power under Nyasaland's new constitution was to be retained in the hands of the Governor, who was to govern the territory with the assistance of a ten-strong executive council comprising three African and two European elected members of the legislature, and five 'officials'. The Africans were to have a majority in the legislative council (20 Africans, eight Europeans and five officials), and the franchise was to be extended to include around 100,000 Africans – only about half the total that Macleod had originally proposed to Welensky and Greenfield. The new qualifications for voting were based primarily on an income of £120 per annum (a figure to which Welensky had attached great importance) and a literacy test.[56]

Macmillan was delighted with the outcome and wrote from Chequers to Macleod, who was spending the weekend in Folkestone, to congratulate him on his 'wonderful success'. 'Of course there will be troubles and difficulties in the future but this is a splendid start and a great relief to us all,' Macmillan enthused. The Prime Minister, like Macleod, was not in the least starry-eyed about the African leaders who were to assume power, although Macmillan's assessment was extraordinarily patronizing: 'Dr Banda, like all these people will be a demagogue one day and something like a statesman another, but this is their nature and we have got to live with it.'[57]

Although Welensky had had no formal status in the talks and remained in Salisbury, Macleod had taken great care to keep him fully informed. After the talks had concluded, the Federal Prime Minister wrote warning that Kaunda would demand the same concessions and asked Macleod to stand firm. But as Macleod later graphically recalled: 'the finger was pointing from then quite clearly at Northern Rhodesia and it was to that problem that after a suitable pause for digestion, I turned my attention.'[58]

Had Macleod had his way, there would have been no pause. In the euphoria of the Nyasaland agreement, he was briefly bullish about progress in the Federation. After dining with the Monckton Commission, he reported to Macmillan on 11 August that:

> all of them, even the granite men from Southern Rhodesia, were openly delighted with the result [of the Nyasaland conference], and their recommendations for Nyasaland, and I suspect for Northern Rhodesia too, are going to follow the same pattern. Even in Southern Rhodesia it is good to see that Whitehead is planning to extend his parliament and bring Africans swiftly into it. So we may yet be in time. It is in any case the best introduction we could have to the Monckton Report.

Four days later, Macleod wrote to Welensky, repeating his argument of the previous May for a Northern Rhodesian constitutional conference to be held during 1961.[59]

The pressure for faster constitutional advance in Northern Rhodesia was about to receive a tremendous boost. On 7 September, Monckton submitted his Commission's Report to Macmillan – a further month was to pass before it was published, during which time the Prime Minister was preoccupied with Welensky's accusation that the recommendation for secession to be allowed in certain circumstances was in breach of the Commission's terms of reference and of assurances given by Macmillan. Of immediate interest to Macleod was the recommendation that the Government should make an early declaration of its intention to proceed with constitutional advance in Northern Rhodesia. On 15 September, Macleod sent Macmillan a secret minute in which he drew attention to this recommendation and reminded the Prime Minister of his (Macleod's) view that it was increasingly difficult to hold to the Government's previously stated position on Northern Rhodesia, and that there was now 'no alternative but to fall in line with this recommendation'. Macleod proposed that soon after the report was published, the Government should say that they accepted that discussion of constitutional advance should proceed as fast as possible. Macleod emphasized to Macmillan the urgency of acting soon because of the 'dangerous position in Northern Rhodesia'. The background was explained in an article that he forwarded from the *Manchester Guardian* – an unusual source for Conservative ministers – headlined, 'Dangers of Delay in Northern Rhodesia', and written by the paper's Northern Rhodesia correspondent, Harry Franklin. As Franklin explained, many of Kaunda's followers 'were trying to hold him to the UNIP plan under which civil disobedience on a major scale (and some said a good deal more than civil disobedience) was to start a week after October 4, UNIP's old deadline for independence'. Kaunda had tried to gloss over this commitment after his meeting with Macleod earlier in the year and had said that he was against violence, but he needed a face-saver. 'There is no doubt', Macleod concluded in his minute to the Prime Minister, 'that a date (whether the 4th or 12th) has been set in October, and that violence may well follow if there is no move by then.'[60]

At a discussion on the Monckton Report the following day, 16 September, Macmillan, Macleod and Sandys – now Commonwealth Secretary in place of Home, who had become Foreign Secretary – agreed that Sandys should take up the question of the timing on Northern Rhodesia with Welensky and Whitehead during Sandys's forthcoming visit to the Federation. In addition, the Governor, Hone should privately tell Kaunda and Roberts (leader of the UFP in Northern Rhodesia) of the likely timetable. However, Sandys did not raise the Northern Rhodesian question with Welensky until he had returned to London, when he explained that Macleod was anxious to make an early statement not only because of the threat of disorder in the territory, but also because the Labour Party were planning to lobby him on his plans. On 28 September, Hone announced that he was beginning informal talks with the parties.[61]

The British and Federal Goverments were set on a collision course over the future of the Federation. Unable to reach a common line on the question of secession, they issued separate statements on the publication of the Monckton Report. When Welensky complained privately to Home that the British Government had never in simple words stated that they were for the Federation, Macmillan felt that an immediate statement should be made to the effect that the Government did support the Federation. Macleod was due to address the Conservative Party Conference at Scarborough the following day, but when Number Ten contacted him about inserting a suitably robust statement in his speech, 'the Colonial Secretary took the point but seemed rather guarded'.[62]

Sandys, who was also at Scarborough, was contacted, and with Macleod devised a suitable formula. In his speech, Macleod recalled that during Macmillan's visit to the Federation earlier in the year, the Prime Minister had said that: 'It was not the purpose of the Monckton Commission to destroy federation but rather that we could see through it how best it could flourish and prosper.' So it followed, Macleod continued: 'that we are very glad to see how much agreement there is in the Report about the value of federation. It is in the light of that conviction, that this recommendation [on seccession] has been put forward.' And, he concluded:

> That is why we make it clear, as we have been asked to do by the Monckton Commissioners, that this and, indeed, any other recommendation of the Report can be fully discussed at the Review Conference when that time comes.[63]

Macleod's last comment on the issue went to the heart of the dispute between the Government and Welensky over the Federal Review. It was an outright rejection of the Federal Prime Minister's view that no discussion of secession should be allowed at the Review Conference. Macleod had fought to keep Macmillan committed to the principle that the recommendation about secession could be discussed. On 4 October he had intervened to object to Macmillan's suggestion to Welensky that the Monckton Report might be treated as 'only a contribution' – the Colonial Secretary counselled that there was, 'great danger in any statement which in African eyes might seem to devalue the Report or to suggest in advance of the Review Conference that we were preparing to sidetrack its recommendations or to pick and choose among them. Sir Roy is only one of the people we must bring to the Conference table'. Any appearance of ministers' hedging on secession would 'have the worst possible effect on the Africans'.[64]

Heading for confrontation

At Scarborough, only nine days before Macleod's 1960 party conference speech, Hugh Gaitskell, Leader of the Opposition, had defiantly told Labour Party delegates after his defeat on unilateral nuclear disarmament that he would 'fight and fight and fight again'. Macleod now warned Conservative representatives that they also faced trouble ahead:

> I cannot promise you, I am afraid, a popular Colonial policy. There will certainly be toil and sweat and tears, but I hope not blood and I hope not bitterness, although in the turmoil that is Africa today of even that one cannot be certain. But this is the road that we must walk, and we can walk no other. The Socialists can scheme their schemes and the Liberals can dream their dreams; but we at least have work to do.

His final, partisan flourish helped win Macleod his ovation. But as he had warned, many people would dislike what he was going to do. His toughest fights in the months ahead would be with the enemies of his policy in the Conservative Party, amongst whom Welensky was able to elicit deep support and sympathy for the Federation.[65]

The risk of bloody confrontation in the Federation was at the forefront of ministers' minds in London and Salisbury during the autumn of 1960. On 11 November, Lord Dalhousie, Governor-General of the Federation warned Sandys of Welensky's threat that if changes in Britain's colonial territories (Northern Rhodesia and Nyasaland) which would lead to break up of the Federation were forced through without prior consultation, 'then we are prepared to defy the British Government and fight if necessary'. According to Dalhousie, this was not the first time that he had heard the word 'fight' used, but he had previously ignored it. However, on this last occasion, 'it came out in a much more cool, calculated and definite form and was used in the context, "I am not going to see all that the white man has built up simply torn down".'[66]

Although Macleod was provoked by Dalhousie's 'very superficial' letter to write Sandys a scathing commentary on the Governor-General's errors and misunderstandings, he recognized that Europeans in the Federation were:

> Frightened, and it is very understandable that they should be so. A way of life that has seemed utterly safe, remote and secure is now brought suddenly into the frontiers of conflict and for the uncertainty that results they blame the British Government and our policies. But in fact our policies are the only ones that can save them . . .

At the heart of this difference in policy lay the problem of political advance for the African majority, of which Dalhousie showed 'no understanding whatever'. Macleod encapsulated the Government's dilemma with crystal clarity:

> On the one side to bring the African away from his very real hatred of federation and of Salisbury and Welensky, and on the other to bring the

European leaders to an understanding that they can no longer ignore the problems of African advance in their own countries.[67]

At Chequers on Sunday evening 13 November – Macleod's forty-seventh birthday – the Colonial Secretary had a private conversation with Macmillan about the forthcoming Federal Review Conference. The Prime Minister reckoned that 'the point was when the British protecting power should be withdrawn', and identified the two main problems facing the British Government as being: '(i) Sir Roy Welensky thinks that all this is a matter between himself and the Government; (ii) but there are Africans.' This latter factor, and the risk it brought of Britain's being drawn into an unwinnable colonial war, weighed heavily with Macmillan and Macleod, as Wyndham's note reveals: 'The Prime Minister and the Colonial Secretary then said that they did not want an Algeria. That was the crux of the matter.'[68]

The Federal Review Conference began, as scheduled, on Monday 5 December at Lancaster House. The Government had also announced their plan for concurrent conferences on Northern and Southern Rhodesia to be held during December. In the event, the Federal Review Conference succeeded only in demonstrating that the gulf between European and African leaders on the Federation's future was unbridgeable. Although Welensky had always claimed that he recognized the need for African political advance, Macmillan was astonished to discover that the Federal Prime Minister had never previously met Banda or Kaunda, the leaders of nationalist opinion in the Northern Territories. During the first week of the Federal Conference, Kaunda demanded dissolution of the Federation; Banda called for secession; and Joshua Nkomo, the Southern Rhodesian nationalist, advocated universal suffrage and a federation of the liberated states of southern Africa. Banda was one of four Africans who walked out when Whitehead addressed the Conference.[69]

Macmillan felt that prospects for the Federal Conference improved over the weekend of 10–11th at Chequers, where Macleod, Sandys, Banda, Kaunda, Nkomo, Welensky, Whitehead, Field and Harper (leader of the ultra-right Dominion Party in Southern Rhodesia) comprised a bizarre guest list – the unlikely duo of Banda and Sandys read the lessons at Sunday morning's church service. But hopes were dashed on Monday 12th when Kaunda, Sipalo, Banda, Chirwa and Chisiza, Nkomo and his compatriot, the Reverend Sithole, staged a dramatic walk out. Whitehead compounded the problem by summarily dismissing Nkomo from his delegation and automatically barring him from the Southern Rhodesian conference. Kaunda subsequently led his colleagues back to the talks, but on Saturday 17th the Government adjourned the conference. At least a complete breakdown had been averted, but it was not much of a face-saver. The conference was never to resume.[70]

Macleod's attitude to the Federal Conference bordered on the dismissive.

As he later acknowledged, he took 'very little notice' of it because he was focusing on the two territories for which he was ministerially responsible:

> It was an exercise that we had to go through but by this time one country [Nyasaland] had become, not independent, but had clearly been shown the door of independence, and I was beginning to move ahead with my plans for the second country, Northern Rhodesia . . . And so, although I listened gravely, and I daresay I said something from time to time, at the Federal Conference, it was nothing like so important to me as the Conference about Malawi [Nyasaland] that had taken place in 1960 and the one in 1961 [on Northern Rhodesia] to which I was looking forward.[71]

Macleod had been pressing a constitutional conference on Northern Rhodesia since the spring of 1960 and although formal talks began in London during December, the troubles that had marred the Federal 'Conference led to its being adjourned on 20 December (along with the conference on Southern Rhodesia) until the New Year. His plans for Northern Rhodesia were to bring him into head-on conflict with Welensky and the traditionalists in the Conservative Party. On 22 December, the Federal Prime Minister described Macleod in a letter to the Marquess of Salisbury, the former Conservative Cabinet Minister and leading traditionalist, as 'the most sinister influence in the British Cabinet today'. Whenever Welensky visited London, he mobilized opposition against Macleod by addressing Conservative backbench MPs at their Commonwealth Affairs Committee, where the Federation enjoyed strong support. Whether or not Macleod would be able to succeed in giving Africans a greater role in the government of Northern Rhodesia and setting the territory on the path to independence would depend ultimately on the extent of Macmillan's continued commitment to African advance when weighed against the depth of opposition among Europeans in Rhodesia and Conservatives at home.[72]

10

'The Brotherhood of Man'

> This is the last thing I shall say as Colonial Secretary . . . I believe quite
> simply in the brotherhood of man – men of all races, of all colours, of all
> creeds.
>
> Iain Macleod, Brighton, 11 October 1961.

The makings of an imperial row

'We have, I think, come through 1960 reasonably well,' Macleod reported to
his colleagues on the Cabinet's Colonial Policy Committee in the memorandum he wrote at the New Year, 1961. Despite the many contrary pressures,
the Government had managed to hold to a pace of change in Africa that he
characterized as being 'not as fast as the Congo and not as slow as Algiers' –
in other words, neither an overnight exodus on the one hand, nor, on the
other, a blind refusal to acknowledge the emergence of nationalism and the
growing demand for independence. 'All the emergencies that existed in the
colonial territories have been ended,' he noted, 'and now for the first time
for thirteen years there is no emergency in any of the dependent territories.'
It was an up-beat assessment of the progress that Macmillan's Government
had made to date, but at the same time Macleod left his colleagues under no
illusion about the gravity of the challenge that lay ahead.

As Macleod warned, the risk remained of a 'Congo' in Kenya and of an
'Algiers' in the Central African Federation. These territories presented a
special problem. 'Although African States have been brought successfully to
their independence,' Macleod explained, 'no one has yet succeeded in
bringing to independence a state which includes a larger settler population.'
If the Government could achieve this, they would have succeeded 'in doing
what the Prime Minister once defined as "turning an Empire into a family".'
But the months ahead were fraught with peril:

> We must also recognize that pressure from the United Nations, now that
> Belgium and France are dropping out as Colonial powers, will increasingly

concentrate on us. And there will be echoing voices from their different viewpoints from both the extreme right and the extreme left in this country. 1961, then, is sure to be a year of drama and decision in the colonial field.

Macleod was soon to find his prophecy coming all too true.[1]

Northern Rhodesia presented the most pressing problem. The constitutional conference on the territory's future had been adjourned during December when the Federal Review Conference had stalled, but Macleod planned to press ahead with a resumed conference during February. Macleod later summed up his objective for the Northern Rhodesian conference:

Ideally I wanted, rather following the parallel of Kenya, to get agreement between the Africans and as many Europeans as I could. If possible, of course, all the Europeans, because there weren't really such extreme right wing Europeans as I remember in Northern Rhodesia as there were either in Southern Rhodesia or in Kenya.

However, the difficulties that stood in the way of making any progress were immense. As Macleod reminded his colleagues, the previous autumn's review of the Federation headed by Viscount Monckton had 'unfortunately' recommended an African majority in the legislative council. It was 'going to be very difficult, if not impossible, to negotiate anything less than this with the Africans. On the other hand it would be almost equally impossible to push the Europeans so far.' Macleod's proposed solution, as he told his fellow Ministers, 'clearly is going to lie somewhere round parity' – an equal number of Europeans and Africans in the legislative council. Indeed, he revealed that he was: 'thinking in terms of a token African majority amongst the elected members while preserving an official and European majority through the official Ministers who would be members of the Council.' The attitude of Sir Roy Welensky, the Federal Prime Minister was crucial. Macleod expected to know by the end of January whether the Northern Rhodesian conference was going to succeed or fail:

And with it whether the Federation has a chance or not, because if Sir Roy is prepared to accept and recommend something like this so I believe we could push the Africans into a reluctant acquiescence. If he doesn't, and the Conference fails, it is hard to see how the Federation itself would survive.

The stakes were high, and the margin for error was very tight.[2]

Macleod's thinking was clear. As he later recalled, he began from the point of view that he should start with 'something like parity', that would 'swiftly resolve into an African majority'. This was to remain his single, overriding 'objective during his difficult final year as Colonial Secretary. By parity, Macleod meant that following new elections, 'the balance would be held by the Governor and by certain sort of cross-benchers, if you can call them that, who I designated as National Members. I was quite clear that the next step after that would be towards – if not, completely – to full African majority and independence.' However, Macleod realized that his basic strategy was bound to bring him into conflict with Welensky because, 'he knew very well that in my mind and in the logic of events parity would last for one parliament and be succeeded by an African leadership. And therefore he fought parity, not because he was against parity, but because he saw clearly enough the consequences'.[3]

Nonetheless, Macleod was determined to hold to his strategy. Whatever the frustrations he suffered as the months were taken up by seemingly endless negotiations on the minutiae of a new constitution, as long as Macleod felt that his basic strategy was still on course, he was prepared to tack and trim on the details. As he later explained:

> I recall once being asked what I was aiming at in the Northern Rhodesian settlement and I replied parity of abuse. And by that I meant that if both Welensky and Kaunda thought it a rotten settlement, and if Welensky thought I was in the pockets of the African nationalists, and if Kaunda thought I was selling him down the river to Welensky, this on the whole was the right posture to be in, and the only one that gave real hope for the future. And this leads to the curious paradox that the Northern Rhodesian settlement, of all the settlements that I have been responsible for, has been by far the most heavily criticized, and from many points of view justly, it is at the same time easily the one that I am most proud of. Because I knew from the very beginning what I was determined to achieve and I was quite undeterred by having to tack and sail and steer strange courses to get there, as long as in the end, both Welensky and Kaunda went to the polls – which they did – with some trouble, and something like a stalemate emerged which would be resolved in the end in the African favour and for months thoughout the intricate and tortuous negotiations that went on this particular guiding line was the only one that I clung to.[4]

However, progress towards majority rule in Northern Rhodesia posed a deadly threat to the old concept of the Federation that had traditionally held sway in the British Conservative Party and that still held good in Salisbury. This deep conflict of interest was now coming to a head. Macmillan would have to decide whether to back his Colonial Secretary, who was responsible to the British Cabinet for administering the Northern territories, or whether to accord Welensky a *de facto* veto over British policy in a British territory. The deep resonance that the Federation still had among many British Conservatives was to prove a powerful factor in this delicate equation.

Macleod had to contend with a further complication within the British Government. Since the Commonwealth Office handled relations with the Federal Government, the Commonwealth Secretary, Duncan Sandys – like Home before him – acted as the closest link between Welensky and the British Government. However, Macleod and Sandys did not agree on policy in Africa. As Macleod recalled, 'he always took a more right wing or slower attitude towards African advancement than I did but he always acknowledged that it was bound to come'. But as Macleod used to argue, in colonial policy, timing was everything. 'Duncan thought I was going on the whole too quickly in Northern Rhodesia', Macleod admitted, while 'I thought on the whole he was going too slowly in Southern Rhodesia'. Although Macleod later claimed that their conflict, 'was never personalized or bitter in any way at all', he acknowledged that: 'We were both, I am quite certain, conscious that the conflict was there and so, of course, was the Prime Minister, Harold Macmillan, who intervenened almost daily on the scene.' With his Colonial and Commonwealth Secretaries often at each other's throats, Macmillan had little choice. But there was an ominous incident for Macleod, that was witnessed by Reggie Bennett, his parliamentary private secretary. Macmillan and Macleod often used to stride together into the Commons division lobby for the evening's ten o'clock vote. The Prime Minister's arm might be round Macleod's shoulder, and they were clearly on best terms. But one evening in early 1961, Bennett happened to enter the lobby with Macleod and noticed Macmillan sitting on a bench opposite. The Prime Minister momentarily caught Macleod's gaze, but then instantly looked away. Bennett realised immediately that Macleod no longer had the Prime Minister's full confidence and had become expendable.[5]

At the start of 1961, Macleod was initially sanguine about the political resistance that had built up to his radical policies. The warning signals of trouble at home surfaced in the British press. In early January, the *Financial Times* accused the Colonial Secretary of advancing too fast, because there had been a marked economic decline in the territories most affected by his reforms. Responding in an interview in the paper on 10 January, Macleod rejected the charge, arguing that rapid advancement had averted the need for emergencies in which businesses would have foundered. Confidence depended on stability and rapid advancement would achieve that. The African leaders wanted to retain European expertise and the rights of the Europeans would therefore only be endangered by acts of folly by one race or the other – but there were many people of both races who were determined to prevent such acts of folly. He doubted that he would be the last Colonial Secretary, though his office might at some stage be merged with that of Commonwealth Relations. However, these reflections of Macleod's stirred up a hornet's nest. In London, the *Daily Express* condemned him as 'the most calamitous Colonial Secretary in History', warning him that his ambition to be Prime Minister was fading. In Salisbury, Welensky was barely able to restrain himself and was deeply worried at the prospect of the leader of the UFP in Northern Rhodesia, John Roberts, whom he did not much respect, negotiating with Macleod in London.[6]

On Monday 23 January 1961, Macmillan, Macleod and Sandys agreed a message that Sandys was to take to the Federal Prime Minister. Macleod told Sir Evelyn Hone, the Governor in Northern Rhodesia, that the note, while seeking to clarify the Government's objectives and approach at the Northern Rhodesian conference, 'leads Welensky back to the problem that the basic choice lies between practical parity or a token majority of African seats' in a new legislative council. At this stage, Macleod was bullish about his prospects both for tabling detailed proposals at the outset of the conference and for moving to a token African majority during the negotiations.[7]

But within forty-eight hours, Macmillan was pouring cold water on Macleod's hopes. Although the Prime Minister was instructing Sandys, who had now arrived in Salisbury, to remind Welensky that the room for manoeuvre in the Northern Rhodesian talks was very limited, and that the new constitution would have to be based on 'parity or something like it', Macmillan had persuaded Macleod not to table his plans for parity at the outset of the conference. However, this concession was of little help. Welensky threatened that the UFP would boycott the conference on the grounds that the proposals for parity were very different from the impression that he had been given by Macmillan. Welensky also claimed that he had not been fully consulted about Macleod's statements. Macmillan strenuously denied the charges, noting that this was 'chiefly significant as showing the mood into which Welensky has got himself', and hoped that Sandys would persuade him that it would be fatal if the Northern Rhodesian conference broke down and a 'great disaster' if the UFP did not come.[8]

Despite Macmillan's efforts, Welensky finally told him that the Northern Rhodesian UFP would boycott the conference. 'I think Welensky believed that Roberts's boycotting it,' Macleod later reflected, 'would mean an effective end of the conference.' However, the Colonial Secretary held a different view:

[Welensky had] rather overestimated the position of the European in Northern Rhodesia. There were other European parties that became of little consequence later, but Sir John Moffat and various other independents were there and were prepared to come, and although it would have been absurd to have a conference without Kaunda, it was sad but not absurd to have a conference without John Roberts and his supporters.

In a remarkably restrained comment, Macleod added: 'This naturally somewhat soured the relationship between Welensky and myself and led to six
or eight months' trouble and argument.' At the end of January, Welensky
wrote to Lord Salisbury and Lord Winterton – two stalwart champions of
the Rhodesia lobby in London – that it was crucial to thwart Macleod in
order to save the Federation, because Southern Rhodesia would secede the
moment that African nationalists gained power in Northern Rhodesia.
'Thus,' notes J.R.T. Wood, the historian of the Federation, 'Welensky said
he wanted Macleod attacked from every quarter.'[9]

The Northern Rhodesian Conference

It was in this highly charged atmosphere that the Northern Rhodesian
constitutional conference began in London at the end of January, 1961.
Macmillan was in a dilemma. As the Prime Minister wrote in his diary, the
Europeans in Northern Rhodesia did not really want African advancement,
but would accept something provided that it fell short of parity. The
Africans sought universal suffrage, but would accept parity or a small
majority. However, if he were to favour the European point of view, he
would destroy African confidence in the British Government and provoke
serious unrest in Northern Rhodesia and perhaps in the Federation as a
whole. The result would be that some of his Ministers – including Macleod
– would resign, dividing his Government and the Conservative Party. If he
supported the Africans, he would demolish the faith of the whites, provoke
Welensky to declare the independence of the Federation and probably bring
about a *coup d'état* in Lusaka. If the Northern Rhodesian Governor defended
himself, there would be a civil war, British ministers would resign and his
Government and his party would be divided. Macmillan could see no
immediate way out of this impasse.[10]

Macleod knew that he could not possibly launch the conference by making
the kind of declaration that he had made at the start of the Kenya conference
– to state that Northern Rhodesia was an African country that was going to
be run by the Africans. As he later explained:

I have no doubt at all that there would have been bloodshed, there would
have been something of a 'coup' by the Europeans in Northern Rhodesia
supported by the Europeans in Southern Rhodesia. And the bloodshed
that would have followed would have been appalling.

In addition, although the UFP had boycotted the conference, Macleod
realized that choosing to ignore them altogether 'would have blown the
powder magazine up'. Since Roberts had come to London and Welensky
had sent Julian Greenfield his Federal Cabinet Minister as an unofficial
emissary, Macleod decided that he should talk with them in order to 'damp

the powder and draw their fire'. Over dinner on 1 February, the Colonial
Secretary floated a possible scheme with Roberts and Greenfield, in which
the legislative council would be elected on two rolls, each electing fourteen
seats. The results were likely to produce an African majority, but parity
would be achieved since the four official members that he planned to appoint
to the new executive would also sit in the legislature. This scheme was
unacceptable to Welensky, but Macleod tried to keep the UFP engaged, even
though they were not participating at the conference.[11]

The Government were now involved in the most arduous and labyrinthine
discussions over the Northern Rhodesian constitution. Macleod later described the negotiations as 'incredibly devious and tortuous', and recalled
that the Cabinet Committee dealing with the problem – the Africa committee – 'sat appalling hours': 'I've never worked so hard in my life as we did
in those months, often to virtually no success at all. I've never seen so many
different formulae produced and examined and discarded.' Macleod later
defended the need to keep lines open to the UFP and the Federal Government and rather glossed over the problems that it caused him at the time.
But as the official papers for the period reveal at one critical moment in
February 1961, Macleod again threatened to resign.[12]

Although progress had been made in the concurrent talks on the Southern
Rhodesian constitution – the nationalists were later to oppose the reforms –
the Northern Rhodesian crisis deepened at the end of the first week of
February. By Thursday 9th, the conference was in almost complete deadlock. Kaunda was becoming increasingly impatient and claiming that the
UFP were 'haunting the talks, and as long as this remains so there is a grave
danger of an explosion at home'. However, there was also growing pressure
on Macleod from his own party. At that evening's Conservative backbench
Commonwealth Affairs Committee, he had faced criticism from almost all
the 50 MPs who attended, and was repeatedly pressed by his critics,
including Frederic Bennett and Lord Lambton, to reaffirm his support for
the 1958 constitution – in effect, a demand to slow the pace of change in
Northern Rhodesia. Despite press leaks that he had endorsed it, the nearest
that he came to doing so – according to the official minute – came in his
reported comment that: 'The general principles laid down in the White
Paper of 1958 were good but their practical application left a great deal to
be desired.' Later that evening, Roberts met Macleod, and claimed afterwards that the Colonial Secretary had been in an abject state of nerves. This
impression, however, is not confirmed by any other source. After the
backbenchers' meeting with Macleod, Conservative MPs showed their disquiet by signing an early day motion, tabled by the former Minister, Robert
Turton, which evoked the 1958 constitution. This had now become code for
opposing Macleod's speed of change. Eventually more than ninety signatures were added to Turton's motion. Macleod was later to be somewhat
dismissive of this backbench pressure, but as *The Times*'s political corres-

pondent noted at the time: 'Nothing that has happened on the Conservative backbenches in the past three or four years compares in interest – and perhaps – significance with the shot that Mr Robert Turton and (so far) 67 others sent whistling across Mr Macleod's bows.' The identity of the signatories suggested that alarm had spread beyond Macleod's usual right-wing critics. The following day, Friday 10 February, the *Daily Mail* published an interview with Welensky, in which he had set out to cause as much mischief as possible for Macleod.[13]

Ministers were also under intense pressure from the nationalists. Kaunda announced that he and his UNIP delegates would stay away from the constitutional talks until Macleod tabled his proposals, warning of the danger of an uprising which 'by contrast would make Mau Mau a child's picnic'. Delegates from the conference called on Macmillan and Macleod and insisted that there should be a majority of Africans over other elected members in the new legislative council. The following day, Macmillan cabled two sets of proposals to Welensky. In very broad terms, the first proposal envisaged that the legislative council should contain 45 elected members, six official and two nominated members – the upper electoral roll would elect 15 members; the lower 15; and both rolls would together elect 15. The alternative scheme proposed a legislature of 46 elected members, six official and two nominated members – the upper roll would elect 16; the lower roll 18; and 12 national members would be elected by both rolls. Welensky rejected both proposals.[14]

The next week, the pressures on the Government intensified. Welensky made a show of force by calling out Northern Rhodesian territorial battalions, while in London ministers urgently reviewed their military preparations – including the use of RAF aircraft based at Nairobi – in the event of trouble in the territory. In London, *The Times* rallied to Macleod's defence in a forceful editorial entitled, 'No Going Back', provoking a predictable, but fierce, reaction from Lord Salisbury. The constitutional talks were on the point of collapse as delegates demanded to know the British Government's proposals. On Tuesday 14th, Macleod made a statement to the conference outlining the broad principles of the Government's thinking, but he had done little more than keep the conference going. The next morning, the dissatisfaction felt by delegates at the continued lack of any detailed proposals led to a 'tense and angry' session, during which they virtually 'exploded' as they demanded something more specific. That afternoon, Macleod sketched an outline proposal for electing 45 members on the 15:15:15 scheme. But whereas Sandys had reassured Welensky that the method of electing the fifteen national members had not yet been finalized, Macleod indicated that the upper and lower electoral rolls would have equal influence. While Welensky was outraged at this idea, the African delegates were infuriated that the details for the upper roll qualifications remained vague and were to be left to further consultation in Northern

Rhodesia – this would allow the UFP a role, despite their having boycotted the constitutional talks.[15]

Disturbed by Welensky's reaction to the proposals made by Macleod, Macmillan now wanted to make a further concession to the Federal Prime Minister. This was almost the last straw for Macleod. The point at issue was the nature of the White Paper due to be published on the Northern Rhodesian constitutional conference. Macleod planned to follow normal practice and issue a summary of the discussions and the documents presented to the conference. However, Welensky's opposition to the details of the proposed method of electing the legislative council and in particular the national members, led Macmillan to suggest that the White Paper should not contain too many details. Macleod strongly disagreed.

Shortly before lunchtime on Friday 17 February, Macleod called on Macmillan at Admiralty House and told the Prime Minister that having seen his minute on the matter, he felt that 'he had no option but to resign immediately'. Macmillan asked Macleod to think it over – he should certainly try to bring the conference to an end while he was still Colonial Secretary. The Prime Minister then asked Macleod why he felt this way. According to the official note, 'Mr Macleod said he was impressed with the sense that we were continually giving in to Sir Roy Welensky and that he was not being allowed freedom in his own sphere of responsibility'. Macleod refused to give way. He could not now amend the documents that had been circulated at the conference, and everybody attending the conference had the minutes. It was not possible therefore for him to turn the White Paper into a mixture of historical survey plus proposals. Having made his point, the two men agreed to discuss the matter further and Macleod left to chair the afternoon session of the conference.[16]

Over the weekend, the Northern Rhodesian crisis dominated the press, with stories that the Strategic Reserve of the British Army had been alerted and reports of a series of meetings at Admiralty House and further last-minute haggling with Welensky. The Monday papers reported the further comings and goings at Admiralty House, included Kaunda's comments following the African delegates' disappointing talks with the Prime Minister. 'I think that Mr Macleod as a person – at least to those of us who were at this conference,' Kaunda observed:

> still remains the only hope in the British Government. The British Government have betrayed us, and it is clear from what we have been seeing that Macleod has been pushed against the wall by the British Government's attitude and giving in to pressure from Salisbury . . . Mr Macleod left to himself could have done the right thing, but he suffers because of his collective responsibility to the Cabinet.

By contrast, Kaunda was critical of Sandys, linking him with 'the Salisbury business'.[17]

The question of whether or not the Government should publish their proposals on the Northern Rhodesian constitution was considered at a specially convened Cabinet on Monday 20 February. As Macmillan explained, the African delegates at the conference had been unwilling to accept the proposals, while Welensky, and also Whitehead, the Southern Rhodesian Prime Minister, were critical. Should the Government nonetheless go ahead and publish, or should they defer, hoping that it might be possible to reach agreement between the Africans and the Europeans by discussion and negotiation? If the Government went ahead, Whitehead might take Southern Rhodesia out of the Federation. Welensky might also declare the Federation independent of Britain and it 'would not be possible for the United Kingdom Government to restore the situation by military means'. However, if they deferred, the Africans might cause disorder in Northern Rhodesia, and possibly other parts of the Federation. On balance, Macmillan now thought they should publish. Macleod agreed, arguing that although the present plan would not be accepted by either side and would evoke strong criticism, there were grounds for hoping that it would not provoke violence. Postponement of any announcement 'would be regarded by the Africans as a betrayal of their interests, would not give any great satisfaction to the Europeans, and would greatly increase the Government's difficulties at home'. The Cabinet agreed that the proposals should be published without any delay.

The terms of Macleod's statement to the House of Commons were then considered by the Cabinet. Ministers were informed that Welensky had made a number of requests about the substance of any statement, including that it should omit any definition of the way in which the national members were to be elected. Macleod was able to meet most of Welensky's points, but argued that it would not be possible to omit his proposed method of electing national members from both the upper and lower rolls. The most that could be conceded was some change of wording – for example, that this was the method that was contemplated. Macleod was also prepared to say that many matters of detail still remained to be settled. The following afternoon, Tuesday 21 February, Macleod made his statement to MPs. 'Before he rose,' reported *The Times*:

> Mr Macleod could be seen listening to what tactical advice came from Mr Macmillan. But when it came to the point, if there were two views about the matter, there could be only one about Mr Macleod's manner. He was concise, lucid and decisive. Nevertheless, we have seen him more relaxed. He had the look and sound of a man in a corner but a man willing to fight for what he believes in.

Although there was 'uncertainty and coolness' on the Conservative benches, the right-wingers who intervened 'produced no murmur from the uneasy ranks around them'. Later that evening, Macleod addressed a meeting of 180 Tory MPs at their backbench Commonwealth Affairs Committee, where 'he had the satisfaction of seeing the first cracks in backbench opposition to the trend of Government proposals'. On the other hand, Macleod was made to realize that there remained a hard core of forty or more backbenchers who were deeply disturbed and who were implacably opposed to his policy. As he was soon to discover, this die-hard rump were capable of delivering a wounding blow.[18]

'Too clever by half'

Welensky reacted furiously to the proposed new Northern Rhodesian constitution, publicly rejecting the proposals, calling up more territorials and recalling the Federal Parliament – like a bull in a china shop, as Whitehead, the Southern Rhodesian Prime Minister, confided to Macmillan. Welensky even considered unilaterally declaring the Federation independent – in effect, launching a *coup d'état* against British rule and almost certainly plunging Central Africa into civil war. In Lusaka, Roberts and other members of the UFP quit the Executive Council in protest at the constitutional proposals – Roberts's place in the territory's Government was taken by Sir John Moffat, a liberal, who had attended the constitutional conference in London. So strong was the talk of a possible *coup* that in the early hours of Thursday 23 February, Sir Evelyn Hone, the Northern Rhodesian Governor, cabled to Macleod, urging the Government to send Welensky a clear warning about unconstitutional action, and – although not asking for any movement of British troops 'at this stage' – suggesting that it might mean reconsidering their decision not to send British troops to Northern Rhodesia against the wishes of the Federal Government.[19]

Macleod advised Macmillan on Thursday 23rd that he thought a coup by Welensky was unlikely, but after a further lengthy session that afternoon at the Conservative backbench Commonwealth Affairs Committee – his second appearance there that week – Macleod attended a meeting in the Prime Minister's room at the House to consider further how to react in the event of a *coup*. By the following Sunday, the 26th, Macmillan was still fretting at what might happen in Northern Rhodesia, and urged Macleod that 'plans must continue to be prepared for this'. The Federal defence chiefs had already become aware of a build-up of British military and air strength in East Africa – not necessarily a threatening move in the light of possible unrest in the Federation and a possible request for assistance from the Federal Government. It was later suggested that at some point during this crisis, Macleod ordered the implementation of the contingency plans designed to prevent a *coup*, and that when the Minister for Air, Julian Amery, learned of this, he saw Macmillan and demanded that the action be stopped. The Prime Minister reportedly complied. However, the evidence suggests that Macmillan was more edgy than his Colonial Secretary about the risk of a *coup*.[20]

On Tuesday 28th, came confirmation in a telegram from the acting British High Commissioner in Salisbury that, despite Welensky's dramatic gestures, the Federal Government were not planning a *coup*. However, his message made clear that: 'the Federal Government (as indeed the Southern Rhodesian Government and most Europeans in the Federation) have the deepest mistrust of the United Kingdom Government and in particular the Secretary of State for the Colonies and believe they will not hesitate to send British troops into Northern Rhodesia to impose a political solution if necessary.' The immediate crisis appeared to be subsiding. Major Patrick Wall, the Conservative MP who was a Welensky sympathizer and had chaired all three of Macleod's meetings at the backbench Commonwealth Affairs Committee, warned the Federal Prime Minister that Conservative MPs were now rallying behind Macleod. Nonetheless, the Rhodesia lobby still had a shot left in their locker.[21]

On Tuesday 7 March, the House of Lords held a debate on Central Africa on a motion that had been tabled a month earlier by the former Labour Colonial Secretary, the Earl of Listowel. The Earl of Perth, Macleod's Minister of State, put the Government's case, and shortly before four o'clock, the Marquess of Salisbury rose to speak. Salisbury was renowned both for his stalwart defence of the Federation and for his passionate commitment to the British Empire – he had resigned from the Cabinet in the spring of 1957 over the release of Archbishop Makarios – but he delivered a speech that was impassioned even by his standards. He caused an immediate sensation and created a sense of drama that has rarely been equalled in the upper House by launching a personal tirade against Macleod.

Referring to earlier speakers who had expressed the 'African view', Salisbury announced his intention to represent the views of 'other sections of the population' in the Federation. Referring to 'the miasma of mistrust' that he claimed had recently developed, he argued that within a few months the 'complete loyalty' of the white Rhodesians had been replaced by feelings 'of suspicion, of contempt, almost of hatred of the home Government'. Answering his own question of how this 'terrible thing' had come about and who was responsible, Salisbury pointed the finger straight at Macleod and delivered one of the most vitriolic attacks ever made against a British minister by a senior figure in his own party. It was not simply that Macleod had pursued the wrong policies: Salisbury's charge went much deeper than that. He attacked Macleod personally, going far beyond the normal bounds of political debate. Arguing that 'the main responsibility must rest on the present Colonial Secretary', he accused Macleod of having, 'adopted, especially in his relationship to the white communities of Africa, a most unhappy and an entirely wrong approach. He has been too clever by half'.[22]

Salisbury was intent on nothing less than character assassination. He elaborated on his damning charge by alluding to Macleod's card playing – while claiming that his remarks were not meant to be offensive to the Colonial Secretary. Recalling Macleod's earlier expertise at bridge, Salisbury commented:

It is not considered immoral, or even bad form, to outwit one's opponents at bridge. On the contrary, the more you outwit them, within the rules of the game, the better player you are. It almost seems to me that the Colonial Secretary, when he abandoned the sphere of bridge for the sphere of politics, brought his bridge technique with him. At any rate, it has become, as your Lordships know, the convinced view of the white people in Eastern and Central Africa that it has been his object to outwit them, and that he has done it successfully.

In response to an intervention from Lord Listowel, Salisbury further accused Macleod of having ignored his duty towards the European community in Africa. Later, he rejected Baroness Summerskill's call on him to withdraw his comments, denying that he had accused Macleod of being disingenuous, but added that he thought he was 'unscrupulous'.[23]

Salisbury's vicious attack ignited a blaze of publicity. His charge that Macleod had been 'too clever by half' struck home, because most people felt, deep down, that there was an element of truth in it. Even Macleod's friends, who thought it unfair, could see what Salisbury, in his malicious way, was driving at. For Macleod was an extremely adroit negotiator, who kept his cards very close to his chest, calculated the odds for the various options in any situation, drove hard bargains and was ruthless in achieving his aims. Liberal he may have been, but Macleod was never 'wet'. That was why he was detested by right wingers. But Salisbury's charge was unfair, since however deeply Macleod disagreed with the leaders of the European settlers in Africa, he genuinely believed that his policies were in their best interests. Unlike the reactionary Lord Salisbury, Macleod saw that striking an ostrich-like attitude towards emergent African nationalism could only bring bloodshed and destruction on the settlers – the people whom he was accused of trying to outwit.

Macleod found Salisbury's attack deeply hurtful. Close friends had never seen him so upset. He greatly appreciated the personal statement made by Lord Perth the morning after Salisbury's onslaught, before the Lords resumed their debate – by convention, Perth was barred from speaking again in the debate, but made it clear to the House that he 'had known about, and been in complete agreement with, every step taken' by Macleod in the African constitutional conferences. After Perth's shining display of loyalty and straightforwardness, it would have been better for Macleod and the Government if the debate had been allowed quietly to fizzle out, but

Viscount Hailsham, leader of the Government in the Lords, stirred up the controversy afresh by launching a robust counter-attack against Salisbury. It was good, political knockabout, but the effect was to give even further publicity to Salisbury's initial accusations.[24]

Salisbury's gibe, 'too clever by half', stuck and was to do Macleod's reputation lasting damage. Macleod made only a mild riposte in a television interview shortly after the Lords debate, when he pointed out that the difference between him and Lord Salisbury was a question of the pace of change and that the anxieties of people living in Africa were very close to him, 'just as they are to Lord Salisbury'. However, when Hugh Fraser, Macleod's Junior Minister, loyally counter-attacked in defence of his Secretary of State, he was cut by members of the Cecil family. Yet Macleod was not interested in perpetuating a personal feud. Lord Perth was an old friend of Salisbury's and by chance the Marquess was due to dine with him a couple of weeks after the row. Perth asked Macleod if he wanted him to find some excuse for calling off their dinner, but Macleod was anxious that Perth should see Salisbury and seemed keen to try and restore some contact with him.[25]

Damaging though Salisbury's assault had been, Macleod faced a much more immediate and serious threat to his proposals for the Northern Rhodesian constitution – Welensky was in town. The Federal Prime Minister had arrived in London a few days before Salisbury's outburst for the March 1961 Commonwealth Prime Ministers' conference and began lobbying Macmillan, other Ministers and Conservative MPs with the intention of securing changes to February's White Paper. Macleod accepted that Welensky should be kept in the picture, but he wrote to Macmillan on 10 March emphasizing the need for further movement towards the African position. 'We cannot afford to have it said,' he warned, 'that we are delaying further in Northern Rhodesia in order to make a deal with Welensky in London.' However, Macleod's fears were soon to be realized.[26]

In mid-March, Welensky presented to Macmillan three schemes for revising the proposals on elections to the Northern Rhodesian legislature. The Prime Minister passed the schemes to Macleod, who examined them and replied that both Schemes 1 and 3 were so clearly biased in favour of the Europeans that neither 'could possibly be presented as coming within the framework of the White Paper'. Scheme 2 was the only one that seemed to open any door for negotiation, but this led straight to Welensky's *sine qua non* that the upper (predominantly European) roll 'should have the controlling influence', since the net result would be to turn ostensible parity into European control of 24 out of the 40 elected seats. 'It is more and more clear,' noted Macleod, 'that to the UFP a "multi-racial approach" means working with Africans they choose: to us it is cooperating with those whom Africans choose and bringing them to recognize the rights of others.' Despite

Macleod's discouraging response, Macmillan replied that the Government must try to accommodate Welensky.[27]

That evening – Thursday 16 March – Welensky gave an extraordinary demonstration of his influence over the Conservative Party, when he addressed about 200 backbenchers at their Commonwealth Affairs Committee. The Prime Minister's Parliamentary Private Secretary, Knox Cunningham, reported to Macmillan that Welensky's reception was warmer and more enthusiastic than his last meeting and that he went all out to get support from the Conservative Party for his policy. 'I think he succeeded in doing so at this meeting,' Knox Cunningham concluded. Similarly Major Patrick Wall told Macmillan that Welensky carried two-thirds to three-quarters of the meeting, adding the surprising claim that the Federal Prime Minister 'will go as far as he possibly can to obtain an agreement and that he will do everything possible to cooperate with the Secretary of State for the Colonies'. This last suggestion surprised the Chief Whip, Martin Redmayne, who nonetheless told Macmillan that Wall was sure that he had not overstated Welensky's message.[28]

However, Welensky's performance had clearly angered Macleod, because of the 'charges, open and veiled, of breaches of faith' that the Federal Prime Minister made. Macleod lunched the next day with the Chief Whip to discuss whether they should make any reply – they concluded that they probably should not. Unknown to Macleod, Redmayne immediately reported their conversation to Macmillan, who had evidently been troubled at Macleod's reaction to Welensky's performance. 'Regarding my meeting with Iain,' Redmayne noted: 'I was at pains to make it clear that I was not your emissary.' And he added: 'You will not want to let him suspect that I reported our conversation to you so promptly.' By Monday, Macleod had thought further about Welensky's accusations and prepared an extremely blunt, point-by-point rebuttal of the five main charges, and suggested circulating it to all Conservative MPs. However, this was too strong meat for the Chief Whip and Number 10 – Tim Bligh, one of Macmillan's private secretaries, suggested some major cuts. In the event, the note was not circulated, although Macmillan used it as a briefing note when he met the executive of the backbench 1922 Committee.[29]

In view of his qualms about African opinion and his anger at Welensky's allegations, Macleod displayed extraordinary forbearance when he replied to Macmillan on Friday 17th about the scope for taking up Welensky's 'Scheme 2'. However, Macleod was nothing if not a realist, and always recognized that he had to try to deal with Welensky. As he explained:

The crux of the matter is that Welensky says that to him upper roll control is a *sine qua non* of any scheme. In other words UFP supremacy must be enshrined in the constitution. No conceivable juggling with words can bring this within the ambit of the White Paper nor the agreed decisions of HMG.

However, Macleod thought there were 'just two possible ways out'. First, with Welensky's agreement:

We should play it long, if possible until Southern Rhodesia is for a time out of the way, and that then we should agree on something very like our own solution. His part of the bargain would be to accept more or less what we had proposed, although we might dress it up a little bit. Our part would be to accept the enormous risks in delay, which would certainly mean increased African pressure and distrust by the Africans, the Chiefs, the liberal parties, not to mention the Opposition in this country, of our intentions.

The second possibility was 'to see if Scheme 2 can somehow, if he really wants a compromise, be made one which we would accept'. Macleod proposed various intricate amendments to the electoral system and some reservation of seats for different racial groups within the national seats. He suggested speaking to Welensky on these lines, making it plain that the Government could not go any further than this – 'And I must add my own personal reservation as to whether I can go as far'. Macleod encapsulated his position in a nutshell:

Our object all along in introducing our proposals for Northern Rhodesia has been to preserve the Federation by showing Northern Africans that it is not a barrier to advance. If we grant to Welensky's prompting upper roll control of the elections, we shall not persuade the Africans and we shall not preserve the Federation except by force – which is unthinkable.

Events came to take on the pattern of a mixture of Macleod's two possible options as the talks between the British and the Federal Government dragged on over the next few months.[30]

On 20 March agreement was reached with Welensky that the British Government would consider proposals on the Northern Rhodesian constitution that were within the spirit and framework of the February White Paper. Two days later, Macleod wrote to Hone in Lusaka instructing him how to handle Welensky – a letter that Macmillan, Trend, the Cabinet Secretary, and Sandys all thought was good:

We have insisted with Roy that the essential thing is that there should be a substantial block of members depending for electoral support upon both races, but we have said that we should be ready to consider any method alternative to the arrangements for the national seats proposed in the White Paper which would have a similar result.

At the end of March, a relieved Macmillan wrote to Trend: 'We have not surmounted the crisis, although we have postponed it.' However, signs of further trouble ahead between Macleod and Sandys could be detected in Trend's note to Macmillan a week later, when he supported the advice of the Prime Minister's Press Secretary, Harold Evans, who had urged:

> Very strongly that *any* important question touching the relationship between ourselves and the Federation should be handled at Prime Minister level, on the ground that nothing else will dissipate the suspicion that the Commonwealth Relations Office and the Colonial Office are running on parallel lines which do not meet at any point.[31]

During the spring, Hone held discussions with the parties in Northern Rhodesia on the basis of the February White Paper. On May 10, Macleod was able to report to Macmillan that Hone, 'has gone much closer to reaching agreement, even with the African parties, than we thought possible.' Indeed, Macleod was anxious that the Government should ensure that more people were aware that even the UFP, which had lost a good deal of ground in the territory, 'would be ready to play if it were not for the intervention of the Federal Prime Minister'. By late May, Hone was telling Macleod that he did not want to appease Welensky any further and that the point might come when he might have to resign.[32]

At the end of May, Sandys visited Salisbury, ostensibly for talks about Southern Rhodesia, but in reality to negotiate with Welensky over Northern Rhodesia. Before he left, Macleod wrote him a detailed eight-page brief, outlining the areas where he thought there was still some room for manoeuvre. The most difficult problem remained the national seats and all manner of devices were now being considered to ensure that these achieved the genuine parity that Macleod envisaged in the legislative council. However, as Macleod had feared, during his talks with Welensky, Sandys agreed that consideration should be given to proposals that would establish a 60:40 ratio of dominance by the upper roll in the election of national members.[33]

Sandys's agreement to allow consideration of a proposal that would give Welensky dominance of the elected national members alarmed Macleod. On Sunday 4 June, he wrote to Macmillan, expressing his unhappiness 'about the emphasis now being put on the scheme that can't possibly be said to be within the spirit and framework of the White Paper and which in particular conceded to Roy the very point we have over and over again denied him'. Macmillan replied sympathetically, saying he quite understood how Macleod felt, and adding that: 'I am still determined to try to find some solution that all of us feel is workable.' However, Macleod was enraged when Sandys had further communication with the Federal Government without consulting him and was insistent that the 60:40 scheme should not be allowed to stand. By 11 June, Macmillan was commenting that Macleod was determined to defeat Welensky; and Welensky was determined to defeat Macleod.[34]

It was not until mid-June that Hone finally reported the rejection of the 60:40 scheme by the other parties in Northern Rhodesia. At Cabinet on Monday 19 June, Ministers were faced with the familiar scenario of a demand from Welensky, backed up by a threat. Welensky was insisting on the 60:40 ratio in order to guarantee upper roll control of the national seats. 'If his demand were not met,' the Cabinet minutes noted, 'Sir Roy Welensky proposed to visit the UK later in the week with the intention of putting his case, not only to the Government, but apparently to parliament and public opinion in this country – and he would then return to the Federation and propose immediate dissolution of the legislature on 26 June.' Welensky might then demand independence. 'A most serious situation would then arise, which might lead to violence and perhaps to civil war.'[35]

However, Macleod won the battle. The next day, Cabinet agreed that Welensky could not have his 60:40 scheme, but he would be allowed some modifications to the February White Paper. In order to try and meet Welensky's concerns, Macleod was prepared to accept the introduction of a race element into the national roll, by requiring that the fifteen national candidates had to secure a minimum percentage of the vote from both European and African voters before they could be elected. This figure was set at 12.5 per cent and the equivalent of 400 votes, whichever was the lower – a requirement that would create the greatest problem for the African nationalists. The draft text of Macleod's statement to the Commons was sent to Welensky, who managed to secure some further tightening of the final details. In addition to the minimum percentages, national roll candidates would also be expected to secure at least 20 per cent of the votes cast on either the upper or lower roll. The fifteen national roll members would also include an Asian elected by Asian and Coloured voters using Northern Rhodesia as a single constituency.[36]

The last few days involved further fraught meetings between Ministers as the final details were settled. Macleod finally made his statement, outlining the new details to MPs on Monday 26 June. He had agreed to modifications designed to help bring the UFP into the elections, but had not undermined the strategy that he had pursued since February. As he later recalled:

The point I was not prepared to yield on was the basic principle of the merging of something like an equivalent balance between the races, and, therefore, the Governor and his nominated officials holding the balance for one more parliament while we moved on. This seemed to me in

February, as it seemed to me in July, to be a key matter. I was, perhaps, wrongly, almost entirely disinterested in what you might call the details. I didn't really care whether this seat was drawn in such a way – these were the sort of things Greenfield felt passionately about, but they didn't worry me at all and I did give way on some of these. If that is yielding to pressure, well then I certainly did. But they didn't affect the main conscious determination to achieve a greater parliamentary parity.

The weeks of argument and debate over the Northern Rhodesian constitution had been a terrible strain for Macmillan, Macleod and Sandys. In Macleod's words: 'there were wheels and wheels and wheels, and the thing was incredibly complicated, far worse than anything I can remember before or since.' According to Macmillan, 'Macleod, with many faults' – he noted that his threatening to resign had become a daily occurrence – 'has been persistent, imaginative, and ingenious. Sandys has been most loyal to me and absolutely tireless.'[37]

Macleod later had fun in the Commons with the mixed reactions to his new proposals. *The Times* headline read: 'Mr Macleod sticks to 50:50 principle. Constitutional proposals for Northern Rhodesia. African majority possible.' Macleod commented that this was accurate, but so too was the *Daily Telegraph*, that declared: 'N. Rhodesia rule left open. European or African majority possible. "Can't work" says Sir Roy Welensky.' The *Guardian* proclaimed, 'Chance of African majority less.' But Macleod noted that it 'would be fair to add that the chance of a European majority was less, too'. And as to 'those who put it in more personal terms', Macleod reflected that: 'The *Daily Express* said, "Welensky Wins", the *Daily Mail* said, "Macleod Wins", and the *Daily Herald* said, "Macleod Wins On Points".'[38]

Macleod was conscious of the keen disappointment that would be felt by Kaunda and his UNIP supporters. They had initially attacked the February proposals, but after a great deal of effort by Hone – helped by Welensky's fierce denunciations of the February White Paper – had been persuaded to accept them as a step forward. Now they were now being asked to accept less than they had been promised in February and would face a tougher battle in the proposed elections. As Macleod later recalled:

When we finally reached harbour – if you can call it that – and we finally tied up the last knots, I asked Kenneth Kaunda to come and see me in my flat at Sloane Court and I told him the details that I was going to give to the House of Commons, I think probably that afternoon. And I said to him in effect – I know this doesn't give you what the Africans got in Tanganyika and Malawi, and indeed, in Kenya. But it does point the way quite clearly for the future. Now you're going to have a very hard job selling this to your party but provided that you are convinced that it is going to be all right in the end, that is to say that you will have a period of – call it what you will – probation . . . And in the end I convinced Kaunda, who realized the doubts he would have, but saw the future clearly enough, and in effect, he went off to see if he could carry this with his party, thinking that he could.[39]

Nonetheless, Macleod realized that the African reaction was very finely balanced from two conflicting responses that he received from African heads of state, via Conservative MPs who happened to be on foreign trips at the time. In Nigeria, Sir Abubakar Tafawa Balewa 'saw quite clearly what the purpose was and thought that Kaunda should accept it and fight the election'. However, Nyerere in Tanganyika was hostile. In the event, Nyerere's reaction was to prove the better guide to the mood among many of Kaunda's supporters in Northern Rhodesia.[40]

End of Empire

'The heart of the Colonial problems,' Macleod had written to Macmillan on 31 May 1960, 'remains in the multi-racial communities in East and Central Africa. If we can solve these problems – and it is a big "if " – everything will fall into place.' Accordingly, Britain's territories in East and Central Africa dominated his time during his two-year tenure of the Colonial Office. He looked forward to their early membership of the Commonwealth, to which he was passionately committed, regarding it as an influence for liberal, multi-racial values and a counter to the ideological spectres of communism – Soviet or Chinese – and racialism that stalked Africa. He was therefore bitterly disappointed when South Africa, then in thrall to the ideology of apartheid, departed the Commonwealth following the Prime Ministers' Conference in London in March 1961, during his travails over Northern Rhodesia.[41]

Shortly before the Prime Ministers' London Conference, Julius Nyerere, who had become the first African Chief Minister in a British colony, wrote to all Commonwealth Prime Ministers urging them to use their influence to secure South Africa's removal from the Commonwealth. On the eve of the conference, he also stated publicly that Tanganyika would not apply to join the Commonwealth if South Africa remained a member – as Sir Richard Turnbull, the Governor of Tanganyika, cabled to Macleod, Nyerere had explained to him that he could not compromise 'with the principles he holds regarding essential brotherhood of all men and so on'. This phrase about the 'brotherhood of all men' was to become the basis of Macleod's greatest speech on colonial policy – and arguably on any subject – but neither he nor most Commonwealth Premiers shared Nyerere's view on South Africa. During the Conference, it became evident that almost all the Prime Ministers wanted South Africa to remain a member. This 'even went for Nehru and Nkrumah', although Macleod reckoned that Canada's Prime Minister,

Diefenbaker, had been the most hostile. Macleod later maintained that if the South African Premier, Verwoerd, 'had been able to make a couple of imaginative moves, I have no doubt that South Africa would have stayed within the Commonwealth'. However, when Verwoerd was asked point-blank whether he would accept High Commissions from his African fellow Commonwealth countries having High Commissioners and residencies in South Africa, he flatly refused. At that moment, Macleod reflected, 'I think we realized that there was no further hope.' If South Africa had been prepared to recognize and treat with their fellow African members of the Commonwealth, not only at Windsor or Marlborough House, but in their own country, Macleod believed that: 'in spite of African opinion, the feeling that South Africa could remain [in the Commonwealth] would have prevailed. And in my opinion it would have been a great help to the African in South Africa.'[42]

Macleod regarded his single, biggest disappointment as Colonial Secretary as being the failure of the West Indies to gain independence as a federation. As in Africa, he quickly seized the initiative in the West Indies, ending the prevarication in Whitehall and speeding their independence. The idea of a West Indian Federation had long been seen by the Colonial Office as a means of enabling the smaller islands eventually to achieve independent status, which – it was felt – they could hardly do on their own, given their small size and lack of resources. A Federation had been formed in 1958, consisting of the ten colonies of Antigua, Montserrat, St Kitts, Trinidad and Tobago, Jamaica, Grenada, Dominica, St Lucia, St Vincent and Barbados. Sir Grantley Adams, the former Barbadian Premier, had been appointed Federal Prime Minister and Lord Hailes – formerly Patrick Buchan-Hepburn, who had previously been the Government Chief Whip – was Governor-General.[43]

In the months before Macleod became Colonial Secretary, Home, the Commonwealth Secretary, became concerned at the embarrassment that might be caused if the forthcoming West Indies constitutional conference resulted in early independence at a time when the Government were about to face the difficult review conference on the Federation of Rhodesia and Nyasaland, at which the African leaders were likely to demand majority rule. Moreover, Julian Amery, the Junior Minister at the Colonial Office who was responsible for the West Indies, questioned whether every other member of the Commonwealth would be willing to accept the West Indies as a member – this was thought to apply to South Africa, against whom Jamaica had recently imposed a trade embargo. The Government therefore sought to do all in their power, through private persuasion, to discourage any early date being set for independence at the West Indies conference during the autumn of 1959. In the event, nothing was settled.[44]

However, when the Jamaican Premier, Norman Manley, indicated that he wanted to visit London in early 1960 to discuss federal issues, Macleod agreed to meet him. Manley was frank in their talks about the growing popular support in Jamaica against the Federation and spoke openly about the risk of secession. The division of authority between the Federal Government in Trinidad and the territorial Governments had given rise to friction and mutual resentment. These problems were exacerbated by the lack of common identity between the Caribbean islands – Kingston in the west was separated by 1,000 miles of sea from Port of Spain in the east. And despite their declarations of support for the Federation, neither of the two most influential leaders – Manley in Jamaica and Eric Williams, Premier of Trinidad – had chosen to enter the Federal Government, preferring instead to remain as leaders of their own relatively large and powerful islands.[45]

Amery had intended to visit the West Indies during the summer of 1960, but was prevented from making the trip by the protracted negotiations on the future of Cyprus. Macleod went in his place. Relations between Britain and its Caribbean colonies were strained. The suspicion had grown in the Caribbean that the British Government were dragging their feet. But Macleod had ended the go-slow on African policy and he now set about transforming the position in the West Indies. He was anxious to take his own 'soundings' in the Caribbean; to resume the political talks that had been suspended during the previous autumn on a new constitution for Trinidad; to agree a joint negotiating position with the West Indies Governments prior to talks with the United States over the future of the leased military bases in Antigua, Jamaica, St Lucia and Trinidad; and to counter the centrifugal forces that were threatening the Federation.[46]

Macleod's West Indian tour had a disastrous start and was dogged by bad luck. Eve accompanied her husband, but on their first full day in Kingston she slipped while visiting a hospital and broke her leg. She spent the rest of the fortnight at the Governor's residence with her leg in plaster while Iain completed his programme of political meetings in Jamaica and then headed on to Trinidad and Barbados, where he had meetings with the Premiers of the smaller islands. In Trinidad, Macleod's private secretary, D.K. Pearson, had to undergo an emergency operation for appendicitis. Finally, Macleod returned to Kingston, to pick up his wife for their flight home to London – on their arrival at Heathrow, Eve had to be lowered in her wheelchair by a baggage fork-lift truck from the Comet airliner.[47]

Politically, the visit began inauspiciously. Shortly before the Macleods' arrival, Sir Alexander Bustamente, former Chief Minister of Jamaica and leader of the Jamaican Labour Party, then in opposition, made his 'bombshell' announcement calling for Jamaica to leave the Federation. Manley, the Premier – who happened to be Bustamente's cousin – countered on 31 May by declaring his Government's intention to introduce a Bill to provide for a referendum on the future of Federation. Although this raised a fundamental constitutional question, the Governor, Sir Kenneth Blackburne, readily agreed to Manley's request without consulting either the Governor-General, Hailes, or Macleod. Hailes always maintained that had Macleod been in a position to postpone or cancel the referendum, the Federation might have been saved, but this is to reckon without the groundswell of popular opposition to the Federation and the reaction that Macleod's deferral or veto would have created.[48]

Macleod negotiated this delicate situation with aplomb. He made it clear from the moment he arrived that he had not come to urge any particular view about the shape of the Federation or the pace of its advance to independence, as these were matters for West Indians to settle. In other words, he was not taking sides in the Jamaican referendum. But after dinner on his first evening, Friday 3 June, Macleod assured Manley that he was certain he had been right in deciding to hold a referendum, since Bustamente's challenge was one which no politician could have afforded to ignore – the alternative would have been possibly years of uncertainty. On Saturday 4 June, Macleod met Bustamente for an hour. The former Chief Minister was inveighing against the evils of Federation for Jamaica, when he leaned forward in his chair and gravely asked: 'Mr Macleod, how would you like it if England were governed by Scotsmen?' Macleod was slightly taken aback for a moment, but then replied with equal gravity: 'Well, Sir Alexander, first, it is; and secondly, I rather like it.'[49]

Stung by Bustamente's secessionist call, Manley had also said that he would not attend Macleod's scheduled meeting later in the tour in Trinidad with the West Indian Premiers and added that if the talks went ahead without him they should not discuss the future of the Federation. Again, Macleod astutely resolved the crisis. When he met Manley and his Cabinet on Monday the 6th, he kept an earlier promise with the Premier and agreed that while he would be quite impartial about the outcome of the referendum, he should state publicly that he agreed with the decision to get the issue of the Federation decided once and for all. Macleod's approach persuaded Manley to change his attitude towards the Trinidad Conference, and he agreed to attend, later dropping all restrictions on the subjects to be discussed.[50]

In Trinidad, Macleod realized that the key to repairing the island's strained relations with Britain lay in establishing a rapport with the island's Premier, Eric Williams. On the morning after his arrival, Macleod had a two-hour tête-à-tête with Williams and won him over. From the first, Macleod showed his determination to reach a quick agreement on Trinidad's new constitution – during his visit, he announced new proposals that provided for full, internal self-government which would be introduced in time for the island's next elections, due to be held in September 1961. He also demonstrated his understanding of William's insistence that the Trinidad Government, and not the Federal Government, should present the case for recovering the area occupied by the leased American base at Chaguaramas in the future negotiations with the US Government. Macleod succeeded in gaining acceptance by the West Indian Ministers concerned, both

Federal and territorial, of a formula that would bring them to a conference table with Britain and the USA, to discuss a revision of the 1941 Agreement later in 1960. The negotiations with the Americans were successfully concluded by his junior minister, Hugh Fraser.[51]

Macleod's message to the West Indian Premiers and Chief Ministers when he met them in Trinidad on Friday 17 June improved relations and lifted the mood of gloom and suspicion. He reiterated his position on the Jamaican referendum, while he believed that Federation provided the best answer to the problems and aspirations of all the islands. The British Government were 'on the tails of the West Indies' and chasing them to early inde- pendence, because it was right and fitting that they should attain this status. The Government had had a West Indies Independence Bill in the legislative programme for a long time, but each time it had had to be deferred because the West Indies were not ready. Macleod hoped that this stage would soon pass. The West Indies, he would say – in marked contrast to some of his Ministerial colleagues in London – 'ought to be independent'. They had much to offer the Commonwealth and the world as an independent nation, not least in the field of race relations, since they were genuinely multi-racial societies. His advice was 'hurry'. At the same time, he reassured them that the British Government would be at hand to advise and assist them into independence – with defence, and also economically and financially. At a final meeting with Manley and Williams on Saturday 18 June, the two Premiers accepted the need to agree on the desirable form of the Federal constitution that should emerge from a reconvened constitutional con- ference.[52]

On 31 May 1961, Macleod opened the West Indian Constitutional Conference at Lancaster House. But with the Jamaican referendum not due to be held until the following September the talks went stickily and dissensions, particularly over the question of 'freedom of movement' within the Federation, threatened to disrupt it. As Macleod observed; 'although one had extremely good personal relationships with West Indian leaders, in the end one couldn't get away from this pledge that had been given by Manley that he would submit the result of a West Indian Federation as a referendum to the people of Jamaica.' Macleod sensed that the more he tried to tie up 'matters like financial control and freedom of movement, the more almost certainly you would swing the referendum against Manley because the resentment would rub off on him.' As a result, 'one was building on sand all the time and perhaps I should have seen this at an earlier stage'.[53]

By the end of the conference, Williams was saying Trinidad might opt out of the Federation, whatever the outcome of the referendum in Jamaica. Although Macleod considered abandoning the plans for federation, he was convinced that to have done so would have been wrong – partly 'because I don't like admitting failure unless it is inevitable, and partly because there still at that time seemed a real prospect of success'. Provided the Jamaicans voted for the Federation, Macleod felt that Williams's concerns were negotiable. Indeed, a potentially strong Federal Government had emerged from the constitutional deliberations.[54]

In the event, on 19 September, less than a month before Macleod's departure from the Colonial Office, the Jamaicans voted by 54 per cent to 46 per cent to reject the Federation. A week later, Macleod advised the Cabinet that it was not possible to contemplate resisting a request for full independence by Jamaica, given the precedents of Cyprus and Sierra Leone, which had both been granted their independence by this stage. The Cabinet endorsed his proposal that Jamaica should have full independence and that the Government should sponsor its membership of the Commonwealth. If Trinidad were to ask for independence on its own, Macleod argued that there would be no alternative but to agree. However, the Cabinet invited Macleod to report on the prospects for establishing an Eastern Caribbean Federation, that might include British Guiana, but nothing ever came of it. In early October, Macleod assured Manley that the British Government accepted the referendum result and were ready to sponsor Jamaican membership of the Commonwealth.[55]

After the Jamaicans had voted to secede, Williams's arithmetic for the Federation was inevitable – one from ten does not leave nine, but zero. Could Macleod have done more to save the Federation? Reflecting on events several years later, Macleod concluded that he had been defeated by two factors – the divisions within the Caribbean, and timing. His misjudgment had been not to read the writing on the wall sooner. As he confessed:

> I should have seen that although I could get over personality differences, and although I could create a Conference success, yet the long-term plan for a Federation simply would not have worked because of the contrast of the big islands and the small ones. I didn't see this and I should have seen it. In many ways I regret this more than anything else.[56]

Timing was also against him, although as he recognized, he had brought this problem on himself as a result of his acceleration of the pace of decolonization:

> In the year from June 1960 to June 1961, what had happened was that there had been such change in the attitude of both colonial countries and of London itself, that the ideas which I had inherited from my predecessors in 1959 simply wouldn't work in 1961. You see, when you were giving independence to a country the size of Gambia, to islands the size of Malta and Cyprus, it's a bit much to expect Jamaica or Trinidad to sink their sovereignty with a whole collection of smaller islands, many of which they would have to help almost as pensioners.

In August 1962, both Jamaica and Trinidad became independent Commonwealth members. Barbados followed in November 1966.[57]

Macleod was unable to make headway in British Guiana, principally because of the political and racial divisions within the territory and the radical left-wing Government led by Dr Cheddi Jagan. At the March 1960 conference, Macleod had allowed Jagan's administration to assume responsibility for internal security, including control of the police. Although the Governor was left no reserve powers, he was still responsible for the armed forces. This situation was to cause trouble later. In the wake of the Cuban coup and Castro's rise to power, the Americans were nervous about instability in the Caribbean, and were especially concerned at the prospect of a Castro-style regime coming to power after independence in British Guiana.[58]

Macleod later recalled his meeting with President Kennedy in the Oval Room at the White House during 1961, when 'he told me some of his anxieties in relation to British Guiana, and in effect said that he understood our policy but hoped that we wouldn't go too quickly towards independence'. The irony was not lost on Macleod, who had had to listen to the Americans pressing for speedy British decolonization, especially in Africa. 'Mr President,' Macleod queried, 'do I understand that you want us to go as quickly as possible towards independence everywhere else all over the world but not on your doorstep in British Guiana?' Kennedy laughed and said; 'Well, that's probably just about it.' Macleod responded, 'Well I understand too, but our policy, of course, remains that the country shall move towards independence.' However, Macleod's desire to move towards independence was thwarted by the near impossibility of securing an agreed constitution between Dr Jagan and the leading opposition politician, Forbes Burnham. Macleod suspected that Sandys' approach after 1963 was largely influenced by the Americans. During the Commons debate on his successor's complicated constitutional proposals in April 1964, Macleod intervened from the backbenches to support the Government while warning against the dangers of trying to block one man – in this case, Dr Jagan – from coming to power. British Guiana finally became independent as Guyana in May 1966.[59]

Inevitably, Macleod had to accord some territories lower priority. In the case of Cyprus, the Foreign Office continued to take the lead and the island achieved independence in August 1960. In other cases, such as Britain's remaining West African colonies, there was no problem with European settlers and their progress to independence was relatively straightforward. 'Here almost all news is cheerful,' Macleod told Macmillan in May 1960. 'We had excellent conferences on Nigeria and Sierra Leone and managed to secure satisfactory defence agreements from both. Sierra Leone will become independent in April next year, and then the only Colonial Territory in West Africa will be Gambia.' Nigeria was independent by the autumn of 1960, and although Macleod briefly had to impose a state of emergency in Sierra Leone, the territory was still able to become independent in April 1961. The Gambia, a geographical oddity that was 300 miles long, 30 miles wide, and almost entirely surrounded by Senegal, proved to be more irksome. Macleod was anxious to press ahead with its independence before pressure mounted at the United Nations, and initially believed that 'the most likely solution is that, in spite of the physical separation, it will federate with Sierra Leone'. In fact, some form of association with Senegal seemed more appropriate, but even this was to prove difficult. The problem of a tiny colony like the Gambia prompted Macleod to propose a plan to the Commonwealth Prime Ministers' Conference in 1961, whereby smaller territories would move to self-government, with a larger Commonwealth state assuming responsibility for their defence and foreign affairs. The larger states, however, were reluctant to take on extra responsibilities, and although the Labour Government in Britain established the Associated States in the West Indies, Macleod's idea was never developed as he had hoped.[60]

Malta had been the first colony that Macleod visited, but only because it lay on the route to Africa. It was an inauspicious visit, since Dom Mintoff, leader of the island's Labour Party, organized demonstrations against Macleod and refused to meet him. Macleod became intensely dissatisfied at the continuation of Governor's rule that had been imposed following the riots of 1958, especially since the islanders had a long tradition of self-government. In May 1960, he indicated to Macmillan his view that although Britain's defence requirements on the island complicated Malta's progress to self-government, they should not be allowed to contradict it. The following year, the Governor, Sir Hilary Blood, devised a satisfactory constitution and the ensuing election was won by Dr Borg Olivier's National Party. Malta finally became independent in September 1964.[61]

Macleod was less successful in Aden, another colony where defence requirements complicated any efforts at political advance. The British Government sought to secure Aden against the threat from Arab nationalism, principally through Nasser's influence in nearby Yemen, by combining political advance for Aden with its entry in to the South Arabian Federation – consisting of the old Protectorates – prior to independence for the whole area. Macleod visited Aden and the Protectorates for a few days in early April 1961, and although the merchant Adenis were ill-matched with the feudal sultans, he pressed ahead with discussions on the proposed merger in London the following July. This shotgun wedding was completed in January 1963. However, neither the workers of Aden nor the tribesmen of the Protectorates were represented in the new South Arabian Federation and their exclusion represented a time bomb ticking away behind the constitutional façade. When the Labour Government announced in February 1966 their plan to withdraw from the Aden base, the bloody battle that ensued gave a taste of what Britain might have experienced on a much bigger scale in Africa had it not been for Macleod.[62]

East African Finale

Tanganyika 'continues to be the brightest spot,' Macleod told Macmillan in his survey of the colonies on 31 May 1960. Elections were due the following October and Julius Nyerere, the future African Chief Minister, had:

Always shown excellent cooperation with us and the Governor and a complete understanding of the economic needs of his country and the need for keeping British administration and Western capital and know-how. There is no reason why Tanganyika should not continue to go forward and prosper.

As Macleod had agreed, Tanganyika's independence conference was held not at Lancaster House, as had become the tradition, but in Dar-es-Salaam at the end of March 1961.[63]

Attending the Tanganyika conference immediately after the Commonwealth Prime Ministers' Conference in London and following the huge row in the Conservative Party over Northern Rhodesia, made a pleasant contrast for Macleod. 'It was an immensely happy occasion,' he later recalled. He was accompanied by Eve and when they arrived, they were greeted by 'enormous cheering crowds waving palm branches, and this made something of a change from the receptions I had in other African countries at the time when Africans were somewhat suspicious of the British Government, and in particular of the Secretary of State.' The conference, held in Karimjee Hall, went smoothly and was unremarkable, except for one amusing incident that arose because of Nyerere's wish immediately to take the title of Prime Minister ahead of independence. Macleod preferred him to remain as 'Premier' during the period before independence, because of the repercussions in other territories where Premiers would demand to be called Prime Minister and were likely to call for the independence associated with being a Prime Minister. A 'splendid argument' developed, with 'references and authorities and precedents being quoted at each other'. In fact, Macleod was not particularly bothered about the matter, and felt that he could handle any repercussions. Finally, he told the conference, 'with a very stern visage and in his fiercest words', that he had come to a decision, there was no question of his changing his mind, and if they did not accept his verdict the conference would have to end at once. This threw Nyerere and his Cabinet into 'absolute consternation'. Macleod then declared that Nyerere's title would be 'Prime Minister'. At that, Nyerere and his colleagues 'burst out laughing and threw all their books in the air with great delight'.[64]

Macleod's gesture 'crowned a very happy and successful conference'.

Nyerere also asked that, on independence, Tanganyika should become a republic but when Macleod pointed out that he could not authorize this personally and would need Cabinet approval, the Tanganyikan leader accepted his argument and persuaded his colleagues to drop this demand. Macleod had initially suggested that independence should be granted in March 1962, in order to allow time for the necessary administrative arrangements, but finally agreed to Nyerere's faster timetable. As Judith Listowel, the historian of Tanganyikan independence has noted, when Macleod announced, during his final speech at the conference, that Tanganyika was to become independent in December 1961:

> his words were drowned by cheers which spread from Karimjee Hall into the garden, thronged with thousands of excited Africans. Their cheers were echoed further down Acacia Avenue, and then in the side streets, in the market place and in all the corners and alleys of Dar-es-Salaam.'

Afterwards, the Macleods and their hosts 'spent a day and a bit in celebrations'.[65]

The significance of Tanganyika was that it had won its independence almost a decade earlier than the 1970 target date that had been envisaged only a couple of years earlier before Macleod entered the Colonial Office. To the charge that he had ushered Tanganyika to independence when it lacked the necessary administrative back-up, Macleod replied that: 'We were conscious that we were putting perhaps too big a burden on the administrative structure. But you see the alternative, of course, was to go on governing.' And, as he added:

> That not only wasn't my policy but wasn't in the judgement of the Prime Minister and myself and the Cabinet, in the best interests of this country. Or indeed, of the countries concerned in Africa. And therefore, you have to accept that, if you go for a solution that leads you to journey's end quicker than you would otherwise plan to go, then there are some problems on the road.[66]

Some of the worst problems were experienced in the island colony of Zanzibar, which was to merge with Tanganyika in 1964 to form Tanzania. The politics of Zanzibar were complicated by the fact that the ruler, the Sultan, was an Arab, and relations between the Arab minority and the African majority were strained. Macleod had been worried about the position in Zanzibar, but had only spent a few days in the island at the end of 1959, and again during the spring of 1961, immediately after the Tanganyikan conference. His decision in 1960 to press ahead with British withdrawal coincided with the death of the old and respected Sultan Khalifa. The elections held in 1961 produced a 'freak' result, putting the Arab minority in control at the time of independence in December 1963 – the first time since South Africa in 1910 that the British had handed over power to a minority. However, within ten days of independence, a revolutionary *coup* saw the Africans seize power. Macleod later felt that had the old Sultan lived a little longer, 'the transition might have been a more peaceful one'. But as he later acknowledged, he should have been more alert than he was to 'the danger of moving towards independence with the Africans as much in the minority as they were'.[67]

While Macleod had hastened independence in Tanganyika as a demonstration that Africans could achieve political advance without violence, he was aware that Kenya represented the real test of his colonial policy. His new constitution, agreed between the Africans and Blundell's New Kenya Party at Lancaster House in February 1960, represented his first step in trying to reconcile the interests of the European community with the African demand for majority rule. But the suddenness of Macleod's accelerated progress towards an African dominated Government had disturbed Conservative backbenchers and alarmed Kenya's settlers. Moreover, during the spring of 1960, Belgium's decision to leave the Congo within a matter of months had terrified settlers throughout Africa. In Kenya, European confidence collapsed. House and share prices tumbled. The prospect of the settlers leaving the country and taking their capital, skills and families with them, threatened Macleod's plans for an economically successful, multi-racial Kenya.[68]

It was against this background that Macleod authorized the Governor, Sir Patrick Renison, to make a statement confirming that the African nationalist leader, Jomo Kenyatta, would not be released from detention. However, Renison insisted on describing Kenyatta in his statement as 'the African leader to darkness and death'. Macleod strongly advised the Governor against using this phrase, 'for the obvious reason that we would sooner or later have to deal with Kenyatta'. Renison 'was very proud' of his phrase about Kenyatta and said that unless he was allowed to use it, he would have to resign. This struck Macleod as 'absurd', but he judged that: 'we had enough troubles in Kenya without another one rising, because he would then be seen as the standard-bearer of the Europeans.' Macleod was only too well aware that Renison's resignation would have provoked a storm of protest against him in the Conservative Party and driven Kenya's panicky white settlers either to exodus, or to extremism – especially when Sir Ferdinand Cavendish-Bentinck was trying to rally the Europeans against the Lancaster House agreement, and bring about what Macleod feared would be 'a return to purely racial politics and racial thinking'. Macleod accordingly 'put up with Renison's extremely ill-judged phrase'. But as he had feared, 'it did a considerable amount of harm' among Africans. Macleod regarded Renison 'throughout as a rather silly man', but tried to comfort himself by remembering the Governor's 'very real compensating qualities' – popularity, integrity and 'a very high record in the Service'. Nonetheless, 'Kenya wasn't the country for him'.[69]

The impact of Renison's ill-advised statement was reinforced at the end of May 1960, when the Kenyan Government published the Corfield Report which set out to prove that the settler view of Kenyatta was right. Again, Macleod thought this ill-advised. These incidents reveal a serious problem for him in Kenya. Although the colony's administrators were 'at all levels head and shoulders above that of any of the others that I saw', they were also among the most difficult to handle. After his first visit to the colony, he had told Macmillan that, despite their high calibre, 'they thought little in the years of emergency of the letter of the law'. As Macleod later recalled: 'The Kenya Government in Nairobi had the sort of idea that it was a Government on its own and could treat on equal terms with the Government in Whitehall.' At times, Macleod barely concealed his contempt for the Governor and his administration.[70]

In the February 1961 election, the Kenyan African National Union party (KANU), in which Mboya and Odinga took leading roles, campaigned on the claim that they would not accept office unless Kenyatta was freed. Although KANU's support among the Kikuyu and the Luo won them twice as many votes as Ronald Ngala's Kenya African Democratic Union party (KADU) that attracted the minority tribes, the Governor was able to form a minority Government of KADU, Blundell's New Kenya Party and Kenyan Asians. This outcome accorded with the strategy that Macleod had mapped a year earlier, when he had realized the need to carry the support of an important section of the European community in his plans for a phased transition to African majority rule.[71]

The return of Kenyatta to public life was central to Macleod's political plans. Macleod began by transferring Kenyatta from 'the entirely inaccessible place that he was, into a place where it was possible for people to consult him and interview him for the press'. This gave Macleod an opportunity to weigh reaction, and to allow the fact of Kenyatta's freedom to become accepted, before he took the final, carefully stage-managed, step. 'The release of Kenyatta,' Macleod later remembered, 'was something so profoundly shocking to so many Europeans that timing became all important . . . and it was of great importance that even though they expected it, that it was done in such a way that this was a decision taken by the Government in Kenya and the Government in London.' Kenyatta was finally set free in August 1961, while Macleod was again embattled with the problems of Northern Rhodesia. After Macleod's departure from the Colonial Office, a second constitutional conference during the spring of 1962 resulted in agreement on a constitution for Kenyan independence and the formation of a KADU–KANU Government, with Ngala and Kenyatta as joint Premiers. Macleod's successor, Maudling, was also able to triple Macleod's Land Settlement Scheme which provided land for African farmers and compensation for the settlers. A year later, KANU won new elections, and Kenyatta was Prime Minister at independence in December 1963.[72]

Macleod chaired his last constitutional conference as Colonial Secretary on another East African colony – Uganda. Although this territory lacked a large settler community, it represented one of his most testing challenges, and until almost the last minute, he was not sure whether he would succeed. As he had explained to Macmillan in May 1960:

> The problem here is an extremely complex and difficult one. In no other territory is the political picture so confused. No national African leader of any sort has yet emerged. In consequence the struggle goes on between the traditional forces represented by the Kabaka and the other Agreement Rulers and the rising power of the political parties.

Macleod tried to keep the balance between the Kabaka of Buganda and the kings on the one hand, and the parties on the other, by keeping to his timetable for new elections while setting up a commission – under the chairmanship of Lord Munster – to advise on the relationship between Buganda, the kingdoms and the rest of the country. 'In this way,' Macleod told the Prime Minister:

> I hope to preserve an uneasy advance. But the situation is in my view potentially very explosive, although because there is no real colour problem involved it does not attract the headlines in the same way as events in Kenya and further south.

The British Government had long feared that Buganda – the Kabaka's kingdom at the heart of the country – might secede. When this occurred in December 1960 and the Baganda abstained in the March 1961 elections, Macleod responded by making it clear that their separatism would not be allowed to obstruct the transfer of power.[73]

In June 1961, the Munster Commission recommended a semi-federal relationship between Buganda and the kingdoms and the rest of the country. During the summer, Macleod held discussions with the political leaders – Ben Kiwanuka, the Chief Minister, and Dr Milton Obote of the Opposition – with a view to convening an early constitutional conference that would move Uganda towards independence on the basis of the Munster report. But the Kabaka remained obdurate. As Macleod later recalled, still exasperated at the memory of the endless negotiations:

> The Kabaka was an extremely difficult man to deal with because he regarded himself as a King and he regarded me as a hireling of the Queen. And he didn't really think he ought to talk to me. He thought he ought to speak to the Queen. A very opinionated person, and he was also easily

the most stubborn man I've ever dealt with, and that's saying something because I have dealt with some of the most stubborn trade union leaders in this country and as Secretary of State some of the most obstinate leaders with different coloured faces that you could possibly find, but none of them came anywhere near the Kabaka for sheer, blind, pig-headed obstinacy.

Nonetheless, Macleod finally forced the issue by announcing to the Kabaka and the other three kings that the Lancaster House Conference was going to start, and – as he later paraphrased his message – 'you will be there. If you are not there it will go on without you, and matters concerning your country will be dealt with in your absence'.[74]

The Ugandan conference was a touch and go affair. The Governor, Sir Frederick Crawford, who was more in favour of African advancement than Macleod had suspected, became his 'main prop and stay'. Macleod had never developed the close relationships with the leading African politicians in Uganda of the kind that he had established in the other British colonies – he hardly knew Kiwanuka, had met Obote only a few times, and could not get on with the Kabaka or any of his advisers. The talks stumbled from one crisis to another, including a walk-out by Kiwanuka and lengthy negotiations with the Kabaka outside the conference. The Kabaka's ministers reported to him on the conference, while the other kings were concerned mainly with 'absolutely absurd matters like how many guns they should have as a salute, how they should rank in precedence', and other trivial matters. At one point Kiwanuka put forward three papers on behalf of his Government, but when invited to speak in support of them by Macleod opposed them all. Macleod deferred attempting any solution to a tricky territorial dispute over the so-called 'lost counties', by setting up a new Commission, consisting of Lords Molson, Listowel and Ward, to investigate the problem. He later reflected that this had been a mistake, although if he had not promised an inquiry he might not have been able to clinch an overall agreement.[75]

The outcome was in doubt until the final day. Macleod sensed that many of the African delegates thought that the British Government would listen to the Kabaka and the kings, and would not contemplate early independence. The tense last session consisted almost entirely of a speech by Macleod, who had been told by Macmillan that his move from the Colonial Office in the Government reshuffle was to be announced later that day. He explained the complicated, formal guarantees that he had agreed separately with the Kabaka, and then announced that elections would be held before the introduction of the new constitution. Obote realized that these would give him the Premiership. Kiwanuka had got nothing, but in almost his next breath, Macleod declared that he would be leaving his post as Colonial Secretary that evening and that Uganda would be independent in exactly twelve months' time – on 9 October 1962. Kiwanuka had always demanded independence and was therefore in no position to object. The independence timetable bequeathed by Macleod was desperately tight, but it was met. Elections were held in April 1962, and the new Premier, Obote, led Uganda to independence.[76]

Macleod's dramatic, last-ditch triumph at the Uganda conference provided the finale to his time at the Colonial Office, but it was developments in the Central African Federation that precipitated his move. In August 1961, Banda won an overwhelming victory in the Nyasaland elections and, as Macleod had counselled beforehand, this immediately spelled further trouble for the Federation. Moreover, Welensky was moving to a plan for future discussions on the Federation that – in Macleod's view – virtually excluded African leaders like Banda and Kaunda from the negotiating table. But the real problems lay in Northern Rhodesia, where the June revision of the February 1961 constitutional proposals was causing renewed trouble.[77]

The Last Straw for Macmillan

Despite Macleod's hopes, it proved impossible for Kaunda to sell the June 1961 revised Northern Rhodesian constitutional proposals to his party. Hone, the Governor in Northern Rhodesia, informed Macleod on 15 July that Kaunda was now demanding changes to the June proposals. Welensky's reluctant acceptance of the proposals was based on the assumption that the concessions were firm, but Macleod indicated to Hone that although he did not want to upset Welensky, 'we should not I think close our minds to some gesture towards the Africans and Asians.' However, Macleod suggested helping Kaunda principally by removing the Asians' proposed separate seat in the legislative council.[78]

The force of African nationalist anger at the concessions made to Welensky in June soon erupted. At the start of August, some districts of Northern Rhodesia were rocked by arson attacks, explosions and violent disturbances. Part of the problem, as always, was the interaction between events in the two Rhodesias. In Southern Rhodesia, a referendum had been held on 26 July on the new constitution that had finally been agreed with Sandys. As Macleod explained to Macmillan, Welensky and his party had therefore also been putting 'about an impression of greater satisfaction' with the constitutional settlement in Northern Rhodesia than the British Government had wanted. In consequence, 'a good deal of the moderate support which we previously enjoyed has slipped. The UNIP hot-heads in the lower levels of the party have begun to take matters into their own hands.'[79]

Macleod's aim was to help Kaunda play a moderating influence on nationalist opinion. The Colonial Secretary was concerned that the Governor should not be manoeuvred into taking security measures prematurely, since this would play into the extremists' hands, but Hone rejected Macleod's suggestion on 6 August that he should see Kaunda. Macleod urged the Governor to reconsider his opinion. 'I am very much afraid,' he argued:

> That if we leave him [Kaunda] completely incommunicado now we shall inevitably force him either to join with the UNIP hotheads at the lower levels in a violent campaign against the Government, or to withdraw from the territory, in which case his political influence for the future is likely to be lost.

The following day, Hone reported that Kaunda had had an interview with the Northern Rhodesian Minister for Native Affairs, who thought that Kaunda wanted peace but hoped that reconsideration would be given to abolishing the reserved seat for Asians and coloureds and reducing the hurdle that candidates had to clear to secure election (this hurdle was expressed as a percentage of the vote). If this was done, he would instruct his organization to take part in elections.[80]

The violence worsened. The Governor now planned to introduce security measures in the provinces of Northern Rhodesia affected by the trouble and Macleod agreed to support whatever action was deemed necessary. 'Meantime,' Macleod reported to the Prime Minister on Wednesday 9th, 'Kaunda himself is in a most difficult position.' Kaunda was clearly anxious to avoid a showdown, and it was 'somewhat encouraging' that for the time being he had publicly shelved plans for an uprising on the grounds that a calmer atmosphere was needed. However, 'pressures may force him over the edge', and Macleod therefore consulted Hone again about the possibility of an approach to Kaunda to try to avoid this, 'despite the obvious difficulties of "negotiation" with him at this juncture'. Although Macleod recognized that 'nothing can or should be done until violence disappears', it was clear that he believed that some change would have to be made in order to help Kaunda. His preference remained for removing the proposed separate Asian seat: 'because this plan was assailed from all sides it seems to be the only place where conceivably we could make a change that would not hurt anybody very much and yet might just give Kaunda enough to bring his people in to contest the elections.'[81]

Macleod's realization that the African unrest necessitated a further revision to the constitutional proposals put him politically out on a limb. For months, the Prime Minister and the Cabinet Secretary had been preoccupied by the minutiae of constitutional formulae, incessant ministerial and departmental wrangling, backbench dissent, and continual manoeuvrings and threats by the various parties in Northern Rhodesia. They had thought that a satisfactory package had finally been agreed in June, but now Macleod was suggesting that it had to be changed yet again. In August the Prime Minister, having laboured so hard and so long for the June settlement, was not yet ready to confront this inescapable fact. Long since wearied by the endless conflicts between Macleod and Sandys, Macmillan finally determined that he would have to move Macleod from the Colonial Office.

Macleod left Britain on Saturday 12 August for a three-week break at what had become his and Eve's favoured holiday haunt of S'Agaro on the Costa Brava. Within days of Macleod's leaving, Kaunda suddenly arrived unexpectedly in London. Lord Perth, who had to be hastily summoned from Scotland, could offer him no constitutional changes. On Friday 18th, Hone reported from Lusaka that there were further disturbances, and that Kaunda, having returned from London, had torn up his identity card and declared that he would not cooperate with the Government. Kaunda's announcement of the continuation of the civil disobedience campaign, while disassociating himself from violence, did not impress Hone. 'In these circumstances,' Hone telegrammed to Perth, 'I see no point in making any further approach to Kaunda, he has made it clear where he stands.' Perth informed Macmillan that he had agreed to Hone's introduction of detention without trial.[82]

In these circumstances, Macleod was likely to press even harder for changes to the June proposals when he returned to London on Thursday 31 August. This prospect greatly alarmed Macmillan. Yet refusing to help Kaunda was likely to drive the Government into a cul-de-sac, as is revealed in a minute to the Prime Minister from Philip de Zulueta, one of his private secretaries. As de Zulueta noted, Trend in the Cabinet Office was:

Concerned lest the Colonial Secretary, when he returns, should propose some changes in HMG's proposals. He feels, I think with every reason, that it would be almost impossible to get agreement to some revised proposals at this stage. But unfortunately at the moment it seems doubtful whether the present proposals will work.

Macmillan was desperate to avoid any direct discussion with Macleod, as is patently evident from his note to Bligh on Monday 28th:

I have no doubt that the Colonial [sic] will wish to discuss this with me. But I am not very anxious to discuss it *alone* [Macmillan's emphasis] with him. Of course, if he does not raise the question of any change in the Constitutional decisions, I will leave it alone. But if he does so, it would be better at either a meeting of the full Africa Committee or a number of Ministers especially concerned, including of course the Commonwealth Secretary.

Macmillan had had enough of Macleod on Northern Rhodesia.[83]

Before Macleod returned, his deputy, Perth, recommended to the Prime Minister that changes should be made to the constitutional proposals, but Alport in Salisbury and Hone in Lusaka were opposed. Macmillan noted to Bligh that he hoped both Secretaries of State would 'agree on *no change*'

[Macmillan's emphasis]. Macleod and Sandys were at least agreed that law and order in Northern Rhodesia had to be restored before any consideration could be given to the constitutional problem. Macleod was to see Sir John Moffat, leader of the liberals and head of the Northern Rhodesian executive council, and Kaunda separately at his flat. The plan was that Macleod should speak to Kaunda in very strong terms about law and order, and then send a letter to Moffat for publication, setting out the Government's position.

However, the apparent agreement between Macleod and Sandys soon collapsed in acrimony. By suggesting a public statement, Macleod had out-manoeuvred Sandys and skilfully found a way, despite Macmillan's desire for 'no change', of keeping open the door to change. His proposed public signal, in the form of a letter to Moffat, would enable links to be rebuilt with Kaunda. But in Lusaka, Hone opposed Macleod's draft letter, arguing that violence would be seen to have won. Even Moffat doubted that the letter would do any good. Macleod was undeterred, and still thought that it was worth sending. As to Sandys, Bligh noted for the record that: 'The Commonwealth Secretary does not seem to be quite sure what he wants to do about all this.'[84]

Sandys became so bitter that he as good as alleged to the Prime Minister's private office that he could not trust Macleod's word. 'The Commonwealth Secretary in speaking to me,' noted Bligh, 'said that he would agree with the draft letter to Moffat if the Colonial Secretary really meant it.' Sandys had been referring to a passage in Macleod's draft, that began: 'Only when the Governor can assure me that law and order has been substantially restored shall we be in a position to turn our minds to constitutional matters . . .' Perhaps out of self-preservation, Bligh reported Sandys's allegation indirectly to Macleod on the private office net. Bligh duly noted, no doubt with equal tact, that: 'The Colonial Secretary said that he did mean it'.[85]

This latest clash prompted Macmillan to call a meeting at Admiralty House on Wednesday 6 September with Macleod and Sandys, and also Trend and Bligh. Rather than send a letter to Moffat, the Prime Minister favoured a statement by the Governor. But Hone was utterly opposed to the idea and it was decided instead that the Government should issue the statement themselves. In the meantime, Welensky had been sounded out and was demanding that no statement should be made on Northern Rhodesia until the Government had heard the views of the Federal Cabinet. At a further Admiralty House meeting between Macmillan, Macleod, Sandys, Trend and Bligh on Monday 11th, Macleod argued that the Government should go ahead and issue their statement on Tuesday 12th, whatever Welensky planned to do about it. Again he was overruled.[86]

Despite the frustrations of the repeated delays, Macleod at last thought that the path was clear. But later on the 11th, Sandys reacted to Welensky's threat to issue his own statement if the Government went ahead, by urging even further delay. Clearly enraged, Macleod fired off a no-nonsense minute to Macmillan. 'We cannot once more be put off from a decision that we have taken,' he declared, 'because of the threat that Welensky will make a speech denouncing it.'

Macleod's anger produced a compelling riposte to those who were prevaricating – this included Macmillan, although the Prime Minister was going to some lengths to hide his own views from Macleod. Macleod's assessment of the crisis caused by June's constitutional proposals was stark:

The whole facts of the matter in Northern Rhodesia are
1. That over 2,000 arrests have been made.
2. That about 25 people have been killed.
3. That we have had to take emergency powers including the right to detain without trial in two of the provinces of Northern Rhodesia.
There is every possibility that the position may get worse and we have certainly failed to achieve the minimum degree of acquiescence which we looked for hopefully in June.

Moreover, Macleod left Macmillan in no doubt of his views on Welensky and his advisers:

The Federal Government's assessment of the security risks have been proved disastrously wrong. You will remember that they urged on us that even if we accepted their proposals African reaction would be slight and easily contained. In fact even on our proposals which were so much more favourable to the African we are barely able to hold the position.

Welensky's reasons for trying to delay even further the Government's issuing their statement were contemptuously dismissed:

There is no question whatever as Welensky suggests of re-opening the Northern Rhodesia Constitutional talks. Indeed our statement specifically makes plain that we would only *consider* changes 'within the limited area where disagreement persists' i.e. in practice on the Asian seat and the percentage for the national seats.

Finally, Macleod emphasized why he believed that 'speed' was of such importance:

If Welensky is going to threaten us with a speech, it will not matter whether we issue our statement on Tuesday or Wednesday or Thursday. But if Kaunda returns and no statement has been made his Executive will urge on him to implement Stage 3 as it is called of their plan which involves disturbances on the Copperbelt. Once this happens the situation in Northern Rhodesia, and indeed the cause of the Federation, could be set back for years.

The Government duly issued their statement on 14 September.[87]

On 27 September, Macleod's private office forwarded to Bligh a copy of Macleod's minute to Perth reviewing the possible options in Northern Rhodesia. Macleod stressed that there was 'very limited room for manoeuvre'. Meeting Kaunda's demands was simply not practicable, while doing nothing at all would mean surrendering to Welensky. The most likely options remained the Asian seat and the percentages. Bligh passed Macleod's minute to Macmillan, with a note suggesting that 'the Colonial Office are approaching this on the right lines'. In response, the Prime Minister scrawled: 'we *must* leave this to after the change. Let it drag on if we can.' His euphemistic reference to 'the change', confirmed that his removal of Macleod from the Colonial Office was imminent.[88]

During the latter part of September, Macmillan discussed with Macleod his plan to move him from the Colonial Office, but with the Uganda constitutional talks due to last into October, no formal announcement was to be made until Monday, the 9th. As Macmillan had hoped, Macleod made no attempt during his final days at the Colonial Office to launch a pre-emptive initiative on Northern Rhodesia. But Macleod saw no need. When the Prime Minister had informed him of 'the change', Macleod had been relieved to hear that he was to be replaced by Maudling, whom he knew shared his liberal views. Indeed, Macleod's judgment of Maudling was to prove better than the Prime Minister's. As Macmillan later admitted, 'had I thought that there would be some relief in the pressure from the Colonial Office, I was doomed to disappointment – I soon found that Maudling was quite as "progressive" as Macleod. Indeed, in some respects he seemed "*plus royaliste que le roi*".'[89]

After a subsequent fact-finding tour to Africa, Maudling concluded, as had Macleod, that in Northern Rhodesia the Government had to help Kaunda. In February 1962, he eventually secured modest constitutional changes of the kind that Macleod had sought. Again, there was a major battle in the Cabinet, but Macleod's overriding purpose was finally realized – Kaunda's and Welensky's parties both went to the polls. As Macleod later acknowledged: 'the aim of getting two people who appear absolutely irreconcilable to the polls in what was genuinely for the first election, a fair fight, overwhelmed everything else.' This objective was achieved within Macleod's original constitutional framework, on the basis of parity between Africans and Europeans. Macleod accepted that technically the new constitution could be shot full of holes, but 'at the end of the day myself and my successor, Reggie Maudling simply had one answer – well, it worked, didn't it!'[90]

Swan Song:

On the morning of Wednesday 11 October 1961, just two days after the announcement of the reshuffle, Macleod delivered his final speech as Colonial Secretary at the Conservative annual conference in Brighton. It was the speech of his life and ranks as one of the great political performances of modern times. It not only set the seal on his two years at the Colonial Office but was the finest justification of the policy of rapid decolonization ever given. As he spoke, any idea that the end of Empire was little more than an inglorious act of expediency was banished from his audience's mind and instead was transformed into an inspirational act of idealism.

The facts were startling. 'At the end of the last war,' Macleod told his audience, 'something like 630 million people lived in the dependent territories of the Crown.' Now, following his latest success in the talks on Uganda, the figure was down to 23 million. But at the heart of the debate was the feeling held by many of his critics in the party that the pace of decolonization was too precipitate. How was he to meet their fear that in the rush to majority rule, the rights of the white settler minorities, notably in Kenya and Rhodesia, were being sacrificed? Macleod met his critics head-on. Instead of seeking to evade the issue of white minority rights, or offer soothing reassurances that meant little in reality, he was brutally frank.

> How is this to be done? Do not, if I may say so, put too much faith just in paper guarantees. Independence to a country means what it says. It means that that country is independent, not just from the Colonial Secretary, but from this country as well. They are free and equal with us in the British Commonwealth of Nations.
>
> Therefore, although there is much to be said for entrenching property rights deeply in the constitution, although there is much to be said for human rights and Bills of Rights, although, above all, you should do everything you can to ensure an impartial judiciary, yet you must realize that the only final safeguard is the good will of the people who live in that country. This can be earned, and is being earned, and we must do everything we can to earn it.

As Macleod observed, it had: 'fallen to me to be Colonial Secretary during two of the most tremendous years of advance the world has ever seen.' For there was one overriding, unavoidable fact that he could not escape as Colonial Secretary and that he was determined to impress upon the party. 'You must be in no doubt that you are watching one of the great dramas of history, as so many countries thrust forwards through nationalism towards their independence.' It was against this background that he had to chart his course:

We in this country have always understood the emergence of nationalism. If we look at the problems of Africa today, which have concerned us so much in this short debate, it is easy enough to point to a country and say, 'There in the Congo you can see what happens when there is inadequate preparation and you go too fast'. I agree. The Congo was a failure of inadequate preparation. But you must also look round the map of Africa and look at Angola, Algiers and South Africa and see the tragedies that can come if you go too slow. Of course the Congo events went too fast. There are other places in Africa where they have gone too slow ... confronted with this choice, as one would never hope to be, there is probably greater safety in going too fast than in going slow.

Macleod then confronted the conference with the dilemma that he had to face daily:

The tightrope of timing which the Colonial Secretary has to walk in every territory every week, sometimes almost every day, is the most difficult of all his tasks – how you try to reconcile the emerging nationalism of these countries with the need for the surest possible protection for the minority. As you walk this tightrope, you must realize that if you fall from it it will bring disaster and perhaps bloodshed to so many people to whom you stand in a position of trustee.

At this point, Macleod lifted the debate onto a different plane, abandoning the traditional Conservative obeisance to statecraft in favour of an avowedly moralistic appeal: 'How, then, do you go forward? On what moral principles should you base your policy, for be very sure that in this field, as in every other field, if your policies are not based on principle they will fail?' Macleod's 'own personal belief' was based on three principles:

First, I believe in the rights and duties of men, and that means of all men. But do not ever fall into the error of assuming that, because you give a man better housing, because you give a man better education, because you improve the health services, somehow that will satisfy his craving for basic political rights. It cannot do. Indeed, it is bound to sharpen it.

Remember also that however great your services may have been to a country ... that will never always be accepted as a reason why automatically you should govern.

Secondly, he believed:

In what our grandfathers would have called the British Imperial mission. It is not yet completed. Since the world began, empires have grown and flourished and decayed, some into a sort of genteel obscurity, some leaving little heritage and culture behind them, some even no more than stones covered by sand. They are one with Nineveh and Tyre, but we are the only empire leaving behind us a coherent political scheme of development. We are the only people who, with all the hesitations and failures that there have been, are genuinely resolved on turning, to use Harold Macmillan's phrase, an empire into a commonwealth and a commonwealth into a family.

Finally, Macleod revealed in a great peroration the fundamental, romantic, and almost mystical, belief, that had been his personal, guiding star during the previous two years. Significantly, too, he found its finest expression in the words of a Scottish poet:

This is the last thing I shall say as Colonial Secretary. The third principle is that I believe quite simply in the brotherhood of man – men of all races, of all colours, of all creeds. I think it is this that must be in the centre of our thinking.

And now what lies ahead in this event? It is perhaps strange to an English and to a Welsh audience to quote the greatest of our Scottish native poets, but nobody has put this in simpler or finer words than Burns:

> It is coming yet for a' that,
> That man to man the whole world o'er,
> Shall brothers be for a' that.

And this is coming. There are foolish men who will deny it, but they will be swept away; but if we are wise then indeed the task of bringing these countries towards their destiny of free and equal partners and friends with us in the Commonwealth of Nations can be a task as exciting, as inspiring and as noble as the creation of empire itself.[91]

Macleod's speech had been 'an almost provocative vindication of his stewardship', the political correspondent of *The Times* reported from Brighton. He had been greeted with a 'warm reception' as Party Chairman-designate and at the end of what Macleod had called 'a personal declaration of faith, he had another ovation which might have suggested to any innocent in the hall that his colonial policy had never attracted the attention of a single critic in the party'. The speech had an amusing sequel at the Colonial Office, when Macleod's successor, Maudling, greeted junior ministers and officials at one of his first meetings by commenting. 'I suppose I'm looking at a lot of people who believe in the "brotherhood of man".' Maudling's actions in Northern Rhodesia were to show that his heart was with Macleod.[92]

Of Britain's nineteen African colonies, only two, Sudan and the Gold Coast, had become independent by the time Macleod entered the Colonial Office in October 1959, and only another one, Nigeria, had a date in view. The other sixteen were all thought to have some way to go. But as a result of Macleod's intransigent radicalism, all of them, except Southern Rhodesia, were independent by 1968. Indeed, the five territories in East and Central Africa, which had presented the Government with the most difficult problems, and where Macleod had concentrated most of his efforts and energies, all gained independence within three years of his departure from the Colonial Office – in East Africa, Tanganyika in December 1961 (Tanzania from April 1964), Uganda in December 1962 and Kenya in December 1963. The Central African Federation was finally disbanded in December 1963, and independence was granted to Nyasaland (Malawi) in July 1964 and Northern Rhodesia (Zambia) in October 1964. As William Roger Louis, the historian of African decolonization, has observed: 'Macleod was to Africa as Mountbatten had been to India'.[93]

Was Macleod guilty of pressing ahead too fast, when Britain's colonies were ill-prepared for self-government? Macleod gave his answer to this charge several years after he had left the Colonial Office:

Were the countries fully ready for independence? Of course not. Nor was India and the bloodshed that followed the grant of independence there was incomparably worse than anything that has happened since to any country. Yet the decision of the Attlee Government was the only realistic one. Equally we could not possibly have held by force to our territories in Africa. We could not, with an enormous force engaged, even continue to hold the small island of Cyprus. General de Gaulle could not contain Algeria. The march of men towards their freedom can be guided, but not halted. Of course there were risks in moving quickly. But the risks of moving slower were far greater.[94]

Macleod was acutely conscious of the need to assist the administrative and economic development of the colonies as they moved to independence. He introduced a scheme that enabled many British colonial officials to remain after independence and he secured additional funding for projects to encourage African agriculture, education and other development projects. But he realized that it would be fatal to defer independence on the grounds that the territories were not ready. Any such delay went totally against the grain, because of his calculation of British self-interest; his recognition of the force of the demand – especially in Africa – for liberation from colonial or minority rule; and his moral commitment to people's right to run their own affairs.

He had no illusions about the possible consequences of independence. He argued this point in his Conservative Political Centre Lecture at the party conference in October 1960:

Too often people seem to think we can dictate the course of events after independence. We cannot. Nigeria is now as independent as Canada or Russia or America. Control has not passed from the Colonial to the Commonwealth Relations Office. It has passed from London to Lagos.

His idealism was limited to a wish that Britain could, 'so lead our territories towards their political destiny that we keep them as friends, allies and partners in our great Commonwealth of nations'. But there was no misty-eyed sentimentality about the prospects for the 'Westminster model' of democracy taking root:

We should not be too disturbed if in the early years of independence some countries feel they need a stronger executive than we would find tolerable here. We should not despair if a new country builds its own traditions and makes its own mistakes. We cannot make them for them. Nor should we get too excited if they make disrespectful noises about us or our allies – it doesn't mean they've joined the Communist bloc.[95]

In view of the atrocities and horrors that we have witnessed in too many countries in Africa since Macleod's day, his comments now appear complacent. But he was being utterly realistic. When he became Colonial Secretary, he faced the very real prospect of bloody colonial and racial wars unless political change was accelerated in British East and Central Africa. He judged, correctly, that British public opinion had neither the desire nor the stomach to defy the growing demands from Africans for their independence – even if the wish to hold on to the African Empire had existed, the cost in blood and treasure would have been unacceptably high. Moreover, as Macmillan was acutely aware, Britain was in no position after Suez to risk further antagonizing its American ally, and an illiberal, colonial policy in Africa would have put an intolerable strain on the special relationship.

The failure of Britain's colonial administration to train more Africans and entrust them with responsibility was one of the reasons behind the increasingly insistent demands of nationalist leaders for their countries' independence. By the end of the 1950s, it was too late to try and put right, over another decade or more, what had not been done in earlier years. Any idea that past omissions could have been rectified during the 1960s in a political climate of peace and stability is palpable nonsense. As Macleod perceived, the alternative to rapid political change in Africa was the perpetuation of rule by decree and detention – threatened or actual. It is no accident that after 1960, only the Portuguese dictatorship among Europe's colonial powers was prepared to continue ruling in Africa.

Britain's strategic interests were undergoing an irreversible shift. In July 1961, less than three months before Macleod left the Colonial Office, the Cabinet took the historic decision to apply for membership of the European

Economic Community. Yet Macleod was concerned that Africa's needs should not be neglected after independence. He was to remain passionately committed to the need for overseas aid – public and private; economic, social and technical. In his 'One World' CPC lecture in 1960, he felt certain that if Disraeli had been alive:

> The theme which would inspire his pen would not be the surviving defects in our domestic arrangements, but the challenge of the Two Nations, rich and poor, white and coloured, in the wider world. By raising living standards and by social reform we are succeeding, if we have not actually succeeded in creating One Nation at home. Now we must carry this policy into the Commonwealth and beyond; for there the gap between the industrialized and the under-developed nations confronts accusingly both our conscience and our plain self-interest.

Macleod could not have been expected to foresee quite the extent of the neglect of Africa's needs, neither the crippling lack of coherent development policies by western governments.[96]

The description of Macleod as probably the greatest Colonial Secretary since Joseph Chamberlain, and perhaps the greatest ever, is fully justified. Chamberlain was inspired by the imperial vision and a closer union between Britain and the colonies; Macleod, by majority rule and independence within the Commonwealth. Macleod had the power of intellect and sheer, ruthless determination to bring about African independence more quickly than almost anybody had thought possible when he first became Colonial Secretary. But although he saved Britain from a fearful fate in Africa, he had to pay a price in the Conservative Party for his part in dismantling the Empire ahead of schedule.[97]

11

Defeats, Drift and Scandal

To say that Macleod oozes complacency would be too rude. Rather, a perspiration of firm confidence exudes from every political pore. Whatever ferments may boil up inside, his outward mask is one of coolness. It is this quality which makes him a highly effective debater and the very man to calm a Party conference inclined to panic.

Michael Foot, profile of Macleod, *Daily Herald*, 8 October 1962.

On the up

The notion that Macleod's drastic hastening of African independence and his running battle with the Conservative right had cost him any chance of ever becoming party leader was not generally held at the time. As a result of the Cabinet reshuffle on 9 October 1961, in which he was moved from the Colonial Office to become Chairman of the Party Organization, Chancellor of the Duchy of Lancaster and Leader of the House of Commons, Macleod appeared to have suddenly broken clear of the pack of potential leadership contenders and emerged as the frontrunner to succeed Macmillan. Not only did it seem that he had stolen a march on his contemporaries – Heath, Maudling and Powell – and re-established himself as the leading Tory of his generation, he had also leapfrogged older contenders, notably Rab Butler.

Just one month short of his forty-eighth birthday, Macleod's star was in the ascendant. Walter Terry in the *Daily Mail* described him as 'the Tories' man of the future', and even the *Daily Express*, no fan of Macleod after his demolition of Britain's African Empire, acknowledged that he was 'the potential new heir'. On the left, the *Daily Mirror* dubbed Macleod the 'favourite to succeed Macmillan', while the *Daily Herald* carried a cartoon of him with the caption, 'Supermac Mark II'. Macleod had emerged, according to *The Times*, 'as one of the strongest men in the Government'. The *Economist* referred to Macleod as: 'the next best Prime Minister we've got ... This is still a precarious prophecy to make but, at the very least,

Mr Macleod has been given his chance.' In the *New Statesman*, Anthony Howard's political column was headed 'Mr Macleod's coronation'.[1]

Although Macmillan had wanted to bring Macleod forward, he never intended a 'coronation'. The immediate press reaction to the reshuffle was largely the result of Macleod's success in wringing a significant concession from the Prime Minister. The episode reveals Macleod's ruthlessness, since it was clear that the victim of his demand on Macmillan would be Butler who, since the October 1959 election, had combined the posts of Home Secretary, Chairman of the Party and Leader of the House. However, Macleod was quite undeterred by the humiliation that would be suffered by his mentor and did not let any feeling of loyalty or sense of sympathy moderate his own political ambition. Macmillan had been pondering on Cabinet changes during the 1961 summer recess. In September he told Butler that he felt that he (Butler) was burdened by too many jobs: there was friction between his role as Home Secretary and Party Chairman, and it was a pity that he had to combine the leadership of the House (a post that he had held with some distinction since 1955) with the party chairmanship. Initially the Prime Minister planned to relieve him of only the party chairmanship, a change that Butler welcomed.[2]

Macmillan had decided that he must appoint as Party Chairman somebody with more fire. Macleod seemed the ideal candidate, since he had passion and was the Conservatives' most compelling debater and effective propagandist. Macmillan therefore offered him the party chairmanship, commenting that although there was a risk that 'a lot of colonels will resign' from the party, he did not mind this. The chairmanship would be combined with the chancellorship of the Duchy of Lancaster, a largely nominal government post that would enable Macleod to retain his seat in Cabinet. However, Macleod insisted that, in addition, he should take another of Butler's jobs and become Leader of the House. Macmillan was never likely to defend Butler's interest and preferred to concede Macleod's demand.[3]

Butler later claimed that he, 'had always known that Iain would like to follow me in my political career and so now I thought perhaps I had better be generous'. But his true feelings were revealed when he added that, 'it was much more of a shock for me than anything that had happened before, even my difficulties at the Exchequer'. Somehow Butler managed to reconcile this admission with his comment that: 'while it may have been sensible to give up a little work, I felt that this must be the beginning of what we wanted to see in the end, namely my own success in the Party and Iain following me.' Yet Macleod had dealt Butler a severe blow. 'One important effect of Mr Macmillan's reconstruction of his Ministry is to leave Mr Butler with one hat instead of three and to give Mr Macleod three hats instead of one,' as *The Times* succinctly reported.[4]

Only when his triumph was complete did it seem that Macleod suffered a twinge of guilt. Writing to Butler, he declared that: 'I have been so long

a lieutenant of yours in my political career that I am particularly delighted
to have the chance of carrying on work you have done with such distinction.'
This did nothing to heal Butler's sense of the hurt. 'Rab deeply wounded
about removal from Leadership of House and Chairmanship of Party,'
Selwyn Lloyd, then Chancellor of the Exchequer, noted in his diary. 'Not
a good word to say for Macleod.'[5]

The fact was that Macleod regarded the quickest route as best. In October
1961, he reckoned that his approach had been vindicated. After the reshuffle,
according to Selwyn Lloyd, Macleod was 'much happier than before'. The
Prime Minister had told Macleod on Monday 2nd, a week before the official
announcement, that he would be appointed to all three posts. That evening,
Macleod visited Hugh Fraser's house in Campden Hill Square to break the
news. When Lady Antonia, Fraser's wife, returned from a televised debate,
she found them drinking champagne. She noted their conversation in her
diary:

> *Hugh*: Iain has something to tell you.
> *Iain*: Yes . . . I'm to be Leader of the House. And Chairman of the Party.
> And Chancellor of the Duchy. I've got the lot.
> Tears of emotion sprang into my eyes, and the first thing that sprang into
> my head (which I said) was: 'Oh, I'd give a thousand pounds, I'd give my
> Marks and Spencer shares to see Lord Salisbury's face when he hears the
> news.' This seemed to please Iain.[6]

The following evening, Macleod and Eve unexpectedly called on Nigel
Fisher at his Westminster house in Lord North Street. Celebrating over
more champagne, followed by dinner at Quaglino's, Macleod 'was in a state
of euphoria'. Fisher had 'never seen him happier or more relaxed' as he
asked the band to play all his favourite tunes and sang 'Don't Fence Me In',
the popular hit song of the late 1940s, 'in his croaky voice, with a beaker of
brandy in one hand and a large cigar in the other'.[7]

Yet Macleod's new status was characterized, to adapt a phrase famous
from another context, by responsibility without power. As Party Chairman
and Leader of the House, he had to bear much of the responsibility for
Cabinet decisions because of his leading role in justifying policy and in
ensuring that the Government got their business through the Commons. But
he had very little power in Whitehall. Macleod's subsequent acknow-
ledgement that to be effective in Cabinet, a minister must have a major
department behind him or her, reflects his own experience at this time. As
the Cabinet papers for the period show, from October 1961 he had no locus
in the key decisions that shape government and was effectively marginalized.
Having been accustomed to a large private office and large numbers of
official advisers, he was now seriously understaffed – as Chancellor of the
Duchy of Lancaster, his staff comprised a private secretary, an assistant

private secretary and a shorthand typist, although officials of the House of Commons assisted in his parliamentary duties.[8]

Macleod sought to make the most of his political locus as Party Chairman and the direct line that this gave him to the Prime Minister. But even this asset would diminish towards the end of Macmillan's premiership. Although Macleod's immediate staff comprised only the chairman's personal assistant, Felicity Yonge and a shorthand typist, he now had at his disposal the full resources of Central Office. In addition, as an old boy of the party's research department and longstanding friend of its director, Michael Fraser, he knew that he could depend on it to help him in his key tasks – presentation of policy; providing the political input to the Prime Minister and Cabinet; and servicing the policy work and drafting the next election manifesto. Official papers and party records for the period reveal Macleod's effectiveness in wielding his political influence.

More pertinent is the question whether Macleod had taken on an impossible task in trying to combine his political role as Party Chairman with his wider duties as Leader of the House. Lady Thatcher sees no incompatibility between the two jobs, although as Prime Minister she did not repeat the example set by Macmillan. However, Viscount Whitelaw, who, at different times, has been Party Chairman and Leader of the House, 'never actually believed that the two jobs can be done together' and regards them as 'mutually exclusive'. Macleod's combativeness had helped him wrest the Leadership of the House from Butler, but it was to deny him the same outstanding success in the post that Butler achieved. As Whitelaw recalls, 'Iain was by nature a very belligerent politician, and the result was that, though he was also very keen on parliament, I never thought that it was one of his happiest times'.[9]

Yet the overriding fact was that the political tide had turned against the Conservatives, who were about to suffer their worst two years since returning to office in 1951. That autumn, for the first time since the 1959 election, Labour edged ahead in the opinion polls as Selwyn Lloyd's July 1961 deflationary measures, including an increase in bank rate from 5 to 7 per cent, took effect. The accompanying pay pause, or freeze, began to bite, particularly on workers in the public sector such as nurses. Resorting to 'stop' after years of economic 'go' not only brought unpopularity, but raised serious doubts about the real state of the British economy. Moreover, the Government lacked a new tune for people to hum. Although the Cabinet had made their historic decision at the end of July that Britain should apply for membership of the European Economic Community, it was virtually impossible for them to reap any political benefit before the Commonwealth had been assuaged and the negotiations on British entry successfully concluded. These deeper, economic and political problems were the real cause of Macleod's difficulties in his dual parliamentary and party role.

Macmillan's announcement of his reshuffle at the start of the Tory conference week in Brighton, gave Macleod the opportunity to make an immediate impact as the new Party Chairman. However, so brilliant had been Macleod's valedictory 'brotherhood of man' speech on colonial policy on the first morning, that it quite eclipsed his brief comments as Party Chairman two days later, perhaps ominously on Friday 13th. The principal victim of the reshuffle, Butler, had to face the party faithful in full cry on law and order, 'shorn of two plumes and retaining only the Home Office'. However, the Home Secretary responded with the best conference speech that he ever delivered.[10]

'It was a famous victory,' as Mollie Butler, Rab's wife, recalls: 'It was also the occasion when Iain Macleod came up to me, tears of emotion on his cheeks, and said, "Tell Rab I have never heard him make a better speech".' Recalling the recent headlines of the 'Butler down, Macleod up' variety, Macleod congratulated Rab with the words, 'Rab up again'. But relations between the two men were still strained. When parliament reconvened shortly afterwards, Butler, in a display of pique, refused to vacate the room traditionally allocated to the Leader of the House and situated conveniently near the back of the Speaker's chair. After an awkward few days it became clear that Butler would not budge and a new room had to be found for Macleod.[11]

A wind of change, or at least a breath of fresh air, was suddenly blowing through Smith Square. This impression was, perhaps, never better exemplified than during Macleod's 'animated conversation' with Kenneth Harris in the *Observer* less than two months after he became Party Chairman. Responding to Harold Nicolson's recent statement that he (Nicolson) hated the Conservatives because they were cruel, indifferent and selfish, Macleod professed not to know:

Why people like Nicolson don't realize that if their picture of the Tory Party had any truth in it, it's now hopelessly out of date. I still can't quite get used to it. Every now and again, somebody on the opposite side of the House gets up and starts ranting about what the Tories did to the workers in the thirties or twenties, in a tone that makes some of us on our side of the House – well, our jaws just drop.[12]

The Conservatives were the masters now, but they were not the bosses' party. This was Macleod's message. He argued that the party had changed fundamentally since 1945 and wanted to take this change further. His vision was a new, model Tory Party that was pragmatic and appealed to the centre ground, and that he believed was now emerging:

Those who want to be empirical and rational, see the virtues of avoiding extremes, and want to discuss everything in moderate temper in the hope of coming to common ground, are becoming more and more influential. That's what I mean by a strengthening of the centre.

There was no equivocation in his commitment to a strong State:

As for the Liberals, I don't like their basically *laissez faire* attitude to politics. I am much more of a positivist than any Liberal could ever be: I believe in the State being powerful, and I believe in *using* it as an instrument.

Macleod's rapport was strongest with young Conservatives, for whom he seemed to take on the guise of a pied piper. As David Wood, political correspondent of *The Times*, perceptively observed in 1961, Macleod's promise that the party's new policies for the sixties would be 'relevant and decisive', should be viewed in the light of the growing number of young representatives at Conservative conferences, 'contemporary in attitude, whose stake is not in the past or in privilege, but in the future and in opportunity'.[13]

A couple of weeks after taking up his new post at Central Office, Macleod set the wheels in motion to develop new policies for the 1960s. Seeking Macmillan's approval to 'set up a policy study group almost at once', in keeping with the practice before the 1955 and 1959 elections, he planned 'the same system of first generating thoughts about future policy, then bringing them together in various drafts for the election manifesto, and finally supervising them by a senior committee under the chairmanship of the Prime Minister.' He proposed that the senior, or steering, committee should again be chaired by the Prime Minister, 'assisted by four or five senior ministers with Michael Fraser as Secretary'. Macleod had no intention of relinquishing either his place on the Steering Committee or his chairmanship of the policy study group. Within two months of his appointment, he had set up his policy study group, now formally reconstituted as the Chairman's Committee, 'to chase ideas around in the hope that one in ten will come to something'. At the committee's first meeting on 4 December 1961, he warned (according to the summary in the official minute) that: 'the fact that we had now been in power for over ten years was the main problem we had to face in the presentation of policy . . . Our long period in office made an appearance of novel ideas in our programme vital.' Although he included on his policy committee high-calibre ministers like Sir Edward Boyle and Sir Keith Joseph, he recruited too many cronies and sympathizers. Among those who agreed to serve were the backbenchers, Lionel Heald, the former Defence Minister, Maurice Macmillan, the Prime Minister's son, and Charles Longbottom, who became Macleod's Parliamentary Private Secretary; Nigel Fisher, later a minister at the Colonial Office and friend of Macleod's; Geoffrey Kitchen, the head of Pearl Assurance and, in the event, the only businessman, who also happened to be another friend of Macleod; William Rees-Mogg, the journalist and former Tory candidate, who was close to Rab Butler; and Sir Toby Low (later Lord Aldington), who predated Macleod at Central Office where he served as deputy chairman and who had also been a member of the 'One Nation' group.[14]

Macleod's selection never had the making of a ginger group. He would have to provide the grit in the oyster himself, but this was more difficult than in the past, since he had to contend with his dual responsibilities as Party Chairman and the Leader of the House. Macleod's mornings were dominated by Central Office and ministerial meetings; his afternoons and evenings were often devoted to seeing the Government's business through the Commons; and his Fridays and Saturdays were consumed by party tours and speaking engagements across the country – weekend visits were particularly trying, since he found most people boring and party workers the most boring of all. His daytime burdens probably explain why the Chairman's Committee always met after dinner and never held more business-like office meetings as Macleod had originally intended. Goldman felt that this was one reason why the group was not more effective, but Rees-Mogg recalls being impressed by Macleod's handling and grasp of the subject matter.[15]

No sooner were Macleod's feet under the chairman's desk than he became preoccupied by the Government's mounting difficulties. The large swing to the Liberals in the Oswestry by-election a month after Macleod had taken up the reins at Central Office, was a precursor of the shattering blow that the Liberals were about to inflict on the Macmillan Government. Also in November, the Government's pay pause suffered a serious breach when the Electricity Council made a sizeable pay award, and were subsequently rebuked in the Commons by Macmillan. The Chancellor of the Exchequer, Selwyn Lloyd, received such a grilling when interviewed on BBC Television's *Panorama* that he wrote to Macleod asking whether it was: 'worth my while or the Government's or the Party's for me to make the effort required for these programmes? I should like to know, however uncomplimentary.' Macleod thought the programme 'went very well except, since you asked me to speak frankly, your answer about strikes'. Lloyd had prevaricated when asked whether he was prepared to stand up to nationwide strikes. 'This did give the impression of ducking,' Macleod commented, 'and I feel that a simple answer "Yes" would have had great effect.' Macleod also passed on the suggestion of Sir Toby Low that Lloyd might visit the television studio at Central Office to receive some practice – an idea, the hapless Lloyd agreed, for which 'there is a lot to be said'.[16]

All Macleod's political skills were put to the test during the last two years of Macmillan's premiership, as he fought to sustain the party while facing a fractious parliament and a press that had scented blood. The appointment of Charles Longbottom, the young MP for York, to work with Dr Reggie

Bennett as an additional Parliamentary Private Secretary, further strengthened Macleod's ties with the younger MPs. Macleod was mostly fortunate in his backbench enemies – the more virulent ones like Crosthwaite-Eyre from Wiltshire and Dudley-Williams from Exeter, were not always popular with their colleagues. Many of his enemies also dated from his days as Colonial Secretary and used to return to the Commons each Monday, refuelled with vitriolic comments about Macleod that they heard in their constituencies from embittered, former white settlers who had fled Africa – typically, 'disgusted of Bulawayo' had retreated to the West Country.[17]

It fell to Macleod, as Leader of the House, to give each Thursday evening's 'off the record' briefing of parliamentary lobby correspondents at Westminster. Although he could not prevent the Tory press turning against Macmillan, among the political journalists he was reckoned to have performed this role 'absolutely brilliantly, probably better than any other Tory'. Above all, Macleod was an excellent phrase-maker, who used his wit to great effect. This natural talent delighted the lobby, who would use Macleod's phrases as though they were their own. Writing a year after Macleod's appointment as Leader of the House, Anthony Howard commented in the *New Statesman* that if he (Macleod), 'was in the business [he] would be the greatest political journalist of them all.' Macleod also used to invite a few trusted journalists to his room at the Commons at about six o'clock on a Wednesday evening for a glass of whisky. Among this 'inner circle' were Harry Boyne of the *Daily Telegraph*, David Wood and Ronald Butt of *The Times*, Walter Terry of the *Daily Mail* and Norman St John Stevas of the *Economist*. While Bennett served the drinks, Macleod would relax and chat freely, giving them some of the ideas that were in his mind. In return, he gleaned intelligence about the political scene and Fleet Street.[18]

Macleod's talent was equally respected in the Commons, where Macleod's brilliance in debate is remembered by two of the most effective parliamentary performers on both sides of the House. In Lord Hailsham's recollection: 'Together with Edward Boyle, Iain Macleod was one of the two left-wingers in the party I most admired and differed from most often.' Moreover, Hailsham has acknowledged that:

Iain had the best mastery of the House of Commons on our side. To hear him wind up a debate on the side of the Government was an education in the parliamentary art. He scarcely had a note in front of him, spoke admirably to the point with hardly a word out of place, and held the House in the hollow of his hand with the sheer enchantment of his debating skill.

In Michael Foot's judgement, whereas Churchill had been an orator, Macleod, like Bevan, was a great debater because he would actively try to persuade his audience, meeting the strongest point in the Opposition case and dealing with it. Macleod was, 'capable of changing people's opinions in the course of a debate' and could 'command the interest of people on the other side of the House'. They respected his approach and 'wanted to know what his opinion was on an issue'.[19]

Perhaps the true measure of the respect in which Macleod's debating skills were held was the fear with which he was viewed on the Opposition frontbench. In his first major speech as Leader of the House, winding up the Queen's Speech debate on the economy, Macleod used his wit to telling effect against Harold Wilson, then Shadow Chancellor, who had spoken immediately before him. Referring to Wilson's speech, Macleod commented that:

> It was, as always, witty, cogent and polished – and polished – and polished – [Laughter.] He paid me the great compliment of saying that to this situation and this debate I had brought a fresh mind. I wish that he would bring a fresh speech.

Wilson regarded this gibe as one of the wittiest made against him in the Commons. He shared Barbara Castle's view, first expressed nine years earlier, that Macleod was the Tory whom Labour should fear most. Around the same time as Macleod's twitting of Wilson, a television interviewer asked the Shadow Chancellor after a broadcast if there was anyone whom he would fear as a Conservative prime minister after Macmillan. 'Only one man,' Wilson is said to have replied, 'and they'll never have the sense to choose him – Macleod.'[20]

Macleod was immediately caught in the political spotlight at the start of the 1961–62 session of parliament. But this attention was far from welcome. Ministers had agonized for years about the sizeable increase in coloured immigration (principally of West Indians) since the mid 1950s. In 1961, they finally grasped the nettle. That year's Queen's Speech confirmed the Government's plan to introduce controls on British subjects entering the United Kingdom from other parts of the Commonwealth. Within government, Macleod had been one of the strongest opponents of every previous call for controls and he was the last minister to be persuaded of the need for some such action. His unease was highlighted by Gaitskell in the Commons, on the first afternoon of the new session. Recalling Macleod's 'brotherhood of man speech' less than three weeks earlier, the Leader of the Opposition did 'not question for one moment his sincerity' and believed that Macleod was 'a determined opponent of racial discrimination'. But, Gaitskell added: 'Let me tell the Rt Hon. Gentleman that we shall be watching him very closely on this issue [of immigration control] in the coming weeks and months.'[21]

Macleod's response was remarkable. Speaking at the end of the week-long debate that follows the Queen's Speech, Macleod made no attempt as a senior minister to disguise his deep, personal regret at what was, after all, a central plank in the Government's programme. 'I detest the necessity for it in this country,' Macleod said of the curb on Commonwealth immigration. 'I say that frankly,' he continued, 'but I believe it to be necessary and I believe that when we have examined it carefully it will commend itself to both sides of the House.' As he reminded MPs, he had 'said almost a year ago that administrative methods alone were becoming no good because this country, with its prosperity, was like a magnet.' The alternative of imposing a housing requirement, he argued, 'would mean that the tap would be turned off altogether', since no local authority would lift unknown people from another country to the top of their housing list. As to the charge that the Government were acting in unseemly haste, Macleod countered that 'We have taken years to decide it'.

But it was Macleod's elaboration of his own change of mind that is most revealing. His speech was transformed into a personal statement:

No one has been closer to this problem than myself other than perhaps the Home Secretary [Butler]. I have seen this when I was Minister of Labour grow from something about which no figures and no problem existed into a problem that flared into the headlines with race riots in this country, of all countries, and I have seen it when I was Colonial Secretary. I came to the conclusion in the spring of this year, looking at those figures, that it was no longer possible to avoid such legislation.

In fact, Macleod cited no figures to the Commons, but the following week told the Tory backbench 1922 Committee that (according to a report of the meeting), 'if steps had not been taken now there might have been 250,000 immigrants next year'. Again, Macleod's defence of the new curbs is redolent of an older, liberal Toryism, that took such action more in sorrow than anger. 'The Bill was a profound departure from the path which the Government would have wished to follow,' Macleod told Tory MPs, 'and had only been introduced with the greatest reluctance because it was our plain duty to do so.'[22]

Securing the passage of the bill through the Commons became Macleod's major concern for the next three months. The day after his muted defence of the legislation in the Commons, he told MPs that the second reading debate would occupy only one day and, since he was advised that it was not a constitutional bill, the committee stage would be taken 'upstairs' and not on the floor of the House. Macleod's understanding of a constitutional bill was questioned by the Tory backbencher, Sir Kenneth Pickthorn. In reply, Macleod commented that he was 'diffident about disagreeing with someone who had tried to teach me at Cambridge the rudiments of constitutional history'. 'And jolly bad you were,' Pickthorn retorted. It was small comfort for Macleod that, as he later revealed, Sir Kenneth had waited for him behind the Speaker's chair as Macleod left the chamber, and confessed: 'I'm sorry I said that, I didn't mean it.'[23]

Under intense pressure from Gaitskell and many Labour MPs to allow the committee stage to be debated on the floor of the House, Macleod undertook to check the advice he had received. He quickly reversed his earlier decision. *The Times* praised Macleod's *volte-face*, commenting that whatever the technicalities, the bill was clearly a constitutional one in spirit, since it struck 'at the very roots of British tradition and Commonwealth ties'.[24]

On the bill's second reading, Macleod's discomfort grew when Nigel Fisher, his close friend, spoke against the bill, concluding his speech with a wounding rebuke: 'I believe my Rt Hon Friend was absolutely sincere in his Brighton speech when he talked of the brotherhood of man. I believe in it too, and it is because I believe in it that I cannot vote for this bill tonight.' As Fisher later recalled, they were 'hard words from a friend and I regretted them in retrospect'. At a party the following evening, Macleod congratulated Fisher on his speech, 'with much of which he had agreed, and only remonstrated gently about my peroration which, he pointed out, had added strength to Gaitskell's criticism'.[25]

In December, Macleod announced his intention to introduce a time limit, or 'guillotine', on both the Commonwealth Immigrants Bill and another Government measure, the Army Reserve Bill. Predictably, he was roundly condemned from all sides. For the Opposition, George Brown described Macleod as a contemptuous Leader of the House, and claimed that in sixteen years he had never known a Leader treat the Commons so badly. 'Cross-bencher' in the *Sunday Express* reported that Macleod's leadership of the House was regarded as feeble by Tory MPs and a couple of weeks later claimed that: 'few reputations have plunged so swiftly as that of Macleod.' Although *The Times* did not mention him by name, its editorial of 21 December reckoned that the first couple of months of the new session had gone badly for the Government, which had created the impression of a weakness of judgment and assurance. But Macleod found an unexpected defender in Jo Grimond, the Liberal leader, who argued that the blame lay with the Government in general and that it was: 'quite unfair to blame him [Macleod] for all that has gone wrong'.[26]

By the new year, Macleod found a surer touch. On 25 January 1962, two days after parliament returned from the Christmas recess, Macleod moved the guillotine motion on the Commonwealth Immigrants Bill. 'It was a day notable mainly for Mr Macleod's deft handling,' reported the parliamentary correspondent of *The Times*:

He scored gently, but well, on one occasion and later deserved some appreciative laughter as he recalled his own reasons for rejecting a course which would have seemed 'too clever by half'. Mr Macleod was observed at one point to be laughing – a rare sight which may signify a new relaxation in the Leader of the House.

In February the bill completed all its stages in the Commons and was sent to the Lords. By April, it was on the statute book.[27]

A sequel to the controversial debates of 1961–62 occurred on the eve of the 1964 election. In the column that he was writing by that time in the *Spectator*, Macleod noted that: 'One of the first issues in the general election turns out to be whether coloured immigrants should be an issue at all.' Regretting the 'unpleasant' reports from Midland and London constituencies, he recognized nonetheless that it was 'unreal to pretend that there are not constituencies where this must force itself as an issue,' and recalled:

> In my first speech to the House of Commons as Leader, I said that I detested the necessity for the Bill which is now an Act. For this, Mr Butler and myself were denounced as hypocrites by Hugh Gaitskell to wild acclaim from the Opposition benches. The Bill was opposed so fiercely that a guillotine motion became inevitable. Now 90 per cent of Socialist candidates would 'detest the necessity for this Bill.' A few would not even be prepared to do this, and the remaining few who cling against all the evidence to an open-door policy have fallen silent as the election comes near. Who were the hypocrites?

Macleod evidently found the charge of hyprocrisy levelled against him almost three years earlier deeply wounding. The memory still rankled.[28]

Raising Old Ghosts

In his new post as Party Chairman, Macleod might have taken encouragement for his career prospects from the example of a politician who, at first sight, appears an unlikely model – Neville Chamberlain. Just over thirty years earlier, Chamberlain had been Party Chairman and later went on to become Chancellor of the Exchequer and Prime Minister. Macleod, shortly after his own appointment as Party Chairman, published a biography of Chamberlain. Yet the Prime Minister's papers for 1961 reveal that its publication caused consternation in Whitehall and provoked irritation among the anti-Chamberlainites who had largely run the Tory Party since the old appeaser's death in the autumn of 1940.

Macleod and Chamberlain were united by a common bond that made them exceptional among Conservatives. Both men had an abiding interest in, and specialist knowledge of, social policy. As Macleod explained in the preface of his book, when he entered politics after the Second World War he had found himself:

> constantly taking up work which Chamberlain had pioneered. He had been the founder and inspiration of the Conservative Research Department where, under R. A. Butler and David Clarke, I worked from 1946

to the end of 1949. I was, as Chamberlain had been, Minister of Health for a long time. I was concerned as Minister of Labour with the ending of National Service, he in the First World War had been its first Director.

But Macleod's curiosity was excited by more than his treading some of the same paths: 'From the study I made of earlier social legislation I began to form of this man I never knew a mental picture that seemed so utterly different from the public image which all but his friends seemed to accept.'[29]

Macleod was only able to write the first half of the book, covering the years to 1931, including Chamberlain's great, reformist period as Minister of Health and his stint as Party Chairman. The remainder had to be completed by Peter Goldman, whose help with planning and research and 'historical sense and political judgment' are acknowledged by Macleod. Despite the trouble Macleod had had in completing his book, in February 1961, nine months before its publication, he accepted a commission from Weidenfeld and Nicolson to write another, *The Last Rung*, comprising bibliographical essays of politicians who never became Prime Minister. Peter Goldman again helped, but Macleod stood no chance of meeting the delivery date of September 1962. Although the deadline was waived, Macleod only ever completed three chapters on Austen Chamberlain, Lord Curzon and Lord Halifax and some time later told Fisher that the last chapter might be an appreciation of Rab Butler.[30]

It was the second half of Macleod's biography – the section mainly penned by Goldman – that attracted most interest. Macleod and Goldman offered a sympathetic assessment of Chamberlain's foreign policy, challenging what was then the almost universally-held view of him as the 'guilty man' of appeasement. This revisionist interpretation was ahead of its time, and Macleod (his was the only name on the title page) was caricatured in the press as a 'man of Munich'. Even before publication, alarm bells were set ringing in the Cabinet Office, because Macleod's use of Chamberlain's private papers threatened to reveal details of government decisions made little more than 20 years earlier – at this time, Cabinet papers and other government documents were not released publicly for 50 years, although even under the subsequent 30-year rule Macleod's disclosures would have been in breach. Sir Norman Brook, the Cabinet Secretary, vetted the text and alerted the Prime Minister to Macleod's revelation that the Cabinet had had a greater part to play in the abdication than previously thought. 'There are good reasons why the cabinet's role in this should not be further emphasized at any rate while the Duke of Windsor is alive.' Neither did Brook want it disclosed that senior civil servants (Horace Wilson and Warren Fisher) had drafted a formal document advising the King 'to reorder his private life'. Instead, the book should say that it had been drafted by Chamberlain. Macleod duly amended his text.[31]

Brook also thought that Macleod should let the Earl of Avon (formerly

Sir Anthony Eden) see what he had written about his resignation as Foreign Secretary in 1938. Avon was deeply upset that (in the words of Brook's minute) 'this apologia for Chamberlain's policy should be published by a minister in office'. In Avon's view, 'the mere fact that Mr Macleod was a member of the Government now in office – even more that he was now the Chairman of the Conservative Party would cause a good many people to think that the book had some sort of official authority.' Avon was concerned that it should be made clear 'by some means' at the time of publication that Macleod had written the book in a private capacity, since (as Brook paraphrased the former prime minister's argument): 'Munich was still an issue which would divide the Conservative Party. And the timing of publication, in the midst of the Berlin crisis [the Berlin Wall had been erected in August 1961] was particularly unfortunate.'[32]

Brook assured Avon that he saw 'no great difficulty' in ensuring that something on the lines of his suggested disclaimer should appear in the press, 'if only in the gossip columns, at the time the book was published'. Macmillan, whose rebelliousness against the Tory leadership over appeasement was unrivalled, readily accepted Avon's proposal. The Number Ten press secretary, Harold Evans, was duly told to let it be known that the book was not official. Macmillan also accepted Brook's advice that Evans should say that Macleod had begun work on the book a long time ago.[33]

'It was a bad book,' Macleod later confessed to Alan Watkins, 'I made a great mistake in writing it. It made me no money, and it has done me a lot of harm.' Michael Foot, himself a politician and writer, judges that 'it was a great shame' that Macleod wrote the biography. However, Macleod's insight as a politician is valuable, and as the Cabinet Secretary appreciated, Macleod had provided revelations. Macleod sought no refuge in Watkins's view that the book 'had been grudgingly and meanly reviewed', and blamed only himself. His claim that it had done him 'a lot of harm' seemed melodramatic, since it was largely forgotten rather than being held against him. But had Macleod, perhaps, been referring to a more secret wound? He had infuriated one old, anti-Chamberlainite, Avon. Was Macleod also aware, perhaps, that another, Macmillan, who always remained acutely conscious of whether other Tories were *Munichois* or *anti-Munichois*, might now have further reason to cool towards him in addition to his disruptive rows with Sandys over Northern Rhodesia? The answer to this question may never be known, but Butler's unabashed championing of appeasement as the senior Foreign Office minister in the Commons after Eden's resignation had always seemed to count against him in Macmillan's mind.[34]

Orpington and the 'night of the long knives'

The Conservatives faced a severe test in the series of by-elections during March and April 1962. They fared badly at Blackpool and Lincoln, in the former only narrowly retaining the seat against a Liberal challenge. At Middlesbrough East, Labour won as expected but the Liberals moved into second place. But by far the most significant result came in Orpington, on the south-eastern outskirts of London and next door to Macmillan's own constituency of Bromley. Although the Conservatives faced the prospect of a sizeable fall in their majority, there had seemed no special danger for their candidate, Peter Goldman, who was confidently expected to crown more than a decade of backroom policy work with a parliamentary and ministerial career. But on 14 March 1962, the voters of Orpington delivered a seismic shock to Macmillan's Government, when a 15,000 Conservative majority was overturned and replaced by an 8,000 majority for the Liberal candidate, Eric Lubbock (the future Lord Avebury). The day after, both the Prime Minister and the Party Chairman addressed the annual meeting of the Conservative Central Council, comprising senior constituency office-holders, in what *The Times* described as 'the spirit of Verdun'. Such was the scale of the turn-round, that the phenomenon known as 'Orpington Man' was invented as a personification of the revolt against the Conservatives. As explanations were sought for Orpington Man's motivation, there were mutterings that Goldman's being a Jew had not helped and that Lubbock, who had briefly served in the Welsh Guards, looked more like the Conservative candidate. Macleod implicitly rejected any such suggestion just a few days after the by-election, on Monday 19 March, when his Chairman's Committee met over dinner at the Commons. Goldman was present, having immediately resumed his policy work, and Macleod opened the proceedings by saying how keenly he felt for him – his only consolation was that nobody could possibly have done better.[35]

But what had motivated 'Orpington Man'? At the end of the Chairman's Committee meeting, Goldman spoke of the 'disgruntled true-blues' who typically complained that the Government were not tough enough on the trade unions, but were too tough on Sir Roy Welensky; that there was no lead from the Government; and that Selwyn Lloyd was not an economist – the middle income group, earning from £800 to £1200 a year, who were buying their own houses and who commuted to the metropolis, were feeling hard pushed financially. Some sense of the unease in the party surfaced when Boyle and Enoch Powell, who had been guest speaker at the Chairman's Committee, both argued that the Government should stick to their tough line on incomes. Joseph wondered if now was not the time, while the Government were already so unpopular, to introduce other tough measures (for example, by pushing up commuter fares closer to their real cost), but Macleod warned that to do so would 'start a slide against you that you will never recover'.[36]

Two days later, Macleod was made aware of how far the 'slide' had already gone against the Conservatives. As he minuted the Prime Minister, he had 'just heard privately that the *Daily Mail* public opinion poll took an immediate nationwide poll after the Orpington result and came up with the following figures: Liberal 35.9 per cent, Labour 30.5, Conservative 27.4, Don't Know 6.2. This result was 'so startling that the *Daily Mail* have decided not to publish it', although they planned to take a further check at the weekend and would probably publish that result. On 28 March, NOP's national survey gave the Liberals 33.7 per cent, Labour 33.5, Conservatives 32.8.[37]

The state of shock felt in the party was made all too clear to Macleod when, the week following Orpington, he appeared before the Thursday evening meeting of the Conservative backbenchers' 1922 Committee. Facing a barrage of hostile complaints from anguished MPs, many of whom suddenly felt that their seats were not as safe as they had imagined, Macleod informed them that he had immediately commissioned a private opinion survey of Orpington – a similar survey had been tried after the Rochdale by-election in 1958. But he thought that the situation was more serious than five years earlier and reminded them of some of the advantages that the Conservatives had enjoyed during 1957–58, especially the London bus strike – it was clever of Macleod to remind Tory MPs of one of his great triumphs that had helped spark the revival in Conservative fortunes before 1959. He had little doubt about the root cause of the Government's unpopularity – the pay pause outweighed all other subjects by nine to one in his post-Orpington postbag. He did not blame presentation, since policies which were fundamentally unpopular could not be presented popularly. His frankness was characteristic, but as Party Chairman he was wise to guard his own back. Instead, he argued that the pay pause was wholly right; but it was unfortunate that the Orpington and Enfield type of constituency was worst hit by it. Recognizing a feeling that the very rich and the unions could opt out, while the middle classes had been sacrificed, Macleod conceded that, frankly, this had been the case – the man earning £1,000 a year, who had no political allegiance, was no longer voting Conservative. By way of giving backbenchers an upbeat message, he reckoned that the policies were beginning to show success, helped by that day's cut in the bank rate. Although there would be rougher water ahead, he reportedly had a 'fierce faith in the mission of the Tory Party', and believed they would come through.[38]

Not all Conservative MPs were convinced. On 30 March, the Chief Whip, Redmayne, minuted the Prime Minister that he had stopped Sir Cyril Osborne, the right-wing MP, from publicly attacking the whole party structure by promising him a private word with Macmillan. Osborne had wanted Macleod to be replaced as Party Chairman by 'another Woolton figure', who could 'inspire and revitalise the party'. But he also went further and told Redmayne that half the Cabinet should be removed and replaced by younger men. As events turned out, Osborne's apparent over-reaction was not all that wide of the mark, although Macleod's own position was safe.[39]

Macleod's assessment of the Orpington débâcle was confirmed in late March when he received NOP's detailed constituency survey. 'One thing that emerges with absolute clarity,' he wrote:

Is that the popular reasons [for Orpington], such as pensions, Schedule A, nuclear disarmament and colonial policy, had nothing whatever to do with the result. Incomparably the leading factor was the dislike of the pay policy and general dislike of the Government which I suspect more than anything else is also connected with this.

Moreover, with Selwyn Lloyd's 1962 budget only four days away, Macleod advised Macmillan that:

A great deal will hang both on the Budget itself and on the words that the Chancellor uses when he speaks. As far as the first is concerned, we must begin, I think, to show the light at the end of the tunnel; and as far as the second is concerned, it is essential to emphasize that what we really wish to see is a policy of growth and that our efforts will be directed towards this.[40]

Despite Macleod's advice to the Prime Minister, the April 1962 budget was a missed opportunity. The unimaginative and uninspiring Selwyn Lloyd failed to provide any economic stimulus. Even his promise to abolish Schedule 'A' tax at some future date – his one sop to disillusioned Conservative supporters – was only inserted after the pre-budget Cabinet as a concession to critics, of whom Macleod was one. In fact, this was the second year running that a revolt at the pre-budget Cabinet had forced Selwyn Lloyd to revise his plans, since in 1961, Macleod, Maudling and Heath had forced the last-minute inclusion of the promise to introduce a tax on short-term gains realized within six months. As to the 1962 budget judgment, Samuel Brittan commented a couple of years later that it 'has ever since been regarded inside the Treasury with embarrassment'. It quickly became clear that the real problem was not excessive public spending, as Selwyn Lloyd argued in his budget speech, but the onset of a deflationary cycle and higher unemployment.[41]

There was an amusing sequel to Brittan's further revelation that during the months after the 1962 budget: 'a number of Ministers wrote personal papers for the Cabinet voicing concern about a possible recession and attacked the Treasury's complacency' – among them Macleod. 'This made me blink,' Macleod commented when Brittan's book first appeared, 'and would, I imagine, put Lord Normanbrook [formerly Sir Norman Brook, the Cabinet Secretary] in grave danger of spontaneous combustion.' Adding that, 'it would be injudicious to comment on whether Mr Brittan is right or wrong,' Macleod quipped, 'Sam, Sam, who told tha? And answer, I suspect, comes there none.' The official documents for 1962 subsequently released under the 30-year rule, show that Macleod did indeed submit personal papers to the Prime Minister expressing his concern and criticizing economic policy.[42]

At the end of April 1962, Macleod was suddenly presented with an opportunity to renew his call for an urgent change of direction on the economy. On the 25th, the Prime Minister left for a visit to the United States, but before doing so minuted Butler that the Cabinet on Thursday 3 May should be devoted to the economic and political situation, with further time reserved for the discussion to continue on Friday 4th. Macmillan copied his minute to Selwyn Lloyd and Macleod. Here were the first straws in the wind of a change in policy. Macleod did not delay in seizing the moment, sending the Prime Minister a 'personal and confidential' minute, to which he attached a ten-page note that analysed the results of the seven by-elections held during the previous two months and showed that: 'Our average loss of the Conservative percentage of the vote was 20.5 per cent'. 'This position has not been altered very much by the Budget,' Macleod warned. Although he noted that 'most Budgets suffer a loss of appeal in the country after a few weeks and not infrequently command more support as time goes on', and thought that this might be the case in 1962, he was to all intents and purposes sounding the death-knell for Selwyn Lloyd's chancellorship. Both the post-Orpington NOP survey and his postbag as Party Chairman made clear that:

> Economic policy is probably more important than all other subjects put together. Our supporters feel that our policy is one of restraint when they are in fact in a mood, rightly or wrongly, for expansionist policies. They feel that even if the policy is right it has not been put over, and they feel that for some people, particularly the nurses, it is plainly unfair. For myself, I believe that the issue of nurses' pay has done us an immense amount of harm. It is really very difficult to project the image that 'Conservatives Care' in the face of this.

Macleod's skilful drafting was designed to hit all the right notes with Macmillan, the arch-expansionist and 'Middle Way' Tory, and persuade him to reassess his Chancellor's approach.[43]

Macleod was 'sure that we must try to get off the hook as far as nurses and perhaps university teachers are concerned', and thought that 'we could start now to steer the first claim towards arbitration, which is almost sure to come in the end and which will result in a much higher award than the offer that we have made'. Secondly, 'if we are to begin, however tentatively, to reinflate . . . one of the best dividends from every point of view would be to do something, which need not be spectacular, in relation to the educational Minor Works programme'. He did not doubt that the Conservatives could seize back the initiative, but: 'The danger is that that we may wait too long before we begin to recover.' The pay pause had ended on 1 April and been replaced by a voluntary 2½ per cent 'norm'. Macleod acknowledged that, 'Restraint must of course remain', but he reiterated that 'it must be the springboard to growth and this is where our emphasis over the next few months must be placed'.[44]

In early May, Butler, who had seen Macleod's minute, suggested to Macmillan that when the Cabinet discussed the economic and political situation, Macleod 'will be able to follow on the Chancellor and make the debate lively'. In their discussion ministers agreed on the need for an incomes policy as a permanent feature of policy, but were equally concerned about the political damage pay control had done to the Government and felt that steps had to be taken to remedy the injustices. The following day, Macleod illustrated for the Prime Minister the political damage caused by the pay pause, sending him a copy of a recent editorial from the journal of NALGO, the local government white-collar trade union. The journal's leader referred to the revolt of white-collar workers at Orpington and cited figures purporting to show that since 1946, NALGO workers' earnings had increased by less than half those of manual workers and had failed to compensate for the rise in prices. 'I am sure,' Macleod commented, 'that the greater majority of our troubles stem from this.' Selwyn Lloyd's performance over the following weeks only confirmed Macleod's call for urgent action. Macmillan was increasingly exasperated by his Chancellor's failure to propose new initiatives or to explain and sell the Government's incomes policy.[45]

On 28 May, Macmillan delivered to the Cabinet what can best be described as a lengthy treatise on the growing complexities of government in Britain's changing political economy. Macmillan saw a permanent form of incomes policy as the key to maintaining the four objectives of postwar economic policy – full employment, stable prices, a strong pound and sustained economic growth – but he had taken heed of the anxieties felt by Macleod at the political damage of pay controls and felt that a package of accompanying measures (a 'new approach') would be needed to sugar the pill and win the necessary public support. Ominously for the cautious Selwyn Lloyd, Macmillan observed that 'in politics you must take some risks, and I hope the Chancellor of the Exchequer will not think me too ambitious'. The Prime Minister then echoed Macleod's argument that the proposed package 'must include not only the promise that growth will come, but some expansionist measures now'.[46]

The rug was being pulled from beneath Selwyn Lloyd's feet, but still the Chancellor did nothing about it. At by-elections in early June in two Conservative held seats, both with majorities above 8,000, the Conservatives barely held West Derbyshire and lost Middlesbrough West. On Sunday 17th, Macmillan discussed economic policy and his plans for a National

Incomes Commission as part of a permanent form of incomes policy with three dinner companions – Macleod, Selwyn Lloyd (who had been able to use Chequers as though it was his country home since his divorce in 1957) and Michael Fraser, Director of the Conservative Research Department (later Lord Fraser of Kilmorack). Selwyn Lloyd had seemed tired over dinner, but afterwards, as the four men sat chatting, he suddenly proclaimed from the depths of an arm chair, 'Floreat Fettesia!' The Prime Minister had not the faintest clue what his Chancellor was talking about and it took some time before he grasped that his three companions were all Old Fettesians. When, at last, the penny dropped, Macmillan merely grunted. The weekend was to be one of Selwyn Lloyd's last at Chequers.[47]

Under renewed political pressure, the Prime Minister grew impatient at having to do his Chancellor's thinking for him. He was angered following the discussions in Cabinet on 20 and 22 June when Selwyn Lloyd gave a chilly response to Macmillan's own proposals for relating the rise in personal incomes to the increase in national wealth. Between the two Cabinets, on 21 June, Macmillan discussed his Chancellor's future with Rab Butler, and later that day pre-empted Selwyn Lloyd in a speech at Luton Hoo in which he indicated that a new approach was afoot on economic policy. Macleod had been asked to comment on an earlier draft of the speech and had written to the Prime Minister that 'although it doesn't let the cat out of the bag, [it] does show clearly that there is a cat in the bag'. In Macleod's view, this was 'all to the good and I am all for it'.[48]

By Friday 6 July, Macmillan and Butler were considering Maudling's qualifications to replace Selwyn Lloyd some time in August. On Monday 9th, Macleod received the party's forecast that the Conservatives would probably lose their deposit and come third at the by-election in the marginal seat of Leicester North East, where polling would take place three days later. Only the previous week Macleod had predicted a two-horse race, but it was now clear that the Liberals would be runners-up to Labour. On Tuesday 10th, Butler and Macleod saw Macmillan to press the argument for reflation. The following day Macleod reiterated his arguments in his 'personal and confidential' letter to the Prime Minister. Warning of 'a bad result, even though Leicester is one of the most prosperous cities in Europe', Macleod predicted that the recent 'pattern of discontent' would force the Conservatives into third place, and surmised gloomily that 'perhaps this result is more disturbing even than the previous ones'. His conclusion proved to be political dynamite. 'I recognize that we are in a period in which it is extremely difficult to produce positive policies,' he wrote, 'but I feel I should urge upon you, as Chairman of the Party, that if you are contemplating making changes in the Government, that these should be made *before we rise for the Recess* [author's emphasis].' Tim Bligh, one of Macmillan's private secretaries, replied: 'The Prime Minister was grateful for your letter of July 11 about Leicester North East, and *the need for the Government to be seen to be doing something* [author's emphasis]'. Within forty-eight hours, Macmillan executed the biggest reshuffle in modern British history, sacking a third of his Cabinet.[49]

Macleod did not expect the Prime Minister to act for another week or so. Even then, he thought that only the Chancellor was likely to be moved, with any other changes announced later. But on the same day that Macleod had written to Macmillan, Butler had lunched with Lord Rothermere and leading executives of the *Daily Mail*. The next morning, Thursday 12 July (polling day in Leicester), the paper carried a front page scoop by its political correspondent, Walter Terry, headlined 'MAC'S MASTER PLAN', predicting an autumn reshuffle. Terry suggested that Selwyn Lloyd, Butler and Macleod would be involved in the changes, and that the Chancellor might be elevated to the House of Lords as Lord Chancellor.[50]

Macmillan was appalled. In what his biographer judges to have been 'a loss of nerve', the Prime Minister decided that he had to act immediately. He had planned to warn Selwyn Lloyd that evening (12 July) of his imminent replacement at the Treasury and, in keeping with Macleod's advice, to announce the change the following week. Instead, he dismissed Selwyn Lloyd peremptorily, although he delayed any public announcement. The deposed Chancellor spent the rest of the evening at the Commons, pouring out his heart to backbench and ministerial friends. In no time, the news of his imminent sacking was circulating round Westminster and Fleet Street.[51]

The next morning, Friday 13th, Macmillan was alarmed to hear that Selwyn Lloyd had suggested to John Hare, the Minister of Labour, that he ought to resign in sympathy and was fearful of a weekend of speculation in the press. The Prime Minister reacted with indecent haste. His proposed August reshuffle was brought forward and completed within a matter of hours. Out from the Cabinet along with Selwyn Lloyd went Eccles (Education), Hill (Housing and Local Government), Kilmuir (Lord Chancellor), Maclay (Scotland), Mills (Minister without Portfolio) and Watkinson (Defence). The main beneficiary was Maudling, who became the new Chancellor at the age of 45, three years younger than Macleod.

The two ministers who had done most to bring about a change at the Treasury, Butler and Macleod, had not benefited personally from the changes. Although Butler was awarded the title of First Secretary of State and unofficial status as Deputy Prime Minister, he was replaced at the Home Office by Henry Brooke, and given the task of handling the insurmountable problem of the Central African Federation. Macleod might have replaced Selwyn Lloyd, but instead Macmillan kept him where he was. The choice of Maudling as Chancellor had some advantages for Macleod, since they were both Keynesians and shared a commitment to full employment. Despite their rivalry, Macleod respected Maudling's first-class economist's brain and, on a personal level, they remained friends. Nonetheless, Maudling's appointment represented a setback for Macleod. Hitherto, he had led the field among his generation of Conservatives and had long been regarded as the most likely future leader. Now he had been leapfrogged. Maudling had become the first Conservative from the 1950 intake to head one of the great offices of state. Having urged Macmillan to take decisive action, Macleod had seen the Prime Minister bring forward another leadership contender, and mishandle virtually every aspect of the reshuffle. While Maudling had scooped the pool, Macleod was condemned to continue carrying the can for any further party disasters.

But were Macleod's prospects really so bleak? One man who did not think so was Michael Foot, who profiled Macleod for the *Daily Herald* almost three months after the 'July massacre', on the eve of the Conservative conference. 'If by some national misfortune,' wrote the left-wing Labour MP, 'the Tories win the next election, the man who will stand very near the top, ready and willing to step into the top place of all, will be Iain Macleod.' As Foot argued:

> Macleod emerged from Macmillan's blood-letting last July with his head still on his shoulders. Macmillan cannot afford another Night of the Long Knives. Next time it would have to be suicide, not murder. So Macleod is safe in his job. If, under his chairmanship, the Tories can scramble from their present doldrums to victory, he will be their hero.

For a while, during the early autumn of 1962, the prospects of a fourth, successive Conservative election victory did not seem entirely fanciful.[52]

Fighting to Revive the Party

How could Macleod, as Party Chairman, knock the party into shape and rally the Conservatives before the next general election, which would probably be held between October 1963 (only fifteen months away) and October 1964? Outwardly, Macleod displayed the utmost confidence in the Conservative Party organization. It was the envy of Labour and Liberal politicians. 'Their machine is superbly efficient and well-oiled,' wrote Michael Foot in October 1962. 'Macleod almost strokes the bonnet like a man who has just acquired a brand new model of a car which has always served him flawlessly in the past.' Yet Macleod knew that there were problems with the engine. While acting the proud owner, he had begun making urgent repairs and seeing whether he needed to order new parts.[53]

As the disastrous run of by-election results during the spring and summer of 1962 had demonstrated, more needed to be done to prevent the Liberals gaining a toe-hold at the constituency level. Macleod had informed the Prime Minister on 2 April that he intended to raise the need to involve young people at the local ward level when he had dinner that week with the National Union's Area Chairmen. He finally wrote to constituency chairman the week following Macmillan's 'July massacre', suggesting that they should replace association and ward officers if they had held their positions for too long. It was insensitive timing when Conservatives were reeling from the shock of Macmillan's bungled reshuffle. Moreover, the voluntary wing of the party (the National Union, to which constituency associations were affiliated) jealously guarded their independence from the professional organ- ization in Conservative Central Office – Macleod was Chairman of the Party Organization, not of the National Union. His letter was bound to cause protests, even though the 1945 model rules for local associations stated that nobody should hold the same office for more than three years. Macleod was attacked for 'ineptitude' and the matter was raised at the 1922 Committee, although critics made little headway as other MPs backed him. Following his letter, the rule governing the re-election of local party officers was followed more closely.[54]

In the summer of 1962 the National Union recognized in their own report that the parliamentary, professional and voluntary wings of the party were not working as closely together as they should. Their recommendation that a committee should be appointed, on the lines of the Maxwell Fyfe committee of the late 1940s, whose report had transformed the party into a modern, election-winning machine, provided Macleod with the opportunity to launch a thorough review of the party's structure. However, he was disinclined to appoint yet another committee, and on 24 September sent a minute to Macmillan suggesting that the task should be undertaken by one man, and that his choice was Selwyn Lloyd.[55]

Macmillan agreed, and on the 28th, Macleod invited the former Chancel- lor to undertake the review. 'I have a feeling,' Macleod wrote, 'that this sort of job, which requires very close knowledge of the Conservative party, can best be done by one man rather than a Committee, and I really believe that nobody could do it better than you.' Macleod's choice of the man whom he had done more than almost anybody else to remove from the Chancellorship was shrewd. Selwyn Lloyd was a senior figure, widely respected throughout the party, for whom there was great sympathy after the events of July. Macleod's invitation also offered him the opportunity to begin his rehabili- tation. Macleod's presentation and timing of this initiative cannot be faulted. In October 1962, the party conference welcomed Macleod's announcement that Selwyn Lloyd would take charge of the new inquiry.[56]

The Selwyn Lloyd Report was published in June 1963, with a summary of recommendations that ran to four pages. Selwyn Lloyd had kept Macleod closely informed as he visited every area in England and Wales and met about 3,000 local party leaders during the fiercesome winter of 1962–63. Although the inquiry was not such an important milestone in the party's history as Maxwell Fyfe's had been, it made a major contribution to future

Conservative election successes, by recommending improved remuneration for party agents and in stressing the urgent need to focus greater effort on marginal seats. Among the Report's more significant, forward-looking proposals were the setting up of a separate Conservative trade union group, the appointment of a third party vice-chairman to be concerned solely with local government, more advertising and more training in the techniques of television presentation (perhaps Selwyn Lloyd recalled the television training session that Macleod offered him in December 1961).[57]

Good organization is crucial to winning elections, but it is only half the battle. Macleod realized more than almost any other Conservative politician that if the party were to win a fourth successive victory, they needed to show that they understood people's concerns in the 1960s and could offer a vision of the better society that Conservatives would create. While the Conservatives were taking a heavy beating in by-elections, council elections, and in opinion polls during the first half of 1962, behind the scenes Macleod began his policy review. By February 1962, when the Chairman's Committee began reviewing the position, various policy committees (under the auspices of the party's Advisory Committee on Policy) were already at work on an array of subjects, although few were concerned with social policy. Macleod had made his career by plugging the gap in the party's knowledge of social policy and between March and June 1962 he put the subject at the top of his Chairman's Committee's ag enda. Neither was it any surprise that Macleod should begin by inviting Enoch Powell, then Minister of Health, to discuss his ideas with the Committee. As Macleod recalled, his immediate predecessor, Crookshank, had been in the Cabinet, but he had not and ten years later neither was Powell. In Macleod's view, this omission had harmed successive Conservative Governments. If it was necessary to have long-term plans for health and welfare services, he wondered, why not appoint a Minister for Health and Welfare Services (including water) to the Cabinet? Reorganization of the ministries responsible for health and social services had been considered before the 1959 election, but had been rejected on the advice of Norman Brook, the Cabinet Secretary. In July 1962, Powell was promoted as Minister of Health to the Cabinet. The changes that had been largely presaged by Macleod were not introduced until November 1968, when the Wilson Government created the Department of Health and Social Security, headed by a Secretary of State in the Cabinet.[58]

Just as Macleod, when he had been Minister of Health, had dismissed any idea of a radical shake-up in the National Health Service, so did Powell. In his judgment, the structure of the NHS was not in any way ripe for reconsideration, neither did he see the time when it would be: the only option for the time being was to pursue a business-like improvement of its efficiency, and tighten up and strengthen its organization and structure. His front-runner for a new policy was replacing the existing system of state retirement pensions (based on national insurance and national assistance payments), by a guaranteed minimum income for the old. The new scheme would involve a means test, but the purchasing power of the very old would be increased. Although Macleod was wary of the political difficulties of means testing, and Boyle was sceptical of the whole idea, Macleod subsequently set up a sub-committee (consisting of himself, Powell, Sir Keith Joseph and Lord Balniel) to develop the proposal.[59]

At the same time, Macleod's interest was attracted by the idea of a 'new Beveridge Report'. The suggestion was initially made by John Rodgers, a fellow founding member of the One Nation Group, who wanted a new survey to look into the social services, the burdens on various sections of the community, and how best Government action might help. Stung into action by the Orpington and Blackpool by-elections, Rodgers believed that Conservatives had to show that they understood that some people, particularly young couples and the very old, were finding it hard to manage. Macleod was generally favourable, because so much had changed in British society since Beveridge, but he also came to appreciate the political risks involved. Any inquiry into the welfare state would be bound to raise widespread, public suspicion ('shooting Santa Claus' was never popular), and many Conservatives failed to appreciate that the middle class benefited from state provision and services, and would resent changes that might affect them adversely.[60]

By May, the Prime Minister wondered how far Macleod had 'got with the proposition for a new "Beveridge" Report'. Although 'it would be "pie in the sky" ' in an election manifesto, Macmillan thought that 'a powerful commission led by a well-known Conservative, perhaps an ex-Minister, would win us credit for new initiative, even if it were unable to report before an election'. Macleod raised the 'new Beveridge' proposal with his Chairman's Committee on 5 June, when their guest was John Boyd-Carpenter, the Minister for Pensions and National Insurance. They concluded that the Government should announce, probably at the same time as they increased national insurance rates, their intention to have a wide-ranging inquiry over the whole of the social services field in the context, in particular, of full employment. Accepting their advice, Macmillan concluded that any announcement 'must follow during 1963'. But by then, the Government were preoccupied with more pressing difficulties.[61]

Only four days after the 'Night of the Long Knives', on 17 July 1962, the Prime Minister attended the Chairman's Committee for what was to be their last meeting until the new parliamentary session in November. As Macleod reported, they had swiftly come to the conclusion that education and housing were the key ministries for the future, so they were delighted that two of their number, Boyle and Joseph, were now the ministers for these two subjects (both men had been appointed during the July reshuffle). Macmillan's *tour d'horizon* made it plain that his overriding preoccupations were the vexed question of how to achieve faster economic growth without inflation, and Europe. But there was a revealing difference of emphasis between Macmillan and Macleod in their view of the party's predicament. Macmillan reckoned that to some degree their problems were caused by having been too successful. As a result, people were no longer afraid to vote Liberal. But even if the Government lost the next election, they had created a country that was not divided by a great gulf between rich and poor. Macleod adopted a less complacent tone. He was concerned that the belief that 'Conservatives care' had been lost, and that the voters thought they had become 'Cotton and Clore men', identifying them with the super-rich capitalists of the period.[62]

Nonetheless, Macleod managed an extraordinary display of confidence in October 1962 when Michael Foot conducted his pre-conference interview for the *Daily Herald*. 'MACLEOD – so cool, so clever: He KNOWS he is the man to rule', ran the headline. Foot told his readers that: 'believe it or not, to judge from the way he talked to me . . . Macleod assumes that electoral victory is almost in the bag.' The Liberal revival would 'falter', and Macleod saw 'the most dismal future for Labour'. Their meeting made a powerful impression on the Labour MP:

> To say that Macleod oozes complacency would be too rude. Rather, a perspiration of firm confidence exudes from every political pore. Whatever ferments may boil up inside, his outward mask is one of coolness. It is this quality which makes him a highly effective debater and the very man to calm a party conference inclined to panic.[63]

In his speech to the 1962 Conservative Conference at Llandudno, Macleod confronted the awkward facts head on. Instead of glossing over the doubts that had surfaced about Britain's newly affluent society, he brought Conservatives face to face with the reaction to the credit squeeze and pay pause, and the feeling that public provision had lagged behind the increase in private wealth. He acknowledged, in a remarkably frank passage, that:

> The people of this country think that the society which we have created is not sufficiently just. They were puzzled, I use a neutral word, earlier this year when their attention was drawn to the disparity between the earning power of public employees like teachers and nurses and the earnings of those protected by large unions who can bargain with private employers. They are puzzled by the fact that still in this twentieth century the child of a skilled manual labourer has only one chance in a hundred of going to the university, while the child of a professional man has 34 chances. They are puzzled that 42 per cent of the people in this country still earn £10 a week or less. I put it no stronger than that.

These home truths were not what was expected from the Party Chairman, whose role at the end of conference week had hitherto been, in Macleod's words, 'a rather pointless summing up of the Conference'. But Macleod would have none of that, as he had informed Macmillan beforehand.[64]

Although Macleod had couched his comments in terms of people's perceptions, the facts and figures that he claimed had 'puzzled' voters implied severe criticism of Conservative Governments for their shortcomings since 1951. His mastery of debating technique allowed him to get away with it triumphantly. Rejecting emphatically the socialist ideal of equality, he offered instead his own, powerful vision of a 'just society':

> There is certainly today no cry for equality. It is not equality for which free men yearn, and that is why we should oppose the word equality with the word justice. My own definition of what people understand by justice in the middle of the twentieth century is that no people or section of people should be deprived of opportunities which can be made available to them. The just society which we seek is a society which can confidently invite the men and women who compose it to make their own way in the world, because no reasonable opportunity is denied to them. You cannot ask men to stand on their own feet if you give them no ground to stand on.[65]

This combination of straight talking to the party and offering a personal vision as their inspiration is usually the prerogative of the Party Leader. Macleod could do it better than anybody. He was also shrewd enough to realize that without a major department of state, the annual conference afforded him, as Party Chairman, what was likely to be his best opportunity to push his claim to the Tory succession. When he had advised Macmillan of his own proposed change of plan for the Party Chairman's speech, Macleod had also suggested that the Prime Minister should 'consider, without giving notice of this to the Conference or the Press, just appearing and listening' to the Friday afternoon debate. Hitherto, the Conservative leader, unlike his Labour and Liberal counterparts, had not attended the annual conference and only appeared afterwards to address a mass rally. But Macmillan was not persuaded. The tradition was not to be broken until the Conservatives again found themselves in Opposition.[66]

Although the Prime Minister failed to take his Party Chairman's advice to put in an appearance during the 1962 Party Conference, Macleod's suggestion for the leader's speech to the mass rally chimed with Macmillan's thinking. 'I am sure,' Macleod counselled, 'it would be wise this year to concentrate on the Common Market rather than to embark on the traditional survey of events both at home and abroad.' Macleod had become increasingly frustrated during 1962 as the negotiations over British entry had dragged on interminably in Brussels, when he desperately needed to find a new, positive message if he were to revive party morale. Macmillan had been acutely aware of the deep anxieties that the prospect of British entry was causing throughout the Commonwealth, but once the hurdle of the Commonwealth Conference had been cleared, Macleod lost no time in preparing the ground for a great campaign to mobilize support for British entry. On 18 September, he circulated to members of the Cabinet a memorandum on public attitudes. The country was evenly divided on British entry, but opinion was volatile with swings of up to ten per cent occurring within a month or two. Although the large majority of floating voters on this issue were slightly more inclined to be opposed, Macleod felt this could easily be reversed, particularly since people complainted about the lack of information and there were indications that the country would welcome a clear lead. Opponents of entry tended to give emotional or political reasons, expressing concern about British sovereignty and links with the old (white) Commonwealth. There were fears that Britain was likely to be outvoted in Europe, or to 'surrender our independence to Frogs and Wogs'. Macleod's conclusion was that the country's head was convinced but its heart was not. This pointed to the need for an idealistic campaign, in which the key targets were opinion formers and young people. Entry into Europe needed to be presented 'with trumpets' as Britain's next, great adventure.[67]

During the same week in which Macleod urged his European campaign on fellow ministers, the Labour leader, Gaitskell, who previously had not committed himself on the issue, declared on television that he was opposed to British entry. 'I think last week was a good week for us,' Macleod wrote to Macmillan on Monday 24th. 'The pro-Common Market press is now in full blast,' he noted, and Gaitskell's television performance, 'although an effective performance in itself, clearly marshals the Socialist[s] on the side of reaction.' After the Labour leader told his party conference at Brighton in early October that British entry could mean 'the end of a thousand years of history', Macleod judged that:

> The effect of what happened at Brighton last week has been to leave only the heavyweights in the ring. There isn't much room for Grimond or the Liberals now – it'll become a personal contest between Macmillan and Gaitskell. And, of course, the clearer cut the issue is in presentation – and the difficulty with this one has always been its complexity – the easier it is to put over.

The Prime Minister delighted the Conservative mass rally by mercilessly mocking Gaitskell's long indecision on the issue, quoting the Jerome Kern song, 'She didn't say yes, she didn't say no'.[68]

For a while, it seemed that Conservative fortunes were reviving. As Anthony Howard reported in the *New Statesman*, a confident Macleod was delighted because he expected that Labour would have to pay a price for

Gaitskell's anti-Common Market stance in lost votes among the middle class. In the Conservative Party Chairman's view:

> I've always told this party that in order to win we have to be able to count our working-class vote by the million. I'm not sure that the converse of that isn't true as well – that the Labour Party today has no hope of power unless it can count its middle-class supporters in millions too. And I just don't see how it's going to be able to do that now.

But by deploying British entry as their rallying cry, the Conservatives were set on a high risk strategy. Too many of the party's eggs had been put in the European basket.[69]

Drift

The early autumn of 1962 turned out to be a false dawn for the Conservatives. Domestic party politics were eclipsed during the last week of October by the Cuba missile crisis, when the world stood on the brink of nuclear annihilation. No sooner had the threat receded than the Government were embroiled in an increasingly embarrassing row over the case of W. John Vassall, an Admiralty official who had been found guilty of spying for the Soviet Union. By early November, wild rumours were circulating about the relationship between Vassall, who was homosexual, and the former Civil Lord at the Admiralty, Tam Galbraith. Although the allegations were groundless, Macmillan nonetheless required that the junior minister, who by then was at the Scottish Office, should resign. That autumn also saw the launch of BBC Television's late-night satirical programme, *That Was The Week That Was* (or *TW3*). Within a matter of months, the conjunction of an alleged, new spy scandal and the satire boom was to rock the Government to their foundations.

The time was ripe for the satirists. The notion that a modern society should be ruled by its elders and betters was increasingly rejected, yet Macmillan's Government had about it the aura of rule by elders and betters. Inevitably, ministers (especially the hapless Home Secretary, Henry Brooke) became the butt of some harsh, satirical comment. But when the Postmaster General, Reginald Bevins, suggested taking action against the BBC over *TW3* following an item about the Prime Minister, Macmillan had the sense to reject this advice. Macleod often found himself in more sympathy with young people and their questioning of society. Like millions of other viewers, the Chairman of the Conservative Party, Chancellor of the Duchy of Lancaster and Leader of the House, became a fan of *TW3*, regularly tuning in to the BBC late on a Saturday night.[70]

What finally shattered the hopes of political recovery entertained by Conservatives during October was the 'little general election' in late

November, when five by-elections were held on the same day. Macleod had persuaded Ian Gilmour, the owner and former editor of the *Spectator*, to put his name forward for the supposedly safe seat of Central Norfolk, and had reassured him over dinner at White's before the campaign began that he would win easily. In the event, Gilmour scraped home by 220 votes after a recount and reckoned that he would have lost had polling taken place a week later. The Conservatives lost two seats to Labour – Woodside, a marginal Scottish seat; and South Dorset, where the Conservative vote was split when the former Conservative MP, Lord Hinchingbrooke, having succeeded to a peerage, declared his support for a former local party officer who stood as an anti-Common Market candidate.[71]

'Unemployment remains a deep anxiety,' Macleod noted in his assessment of the results for Macmillan (the jobless total had risen from 259,000 in July 1961 and was to reach a postwar peak of 878,000, or 3.9 per cent, in February 1963): 'It lost us Middlesbrough West in the summer and it lost us Woodside, but it affects areas other than those of heavy unemployment just as those who were not nurses felt deeply about the way we treated the nurses' pay claim.' Macleod could detect a silver lining, of sorts. Had the by-elections been held in the summer, he reckoned that the Conservatives would have lost all five. And although the Conservative vote had fallen, Labour had only managed to increase their share of the poll in one seat. 'On the other hand,' he added: 'The country, if not actively hostile to us, is at least suspicious and neutral, and we have a long way to go to re-establish fully the image that Conservatives care and that Conservatives are competent.' Macleod echoed Gilmour's report that opinion shifted against the Government during the last week of the campaign. But unlike most observers, he doubted that it had been caused by the Vassall case and instead thought 'it much more likely that it was our underground [H-Bomb] test'. On his visits to the four English by-elections he found: 'that this did disturb even Conservative opinion a great deal and was regarded by our opponents, however wrongly, as being a slap in the face to disarmament.' His conceding to Macmillan that he was 'being wise after the event because I might have protested at the time about this announcement', shows that he possessed a party boss's unhesitating readiness, whenever necessary, to manage the news.[72]

As to the 'lessons for the future', Macleod warned that despite the similarities with the Government's position in 1958–59, 'two new factors tell very much against us now'. Because the Conservatives had been in power four years longer, they had 'no margin of error left, and the smallest slip by any Minister becomes a liability out of all proportion to its worth'. In addition, they were still 'awaiting Brussels'. As a result, industry was keeping many proposals in its pending tray until it knew the outcome, 'and this in turn means that reflation does not move as swiftly as we were able to make it hum in 1958/59'. Despite 'our success at Llandudno, we still cannot give out the trumpet call that would, I believe, gather people to us'. The party's propaganda for the early spring needed to be 'much more positive' than 'Don't let Labour ruin it' had been in 1959. Macleod was toying with the two keystones, 'Conservatives Care' and 'Efficiency', but had not yet developed his ideas.[73]

Like most Conservatives, Macleod was relying on Europe to come up trumps in the New Year. But the omens for Macmillan's realizing his 'Grand Design' were not good. During December, the immense difficulties of simultaneously maintaining the 'special relationship' with the United States, becoming a part of Europe and retaining the leadership of the Common-wealth, seemed to be becoming insuperable. It was deeply embarrassing to Macmillan that, at the start of the month, Dean Acheson, the respected former American Secretary of State, should say as much when he com-mented that 'Great Britain has lost an Empire and has not yet found a role'. Worse followed when the Americans decided to cancel the development of the Skybolt long-range missile, on which the future of Britain's independent nuclear deterrent depended. The result would have been tantamount to British unilateral nuclear disarmament, totally destroying the Government's defence strategy. Macmillan finally avoided this ignominy by persuading President Kennedy at their Nassau talks that Britain had to have the Polaris missile. But the Skybolt crisis exhausted Macmillan and the new Anglo-American agreement inevitably antagonized the French President, de Gaulle.[74]

On 14 January 1963, de Gaulle delivered a shattering blow to Macmillan when he proclaimed his opposition to British entry to the Common Market. Negotiations in Brussels were broken off, but had not yet formally broken down. The Prime Minister sought his Party Chairman's political assessment of the line to be taken in the event of a final collapse. In the face of such a bitter disappointment, Macleod's response, drafted after consulting his senior advisers at Central Office and many MPs, was a model of reasoned analysis and responsible advice. Suggesting that 'we should not minimize the blow to our [British] hopes, and to the hopes of our friends in Europe', Macleod counselled:

Many people may feel some relief at the ending of worrying negotiations and the fear of a plunge into the unknown. But the building of a united and outward-looking Europe is felt by many of the best elements in our society, and by centre opinion generally, as the great task and adventure that faces us. To shrug it off, turn our backs on what we have been trying to do (and indeed on much that has been achieved since the war), or turn to some second-best alternative, would be politically damaging and would involve the hazard of leaving the Liberals as the only 'European' Party in Britain.[75]

He warned:

> There is a real danger that the latent xenophobia and jingoism of the Parliamentary Party and in the constituencies will rise to the surface. This might rally our confirmed supporters for a time, but would be damaging over a far wider field, and should be firmly discouraged.

Since Labour would 'try to make political capital out of these events,' it was important:

> To rebut the 'we told you so' argument; to keep the blame for the breakdown firmly where it belongs and where it is at present clearly recognized to be; and to point out that, but for the French attitude, acceptable terms might well have been obtained.

It was still, just possible that the negotiations might resume. If this were to happen, Macleod advised:

> Success, if we can achieve it, would be very sweet, but if fail we must let it be now. Banquo was right in Macbeth: 'If it were done when 'tis done then 'twere well it were done quickly'.[76]

Just four days later, on 29 January, the French formally vetoed British entry. Although Macleod had endorsed the Banquo school of politics, Enoch Powell 'was struck by the extent to which he [Macleod] regarded de Gaulle's brush off as disastrous to Macmillan'. Searching for a new theme for the Government to replace the European dimension, Macleod suggested to the Prime Minister that 'We have consistently stressed the need for efficiency, modernization, readiness to change, whether we go into the Market or not. The need now is not new: it is more urgent.' But it sounded unconvincing, as if his heart was not really in it. Macmillan lost his impetus and sense of direction, paralysing the Government and the party. In Powell's recollection, during January to March Macleod 'was of the opinion that Macmillan was disintegrating'. Macleod was to suggest twelve months later that de Gaulle's veto had provided the party with a valuable shock and that exclusion from the Common Market had been good for the Conservatives, since the party could not stand bickering and were exceedingly unhappy about Europe. Yet this argument ran totally counter to his attitude and behaviour during 1962 and 1963.[77]

The New Year of 1963 brought a peculiarly sombre time in British politics. Gaitskell died on 18 January. 'The word that first came to my mind was courage,' Macleod commented in his tribute to the Labour leader. 'He was a very courageous man,' Macleod continued, 'and I remember what Sir James Barrie said forty years ago in his rectorial address to St Andrews:

"Courage is the thing – if that goes all goes." ' Because of Macleod's disability, and the disability that had afflicted Eve, there was nobody better qualified to speak about courage, or to recognize it.[78]

Scandal

It was a measure of the Macmillan Government's fragility by 1963 that a junior defence minister's affair almost became the straw that broke their back. Macleod, as Leader of the House, was one of five ministers at the fateful meeting with John Profumo, the War Secretary, on the night of Thursday 21 and the early hours of Friday 22 March, at which his personal statement to the Commons was agreed. This statement proved to be Profumo's, and nearly Macmillan's, undoing. Within three months, Profumo confessed that he had lied to Parliament in denying any impropriety with Christine Keeler, and resigned. A naval attaché at the Soviet Embassy, Captain Yevgeny Ivanov was also said to have been involved with Keeler, and the Opposition, under their new leader, Harold Wilson, launched a furious assault, claiming, disingenuously, that they were not interested in the morals of the case, but only in British security.[79]

During the autumn of 1962, Macleod was briefly touched by the web of intrigue and rumour that eventually ensnared Profumo. On the night of Wednesday 31 October 1962, in the immediate wake of the Cuban missile crisis, Macleod learned from William Shepherd, a Conservative back-bencher, that he (Macleod) was being implicated in the attempted infiltration by Ivanov of the upper echelons of government. The man helping Ivanov was Stephen Ward, who had approached Shepherd and invited him to his flat for a drink with Ivanov earlier that evening. Shepherd and Ivanov had an argument and as Shepherd left, Ward announced that he and Ivanov were dining with Macleod later that evening, implying that they knew him well. Macleod seemed 'unperturbed' by Shepherd's information, and wrote to Lord Home, the Foreign Secretary, explaining what it was all about, and also spoke to him about what had happened.[80]

Although there was no truth in Ward's boast about knowing Macleod, he had some reason to hope that he and Ivanov would meet him that night. Macleod's daughter, Diana, was giving a party at the family's Chelsea flat and one of her guests had asked whether he could also bring somebody else – this extra guest turned out to be Stephen Ward, accompanied by someone from the Russian Embassy, whom, it was later assumed, must have been Ivanov. Diana and her friends eventually finished their evening at a night-club, where both Ward and Ivanov were again present. The next day, Diana was interrogated at length by a security service officer to find out what she knew about Ivanov and how he had come to be invited to her party. Macleod had not been present at the party, had never met Ward or Ivanov, and no further attempt was made to contact him or any member of his family.

However, the incident was referred to the following summer by the Prime Minister in a note to the Cabinet during their discussions on the implications of Profumo's resignation. 'It may be safely presumed,' Macmillan wrote, 'that the intention was to press on Mr Macleod the same points in relation to Cuba as had been put to the Foreign Secretary'.[81]

By the autumn of 1962, rumours of Profumo's affair with Keeler, and Ivanov's involvement with Keeler, were circulating in London's clubland, Fleet Street and Westminster. It is inconceivable that Macleod had not heard these rumours. But as Macleod later told the Commons, he had not discussed the matter directly with Profumo before the night of 21–22 March. From the moment the rumours took hold until almost the day Profumo resigned in June 1963, ministers, including Macleod, seemed to will themselves to reject whatever else they heard and believe the beleaguered War Minister. Their attitude went beyond the bonds of party and ministerial loyalties. The rumours rose to a crescendo while Whitehall was shuddering at the ramifications of the Vassall case. Politically, the Government could not afford the revelation of another spy and sex scandal. Ministers were also deeply angry that Galbraith, who was subsequently shown to have been blameless, had been forced to resign as a result of press innuendo and gossip. Relations with the press had been poisoned as a result of the imprisonment of two journalists who refused to reveal their sources in the Vassall case. Many Conservatives had initially been delighted that some punishment had been meted out to Fleet Street after the papers' behaviour during the Vassall affair, but Macleod had realized that the press would become even more hostile towards the Government. In addition, the Conservatives' poor showing in the November 1962 'little general election', the Skybolt crisis the following month, rising unemployment during the winter and de Gaulle's veto in January 1963, all combined to create something of a bunker mentality.[82]

Even so, ministers' readiness to suspend any disbelief as the Profumo rumours intensified, now seems incredible. Redmayne, an unimaginative military figure, later confessed to having initially harboured doubts about Profumo's denial. Macleod never mixed in the same night-club set as Profumo, but it would have been extraordinary if he had not suspected at some point that the rumours might be true. But there was also an additional factor at work. Macleod and Profumo, like many other members of the Macmillan Government, were members of the generation of Conservatives who had served as officers in the War and who entered politics afterwards imbued with a strong sense of duty. They were inspired by a desire to create a modern Conservative Party and to build a better society, but they also tended to see themselves set apart from others – the officer class as the new ruling class. At one and the same time, they could do much as they liked while being regarded as an officer and a gentleman. Moreover, when Profumo gave his word to his fellow

Ministers and to the House of Commons, it was surely proof of his innocence.

Matters began to come to a head during January 1963. Keeler was told that she would be called as a witness in the trial of Johnny Edgecombe, a former lover, who was on trial following a shooting incident at Stephen Ward's flat in December. She tried to sell her story, including an account of her affair with Profumo, to the press. Although she failed, it remained possible that she would refer to the affair when she gave evidence during Edgecombe's trial. As the threat of a scandal loomed, Moscow recalled Ivanov. Reflecting on his friend's abrupt departure, Stephen Ward later observed that whatever else had happened, Ivanov's bridge had improved while he was in Britain, 'and I hope that he profited from the book I gave him, *Bridge is an Easy Game*'. The author, of course, was Iain Macleod.

In late January and early February, Profumo was questioned by the Attorney General, Sir John Hobson, and the Solicitor General, Sir Peter Rawlinson. Profumo denied that he had had an affair with Keeler. He also instructed his lawyers to sue anybody who published the libel and informed the Director of Public Prosecutions that he was ready to give evidence in any criminal proceedings that might arise from blackmail proceedings. His robust stand reassured the law officers and helped hold the press at bay.[83]

Nonetheless, the rumours were published in early March by Andrew Roth in his newsletter, *Westminster Confidential*, subscribed to mainly by MPs, journalists and embassies. Profumo was apparently advised not to sue, because the paper's circulation was small and a libel action would draw further attention to the rumours. On 14 March, the news of Keeler's disappearance on the eve of the Edgecombe trial stirred a fresh wave of speculation. A week later, on the night of 21 March, this speculation was raised on the floor of the House of Commons during a debate on the imprisonment of two journalists for contempt of court in the Vassall case, by three Labour MPs, George Wigg, Richard Crossman and Barbara Castle, speaking under the protection of parliamentary privilege. It was clear to anybody who had heard the rumours that they were referring to Profumo.[84]

Their intervention almost backfired. Hobson and Rawlinson, the Government's law officers, and Deedes, the Minister for Information, had been on the Government frontbench for the debate. Macleod heard the end of the debate, which continued until around 1.30am, and immediately consulted the Chief Whip. The law officers in particular felt that Profumo had been handed a golden opportunity to state in public what he had maintained in private and scotch the rumours once and for all. The ministers also feared that unless they acted quickly, the weekend press would take up the Labour MPs' comments and develop the story further. The Chief Whip consulted Macmillan, who agreed that Profumo should make a personal statement in the Commons when the House met at 11.00am the following morning, as was then customary on Fridays.[85]

Had Butler still been Leader of the House, and not Macleod, it is probable that Profumo would not have made his fateful statement. When Butler was telephoned on the Friday morning and asked by Macmillan to 'hold his hand' on the frontbench while Profumo made a personal statement, Butler immediately exclaimed, 'Not on a Friday morning surely!' According to Butler's biographer, Anthony Howard, Butler thought that Profumo should have been given more time, and should have withdrawn from his ministerial post while an inquiry was conducted. If this advice had been followed, the Government, Macmillan and Profumo would have been saved great embarrassment.[86]

Although Macleod and the other four Ministers acted on assurances by Profumo and were concerned to prevent the weekend press having a field day, the Cabinet's subsequent inquest into their action further strengthens the impression that they were almost willing themselves to believe Profumo. The Ministers knew that Profumo – as he had admitted to the Chief Whip as early as 4 February – had couched his letter to Keeler of August 1961, terminating their relationship, in affectionate terms; and that he had admitted to having bought her a present and to having been alone with her in Ward's flat. However, they had continued to take Profumo's word about his relationship with Keeler and had even failed to ask him for a copy of his letter to her in order to judge for themselves whether it implied any impropriety. In mitigation, Macleod and his colleagues maintained that they had no grounds for doubting Profumo's word that the letter was entirely innocent – Macleod himself had penned affectionate, personal letters to women friends on departmental notepaper. Also, on the afternoon of the late-night meeting, Deedes, the Minister without Portfolio, had been told by several 'representatives of the press' who had seen the letter that they regarded it as of no great importance. Moreover, Profumo had continually denied that there had been any impropriety.[87]

On the night of 21–22 March, Profumo and his solicitor were called at about 1.30am and met with the five ministers (Hobson, Rawlinson, Redmayne, Deedes and Macleod). The statement was hammered out during the small hours – a process that transformed it into something other than a 'personal statement'. Skilfully concentrating mainly on the issue raised by Castle's comment about 'a perversion of justice' and her reference to 'people in high places', the statement denied Profumo's being 'connected with or responsible for Keeler's absence from the trial at the Old Bailey'. Had the statement not gone any further, that might have been the end of the matter. But the whole purpose of the exercise was finally to squash the rumours. As Macleod revealed later to the Commons, Profumo disliked the phrase, 'Miss Keeler and I were on friendly terms', as this – to quote Profumo's words – 'sounds so awful'. But Macleod added that he and his fellow Ministers 'insisted that that must be included because it was part of the truth, and an important part, as he [Profumo] had consistently said'.[88]

Macleod said no more in the subsequent Commons debate about the drafting of the key section of Profumo's statement. But the five ministers had felt that Profumo had to repeat the assurances that he was giving privately – while acknowledging that he had known Keeler for two years, he should deny emphatically that he had had an affair with her. Macleod later told a journalist colleague on the *Spectator* that he had been blunt with Profumo: 'Look Jack, the basic question is, "Did you fuck her?" ' Profumo reportedly replied that he had not. Although Macleod's reollection has him putting a characteristically blunt question to Profumo, their exchange is not corroborated by others who were present. In any event, Profumo agreed the draft, including the sentence: 'There was no impropriety what-soever in my acquaintanceship with Miss Keeler.' It was the only lie in his statement.[89]

Profumo delivered his statement with the Prime Minister seated on one side of him and Macleod on the other. The Labour MPs who had raised the rumours appeared to have been routed. The mood on the Government benches was, for the most part, euphoric. Profumo had categorically denied any misconduct and, as Jim Prior, one of the 1959 intake of MPs, has recalled, backbenchers were impressed because 'an experienced lawyer (Sir Peter), an army man (Redmayne), and one of the brightest brains in the Party (Iain), [had] grilled Jack assiduously and declared him as clean as a whistle'. Profumo followed the threat of libel suits, with which he had concluded his statement, by actions against *Paris Match* and *Il Tempo*.[90]

However, some Conservatives were not convinced. Macleod was quickly aware of the continuing doubts. Lord Aldington, the Deputy Chairman at Central Office, with whom Macleod worked closely and well, went to see Redmayne and Macleod, and told them that he was convinced that Profumo was lying. Redmayne would not take this and told Aldington to leave the room. When Macleod's Parliamentary Private Secretary, Charles Long-bottom, sought to relay to him the reaction of journalists to Profumo's statement, Macleod reacted even more fiercely than had the Chief Whip. Longbottom had accepted Profumo's denial, but immediately afterwards was told by two lobby correspondents that Fleet Street knew that Profumo was lying about his relationship with Keeler. Shocked, Longbottom made straight for Macleod's room and reported what he had been told. Macleod's response shook Longbottom. He had never seen Macleod look so ferocious as he exploded, bawling him out and telling him never to come back to his room repeating press title-tattle.[91]

Profumo's lie was a time-bomb. In May, Macmillan asked the Lord Chancellor, Lord Dilhorne, to begin an inquiry into the case. On 4 June, Profumo was summoned from holiday in Italy. The following day, having confessed his lie, he resigned his office and his seat. Macleod had every reason to be furious with him, since his assurances had proved worthless. In addition, along with the other ministers who had attended the meeting before Profumo's March statement, Macleod now found himself in the dock. This hapless five were accused of having been either – in the words that Macleod later used in the Commons – 'conspiring knaves', or 'gullible fools'.[92]

Nonetheless, Macleod realized what the Profumos were going through. He and Eve were in the United States, taking advantage of the Whitsun recess, when Profumo resigned. 'I was, and am, a friend of Jack and Valerie Profumo,' he told a questioner at the Washington Press Club. 'I think it is a personal tragedy that this should have happened.' It was a fearless and honest comment to make at that time, and echoed his reaction five years earlier, when he had made a similar comment about Ian Harvey, his friend from Fettes, who had also had to resign as a Minister following a personal scandal. It was also quixotic, but Macleod was not exaggerating his friendship with Profumo, as has sometimes been suggested. The two men had known each other since they worked as backroom boys in the late 1940s – Profumo as Director of Spoken Word Propaganda in Conservative Central Office, Macleod at the Research Department. After they became MPs, they often mixed in the smoking room and talked politics. Indeed, Macleod made such an impression on Profumo that the latter was often a willing listener during their conversations, regarding Macleod as a political giant from his own generation and a likely future Prime Minister. Their families also got to know each other. Perhaps more importantly, Macleod's comments in the wake of Profumo's resignation reflected a sense of proportion – the Government had been severely embarrassed and Macmillan brought to the brink of resignation, but the real tragedy was personal.[93]

Yet Macleod inadvertently had a hand in the most notorious ministerial outburst about Profumo. Prior to the Commons debate on the Profumo case on 17 June, John Grist, editor of BBC Television's specialist political programme, *Gallery*, telephoned Macleod to invite him to appear on the edition of Thursday 13th. Macleod replied that he could not, because he was winding up the debate for the Government the following Monday – out of respect to the House, he should not pre-empt his speech by appearing on television first. However, he would arrange for Lord Hailsham to appear in his place. A further invitation to Macleod to appear on BBC Television's *Tonight* was also declined by Deedes on the grounds that only one person should speak for the Government and in one place. When Hailsham arrived at the studios, he told Grace Wyndham Goldie, then the BBC's head of talks: 'I came because I was asked to come by the Chairman of the Party'. But his approach was in marked contrast to Macleod's. During the interview, Hailsham became irritated by Robert McKenzie's questioning about the implications of the case for the Conservatives and their leadership, finally snapping intemperately that: 'A great party is not to be brought down because of a scandal by a woman of easy virtue and a proved liar.' This outburst was soon to have repercussions on Hailsham's career and the leadership of the Conservative Party.[94]

Macmillan would almost certainly have fallen had there been another ministerial resignation. The Prime Minister had refused Redmayne's offer to resign immediately after Profumo's demise, but it was touch and go whether others might quit. At Cabinet's inquest on the scandal on Tuesday 12 June, the Prime Minister expressed his deep concern at the widely held belief that the five ministers who had been involved in helping draft Profumo's statement 'must themselves have suspected at the time that the statement disclosed less than the full truth'. It proved impossible to complete their discussion in one meeting and before ministers met again the following morning, the tension was heightened by a story in the press that named Powell as the ringleader of a demand that Macmillan must go – Powell was 'in the end satisfied that Macmillan was not personally, dishonourably to blame'. Although the Prime Minister stated that the five ministers had 'acted in good faith on 22nd March', they faced further criticism from other ministers for having failed to verify from the security service that there was no security risk in Profumo's association with Keeler. By the end of the Cabinet discussion, it was clear that much depended on the outcome of the Commons debate.[95]

The potency of the Profumo scandal was that it confirmed the satirists' cruel image of Macmillan as outdated and out of touch. He was revealed as ignorant of the modern world and the company that his ministers kept and pitifully incapable of dealing with the rumours when he first heard of them. Macmillan was worsted by Wilson at the opening of the Commons' censure debate. Winding up for the Government, Macleod attempted to meet the Cabinet remit of earlier that day by dealing in particular with ministers' actions regarding Profumo's statement. But by going into detail about the late-night meeting, he inevitably highlighted the active participation of five ministers in helping draft what was supposedly a personal statement. At the end of his speech, he conceded that during Profumo's affair with Keeler in 1961, 'a real security risk obtained', although he added that it did not follow that there had been a security breach. At the end of the debate, the Government's majority fell by nearly 30. It was almost, but not quite, fatal for Macmillan's premiership.[96]

The Government came desperately close to collapse during June 1963. The Conservative Party were in a state of panic. People were in a mood to believe anything. Wild rumours about sexual scandals involving the aristocracy – the Duchess of Argyll's divorce case had scandalized the country – ministers, judges and other eminent figures, swept the country while the British public indulged in one of their periodic fits of morality. Arguably Macleod's most crucial intervention – and possibly life-saving as far as the Government were concerned – came at the end of one of the more bizarre Cabinet discussions during that fraught month. Sandys, the Colonial and

Commonwealth Secretary, whose name had been mentioned in rumours arising from the Argyll case, actually arrived at Cabinet with a resignation letter in his hand, but was dissuaded from delivering it. Such was the intensity of the rumours about scandals involving ministers and other senior figures, that a number of them chose to confess their indiscretions. Macmillan was horrified. Immediately after the meeting ended, Macleod went straight to the office where the Prime Minister's private secretaries worked. 'This way lies madness!' he declared, telling them that the Prime Minister must reconvene the Cabinet and instruct ministers to desist from any such talk. Macmillan duly did so.[97]

Macleod's conviction that no credibility should be given to any further rumours led to a row with Macmillan. Macleod had left open during his speech the form of any inquiry into the security aspects, but a few days after the debate the Prime Minister told him that he planned to appoint Lord Denning to conduct a judicial inquiry into the security aspects and the rumours and allegations. As Macleod later recalled:

> I was against it [the Denning inquiry] from the start and believed we ought not to give an inch to the filth-mongers. But I can remember now going to see him [Macmillan] on the Thursday before he announced it. He was in a terrible state, going on about a rumour of there having been eight High Court judges involved in some orgy. 'One,' he said, 'perhaps two, conceivably. But eight – I just can't believe it.' I said if you don't believe it, why bother with an inquiry? But he replied 'No. Terrible things are being said. It must be cleared up'.[98]

As well as becoming a bestseller, the Denning Report prompted a sequel for Macleod to the Profumo case. When the report was published in September 1963, Macleod seized on the reference to the comments that had been made by the three Labour MPs, Wigg, Crossman and Castle in the Commons on 21 March. Denning had failed to distinguish between the specific point made by Castle and the more general references to 'rumours' made by Wigg and Crossman, and stated that all three speeches had 'clearly imputed that Mr Profumo had been responsible for the disappearance of Christine Keeler'. Nonetheless, Macleod called on the three MPs to withdraw what they had said. Crossman and Wigg strongly objected and jointly wrote to him saying that they had nothing to withdraw and he should apologize. Macleod sent a robust reply on 7 October. Crossman and Wigg sought legal advice from Arnold Goodman and threatened legal action. But the matter went no further. As Crossman's biographer, Anthony Howard, concludes, it was probably just as well for Crossman that the issue ran into the ground, for a libel jury might well have decided that just as important as the words people use are the meaning they intend to have attached to them. 'And on that latter point,' observes Howard, 'Lord Denning may well have formed a legitimate judgment.'[99]

The Profumo case did the Government irreparable damage. Not only had the scandal dealt a near-mortal blow to the Prime Minister's authority, it had distracted Macmillan and his ministers from developing future policy. During the summer of 1963, survival came to take precedence over longer term thinking. The Chairman's Committee had virtually completed their work by February 1963. The time had come to prepare a policy document, with a view to the next manifesto. The Research Department began compiling possible material for inclusion, and a draft document, *Britain in Top Gear*, was prepared by the summer. However, the key, strategic policy-making group, the Steering Committee, chaired by the Prime Minister, had met for the first time on Monday 18 March only three days before the Profumo scandal broke in the Commons. On Sunday 28 April, ministers (including Profumo) attended a strategy session at Chequers, at which Maudling, Macleod and Heath respectively chaired discussions on industrial and economic policy, social questions and government reorganization. None of these three younger leadership contenders distinguished himself. Macleod's session was largely dominated by an over-technical discussion about Powell's proposal for a guaranteed minimum income in old age. But it was not until 26 July that the Steering Committee met again, when Macleod's paper on a minimum income in old age prompted concern about the likely short-term costs. The group also agreed with Butler's view, endorsed by Macleod, that the draft document, *Britain in Top Gear*, should not be published as a party conference pamphlet. The summer's distractions had left the Steering Committee with much to do during the autumn.[100]

Macleod had suspected beforehand that Blackpool's 1963 gathering would be 'a rather dull conference'. He could not have been more mistaken. A week later Macleod had left office and could no longer shape party policy. His chairmanship had coincided with a disastrous two years for the Conservatives. After Lord Aldington's resignation in the spring of 1963, Macmillan appointed Lord (Oliver) Poole, who had been Chairman when he became Prime Minister, as Joint Chairman alongside Macleod. Aldington and Macleod had worked closely together, but Macleod and Poole never got on. Macmillan had intended to replace Macleod with Poole, but Poole had dissuaded him, pointing out that the Chairman should not be blamed for the party's unpopularity. Nonetheless, the Conservatives' travails during his chairmanship did Macleod's prospects no good at all when the party's attention suddenly turned to the issue of who should be Macmillan's successor.[101]

12

The Tory Leadership: Bedlam at Blackpool

> The truth is that at all times, from the first day of his premiership to the last, Macmillan was determined that Butler, although incomparably the best qualified of the contenders, should not succeed him.
>
> Iain Macleod on the October 1963 struggle for the Tory leadership, the *Spectator*, 17 January 1964.

The Contenders

Macmillan's premiership had survived the summer and, as the party conference season approached, Macleod had moved to kill speculation about an autumn election. But the Prime Minister's authority had taken a terrible mauling and the question remained whether he should now stand down and allow a new leader to take the Tories into the 1964 election. This Tory dilemma suddenly had to be resolved during October 1963 in circumstances varying between the chaotic and the farcical. The ensuing eleven-day struggle was one of the most controversial and dramatic episodes in the Party's long history. At the end of it, Macleod, after more than eleven years in office and accompanied only by Powell, headed into the political wilderness. Several months later, he was provoked to publish his own explosive account of the crisis, blowing the whistle on the conspiracy that had secured the Tory succession for Home and bringing down on his head even greater opprobrium from his own party than he had received for refusing to serve the new Prime Minister.

Macleod's approach to the 1963 leadership crisis has long remained a puzzle, even to his closest political allies. How could such a shrewd, political operator allow himself to be so completely out-manoeuvred? From Macleod's point of view, the episode was an unmitigated disaster: the Party were lumbered with the wrong leader; Macleod felt compelled to leave office although Butler, his preferred choice, had agreed to serve Home; and, to add insult to injury, he was portrayed as one of a small number of conspirators whereas many others had plotted more actively and success-

(*left*) Annabella Macleod, née Ross, on her wedding day

(*below*) Dr Norman Macleod with Iain in his arms

(*left*) Iain and sister Rhodabel having a holiday at Intake Farm, Skipton

(*above*) Iain Macleod, when his ambition was to play scrum-half for Scotland

(*right*) Iain
Macleod marries
Eve Blois,
Halifax, January
1941

(*below*) The
Macleods hit the
campaign trail,
Enfield, 1950 –
Eve with
Diana and
Torquil

The new Minister of Health, May 1952 – Eve was stricken with polio the following month

(*left*) Macleod with Aneurin Bevan watching their rugby teams, Saracens vs. Ebbw Vale, January 1953 – the Tory MP, Beverley Baxter, in trilby and glasses, sits between them

(*below*) Frank Cousins, the union boss who became Macleod's adversary in the London bus strike, 1958

(*above*) Visiting a day nursery, Camberwell, London, July 1952

(*right*) Macmillan's playing to the gallery denies Butler the Premiership in January 1957 and rallies the Tories after Suez

(*left*) Newcomer in Africa – Macleod inspects a camp for Mau Mau detainees in Kenya, December 1959

(*below left*) Planning Nyasaland's independence with Dr Hastings Banda

(*below*) Setting Tanganyika free with Julius Nyerere in Dar-es-Salaam

(*above*) Sir Roy Welensky, Prime Minister of the Federation of Rhodesia and Nyasaland, who opposed Macleod's plans in Central Africa

(*left*) Leaving church with the Rhodesian nationalist leaders, Joshua Nkomo, left, and Kenneth Kaunda, centre, during their weekend at Chequers, December 1960

(*above*) Punching home the Tory message, Blackpool, October 1963

(*left*) Enoch Powell joins Macleod and Christopher Soames in Macmillan's Cabinet after the 'night of the long knives', July 1962

(*below*) Soon-to-be rivals for the Party leadership Lords Hailsham and Home, le applaud R. A. Butler's speech at the rally after the 1963 Party Conference, with Macleod clapping on right

(*right*) Tory Chairman, Macleod, and the Chancellor, Reggie Maudling, leaving Number Ten in October 1963, still in the dark about who would win the Tory crown

(*below*) Butler, the favourite, with Home, the late entrant who beat him to Number Ten

(*foot*) In the editor's chair at the *Spectator*

(*left*) Iain, with Torquil, Diana and Eve

(*below*) A ritual of Conservative conferences in the late 1960s, as the 'little Scotsman' rallies the party with his own brand of Toryism. Sitting uneasily on either side of Macleod are Tory leader, Edward Heath, left, and party chairman, Anthony Barber, right

(*foot*) The spoils of victory – arriving at Number Ten to be appointed Chancellor of the Exchequer, June 1970

fully. Why had Macleod apparently done so little, until it was too late, to organize for Butler? Why did he seem badly misinformed and out of touch? Or was he, perhaps, playing a deeper game, hoping that in the event of a deadlock between the main contenders, he might emerge as the dark horse candidate and capture the Tory crown?[1]

Interviews with the surviving participants and witnesses of the 1963 leadership crisis, together with a careful reading of Macleod's published account and comparison with the other versions of the events now available, provide a fuller picture of his motivations and actions during the crisis than has previously been possible. Undoubtedly Macleod allowed himself to be out-manoeuvred. After the event, he had no doubt that the selection of Home was a conspiracy. Knowing the beast that is the Conservative Party, Macleod perhaps should not have been so surprised – especially since he was aware 'that at all times, from the first day of his premiership to the last, Macmillan was determined that Butler should not succeed him.' Why then did Macleod not play the leadership struggle differently?[2]

Although Macleod became one of Butler's most committed supporters, he only did so relatively late in the day. His position on the leadership, and whether there should be a new leader at all, shifted during the preceding months. In his subsequent account, Macleod traces the background to the October crisis from the Chequers' meeting of ministers on the modernization of Britain, held during the weekend of 27–28 April 1963. But he does not reveal his own change of mind during this six-month prelude. Macmillan thought that three members of his Cabinet in the Commons were, in Macleod's words '*papabile* and of sufficient authority to be considered as possible contenders'. The three were Heath, Macleod and Maudling. Unlike Macmillan and Butler, and, in the Lords, Viscount Hailsham and the Earl of Home, they were all products of the postwar generation of politicians, being members of the impressive Tory class of 1950. As Macleod explained:

> It was not by accident that he [Macmillan] brought forward these three to be Chancellor of the Exchequer [Maudling], Minister in charge of our bid to enter the Common Market [Heath], and Chairman of the Party and Leader of the House of Commons [Macleod].

Macmillan 'hoped that one of the three would show himself clearly as the future leader'. Neither was it any accident that the three sessions of the Chequers weekend 'were presided over by the same three'. Macleod could not resist pointing out that Home was not even at the weekend conference, having left Chequers that very morning for an engagement abroad. The damning observation that 'no one commented on his absence' made it clear what Macleod thought of Home's leadership credentials. As to the three younger contenders: 'Macmillan's private preference between the three of us is known to have varied,' Macleod reported, 'but when the time came he was clear that none of us had emerged with the necessary decisive lead.'[3]

Macmillan had begun, from February 1963, to mention Hailsham as his possible successor (Hailsham did not learn of this till later). In June, Macmillan told Hailsham that he believed that he was the right man to succeed him, if he (Macmillan) decided to quit before the election: he had previously approached Home, but the response had been unenthusiastic, and in any case Macmillan now preferred Hailsham. Lord Poole, by then Joint Party Chairman with Macleod, also tipped off Hailsham to prepare himself to become the next Tory leader. Hailsham, for his part, still expected Butler to succeed Macmillan, with Macleod as a possible outsider. As Macleod pointed out, 'Macmillan had treated Hailsham with scant courtesy after the 1959 election'. However, Macleod added, somewhat sniffily, that: 'Hailsham had always had (and still has) a strong hold on the affections of the right wing and of many key party workers.' During the early months of 1963, there was a surge of support for Hailsham in the constituencies. At the same time Macleod felt that Macmillan had lost his grip. In addition, the Prime Minister no longer treated Macleod as his confidant, or 'trusty'. Macleod was enough of a realist to see that his own chances of the leadership had receded, since he was paying the price of being Chairman while the party's fortunes had ebbed disastrously during 1962. Briefly, he came to regard Hailsham as more likely than Macmillan to lead the Tories to a fourth election victory, but such was his lack of enthusiasm that he was not seen as a supporter in the Hailsham camp. Ironically, it was Macleod who helped to undermine Hailsham 's prospects, in the process weakening his own regard for Hailsham's suitability as Prime Minister. Hailsham's outburst about Profumo on BBC television was to count against him in any leadership struggle. Macleod, who had volunteered him for the interview, now finally cooled towards him as a contender.[4]

During the summer, Macleod came to the view that Macmillan should lead the party at the next election. Speculation about the leadership intensified following the Government's reduced majority at the end of the debate on the Profumo affair. Butler and Maudling were thought to be the front-runners – most Tory MPs favoured the younger man, as the chairman of the backbench 1922 Committee, Major John Morrison, told Butler. But instead of turning to one of the younger contenders, Morrison approached Home and insisted that he should become Leader. Hailsham was still in with a chance, and Heath, Home and Macleod were all being mentioned as outsiders. In this situation, it would suit Macleod best if Macmillan opted to soldier on. If the Prime Minister could lead the Tories to a fourth election victory, Macleod, as Party Chairman in a victorious campaign, would be well placed. Macmillan could be expected to retire after a couple of years (he would then be in his early seventies), by which time Macleod could expect to have occupied one of the major offices of state. Macleod's Joint Chairman,

Poole, who was travelling the country rallying the party behind Macmillan, found wide backing for the Prime Minister and passed this news to Macleod and Macmillan. When, in early July, Macmillan's main challengers fuelled speculation over the leadership, Macleod seized the opportunity to make public his personal support for Macmillan. Maudling, in a weekend speech, and Butler, during a television interview, both implied that there should be a change of leader before the next election. But they were rebuffed by Macleod on 13 July, in a stalwart defence of the Prime Minister. Macleod had become a Macmillan man and would remain so until fate intervened in early October. If Macmillan did finally decide to step down, Macleod hoped that he still might emerge, but he realized that his hopes were slim.[5]

Amidst all the intrigue and recrimination of the spring and summer, there occurred an important development that would have a crucial bearing on the Tory leadership. The Government's bill enabling peers to disclaim their titles passed through the Commons and the Lords. It was a reform for which the Labour politician, Tony Benn, had vigorously campaigned since the death of his father, Viscount Stansgate, in November 1960. Hailsham, who had likewise succeeded his father as the second Viscount in 1950, had also been a reluctant peer, but his plea for reform had been rejected by Attlee. Butler, who was Leader of the Commons when Benn began his campaign, had been unsupportive. Whatever the motivation for his stance, it angered his natural supporters among younger Tory MPs. Finally, he agreed to set up a joint committee of Lords and Commons to examine the matter.[6]

The joint committee eventually reported in December 1962, having agreed by the narrowest of majorities to extend the right to disclaim a title to existing hereditary peers like Hailsham and Home. Home was not a reluctant peer by any stretch of the imagination, but any provision designed to help the likes of Hailsham would inevitably be available to any hereditary peer. When the joint committee's report appeared in late 1962, Anthony Howard, writing in the *New Statesman*, pointed out that it offered Home his only chance of defeating Butler for the leadership, but this would depend on Macmillan's backing Home and timing his resignation right (ie in October 1963, before a 1964 election).[7]

As Leader of the House of Commons, Macleod told MPs on 28 March 1963 that the Government were 'taking note' of the joint committee's recommendations, and that he intended to introduce the necessary legislation before the next election. However, when the Government's bill was published in late May, it granted the right of immediate disclaimer only to the *successors* of hereditary peers, whereas peers who had taken their titles would have to wait till the dissolution of parliament, i.e. the next general election. As a result, Benn, who had not taken his title and had stood for election to the Commons although he was barred from taking his seat, would be free to disclaim straight away, whereas reluctant peers like Hailsham, who had complied with precedent and sat in the Lords, would have to wait.

Unless the 1963 bill was amended, Hailsham's hopes of returning to the Commons and any hope that he might take over the leadership before the next election would be stymied. Just such an amendment was moved in the Commons on 27 June by Labour's Patrick Gordon Walker, who wondered whether the motive in drafting the bill as ministers had had been to keep Hailsham 'out as long as they possibly can', adding that Macleod, who was responsible for handling the bill, could not 'altogether escape suspicion'. However, the Government's acceptance of this amendment, when Macmillan's authority was at a low ebb, would have been taken as a signal that his days as Prime Minister were numbered. Macleod, who by this stage no longer favoured Hailsham, led the Tories into the division lobbies, where the amendment was defeated by 174 votes to 113.[8]

In a further twist, the Government were defeated on 16 July in the Lords, when the amendment (moved by Lord Silkin) was passed by 105 votes to 25. Among those supporting the amendment were the former Tory Cabinet ministers, Salisbury, Swinton and Stuart. When the peers' amendment came before the Commons on 30 July, the Government abandoned their earlier objections and accepted it virtually without demur. Between the Lords' revolt and the Commons' compliance, Macmillan's standing had been boosted by the news of the initialling in Moscow, on 25 July, of the Nuclear Test Ban Treaty, and shortly afterwards, by the remarkably warm reception to his 'end of term address' to Tory backbenchers at the 1922 committee. There was now less political risk for the Prime Minister in accepting the amendment, and, should the need arise, it would enable him to call on his potential successors in the Lords. From the moment that the Peerage Act received royal assent the following day, Hailsham and Home were free to enter the leadership lists if Macmillan quit.

The Peerage Act suited Macmillan most and Butler least. It was not welcome to Macleod, but there was a minor consolation in that existing hereditary peers who wanted to exercise their right to disclaim had to do so within twelve months. If, as Macleod hoped, Macmillan decided to lead the Tories at an election in 1964 (possibly as late as the autumn), the onus would be on any leadership contender in the Lords to declare his hand by the end of July 1964. Hailsham and Home had discussed, earlier in 1963, the matter of disclaiming their titles (Hailsham thinks at Home's suggestion) and agreed on 'the absolute impossibility' of them both disclaiming their titles because of their role as the party's leading spokesmen in the Lords, and that each would consult the other should the possibility become real.[9]

It was still not certain that Macmillan would continue as Prime Minister. Many backbenchers and ministers wanted a new leader before the next election. Despite his own views, Macleod appears to have had some general discussions with Butler and Maudling. However, William Rees-Mogg, then writing for the *Sunday Times*, who was close to Butler, does not believe that Butler and Macleod had clearly agreed their positions in the event of

Macmillan resigning. Macleod was also close to Maudling, and they would reach an understanding, although the evidence suggests that they did not do so until the Tory conference at Blackpool.[10]

Meanwhile, the third of the younger generation of Tory hopefuls, Heath, had realized that he stood no chance of winning the leadership in the immediate future. He was against Hailsham becoming leader and initially favoured Butler, but during the summer changed his mind. Heath's own best hope lay in securing a senior Cabinet post from which to build his own leadership bid later. During September he visited the Isle of Islay retreat of Major John Morrison, Chairman of the 1922 committee, who was already a supporter of Home. Heath hoped that by securing Number Ten for Home, he would succeed him as Foreign Secretary, thereby improving in the longer term his own leadership prospects. As a former Chief Whip, Heath's strong backing for Home would weigh heavily in the whips' office, where the Chief Whip, Redmayne, was to play a key role in the drama that soon began to unfold.[11]

The unexpected intervenes

During the long summer recess, Macmillan fretted indecisively about his future. Over the weekend of 5–6 October at his home, Birch Grove, in Sussex, he confided his doubts about soldiering on to his son-in-law, Julian Amery, Minister for Aviation and to his son, Maurice Macmillan. They urged him to continue and he began to move towards staying on – for another two or three years. This outcome would have suited Macleod. But after Amery and his son left, the Prime Minister dined alone with Home. The Foreign Secretary argued that Macmillan should keep to his original plan of resigning early in 1964, although both men were concerned at the risk, in the run-up to an election, of a divisive struggle for the leadership.[12]

On Macmillan's return to Number Ten on Monday 7 October, he was told by his Private Secretary, Tim Bligh, that most of the Cabinet were rallying to him. He saw Butler, and other senior ministers, including Redmayne, the Chief Whip, and Dilhorne, the Lord Chancellor. The latter two 'declared themselves ready to do battle for Macmillan', but Poole was now convinced that the Tories were bound to lose the next election and urged Macmillan to stand down. The political assessment of ministers' views given to the Prime Minister by Bligh (a civil servant) is flatly contradicted by Macleod's comment that he (Macleod) was 'at the end, perhaps the only member of Macmillan's Cabinet to hold steadily to the view that the Tory party would do better under Macmillan's leadership at the polls than they would under any of the possible alternatives'. Hailsham recalls that when he saw Macmillan that day, the Prime Minister told him 'formally', that he wished Hailsham to succeed him, and led Hailsham to understand that he expected to retire about Christmas.[13]

According to his biographer, Alistair Horne, Macmillan had decided by the evening to stay on as leader. However, in the early hours of Tuesday 8th, he was taken ill. His prostate trouble had flared up. In obvious discomfort, he managed to chair the morning's Cabinet meeting. At noon, the Prime Minister cut short the lengthy agenda of official business, seemingly in order to let his colleagues know his intentions for the future. However, the most that he apparently said was, 'there has to be a decision and I shall announce it at Blackpool'.[14]

What followed was to have a crucial bearing on Macleod's conduct over the following eleven days. Macmillan left the room to allow the Cabinet the opportunity to discuss the position freely. Ministers were bewildered. Redmayne later told the Prime Minister that all the Cabinet except Powell had agreed to back him fully if he decided to lead the party at the election. But there was little time for discussion, because most of the Cabinet had to leave for Euston to catch the special train to Blackpool. However, the sense of unease about Macmillan's health prompted Dilhorne to say that in the event of the Prime Minister's being unable to stay on, he (Dilhorne) would be available to help in any Cabinet consultation on a successor. Home then intervened to say that since he was in no circumstances a candidate, he would also be ready to assist. Macleod alluded to Home's self-denying ordinance when he wrote in the *Spectator* that 'the Cabinet left for Blackpool assured that Home was not a contender.' Dilhorne and Home appeared to have cast themselves in the roles played by Kilmuir and Salisbury six years earlier. In these circumstances, it was reasonable for any Cabinet minister to assume that if Macmillan stood down, Dilhorne and Home would be the umpires, or honest brokers. In the event, this was not valid.[15]

Almost immediately after he had arrived in Blackpool, at about 7.00 pm on Tuesday 8th, Macleod told the press that he was 'quite certain that the Prime Minister on Saturday will make the position about the leadership absolutely clear'. Yet even these somewhat delphic words would soon have to be eaten. Shortly before 9.00 pm, while he was performing one of his traditional functions as Party Chairman, attending the Conservative agents' eve of conference dinner, he was told by a waiter that there was a call for him from London. Apparently his sister was ill – an obviously false message since his only sister, Rhodabel, had died a year earlier. By the time that Macleod reached the telephone, Number Ten had been cut off, but contact was quickly reestablished. Macleod was told that Macmillan had to have an operation and would not be able to make his speech on Saturday, and that during his absence Butler would take charge of the Government. Number Ten was about to issue a press statement to this effect.[16]

So began the almost surreal farce, mingled with tragedy, that was to envelop Tory politics during the following fortnight. Macleod had scarcely returned to his seat when he was again called to the telephone. Quite by coincidence it was Randolph Churchill calling from Washington. Macleod 'greeted him, apologized for not being able to talk at length to him, and rang off'. As Macleod later recalled:

> With Randolph in Washington, I thought the news was safe for at least an hour. I underestimated him. Randolph was immediately suspicious and concluded from my reluctance to exchange gossip with him that something was going on.

After two further transatlantic calls, Churchill 'put together what he was told', and then rang President Kennedy and the British Embassy 'and gave them a complete account of what was afoot before the offical news was released'.[17]

In Blackpool, Macleod summoned his Cabinet colleagues who were attending the agents' dinner and informed them. Bill Deedes, Minister for Coordinating Information recalls that Macleod was clear that they should call a press conference to follow the release of the press statement in London. At about 9.40 pm, as soon as Macleod knew that the announcement had been made by Number Ten, he told the Tory agents of the news. To Deedes's immense relief, Macleod fielded the questions at the press conference that followed at the Imperial Hotel. Referring to the morning's Cabinet meeting, Macleod thought that perhaps Macmillan 'did not look very well, but this did not occur to me at the time'. He told journalists that no decision about the leader's speech on Saturday would be made until Butler arrived early the next evening (Wednesday 9th), and would say nothing about whether Macmillan would remain leader.[18]

Although everybody at Blackpool assumed that Macmillan's days as leader were now moving to an early end, possibly in a matter of weeks rather than months, nobody seriously expected that his resignation was imminent. However, Macmillan had concluded (wrongly) from the medical diagnosis that he would have to resign soon as he would not be able to continue in office and might even have cancer. Alistair Horne, his biographer, believes that Macmillan's decision might have been different if his personal physician, Sir John Richardson, had not been on holiday, but the Prime Minister's mind was apparently made up by the time that he reached Number Ten on Tuesday evening. In fact, there was still time for Macmillan to change his mind during Wednesday. He would not be operated on till Thursday and although he was also insistent that he should write to the Queen, who was at Balmoral, informing her of his decision no public announcement was to be made until she had signalled her approval. However, any chance for second thoughts quickly disappeared.[19]

The key to understanding Macleod's attitude during the ensuing leadership struggle is that Macmillan had come to rely on a narrow range of advice. Outside the immediate family circle, the only ministers whom Macmillan saw on Wednesday 9th were Dilhorne and Home, although Butler was still in London. Even before his illness, Macmillan had largely shut himself off politically from Butler and the younger generation in the Cabinet, and had come to depend for political advice almost entirely on his family and the older generation, drawn predominantly from the traditional right of the party. While Dilhorne, Home, Poole, Morrison and Redmayne were more likely (though not invariably) to find a receptive ear in Downing Street, others whose standing in the Cabinet and the party qualified them as senior advisers – Butler (First Secretary), Maudling (Chancellor of the Exchequer) and Macleod (Leader of the House and Joint Party Chairman) – were systematically excluded. This state of affairs underlies Macleod's intense anger at the outcome. His eventual, public vilification of Macmillan's cabal as 'the magic circle' reflected what he was saying privately. Later, Butler said of Macleod's explosive account that 'every word of it is true'.[20]

One other crucial factor about Macleod's state of mind must be taken into account. During the leadership struggle, he and Eve were having to cope with a harrowing family crisis. Diana, their daughter, had had an operation for appendicitis in mid-September and had returned home in time for her nineteenth birthday on 8 October. But after a week she suffered a serious relapse and had to be rushed back into hospital. She became so desperately ill that during October her life hung in the balance – on at least one occasion it seemed that she was about to die and Macleod was summoned to her bedside. His friend, Nigel Fisher acknowledges that his daughter's illness 'would itself have been sufficient to unbalance the judgement of most ordinary men', but adds that 'it was quite unlike Macleod not to be able to discipline his mind. He would usually have been able to assess and compartmentalize the political priorities and separate them from the domestic strain'. Fisher knew Macleod well and considers that it was 'unlikely' that this anxiety clouded Macleod's judgment. But Macleod was devoted to Diana and although he could 'compartmentalize', he was a deeply emotional man. It is inconceivable that the very real possibility that Diana might die did not affect and distract him.[21]

Under such personal strain, the brouhaha that enveloped Blackpool, with its backbiting and rumour-mongering among people whose excitability and delusions of their own self-importance were only exceeded by their irrelevance to the leadership struggle, was rendered even more grotesque for Macleod. He found the atmosphere in the bars and around the main hotel, the Imperial, distasteful and spent his limited free time in his hotel room. Amery, who with Maurice Macmillan, was busily promoting Hailsham's cause, has no recollection of having even seen Macleod. Moreover, because of Diana's illness, Eve, who was better at socializing, was only able to attend the conference for one night. Eve's absence denied Macleod an important source of intelligence, gleaned from the wives of senior Tories (this source would later provide a vital tip-off) and also party activists, with whom Macleod never mixed easily (with the exception of many Young

Conservatives). Macleod's sociable friend and Parliamentary Private Secretary, Dr Reggie Bennett, acted as his ears and eyes for the week, the only Tory conference that he ever had to attend during his twenty-four years as an MP. To the extent that Macleod put in an appearance in the bars, he was usually seen chatting with Bennett.[22]

Although there was no need to make public Macmillan's decision to resign during the party conference, the process for doing so was quickly set in motion. The impact of such an announcement was bound to be electrifying, creating a frenetic atmosphere akin to an American-style presidential convention. Macmillan's overriding motivation was undoubtedly his determination to block Butler from the succession and his consequent wish to do all that he could to secure the leadership for Hailsham. As a former Party Chairman, Hailsham's rumbustious style had enthused party activists before the 1959 election triumph and made him popular among the Tory faithful. There was no better opportunity, or so it seemed, to set the Hailsham bandwagon rolling than at Blackpool. On Wednesday morning (9th), Macmillan told Amery, who was still in London, to go north and 'make sure that they get Quintin in'. This prime ministerial order was never countermanded.[23]

Of even greater significance was Home's visit to Macmillan in hospital on Wednesday morning, particularly since the Prime Minister did not see Butler. Home was Macmillan's other preferred candidate, besides Hailsham, to block Butler. Home had been arguing consistently for a month that the Prime Minister should retire before the next election, most recently over their private dinner the previous Sunday, and he was unlikely to say anything that might cause Macmillan to have second thoughts about resigning.

Home had ruled himself out as a contender at Tuesday's Cabinet, but Macmillan later amended Randolph Churchill's account and made it clear that later on Tuesday, before entering hospital, the Prime Minister had told Home 'that in some circumstances it might be necessary for him to lead the Party. Home had then replied that if enough time were allowed someone would emerge.' Home would later claim that when he visited the hospital on Wednesday morning 'the question of my succession to Macmillan had simply not crossed my mind'. In addition, according to Home, when the Prime Minister mentioned the possibility of his becoming leader, Home demurred and Macmillan expressed his preference for Hailsham. Macmillan subsequently claimed that he told Home 'no one was emerging and it would almost certainly be his duty to disclaim his peerage and slip into the front line. Home was still reluctant but said if no one did emerge he would accept a draft.' However, Wednesday was far too early for anybody to have emerged, and Macmillan's recollection therefore seems unreliable.[24]

Was Home, perhaps, less of a reluctant draftee and more ambitious than is generally assumed? Anthony Howard, Butler's biographer, states that there is no evidence of undue pressure being brought to bear on Macmillan, but he reveals that Butler had his doubts. Butler suspected that Home had encouraged Macmillan to resign and then extracted a resignation statement from him. Later in the week, Home read the Prime Minister's announcement to the Tory conference. 'A statement of the facts,' Butler wrote privately, 'cannot stress too strongly that Alec Home obtained this and himself read it out.' The conference is the National Union's, and in 1963, Home happened to be President of the National Union. Yet it was highly irregular that a prime minister's resignation should be announced to a party conference instead of by Downing Street. Since most political journalists were at Blackpool, any announcement should either have been delayed until the following week, or, if it was to be made at Blackpool, should have been made by Butler, who was now in charge of the Government. But Home's presidential intervention brought into the limelight another contender who might block Butler if Hailsham's bandwagon became bogged down. Yet as far as Macleod and most of the Cabinet were concerned, Home was simply not a runner and when he read out the Prime Minister's announcement they assumed that he was fulfilling the duties for which he had volunteered as umpire or honest broker.[25]

In Blackpool, Home was already being mentioned as a possible contender as early as Wednesday morning. The question of the succession to Macmillan was on everybody's lips as Tory representatives thronged the Winter Gardens for their opening session. Having claimed his seat at the press table, Harry Boyne, political editor of the *Daily Telegraph*, went for a walk round the hall at about 10.30am. At the back, he met Sir Cyril Osborne, the traditionalist Tory MP, who declared himself for 'Alec'. 'Alec who?' enquired Boyne. 'Home', came the reply. 'But he's an earl,' commented Boyne, prompting the reminder from Osborne that Home was now able to disclaim his peerage. Later in the morning, Boyne was approached at the press table by Elizabeth Sturges-Jones, a Central Office press officer. 'Don't forget Alec Home,' she told him. She had heard Home mentioned by local party representatives. In Boyne's view, the person spreading Home's name was the Chief Whip, Redmayne.[26]

Had Macleod not been as quick as he was to discount any reference to Home as a contender, he might have realized what was afoot. His readiness to accept what Home had said surprises some of Macleod's friends. Although Home was regarded as one of the most trustworthy politicians, Macleod was a realist and they would not have expected him to take such a remark as a moral commitment. Macleod was usually among the first to recognize that circumstances can change quickly in politics and that whatever Home had told his colleagues on Tuesday morning, he might be tempted by the leadership. However, Macleod was certainly not alone: Hailsham, too, explicitly believed what Home had told the Cabinet and refused to accept the warning of Ian Gilmour and Dennis Walters that the Foreign Secretary was in the running.[27]

Macleod also assumed that the Prime Minister's resignation would not occur until some time after the froth of the conference had faded. By Wednesday, only Butler and Home already knew that the first moves in the leadership struggle were about to be made at Blackpool. Butler, on his arrival in Blackpool late that afternoon, immediately moved to demonstrate his preeminence by occupying the prime ministerial suite, while the National Union's powers-that-be were persuaded to invite him to address the Saturday afternoon rally in the Prime Minister's place. Ominously for Butler, he had more difficulty in persuading a dozen Cabinet ministers to allow him to accept the invitation and, by way of a barter, had to sacrifice his planned speech at the close of Thursday morning's session on party policy (the Saturday address became his only speech of the week). His close colleagues, Boyle and Macleod, still unaware of the storm that was about to break over the conference, were surprised at Butler's insistence that he should address the rally. It was only later on Wednesday evening that Macleod first learned that Macmillan's intention to resign was to be announced on Thursday afternoon, assuming that his operation that morning had been successful.[28]

The Balloon Goes Up

On Thursday morning, the 10th, Macleod delivered his speech to the conference. Rallying the party faithful on this occasion presented a major challenge, even for a proven master of the conference platform. Not only had the 4,000 representatives arrived in Blackpool after a dismal year for their party, worse even than the disasters of 1962, but now the Tory leadership was uncertain.

Macleod needed no encouragement to see that the most effective way to banish the uncertainties over the Tory leadership was to mock the opposition leaders. The previous month, Grimond had delivered the speech of his life when he urged his Liberal troops to march towards the sound of gunfire, a bravura performance that Macleod now dismissed: 'We need not waste time on Mr Grimond's Fred Karno effort about marching his troops towards the sound of gunfire – "It's a long, long way to Tipperary".' And as for the new Labour leader, Macleod recalled that when Wilson had resigned in 1951 after four years at the Board of Trade, he (Wilson) had spoken of British industry standing 'disorganized and threatened by partial paralysis'. 'That is what four years of Mr Wilson does for you,' declared Macleod. 'This is not a Daniel. This is Ethelred the Unready come to judgment.'

In his stirring peroration, Macleod roused the conference with a memorable declaration:

And will we win? Yes, of course we shall. The Conservative Party is like dry tinder, and a spark will set it ablaze. Let us start now from this great conference, as we did at Blackpool in 1950, 1954 and again in 1958. Let the faint hearts go their ways. Whoever they be, there is no room for them in our party. We are better without them.

It was a thrilling finale, although in ten days' time his attack on 'the faint hearts' would be turned against him by his enemies. But now he had given Tory loyalists a moment to savour for which they had long yearned. They rose to their feet to applaud – standing ovations were not then as common as they later became.[29]

Yet even Macleod's spell-binding performance was eclipsed by the drama that began to unfold later that day. During the afternoon session, the crowded conference hall was told that an important announcement about Macmillan would be made at the end of the day's final debate. Poor Boyd-Carpenter, Chief Secretary to the Treasury, whose speech on the rating system (the result of months of detailed work) immediately preceded this statement, found that his words fell on deaf ears. Eventually, at 5.05 pm, the Earl of Home, as President of the National Union, rose to address the conference from the platform, and donning his then unfashionable and antiquated-looking half-moon specs, read Macmillan's letter. Writing on Wednesday, before he underwent his operation, the Prime Minister explained that even if the operation was successful, he:

> Would not be able to face all that is involved in a prolonged electoral campaign. Nor could I hope to fulfil the tasks of Prime Minister for any extended period. I have so informed the Queen. In these circumstances I hope that it will soon be possible for the customary processes of consultation to be carried on within the party about its future leadership.

Beside Home on the platform as he read the letter a bevy of ministers sat like stones, as *The Times* reported:

> Only Mr Macleod betrayed the strain that many of them must have felt. He sat looking straight ahead, unseeing, and in his eyes there rose a tear, which glistened for an instant in the television lights.[30]

The emotion of the moment did not cause Macleod to lose his sense of ironic detachment. As Watkins recalls, when he enquired of the Party Chairman what he thought would be the outcome of the leadership struggle, Macleod responded to the effect that the Conservative Party would 'do the right thing, as it always does. It will come to a considered decision, which will be the right one'. This was said with a twinkle in his eye. But Macleod neither had any inkling of what would follow, nor did he imagine that 'the customary processes of consultation' would be brought into utter disrepute.[31]

Hailsham had already been sought out by Amery and Maurice Macmillan. 'Their joint message was clear and was conveyed straight from Harold himself,' Hailsham has recalled. He was to act at once. Their message was confirmed by Poole, who urged Hailsham that his announcement should be irrevocable and unequivocal. Hailsham had already spoken with Home, reminding him of their earlier conversation about the impossibility of their both disclaiming. Hailsham now told Home that he (Home) did not have adequate experience of home affairs to become Prime Minister. On Thursday evening, when Hailsham told Butler of his plans to disclaim, the acting Prime Minister, not unnaturally, sought to dissuade him.[32]

Hailsham announced his intentions later that evening, in the unlikely surroundings of the Baronial Hall in the Winter Gardens, where he delivered the prestigious, annual CPC lecture, something of an intellectual high-point of each year's conference. Hailsham kept to his prepared text. Major Morrison, who left before the vote of thanks, was soon telling people at the Imperial Hotel what a boring, dreary speech Hailsham had made. However, immediately after the vote of thanks this decorous occasion became bedlam. Hailsham began to make a personal statement, and to cries of 'Declare yourself!' from one of the boxes high above the auditorium, the Macmillan family candidate proclaimed that it was 'his wish to say tonight that it is my intention to disclaim my peerage'. This declaration was greeted by loud applause and shouts of 'We want Hailsham!' But many were shocked by the raucous scenes. Unfortunately for Hailsham, instead of demonstrating his popular appeal, the episode reminded Tories of his showmanship and other incidents – his ringing the bell at the 1957 conference and his outburst on television over Profumo – that raised doubts over his temperamental suitability for the highest office.[33]

Reggie Bennett, Macleod's 'eyes and ears', quickly learned of Hailsham's dramatic declaration and passed on the news to Macleod. For the next forty-eight hours the Imperial Hotel, where ministers and party bigwigs were staying, became the focus of intense canvassing and lobbying. But Macleod remained aloof, much to the consternation and puzzlement of his political allies and press contacts. Patrick Jenkin, one of Macleod's 'young Turks', who had been Tory candidate for Labour-held Enfield East before his adoption to fight Sir Winston Churchill's former seat, 'was becoming increasingly concerned that he (Macleod) was falling behind in the race'. After Macleod's speech on the Thursday morning, Jenkin approached Macleod and asked him:

'Iain, are you in this race?'

'Yes, of course I'm in it,' replied Macleod.

'Well, you've got to get moving, because the forces for Rab and Alec and so on, are all gathering strength, and people are not talking about you as being among the front-runners. What are you going to do?'

'Oh, I've got my people working. My hat is in the ring.'

Although Macleod appeared to be 'quite determined' in what he told Jenkin, 'his people' were not being organized to work for him and were conspicuous only by their absence. It was not clear who they were, since all his friends and advisers profess to having been as concerned as Jenkin about Macleod's apparent inaction.[34]

Like most other witnesses of events at Blackpool, Rees-Mogg recalls little of Macleod during the conference: 'it was a characteristic defect of Iain as a practical politician that he played his cards far too close to his chest . . . The result of that was that he didn't mobilize the people who were sympathetic to him in the way that he could have.' Macleod's attitude appeared to be that since the leadership would not be settled at Blackpool, and the Cabinet would have the last word, there was no point running a campaign during the conference. It might even prove counter-productive. His old foes on the right from his days as Colonial Secretary would more easily be able to mount a vociferous campaign against him at Blackpool and he might find himself being ruled out too early. He was a very long shot for the leadership and his only chance lay in a deadlock between the main contenders, when he might be able to come from the back of the field.[35]

The upshot was that Macmillan's chicanery left Macleod standing. Dilhorne and Redmayne immediately set in motion 'the customary processes' for selecting a new leader, although the Prime Minister had only said that he hoped that 'it would soon be possible' to do so and did not formally commission soundings of party opinion until the following Tuesday. Some ministers recollect visiting Dilhorne in his small back bedroom in the Imperial and sitting on the edge of his unmade bed while responding to the Lord Chancellor's questions about their preference for the next Prime Minister of the United Kingdom. Amery recalls, when he was asked, saying that he wanted Hailsham and was against Butler, but would be prepared to accept a compromise candidate. Meanwhile, Redmayne was busily summoning backbenchers to his room. This was a daunting experience in those more deferential days, when the Imperial remained the preserve of ministers and party grandees, while a relatively small media retinue frequented the bar. Admitting to 'some trepidation', Jim Prior found himself in the Chief Whip's presence:

'Who do you favour?'
  'Reggie Maudling as first choice, but if not, Rab, of course.'
  'Not Quintin.'
  'No, not Quintin.'
  'Thank you very much.'
Then:
  'By the way, what about Alec if he decides to stand?'

'I don't really know him, and in any case he's in the House of Lords.'
'So he's not a runner?'
'Well, we don't know yet, do we?'
'But if he does renounce?'
'I suppose he would be possible.'

Prior had 'little doubt that even at that early stage I was put down as an Alec supporter'. His experience was shared by other backbenchers and junior ministers at Blackpool and in London the following week.[36]

Like many others, Prior was baffled why Macleod, 'who after all was Party Chairman, ever allowed the Home bandwagon to gather momentum'. Bennett had a blazing row with Macleod about it. After Hailsham's declaration, Macleod told him 'in no uncertain terms that the Cabinet had gone on strike and would not have Quintin'. But Bennett had learned that Home was being promoted as a compromise candidate.

'There's a dark horse, and he's coming up on the rails,' Bennett said.
'Who?' asked Macleod.
'Alec.'
'Don't talk nonsense'.
'I'm not inventing this. I'm hearing it everywhere, I assure you.'
'Absolute rot; it's not a possibility.'
'But it's being said.'
'Quite impossible. I have heard him affirm categorically that he was not a candidate.'
'Maybe he isn't or wasn't; but that doesn't say that he hasn't been drafted.'

This news did not accord with Macleod's belief that he had the word of an honest man. He not only rejected what Bennett was telling him, but appeared deaf to the growing clamour of right-wing support for Home from the likes of Nigel Birch, the former Treasury minister, who arrived in Blackpool noisily championing the Foreign Secretary's cause. When David Butler, the Oxford political scientist, gave his appraisal of the candidates' prospects during a television broadcast, and afterwards (off screen) asked Macleod for his comment, Macleod replied (as he wrote three months later):

that it was a fine analysis and only obviously wrong in one assessment. I promised to tell him 'when all this is over' what was wrong. Lunching with him recently I explained my comment. Home, I told him, was at the time of the broadcast in no circumstances a contender.

However, Macleod did not reveal in his subsequent exposé that before the end of the October conference, he would make an important move to head off Home's challenge.[37]

Macleod was more active behind the scenes than has generally been realized, but not in his own cause. With Hailsham's bandwagon stalled, Maudling and Butler had emerged as the principal front-runners. Hailsham, who held Macleod's 'mastery of the House of Commons' in highest regard, 'never quite knew why Reginald Maudling and not Iain was, with Rab Butler and myself, the third contender for the succession to Harold Macmillan'. However, by 1963, Maudling, the 46-year-old Chancellor of the Exchequer, clearly enjoyed stronger support among young Tory MPs and ministers. They hoped that by jumping a generation the party would meet the challenge from Labour's new 47-year-old leader, Wilson. Maudling's prospects were further boosted, since even some of Butler's natural sympathizers doubted Rab's suitability as a Prime Minister, primarily because of his alleged tendency to sit on the fence when decisions had to be made. Although Butler's postwar vision of Toryism had inspired the 'One Nation' group of backbenchers, they failed to back him when they met privately at the Imperial to discuss the leadership.[38]

Initially, Macleod wanted the succession to pass to his own generation. He readily agreed a 'non-aggression pact' with Maudling, to the effect that whichever one of them had the best chance of securing the Tory succession, neither would stand in the way of the other. This meant that at Blackpool Macleod backed Maudling. It seemed propitious for Maudling that his speech to the conference should fall on the Friday morning. Although Maudling was no orator, Macleod gave him all the help he could and tried to ensure that he would at least follow the basic tenets of speechmaking. 'For God's sake, give them time to clap,' Macleod urged, 'and when you get to your peroration, belt it out with all you've got.' Macleod sat next to Maudling on the platform to give him moral support and, as Wilfrid Sendall reported in the *Sunday Express*, when the Chancellor rose to speak, 'Iain Macleod generously whispered to him: "Go on Reggie, this is your chance".'[39]

Tragically for Maudling, he failed to rise to the occasion. His speech concluded with 'a peroration which Churchill would not have disdained', as the Chancellor proclaimed the noble purposes of economic policy, but, as Sendall lamented:

> If only the delivery could have matched the words. But, alas, it fell abysmally below them. Handed to Churchill, or to Macmillan, or to Macleod, this text would have produced a famous speech. Maudling himself wrecked it.

With it was wrecked Maudling's hope of the leadership. 'How could Reggie do it?' Macleod asked despairingly afterwards. Harry Boyne found that Macleod 'was practically in tears' over Maudling's failure and spoke of it as 'the lost chance'.[40]

The inauspicious omens became stronger during Friday when Home delivered his conference speech to conclude the foreign affairs debate. He was well received despite giving the impression that he had not made any great effort to rouse the conference, even commenting 'I am offering a prize to any newspaperman who can find a clue in my speech that this is Lord Home's bid for the leadership.' Perhaps it was Home's triumph, in contrast to Maudling's wretchedly disappointing performance, that finally persuaded Macleod to act.

In his room at the Imperial, in the very early hours of Saturday morning, Macleod gave two of the most respected lobby journalists of their day, David Wood of *The Times* and Harry Boyne of the *Daily Telegraph*, an off-the-record briefing. Over 'long thin scotches', served by Reggie Bennett, Macleod confirmed the rumours that Home was in contention. Was he, perhaps, talking up Home's prospects in order to convey that a deadlock was developing between Butler and Home, in the hope that he would emerge from the back of the field? Neither Wood nor Boyne subscribe to this theory. Wood had no doubt that Macleod was determined that the party should not disperse the next day without knowing what threatened (a real challenge from Home) and he also hoped that in doing so, he would help Butler achieve a groundswell of support in the conference and promote his claim. Sir Harry Boyne confirms Wood's interpretation.[41]

It is worth reiterating what Macleod stood to gain if Butler won: in Butler's words, he and Macleod 'had a secret . . . he always said he hoped that I would be Prime Minister, and he wished himself to succeed me.' Moreover, as Butler also subsequently revealed, had he become Prime Minister, he would have appointed Macleod Chancellor of the Exchequer. Macleod was aware of this, since Butler also disclosed that he 'had already discussed with him [Macleod] the names of some economists who could have been brought in to help'. As soon as Maudling had failed to seize the crown for the younger generation, Macleod hoped that Butler would be selected.[42]

In Macleod's own, subsequent account of the leadership struggle, he claimed that neither he nor Maudling had thought of Home as a contender until they first heard of his selection the following Thursday (17th), 'although for a brief moment his star seemed to have flared at Blackpool'. On the night of Friday the 11th, Macleod suddenly seemed to have spotted a *super nova*. His mistake was in assuming that it would fade as quickly as it had 'flared'.[43]

Before Butler's address to Saturday afternoon's Tory rally, Rab and Mollie, his wife, lunched with the Homes, who, as Mollie has recalled, 'were friends, not rivals, in our eyes'. To the Butlers' amazement, Home informed them that he would be consulting his doctor to check on the state of his health. This could mean only one thing: Home was about to throw his hat in the ring. The news threw Butler off his stride. In addition to Dilhorne and Redmayne, Home's name was already being pressed by a number of senior Tories, notably Selwyn Lloyd, the former Chancellor and Foreign Secretary, Duncan Sandys, the Commonwealth Secretary, John Hare, Minister of Labour, Nigel Birch, the former Treasury Minister, John Morrison, Sir William Anstruther-Gray and Sir Charles Mott-Radclyffe.[44]

'We choose a leader not for what he does or does not do at the party conference,' Home declared as he introduced Butler at the afternoon rally, 'but because the leader we choose is in every respect a whole man who in all circumstances is fit to lead the nation.' As Fisher notes: 'It was a curious and unlikely remark if, at that time, he considered himself a candidate.' But depending on his doctor's report, Home intended to enter the contest. Butler's speech disappointed his supporters. One incident was particularly telling. As Butler spoke, he was heckled by some Empire Loyalists in the audience. When Butler paused to mop his brow, Home, in his capacity as President of the National Union, intervened to restore order.[45]

13

The Tory Leadership: 'The Magic Circle'

It is some measure of the tightness of the magic circle on this occasion that neither the Chancellor of the Exchequer nor the Leader of the House of Commons had any inkling of what was happening.

Iain Macleod on the October 1963 struggle for the Tory leadership, the *Spectator*, 17 January 1964.

The Drama Returns to London

After Butler's speech on Saturday afternoon, Tory representatives, MPs and ministers went their separate ways. But any hopes that the heady atmosphere generated during the conference would quickly evaporate were dashed by the continuing speculation in the press. The canvassing and lobbying by contenders and supporters transferred to Westminster and Whitehall – Ian Gilmour, one of Hailsham's supporters, met Macleod in White's one night and suggested that he might join the 'Quintin bandwagon', but Macleod replied, 'No, I'm not going to row in that boat'.[1]

Because Parliament was not sitting, ministers and MPs were denied the regular source of information and gossip that flows though the corridors, lobbies and tearooms when the Commons is in session. Many junior ministers were quickly submerged in their departmental work and many MPs were not in London – Bennett, for example, was no longer in close touch with Macleod. This helped Macmillan control the succession from his sick-bed. His interest lay in bringing matters to a head as quickly as possible and certainly before Parliament resumed on Thursday 24th, when the main contenders in the Commons, Butler and Maudling, and possibly even Macleod, would more easily be able to rally their support. Macmillan's great *coup* was to fool the contenders in the Commons into believing that the 'customary processes' would take time, whereas in fact he was planning to settle the succession within a matter of days, as the Prime Minister divulged to the Queen but not the Cabinet.[2]

On Monday 14 October, Home received a clean bill of health from his doctor. That evening Macmillan heard the result of informal soundings of the party from his son, Maurice, and Poole, the Joint Party Chairman: the party in the country wanted Hailsham, MPs wanted Maudling or Butler, and the Cabinet wanted Butler. This confirmed that the Prime Minister could best block Butler by consulting all sections of the party before the return of the Commons. Macmillan prepared a minute outlining his plans for the soundings of party opinion, which was read to the Cabinet by the hapless Butler, as acting Prime Minister, on the morning of Tuesday the 15th: the Cabinet's views would be taken by Lord Dilhorne, the Lord Chancellor; those of Tory MPs and junior ministers by Redmayne, the Chief Whip; those of active Tory peers and ministers in the Lords by Lord St Aldwyn, the Whip in the Lords; and those of the constituency parties by Lord Poole, Mrs Peggy Shepherd and Lord Chelmer 'as best they can'.[3]

Macleod's exclusion from any role in taking soundings indicated that he was not one of the 'magic circle', but it could also be taken as signifying that he remained an outside contender. This was what Macleod appeared to think, since he told Randolph Churchill on Monday the 14th:

'Keep your eye on the back of the field.'
'You mean looking for a dark horse?' Churchill queried.
'That's it.'
'Would the dark horse be called Macleod?'
'That's about it.'

'But he must have known in his heart,' Nigel Fisher judges, 'that the prospects of this were poor.' Of considerably greater importance than Macleod's exclusion from Macmillan's list was Home's (Dilhorne was to be solely responsible for sounding out the Cabinet). Macmillan had switched to promoting Home as 'he would be the best able to secure united support'. Significantly, no formal provision was made in Macmillan's minute for the Cabinet to have any further role before advice was formally tendered to the Queen. Although Macmillan's minute stated that 'These consultations may take a day or two', suggesting that the selection process might be concluded swiftly, it did not occur to ministers to insist on meeting again after the 'customary processes' had been completed. As a result, Macmillan was able to retain complete control from his sick-bed.[4]

Although Macmillan saw members of his Cabinet during Tuesday and Wednesday (Macleod was among those who attended on Tuesday afternoon), he regarded their visits as courtesy calls. Randolph Churchill's narrative, vetted by Macmillan (and described by Macleod as 'Mr Macmillan's trailer for the screenplay of his memoirs'), is perhaps more revealing of the Prime Minister's ploy than either Churchill or Macmillan realized. According to Churchill, Macmillan greeted any suggestions from ministers about the leadership during their brief conversations by referring:

To the Cabinet decision on Tuesday that the four separate 'soundings' should be carried out. They (ministers) realized that they could do or say nothing that could affect the issue until the enquiries had been completed.

Macmillan's plan had now been elevated to the unchallengeable status of a 'Cabinet decision'. There was an implication that ministers would have some further opportunity to 'affect the issue' after 'the enquiries had been carried out'. It was this opportunity that Macmillan was anxious to deny his ministers. 'The Prime Minister,' Churchill added in an infelicitous turn of phrase, 'having thus sewn up the situation in a bag, nonetheless continued to take an active interest in the situation. . . . He was determined to see the matter through. And see it through he did.'[5]

Yet not every minister was happy at the way the Cabinet were being sidelined. As Macleod relates, on the very day that the Cabinet had heard Macmillan's plan for soundings to be taken:

> a member of the Cabinet came to see me. He had been trying without success to have a meeting of the Cabinet called to consider the situation. I gave him splendidly ironical advice in the light of what was already afoot. 'Try Alec,' [Home] I said, 'he's not a contender, and he ought to be a kingmaker.' He took my advice, but not surprisingly without result.

The moral of this anecdote is that if Butler, as acting Prime Minister, and Macleod, as Party Chairman and Leader of the House, had been alert sooner, they might still have thwarted Macmillan. Indeed, Boyle, one of Butler's strongest supporters, was in a position to raise the alarm twenty-four hours before Macleod first heard the name of Macmillan's successor. Immediately after his interview with the Prime Minister on Wednesday 16th, Boyle had been told by Bligh, the Prime Minister's Private Secretary, that Home was the likely winner. Had Boyle thought to pass on this inside information, the moves to organize Butler's support might have begun a crucial day earlier. Even so, Macleod still came within an ace of securing the Tory crown for his mentor.[6]

The soundings of party opinion were conducted following Tuesday morning's Cabinet and during Wednesday. These soundings and the presentation of advice to the Queen as to whom she might ask to become her next First Minister were portrayed as objective assessments, impartially applied. They were no such thing. This was at the heart of Macleod's subsequent attack and explains why he could not allow Randolph Churchill's apologia of the selection process, and of Macmillan's role, to stand unchallenged.

Macleod's criticism is not primarily focused on the soundings of Tory peers or the party in the country. Of the peers, who were reported to be the strongest (two to one) in their support for Home, Macleod pithily observes, 'I'm sure they were.' He was reminded of 'the verse composed in epitaph for Tom Harrisson who with Charles Madge founded Mass Observation – Dr Gallup's forefather:

> They buried poor Tom Harrisson with his Mass Observer's badge
> And his notebooks: there were twenty thousand odd.
> And he'd not been gone a week when a report arrived for Madge:
> Heaven's 83.4 per cent pro God.

The constituencies were reckoned to be split 60 per cent for Hailsham and 40 per cent for Butler. 'This doesn't seem to leave much room for the rest of us,' Macleod notes tartly, since 'the spread was much wider.' But what most concerned Macleod were the soundings of junior ministers and MPs and also of the Cabinet.[7]

In Macleod's view, Macmillan was not the only key player in the drama – the Chief Whip was also central: 'Churchill wholly underestimates the significance of the fact that Redmayne believed that Home was the right man.' Macleod does not dispute that Redmayne had sought to fulfil his duty as Chief Whip:

> to consider which man is 'best' for the party, and if he comes to a clear conclusion to do all in his power to achieve that result . . . His judgement may have been right or (as of course I believe) wrong. That it was sincere is beyond argument.

Likewise, Macleod readily accepted that: 'In a still higher sense the same duty applies to an outgoing Prime Minister, and I can accept that Mr Macmillan discharged it with equal sincerity.' In Macleod's view, Macmillan judged:

> And it is only honest to admit that many others shared his view, that Butler had not in him the steel that makes a Prime Minister nor the inspiration that a Leader needs to pull a Party through a fierce General Election.

It was Macleod's contention that although Redmayne and Macmillan had acted in what they saw as the party's best interest, Butler's rejection and Home's selection had only been achieved by considerable manipulation and management of the selection process, or what he called in his exposé, 'contradiction and misrepresentation'. Was Macleod right?[8]

Less than a week after the leadership struggle was over, and stung by criticism in the press of the selection process, Redmayne attempted to prove in a speech at Bournemouth on 25 October that Home had not been a compromise candidate – although as we now know from Macmillan's diary, the Prime Minister referred to Home as a 'compromise candidate'. In Macmillan's plan, the whips were supposed to ascertain from Conservative MPs their first choice as the next Leader, their second choice, and who they would least like to see as Leader. Redmayne claimed that even on the first preferences of Tory MPs Home had a very small lead, a point that he would repeat during a radio interview two months later. 'I am neither impressed nor surprised,' Macleod commented in his own account:

> The Chief Whip and I imagine the Whips Office had been working hard for a week to secure the maximum support for Lord Home. So had many of the leading figures on the backbenches. That in such circumstances Lord Home had achieved a majority of one or perhaps two will amaze few people.

As Churchill acknowledged, 'Home led in popularity' among junior ministers and backbenchers, 'but only narrowly. There was no clear-cut overall majority for him'. Among the senior backbenchers to whom Macleod alluded were Selwyn Lloyd, the former Chancellor and Foreign Secretary, and Major John Morrison, Chairman of the 1922 Committee. Macleod might also have pointed out that although Morrison was accorded no role in the procedure laid down by Macmillan, Churchill reports that the Major accompanied Redmayne to the hospital on the morning of Thursday 17th, in order to present 'their combined report of feeling' among junior ministers and Tory MPs. During the presentation of their 'combined report', Churchill adds that 'Morrison personally expressed himself strongly in favour of Home' – Morrison had been backing Home since the summer.[9]

But are Macleod's allegations about the whips true? Redmayne had already approached many junior ministers and MPs during the Tory conference, before the Prime Minister had laid down the formal procedure. And as at Blackpool, the Chief Whip's exercise continued to favour Home. Viscount Whitelaw, who was then a junior minister, but had served in the Whips' Office and would later succeed Redmayne, vividly recalls his experience of the selection process. Whitelaw was telephoned by one of the whips, asking him who he wanted. Whitelaw wanted Butler, with some misgivings. He was then asked, 'But if Alec Home was available would you be prepared to support him?' As Whitelaw recalls, it was 'a totally irregular second question'. Sir Reginald Bennett also recalls that he was asked, 'If Home was nominated, would you vote against him?' Similarly, Berkeley has recalled that:

> A vital question was put to those who were verbally consulted, including myself, namely that 'If there is a deadlock between Rab and Quintin would you accept Alec Home?'

Berkeley declined to answer 'this hypothetical question', but he is convinced that many other MPs 'fell into the trap and, in this way, Mr Macmillan got the answer that he wanted'.[10]

Half a dozen surviving members of the 1963 Whips' Office later denied that they were instructed to use the hypothetical question quoted by Berkeley, but were left to consult MPs 'in any way they thought fit'. However, Redmayne let the cat out of the bag during his radio interview when he revealed that his 15-strong team of whips provided him with:

> A simple note of the preference of each man, [sic] of any second or third preference, and of any particular objection he might have to any of the known candidates, plus a great deal of other detail, some of it personal, some of it political and so forth.

In other words, the whips' exercise was not a straightforward, head-counting exercise, and embellished even the survey of MPs' preferences apparently envisaged by Macmillan. Redmayne also claimed that Home 'was outstandingly the leader as you took it further through the field'. This calculation was biased. When asked whether he attached more weight to the opinion of some MPs than to the opinion of others, he acknowledged that 'in every organization there must be people of whose opinion one would more strongly rely than on others'. Secondly, although he rejected press allegations of having organized a 'black-ball system', he immediately confirmed that this was precisely what had been done:

> Since the object of the exercise was to find out under what Prime Minister the party could most unitedly and enthusiastically move on in the pre-election period, *one had obviously to think with which man there would be the least number of dissidents* [author's emphasis].[11]

In one of Macleod's most damning comments on the Chief Whip's role, he suggested that 'if the recording of opinions approached the confusion known to have been engendered by the method of sounding the Cabinet the margins of error must have been enormous'. Responsibility for sounding the Cabinet lay with Dilhorne, but as Macleod argued:

> The lobby correspondents have been shown by events to have made a more accurate assessment of opinion in the Cabinet than the one attributed by Churchill's book to the Lord Chancellor. For it is with the revelation of the Cabinet's opinions that we reach true absurdity.

According to Churchill's account (vetted by Macmillan), on the morning of Thursday 16th:

Dilhorne arrived at the hospital at 10.56 and he reported to the Prime Minister that most of the Cabinet were very strong for Home. Whereas originally there had been six adherents of Butler and six of Hailsham, Dilhorne had to report that the overwhelming consensus pointed to Home. Home had the best chance of uniting the Cabinet if he could be persuaded to disclaim his peerage.

'I cannot imagine,' noted Macleod, 'what "originally" means unless it is suggested that there were two or more polls by the Cabinet.' Plainly Macleod was unaware of there having been more than one 'poll'. The Lord Chancellor had begun his soundings at Blackpool and continued (and possibly repeated some of them) in London the following week. 'With the benefit of hindsight,' Dilhorne wrote shortly before his death in 1980 to Alistair Horne, Macmillan's biographer, 'I think it was a mistake to try to obtain views during the hurly burly of that Blackpool conference. It should have been done when things were calmer and people had more time for reflection.'[12]

Yet a bigger mystery concerns Dilhorne's assessment that the Cabinet supported Home. His detailed report to Macmillan, which was only revealed in 1989, claimed that the Cabinet's first preferences were: Home 10, Maudling 4, Butler 3 and Hailsham 2 (Home was not counted as voting). Yet long before these details were available, Macleod had challenged Dilhorne's conclusions with his own estimate. 'On Friday, October 18th,' wrote Macleod:

five members of the Cabinet met for a sandwich lunch. None thought Lord Home the first choice. Butler, Hailsham and Boyle were not present. That makes eight. Of the others I only know the point of view of five: two for Home, three against. From my personal knowledge then eleven were against Home and two for. There were some half a dozen others. But even if there wasn't a single one of these for Butler or Maudling or Hailsham, the figures in the [Churchill] book (as other reviewers have pointed out) are simply impossible.[13]

Macleod's estimates have been supported by Powell and by Lady Butler, who published the list of eight Cabinet ministers who telephoned her husband on the evening of the 17th and morning of the 18th to say that they were supporting him. Seeking to 'explain the inexplicable', as Macleod described Dilhorne's arithmetic, he concludes charitably (but one suspects with his tongue in his cheek) that during the separate conversations between Dilhorne and each member of the Cabinet, 'the expressions of genuine regard for him [Home] somehow became translated into second or even first preferences'.[14]

The biggest puzzle is that Dilhorne listed Macleod among the ten

Ministers who declared their first preference for Home. Yet when Home became Prime Minister, Macleod refused to serve in his administration. Horne speculates that Macleod may have changed his mind, suggesting that this can be inferred from Macleod's comment that the 'key day' for him was Thursday 17th, 'which began as an ordinary working day and ended with my firm decision that I could not serve in the Administration that I knew Lord Home was to be invited to form.' But this is to take the sentence out of context and stretch Macleod's meaning too far.[15]

But is Dilhorne right about Macleod's having backed Home? The Lord Chancellor's record of preferences is written down in black and white, and in the absence of any Macleod diary, there is no known, surviving documentary evidence written at the time in which Macleod states precisely what passed between him and Dilhorne. Dilhorne later assured Horne that 'It is not a thing about which I would make a mistake', and Horne comments that the Lord Chancellor was a lawyer trained 'not to get things wrong' – although another former minister was prompted by the revelation to observe that 'Reggie [Dilhorne] got it wrong – he often did.' Butler professed himself 'not at all surprised' at Dilhorne's note, since 'Macleod was very shifty, much more than you think', while Macmillan commented cryptically, 'Well, you know . . . Macleod was a Highlander . . .!' Those inclined to take Dilhorne's written record at face value discern two possible motivations for Macleod's choice – either that he opted for Home because he underestimated the Foreign Secretary's support in Cabinet and by supporting him hoped to bring about the deadlock from which he might emerge as leader; or that he voted tactically for Home in order to block Hailsham. Yet neither theory accords with the recollections of those who were closest to Macleod at the time, or with his subsequent actions.[16]

The evidence that Dilhorne had got it wrong is compelling. Gilmour, who discussed both the crisis and the *Spectator* exposé with Macleod, hits the nail on the head when he writes: 'If for whatever reason Macleod had voted for Home, it is not within the bounds of possibility that he would have refused to serve in Home's government.' Like Gilmour, Powell, who was closest to Macleod during the leadership struggle finds it 'inconceivable that Macleod at that stage was playing a devious game' and quite impossible that Macleod could have changed his mind. Similarly, Lord Aldington (who attended meetings at both Macleod's and Powell's flats on Thursday 17th), Lord Eccles (a Cabinet colleague until 1962) and Lord Fraser of Kilmorack (formerly Sir Michael Fraser, who had known Macleod since school days and who, as head of the research department, was extremely well informed during the leadership crisis) all dismiss the idea that Macleod had backed Home. Eve Macleod is adamant that her husband could never have supported Home.[17]

Dilhorne is condemned as an unreliable witness by his own written record, for he also lists Boyle, a card-carrying Tory left-winger, among the first preferences for Home. Boyle recalled privately less than four months after the leadership struggle that when Dilhorne had asked him about Home, he had replied that Home was not on and had reserved his position about serving. As Gilmour argues, although 'Macleod might just conceivably have voted tactically for Home . . . it is inconceivable that Boyle would have done so'. So much for Dilhorne's score-keeping. Moreover, when Macleod's narrative flatly contradicted the accuracy of Dilhorne's figures only three months later, the Lord Chancellor did nothing to rebut the charge. Gilmour is surely right to conclude that 'Dilhorne's silence shows that he knew his figures were phoney'. Had it been true that the majority of the Cabinet had declared for Home as their first choice and that Macleod was one of that majority, Dilhorne could have destroyed Macleod's argument and his credibility at a time when Macleod's stock in the party was at rock bottom. Macleod would have realized the weapon that he was handing Dilhorne, and it is beyond the bounds of possibility that he would have put his career at Dilhorne's mercy.[18]

The 'midnight meeting'

On Thursday 17th, Macleod and the main contenders – except, of course, Home – were to discover their folly in allowing Macmillan to remain in control of events. That morning, as Macleod noted in his narrative, his wife:

> came back from a long telephone conversation with one of our oldest friends . . . to say that the succession was to be decided that afternoon. The information was third-hand, but the links were strong, and the original source the one man who would certainly know.

The 'friend' was Viscountess Monckton, with whom Eve had been discussing the hospitals' League of Friends; the Viscountess's informant was Lady Dorothy Macmillan; and the 'original source' was none other than the Prime Minister. The Tory wives' network had again proved its effectiveness. Macleod 'was surprised but not disturbed' by the news:

> To me it seemed clear that if the situation was going to gell swiftly, the choice must be Butler: if there was deadlock, it would surely come back to the Cabinet. I had not of course appreciated then that it was in fact an essential part of the design that the Cabinet should have no such opportunity. Churchill's book makes this plain.[19]

Still unaware of Macmillan's real design, Macleod attended a morning meeting at Number Ten on the difficult closing stages of the Kenya conference. Both he and Maudling were present as former Colonial Secretaries, and afterwards Macleod accompanied the Chancellor back to his room in the Treasury where, over a drink, Macleod told of his wife's telephone conversation. They were soon joined by Frederick Erroll, President of the Board of Trade and Maudling's closest friend in the Cabinet. As a result of their talk, shortly before one o'clock Maudling telephoned Dilhorne. 'To all suggestions that the Cabinet (or the Cabinet less the chief contenders) should meet,' Macleod added, 'Dilhorne was deaf.' Maudling first suggested that the Lord Chancellor should convene a ministers' meeting to discuss the whole question of the leadership, an idea that Dilhorne resisted, revealing that he was due back at Macmillan's bedside, where he had spent much of the morning. Ten minutes later, Maudling called Dilhorne again, urging that the Cabinet should have an opportunity to review the procedures the Prime Minister was planning to use in preparing his assessment of party opinion to the Queen. Dilhorne still refused. Macleod later learned that the Lord Chancellor had already turned down one such request: 'No doubt he thought he was acting wisely.' Yet the failing surely rests with Butler. Although Dilhorne was supposedly holding the ring during the leadership struggle, Butler was acting Prime Minister and he had every right to call a Cabinet meeting for Thursday morning, which would have given him and other like-minded ministers the opportunity to prevent what followed. That morning he, too, had learned of the imminence of a decision on the leadership, but he failed to act.[20]

Although Macleod's suspicions had been raised, he still had no inkling of what was about to happen. He joined Maudling and his wife, Beryl, for lunch. They 'discussed Butler a good deal', referred to Hailsham once, but 'never mentioned Home in any connection'. Afterwards, Macleod returned to Conservative Central Office to clear some papers. It was there that Macleod first learned, indirectly, just how wrong he and Maudling had been about the likely choice:

> In mid-afternoon the telephone rang. It was a senior figure in Fleet Street. He told me the decision had been made, and that it was for Home. He himself found this incredible, but he was utterly sure of his source.

Macleod's informant was Rees-Mogg of the *Sunday Times*, who was telephoning Macleod, as Party Chairman, for confirmation of the story and was astonished to discover that Macleod was 'genuinely surprised' at the news.[21]

Macleod immediately telephoned Maudling and Powell and arranged to meet them as soon as possible at his Chelsea flat (all three then lived near one another in neighbouring Chelsea and Belgravia):

> Almost at once the phone calls started from the leading newspaper political correspondents. Each of them had the same story. Someone, I

presume, thought it proper even before the Prime Minister had resigned to prepare the press for the (unexpected) name that was to emerge. News management can be taken too far.

Before 'any action could be contemplated' by the three dissident ministers at Macleod's flat, they had to confirm the story 'beyond doubt'. Macleod did some telephoning of his own. Desperately trying to confirm the report, he called Harry Boyne at the *Daily Telegraph*. Boyne wondered what Macleod had heard, but first Macleod asked him whether he had heard 'that it's all come down to Alec, he's their man'. Boyne said that Redmayne, the Chief Whip had mentioned Home, and had made an exception to his usual line of saying that he couldn't say any more by adding the cryptic comment, 'Don't forget Goschen.' It had been Lord Randolph Churchill's great error to 'forget Goschen' when he offered Lord Salisbury his resignation as Chancellor of the Exchequer in December 1886: Salisbury called Churchill's bluff by accepting his resignation and appointing Goschen, the Liberal Unionist, in his place, consigning Churchill to political wilderness on the backbenches.[22]

But what was Redmayne's purpose in alluding to this incident? He was unlikely to do so merely to point to the failure of Randolph Churchill (grandson of Lord Randolph) to promote Hailsham's cause successfully. Instead, the Chief Whip was issuing a warning by the 'magic circle' against any attempt to organize against Home. Any dissidents would face the same fate as Lord Randolph – their bluff would be called and they would face political oblivion. Meanwhile, Maudling had left Macleod and Powell for half an hour to check the story, and eventually telephoned them with confirmation. Maudling then returned, and the dissident threesome were joined by Lord Aldington as the stream of telephone calls from the press continued.[23]

What happened at this juncture is critical to Macleod's refusal to serve. As Macleod explains, if he, Maudling and Powell 'were going to make any serious protest against an invitation being extended to Lord Home, it was essential that he should know about this at the earliest moment'. Powell and Macleod each decided to speak to him direct. Macleod had a dinner engagement, but telephoned Lord Home, who was out, and made an appointment for Powell and himself to see the Foreign Secretary after dinner. Macleod's reasoning gives the lie to suggestions that he may have changed his mind about serving Home during the course of the day. He had only heard that Home had emerged as the prospective leader that afternoon. As he makes clear in his article:

> From the beginning I was in no doubt that if, as Joint Chairman of the Party and Leader of the House of Commons, I felt strongly enough to tell Lord Home that I thought it wrong for him to accept an invitation to

form an administration, I could not honourably serve with him in that administration.

Macleod 'slipped away for a moment' to tell his wife what he 'thought the end might be'. And he 'felt clear that in the true interests of the Tory Party another point of view must be put'. Eve agreed 'at once', and continued to back his decision 'through all the unpleasantness, local and national, that we knew we must face'. The Macleods then went to the St Stephen's Club in Queen Anne's Gate, off Birdcage Walk, where he 'made as gay and confident a speech' as he could to the club's political committee. After the dinner, Macleod telephoned Powell and went round to his house in South Eaton Place. So began the so-called 'midnight meeting' that has become part of Tory mythology.[24]

Before Macleod and Powell telephoned Home, as they planned, they received a call from Hailsham, who had heard the reports of the intended nomination of Home. Hailsham kept in touch with the anti-Home, pro-Butler movement at South Eaton Place during the night from his Putney home, where his closest supporters had gathered. The telephone became Hailsham's source of intelligence and his principal weapon. He told Home, who confirmed the news of his nomination, that it was 'disastrous' and 'the most awful thing I have ever heard'. And speaking to Butler's wife, he remarked of Home's selection, 'Mollie, this simply will not do.'

When Macleod and Powell rang Home, it was apparent that they could not see him without 'running the gauntlet of the reporters who had already encased him'. Instead, they spoke on the telephone. As Macleod relates:

I spoke first. I told him that there was no one in the party for whom I had more admiration and respect; that if he had been in the House of Commons he could perhaps have been the first choice; but I felt that those giving advice had grossly underestimated the difficulties of presenting the situation in a convincing way to the modern Tory Party. Unlike Hailsham, he was not a reluctant peer, and we were now proposing to admit that after twelve years of Tory government no one amongst the 363 members of the party in the House of Commons was acceptable as Prime Minister. I felt it more straightforward to put these views to him tonight rather than perhaps have to put them in other circumstances tomorrow.

Macleod did not hear what Powell said to Home, but his assumption that he spoke on similar lines is confirmed by Patrick Cosgrave, Powell's biographer. In fact, by this stage the dissidents' objections should not have come as a complete surprise to Home, since his private office had been warned of likely dissension by Rees-Mogg, who telephoned his private secretary at the Foreign Office to warn that Home would be 'wholly unacceptable to a part of the younger section of the party, and the party will be split'.[25]

One by one, Maudling, Aldington and Erroll joined Macleod and Powell at Powell's house after their evening engagements. This gathering was only one of several feverish, ministerial conclaves that night. Macleod reckons that there were at least three 'and there may well have been others' – at Putney, Hailsham had been joined by Amery and Peter Thorneycroft, who were trying to persuade him to serve Home. Butler himself played no part, other than taking calls from his agitated supporters in his suite at St Ermin's Hotel, where he and Mollie were staying because of dry rot in their Smith Square home ('as well as in the body politic' in Mollie's sharp comment). The South Eaton Place meeting was discovered when Henry Fairlie, a political journalist, rang Maudling's home and was given another number that he traced as Powell's. Derek Marks of the *Daily Express* acted on a hunch and went to investigate. 'He deserves whatever award there is for the scoop of the year,' acknowledges Macleod, somewhat ruefully. Boyne came within a whisker of unearthing them. As had been agreed that afternoon, he telephoned Macleod's flat at 11.00 pm, but Eve told him that Macleod was not yet back. Boyne rang off, but when he picked up his receiver to call his news editor, he found that the operator had not yet disconnected his line and was astonished to hear Eve's voice saying, 'Harry Boyne's onto something, but I haven't told him anything. I've told him you'll ring him when you get home.' She had called her husband, but Boyne had no idea that Macleod was by then at Powell's.[26]

The anti-Home lobby soon had cause for optimism. 'Before long,' according to Macleod:

> It was established that Maudling and Hailsham were not only opposed to Lord Home but believed Butler to be the right and obvious successor and would be ready and happy to serve under him. The rest of us felt this understanding between those hitherto the three principal contenders was of decisive importance: the succession was resolving itself in the right way.

It meant that most of the Cabinet were against Home and prompted Aldington to inform the Palace of the opposition to Home. A similar warning came from Lord Lambton, one of Macmillan's fiercest backbench critics who had rallied to the Butler cause and who telephoned the Palace at the suggestion of John Junor, editor of the *Sunday Express*, to warn that the Cabinet had not been consulted. Early the following morning, Walters from the Hailsham camp also telephoned to suggest that it would be unwise for the Queen to call Home without knowing how the other four (Butler, Hailsham, Macleod and Mandling) stood. This was probably the high-point of the dissidents' hopes. The fact of their alerting the Palace to the difficulties that would follow if the Queen were to ask Home to form an administration raises the constitutional question of the advice that she received during Friday 18th, particularly since it was later claimed privately by her private secretary that he had been quite unaware on this crucial day of the weight of the meeting at Powell's house and the force of the opposition to Home.[27]

But the dissidents were aware on Thursday night of the determination of the party establishment to nominate Home. The Chief Whip was telephoned and rather than embark on a discussion over the phone went to Powell's house. He was obdurate in backing Home. 'He naturally did everything he could to persuade us to accept the situation as he saw it,' recalls Macleod diplomatically, 'but we finally asked him to report to the Prime Minister the fact of the understanding which had arisen between Butler, Maudling and Hailsham. He promised to do this.' This again raises the question of which facts were subsequently communicated to the Queen. Before the dissidents left Powell's house, Macleod, Maudling and Powell 'spoke to Butler himself, told him what had been agreed, and assured him of our support.' Butler was in a mental torment – all night, Butler's wife, Mollie, was imploring him to stand firm against Home's becoming Prime Minister.[28]

End-game

Early the next morning, Friday 18th, Macmillan learned of the overnight rebellion. Nonetheless, by 8.30am the Prime Minister had decided to press ahead. But his newly chosen successor had become nervous when he heard of the agreement reached between the other main contenders: 'Well, I thought I was coming in to heal, not to wound,' Home fretted. 'Look, we can't change our view now,' said Macmillan, rallying him. 'All the troops are on the starting line. Everything is arranged. It will just cause ghastly confusion if we delay'.[29]

Butler meanwhile telephoned Dilhorne 'urging him to seek the Prime Minister's authorization to convene a meeting of the three other main candidates for the succession before any final decision was made for Home.' No reply was forthcoming. By 9.30am, the Prime Minister had tendered his resignation in a letter to the Queen. As Powell later pointed out, 'a Butler government enjoying general acceptance was available by the time Macmillan's resignation reached the Queen'. By Friday morning, Powell recalls:

> The following declared, to Mr Butler and to one another, that they did not consider Lord Home should be Prime Minister, that they would serve under Mr Butler, and that they would not serve under Lord Home unless Mr Butler had previously agreed to do so.

Those listed by Powell are: Macleod, Maudling, Hailsham, Boyd-Carpenter, Erroll, Boyle and Powell.[30]

Macleod was convinced that Home could still be stopped. The Queen visited Macmillan at 11.15am, and he read to her the memorandum of advice that he had carefully drafted following receipt of the various soundings during Thursday. In Macleod's words, this memorandum 'purported to be not the advice of one man, but the collective view of a party'. At 12.15pm the Queen asked Home to the Palace and followed earlier precedent by asking him first to consult his colleagues and see whether he could form a government before formally appointing him Prime Minister. While Home was on his way to the Palace, the meeting organized by Macleod between the other three main contenders – Butler, Hailsham and Maudling – finally took place in Butler's office, with Macleod present in his capacity as Chairman of the Party. Maudling and Hailsham agreed to serve under Butler.[31]

Everything now depended on the talks with Home and the determination of Butler's allies and, crucially, on Butler's own resolve. Butler lunched with his wife, Mollie, at the Carlton Club, where Rees-Mogg and Berkeley, who had also been in the dining-room, approached the Butlers as they left, Rees-Mogg saying to Rab, 'I do hope, sir, that you are going to refuse to serve.' The Butlers then drove straight to Number Ten, where, as Macleod relates: 'Butler himself reserved his position, intimating that he would not serve under Lord Home unless satisfied that it was "the only way to unite the party".' In this comment lay the seeds of Butler's defeat. 'Maudling and Hailsham kept to their agreement with Butler,' Macleod reports, 'and refused to serve unless Butler did.' During Friday afternoon, Home also faced a threat from a smaller group of hard-line opponents who had emerged during his first round of talks with the old Cabinet. Macleod identifies himself and Powell: the third unnamed hard-liner was Boyle. These three 'used their influence towards what they believed the right solution by answering Lord Home's enquiry in the negative'.[32]

Home had the great advantage of having been to the Palace and hosting his consultations at Number Ten – any move to prevent his succession was more easily portrayed as a threat to party unity. It was in these circumstances on Friday evening that the key 'quadrilateral' meeting took place at Number Ten between Home, Butler, Hailsham and Maudling. By this stage, Hailsham had moved towards serving Home, having been warned by Selwyn Lloyd, one of Home's strongest supporters, that his refusal would look like sour grapes. Senior sympathizers of Hailsham, including Amery, Poole and Thorneycroft, also counselled that he should serve Home. Hailsham now decided that he would do so if Butler and Maudling did. Butler returned to St Ermin's on Friday night telling Mollie, Geoffrey Lloyd, his friend from Cambridge who had served in government with him, and Junor, who had joined them, that it was all over. Home had won. They tried to rally Rab, hoping that if he held out over the weekend the anti-Home forces would muster. But on Saturday morning, Butler saw Home and agreed to serve in the interests of party unity. Maudling was easily persuaded to follow suit, to Macleod's intense irritation, and Boyle, despite strong reservations, did likewise.[33]

By lunch-time on Saturday 19th, Home had kissed hands as Prime Minister. Only Macleod and Powell refused to serve. Other ministers and senior backbenchers tried in vain to persuade Macleod to reconsider his position. Boyd-Carpenter recalls telling Macleod that the failure of the Party Chairman to serve would be particularly damaging for party unity. Some, like Whitelaw, suspected that Powell's influence was decisive with Macleod, as it was alleged to have been with Thorneycroft and Birch when they resigned from the Treasury in January 1958. When Watkins later asked Macleod why he had not served, Macleod replied, 'I'd given my word that I would not, and I kept my word.' From the nature of Macleod's conversation with Home on the Thursday evening, Home cannot have been in any doubt that Macleod, like Powell, would find it impossible to serve under him. This is borne out by Macleod's description of the *dénouement* at Number Ten, where he:

Had two short interviews with Lord Home, one before and one after he became Prime Minister. Both were very friendly but brief. I am sure he would have liked me to change my mind. I like to think that he knew that I could not. For myself and Powell it become a matter of 'personal moral integrity'. The words are those of another member of the Cabinet.[34]

As had happened in 1957, the Tory crown had been seized from Butler's hands moments before his expected accession. Macleod commented to Powell that they had 'put the golden ball in his [Butler's] lap, if he drops it now it's his own fault'. Powell himself later spoke of having handed Butler 'a loaded revolver and told him all he had to do was pull the trigger', but Butler had not wanted to use it if it would make a noise or hurt anyone. Butler lacked the mettle of his younger supporters: had Macleod been in Butler's position he would neither have dropped the 'golden ball', nor hesitated to pull the trigger. That is why the Tory right always regarded Macleod as their most dangerous enemy.[35]

Macleod was to spend the next six and a half years out of government, finally returning for only one month, and Powell was never to hold office again. Macleod's hopes of serving as Chancellor under Butler and eventually succeeding him as leader had been smashed. Butler became Foreign Secretary – to the chagrin of Heath, who had hoped for the Foreign Office in succession to Home – before retiring in 1965 'to endless port and dignity' (in Rab's felicitous phrase) as Master of Trinity College, Cambridge. Of the other anti-Home ministers, Hailsham remained Lord President and Minister for Science, Maudling stayed at the Treasury and Boyle at Education, while

Erroll was moved to the Ministry of Power to make way for Heath at Trade.[36]

Home was deeply stung by Macleod's and Powell's refusal to serve. He remained bitter at their action and was scathing about their motives. 'The reason which they gave to me,' Home wrote thirteen years later, 'was that they did not believe a man with my social background could win a General Election for the Conservative Party at that time in the twentieth century.' And, with an unaccustomed acerbity, Home added that he 'had a feeling that at the back of their minds was the calculation that, although we might lose in 1964, the next opportunity would not be long and that then we would win under another leader'. In other words, Macleod and Powell were already jockeying for the next leadership struggle. This was the view taken of Macleod's motives among Tory MPs in the smoking room when the Commons reassembled in November. The view of traditionalist Tories is recalled by Whitelaw: 'Here was the great traditional Tory, Alec Home, come to save the party at the next election, and what does Iain do as Chairman of the Party, someone who could have done so much to save the election for the Party? He refuses to serve.' Macleod's parliamentary enemies on the traditionalist right had a further pretext to vilify him. 'Iain had betrayed Alec. We always knew what this man was like – look what he did to our kith and kin in Africa.' Whereas Macleod was seen as scheming and was 'getting off the boat', Powell was seen as an eccentric, former professor, possessed of an erratic brilliance and liable to act entirely by his own lights. Powell was reckoned to be dotty, but Macleod was held to be devious.[37]

What were Macleod's motives? At least half a dozen can be deduced. Although Home was right that Macleod judged that the Tories faced defeat at the next election, he omits to say that Macleod regarded Home's leadership as the major contributory factor to such an outcome. Yet this was the main reason that Macleod resisted Home's selection so stoutly. As far as Macleod was concerned, Home inflicted irreparable damage on the party's prospects in taking on a job that he should never have contemplated. Home was not a 'reluctant peer'. The Tories' admission that they could not find a Tory Prime Minister from the Commons ran counter to Macleod's commitment to establish the Tories as a modernizing force. Macleod had told Home that he (Home) knew nothing of the economy, the social services or domestic politics, and yet understanding these areas was central to modern politics. Home seemed, deep down, to share Macleod's assessment. His underlying lack of confidence in his capacity to be a modern party leader helps explain why, less than two years later, he gave up the leadership so easily.[38]

As to the charge that Macleod's refusal to serve was motivated by a calculation of his own leadership prospects, there was no doubt an element of calculation in his mind. But this was not the main reason, and to the

extent that it was a factor, Macleod badly miscalculated. His refusal to serve
Home made him deeply unpopular in the party, as he had been warned
would happen by friends and ministerial colleagues who pleaded with him
to serve. He even faced hostile criticism within his constituency party, where
some of those who had been the most fawning became the most hostile.
Macleod appeared to have permanently blighted his leadership prospects.
Indeed, such was the ferocity of Tory reaction that in the view of Carr,
Macleod's long-standing friend and colleague, his refusal to serve:

> really did set a lie to the view that some people held of Iain – I never did
> – that he was so overweeningly ambitious that every card he played was
> like a bridge player calculating to make sure that he succeeded. I just do
> not believe that was true and I never did. But if you need proof, he really
> could not have done himself more harm.[39]

Macleod simply could not stand Home's politics. It counted deeply with
Macleod that, as he would write in his subsequent account, 'the Tory Party
for the first time since Bonar Law is now being led from the right of centre'.
Macleod did not doubt that 'this chimes with the wishes of many good
Tories who were disturbed and angered by some aspects of our policies these
last twelve years'. Macleod strongly disagreed with Home's archly tradition-
alist approach on Africa, which then occupied centre-stage in British
politics. In Gilmour's opinion, 'Africa was then much the closest subject to
Macleod's heart', and this further militated against his serving in Home's
Cabinet.[40]

Macleod's dismissive judgement of Home explains one aspect of his
principled refusal to serve. As Bennett recalls, since Macleod and Powell
had told Home directly 'that he (Home) was no good at all for Prime
Minister, they could not simply fall in line, and meekly say, well now you've
got it, yes, we think you are wonderful'. Macleod and Powell had told Home
why he should not be Prime Minister, whereas other dissidents had not
expressed their views directly to Home. In Bennett's words, 'this rather
quixotic gallantry spelt ruin' for Macleod and Powell. Although Macleod
was later to admit that his refusal to serve had been a mistake, he was deeply
disappointed that other pro-Butler ministers, particularly Maudling, agreed
to serve. However, he was not altogether surprised: 'You don't expect to
find too many people in the last ditch with you,' he told Gilmour. Indeed,
Barney Hayhoe perceives that Macleod held a fatalistic, celtic view of the
whole episode.[41]

On any realistic view, Macleod was released from any commitment not to
serve Home the moment that Butler accepted office: after all, nobody can be
expected to remain more royalist than the king. But in the final resort,
Macleod could not tolerate the rigging of the selection procedure and was not
prepared to condone the conspiracy by serving under the victor. This became

apparent three months later when, in the eyes of most Tories, Macleod compounded his sin of refusing to serve by publishing a blow-by-blow account that revealed Macmillan's manipulation of the selection procedure. Even if Macleod had accurately foreseen the self-destructive consequences of his actions, J.W.M. Thompson, who worked with Macleod on the *Spectator*, believes that Macleod's basic judgement would not have been any different.[42]

Macleod became the main target of Tory fury because he was seen to have provoked a row that shattered any semblance of party unity, so crucial in the run-up to a general election, and because he was held to be more devious than Powell. Indeed, the row over the leadership was deeply damaging to the party's prospects, but the real culprit was Macmillan. It was his handling of the succession – first backing Hailsham, then switching to Home, and blocking Butler at all costs – that caused the trouble. The argument that Macmillan was right to back Home, because only Home could unite the party is plainly wrong. As a result of Macleod's actions, it was established that the other contenders were prepared to support Butler. With their backing and with an election at the most a year away, the party would have united behind Butler. The argument that Macmillan's system of consultation was more democratic because all sections of the party were consulted ignores the scope for bias and incompetence, which clearly occurred in October 1963. The manner of Home's selection totally discredited the 'customary processes'. There was also an extremely important constitutional point: the Tories claimed that their method upheld the Royal Prerogative, but the 1963 crisis raised questions about the role of the Palace in so readily acceding to Macmillan's scheming.

Ironically, almost two years later and only after Home himself had quit as leader, Macmillan would come to share Macleod's critical judgement of Home. 'Alec did his best – with courage and dignity,' he wrote to his confidante, Ava, Lady Waverley, in September 1965, 'but he could not impress himself on Parlt. [sic] or people enough for a PM.' And towards the end of his life, Macmillan admitted, as his biographer writes, that 'perhaps it would have been better for the Party if Rab had been his [Macmillan's] successor after all; "then we could have won the election in '64 . . . though we would have lost the next one." ' Perhaps it was just as well for the mental composure of Butler and Macleod that, after all that happened in October 1963, and the consequences for their political careers, these belated, second thoughts of Macmillan's were not made public during their lifetimes.[43]

14

Editor

And Quoodle here discloses
All things that Quoodle can.
G.K. Chesterton, quoted by Iain Macleod in the 'Tailpiece' of
'Spectator's Notebook', the *Spectator*, 13 December 1963.

Until Mr Randolph Churchill's book appeared there had been an unspoken agreement that the less said about the recent struggle for the Tory
leadership the better. 'Macleod and Powell,' wrote a political commenta-
tor, 'have been reticent to a tactical fault.'

Iain Macleod's opening words of his article, 'The Tory Leadership,'
the *Spectator*, 17 January 1964.

An Almighty Row

Although Macleod was consigned to the political wilderness after eleven and
a half years in government and almost eight in Cabinet, he was back in the
headlines within a fortnight of his return to the backbenches. On Thursday
31 October 1963, before the dust had settled on Macleod's and Powell's
refusal to serve Home, the *Evening Standard* ran a scoop in its 'Londoner's
Diary' suggesting that Macleod was about to become editor of the *Spectator*,
the prestigious, long-established weekly. Macleod's startlingly rapid move
from Cabinet table to editor's desk caused a sensation.

At the end of October 1963, the attention of the political press was focused
on what they believed would be the last, bizarre instalment in the Tory
leadership saga. The new Prime Minister, Sir Alec Douglas-Home, having
renounced his peerage, and with it his membership of Parliament, had
delayed the state opening of the new session for a fortnight until 12
November while he sought to return as an MP in the Kinross and West
Perthshire by-election where polling took place on Thursday 8th. This
rock-solid Tory seat in Scotland, a commodity less rare then than it
subsequently became, was vacant because of the death during the summer

recess of the sitting MP, Gilmour Leburn, and the felicitous action of the recently adopted Tory candidate, George Younger, who stood down. Among the political correspondents hastily despatched to Perthshire, George Gale, of the *Daily Express*, was one of the first to learn of Macleod's appointment. No sooner had Gale heard the news from London than he rushed into the bar where his fellow journalists were gathered and exclaimed, to their astonishment: 'You'll never guess what – Iain Macleod has been made editor of the *Spectator*!'[1]

Macleod had been offered the job, without any prior warning, the previous Sunday evening, 27 October, when Ian Gilmour, the paper's owner since 1954, had telephoned him at his home. Macleod was considering his future, and it was natural that he should talk things over with Gilmour, who had become a friend and political ally. As they chatted on the phone, Gilmour made a suggestion that interested Macleod immediately: 'This might seem a strange idea,' ventured Gilmour, 'but would you like to edit the *Spectator*?' They agreed to discuss the proposal further the next day, Monday 28th, over lunch at a favourite haunt, La Speranza, an Italian restaurant near Harrods on the Brompton Road, Knightsbridge. They first considered Macleod's reasons for refusing to serve Douglas-Home, and then turned to the question of the editorship. In Gilmour's recollection, Macleod 'more or less accepted on the spot, subject to considering it'. Two days later, on Wednesday 30th, Macleod confirmed his acceptance.[2]

There were those, however, who doubted the wisdom of Macleod's decision. J.W.M. Thompson, who heard Gale pass on the news in Perthshire and who would later become Macleod's deputy editor, recalled that the political journalists were astonished that an ambitious politician had taken on the editorship of a weekly. Although there was nothing unusual about a politician taking up the pen, Macleod was entering journalism not as a freelance contributor but as an editor and, unlike his counterpart at the *New Statesman* – John Freeman, the former Labour MP and minister – he remained an active party politician with every prospect of returning one day to high political office.[3]

The paper that Macleod would edit had long prided itself on its independence of any political party, a tradition dating back to 1828 when its first owner-editor, Rintoul, established the *Spectator* to fight for the Reform Bill. It had remained radical or Whig until the rise of the Labour Party pushed it towards conservatism. Its owners, however, preserved the paper's independence from party ties. Wilson Harris, its editor until 1922, though conservative by temperament, sat in the Commons as an Independent. Wrench, who took over from Harris as owner-editor, and Wrench's successor, Gilmour, had continued the tradition. Although the *Spectator* endorsed Eden at the 1955 election, it was bitterly opposed to Suez, did not back Macmillan in 1959 and criticized his Government's colonial policy, particularly in Central Africa and Cyprus, and also their approach to capital and corporal punishment.

How could Macleod the politician be reconciled with Macleod the editor? Enoch Powell, Macleod's ally in refusing to serve Douglas-Home, urged Macleod not to take it on, regarding 'it as a dangerous thing for an active politician and an ambitions politician to sit himself down in an editor's chair'. Instead of Macleod being able carefully to select on which subjects, and when, to nail his colours to the mast, he would be obliged to state publicly his views on different issues virtually every week. But it was the paper's independence of party ties that attracted Macleod: he would never have contemplated editing a tame party rag. The clichés often uttered about the reputations of Macleod and Powell – the former, a cunning tactician, the latter, a fearless maverick – are contradicted. On this occasion, Powell appears as the cannier operator.[4]

Editing the *Spectator* involved risk, but it brought opportunities that would help Macleod confront his political exile. He did not disguise his dislike at being out of office, telling David Butler and Anthony King, the Oxford academics, in December 1963, a couple of months after leaving the Cabinet, that running the country was the only thing worth doing. He was acutely conscious of his exclusion from the party leadership for the first time since he entered the Parliamentary Secretariat in 1946. On occasion, usually over an evening drink or dinner, he would talk to a close friend, like Nigel Fisher, about giving up politics altogether, but Fisher never thought that he was serious. Macleod said the same to J.W.M. Thompson, who felt that 'such prognostications never sounded convincing':

> It seemed unthinkable that he would ever turn his back on political life voluntarily. He was in love with the whole drama of it. The unexpected-ness of it all, the sudden shifts of fortune which come as trials and burdens to many men, [he] seemed to relish.

Peter Walker, who shared an office with Gilmour in Gayfere Street, Westminster, and likewise had entered the Commons at a by-election during Macleod's period as Party Chairman, sensed Macleod's depression. Gilmour and Walker made a point of seeing him regularly and making it clear that in their view he had a considerable political future. But it was the editorship of Gilmour's paper that offered concrete help. It provided a platform for his radical Toryism and would help him stay in the swim of public debate as the months passed and Fleet Street lost interest and turned its attention from former ministers to new personalities.[5]

Financial considerations were also important. Macleod had no private means. After the loss of his ministerial salary of £5,000 a year he was left with only his MP's annual pay of £1,750, and the Macleods had been left out of pocket following his stint as Colonial Secretary. Macleod's life-style was not expansive or extravagant, but he liked to eat at the best restaurants, and he enjoyed the theatre and entertaining guests at White's. Gilmour offered him £5,000 a year, 60 per cent more than Macleod's predecessor received. But the money was not the only factor. He received other offers, and accepted a non-executive directorship from the Chairman of the Lombard Bank, Eric Knight. In addition to a seat on the board, Macleod gained the use of a chauffeur-driven Daimler that he enjoyed for the next six and a half years and regarded as being more of a necessity than a perk. 'Frankly, it's the car,' he told Harry Boyne, who asked why he took a directorship with Lombard. Macleod was only half-joking: he explained that ministers were not only driven everywhere but 'the most attractive thing of all is what the chauffeur can do for you'. A minister's driver served, in effect, as a personal batman, running all sorts of errands. In Macleod's case, although he never mentioned his worsening disability even to close colleagues, not having to worry about his travel arrangements or to struggle in and out of taxis, was an immense relief to him.[6]

Above all, the idea of editing the *Spectator* appealed to Macleod. He had served a lengthy spell in government, including two exhausting years as Colonial Secretary. His political prospects were uncertain. He would have to await the next election, possibly not due for another year, before any longer-term assessment of his likely position in the party could be essayed. Until a new parliament was elected, and the composition of the party and strength of Douglas-Home's leadership were established, it was impossible to know when, and on what terms, Macleod might return to the Tory front bench. There was no doubt that Macleod wanted to return. Shortly after he had accepted the editorship, he dined at Nigel Fisher's house in Lord North Street, Westminister, and over a pre-dinner whisky and soda his eyes lighted on his friend's ministerial red box. In response to Fisher's ribbing about his wanting to have a red box again, Macleod conceded 'Yes, you're right. I shall have to come back.' As Fisher recalled, 'he added with a touch of defiance: "And I don't run in a race to run second".'[7]

The unexpected opportunity to edit an independent paper provided an immediate antidote to the boredom of the political wilderness. What appealed to him was the testing of his talents and the pitting of his wits. He would still be able to argue his political corner and exercise his skills – in which he was totally self-confident – as a manager and leader of a team, and he would also be tackling a new role and operating in an evironment very different from the ministerial milieu that he had known since 1952. Lord Aldington, who used to dine with Macleod during his period on the paper, found that he seemed happy with his life: 'He had influence as editor, he was resting after an exhausting and solid spell in Government, and he seemed to enjoy the *Spectator*.'[8]

The astonishment expressed at Macleod's appointment by the journalists in Perthshire was mild by comparison with the shock felt in the office of the

Spectator's editor at number 99 Gower Street, Bloomsbury. The first that the unfortunate incumbent, Iain Hamilton, heard of his sacking was in a phone call from the *Evening Standard* shortly before lunch on the day of its scoop. The botched replacement of Hamilton sparked 'the most imperial row' that enveloped virtually everybody on the *Spectator* – owner, directors, editors (past, present and prospective), editorial staff, staff writers, contributors, messengers and readers. Macleod was not directly responsible, but his insouciance gave the first impetus to what denizens of Gower Street felt was a 'tidal wave' that came crashing though the front-door of number 99.[9]

Gilmour had intended to announce Macleod's appointment in time for the Sunday papers of 3 November. But he had first to explain his decision to Hamilton and discuss with him his future. Accordingly, he had invited Hamilton to meet him for a drink at his club, White's, on Thursday evening, 31 October, when that week's issue had been printed and was already being distributed. But his plan soon went awry. Unwisely, Macleod had already mentioned Gilmour's offer to Bill Deedes, a former journalist and, at the time, the minister responsible for the Government's press relations. Although Macleod was no longer a member of the Government, Deedes tipped off the Sunday papers. The story leaked to the *Evening Standard*, who duly told Hamilton and published their scoop, several hours before proprietor and editor were due to meet.[10]

Hamilton claimed afterwards that the news had come 'like a bolt out of the blue'. In fact, Gilmour had decided several months before that he would have to replace Hamilton as editor because 'the paper was in difficulties and it clearly needed a change'. The paper's circulation had declined, its cover price had had to be increased from ninepence to a shilling, and by the summer of 1963 there was a growing sense of malaise at Gower Street. During September, Gilmour and the paper's managing director, H.S. Janes, had discussed with Hamilton, on separate occasions, a possible change of editor. Hamilton, however, had reason to be both angered at the manner of his dismissal and surprised at the identity of his successor. Only a week earlier, on Thursday 24 October, he had written to Macleod, inviting him to become one of the paper's contributors. Macleod's reply did not suggest a man itching to take up the pen: 'Thank you, but not yet. And probably not for a fairly long time.' As Hamilton told the press conference he assembled at Gower Street on Friday 1 November, the day after the news broke of Macleod's appointment, these letters provided 'a curious irony' to the situation.[11]

Hamilton also revealed that when he had arrived at White's Gilmour greeted him by saying that he could not begin to apologize 'for the unspeakable way' in which he (Hamilton) had been treated. According to Hamilton, Gilmour then added, 'Before we talk any more are you willing to do an Oliver Poole?' Hamilton took this as a reference to the readiness of Lord Poole, who had served with Macleod as Macmillan's Joint Party Chairman, to accept demotion and become Vice-Chairman under Douglas-

Home's appointee as Party Chairman, John Hare. But Hamilton was not Poole. Having revealed enough of their conversation to dash Gilmour's fond hope that he would happily serve as Macleod's deputy, Hamilton thought that the rest of their talk 'had better remain private'.[12]

The circumstances of Macleod's appointment became a *cause célèbre*. Fleet Street, obsessed with the *Spectator* washing its dirty linen in public, was transfixed. The *Spectator*'s small editorial staff had issued a statement shortly before Hamilton's revelatory press conference, 'vehemently protesting' at what they described as the 'shabby treatment' of their editor. According to the Pendennis column in the *Observer*, contributors and former staff-writers of the *Spectator* were being approached by Kingsley Amis, the novelist and himself a contributor, and by Bernard Levin, a former parliamentary correspondent under the pseudonym 'Taper', to put their signatures to separate letters of protest to *The Times*. Letters and phone calls flooded in to Gower Street. Many were abusive or aggressive, but they were evenly divided in their opinions. Visitors to number 99 who had contacts with *Private Eye* loitered in the corridor in an ill-disguised attempt to eavesdrop on the debate within the office. The satirical magazine added its barbed comment by offering Enoch Powell a £5,000 post, matching Macleod's salary as editor, explaining that they 'were afraid he [Powell] might feel he was out in the cold'.[13]

The charge that Macleod's editorship would imperil the paper's independence was advanced with greatest vigour by Hamilton's predecessor, Brian Inglis, who had become editor in 1958, when Gilmour abandoned his dual role as owner-editor, and who still served on the board of directors. The fact was that Macleod's appointment would consolidate a shift in the *Spectator*'s editorial stance. By 1962, under Inglis's editorship, the paper seemed less radical Tory and more Gaitskellite. Although its owner knew both the Labour leader and the Liberal leader, Jo Grimond, socially, he was closer politically to Macleod. When Gilmour's adoption as the Tory candidate at the Central Norfolk by-election in 1962 prompted Inglis to resign, Gilmour appointed Hamilton, a former assistant editor, who shared Gilmour's radical Toryism, to the editorship. Unfortunately, Hamilton's eighteen months in the post, during 1962–63, coincided with the Tory Government's deepest period of unpopularity.[14]

The argument over Macleod's appointment came to a head at the meeting of the *Spectator*'s board of directors, called on the morning of Thursday 7 November to confirm Macleod as the new editor. Directors arriving for the meeting were greeted by a crowd of reporters laying siege to the front door of number 99, and a lone policeman strolling up and down supposedly keeping the peace. Macleod was endorsed as editor by a majority of four against two. The board maintained that 'independence does not mean that a paper should not have strong political views. True independence means that a paper's views are not dictated from outside its office.' And they reiterated that 'the independence of the *Spectator* has been plain for all to see' since Gilmour acquired his controlling interest in 1954. And as for the new editor, the board stated that 'Mr Iain Macleod has recently demonstrated his independence in the most convincing manner.' Yet the board's response to the doubts about Macleod's role as editor was not wholly convincing. There was no question of the directors applying the 'Caesar's wife' argument – that it was not sufficient for an editor to be independent of party political ties: he must also be seen to be independent. The board were simply 'content to be judged by the quality of the paper under Mr Macleod's editorship'.[15]

Inglis immediately resigned his directorship, declaring as he left 99 Gower Street that 'the *Spectator* may do well, but it is the end of the *Spectator* as I know it.' Hamilton, sacked as Editor, was promised compensation but nonetheless issued a writ for breach of contract against the *Spectator* and another against Gilmour. Within a month, Hartley, the deputy editor, who had been with the paper ten years, also resigned, declaring that 'A prominent politician should not edit an independent paper'. But what kind of an editor would this dispossessed Tory minister be? Clearly one with wit: in one of his earliest contributions to the weekly 'Spectator's Notebook', he could not resist the opportunity unwittingly provided by the paper's chess correspondent, Philidor. Under the sub-heading, 'Inglis was Right', Macleod wrote:

> Those who have been watching tensely for signs of Tory infiltration even into the special articles will find their darkest suspicions confirmed by Philidor. His article this week contains a shameless plug for the great Moslem chess player Rabrab.

Whatever the effect Macleod's editorship might have for his political career, it heralded an entertaining and fascinating interlude in weekly journalism.[16]

In the Editor's Chair

It was almost a month after the board's confirmation of his appointment that Macleod edited his first issue of the *Spectator*. In the interim he met members of the paper's small editorial staff, in most cases individually at his Chelsea flat, and towards the end of November visited Gower Street several times to acquaint himself with the office. Macleod was anxious to replace Hartley by an experienced journalist with know-how about producing a newspaper, a role soon filled by J.W.M. Thompson who was recruited from the *Evening Standard*. Otherwise, Macleod retained the staff bequeathed him: David Rees, a quietly spoken Welshman, and David Pryce-Jones as joint literary editors; David Watt, an authoritative and waspish political correspondent; Malcolm Rutherford, a young foreign affairs specialist and drama critic; Joan Baylis, the editor's secretary; and Charles Seaton the backroom factotum and librarian.

Macleod's self-confidence in his intellect and skills as a manager had made him a decisive and effective minister, but one who sometimes seemed brusque and impatient. He was no different as editor, displaying a directness that could be disarming. Soon after Macleod's appointment, Rutherford was summoned to see him at Sloane Court West. Macleod asked him what he was paid. Rutherford said £900 a year, to which Macleod retorted that it was nothing like enough and immediately doubled it. But paying a decent salary did not betoken editorial possessiveness. When Rutherford asked whether there was any objection to his taking on other commitments, Macleod made clear his view that nobody worth their salt should regard writing for a weekly paper as their sole work.[17]

Macleod adopted much the same manner with Alan Watkins who was encouraged the following summer to apply for the post of Political Correspondent when David Watt left to become Washington Correspondent of the *Financial Times*. After a first, friendly, meeting Macleod suggested lunch at White's 'to complete the arrangement'. Watkins arrived at one o'clock and found Macleod, with a large dry martini in his hand, seated before a television set watching the Test match between England and Australia. As Watkins has recalled, 'Macleod bought me a drink and said somewhat peremptorily: "I forbid any further conversation until after 1.30" ' – the time at which play stopped for luncheon in those days. After that, Watkins found Macleod 'gruff but friendly enough'. ' "How soon can you join us?" ' Macleod asked Watkins, 'almost in a rasp'. Watkins explained that he was on a three-month contract with the *Sunday Express* but could, if necessary, give in his notice that afternoon. ' "You do that at once," Macleod said decisively.' The impression left with Watkins was that Macleod was 'trying to give an imitation of Lord Beaverbrook, or at least of a tough editor, of few words, at any rate spoken ones'. But Macleod was not imitating anybody. That was what he could be like.[18]

Yet Macleod showed immense consideration towards those with whom he worked closely. It might be said that this was merely part of being a good manager, but it rang true to those who experienced it. Joan Baylis differentiated him from other editors, who treated her as 'a piece of furniture to be passed from editor to editor', characterizing him as 'friendly, yet reserved too', and capable of gestures of support that 'warmed the heart'. At the time of Macleod's appointment she felt on the verge of a nervous breakdown, having borne the brunt of the messages of protest and office arguments over Hamilton's sacking. She had also convinced herself that a politician of Macleod's rank would replace her with his own personal secretary. She felt so highly-strung that she 'dissolved into tears' when told that she was expected to see Macleod at his flat, and 'in desperation swallowed two tranquillizers' to calm herself for 'the supposed ordeal'. On her arrival, however, she discovered that: 'My fears were unfounded, for as I walked into the lounge and was greeted in the way I came to know so well – the outstretched hand, the cheery smile, and the clear high, voice – tension eased in the calm and welcoming atmosphere.' Baylis volunteered her readiness to make way for somebody else, but Macleod reassured her that that was not necessary and immediately set about discussing office business and tackling the correspondence already being delivered to his flat.[19]

When Macleod assumed his full editorial duties, he was greeted on his first day at the office – Monday 2 December 1963 – by a throng of reporters, photographers and film crews. Macleod at once took the boardroom at number 99 as his office, a larger, more comfortable room than the old editor's office, possessing a leather armchair and decorated with prints of 'Spy' caricatures. Gilmour, who had previously worked there, willingly moved to the smaller office. On Macleod's first day, persistent demands from the press to photograph the new editor at his desk were rejected. Those who saw him there that day, and during the rest of his tenure at the *Spectator*, recall the striking impression that he made:

> sitting at his desk with this impressive domed head, rather a hunched person as he sat there, and with a half-secret smile on his lips, and his unusual tenor voice – but it was strong tenor, which had power, and was one that could fill a whole hall if necessary. But when he moved, he was quite a small man and it immediately became clear how badly disabled he was.

From time to time on his first day, Joan Baylis visited the boardroom 'to see if all was well, hoping the harassment was not upsetting the newcomer. It was not, for he took it in his stride, long being used to such phenomena.' And as she recalled: 'Late that afternoon my internal office telephone rang: the voice of the Right Honourable Iain Macleod, PC, MP, ex-Leader of the Commons, ex-Secretary of State for the Colonies, asked: "Can I go now?" '[20]

A daily routine was soon established. His chauffeur-driven car would deposit him at the office between 10 o'clock and 10.30am and would whisk him away again around 4.30pm. He also found time during his truncated day to play long-distance chess on a miniature board in his office with C.H.O'D. Alexander, the paper's chess correspondent, who lived miles away. Often, his day was punctuated by a lunch, and sometimes he did not return to Gower Street but instead went straight to the House of Commons. On occasion, lunch with his deputy, J.W.M. Thompson, would serve as an editorial planning meeting. Favourite restaurants included Quaglino's and The White Tower in Percy Street, off Tottenham Court Road, a couple of blocks from Gower Street, where every Tuesday he ate with Ian Gilmour, rarely returning to the office afterwards. Editor and owner would 'survey the world scene', rather than discuss the paper in any detail, since Gilmour believed in allowing his editors a free hand. Another regular haunt, whenever he lunched with Alan Watkins, was L'Epicure in Frith Street, Soho, and frequently he would invite guests to White's.[21]

His short working day reflected Macleod's extraordinarily efficient despatch of business. He was not a figurehead, as was commonly supposed by people who did not work on the paper, but 'had a natural feeling for the journalism and went about the job with wholly unpompous zest'. As Baylis has recalled, Macleod gave all his editorial duties: 'Due weight and attention, clearing up in half a day what had taken various predecessors long hours to achieve or to decide. This is not necessarily any reflection on them; it is a tribute to his own disciplined mind and power of concentration.' She suspected that part of the reason for his speed of work was because it must have been 'small beer to a leading politician who had held the reins of government in his hands'. But she was underestimating Macleod's ability to work much more quickly than most ministers:

> Everything was dealt with as it came in; the desk was clear, the trays were emptied as rapidly as they were filled; delegation as practised by the editor was a fine art. Correspondence was brief and to the point. Thus, though we were industrious, we were also efficient and the work never overwhelmed us. The boardroom became a haven of tranquillity and efficiency in which I could breathe.

Given Macleod's self-belief in himself as commander class, there was no doubting who was in charge of editorial and managerial policy. Within six months of his arrival, it became clear that 'all was not well with the literary "twins" along the passage', and in April 1964, Rees was confirmed as sole literary editor.[22]

On Wednesdays, when the *Spectator* went to press, Macleod would visit the printing works of Gale and Polden, in Aldershot, to oversee the checking of the page-proofs, and deal with last-minute problems – in newspaper parlance 'on the stone' – in the composing room where the pages were made up by the paper's aptly named printer, Len Stone. Macleod often gave staff-writers attending the printers a lift in his chauffeur-driven car. During these journeys, that could take anything up to two hours, they quickly discovered that Macleod was far from being unapproachable and would chat happily about politics, the theatre, and cricket and rugger. These interests enabled him to display his formidable memory. Macleod explained to Thompson that this facility for memorizing 'was a purely visual thing, like having lots of reels of film in his head. If he wanted to recall a letter, poem, or whatever, he would see the page exactly as if it were in front of him.'[23]

The passion and single-mindedness with which Macleod pursued his interests were less agreeable for those who did not share them. J.W.M. Thompson found that he and Macleod had virtually nothing in common.

As far as Thompson was concerned, racing was the one topic on which Macleod could be boringly predictable. Thompson also found it distracting, when he wanted to talk with his editor during the summer months, that Macleod would have a transistor on his desk, or the radio in the adjoining room at full blast, tuned to the ball-by-ball Test match commentary and cricket scores. Thompson was astonished that it never seemed to impair Macleod's concentration, but at least when he asked Macleod to switch it off, it was always done without any fuss.[24]

Macleod loved going to the theatre and particularly enjoyed seeing good actresses perform, not necessarily women who were conventional beauties. A great favourite was Beryl Reid in 'The Killing of Sister George', in which she played a lesbian actress whose character, Sister George, was about to be written out of a fictional radio series. Macleod's judgement of a play, however, could be prejudiced by his deep antipathy towards any review written by Bernard Levin, a former staff-writer on the *Spectator*. A favourable review by Levin made Macleod almost invariably take against the play; likewise, a panning from Levin virtually guaranteed Macleod's approval. Macleod's disagreement with Levin's judgement appeared to date back at least as far as the heyday of the satirical BBC television programme, *That Was The Week That Was*, or *TW3*, when Macleod was still a minister. His long-time verbal sparring partner, Randolph Churchill, had also contrived to intervene. Although Macleod 'had long been an admirer of the programme', he had commented

> in a debate in the House of Commons, when winding up for the Government, that I was a fan 'with one exception'. Bernard Levin in the next edition of *TW3* made great play with this. He ended by asking in his mock menacing voice what my exception was and when I was going to disclose it. A few moments later the phone rang. I knew who it was before I answered.
> 'Hello, Randolph.'
> 'Ho,' said Randolph, 'and what is your one exception?'
> 'Bernard Levin. I think he is a brilliant writer, but hopelessly miscast on that particular programme.'
> 'Can I send them a telegram to tell them?'
> 'Certainly,' I said.
> And I suppose Randolph did.[25]

Macleod's professional relationship with Randolph Churchill provides the most glaring example of how Macleod's pride in his ability to strike deals and establish a hold on people, and his quixotic sense of loyalty, proved his undoing. Setting his face against all advice to the contrary, Macleod contracted Churchill to write a weekly column about the press. Warnings, from those with professional experience of dealing with Churchill were determinedly ignored. 'Randolph is Randolph is Randolph', was all that Macleod wrote by way of introduction when his new contributor's first column appeared. Their working relationship lasted a year. When Churchill failed to file copy 'in two weeks out of three', Macleod sent him what he termed 'the gentlest of remonstrances'. But his errant correspondent proceeded to claim during an interview on American TV that he had been sacked and handed Macleod's letter to the press. 'Like Clive, I stand astonished at my own moderation,' lamented Macleod, writing of the affair under his pen name in the *Spectator*, 'Quoodle'. 'Still, that's my boy!' he opined, trying to explain why he found such an impossible character as Churchill so appealing:

> Being without Randolph is like being without an aching tooth, a gentleman at arms, a torturer, and a trumpeter. Randolph is a bladder of lard, and the stoutest of friends. He talks better (and louder) than anyone I know. I have a wholly irrational affection for him, which has survived everything. With a little bit of luck it should survive even this paragraph.

But Churchill, acting entirely in character, refused to let the matter drop, and sought to portray himself as the wounded, wholly innocent, party. 'Your contributor Quoodle seems to be luxuriating in his career of Quoodlefaking,' began his petulant letter, published the following week. 'What Quoodle calls "the gentlest of remonstrances" was in fact the sack,' Churchill fumed. Raking over the coals of Macleod's own appointment, Churchill concluded with a final, malevolent thrust: 'It was with this knowledge in your mind that you dismissed me from your paper without notice or compensation. Your predecessor, Mr Iain Hamilton, at least received compensation.' The *Spectator*'s press column was resumed, with Christopher Booker as its regular contributor. But Randolph Churchill's behaviour left Macleod feeling very badly let down.[26]

Macleod's occupancy of the boardroom might have betrayed a certain grandness on the part of a senior politician-cum-editor, or a desire to set himself apart from the paper's writers and contributors. Inevitably, it was taken that way by some of his critics, who wrote of his being treated 'with a great deal of deference by fellow journalists'. In fact, everybody was on first name terms with him, whatever their position on the paper, and his door was open at all times, with no need to knock. Whoever wanted to see him was usually accommodated at the briefest notice. He was also said to have transformed the paper from the lively and amusing 'gossip shop' to one of 'dour industry'. While the long lunches at the *Spectator* ceased, they had begun to hobble inspiration instead of encouraging it, and in Baylis's recollection 'there was no dourness either'. Ian Gilmour, found that Macleod 'was totally unstuffy and gave full freedom to his writers, though a good deal of the political writing in the *Spectator* was, to say the least, inconvenient to him'.[27]

Yet Macleod could be a difficult person to engage in conversation. The impression he created on such occasions was that he was holding something back, or did not want to become involved. It was not a question of Macleod's having any side to him or being uninterested. In part, it was because at the office he wanted to get on and deal with the work in hand and inevitably that required keeping control over his time. 'There was no time-consuming interminable talk,' is Baylis's recollection, 'but there *was* talk of a pertinent and useful kind.' Macleod would readily exchange pleasantries with genuine sincerity, and 'was never less than wholly courteous', but at the same time contrived to signal by his demeanour a desire to avoid anything more than a brief word unless it was absolutely necessary.[28]

The second of the paper's two political correspondents during Macleod's editorship, Watkins, found him 'not so much distant as uninformative', and soon discovered that it was a mistake to try and engage Macleod at greater length. Macleod's dealings seemed to be governed by a wish to tell Tory colleagues 'he had nothing to do with whatever it was his political correspondent had written. Perhaps again he did not want me to feel I was being pointed by him in any particular direction.' Although Watkins concluded that 'the principal reason' for Macleod's approach was that he 'saw his period as an editor not as a continuation of politics by other means but as a respite from them'. However, Macleod was a political animal to his fingertips, and his journalism was inseparable from the man's politics.[29]

Macleod also seemed embarrassed to talk about the convictions that informed his politics, even though his speeches, notably at party conferences, inspired his audience precisely because he was able to infuse the business of modern politics and government with idealism, even romanticism. Elizabeth Sturges-Jones, a press officer at Conservative Central Office recalls Macleod leaving the platform after one of his great conference performances and, as some of his strongest admirers among the Young Conservatives looked on, responding to the flood of congratulations by dismissing his speech as though it was all an act. She was horrified that he should appear so cynical in front of his young admirers, but the explanation lies in his diffidence, both in a social gathering when he did not know the people well and in talking about the idealistic well-springs of his politics.[30]

Macleod personified a pronounced duality: controlled yet passionate, pragmatic yet romantic, down-to-earth yet visionary. His self-control did not suggest an inner iciness, but in the words of a contemporary of Macleod's, 'There is something volcanic about Iain.' As Thompson has recalled, 'there was always about him, even when gay and relaxed, some sense of latent fire', and although he 'never saw Macleod get mad with anybody', he nonetheless sensed 'emotional turmoil within, going on behind the controlled exterior'.[31]

Many felt, like Watkins, that he never seemed completely relaxed: 'He wouldn't sit easily, he would shift his body into positions at times during a conversation.' His usual 'wary' countenance rather reinforced this impression: 'it may just have been his natural appearance, but it was as if he was thinking "What's this bloke up to?" This was possibly accentuated by his very dark eyes – not that they were small, but they were polished, very quick.' Quite often, he would talk sitting on the edge of his desk in the boardroom instead of in his chair, and sometimes put his hand to his back, suggesting that he was in discomfort and pain.[32]

Undoubtedly, by the time he joined the *Spectator*, Macleod's disability influenced the impression he made on others. 'He was a man of great self-control,' Thompson has recalled, 'a characteristic that possibly he had learned through his continual pain.' Thompson discovered his hatred of having any fuss being made about his disability when he visited Macleod in hospital:

> He had been undergoing treatment for his arthritic condition, and the doctors' verdict had not been what he had hoped for. He talked about it in a rather depressed way for a few moments and then he cut himself short. 'Damn it, get the whisky out,' he said, and in the recess of some medical cupboard I found a bottle and we drank from unappetising hospital glasses. Then he began to tell me some joke that had just come his way, and never spoke of his illness again.[33]

Macleod's worsening disability left him more obviously crippled by the mid-1960s. His wartime friend, Alan Dawtry, who had only seen him intermittently over the preceding years, saw him again following a memorial service at St Paul's in the autumn of 1963. As they were walking down the steps outside the cathedral, Dawtry approached Macleod from behind and tapped him on the shoulder. To Dawtry's dismay, Macleod could no longer just turn his head to see who was over his shoulder and had to turn his whole body round. This sometimes made Macleod seem rude. Roy Hattersley, the young Labour MP from the 1964 intake, who became a fairly regular contributor to the *Spectator* during Macleod's editorship, recalls one such occasion, when he happened to spot the Macleods ahead of him at a motorway filling station. He naturally went to have a word with Macleod, who would always greet him at the Commons, and was sitting in the front passenger seat with the door open. As Hattersley approached from behind, he cried to his editor, 'Hello, how are you?' The reply was terse. 'Very busy,' said Macleod, and pulled shut his door. Hattersley, taken aback, did not persevere. But he learned from this incident the extent of Macleod's infirmity. Macleod had been unable to glance round to see who was approaching and, not unreasonably at a motorway filling station, had assumed that it was one of those tiresome people who impose themselves on public figures at any opportunity.[34]

Hattersley's anecdote also shows that unlike many politicians Macleod 'was not a "glad-hander" at all'. He was simply not a socializer, and was 'not one for the small talk of parties', only turning up briefly at the renowned annual summer parties thrown by the *Spectator*. Neither was he ever wholly absorbed, as so many politicians are, by the gossip and speculation of politics. He might talk about 'who's up or down, in or out, what the opinion polls really mean, Randolph Churchill's latest enormity', but he preferred to recount specific incidents or events that had amused him the previous night at the Commons. 'Of small talk, as usually understood in the Conservative party,' Watkins has recalled, 'he had little. He showed no interest in one's garden, car or children's education.' This trait might have indicated 'an egotism which dismissed everything outside himself and his political concerns as of no importance'. Yet, on Macleod's own confession, he was fascinated by people and he was popular at the *Spectator*, where he was regarded as 'a very interesting person . . . who was cheering, uplifting to be with. You felt the day had been improved if you came into contact with Macleod.'[35]

Perhaps the paradox of Macleod – a non-socializer fascinated by people, and a man who could be blunt to the point of rudeness, yet who was also able to cheer and inspire – is more apparent than real. After all, small talk can quickly bore anybody who is genuinely interested in people: far more enjoyable to talk with somebody who says something novel or sees things differently. Macleod took evident pleasure in talking with young people and happily taught Gilmour's children to play bridge. His enjoyment derived from hearing what the younger generation thought and in particular learning how they saw things. Whenever he visited Yorkshire he would delight in visiting his niece, Ethne Bannister and her husband, Mike, at their home near Skipton, talking till all hours with their children and friends. Discovering a new angle or different way of seeing a problem intrigued Macleod. It was fitting that the hope and idealism that the young could bring to government and their country was a theme of Macleod's first leader in the *Spectator*. The subject was close to his heart, but its choice was prompted by the most tragic event.[36]

Personal Testament

Suddenly, every other event that late autumn of 1963 was diminished and overshadowed by the assassination, on Friday 22 November, of the American President, John F. Kennedy. The news of his shooting and death reached Britain during the evening. The next morning Macleod addressed a students conference and delivered a moving eulogy to Kennedy and the idealism that his presidency had appeared to symbolize, conjuring up 'the whole Camelot image'. No British politician was better qualified through his affinity for the young and as an orator, to address that particular audience, that weekend. Never one to waste a good speech by using it only once, Macleod's eloquent performance provided the basis for his first editorial in the *Spectator*, published a fortnight later, on 6 December.[37]

The theme of Macleod's speech and first editorial encapsulated his radical Toryism which encompassed certain aims common to the Roosevelt and Kennedy tradition of American liberalism. Equality of opportunity, racial equality, a citizen's duty to serve, the strong helping the weak: these were the political ideals that Macleod and Kennedy espoused. As Macleod understood, the Second World War had been the formative influence that had caused them both to enter politics:

> That President Kennedy should have become the spokesman of those who fought in war and yearned for peace was natural. But he became also a symbol of youth and hope to a whole generation that was too young to fight and that also yearned for peace.

'It is now our duty,' proclaimed Macleod, 'to be more urgent in our support of the causes for which Kennedy fought. To be more contemptuous of the bigots of right and left alike.' And he reiterated the theme that he had made his own at the Tory conference two years earlier:

> It is necessary to be more urgent in insisting on the brotherhood of man – in Africa, Asia, Alabama or Britain . . . In Africa and Asia the surge towards independence is both inevitable and desirable. In America the new President has pointed to the first task, to pass the Civil Rights Bill.

Although Macleod argued that Britain had no need of legislation on race, he provided a sketch of the kind of Tory radical manifesto for which he would have fought in the party's Steering Committee had he continued to hold a key policy-making role:

> Education, especially higher education, housing and slum clearance, aid both at home and to the Commonwealth: these are the priorities. Conveniently they are probably also the most popular policies. Heart and head for once can make the same appeal.[38]

In what amounted to a personal testament, Macleod had left no room for doubt about where the *Spectator* would take its stand under his editorship: certainly not as some tame lackey of Conservative Central Office. But there was no sign of quite how far – and how soon – he would go in demonstrating his independence and in testing party loyalty almost to breaking point.

During his first three months as editor, Macleod wrote only about half a dozen leaders, a surprising statistic, but one that bears out Thompson's recollection of Macleod's complete lack of possessiveness. Editorial conferences were scrapped, but Macleod would discuss the proposed line with colleagues: thereafter, whoever wrote an editorial was very much left alone by Macleod – there would be no interference or attempt to dictate the line. The subjects chosen by Macleod for the leaders that he wrote himself reveal the importance he attached to the Commonwealth in general, and to Africa in particular: three were concerned with Africa, and one, that he co-authored, was about Cyprus. These matters inevitably loomed larger in British politics than in subsequent decades, but Macleod's interest was rare even for his day.[39]

From the outset, Macleod's written contribution to the paper was not limited solely to the leader page. The week following his leader on Kennedy's death, Macleod made his debut as 'Quoodle', the eponymous author of the 'Spectator's Notebook'. He had 'thought finding a pen name would be easy' but it proved more difficult and the previous week his own name had appeared as the Notebook's by-line. Macleod had ransacked 'Disraeli's novels and Lord Randolph Churchill's speeches to find some suitable title that hasn't been used. And then I remembered Chesterton. After all, the Notebook should be revealing but not all-revealing.' And then, quoting the two lines that appeared at the head of this chapter, he declared, 'That's it'. The by-line that followed read simply 'Quoodle'. But a year later, he was still receiving 'a drizzle of letters' inquiring 'Why Quoodle?' Explaining that his alter ego 'was half-Cairn, half-Aberdeen, and belonged to G.K. Chesterton', Macleod admitted to having 'always been enchanted by The Song of Quoodle', and proceeded to quote its opening:

> They haven't got no noses,
> the fallen sons of Eve;
> Even the smell of roses
> Is not what they supposes;
> But more than the mind discloses
> And more than men believe.

Chesterton's poem concludes with the two lines quoted by Macleod when he chose his pen name. He quoted them again, this time adding 'Not everything, you understand. I am, I take it, still bound by the Official Secrets Act. But "all things Quoodle can . . ." '[40]

Macleod immediately proved himself to be a good columnist. As Gilmour has recalled, 'He was not free from the politician's egotism but he was far more egotisical in print than in private. This made his journalism unrepresentative of the man but it made his column marvellously readable.'

Whereas Macleod's leaders at times tended to read like speeches, Thompson felt that Macleod:

> had a natural talent as a journalist and produced a good weekly column. If he had a fault – and it was an unusual one among people who write but are not journalists – he tended too much towards brevity. He would write in short, sharp paragraphs, make his point, and then stop.

Macleod 'was a good, fast writer', and the paper's weekly Notebook, comprising around half a dozen items, was an ideal vehicle for his pithy observations that combined, in about equal measure, barbs and wit. He 'would write his copy in hand, very often in bed over the weekend, bringing in his copy with him on a Monday morning'. During his first month he was sole author of the Notebook, but he would accept contributions from others so that it sometimes seemed he had suddenly developed a new interest, to the amazement of his friends. As Thompson has recalled:

> Macleod was greatly amused at the ribbing that he received from the members at White's after an item had appeared [in the Notebook] about attending an art exhibition: his cronies at his club knew him too well to believe that he would ever have gone anywhere near such an event.[41]

Writing a weekly column brought its author 'a number of unfair advantages', since he was able to 'inflict his enthusiasms and his prejudices on his readers'. Macleod's 'enthusiasms' included, depending on the time of year, Scotland's chances in the Calcutta Cup rugby match against England, when he hoped that he would 'be a spectator at Bannockburn' having been 'a witness of so many Floddens'; the prospects for the Epsom Derby; and the cricketing fortunes of Freddie Trueman, the Yorkshire fast bowler. Among 'his prejudices', the principal butts of attack were the BBC and its then Director-General, Sir Hugh Greene; 'the Nanny State', the term that Macleod coined to describe unthinking bossiness or intrusion into people's lives by any branch of government; and Harold Wilson, then Leader of the Opposition. Tories commonly regard the BBC as being run by leftists and Macleod was no exception, notwithstanding the fact that he was an avid viewer and self-confessed admirer of *That Was The Week That Was*, which he felt 'was rarely dull and it was salty, malicious, arrogant and often very funny'.[42]

In his eyes, the BBC epitomized the worst aspects of near monopoly, while its bosses personified an arrogance and ineptitude born of guaranteed funding and the BBC's heavily protected status, notwithstanding the Tories' introduction of independent television in the mid-1950s. This hatred of the BBC and government bossiness was rarely better demonstrated than in Macleod's early championing of commercial radio stations in the early 1960s.

'Excellent. Another victory against the Nursemaid State,' he declared in May 1964, when the Government finally decided to allow the pirate radio station, Radio Caroline, to continue. But he was angered that a Tory Government had originally planned to ban its broadcasts: 'Naturally the Labour Party wanted to stop people listening to what they choose to, but it passes comprehension how Mr Bevins [Postmaster-General] thought he could get a similar policy through the Tory Party.' In Macleod's judgement, 'The best solution of course, is to abolish the BBC monopoly of sound radio. The second best is to abolish the BBC.'[43]

Narrow party politics rarely intruded into Quoodle's weekly observations. His dislike for Wilson reflected a deep personal antipathy, that was, as he freely confessed to Alan Watkins, 'irrational. He simply did not care for the man'. But there was more to his hostility than this. He would refer to Wilson as 'that little man', but this was not a reference to the Labour leader's stature, since, if anything, Wilson was slightly taller than Macleod, but signified Macleod's judgement of Wilson as a politician incapable of thinking beyond the short-term, tactical fix, and lacking any stature as a statesman. For his part, Wilson had a wary respect for Macleod. However, some of Wilson's coterie were less respectful and would refer to Macleod as 'the poison dwarf'. Macleod's personal disrespect for the Labour leader was complete following an incident that he witnessed in Edinburgh on the day of the March 1964 rugby match at Murrayfield, when 'at last it was Bannockburn':

> Never have I seen anyone look so absurdly out of place as did the Leader of the Opposition when, followed by a dour crowd of retainers, he came into the jampacked North British Hotel before lunch on Saturday. There was a moment of disbelief as the incredible news was passed round that he was going to make a speech in the Usher Hall on the afternoon of the Calcutta Cup game. 'He'll lose every vote in Scotland,' said one of Scotland's most capped internationals.

Yet Macleod had very different feelings towards other leading Labour politicians. He had affection for George Brown, admired Jim Callaghan personally, and when Michael Foot and his wife, Jill Craigie, narrowly escaped death in a car crash in late 1963, Quoodle composed an appreciative thumbnail sketch of a fellow editor and back bencher: 'Soon he will be thundering again from *Tribune*. He brings passion into a grey age of politics. He has a biting original wit. He rasps in public and is gentle in private . . . It is wholly appropriate that he is both the Member for Ebbw Vale and Aneurin Bevan's biographer.'[44]

On Quoodle's debut, Macleod took up the arguments he had advocated to the BBC in 1962, as Leader of the House and Party Chairman, in favour of televising parliamentary proceedings. Unequivocally a 'House of Commons man', Macleod wrote:

The arguments against allowing at least an edited version of the proceedings in the House of Commons to be shown daily on television are much
the same as were once used to stop newspapers reporting. Members, it is
said, will posture to the cameras: the same argument has been disproved
at the three party conferences. It will be against ancient tradition: the same
argument was used against the televising of the Coronation inside Westminster Abbey. It will show the House of Commons warts and all – as it
is, not as one likes to think it is: so much the better. There are no
insuperable technical problems. The danger of doing nothing is that the
House of Commons may become a secondary forum of political debate. If
every seat in the Public Gallery was filled twice every sitting day 100,000
people could watch the House of Commons in action each year. Eight and
a half million people watch Panorama every Monday night.[45]

The nearest that Macleod came to blimpish traditionalism was in his
decided coolness (but not outright opposition) to the proposed admittance
of women students to men's colleges at Oxford. Macleod's 'One Nation'
Toryism permeated his column as much as it did his leaders. Reporting an
Anglo-American weekend conference at Ditchley Park, Oxfordshire, attended by senators and congressmen, he found 'as usual [that] the hours out
of school were at least as valuable as the more formal discussions. Quoodle
spent most of his spare time arguing in favour of "socialised medicine".'[49]
His visit to Ditchley Park occurred immediately after he had trailed his
intention to write about the Tory leadership crisis: 'In next week's *Spectator*
Iain Macleod reviews *The Fight for the Tory Leadership* by Randolph S.
Churchill.' But not everybody noticed his trailer, the *Sunday Mirror*'s
Sydney Jacobson for one. 'How much longer is Mr Iain Macleod going to
keep up his baffling silence?' the hapless Jacobson inquired in his column
that weekend. 'You've got to hand it to the *Mirror*,' Quoodle chortled the
following Friday. 'They certainly pick up the news'.[46]

Although Macleod kept his counsel about the events of October 1963 during
the first six weeks of his editorship, Quoodle showed that even on this topic he
had not lost his wit. Neither had he lost his bite. Macleod detected the 'irony
in almost every aspect' of the ceremony held in December 1963 for the unveiling
of the statue of David Lloyd George in the House of Commons:

> Ll.G., after all, was a Commoner who became an Earl; his statue was
> unveiled by an Earl who became a Commoner. More than half a century
> has passed since Ll.G.'s great onslaught on the landed peerage; his statue
> was unveiled by a Prime Minister drawn from the landed peerage.

Similarly, quipping about his own exile on the backbenches in the paper's
last edition of 1963, Quoodle wrote:

An anxious friend asks me what the difference is between sitting on the third and sitting on the front bench. Only the difference between economy and first-class air-travel: there is less room for your legs.

This item was headed, 'Tourist', reflecting Macleod's hope that his sojourn on the back benches would be temporary. But within a month he feared that he would never return to the first-class seating.[47]

'The establishment will be livid'

On 17 January 1964, the *Spectator* published Macleod's sensational exposé of what had happened behind the scenes only three months earlier during the Tory leadership crisis. Macleod's decision to break his vow of silence over the events of October 1963 was triggered by the publication of Randolph Churchill's hastily written paperback, *The Fight for the Tory Leadership*, whose selective revelations and highly partial account of Douglas-Home's victory barely disguised the guileful brain of its main source, Harold Macmillan. Macmillan would later claim that although he had talked freely to Churchill, he had tried to dissuade him from writing the book. However, this claim and Macmillan's protestation that he had been rather casual about reading the proofs, leading to one or two minor inaccuracies, were made some months after Macleod's 'frank and detailed narrative' had debunked both Churchill's account and that offered by Redmayne, the Chief Whip.[48]

Macleod's alternative version was profoundly shocking: the party leadership was revealed as a self-selecting, tightly-knit group, which had abused its power and rigged the selection of the new leader and Prime Minister. Although 'he was under no illusion that such an article could only further enrage some of the Tory Party', the depth of hostility that it provoked towards him caused him to confess privately to close colleagues that he thought it had ended his political career. The article's impact was 'explosive'. 'Macleod Spills The Beans', 'Macleod Angers Tories', 'Macleod Flare Up', 'Storm Over Macleod', read the front-page headlines in the popular press on the morning of its publication. Even *The Times* devoted its leading domestic story to the furore, announcing, 'Article dismays Conservatives: "Hardly a Loyal Action" '. As Joan Baylis recalled:

The *Spectator*'s Gower Street office was once more besieged: Orders for copies of the paper were such that the circulation shot up like the chart of a high fever; London, provincial and even overseas newspapers sought permission to reprint; others showed less than courtesy by publishing pirated versions without payment; journalists once again sought interviews and photographs.[49]

Macleod's extraordinary revelations were guaranteed to attract headline coverage, but even so he had assiduously courted maximum publicity. In many papers, the dramatic headlines were accompanied by the same, staged photograph of Macleod, taken the day before as he left number 99, and showing a billboard for the *Spectator* attached to the outside of the building and visible over his shoulder, declaring, 'Iain Macleod on The Tory Struggle'. Having trailed his article the previous week, the paper's front-cover made clear what its editor judged was his main selling point. Most weeks, the cover included a list of the main contributors to that edition, but on this occasion only one author received star billing: 'IAIN MACLEOD: WHAT HAPPENED.' There was no need to explain his subject. Above the headline were arranged five passport-sized photographs of the *dramatis personae* – Maudling, Heath, Macleod, Butler and Hogg (formerly Lord Hailsham); and below, at the foot of the page, was a snap of the Prime Minister. What followed inside the paper did not disappoint a much-enlarged readership. Although Macleod's 4,000-word article, entitled simply, 'The Tory Leadership', was technically a book review, its positioning near the leader page instead of towards the back of the paper indicated that it had not been written primarily with the *Spectator*'s literary aficionados in mind.[50]

Macleod faced the immediate charge that he had merely been waiting his opportunity to cause further trouble for the leader whom he had refused to serve. As the political correspondent of *The Times*, David Wood, reported: 'Mr Macleod has found the opportunity, for his personal statement in a long review . . . of Mr Randolph Churchill's new book . . .' The implication, that Macleod was looking for such an opportunity, was hotly denied in a letter to *The Times*, from Lord Aldington, one of the senior Tories who had attended the 'midnight meeting' with Macleod at Enoch Powell's house. 'I know from personal experience,' he stated, 'that Mr Macleod was doing no such thing.' According to Aldington: 'In spite of the enormous pressure that had been applied to them both and the personal embarrassment to them in their constituencies, Mr Macleod and Mr Powell had held to their original decision to make no statement.' As a result, in Gilmour's recollection, 'nobody quite knew why he hadn't agreed to serve Sir Alec'.[51]

Once Churchill had published, Macleod was bound to have written a rebuttal 'somewhere', whether or not he had been editing the *Spectator*. Thompson, who at this stage was still working for the *Evening Standard*, remembered its earliest beginnings:

We were having dinner together and discussing his new role as editor of the *Spectator*. It was a cheerful and convivial occasion, as meals with him usually were. The subject of Randolph Churchill's new book on the Tory leadership came up. 'Why don't you redview it?' I asked, without pre-meditation. 'You can't stay silent for ever on why you left the government, and that would give you a chance to have your say.' He beamed across the table with that characteristic look suggesting agreeable mischief ahead. 'But I'm going to,' he said. 'Macleod Speaks! – that sort of thing. There'll be a row.'[52]

On the day that his article went to press, Wednesday 15 January, Macleod gave his reasons for breaking his silence in a personal, hand-written letter to Butler, sent from his Chelsea address with a copy of the uncorrected galley proofs. Macleod warned of the likely reaction of the party leadership, that he mockingly called 'the establishment':

Dear RAB,
I had not intended to write anything of last October until Randolph's book appeared. It is sadly inaccurate and grossly unfair to you. I think now (although the establishment will be livid) that the truth should be told, and it must be made clear that you were in fact the rightful choice. I have checked every detail with Reggie Maudling, Enoch [Powell] and Toby [Aldington] all of whom agree. With luck people will now see something of the whole picture.
Love to Mollie from us both,
Ever,
Iain.

Although Butler had ignored an advance copy of Randolph Churchill's manuscript, he wrote across the top of Macleod's letter for his private secretary at the Foreign Office, 'Please put in weekend bag'. Butler would keep his counsel at the time, but in his memoir of Macleod published in April 1982, shortly after his own death, Rab confirmed that 'every word' of Macleod's *Spectator* article 'is true'. Powell issued a brief statement on the evening of Thursday 16th in response to inquiries about Macleod's article: 'I can confirm the accuracy of Mr Macleod's narrative on all matters within my knowledge, and I agree with his general assessment of those events'.[53]

Underlying Macleod's rebuttal of Churchill was the same motivation that led him to accept Gilmour's offer to edit the *Spectator*. He had seen Butler subordinate his personal ambition entirely to the party interest only to be twice denied the highest office because he was said to lack 'inner steel' or 'robustness'. Nobody was ever going to be allowed to make the same accusation of Macleod. Failure to challenge Churchill's account would be taken as a tacit admission on Macleod's part that he agreed with it and, in effect, that his leaving the Government had been a purely cynical act. Macleod was as likely to damage his own position if he kept quiet about the leadership crisis as if he made fresh disclosures. Instead of eventually being rewarded for his loyal silence, his refusal to serve would never be easily forgiven and he would only have compounded the problem by failing to defend himself publicly. He would be damned if he didn't, and damned if he did. 'So he published and was damned.' There was no alternative except to publish a detailed account in order to reveal the 'contradictions and misrepresentation' which Macleod and other senior Tories knew had distorted the selection procedure the previous October. What chance would there be of forcing the leadership to put their house in order if the Churchill version was allowed to go unchallenged?[54]

An immense sense of relief was understandable once Macleod had decided that he would give his version of events. As Gilmour was to recall: 'The article was written in a hurry and some of the phrases in it would have been altered, had he foreseen the interpretation that was put upon them.' Although his draft typescript does bear a few hasty amendments, made in his own hand, these made no difference to its reception. But one phrase was to haunt him for the rest of his political career. Having supplied a list of the key people involved in the selection of Douglas-Home, Macleod added that, 'Eight of the nine people mentioned in the last sentence went to Eton.' As Gilmour later noted, '*Floreat Etona* was never one of his mottoes, but his remark about Old Etonians was a witty crack and was not intended to have deadly significance.' But as Anthony Howard has noted and as Macleod should have realized, 'that was considered a rather low blow for one Conservative to deliver against colleagues in those days'.[55]

Part of the problem was Macleod's tone, another was that his chosen targets were far more important than the author of the book that was supposedly under review. Macleod's initial draft had begun with a fierce condemnation of Randolph Churchill: 'This is a bad book and to have written it is a major disservice to the Tory party.' Although Macleod deleted this opening sentence at typescript stage, he argued that Churchill's work was not an entirely objective piece of journalism. 'Its importance,' claimed Macleod, 'comes from the fact that this is Mr Macmillan's trailer for the screenplay of his memoirs':

Originally, Mr Churchill's preface said that he had been given full assistance by everyone except Mr Iain Macleod. This had to be altered. Among those who either haven't been asked for or have refused comment on this book are the Lord Chancellor [Dilhorne], Mr Maudling, Mr Powell, Sir Edward Boyle, the Chief Whip, Lord Blakenham, Lord Aldington and myself.

Churchill subsequently acknowledged that 'My information for the most part came from the winning side who had no need to whine.' But neither did they have any need, as Churchill might have been expected to recognize, to present an objective account of events. Macleod was at pains at the outset of his article to demonstrate that he wrote more in sorrow than in anger: 'Until Mr Churchill's book appeared there had been an unspoken agreement that the less said the better about the recent struggle for the Tory leadership.' But Macleod's mask soon started to slip and the apologetic tone vanished completely.[56]

Reaction was bitterly divided. Macleod was deluged by a flood of messages and letters. Telegrams sent to the *Spectator* demonstrated the depth of feeling generated by his article. From one outraged reader:

> WHAT A NASTY LITTLE BIT OF WORK YOU ARE STOP FIRST NOTICED YOUR EYES AT THE BLACKPOOL CONFERENCE ON TELEVISION STOP THANK GOD YOU'RE NOT PRIME MINISTER

But from the Boulting brothers, the film producers whose campaign to secure the independence of the film company, British Lion, had been endorsed by Macleod in the *Spectator*:

> WARMEST CONGRATULATIONS STOP YOUR ARTICLE BOTH COURAGEOUS AND NECESSARY IF THE WORD TORY IS TO BE RE-IDENTIFIED WITH THE WORD INTEGRITY

Varying degrees of 'deprecation, annoyance and surprise' were voiced in response to Macleod's article among 'ministerial and Central Office quarters'. His enemies were determined that his action would never be forgiven or forgotten.[57]

Scarcely any Conservatives publicly supported Macleod. One who offered his backing, Peter Tapsell, then the young MP for Nottingham West, read the article while travelling to his constituency and immediately issued a hand-written press release, but he soon discovered that he was almost alone. On the same day (Friday 17th) at Westminster, most Conservative MPs were still reported to feel 'anger and resentment' at Macleod's revelations. It was ironic that the Tory reaction was best captured in public print by David Watt, writing in the *Spectator*, the week after Macleod's article:

> That the beloved leader should be accused of meeting his crown by by-paths and devious crook'd ways, at the very moment when he was about to sally into the field, seemed to the party a monstrous treason and touching protestations of loyalty were imperative.

Three Birmingham Tory MPs, Messrs Cleaver, Gurden and Hollingworth, who were due to appear with Macleod at a party 'brains trust' meeting the following week, called for the cancellation of his invitation, and many more were planning to ostracize Macleod 'by banning or cold-shouldering his platform appearances for the party'. For some days, the situation 'was quite dicey', but the whips saw the dangers for the party in allowing a bloody vendetta against Macleod. There was 'choice irony', noted by the political journalist, James Margach, 'In the role of Mr Martin Redmayne, whose soundings and accountancy methods were impugned by Mr Macleod, in persuading the hunt to be called off and protecting Mr Macleod from the wrath of party loyalists!'[58]

Many rank and file Tories were infuriated. According to a senior party official in Yorkshire, Macleod had not been forgiven by party members even in Skipton, his home town. Macleod also came under increased fire in his own constituency association, although before he wrote the article he had been under pressure to give a full account of his reasons for refusing to serve Douglas-Home. A resolution expressing lack of confidence in Macleod was passed in the North Ward, and although the Potter's Bar association rejected a 'no confidence' motion, the meeting approved a resolution 'regretting publication of the views expressed by Mr Macleod on the Tory Party leadership in the *Spectator* article.' He was censured by his constituency party executive by fifteen votes to fourteen, with seven abstentions, but a no confidence motion was defeated by 29 votes to 7.[59]

Yet Macleod was not completely without support. Powell, visiting Nuffield College, Oxford, on the Wednesday after the article's publication, denied vehemently that the whole Tory Party had turned on Macleod. He maintained that Macleod's critics were vocal but his many friends were silent. 'Here and there,' according to *The Times*, Tory MPs suggested that the fault lay more with Macmillan and Randolph Churchill for having raised the controversy in the first place. Harry Legge-Bourke, a senior backbencher, was one of the few prepared to say as much on the record, but it was a view shared privately at Central Office by Poole, the Party Vice-chairman. Moreover, Macleod's friends were reportedly 'not shy in suggesting that if the Conservative Party goes into Opposition it will need Mr Macleod on the front bench to hammer the Labour Government'.[60]

The line taken by the Tory whips, in an effort to limit the damaging row that had erupted – 'Least said, soonest mended' – proved totally ineffective. On the Monday following Macleod's article, 20 January, the political correspondent of *The Times*, David Wood, in his weekly column published a further account of the leadership struggle that could only have come from one of the leading contenders. In fact, Wood's version had come from Maudling, who had approached the columnist on his (Maudling's) own initiative. Although Maudling's version marginally modified Macleod's account, it further confirmed the extent of Cabinet support for Butler. Macleod also found that some of his enemies were his best recruiting sergeants. He refused to withdraw from the party 'brains trust' in Birmingham as three of the city's MPs had demanded and the formidable local party machine, created by the Chamberlain family, was brought in to end the feud. The three hostile MPs stayed away in protest, but as *The Times* reported: 'There is nothing like a good boycott for whipping up a good audience and tonight's totalled 450. Mr Macleod's appearance on the platform produced avid applause, some stamping and even a few faint cheers.'[61]

Macleod's position was not helped by the furore that erupted simultaneously over the Government's decision to press ahead with the abolition of resale price maintenance – a reform that Macleod had opposed as Party Chairman, when it had first been mooted in 1962. Edward Heath's proposed reform caused widespread dissension in the party, with many backbenchers subjected to intense lobbying against the reform by opinion-forming small shopkeepers and publicans. But instead of distracting attention from Macleod, the two problems were bracketed together. In the *Spectator*, Watt quoted 'a very august politician', as having 'remarked with some bitterness at the beginning of the rumpus, "We were doing fine until Ted Heath came along with his resale price maintenance and your Editor came along with his article".'[62]

Macleod became deeply depressed. His supporters in the parliamentary party were drawn almost entirely from the youngest and least experienced MPs. They tried to do what they could to rally him. Humphry Berkeley, who had been in Switzerland when the article appeared, returned to London two days later and the following week invited Macleod to lunch at the White Tower. Berkeley:

> Found him in the depths of despair. The reaction to his article had been ferociously hostile and he talked to me about giving up politics altogether and concentrating on writing. I told him that this was quite unreasonable and that if he left politics, he would betray a large number of younger members who saw him as the only leader who would preserve the radical future of the Party.

Tapsell also lunched Macleod at the White Tower, having been encouraged by Gilmour. Tapsell had expected to discover that Macleod's diary would already be full with more important lunch engagements, but to his astonishment, Macleod instantly accepted. 'I'm finished,' Macleod said several times during their lunch, while Tapsell tried to be encouraging. But as *The Times* had forewarned, Macleod could 'expect an icy reception when he next meets some of his colleagues: he will certainly continue to be strongly criticized in private'. The behaviour of his colleagues shook Macleod, as Gilmour has recalled: 'Highly sensitive, he was hurt by the enmity of those who in theory were his political allies. He could not understand the behaviour in early 1964 of a then Cabinet Minister who cut him at a party.' At Westminster, Nigel Birch, the right-winger and former Treasury minister, who had been an early supporter of Douglas-Home's cause, was specially offensive. The iciness of Macleod's reception has been vividly recalled by Berkeley:

> He [Macleod] said that he couldn't bear to be near the House of Commons – he was being shunned by everybody. And there was a period of two or three weeks when he didn't go to the House of Commons. I said to him: 'Look, you can't abandon us.' He replied: 'I can't bear that smoking-room.' So I said: 'OK, after a ten o'clock vote we'll go and have a drink there.' We went and had a drink there and were cut by every single person in the room.[63]

Macleod had badly miscalculated the extreme hostility that his disclosures would provoke in the party. With the most closely fought and difficult election campaign since 1951 only months ahead and the Government already on the defensive, most Tories – whatever private misgivings they held about the leadership crisis – placed a premium on loyalty to the leadership. The next general election was the limit of their political horizon. He would never be forgiven for using the phrase, the 'magic circle'. In Whitelaw's view Macleod: 'was a much more emotional man than many people thought, and could at moments be guided by his emotions: the article in the *Spectator* was the emotion of Iain.'[64]

Macleod's evident gusto, bordering on the point of recklessness, in launching such disturbing accusations against a former Prime Minister, the Lord Chancellor and the Chief Whip, confirms Whitelaw's view. The Tory right maintained that he was motivated by pique, as Peregrine Worsthorne cuttingly remarked in the *Sunday Telegraph*:

> What is boring and irrelevant is the suggestion of an upper class conspiracy, particularly coming from a man who has sedulously and successfully modelled himself on that class, and whose complaints against the magic circle only began when he failed to square it in his own interests.

But this is to misunderstand everything about the man and his politics. There was no doubt that Macleod was intensely ambitious and had been convinced, ever since attending staff college during the Second World War, that he was 'commander class'. He clearly enjoyed belonging to White's, but this appealed to the romantic side of his Toryism. The implication that Macleod was a social climber was particularly odious, since it was an indirect way of drawing attention to the fact that his background was not top-drawer and, in effect, castigated him for daring to move in the same circles as the class that had traditionally ruled the Tory party. Yet anybody with ambition in the Tory Party in the 1950s had no option but to work within its prevailing ethos and seek to join its higher echelons. Patently, Macleod was a member of the inner circle of trusted confidants on merit, as demonstrated by his undoubted political skills behind the scenes prior to each of the three successive Conservative election triumphs during the 1950s.[65]

What had angered Macleod about the selection of Douglas-Home had been Macmillan's rigging of the consultation process. But his special sense of outrage stemmed from the conviction that stirred him more than almost anything else in politics: he was an impassioned meritocrat. As Rutherford found during their frequent conversations, he was probably the Tory who came closest to having a chip on his shoulder against the privileged. He deplored the fact that in Macmillan's determination to prevent Butler succeeding him, the former Prime Minister had depended on an out-dated, self-selecting establishment. The party that Macleod and others of his generation had fought to modernize, following Butler's lead, was in danger of becoming as badly out of touch in the mid-1960s as it had been when Macmillan himself had railed against the leadership in the 1930s. Macleod's article was a dire warning to the party not to repeat the same mistake. Macleod 'felt that whatever else happened, he had done his party a service'.[66]

But Macleod had touched a raw nerve and was not thanked for it, although Tory support increased by two percentage points in the Gallup political index the month after his revelations. 'The Tory party can never be quite the same again' was the prophetic comment in the 'Crossbencher' column in the *Sunday Express*. Macleod had delivered the *coup de grace* to the 'magic circle', although he had not objected to the system of consultation *per se* but to its abuse in 1963. He did not address the question of how such malpractice could be avoided in future, an issue that perturbed Tories like Tom Iremonger, who had objected to the selection system since Macmillan's emergence in 1957, and Macleod's young acolyte, Humphry Berkeley, who had been campaigning to reform a system that he described as more appropriate for the 'enstoolment' of an African chief. Some weeks before Macleod's article, Berkeley had approached Douglas-Home 'with the suggestion that some study should be given to preparing a more formal method'. Following the furore over his article, Macleod endorsed Douglas-Home's response to Berkeley:

> The Prime Minister some weeks ago replied that it would be right for the Tory Party to look at this, not in relation to the events of last October or the general election, but as a matter of internal democracy of the Tory Party. Perhaps a year from now the Party should study this matter. I am sure we would be wise to postpone it until then[67]

However, Macleod's article had provided the vital catalyst needed to bring about reform.

'And what of Mr Macleod himself?' asked the weekly political columnist, 'Crossbencher', on the Sunday after Macleod's article, before adding his own speculation: 'One thing is certain. Mr Macleod does not plan to spend the rest of his life as editor of the *Spectator*. He still believes that one day he can become Prime Minister.'

Macleod thought that he had ruined his chances. Powell did not agree. The following week, he was arguing that Macleod had actually gained in strength and stature. Within a matter of months, Macleod was to recover from his depression and come to share Powell's more optimistic assessment of his prospects. In the meantime, he had kept to the maxim of his *alter ego*, Quoodle, to devastating effect:

> And Quoodle here discloses
> All things that Quoodle can.[68]

15

Poisoned Chalice

The Conservative Party always in time forgives those who were wrong. Indeed often, in time, they forgive those who were right.
Quoodle, *Spectator*, 21 February 1964.

Impatient with the Old Guard

Almost from the moment he left the Cabinet in the autumn of 1963, Macleod was frustrated at being out of office. To make matters worse, the uncertainty about his future could not be resolved until the forthcoming election was finally over. In the meantime, he 'clearly had no high opinion of [Douglas-] Home.' Macleod reckoned privately that the bookmakers' odds of 2–1 on Labour winning were about right. But, as he pointed out, that still gave the Tories a one in three chance and he continued to maintain, as he had done in October 1963 and again in his *Spectator* article on the leadership in January 1964, that Macmillan would have won the election if he had stayed on.[1]

As Macleod observed of Douglas-Home's leadership in his *Spectator* article, 'the Tory Party for the first time since Bonar Law is now being led from the right of centre'. But unlike Bonar Law, Douglas-Home was of the traditional right: the cutting edge of the Canadian-born, Glaswegian iron merchant was entirely lacking in the landowning, fourteenth Earl. Douglas-Home would later recall of his premiership, 'we had finished our programme and you couldn't do anything except await the election', revealing an insipid approach that exacerbated Macleod's sense of frustration.[2]

Privately, Macleod was scathing about the Prime Minister: Douglas-Home understood little – if he were asked about unemployment, he would probably think his questioner was referring to a shortage of ghillies. In short, the Prime Minister was a traditionalist, out of touch with the modern world, and incapable of catching up. It would be hard to think of a more damning indictment from Macleod's point of view, or a starker contrast to the leadership that he believed was urgently needed in order to create a modern, forward-looking Tory Party. As Macleod began to emerge from his deep depression, his mind began to turn to how he might realize his vision for a radical Tory Party. Editing the *Spectator* gave him a platform, but it was no substitute for wielding power. The only sure way to achieve his ambition for the party was to regain his position as one of the key figures in the leadership.[3]

But some fences in the party would always remain beyond repair. Only two weeks after his explosive comments on the leadership crisis, Macleod's long-running battle was resumed with his most bitter Conservative adversary from his days at the Colonial Office, the senior Tory peer, the Marquess of Salisbury. Again, Macleod was responding to a highly partial and provocative version of events in which he had been centrally involved. Salisbury had reopened old Tory wounds in late January 1964, when he wrote in the *Sunday Times* what the paper billed as 'a personal protest' by the Marquess, who 'has always opposed "the winds of change" '. 'It is a serious charge and demands a serious answer,' retorted Macleod, taking the unusual step of signing his editorial, an action that was appropriate since Salisbury's attack demanded a defence of his record as Colonial Secretary. The philosophical divide between the two men was never more vividly demonstrated than in their opposing views on the motivating force behind African self-rule. According to Salisbury: 'A large proportion of the new electors did not want power. They did not want to govern. They had always been governed, and they preferred it that way. And that, I believe, is still true, even in this country.'

To which Macleod replied:

> I read those words with honest admiration for a man who in 1964 can still put forward his paternal philosophy in such uncompromising terms. And also with profound relief that, at least since 1959, the British Government has followed another road in Africa.

The clash between Tory right and left persisted on the letters page over the following fortnight. Salisbury's further accusation that Macleod's arguments were tantamount to 'our old friend the policy of Appeasement through weakness in a new form,' was countered by Barney Hayhoe, a prospective parliamentary candidate and one of Macleod's acolytes: 'Too late now to retire gracefully, but please, Lord Salisbury, not too late to retire.'[4]

In view of his continuing battles with the champion of the Rhodesia lobby, Macleod might have been expected to adopt a radical stance when the long-simmering crisis in Southern Rhodesia appeared to be coming to a head. In February 1964 the Southern Rhodesian Prime Minister, Winston Field, rejected the terms privately offered by Sandys, the Commonwealth Secretary, for reforms to the 1961 constitution that were designed to pave the way for eventual independence. In the eight months leading up to the October 1964 general election, Macleod devoted five editorials primarily to the question of Southern Rhodesia, more than twice as many than on any other subject.

As a former Colonial Secretary, he was acutely conscious of both the unique responsibility that rested with British ministers to find a solution and of the costs of failure to African and European alike in southern Africa. His cautious approach was to put him at odds with many of his natural supporters on the left of the Tory Party for the remainder of his life. Although the 'traditional solution' that Macleod had deployed in other territories – 'a Conference leading to rule by majority on a wide franchise at an early date' – was favoured by some left-wing Tories, Macleod rejected it.' As he argued, 'The Southern Rhodesian Government would certainly decline to attend, and the British Government could hardly hold bilateral Constitutional discussions with a (divided) African nationalist party.' At 'the other extreme,' the notion held by some on the right that Southern Rhodesia could somehow be granted independence outside the Commonwealth was derided by Macleod, since the Australian, Canadian and New Zealand Governments would oppose it as strongly as the new Commonwealth states. Probably its only support would be found in the remaining territories under Portuguese rule, and 'although it is of course inconceivable that Britain would take up arms against her or encourage others to do so, an independent Southern Rhodesia would surely be the target for a new crusade'.[5]

Macleod's preferred, 'best solution' was, in his own definition, an 'armistice':

> If the Southern Rhodesian Government could have been persuaded not to press its demand for independence and instead concentrate on a review of the repressive legislation that had done so much to alienate both African and liberal opinion; if the African nationalists could concentrate first on resolving their own internal divisions; if the British Government, with the help perhaps of senior Judges, say from Nigeria and New Zealand, could produce reliable independent estimates of when the present Constitution might produce an African majority: then the way after a few months might be open to a Constitutional Conference which had some hope of success.

Macleod feared that it was already too late. Two months later, Field was ousted for being too moderate and replaced by his Finance Minister, Ian Smith. Speaking at the Oxford Union in May with Garfield Todd, the former, liberal Southern Rhodesian Prime Minister, Macleod recalled that Todd had been rejected because he was too moderate, and that the prime ministers who had succeeded him were also rejected for being too moderate. 'How long can this madness go on?' Macleod wondered. 'How near must this boat go to the weir before a really determined attempt is made to stop it? Sooner or later men must get round a table and thrash out their differences.'[6]

Macleod's practical proposal was to suggest that a way should be found, before the Commonwealth Prime Ministers' Conference in July, for Smith to be admitted to the sessions on Central Africa. By the same token, Macleod felt that it would be 'unreal' not to invite Dr Kaunda to those sessions. After all, Dr Banda would attend as leader of a newly independent (by one day) Malawi, and Kaunda would become the Prime Minister of an independent Commonwealth country long before there was any prospect of a Prime Minister from Southern Rhodesia being in that position. 'Dr Kaunda may well prove one of the leading statesmen of Africa, and it is certain that his voice will always be heard on the side of peace.'[7]

The Commonwealth Prime Ministers failed to take up Macleod's suggestion. During the summer of 1964, statements from the Smith Government became more intransigent. Macleod held to three basic themes. First and foremost, there remained the need to resolve the question of 'whether the present constitution is acceptable as a springboard for advance, or whether it must now be scrapped': in short, 'how quickly it would produce a genuine African majority.' Estimates had varied from eight to thirty years. Macleod published in the *Spectator* a detailed article by Leo Baron, the liberal Southern Rhodesian lawyer, that concluded, 'The African people know that the 1961 constitution cannot take them to majority rule in any period that would be acceptable.' In his editorial in the same issue, he spelt out the implications in a message clearly directed at his old adversaries on Africa, Douglas-Home and Sandys:

It is now necessary to warn against the easy assumption that all that Britain need do is sit back and wait until the 1961 Constitution grinds out an African majority, and in the meantime, by multiplying economic aid hasten the process. It cannot be stated too simply that in 1964 aid is no substitute for political freedom.[8]

Secondly, Macleod was at pains to emphasize the paramount need to preserve Commonwealth unity in the face of a divisive threat. He endorsed the idea that had first been put forward some twenty years earlier for a Commonwealth Secretariat to be established, in the hope that it might help realize the Commonwealth's potential for playing a key role in helping to resolve precisely the sort of crisis that had developed in Southern Rhodesia. Finally, Macleod was convinced of the need to make Southern Rhodesia's Europeans fully aware of the real position and of the consequences if the Smith Government tried to go it alone. Hardly any British politician would contemplate the use of force, and neither would Macleod, but 'it is vital to banish any comfortable thoughts there may still be in the minds of the Government of Southern Rhodesia that rebellion against the Crown would be treated as a weekend wonder and forgotten'. In the event of an unilateral declaration of independence, limited economic pressure by Britain was as far as he proposed going: 'We can and should remove their Commonwealth preferences and refuse to purchase their tobacco crop. It is neither provocative or high-handed to make this clear now. It is plain common sense.'[9]

Macleod's relatively moderate stance on Southern Rhodesia raised few eyebrows compared with reaction to the new line that he adopted on another controversial subject for which he had also held ministerial responsibility. Suddenly, in February 1964, 'to everyone's great surprise', Macleod put his name to a Commons' motion, along with around 140 other backbench Tory MPs, calling for a Royal Commission to investigate trade union reform. This action represented a considerable change of heart but in early 1964, as a result of the House of Lords ruling in the case of *Rookes* v. *Barnard*, union reform ceased to be the preserve of right-wingers like the reactionary, Captain Henry Kerby, a Tory backbencher, or Edward Martell of the self-styled 'Freedom Group'.

In a case that had begun almost eight years earlier at London's Heathrow airport, the Law Lords finally ruled that a worker (Rookes) was able to sue the union, whose officials (Barnard and others) had induced his employers to sack him by threatening to strike unless he was dismissed. By undermining the far-reaching legal protection, or immunity, that had been extended to trade unions by the 1906 Trade Disputes Act, the Lords judgment provided the 'peg' for union reform that an increasing number of Tories had come to feel was long overdue. An inquiry into union law no longer seemed like a political bombshell, and could plausibly be presented as being as likely to assist the unions as to impair them. The subject was immediately raised at Tory backbench committees, and it was made known that Rab Butler and younger ministers charged with formulating policy were considering the idea. The 'One Nation' Group, seeing that the pressure for reform was becoming irresistible, but concerned that right-wingers should not claim the kudos nor be allowed to make the running with their extreme demands, drafted its own Commons motion calling for a Royal Commission. It was this motion to which Macleod, 'wearing presumably his "One Nation", rather than his ex-Minister of Labour hat', added his name. Its importance, compared with earlier, more right-wing, motions, was explained by Macleod:

> It is the voice of all wings of the party. The leading signatories are a coalition of the 'One Nation' Group and the officers of the [Tory backbench] Labour Committee, in short the Tories who have been over the years the most sympathetic to the trade unions.

Most remarkable of all was the urgency of Macleod's demand. Noting that it would be 'tempting for both of the main political parties to postpone action until after the general election', he asserted that: 'This would be the worst of all courses. A new Tory Government would probably do nothing: a Labour Government would simply entrench the abuses.'[10]

Six months later, on the eve of both the TUC's annual congress and the long-awaited 1964 general election campaign, Macleod castigated the continued failure of union leaders (he exempted from blame George Woodcock, the TUC General Secretary) to address the need for reform. Government and Opposition agreed that 'the law should be re-examined and almost certainly changed', but most Tories wanted 'an inquiry (preferable a Royal Commission) not just into trade union law, but into the whole role of the trade unions.' Macleod had no appetite for swingeing anti-union measures, but wanted to establish an up to date system of industrial relations without imposing, at the same time, a great new edifice of impractical restrictions. Some commonly suggested reforms found little favour: 'those who have given careful study' to the problem had 'no enthusiasm for secret ballots, cooling off periods or compulsory arbitration'. Moreover, notwithstanding the need for reform, Britain still had 'one of the best records among the industrial nations of the world as far as time lost in disputes is concerned'. He would still have preferred the TUC to put its own house in order, but 'it cannot be allowed to contract out of the modernization of our society which will be the most urgent task of the next Government whether Conservative or Labour'.[11]

A few days before he left for Africa to attend Malawi's 1964 independence celebrations, Macleod had confided that he had largely recovered his position in the party. He was recorded as claiming that he had been forgiven not only for quitting the Government but also for the *Spectator* article. Such was his confidence that he believed he was even back in the running as a future Tory leader. Of his rivals, Macleod reckoned that Hogg was finished, Maudling had declined fast, and Butler was ageing and no longer a serious contender. Despite all that had happened, his chances of becoming party leader had considerably improved: only Heath, he believed, now stood in his way. This confident self-assessment was indirectly confirmed in early July by the bitterness being voiced privately among Douglas-Home's advisers at Macleod's alleged activities. It was said that Heath's political difficulties owed something to Macleod, who was strenuously trying to build links with Maudling, and with younger people in the party and at Central Office.[12]

Macleod's political recovery seemed to vindicate one of Quoodle's mischievous aphorisms, penned in February 1964, when his prospects had been at their gloomiest. It was prompted, in fact, by the difficulty experienced by Lord Hinchingbrooke in finding a seat after having helped Labour win the 1962 Dorset South by-election when, as the former MP, he backed an anti-Common Market candidate against the official Tory, Angus Maude. But, as Quoodle observed, in the words quoted at the head of this chapter, 'the Conservative Party always in time forgives those who were wrong. Indeed often, in time, they forgive those who were right.'[13]

Campaign Solo

Douglas-Home's statement on 9 April 1964, after months of prevarication, that he would defer the election until the autumn followed advice from Central Office suggesting a Labour majority of 30–60 seats in a spring poll. But there was a chance of victory if he soldiered on and completed the full five–year term of the parliament. As a result, Macleod had to endure an increasingly frustrating year on the backbenches, before the announcement on 15 September that polling day would be held a month later finally heralded an end to his political purgatory. At last, much of the uncertainty that clouded his future would be removed.

If, against the odds, the Tories were to win a fourth term, Macleod's prospects would be bleak. Douglas-Home would have stamped his authority on the party and achieved a signal triumph entirely without Macleod's help. In such circumstances, it was difficult to see any role for Macleod. However, a Tory defeat would spell the end of Douglas-Home as leader. Some Tories, of course, would always hold Macleod and Powell responsible for any defeat, but if the party were to face four or five years in opposition, past divisions would quickly be subordinated to the party's need to regroup and rebuild. The key criterion for a new leader – assuming that Labour won a decent majority – would be the ability to deliver victory in the 1968 or 1969 election. There was at least a chance that in such circumstances the Tories might turn to Macleod. That was certainly his view.[14]

There was no alternative open to Macleod except to work – and, even more importantly, to be seen to work – for the re-election of Douglas-Home's Government. Long before the 1964 campaign began, Macleod discounted any suggestion that he might be less involved in the campaign than previously, pointing to the alacrity with which he accepted a last-minute invitation to speak at the Dumfries by-election in the autumn of 1963, when it seemed that the Tory campaign was in trouble. Indeed, he was expecting to play a central role at the general election, not only in speech-making, but also in planning the campaign, as he had done in elections during the 1950s.[15]

But the call from Central Office never came. Macleod had to resort to a one-man-band campaign on the hustings and in the columns of the *Spectator*. On the day that the old Tory-dominated Parliament was dissolved, Macleod fired his first campaign salvo, attacking Labour's proposed nationalization of steel in a signed editorial, entitled 'Mr H. Dumpty'. Wilson's evasive comment, 'When we say steel we mean steel,' which left nobody any the wiser about the precise scope of his party's nationalization plan, was likened, with telling effect, to Humpty Dumpty's immortal declaration in

Alice Through the Looking-Glass: 'When I use a word, it means what I choose it to mean – neither more nor less.' Macleod welcomed the 1964 Tory manifesto pledge that Richard Thomas and Baldwins, the nationalized steel firm, was to be returned to private ownership. But this endorsement did not betray any shift towards right-wing, *laissez-faire* economics on Macleod's part, since it was 'one of the few items of unfinished business from the last general election mandate' of Macmillan's in 1959. As Macleod argued, opinion poll evidence showed that less than a fifth of the electorate wanted further nationalization, with even a large majority of Labour voters opposed to the idea. Macleod concluded that Labour's determination to nationalize steel was proof that the Socialists, 'for all their brave and borrowed words about modernizing Britain, are incapable of modernizing themselves. Mr H. Dumpty is in charge'.[16]

Macleod was clear where the Tories needed to direct their appeal to the voters: 'The main assault, and the only one with any prospect of success, must be on the uncommitted centre.' The Tories, he acknowledged, had been estranged from the 'centre' since the introduction of the pay pause in 1961. Although it had been 'an honest attempt to underpin prosperity, it was skilfully exploited by the Socialists and was badly presented. In the end it seemed to many people that the Conservatives didn't care.' In Macleod's view, the 'centre' cared about 'All sorts of people, with all sorts of abilities and incomes and with all sorts of different skins.' It followed that the party had to re-examine two key policy areas in preparing its election manifesto: housing, where the anxiety was 'in one sense as much a reflection of prosperity as the crush of cars on the road', but on which the Government's task was 'nowhere near completion'; and overseas aid, which Macleod saw as 'an inspiring theme', urging 'much greater contributions and assistance to Voluntary Service Overseas and the other bodies who bring help to the new and poorer countries'.[17]

Idealistic though it was, Macleod's appeal to the 'uncommitted centre' was certainly not soft, nor complacently accepting of the status quo. Proposals for radical reform were a central ingredient at a time when, as Macleod acknowledged, ' "Modernization" has become a boss word'. As proof that only the Tories were determined to take the necessary tough measures needed to modernize Britain, Macleod cited two highly controversial measures taken by the Macmillan Government in the teeth of fierce opposition: the implementation of the Beeching Report, which entailed the closure of many branch railway lines, and the creation of the Greater London Council. Moreover, during the campaign Macleod highlighted the urgent need for reform in two key policy areas that had been side-stepped by politicians for twenty years – the welfare state and the role of the unions.[18]

Macleod seized on the manifesto's proposals in these two areas as the keynote of his appeal to the 'centre'. 'In the Conservative Manifesto,' he noted: 'An unexciting phrase clothes one of the key decisions: "we therefore propose to institute a full review of social security arrangements so that their subsequent developments may be suited to modern conditions".' According to the *Economist*, this proposal was 'cold porridge' – the very phrase that Macleod had deployed to mock Labour and Liberal policy – compared with the prospect that he had held out to the Tory conference at Blackpool the previous year. But this caustic observation invited Macleod's retort: 'to confuse the metaphor still further, cold porridge in this case is three-quarters of a loaf . . . Carefully worded though it is, the pledge is made'.[19]

There can be no doubting Macleod's commitment to the principle of selectivity as the basis for allocating state benefits. 'In fact,' he maintained:

> We abandoned universality long ago, and each advance has met with general approval. We have given preferential treatment to widows and will continue to do so. We have introduced a graduated pension scheme which links retirement more closely with individual earnings. We have made and will continue to make 'special provision for war widows and those disabled in the service of their country'. The Manifesto promises special recognition of the needs of the older pensioners. And in the Manifesto is the undertaking to extend the graduated principle to the early months of unemployment and sickness.

But Macleod's challenge to Beveridge was not motivated by a desire to demolish the welfare state: quite the reverse. As he argued:

> Brilliant State paper though it was, it was essentially an expression of determination in the 1940s to conquer the problems, especially the unemployment of the Twenties and Thirties . . . . Beveridge assumed an average level of 8 per cent unemployment. Last week's figures showed it at 1.5 per cent.

Macleod also acknowledged that inflation in the postwar years had added to the problems of the Beveridge Report, killing the dream that the amount of assistance paid would be sufficient for maintenance. He ridiculed Labour for going further than Canute ever went with the claim in their 1964 manifesto that the community 'must no longer be ruled by market forces beyond its control', but he saw the welfare state as a crucial cushion to the vagaries of the market.[20]

It was on trade union reform that Macleod was most radical. 'The more one studies the problem of how to get this country faster and more evenly,' he believed, 'the more clear it becomes that the attitude of the political parties towards restrictive practices is the true key.' The problem of trade union law, raised by the *Rookes* v. *Barnard* judgment, was only a small part of a much more important question,' that Macleod idenified: 'Are the trade unions really prepared to play their part in modernization? Are they prepared to cooperate with a full inquiry into their role in our modern society?' His reasoning was uncompromising:

> Without a ruthless attack on restrictive practices modernization is impossible. Without genuine reform of the trade union movement in this country modernization is impossible. Much better, of course, to go forward with the agreement of the TUC to a full reappraisal. But agreement or no, we must go forward.[21]

Denied any official role by Central Office, Macleod was free to give a personal, often light-hearted, sketch of the campaign through the pen of Quoodle, whose 'Spectator's Notebook' was appropriately retitled, 'A Participant's Notebook'. At the end of the first week, Quoodle recounted his agent's splendid advice when he urged Enfield Tories to take a bundle of posters and car stickers as they left Macleod's adoption meeting: 'We want to see our candidate plastered all over the constituency.' As Quoodle mused, 'Once more unto the breach . . .' Later that week, on the Saturday afternoon before his evening speech in Wilson's constituency, Macleod accompanied the Tory candidate, Keith Speed, to watch the rugby league match between St Helens and Workington:

> The game got roughish and the referee sent off no fewer than four players. He was not the most popular man in St Helens. His name was Wilson. And as he ordered off the Saints' most brilliant player, international scrum-half and captain Murphy, a supporter, goaded beyond endurance, bellowed from behind me in the stand, 'Nay, tha's worse than t'other beggar.' Well, that's one vote.

Later in the campaign, a visit by his old adversaries, the League of Empire Loyalists enlivened one of Macleod's constituency meetings. Although they were 'very noisy', they were, 'as usual, brave as lambs', the most hilarious incident occurring after the three ringleaders had meekly complied with the Chairman's request to leave:

> One of the smaller fry, sitting in the second row behind my wife, tapped her on the shoulder and said, 'Mrs Macleod, I do really want to assure you that there is nothing personal in this.' And then raising her voice a whole range of octaves she shrilled at me, 'You bloody murderer.' Nothing personal, of course.[22]

But to all intents and purposes, Macleod was marginalized. His interventions merited only three brief references in *The Times*. Without the challenge of a major role in the campaign to give his performance an edge, he was not at his best. Macleod had seemed the ideal speaker for the climax of the campaign in Lewisham, South London, where the Tories, Christopher Chataway and Patrick McNair Wilson, held two of the three constituencies, all of which were marginal, with Barney Hayhoe standing in the third. But Macleod was a big disappointment. Addressing a packed and noisy meeting at Lewisham Town Hall, he spoke interminably, responding to the persistent heckling by expressing his regret that electoral hooliganism should have blanketed serious discussion of the great issues, and accusing Labour of being indirectly responsible: 'You have only to ask yourselves which party has the most to gain by stifling argument.' When he finally ended his speech, he forgot to give the customary endorsement to the three Tory candidates. Afterwards, Hayhoe's wife, Anne, tackled Macleod about his speech, only to be told that he had deliberately spoken at excessive length in order to 'wear out the hecklers'. But his lacklustre performance reflected the frustration of a star performer who had been denied his role at the top of the bill.[23]

The election was much closer than had seemed likely during the preceding eighteen months or even on election night. Computer predictions from the early results suggested an overall Labour majority of 30, but when the remaining, mainly rural, seats were declared the following day, Labour failed to make the expected gains. The election hung in the balance until early on the Friday afternoon. When the last of the 28 million votes cast had been counted, Labour pipped the Tories by only a shade over 200,000, winning 44.1 per cent of the popular vote against the Tories' 43.4. Translated into Commons seats, the margin was sufficient to secure 317 seats for Labour, against 304 for the Tories and 9 for the Liberals, giving Wilson an overall majority of 4.[24]

One spectacular Tory success that bucked the swing to Labour caused Macleod 'no joy'. As Macleod recognized, 'like it or not, coloured immigration [was] the main issue' in the West Midlands town of Smethwick and had brought about the defeat of the Labour frontbencher, Patrick Gordon Walker. But this did not mean that Gordon Walker 'should be made into a hero'. Endorsing Enoch Powell's view that Gordon Walker was 'not a martyr' but was 'much more like a humbug', Macleod criticized Labour's putative Foreign Secretary for not having defended his views more openly, as Fenner Brockway, the radical Labour politician ousted at Eton and Slough, had done. But Macleod was evidently discomfited by the Tory campaign in Smethwick, despite the Tory candidate, Peter Griffiths, having disassociated himself from the racial insults hurled by some of his supporters. Macleod confessed to having the same reaction to the result as he had to a key by-election in Southern Rhodesia a few weeks earlier in which Macleod's old enemy, Welensky, was defeated by a right-wing candidate: 'I did not want either of them to win.'[25]

But Griffiths had won in Smethwick. On the first day of the new parliament, Harold Wilson outraged Tory MPs by breaking the parliamentary tradition that affords protection to new members until they have made their maiden speech: in his first Commons speech as Prime Minister, Wilson denounced Griffiths as a 'parliamentary leper'. Such was Macleod's contempt for Wilson that he savaged him in his next editorial, bitingly entitled, 'Rattle of a Vicious Man'.[26]

The Conservatives had made a significant recovery from their low point of 1963. But the narrowness of the final result in 1964 tended to overshadow the calamitous collapse in the Tory share of the vote by 6 percentage points (a loss of almost 1,750,000 votes) since Macmillan's 1959 triumph, 'the biggest drop of any major party since their own 1945 débâcle'. The scale of the slump in Tory support puts in perspective the argument that had Macleod and Powell not refused to serve in Douglas-Home's Cabinet, the Tories would have won.[27]

Many years later, John Grigg, the writer, went so far as to suggest that Douglas-Home might have won but for Macleod's article on the Tory leadership. However, the Tories might have won but for any number of reasons, including Douglas-Home's all-too-evident lack of understanding of economics; his gaffe during the campaign in talking about a 'donation' instead of an increase for older pensioners; and his Government's abolition of resale price maintenance, that alienated many small shopkeepers. A group of university Tories blamed defeat on the party's sectional 'one-class' image and 'intellectual sterility'. Any of these factors seems more likely to have had an impact on the election than an article, however sensational, written nine months earlier.[28]

The Conservatives would almost certainly have fared better under a different leader. Butler would have been more popular with non-committed voters. Hailsham would have inspired the party faithful. Maudling would have dealt far more effectively with Wilson's attacks on the Tories' economic record. Hailsham is convinced that the Tories would have won if either he or Butler had been leader. Had Butler succeeded Macmillan, he would have appointed Macleod Chancellor, and Butler later revealed that Harold Wilson, James Callaghan, Douglas Houghton 'and many other Labour leaders' had told him 'that, in their opinion, under those circumstances we should have won the 1964 election'. Butler would then have led the Tories for three or four years, by which time he expected that the country would have become bored with his generation of leaders, stepping down before the next (1969) election in good time to allow his successor to establish himself. Macleod would have been ideally placed to become Prime Minister by 1966 or 1967, in his early to mid 50s.[29]

Back From the Wilderness?

The 1964 election had failed to resolve the political uncertainty. The final outcome was so close that few observers believed that Labour would be able to govern for very long with a wafer-thin majority. The prospect of an early second election put the Tories in a dilemma. Douglas-Home was plainly unsuited for the role of Leader of the Opposition and the political hurly-hurly that lay ahead. But however much the Tories might yearn for a new leader 'next time', it would be quite impractical to replace Douglas-Home only a matter of months before another election campaign. No obvious, alternative candidate had emerged, and memories were still fresh in Tory minds of the damage done by the leadership crisis only a year earlier, when – as was again the case in 1964 – there had been no heir apparent and no formal means of resolving the contest. The Tories had no option except to back Douglas-Home for the immediate future.[30]

For his part, Douglas-Home realized that he had to take immediate action to strengthen his team and invited Macleod and Powell to return to the frontbench. But they were able to extract a price for their acceptance. Their terms were to have a profound impact on their role in Opposition. As Powell recalls, he and Macleod had 'agreed that we would not rejoin the Shadow Cabinet unless we had a liberty not restricted to our assigned subject'. Douglas-Home was not in a position to resist.[31]

The two key Shadow Cabinet posts were allotted to Maudling and Heath, the former as Shadow Chancellor with responsibility for coordinating home affairs, the latter shadowing Labour's newly created Department of Economic Affairs and taking charge of future policy work. Macleod asked Douglas-Home to let him lead the attack on Labour's plan to nationalize steel – his coruscating editorial against Labour's nationalization policy, written at the outset of the election campaign, had served as his return ticket to the frontline of the party battle. The steel portfolio was not a senior post in the Shadow Cabinet, but as Macleod told Berkeley, it 'would be in the forefront of parliamentary controversy and his magnificent debating power would be fully utilized in the House'. As far as Douglas-Home was concerned, it solved the immediate problem of allocating Macleod a suitable shadow portfolio, and it appeared to make sense for the party, since the Tories' most effective debater would lead the fight where the ideological difference between Labour and the Tories was at its sharpest.[32]

If there had been a campaign during the first half of 1965, steel nationalization would have been a major issue, possibly the major issue, dividing the two main parties. Macleod had therefore apparently placed himself in the forefront of the political debate. In an election that the Tories seemed certain to lose, there were few better ways open to him of staking his claim as a leadership contender. After a probable Tory defeat, Macleod would have few rivals as the person best qualified to rally the party in opposition and to lead them back into office in 1970 or 1971. If, however, the Tories won, Macleod would reap much of the credit and would stand a good chance of being rewarded with a major Cabinet post. Either way, it seemed, Macleod would be well placed.

However, everything depended on the timing of the next election. As Macleod warned the Tories in his first editorial after the election, they no longer held the political initiative, despite the narrowness of Labour's majority. 'From now on,' he counselled, 'Mr Wilson calls the tune. He decides when there is to be a general election.' It was sound advice, and a warning that Macleod himself would eventually have greatest cause to rue.[33]

A bout of influenza in the last week of October 1964 caused Macleod to miss the first meeting of the 'leader's consultative committee', as the Tory Shadow Cabinet is properly called. But in the late afternoon of Monday 2 November, on the eve of the state opening of the new parliament, the editor of the *Spectator* made his way along the narrow Commons corridor behind the Speaker's chair and, in the unfamiliar surroundings of the Leader of the Opposition's room, attended his first formal frontbench gathering for more than a year. The challenge that faced Macleod and other shadow ministers was formidable. Labour's narrow victory represented a call for change, a demand that would become increasingly insistent as the decade progressed.

Macleod was under no illusion about the urgent need for change in Britain. Neither was he in any doubt that the Tories were ultimately better equipped to respond than Labour, notwithstanding Wilson's exploitation of the disillusion felt towards the Conservatives after their long spell in power. He had proclaimed his 'Tory Radical' convictions in the issue of the *Spectator* that had reached the news stands on polling day, when he counselled that the true test for the new Prime Minister, 'will be whether he is or is not prepared to lead the agonizing reappraisal of Britain's role in the world that is the first prerequisite for our advance'. The sting of Macleod's message came in the tail. 'No man can or should lead this country,' he wrote, 'unless he is prepared to bulldoze his way through the road blocks to progress.' It was clear that in Macleod's judgement Wilson signally failed to measure up to the task. Equally, however, it was straining the bounds of credulity to imagine that Douglas-Home, quintessentially a Tory traditionalist, could ever fit the bill. Macleod's job specification for the prime minister was tailored for a Tory Radical. The battle for the Tory leadership was rejoined.[34]

But what would Macleod's Tory Radical 'declaration' mean in practice? The following week – and only a week before his recall to the frontbench – Macleod's editorial, entitled 'A Call to Work', amounted to a prospectus for the Tories in opposition. Despite Labour's victory the close outcome of the 1964 election had demonstrated that Britain did not want to be a 'socialist country', but 'the Tories must not rely on the turn of the tide to carry them again into harbour'. The political centre-ground had to be recaptured. Macleod's strategy demanded a new Tory radicalism. The party 'must show itself more closely in sympathy with the young marrieds and the new middle class. It was exactly where the Tory appeal should have been strongest that it was in fact weakest. This must be put right.[35]

When the new parliament met, Macleod's acerbic commentary in the *Spectator* was not always comfortable reading for his shadow ministerial colleagues. 'Some parts' of Labour's Queen's Speech, he readily acknowledged, were 'admirable'. The new section on Social Security was singled out for special praise. The 'immediate increase in benefits (and one hopes in contributions) plus a long-term review', was 'exactly the policy that one would have liked to see in the Speech if the Tories had won.' The lack of reformist drive that dogged the Tories' final year in office was neither forgotten, nor forgiven: 'If here the Labour party steals the Tory Party's clothes, it will be the reluctance of the Tories to accept the case for radical change in the Beveridge concept that will be to blame.'

Labour's plans 'for public ownership and control of the iron and steel industry' were dismissed by Macleod as 'both irrelevant to the theme of modernization and harmful to British industry'. Making 'free medicines' a 'first priority' was not the action of 'any sensible Minister of Health'. Much of the extra expenditure envisaged by Labour would be 'inflationary', when the economy was already 'moving fast into an inflationary wage situation'. On union reform, 'the legislation proposed to deal with the *Rookes* vs. *Barnard* case' had 'exposed a dangerous flank', while it seemed that 'the TUC had won its first concession – no inquiry: no dragging of the trade unions into the light of the present day'. Although Wilson established a royal commission, chaired by Lord Donovan, on the reform of trade unions and employers' associations, Macleod was prescient when he wrote in November 1964, that if Wilson failed to meet the challenge of union reform 'he will certainly be rejected by the electorate'. He applied the same, reformist pressure against his own party, urging that they 'must not wait on events'.[36]

Staking out a position for Tory radicalism was bound to ruffle feathers among party traditionalists, but any criticism of Macleod's approach would be countered by his high profile attacks on Labour's implementation of the outdated and unpopular socialist shibboleth of state ownership. It seemed a promising political strategy and it was even possible that his new role leading the Tory attack on the proposed nationalization of steel might bring him rich political dividends. But events did not conspire quite as conveniently for him as he had hoped. It soon became clear in the course of his first Commons assault on Labour's proposed state takeover that the issues were not as cut and dried as Macleod envisaged when he sought the steel portfolio.

The mist that shrouded the country on Monday 9 November 1964 when Macleod rose to move the Opposition's censure amendment to the Queen's Speech, 'was fated to play a major role in the day's proceedings'. As *The Times* commented rather acidly, 'Not only did it threaten the arrival of Mr Wilson's slender majority from north of the border, but in a less literal sense it filled the Chamber and fogged the issues on both sides.' Macleod began 'in fine style', stirring the Tory benches with his declaration that there would be no half measures in his party's opposition to steel nationalization. They would fight it at every stage. The country did not want it. And he suspected that large sections of the Labour Party did not want it either. Thereafter Macleod's speech began to flag. Neither his use of quotations from *Der Spiegel* as evidence that the British steel industry was efficient, nor his reading of extracts from the report of the restrictive practices court were particularly effective. And when he conceded that the steel industry's continued price fixing agreements were a problem, he prompted disbelief among Labour MPs with his fond hope that they would shortly vanish of their own accord while admitting that if the Tories had won the election they too would have had to deal with the matter.[37]

Macleod's performance had disappointed his own benches, an impression reinforced at the end of the debate when the Government survived its first division by seven votes, two more than its nominal majority in the House. When it transpired that the Tories were one vote short, speculation ensued about the true extent of the Shadow Cabinet's commitment to defeating Labour and their appetite for an early election. However, by the end of the week, Quoodle was able to note that: 'The curious affair of the missing Tory voter in the steel division was solved by the discovery that he was there after all. The Government whip couldn't count.' In the meantime: 'Largely on the strength of this counting error columns of print have been devoted to the assumption that the Tories didn't want to win on Monday in the Division lobby. Well I did!'[38]

Nonetheless Macleod's unsatisfactory speech had helped provide the fertile soil in which rumours about Tory tactics flourished. On the Government frontbench, Dick Crossman felt that Macleod had 'made a very disappointing return to the Tory front bench because he had chosen to do a very technical, quiet, non-obvious speech'. However, the root cause of Macleod's difficulty lay in the confused politics of steel, a factor that was also adding to the Government's problem of their wafer-thin majority and the known opposition to outright nationalization of at least three Labour MPs, Desmond Donnelly, George Strauss and Woodrow Wyatt. Only a week after the election, the Minister for Power, Fred Lee had submitted a paper to the Labour cabinet proposing that, because of the technical difficulties in nationalizing such a diverse industry, legislation should be postponed to the second session'. But deferral was strongly opposed by George Brown, Secretary for Economic Affairs, and Lee received scarcely any support from other ministers. The Cabinet remained determined to introduce a Steel Bill until well into the new year. Indeed, by January 1965 Macleod was advising the Shadow Cabinet that in his judgement, despite the Government's difficulties, 'we will be faced with an out-and-out measure of nationalization'. Macleod's fox was not finally shot for many months. Indeed, it was widely assumed during the winter of 1964–65 that the most likely cause of a failure on Labour's part to introduce early legislation on steel would be another election in the spring of 1965. In that event, Labour would undoubtedly have stood by their pledge to nationalize steel and Macleod would have been in the campaign spotlight. His choice of the steel portfolio would have been fully vindicated.[39]

The steel companies' bitter opposition to state ownership yet equally steadfast commitment to preventing competition was ultimately untenable. But in the short run it seriously weakened Macleod's position. If the steel companies were to continue to enjoy protection and to run a cartel, it was difficult to defend their remaining in private hands. Yet if the Tories were enthusiastically to advocate subjecting the industry to the shock of deregulated competition, they would cause serious concern among the large numbers of people whose livelihoods still depended on steel and who would, for the most part, be voting in the industrial heartlands of Scotland, Wales, the West Midlands and Yorkshire, where many marginal seats hung in the balance. It was this tricky political calculation that put Macleod in a more awkward position than he had expected and helped explain his strangely mixed tone in the Queen's Speech debate. It was a misjudgement that ultimately proved fatal to any slim hope that he still had of winning the Tory crown.

Plotting for the Tory Crown

From the outset of his return to the front bench, Macleod's Tory Radical impatience with Douglas-Home's easygoing, traditionalist leadership was barely concealed. As the minutes of Shadow Cabinet meetings testify, Macleod was more determined than any of his colleagues to ginger up the party's performance in Opposition. At the same time, he was equally determined to enhance his own prospects of becoming Tory leader, and soon embarked on what had the makings of a presidential-style leadership campaign.

Douglas-Home's failure to organize a combative Opposition soon prompted a response from Macleod. At the first Shadow Cabinet after the six-day Commons debate on the Queen's Speech he demanded urgent action to improve briefing and 'coordination of the Shadow Cabinet.' The following day, Macleod also asked to be made available for 'general duties, whatever they may be'. He was plainly concerned to overcome the potentially serious blow to his prospects if steel nationalization were seriously delayed or dropped altogether. Macleod favoured a return to Churchill's practice between 1945 and 1951 of allowing frontbenchers to range relatively freely across different subjects, but Douglas-Home's approach as Leader of the Opposition conformed with that of his Labour counterparts before 1964: each member of the frontbench team was allocated to 'shadow' a specific government department. It was already difficult enough in the wake of an election defeat and the inevitable weakening of the leader's authority to ensure that shadow ministers followed an agreed line, without returning to Churchillian laxity.[40]

Macleod sought a means of organizing an effective Opposition, while preserving some leeway for shadow spokesmen to express their opinions and avoid the restrictions that bind ministers to their departmental ambit. At the Shadow Cabinet's next Wednesday afternoon meeting, on 2 December, Macleod renewed his demand for changes in the way the party conducted their business in Opposition, in order to achieve greater coordination. In addition to the regular Wednesday meetings of Shadow Cabinet, at which the forthcoming week's parliamentary business inevitably dominated the agenda, Macleod suggested that there should be a second meeting each week, in order to hold more informal, discursive discussions, based on a paper prepared either by a shadow minister or by the research department. Macleod's proposal was taken up by Douglas-Home, who maintained in his summing up that the daily committee meetings could provide a tactical line, while Macleod's proposed additional Monday Shadow Cabinet meetings could discuss the party's position on controversial subjects, such as incomes policy and the death penalty, and in due course the work of Heath's policy review could be tied in. Macleod was less successful with his radical proposal that the party should end the undemocratic custom whereby frontbench spokesmen in Opposition, who were, after all, the leader's appointees, invariably chaired the relevant backbench committees.[41]

Yet a much more fundamental democratization of the party's archaic procedures was about to be forced on the Tory leadership. Honouring his earlier commitment to Humphry Berkeley that the rules for selecting the party leader would be examined after the 1964 election, Douglas-Home told the Tory backbench 1922 Committee on 5 November that he was instituting a review. The small review committee, chaired by Douglas-Home, consisted of senior frontbenchers, including Macleod, who thus found himself discussing how to prevent any repetition of a leadership crisis not only with two of the defeated contenders in 1963, Butler and Hogg, but also with two of his most bitter adversaries, Dilhorne and Redmayne.[42]

There was general acceptance that a new system must be devised because the old system had fallen into disrepute. The review committee agreed that the selection should be settled in a ballot, but the question of who should be entitled to vote was more difficult and enormous effort was expended trying to devise a method that would involve all sections of the party. However, Berkeley submitted a memorandum proposing election of the leader by Tory MPs only. On 10 December, Macleod wrote privately to reassure Berkeley of his support for his proposal 'in principle and in detail' and his belief that it was 'gaining ground so fast that it must win'. Four days later, sending his apologies to Douglas-Home for having to miss one of the many meetings on the subject, he gave his reactions to the latest detailed draft by the Conservative Research Department, and concluded:

> The correct procedure is a vote of the Party in the House of Commons, using the transferable vote system. It might be desirable to add the peers who are members of the Cabinet or Shadow Cabinet and perhaps the area chairmen [of the constituency associations] but I would not myself consider it right to go beyond this.

Macleod's view on the general principle of restricting a leadership ballot to MPs was shared by the committee: there was no answer to the objection that any form of electoral college incorporating other sections of the party 'either runs the risk of imposing on the party in the House of Commons a leader whom a majority of them would not have chosen or else gives those outside the Commons no more than a derogatory token role'. The need to ensure that the new procedure would not risk undermining a leader's visible authority in the Commons had finally ensured that Berkeley's proposal was recommended.[43]

The proposal that leadership contests should be settled by balloting MPs was approved during February 1965 by both the Shadow Cabinet and the 1922 Committee, whose honorary secretary, Peter Emery, completed the detailed arrangements that were finally endorsed three months later. Macleod's support for a system of proportional representation in leadership elections had been rejected in favour of a voting system that allowed up to three ballots.[44]

Ironically, the *Spectator* was one of the few papers to raise any doubts about the new procedure. Its political correspondent, Watkins, observed that the second ballot, by allowing new candidates to come forward, was in reality an entirely new election. However, Watkins's editor did not allow his political correspondent to go wholly unanswered. Writing in the same edition, Macleod heralded the new system as 'an admirable solution', citing as one reason the very point that Watkins had queried, i.e. the provision for new candidates to stand on the second ballot. Arguing that 'if it is a victory for anyone it is a victory for Bonar Law', Macleod recalled the stalemate between Austen Chamberlain and Walter Long in 1911 over the succession to Balfour. Eventually, they both stood down in favour of Bonar Law. But had there been an election according to the rules used by the Labour Party during the 1960s, in which the least popular candidate was eliminated from each ballot in turn until one candidate finally secured an overall majority, 'Law would have been eliminated after the first ballot.' Macleod argued that the new Tory system 'could, indeed would,' have enabled Law to be chosen as leader. 'The gain is considerable,' claimed Macleod. 'The price is a slightly more complicated system. With a respectful nod to Mr Alan Watkins, I think it seems a good bargain.'[45]

Although Macleod was at pains to avoid any repetition of the 1963 shambles, and saw the democratization of leadership contests as the only solution, he was opposed to change for change's sake. 'The ideal answer is always that there shouldn't be a contest at all,' he wrote to Douglas-Home during the review: 'As for example when Eden followed Churchill, or Chamberlain followed Baldwin. There should be some provision to take account of this circumstance. Clearly we shouldn't launch into a complicated election unless one is inevitable.'[46]

Yet Macleod was already planning a campaign to establish his own credentials as a future leadership contender. In view of his past battles within the party, it is inconceivable that he would ever have emerged as heir apparent and become leader without a contest. He might have succeeded in doing so had Rab Butler ever become leader, but three weeks before the new selection procedure was formally announced at a meeting of the 1922 Committee, Butler made public his decision to accept the offer of the Crown Appointment of the Mastership of Trinity College, Cambridge. Macleod's mentor had finally bowed out. Macleod would attempt one final effort to achieve the highest office in the Tory Party, but he had known since the autumn of 1963 that he could no longer hope to be carried there on Rab's coat-tails and would have to beat his own path to the summit.

It was not merely as a result of changing the procedure for selecting the party leader that the autumn and winter of 1964–65 seemed to mark the end of an era in Tory politics and the start of another. Within four days, at the end of January, came the State Funeral of Sir Winston Churchill and the memorial service to Lord Woolton, in addition to the announcement of Rab Butler's retirement from party politics. As Quoodle lamented, 'The C-in-C, the Adjutant-General, the Chief of the Policy Staff of the Conservative Opposition from 1945–51 have all gone.' Earlier in the month, he had mourned the death of Monckton, Churchill's emollient Minister of Labour. While Macleod regretted the passing of the leadership that had rebuilt the party, a profound change was sweeping through the Tory ranks in the Commons during the mid-1960s which was more encouraging for his hopes of converting the party to his Tory Radical beliefs. The old-style, paternal-ist, 'knights of the shire' – the likes of Sir Hubert Ashton, Sir Robert Grimston and Sir Anthony Hurd – who had long provided the traditionalist backbone of the parliamentary party, had stood down at the October 1964 election. In their place came an entirely different breed of politician, mainly from the professions, who had made their mark in university politics and through the Bow Group as Tory reformists, and who tended to be liberal on social policy – among them Mark Carlisle, Terence Higgins, Geoffrey Howe, Patrick Jenkin and Norman St John Stevas.[47]

Macleod was an attractive character to the new generation of Tory MPs. He had won their admiration before they entered the House principally for his radical approach as Colonial Secretary, but most of those who encountered him in the Commons after 1964 also found him socially engaging. Although he desperately missed ministerial office, he was a House of Commons man who leavened any gathering in the smoking room, where he happily mixed with most Tories, except a few right-wing reactionaries, and liked to relax with a cheroot cigar and a drink. His fascination for politics and his conviction that Opposition for the Tory Party was an unnatural state that would be shortlived naturally appealed to younger Tories. Equally alluring was his talent as a stimulating conversationalist, setting him apart from many of the career-politicians who have steadily come to dominate the Commons.[48]

Macleod, however, was excluded from the major posts and would always remain something of an outsider as long as Douglas-Home continued as leader. If he was to stand any chance of winning the Tory succession, he had no alternative but to campaign as an outsider, barnstorming the country in the manner of an American presidential candidate. But since it would take time to build up his support, he found himself in the paradoxical position of wanting Douglas-Home replaced as leader while not wanting an early leadership contest.

Shortly after the 1964 election, Humphry Berkeley approached Macleod to suggest forming a small group of MPs who would assist him to improve his standing in the party and eventually become a contender for the leadership. As Berkeley has recalled:

At no time did we contemplate the overthrow of Alec Douglas-Home by Iain but we worked to ensure that if and when Sir Alec went (and we hoped that his departure would be later rather than earlier), Iain would be in a strong position to gain the succession.[49]

The membership of the group reflected Macleod's support among the younger, reformist Tories: like Berkeley, William van Straubenzee had entered the Commons in 1959; Gilmour in 1962; Mark Carlisle in 1964; and David Howell, formerly a journalist on the *Daily Telegraph* and Director of the CPC, was to become an MP in 1966. Others who attended, some more often than others, were a combination of trusted political advisers and people in the media – Reggie Bennett, Macleod's former Parliamentary Private Secretary; William Rees-Mogg, a former Tory candidate, an acolyte of Rab Butler and a columnist on the *Sunday Times*; Peter Goldman, formerly of the Conservative Research Department and the CPC, who had joined the Consumers' Council; Robert Polendine, who ran the London Press Exchange; and two friends of Berkeley's, Anthony Sumption, his fellow director of a merchant bank, and Colin Harris, formerly Goldman's assistant at the CPC, who was a BBC current affairs producer. Polendine had been keen to arrange the services of a full-time researcher for Macleod, and initially Harris had been earmarked for the post. But when he joined the

BBC, Berkeley recruited David Rogers, who had worked for Chris Chataway at Lewisham during the 1959 election. Rogers began working for Macleod at the start of 1965 as one of the first ever full-time researchers to an MP at the House of Commons; his salary was paid by the Berkeley Sumption bank.[50]

In addition to Berkeley's group, Macleod greatly valued the advice of another small group of Young Conservatives, of whom Nick Scott, the YCs' National Chairman, was already a supporter of Macleod. At their weekend conference in mid-November 1964, the YCs' National Advisory Committee suggested that there should be a review of the YC organization and role in the party. The party chairman, Lord Blakenham, agreed and suggested setting up a small working group chaired by Sir Edward Boyle. But at their next meeting, on 12 December, an 'overwhelming majority' of the YCs' national committee backed Macleod as chairman. The Macleod Report, considered by the YCs' National Committee at the end of 1965, reformed the YCs into an effective and modern political youth organization, and although the task imposed an onerous burden of meetings and visits to all parts of the country, it became an important element in Macleod's campaign to build up his standing in the party. Moreover, through the working party Macleod was able to cement his close links with the YCs' high-flyers: among those whom he regularly consulted were Nick Scott, Sidney Chapman, Alan Haselhurst, David Knox, Keith Speed and John MacGregor, all of whom later became Tory MPs.[51]

The existence of the Berkeley group and of Macleod's gatherings with his YC supporters was kept a closely guarded secret, although on one occasion Macleod was infuriated when the *Evening Standard* 'Londoner's Diary' reported his thinking after he had been chatting with a few of his younger advisers, and he asked David Rogers to investigate. Any more serious leak about the meetings would have been construed as a plot to oust Douglas-Home and would have spelt immediate ruin for Macleod's chances. Berkeley's group met each week in the ground-floor mansion flat, at 7 Park Place, St James's, which had been provided for Macleod by the Lombard Bank as a London base after he and Eve had left Sloane Court West to live in the White Cottage at Potter's Bar, a National Trust property in his constituency. Berkeley's initiative soon took on the trappings of an American-style campaign for the presidential primaries. Working breakfasts in Park Place became a regular feature. Macleod and Rogers would meet early on Tuesday and Thursday mornings to liaise over the hectic schedule of speeches, an arrangement that became almost impossible for his researcher when Macleod could not face his breakfast and would pass his plate across the table insisting that Rogers eat it. The informal group of confidants sometimes gathered for breakfast, or lunch, or in the early evening, depending on Macleod's diary. At these meetings, his advisers would tip him off about forthcoming party meetings at which he should try to speak; suggest possible themes for his speeches or for his party political broadcasts; discuss drafts that had usually been prepared by one of the group; and serve as a sounding board on which Macleod could try his thoughts.

Those who briefed Macleod at Park Place recall that he 'was very good to work with' and 'really knew how to get the best out of you'. He 'was always very friendly' and, despite his constant pain, 'would leap from his chair to greet you with great enthusiasm'. Although his closest advisers sometimes sensed the pain he was suffering, Macleod never let it intrude more than making an occasional comment that he had had 'a really bloody awful day', or that he would like to have been more active, adding as he pointed towards his back, 'if it wasn't for this'. But Macleod remained capable of despatching his work at a formidable pace, and his trust in his remarkable memory never faltered, obviating the need to hoard paperwork. When Macleod asked Rogers to collect his papers from his office at the Commons, Rogers was astonished to find that 'in total they amounted to one very thin file with almost nothing in it'. Macleod's extraordinary ability to memorize whatever he wanted was responsible for his eccentric method of speech-writing: Rogers would provide a draft as mapped out by Macleod, and quite often Macleod would take it, work on it, and then throw away the final version, relying when he spoke entirely on his memory and only a few odd notes.[52]

Macleod's campaign was off to a flying start in the new year of 1965 as a result of Wilson's eagerness for Gordon Walker, who had been defeated at Smethwick, to continue as Foreign Secretary. But Wilson's scheme depended on Gordon Walker being re-elected to the Commons as soon as possible, and the veteran Labour MP for Leyton, in East London, Reginald Sorensen, was created a life peer in order to provide Gordon Walker with what was thought to be a safe seat. During the first week of the Leyton by-election, Macleod took the opportunity to appeal to the voters of the centre-ground, where he believed the Tory appeal had been weakest in 1964. Attacking Labour's proposed land commission as bureaucratic and unworkable, he sought to meet public concern about profiteering from land development by saying that he wanted a future Conservative government to introduce 'a tax on the appreciation of building land values collected for the community, and the proper trigger should be the grant of planning permission.' But his second proposal was an even more blatant attempt to woo the voters whose desertion had sealed the party's fate:

I advocate direct help to those buying their own home. Help should be concentrated on those in the middle income brackets, and if this means an open subsidy I do not shrink from it. It would indeed be cheaper to encourage those whose earnings are around and above the national average to become home owners, than to have to provide them with council houses.

Macleod had expressed in blunt fashion the thinking that presaged later Tory drives to boost home ownership. Its subsequent implementation would provide the political bedrock of future Tory election triumphs, but at the cost of a massively subsidized and distorted housing market.[53]

Showing the party how it could win back power, and demonstrating that he was the man best qualified for the task, lay at the core of Macleod's strategy. Four days after his Leyton speech Macleod displayed a rare talent for savaging opponents, as *The Times* acknowledged. 'Continuing in the role of a huntsman who shows the Conservative rank and file plenty of sport,' wrote its parliamentary correspondent, Macleod's 'pursuit of the Secretary of State for Economic Affairs, whom he called "Bluffer Brown" . . . had the Young Conservative pack at Enfield running on a breast-high scent.' Having contemptuously dismissed Brown's warnings to industry to control their costs, Macleod offered some 'positive proposals', including legislation against monopolies and restrictive practices and the dropping of steel nationalization. But singling out Brown for attack was an example of the kind of tactics that he wanted the Tories to adopt in Opposition, as he revealed later in the month in the columns of *Crossbow*, the Bow Group's quarterly magazine. Declaring that he was not a member of either the 'give-them-enough-rope school', nor a believer in all-out attack on all fronts, he urged instead 'guerilla raids, in concentrated assaults on weak ministers, in occasional carefully planned set-piece attacks on the Labour Party in general and the Prime Minister in particular'.[54]

Macleod's address to the Greater London Young Conservatives at Eastbourne in mid-January was billed in the press as 'the first full-scale attempt to propound a theme for the Conservative Party in Opposition'. The new political significance of middle-income couples, or the 'salariat,' was a theme developed by David Howell among Berkeley's group. Arguing that 'Affluence has not yet really come to this country, but it is coming', Macleod went on to explain the political implications:

> The key figure here is the younger married woman. She feels that the whole business of shopping and getting her repairs done and making her gadgets work, is plain drudgery. And she has the vague feeling that all the people with whom she spends money are not competing vigorously enough in serving her. She is reaching for a better life. She feels that the local schooling is not good enough. She doubts whether the health service is good enough.

Adding to the list of woes of young married couples, Macleod cited the feeble pensions offered by a tax-gobbling State machine and housing difficulties – if they had a house they found the costs of living cruelly high, and if they were seeking a house they knew their chances of getting it were remote. It was to these people that the party's new programme must speak directly. The answer for shopping and service problems was a new competition policy, building on the resale price maintenance initiative. The answer on education and health was simply more provision. The answer on pensions was a wider choice between state and private schemes. 'There is not enough choice in people's lives,' Macleod concluded. 'It must be part of a Tory philosophy to provide and believe in choice as well as opportunity'.[55]

However, Macleod's performance plainly got under the skin of the party hierarchy. Accounts of their hostile reaction were made public in time to accompany the press reports of his speech. 'Party Chiefs Upset', declared *The Times*, reporting that Macleod 'has once again annoyed some party managers by the implications of his speech. The argument is resented that party policy needs to be thrown open to public discussion, with the implication that this has not been done.' 'If only,' one critic was reported as having muttered, 'Mr Macleod would attack Labour instead of his own party.' Although Macleod's critics chose to remain anonymous, their designation as 'party managers' and the detailed accounts of the steps taken by Central Office and the policy review team since the election indicated that the attack on him was sanctioned at the highest level. Perhaps what most irritated the leadership was that Macleod had stolen a march on Heath by usurping the task of presenting the policy agenda that properly fell to him as head of the policy review. Macleod had regarded Heath since October 1963 as the strongest contender for the leadership, and since the previous July as his main rival. Further provocation came the week after the Eastbourne speech, with the publication of Macleod's article in *Crossbow*, in which he renewed his attack on having Tory backbench committees chaired by the relevant frontbenchers.[56]

None of Macleod's comments were helpful to a leader whose authority had been weakened to such a degree that he felt it necessary during a speech in Hampstead at the start of February, 1965, to confirm his intention of leading the Conservatives at the next election. The statement was a mixed blessing for Macleod: the longer that Douglas-Home remained leader, within reason, the better for Macleod's prospects of the succession. But the fact that such a statement was deemed necessary suggested that the leader's grip on the crown was slipping. A fortnight later, Douglas-Home dealt what proved to be a fatal blow to Macleod's chances of winning the Tory succession. Macleod's political fate was effectively sealed as a result of a reshuffle in the Shadow Cabinet caused by the withdrawal from politics of his old mentor, Rab Butler. Maudling was granted his request to replace Butler as Shadow Foreign Secretary, but although he remained Deputy Chairman of the Shadow Cabinet, the main beneficiary of the changes was Heath, who was awarded an even stronger role than he already enjoyed. In addition to retaining his responsibility for reviewing party policy and opposing Brown at the Department of Economic Affairs, Heath also took over Maudling's former duties as Shadow Chancellor. With Callaghan due to present Labour's first full budget within a couple of months, the man whom Macleod regarded as his main rival had been given a golden opportunity to steal the limelight and to enhance his reputation by leading the Tory attack on taxation and the economy.

Insult was added to injury for Macleod by the appointment of Hogg to what were described as 'special duties' and Douglas-Home's intention of giving Hogg plenty of opportunity to use his debating powers on *ad hoc* subjects. Hogg's new role was the assignment that Macleod had sought three months earlier. It was a bitter pill coming only days after Macleod had yet again demonstrated his considerable debating skills at the Young Conservatives' annual conference, treating them to 'a scalp-tingling, pulse-racing speech, as inflammatory as Anthony's'. Likening Wilson to Brutus as an 'honourable man', he added by way of explanation, 'When he says something he means it – for a time . . .'[57]

But it was the struggle for the Tory succession that had more in common with a Shakespearian tragedy. Macleod had tried to row his way back, but he had run aground while Heath received preferment. Douglas-Home's promotion of Heath, one of his staunchest advocates during the struggle for the leadership in 1963, had given an enormous advantage to the man whom Macleod saw as a much stronger rival than Maudling. But Douglas-Home had also created his potential Brutus, except that Heath would not need to wield the dagger himself: there was no shortage of ambitious young Tory MPs ready to strike against the old regime as soon as the time seemed right.

Macleod was aware from February 1965 that his hopes of winning the Tory succession, already slim, had become even more slender. Any possibility that he might be thrown a political lifeline by steel nationalization steadily became more remote as ministers confronted the complexity of legislation and the real threat of defeat with a majority, post-Leyton, of only three. On 1 February, Macleod advised the Shadow Cabinet, in the first paper to be considered at one of their innovatory Monday meetings, of the Government's difficulties with the Steel Bill. The earliest that he thought they might be able to publish legislation would be the third week of February, but this prediction assumed that legislation would merely extend the powers of the existing Iron and Steel Board: on the other hand, if ministers opted for outright nationalization of the largest companies, the drafting of legislation would be complicated and a Bill might not even appear before Easter.[58]

However, a month later, Quoodle was wondering whatever had become of the bill: 'It was to have appeared in January, then in February, then (as a positively final date) by March 15. The Ides of March have come and gone. Still no Bill, not even any new date for one.' His comment that, 'the Bill is now at the back of the queue, and that is excellent news,' gave no hint of Macleod's mixed feelings. Denied his opportunity to lead a parliamentary assault on nationalization, Macleod also saw his expectation dashed of a

March 1965 election. Thereafter, he reversed exactly his previous 'ratio of two think-speeches to one attack-speech', a tactical decision that reflected both his desire to see the Tories trying to bring down the Government and his natural relish for savaging opponents.[59]

The Tory defeat on Thursday 25 March in the Roxburgh, Selkirk and Peebles by-election at the hands of David Steel, the 26-year-old Liberal candidate, renewed the rumblings of Tory discontent with Douglas-Home's leadership. As Watkins noted in the *Spectator*, 'How much longer can Sir Alec Douglas-Home continue as leader of the Conservative Party? After the loss of Roxburgh the question does not really have to be asked. It asks itself.' The cool reception accorded to Douglas-Home at the annual luncheon of the 1922 Committee and the Party Chairman's public acknow-ledgement that the leader's television image was appalling, were evidence of Douglas-Home's dwindling authority in the party. But would the murmurings be translated into active pressure on him to resign? The seriousness of the leadership crisis prompted Douglas-Home to broach the 'Leadership Position' at Shadow Cabinet and seek their 'unanimous and whole-hearted support'. Douglas-Home claimed that the press had little to write about and were deliberately slaying him. But Macleod again demonstrated his dissatisfaction with his leader's performance by pointing out, accord-ing to the summary in the official minute, that 'the press have to write news and we must make sure of victories and they will be reported as such'.[60]

Events were moving fast, but time was not on Macleod's side. He had lunched with his advisers earlier on the day that Douglas-Home had raised the question of his leadership. Although Berkeley thought the lunch a success, his comment to Macleod that 'at last . . . our various close advisors are getting to know each other and working as a team' suggested that there was still much work to be done. But by the time that Macleod and his advisers next met at his flat on Budget Day, Tuesday 6 April, Macleod was again in high dudgeon with many Tories. His sin was entirely in character, reflecting his delight in debate and wit. Never one to abide by the code of the career politician and always play it safe, Macleod happily accepted at the start of March an invitation to appear with Patrick Campbell, the celebrated stuttering humourist and an old crony from the Thursday Club, on BBC television's weekly late-night satire programme and successor to *TW3*, *Not So Much A Programme More A Way Of Life* (or *NSMAPMAWOL*). After his first appearance, a more calculating politician would have seen the storm signals and declined any further invitations. A row erupted over a sketch that offended Roman Catholics by mocking the Church's teachings on birth control, although Norman St John Stevas had defended the Church's approach on the same programme. However, as Macleod observed: 'Behind this protest . . . is a dislike of satire itself.' It was not a prejudice that he shared, declaring himself a fan of *TW3* and *NSMAPMAWOL*:

Last week on this programme I discussed power with Malcolm Mugge-
ridge. He held that all power was evil: I replied that both President
Kennedy and Hitler had sought power and sought to use it, and that
therefore what mattered was not the fact of power, but whether it was
used for good or evil ends. In any setting that is a serious argument and
everyone (including the audience) took it seriously.

Typically, Macleod also adduced a partisan defence of satire: 'Satire is
always against the Establishment, and so is part of the Opposition. The more
the merrier, then, say I – but at least I also said it when I was a Minister of
the Crown.'[61]

But when the Tory leader became a target three weeks later during
an edition on which Macleod was again appearing, *NSMAPMAWOL*'s
strongest fan on the Tory frontbench found himself in very hot water. It
was Bernard Levin, whose participation he had disliked on *TW3*, who caused
the furore, when he described Douglas-Home as a 'cretin'. Some Tories had
been annoyed with Macleod for having agreed to appear on *NSMAPMAWOL*
in the first place, and they were furious that he had not walked out. Quoodle
was unrepentant, although his imagery acknowledged that whatever he said,
in some quarters he would always be held guilty:

Before sentence is passed, could the prisoner in the dock say a word?

First, there is surely little point in holding the view that too many
left-wing sympathisers appear on television and at the same time frowning
on Tories who do appear.

Second, my (enormous) mail was about 90 per cent in favour and
half the remaining letters began, 'Of course I did not see the programme,
but . . .'

Third. Even if it made sense to do so you can't walk out of a discussion
programme. You are noosed by a throat microphone, and all you would
succeed in doing would be to strangle yourself. About 1 per cent of my
correspondents seemed to be in favour of this.[62]

Macleod's enemies were quick to pounce. 'I do not believe,' protested the
right-winger Patrick Wall:

That a man who made a brilliant speech at the last [1963] Tory conference
asking for party unity and loyalty and a few days later refused to serve under
the selected leader, followed this up with the famous article in the *Spectator*
and, only last week, allowed himself to become involved with such boring
lightweights as David Frost and Bernard Levin, can ever hope to command
the support of the majority of the Conservative Parliamentary Party.

The incident could not have come at a worse moment. The following week would see the start of the budget debate, and Heath, his rival for the leadership and Douglas-Home's strongest supporter in 1963, would occupy the parliamentary limelight and remain there for the rest of the spring and summer.[63]

By the end of April 1965, however, it seemed that Macleod might share some of the parliamentary limelight with Heath. Returning from a visit, during the Easter recess, to the United States, he found that at long last the Government were about to try to seize the initiative on steel. Wilson planned to publish a White Paper on nationalization, followed by a Commons debate. If Labour were defeated, he could consider either an early election or dropping the plans for steel.

The White Paper was delayed until after Easter, but Labour's subsequent, belated rush to hold a parliamentary debate within six days of its publication infuriated the Opposition, particularly since the Commons vote was to be held on the day of the by-election in the safe Tory seat of Birmingham, Hall Green, caused by Labour's appointment of its former MP, Aubrey Jones, to head their newly created Prices and Incomes Board. By arranging the debate before the new Tory MP could take his place, Labour had increased their majority to four, and if the two steel rebels, Donnelly and Wyatt voted against the Government, the result would be a tie instead of a defeat. In this event, convention decreed that the Speaker use his casting vote to keep an issue before the House, and he would therefore vote with the Government. At Shadow Cabinet on Wednesday 28 April, Macleod urged that when the date of the steel debate was announced the next day, Tory MPs should make it clear that that the House was insulted by the lateness of the White Paper and its coming out after the date of the debate had been set less than a week later. When Douglas-Home chose to level this charge against the Government, it appeared to signal a tougher line by the leadership.[64]

Prior to the steel furore, Macleod had taken up a widespread feeling on the backbenches that Labour were being allowed too easy a ride. In Macleod's view, the Tories were 'letting Mr Wilson get away with a full and crowded programme on a majority less than half the one that Mr Attlee had' during 1950–51. At Shadow Cabinet on 4 May, he urged a more aggressive approach: they should fight the Government over its handling of the committee stage of bills, on which Labour only maintained their small majority in committees 'upstairs' by deliberately under-representing the number of Tory MPs; and they should deploy all manner of devices to consume as many days as possible that remained for Government business before the summer recess. Macleod's plan, designed to force Labour to crack under the pressure, was a call that he would press repeatedly on the leadership during the summer.[65]

The steel White Paper, finally published on Friday 30 April, betrayed its origins as a gambit in Wilson's parliamentary manoeuvring, and was easily dismissed by Macleod as a 'naive document merely asserting that nationalization was more efficient than private enterprise' and which showed 'pathetic faith in the merits of centralization'. But as he had found in the autumn, the subject was less black-and-white than many Tories had assumed, and the difficulties for the Opposition were highlighted at a well-attended backbench meeting. As he reported to Shadow Cabinet on Wednesday 5 May, the eve of the debate, the prevailing mood among backbenchers had been: '1. That we must declare our outright opposition to nationalization; 2. That our attitude should not be wholly destructive.' Macleod advised that: 'These points are not at all easy to reconcile in a short statement'. He argued that it would be best in his speech to say quite categorically that if steel were nationalized the Tories would denationalize it. But his radicalism was questioned by Douglas-Home, who pointed out that some members of the party hoped the Tories would not promise denationalization again. In the ensuing discussion shadow ministers backed Macleod, recognizing that although denationalization could be very difficult, it must be promised. As a result, the draft statement that Macleod had circulated was strengthened, so that he was authorized to state that: 'We are wholly opposed to the nationalization of the iron and steel industry, and if the industry is nationalized we will denationalize it.' [66]

Macleod's speech the following day, Thursday 6 May, was his great chance to advance his claim for the succession. That week, Tory rumblings about Douglas-Home had revived, leading to speculation in the press that if there was no early election, Douglas-Home would soon be replaced as leader. But Macleod again signally failed to rise to the challenge. His speech was a severe disappointment, and was regarded by his close advisers to have been one of the worst he ever made in the Commons. It cannot have helped that he was in some discomfort from a burst blood vessel in his left eye, a mishap, he told the House, that he suspected 'had happened when I read the White Paper'.

He began his speech hesitantly and never got fully into his stride, although he later stirred the Tory benches with some political knockabout, dismissing Fred Lee as a 'Labour Party primitive, a sort of political pterodactyl'. Alluding to the power of the union bosses, epitomized by the presence of Frank Cousins, former leader of the Transport and General Workers' Union, in the Cabinet, he taunted George Brown as a man whose policy had been 'ruined by his brothers and his Cousins'. But Macleod was worsted as he began his final assault on the Government by an intervention, not recorded in the official report, that suddenly turned the spotlight on the jockeying on the Tory frontbench over the succession to Douglas-Home. Macleod's claim about the debate on the White Paper, that there were 'two reasons that we have to go through this exercise', provoked an instantaneous cry from the Labour benches, 'Reggie and Ted?'[67]

The root cause of Macleod's debating failure had been twofold. He was still not happy with the subject, although he was helped by the abandonment of common pricing agreements by the steel companies – in line with the report of the restrictive practices court – a development that he had predicted the previous November. Also, he hated being in Opposition, as he revealed to a Labour minister a week after the steel debate. On Thursday 11 May, Macleod spoke in a debate on racial discrimination at London University, where his opponent was Dick Crossman, Minister for Housing and Local Government. The occasion is now remembered for what occurred afterwards: Crossman went on to dine alone at Prunier's, in St James's, where he absent-mindedly left his Cabinet papers which were then found by another customer and passed straight to the *Daily Express*. Macleod had no sympathy since he recalled that Crossman had been carrying his papers round loose: 'Scores of people must have seen them and been aware that some of them were classified.' But the evening was also significant because of the exchange that occurred when Crossman happened to tell Macleod how much he enjoyed being a minister. 'Of course you do,' replied Macleod. 'Being a minister is the only thing worth doing in the whole world.' And to Crossman's response that he wouldn't go as far as that, Macleod came back: 'Of course you and I are politicians. A minister's life is the only thing in the world worth having.' It was then that Crossman realized Macleod really meant it.[68]

On 24 June, Macleod pressed Wilson to say whether he still stood by his promise of the previous March that steel would be nationalized before the end of the session. Wilson dodged the question, responding with a gibe at Macleod's frustrated leadership ambitions by assuring him that the bill would appear in good time for him to shine. However, Wilson was about to deliver what was, in effect, the *coup de grâce* for any lingering hopes that Macleod held of becoming leader. Two days later, the Prime Minister stated at a Labour Party rally in Glasgow that he had no intention of calling an election during 1965. The hapless Douglas-Home had also claimed on the same day, 26 June, that there would be no Tory leadership election that year. But Wilson had trumped him. Clearly, it would be possible after all for the Tories to replace Douglas-Home and make their new leader known to the public in time for the next general election. The question suddenly became whether Douglas-Home, not the Labour Government, could reach the haven of 30 July and the long, summer recess.[69]

16

From Lost Leader to Prodigal Son

Revolutions in this country, and especially within the Tory party, are rarely plotted. They just happen. This week's election for the Tory party is just as surely 'the changing of the guard' as John F. Kennedy's nomination was as Democratic candidate in America. Only the Conservative members of the House of Commons voted. The role of the Tory peers is now confined to joining in the applause for Edward Heath at the full endorsement meeting next Monday. A new era begins.

> Quoodle, commenting on the 1965 Tory leadership election, 'Spectator's Notebook,' the *Spectator*, 30 July 1965.

Lost Leader

The ambivalent attitude of Macleod and his supporters towards Douglas-Home – not wanting him to resign as leader until Macleod's standing had improved, but impatient at his poor leadership – was reinforced after Wilson's deferral of an election. The report in the *Sunday Express* on 27 June 1965 that one hundred Tory MPs wanted Douglas-Home to make way for Heath as leader and the calls voiced the following Thursday, 1 July, at the 1922 Executive Committee of senior Tory backbenchers for Douglas-Home to stand down were almost as unwelcome in the Macleod camp as in the leader's office. But within a week, Macleod was again frustrated by the failure of the leadership to pursue more aggressive tactics when the Shadow Cabinet decided, after two meetings on 5 and 7 July, that the Tory peers should not press an amendment they had tabled to the Trade Disputes Bill, introduced by the Government to reverse the judgment in the *Rookes* vs. *Barnard* case. Macleod had disagreed, arguing that the Tory peers should stand firm: if they did not, people would ask whether they would ever be prepared to make a stand on anything, and would accuse them of being under Wilson's control.[1]

While Macleod was raising the temperature in Shadow Cabinet, Heath's attack on Labour's Finance Bill in the Commons resulted in three defeats for the Government in one day, 'Black Tuesday', 6 July. Heath was reaping the benefits of having masterminded a thoroughly professional operation against the Finance Bill at precisely the right moment. The pressure on Douglas-Home to resign had increased the previous day when the 1922 Executive Committee were divided on his leadership, despite his statement that he had no intention of resigning. However, by mid-July it looked as though Douglas-Home would confound his critics as the press reported his intention to reaffirm that he would lead the party at the next election during the leader's customary annual address to Tory backbenchers on the evening of Thursday 22 July.

But by the time that Douglas-Home appeared at the 1922 Committee, his already vulnerable position had been fatally eroded. Exactly a week before-hand on 15 July, an opinion poll conducted by NOP found not only that Labour's lead had increased from 2 to 4.6 percentage points, but that Wilson was regarded as much more 'sincere' than Douglas-Home. It was a bitter blow for a man whose principal claim to retain the leadership had been that, despite his other shortcomings, he was at least somebody whom people would trust more than Wilson. That weekend, on 18 July, the *Sunday Times* published an article by William Rees-Mogg under the headline, 'The Right Moment to Change'. Rees-Mogg congratulated Douglas-Home on having played a 'captain's innings', but added that it was hard to resist the widespread view that the Tories 'will not win a general election while Sir Alec remains their leader'.[2]

Rees-Mogg's article prompted a flood of messages to Central Office and the Whips' Office calling on Douglas-Home to stand down. Whitelaw, the Chief Whip, and du Cann, the Party Chairman, advised Douglas-Home to resign; his strongest supporters, including Selwyn Lloyd and Boyd-Carpenter, urged him to stay on. Douglas-Home privately made the decision to quit on Tuesday 20 July following a poor performance in a Commons debate on foreign affairs – supposedly his forte. He informed the Shadow Cabinet on Thursday 22nd, before his attendance at the 1922 Committee. Late that afternoon, Macleod hurriedly consulted his advisers at his Park Place flat to decide whether he should declare himself a candidate. His own mind was already largely made up not to stand, but he wanted to hear what others thought. Events had moved so fast that Berkeley, the strongest advocate that Macleod should stand, was still on his way back from a visit to the Seychelles. Macleod's soundings with his advisers confirmed his view that he would not progress beyond the first ballot: a careful calculation indicated that Macleod might get about 40 votes, perhaps up to 45, but far fewer than either Heath or Maudling. His controversial record in the party and the persistent campaign against him by a hard core of bitter enemies on the reactionary right of the party, ruled out any possibility of his emerging as a compromise candidate in the event of a dead heat between the two front runners.[3]

At six o'clock that evening, Douglas-Home, 'looking terribly drawn and ill', appeared before the packed meeting of Tory backbenchers in Committee Room 14 and read a short statement declaring that he would resign as leader. The Tory Party would be choosing a new leader in Opposition for the first time for more than 50 years, since Arthur Balfour resigned in 1911, and for the first time ever by its new electoral procedure. Immediately after Douglas-Home's statement, Macleod – in the tactful phrasing of *The Times*, 'facing the current facts of the situation in the parliamentary party' – made known that he would not be standing for the leadership. He had told the Chief Whip, Whitelaw, of his decision, without offering any reason, and penned a private note to his leading campaigner, Berkeley, who arrived back from the Seychelles the following day:

My dear Humphry,
I'm sorry you weren't with us when the decisive moment arrived yesterday: I wanted to talk to you very much. But I'm sure I did the right thing and I think you agree. So there it is. And most particularly I want to thank you for so much help and loyalty and friendship. I am very grateful indeed.
See you soon,
Ever,
Iain

In fact, as Berkeley later recalled, he 'did not agree that it was right for Iain to withdraw from the contest and I told him so, but since he had already announced in public that he would in no circumstances be a candidate, it was too late.' Berkeley did not think that there was any chance of victory, but 'wanted him to stand if only to establish a future claim'.[4]

In the event, it was Powell who sought to establish a future claim by adding his name to those of Heath and Maudling in the first ballot – in Powell's words, 'to leave my visiting card'. But as Powell discovered, Macleod was surprised by Powell's decision. Only the previous week, before the question of a leadership contest, let alone Powell becoming a candidate, had occurred, Macleod had been prompted by the publication of a collection of Powell's speeches and articles to write a profile of his long-time political colleague for the *Spectator*. 'I am a fellow traveller,' Macleod wrote, 'but sometimes I leave Powell's train a few stations down the line, before it reaches, and sometimes crashes into, the terminal buffers.'[5]

It was widely assumed when Macleod declared himself a non-runner that he would hop on board Maudling's train. Like Macleod and Powell, Maudling was an old boy of the Conservative Parliamentary Secretariat, where he and Macleod were congenial companions. Later, Macleod had been delighted when Macmillan appointed Maudling to succeed him at the Colonial Office. Moreover, in 1963 they had reached an informal understanding that in the event of a leadership contest only the one who seemed to have the best chance of winning should enter the lists.[6]

However, even before the 1964 election, Macleod had thought that Maudling's standing in the party was in decline. Although they again served together on the frontbench after the Tory defeat, Macleod seemed to view Maudling more as a rival than an ally. As the Chief Whip, Whitelaw, recalls, Macleod 'was pretty critical of some of Reggie's time as Chancellor'. In the eyes of many Tory MPs, Maudling was seen to have ducked the task of harrying Labour over their 1965 Finance Bill. Heath had gratefully accepted this challenge, and skilfully delegated specific sections of the bill to the team of bright, young financial experts whom he recruited, like Patrick Jenkin, Terence Higgins and Peter Walker, who were also admirers of Macleod. Such professional tactics have since become more commonplace, but Heath and his young high-flyers made a great impression at the time.[7]

But could Macleod vote for Heath, whom he had disparaged after the 1963 leadership crisis and had regarded for at least a year as his main rival? Heath, like Macleod, had been a founder member of the 'One Nation' Group. There was less to choose between Heath and Maudling on policy than between Powell and either of them. Like Macleod, they were unequivocally committed to upholding the postwar settlement – the mixed economy, the welfare state and the maintenance of full employment through the application of Keynesian economics. The differences between the two main contenders were probably most pronounced on the questions of incomes policy and Europe: Maudling was deeply convinced of the need for some form of incomes policy, whereas Heath tended to lay greater stress on union reform and greater competition; and Heath was passionately committed to British entry into the European Economic Community, whereas Maudling was more sceptical without being an outright opponent. For what it is worth, Heath, like Macleod, also supported the abolition of capital punishment, whereas Maudling remained a 'hanger'. But on major questions of party policy, Macleod had no reason to man the barricades against either of the frontrunners.[8]

Yet perhaps the greatest point of distinction between Heath and Maudling was their approach to politics and the style of leadership that they offered. There was no doubt which Macleod preferred. He was convinced that the party 'needed something rather tougher' than Maudling could provide, a judgement shared by Butler, who had also been closer personally to Maudling. The contrasting campaigns epitomized the different styles of leadership that Heath and Maudling represented. Maudling was deliberately low-key in his canvassing, partly because that was the way he thought the ballot should be conducted but also hoping to benefit from the backlash against Heath's supporters for the part they had played in Douglas-Home's downfall. By contrast, Heath's campaign personified the kind of aggression and drive that Macleod had been urging on the party. He had a more youthful and radical campaign team, including several of Macleod's closest political associates, notably Walker and Gilmour. As the *Spectator* noted after the election, 'the division between the supporters of Heath and Maudling was in part at least between the younger and the older members of the Conservative Party, between those who wanted to live dangerously and those who wanted a quieter life.'[9]

Emotionally, it was a difficult decision for Macleod, nonetheless. He had been close personally to Maudling, and could never relate to Heath other than on a purely professional basis. Maudling was therefore the last person that Macleod wanted to see on the morning of Tuesday 27 July when he went to cast his leadership vote. But, to his great embarrassment, it was Maudling whom he met as he arrived at the Palace of Westminster and who proceeded to accompany him all the way from the entrance to the upstairs committee corridor and along to Room 14, where the ballot was being held. As they were about to enter and collect their voting slips, Macleod simply wished Maudling 'Good luck!' If Maudling had not already guessed from Macleod's awkwardness and his failure to give any indication that Maudling could rely on his support, it became clear at that moment that Macleod was about to vote for Heath.[10]

A much greater shock awaited Maudling. When the result of the first ballot was declared at 2.15pm. Heath had won 150 votes, Maudling 133 and Powell fifteen. Although Heath had won an overall majority, he was short of the required 15 per cent margin of the votes cast over the runner-up. Nonetheless, Maudling, who was contacted by Robert Carr at a city lunch with the news, saw that his position was hopeless and decided that, like Powell, he should withdraw. However, he delayed announcing his decision for a few hours, so as not to be seen as a pushover, and this brief postponement gave rise to an incident that further illustrated Macleod's edginess about not voting for Maudling. On returning to the Commons, Maudling happened to see Alan Watkins in the Members' lobby and commented, 'That was a turn-up for the book.' Indeed, Maudling's camp had overestimated his support by 30 votes, and to his evident dismay Maudling also discovered that Whitelaw, who he had assumed would vote for him, had also voted for Heath. In his affable way, Maudling vouchsafed to Watkins that he would concede later that day. Watkins returned to his paper's office in Gower Street, where he found Macleod, who knew the result but not Maudling's intention to stand down. But when Watkins told his editor that he had just met Maudling and related the news of his withdrawal, 'Far from commending his political correspondent for zeal, he looked exceedingly angry,' Watkins has recalled. Macleod responded, 'I hope you haven't been telling Reggie anything of what I've been saying. It could be very damaging.' Since Macleod 'had not said anything of any substance about the Conservative election', Watkins was therefore 'able to assure him with complete sincerity that on this matter I had been silent'.[11]

The bulk of Macleod's supporters also voted for Heath. The Macleod vote denied Maudling the victory that he thought was his for the taking. Had Macleod and most of his supporters backed Maudling, the final figures would probably have been reversed: 150 for Maudling to 135 for Heath. Yet there never was a Macleod group in the sense of a caucus ready to vote *en bloc* on the instruction of their leader. Some of his closest supporters did not know how he had voted.[12]

But should Macleod have stood in the first ballot, as Berkeley wanted? Macleod would almost certainly have polled more votes than Powell's derisory fifteen votes, although his support might have been 'squeezed' as some of his followers realized that he stood no chance and switched to one of the frontrunners. Powell's participation was intended to put down a marker for the future, but it backfired badly by demonstrating his lack of support: no longer could his speeches be said to represent the views of a significant number in the parliamentary party, or that his support on the backbenches demanded his presence in the Shadow Cabinet. From that point on, Heath always knew that, in the last resort, he could call Powell's bluff. Even if Macleod had maximized his potential vote, it is difficult to see how he would have benefited from entering the contest. He did not need to stand in order to force his way back into the inner circle, since it was clear that either Heath or Maudling would include him among their most senior advisers. It followed that neither was there any need for Macleod to put down a marker as a future leadership contender: his return to the top rank of the party would provide sufficient launch-pad should the occasion arise, although such an eventuality seemed unlikely for the foreseeable future since Heath was 49 years old, and Maudling 48, whereas Macleod was 51. When another leadership contest eventually occurred the party would probably look to a younger generation for a successor.

The explanation for Macleod's backing for Heath was given in the *Spectator* immediately after the leadership election: 'There can be no doubt that Mr Heath's takeover indicates that a radical alteration in the Tory ethos is in the making.' Macleod welcomed this development as providing the opportunity for the shift in Tory appeal that he was advocating for the centre-ground voters – not those voters whom he characterized elsewhere as 'vague liberals', but the centre in the sense of 'uncommitted voters', the 'salariat' or 'new competitors', the younger, new middle-class couples, whom he had identified in his own constituency. 'If the logic of his [Heath's] election is carried through,' ran the *Spectator*'s argument: 'It is possible to foresee a significant change of attitude among a massive public which has been alienated from old-style Conservatism. And Mr Heath is not the man to let the impetus towards change slacken off now.' Most pleasing for Macleod was the thought that:

The decisive section of the electorate which harbours no enthusiasm for socialism, but which shrinks from the strains of the 'Eton Boating Song' and all that nonsense about grouse moors is due to come under a new influence. The party battle lines will never be the same again.

Having found that the leadership election 'turned out to be both efficient and painless', Macleod concluded that the Tory Party: 'Is going to be asked by its new leader to embark on policies that may seem, electorally dangerous, and will certainly be uncomfortable. It will find, and, again perhaps to its surprise, that the experience will not be as unpleasant as some of them fear, and will be politically rewarding. Courage is all.'[13]

Macleod's part, and that of his acolyte, Berkeley, in the dramatic changes wrought in the Tory Party in less than two years since the fall of Macmillan merited a passing, wry, reference: 'This week has brought evidence of the Tory party's ability to evolve and adapt, once it has been given a helpful shove or two from within.' But in linking Heath with the Tory revolution, the new leader was put on notice to live up to his credentials as a Tory Radical:

Mr Heath is by nature very willing to shove mightily . . . Perhaps we may offer him a thought which appeared on this page on polling day last year: 'No man can or should lead this country unless he is prepared to bulldoze his way through the road blocks to progress: not for the sake of change, but because change is our ally.'[14]

Prodigal Son

It was not in Macleod's temperament or perception of why he was in politics to settle for an epitaph as the Tories' lost leader. Butler had never become leader yet had done more than anybody to create a modern Tory Party: similarly, Macleod knew that many battles would have to be fought to fashion a party that reflected his Tory Radical ideals and was capable of winning power in order to put them into effect. Almost immediately after the leadership election he was handed the challenge that would define his political ambition until the end of his life. On Wednesday 4 August 1965, two days after the traditional Tory Party meeting at which their new leader was formally endorsed, Heath announced his new Shadow Cabinet, appointing Macleod to the key role of Shadow Chancellor. From this moment on, Macleod's sights were set on Number Eleven Downing Street, as the summit of his ministerial career. His intention was to become a great, reforming Chancellor.

First, of course, the Tories would have to return to office. But the new leadership realized straight away that it would not now be as easy to oust Labour as it might have been at times during June and July. The source of the Government's summer crisis was the renewed pressure on sterling. This problem had bedevilled Labour since they returned to power and were faced with an annual deficit in the balance of payments approaching £800 million, then unprecedented in peacetime. Although years later economists calculated on the basis of more up to date figures that the deficit was £355 million, it was still bad – and decisions had to be made at the time without the benefit of the revised figures. Wilson, who still bore the psychological scars of having been a minister when Attlee's Labour Government had carried out the last devaluation of sterling in 1949, eschewed the remedy of further devaluing the pound to a more realistic level against the dollar. While George Brown at the newly created Department of Economic Affairs tried to reduce the rate of pay and price rises through a voluntary policy, the Chancellor of the Exchequer, James Callaghan, introduced an imports surcharge and export rebates to improve the balance of payments without resorting to full-scale deflation. Nonetheless, the Government was forced to seek further loans from central banks and the International Monetary Fund (IMF) and also to extend its economic measures to include increased interest rates, a curb on bank advances and tighter exchange controls.[15]

The wider problems of the economy came to dominate the political debate, but this did not work to the Opposition's advantage as much as might have been expected. There was a feeling that Labour had not yet had a proper chance to see what they could do and Wilson rarely missed an opportunity to press his claim that the pressure on sterling resulted from the soaring balance of payments deficit that had arisen under the Tories' economic stewardship. The Tories were in an awkward position. They had not had sufficient time since their defeat the previous October either to distance themselves from responsibility for the difficulties that were besetting the country or to develop convincing and distinctive policies. Uncertainty over the date of the next election added to their predicament. How much should they reveal of their plans in those areas on which Heath's policy teams had already drawn up detailed proposals, such as personal taxation? Quite reasonably, they feared that commitments made only months after leaving office might soon prove irrelevant or misguided.

Playing his new hand as Shadow Chancellor was already tricky enough, but Macleod was also having to learn the game as he went along. He was no economist: he had not studied economics and neither had he ever specialized in the subject as a Tory backroom boy, MP, or minister. He had, of course, been party to Cabinet discussions on the economy for almost eight years from December 1955, and in his first Cabinet post as Minister of Labour had been thrust into the front line of the intermittent and escalating war by successive governments against what were deemed to be excessive wage rises. But he had been a field commander implementing only part of the grand strategy designed in Numbers Ten and Eleven, Downing Street: he had never served on the central staff as a Treasury minister. 'I have much to learn quickly,' he wrote to David Howell shortly after his appointment, 'but then I learn quickly.' He tackled economics as an intellectual challenge, rather as he had once set about mastering bridge. He began appearing at the

Spectator with a copy of the *Financial Times*, which the weekly did not take, and would clip from it the latest table of economic indicators. As part of his crash course, Macleod recruited Peter Walker, who had advised him since his refusal to serve Douglas-Home and, as well as serving as Heath's campaign manager, had been one of Heath's deputies on the Finance Bill. Each week for about ten weeks during the late summer and early autumn of 1965, Walker would prepare a paper on a particular subject and send it to Macleod for him to read before their regular briefing session every Sunday morning at about ten o' clock at Macleod's Potter's Bar home. Before joining Eve for lunch, they discussed for three hours or so their chosen topic, such as the international currency scene or company taxation. Walker quickly discovered that Macleod had no knowledge of economic affairs or financial affairs and although he was trying very hard, was bored by some of the terminology.[16]

Before Macleod had any time to play himself in he was confronted, in mid-September, by the Tories' central dilemma: how to respond to positive initiatives by the Labour Government. In what seemed at the time a highly significant event for the country, George Brown, Secretary of State for Economic Affairs, amidst a blaze of publicity, published the Government's National Plan on Thursday 16 September. This much-heralded document incorporated predictions about overseas trade and the world economy, along with industries' forecasts of their likely scale of expansion. It provided useful information about Britain's industrial performance but its main significance was the Government's prediction of an increase of 25 per cent in the economy's total output between 1964 and 1970, an average annual growth rate of about 4 per cent.

Macleod was put on his mettle even before publication by George Brown's extraordinary high-handedness in claiming that he should be allowed by the BBC to make a ministerial broadcast and that since the document was being issued on behalf of the nation there should be no reply by the Opposition. Macleod was furious. He insisted immediately that he must be allowed to give the Opposition's response, a demand supported by Heath. Brown was equally vehement in refusing to give way. It fell to Willie Whitelaw, as Opposition Chief Whip, to resolve the conflict with the BBC. Having held the post for less than a year, Whitelaw knew that his standing with Macleod, and also with the new leader, depended on securing the Opposition's right of reply. Macleod's instruction to Whitelaw was blunt: 'You will arrange for me to broadcast.' Whitelaw replied that he was not sure that he could because the BBC might refuse, but Macleod simply repeated his command as though Whitelaw had said nothing: 'You will arrange for me to broadcast.' Fortunately for Whitelaw, Hugh Greene, the BBC Director-General, accepted his argument and Macleod made the broadcast. In view of Macleod's general contempt for the BBC and his previous spat with Greene, whom he had annoyed by referring to him in the weekly 'Spectator's Notebook' as one of the country's leading socialists, it was ironic that it was Greene's support for Macleod's position in this incident that began the steady deterioration in the Director-General's relations with the Labour Government.[17]

Macleod was on strong ground in his immediate reply and in his broadcast the next night when he highlighted the glaring contradiction between Brown's claims for sustained, rapid growth and Callaghan's increasingly restrictive measures. 'After July the plan could not make sense,' declared Macleod, 'Mr Brown proposes and Mr Callaghan disposes. Mr Brown sees light at the end of the tunnel and Mr Callaghan promptly blocks up the tunnel.' Not only had industry been required to draw up plans to 1970 before the July measures. 'It is quite clear,' he told viewers of his television broadcast, 'that the arithmetic is faulty. Industry was given the answer and then told to work out the problem. And if you remember your school days, it seems a curious way of doing sums.' But he was not entirely convincing, since he did not oppose outright the document's publication, commended industry's readiness to cooperate and accepted that much of the document was 'helpful, even interesting'.[18]

The Tory dilemma over the National Plan surfaced in Shadow Cabinet prior to the Commons debate, held in the closing days of the 1964-65 parliamentary session. The upshot was a muddled remit for Macleod, as shadow ministers agreed that he should give the plan a 'cool reception, welcoming it as a document on the one hand and condemning its deplorable handling on the other'. The Opposition would not even force a vote at the end of the debate. A few weeks earlier while wearing his editorial hat, he had exposed the reason for the Tories' awkward predicament:

> The case will no doubt be argued on the basis of Socialist 'planning' versus Tory 'freedom'. The argument is sterile and unreal. It was Mr Selwyn Lloyd, not Mr George Brown, who set up the [National and Economic Development Council] NEDC, and it is hard to find a single new proposal in the whole 492 pages.

Macleod would not gainsay the precedent of economic planning set by the Macmillan administration and distanced himself from the challenge to frontbench orthodoxy being mounted by Enoch Powell and his small band of followers, who were calling for the party to put their faith in market forces. When Macleod acknowledged that, 'Of course, it is right to have a certain amount of planning', a Labour MP pointedly inquired, 'What about Enoch?' Macleod's reply seemed to be directed as much to his own benches as those opposite, reminding MPs that it had been Powell 'who produced the two longest-term social plans in this country, the ten-year plan for hospitals, and for local welfare services'.[19]

A combination of the Macmillan legacy, policy differences and the political uncertainties of the autumn of 1965 – how soon would there be an election? – made it very difficult for the Tories to keep the initiative. Doubts were raised in Shadow Cabinet about the advisability of publishing any kind of policy document, but Macleod and Maudling pointed out that they were committed to do so' and, as Macleod explained in the *Spectator*: 'The faithful had to be fed.' Published the week before the October 1965 Tory conference, much of the diet offered in *Putting Britain Right Ahead* would become staple fare during the Tory years in Opposition. But at the time its overall stance was hard to define. Macleod thought it:

Possible to argue that the document (trades unions – immigration) represents a move to the right. Equally possible to argue (Europe – social services) that it is a victory for the left. These terms have very little meaning inside the Tory party. Basically the document is an expression of the thinking of the party's new leader.

Heath's radical approach to Europe and the unions was particularly welcomed by Macleod. The 'commitment not only to Europe but to a European view of many policy decisions is satisfying and complete', while the 'major departure from traditional bipartisan policies' on the unions was 'not the flat out attack on the trade union leaders, official and unofficial, in London and on the shop floor, which some Tories wanted and some Tories feared'. The document's call for unions that were strong and properly constituted with rules that were just in themselves and which were binding on their members, was in accord with the Tory Radical line that Macleod had pursued publicly since early 1964. But prior to publication he had argued that since this section was likely to attract most attention, the work of Sir Keith Joseph's policy group on the subject should not be watered down.[20]

On the central questions of economic policy – for which Macleod had assumed responsibility only a couple of months earlier – *Putting Britain Right Ahead* offered at best only scraps or nothing at all. Government intervention was said to be justified where competition had been suppressed: the NEDC would be used for this purpose and for seeking out industrial inefficiency. There was no reference to incomes policy, but when Heath was pressed on this apparent omission at the document's launch he claimed that the whole section on employment constituted an incomes policy: it did not consist in just setting a norm – people would receive higher returns by ending restrictive practices, and those who could not take part in productivity bargaining would be dealt with by the Government. Perhaps most striking is that as the new Shadow Chancellor, Macleod chose to quote in the *Spectator* the words that Heath wrote in a personal foreword distancing himself from Maudling's 'dash for growth'. Heath advocated:

the need for the closest scrutiny and rigorous control of all branches of public expenditure, the need for our business activity to be kept free from the distortions of excessive demand and for an expansion to be achieved without the inflationary consequences of an overstrained economy.

To which Macleod, mindful of the demands that he would face for extra spending, added: 'This is the reality of policy-making today.'[21]

Yet Macleod had raised expectations that the Tories would make detailed promises on taxation. In the course of his broadcast reply to the National Plan in September, Macleod claimed that Heath 'has been working out the sort of incentives that we are going to provide', and added, 'he will be putting them before you very soon: incentives to earn, incentives to save. But I promise you they will be practical proposals, not just paper plans'. At the next Shadow Cabinet meeting that by chance Macleod was unable to attend, Heath suggested that in view of Macleod's statement there seemed to be an omission in the document, and wondered whether it was possible or desirable to include details on incentives. At the last Shadow Cabinet discussion before publication Macleod felt they were being specific enough and cautioned against the very approach that he had appeared to promise only weeks earlier:

On taxation the dilemma of an Opposition is at its most acute. How, without unveiling the next Tory Budget, do you show that you mean to change course? Here the document manages to be both imprecise and prophetic. The aims are to reward initiative, to lessen the burden of taxation on rising earnings, to start building both a property-owning and a capital-owning democracy.[22]

Whatever the constraints on setting out detailed policies, Macleod would not let slip the opportunity of his 1965 Conference speech at Brighton to celebrate his return to the party's highest counsels. Before the annual conference, Sewill, then Director of the Research Department, would visit the frontbench spokesmen to check that they had everything they needed for their speeches. Invariably, they would want paragraphs drafted on this or that issue, or drafts for sections of their speeches that would deal with particular aspects of their area. These drafts were then cobbled together, with or without the help of the research department. Macleod's approach was entirely different. He would always decline any offer of help with his speech, telling Sewill that he hadn't written anything for his speech until the night before. Only then would he finally sit down and compose his speech, without any research department help. Neither would he ever show his speech to anyone before delivering it. Whereas others delivered lectures and read out carefully drafted formulae with little care for the sound of the words on their audience's ear, Macleod's speeches were near to poetry. He saw a speech to a great audience as an art form in its own right.[23]

Within minutes of opening his speech at Brighton, Macleod's wit delighted his audience. Setting out to 'explain and expand the policies, the beliefs and the thinking that lie behind' the policy document, he commented: 'And many of them of course, come back to money'. Almost as an afterthought he added: 'Money is (pause) the root of all progress.' The party faithful loved it. Reminding those who had heard him speak in their constituencies that: 'The phrase of all phrases that is most often on my lips is one of Lord Randolph Churchill's – "Trust the people" – Why then . . . should they not be trusted with more of their own money?' The prospect of lower taxes drew instinctive applause, but Macleod immediately offered a vision that transcended both tax-cutting populism and the prosaic style of *Putting Britain Right Ahead*. Recalling that at Blackpool in 1946 – 'the first Conference we held in defeat' – Anthony Eden had put forward the idea of a nationwide property owning democracy, Macleod told his audience that: 'the time has now come in the first and I hope the only Conference that we hold in Opposition, to put a new concept to you.' Quoting from the 1965 document on the 'opportunity . . . to save up a bit of capital', he asked, 'What does 'save up a bit of capital mean'? It means to me the creation of a nationwide capital owning democracy.' His declaration prompted prolonged applause. 'Is this a dream?' he continued. 'Yes, of course it's a dream under Socialism. Of course it's a dream with the present levels of personal taxation.'[24]

Here was Macleod the speechmaker in top form, his use of language, his delivery, his voice, his wit all concentrated on one objective: to captivate his audience so totally for every second of his fifteen to twenty minutes performance of partisan point-scoring and idealism that the experience would inspire them throughout the political battles that lay ahead. Thrilling the party faithful with his pledge that a future Tory government would bring down taxes, Macleod viciously savaged Wilson for having accused the Tories of being 'unpatriotic' in opposing Labour's economic measures, with all the contempt that a veteran of France in 1940 and D-Day – which Wilson was not – could muster:

I say, first, that any wise measures that are taken in support of sterling will always have – and always have had – the full support of the Tory Party and, secondly, I say that in peace – and for those of us who are old enough in war – we have gone where we thought duty took us on behalf of this country, and there is nobody in the Tory Party who thinks that he needs lessons in patriotism from Mr Wilson.

Having dismissed Wilson, Macleod returned straight away to the political high ground, concluding with a rousing reiteration of his vision of what the modern Tory Party should stand for – and what he was determined that it would stand for – and a rallying cry for the battle that lay ahead:

> Before we meet again in Conference we shall be called upon to convince the electorate that we stand for humanity as well as efficiency; for compassion as well as competition, and that for us even the pursuit of excellence is but part of the pursuit of happiness. It is because I believe that we can meet this double challenge, to heart as well as to head, that I long for confrontation at the polls, and when that is behind us, I look forward with relish, but with humility, to the chance that our Party will have of placing itself, hand and head and heart in the service of our people and of our country.

It was a bravura performance, best described by the conference report that appeared in the *Economist:*

> In the economic debate the conference was swept off its feet by that great voice of Mr Iain Macleod's promising a decrease in taxation and lambasting Labour's policy. Here was one of Mr Heath's hard-headed pacemakers, but with an additional gift of being able to point out some promised land to the faithful. No wonder Mr Heath beamed on him and no wonder that he beamed back in sheer happiness at his reception by the conference. It was the hour of the prodigal son.[25]

Farewell to the *Spectator*

On Monday 11 October 1965, just three days before this triumphant performance, Macleod announced his resignation as editor of the *Spectator*, though in fact, he would continue in post for almost three more months. He had been a good editor, earning respect as a fast, effective writer and a quick decision maker, who appeared to take the transition to journalism in his stride. He was certainly better at the job than Dick Crossman, his counterpart on the Labour frontbench, who later edited the *New Statesman*. Yet the *Spectator* which Macleod passed on to his successor, Nigel Lawson, a former financial journalist and aide to Douglas-Home, was, to all intents and purposes much the same paper that he had inherited a little over two years earlier. Gilmour's hope that the appointment of a prominent and controversial politician as editor would boost circulation was confounded. The massive publicity and leap in sales attracted by the revelations on the Tory leadership in January 1964 had no lasting impact; and – perhaps less surprisingly – neither did a 1965 television commercial, featuring Macleod, shown on Independent Television during their day-time educational broadcasts.[26]

Fears that Macleod's editorship would reduce the *Spectator* to a Tory house journal were equally confounded. It was true, as J.W.M. Thompson, his deputy editor, observed, that Macleod the journalist and the politician were indistinguishable, but Macleod's politics were never cosily conformist. Neither was his journalism. It helped that Macleod did not write as politicians customarily do. Watkins's assessment of Macleod the writer, coming from a journalist who takes particular care over his words, is worth noting:

> Real writers write in words; most literate people in ready-made blocs of words; and politicians commonly in whole prefabricated sentences or sometimes paragraphs. By this test Macleod was very close to being a real writer. Certainly he was a journalist of considerable technical accomplishment, being able to pen short and easily understandable sentences without producing a jerky or staccato effect.

'He wrote well and frequently' according to J.W.M. Thompson and was ready to take on almost anything. Macleod's account of his experiences in the D-Day landings, written for the twentieth anniversary of 6 June 1944, is a compelling read. His reviews are no less readable, although they were often highly personalized essays spiced with revelations about the characters and events involved. His portraits of Roy Welensky, Michael Blundell and Enoch Powell were full of insight and in turn devastating, sympathetic and perceptive.[27]

Macleod restricted his writing on current politics to his editorials and the odd, often acerbic, paragraph or two in his weekly column. The principal exceptions stemmed from his fascination with the Commons. In 'First Thoughts', he cast a sceptical eye over the convention and practice of maiden speeches in the new parliament of November 1964 – the first 'maiden', who began with the ritual expression of humility was, as Macleod noted, 'a Mr. Robert Maxwell', although the full irony of this happenstance would only become apparent many years later. His account was enlivened by the one aspect of the ritual that Macleod found irresistible:

> The most fascinating question is, of course, whether one can spot future classic winners from watching these first trial gallops. The answer is probably 'no'. Not because the winners aren't there, but because early-season form is apt to be as unreliable a pointer to Cabinet office as two-year-old racing has become to the Derby.

Light-heartedly applying a 'decibel applause measurement' by noting which maiden speakers had attracted the bracketed words '(Cheers)' or '(Loud Cheers)' at the end of the précis of their speeches in *The Times*, Macleod found that four maiden speakers had received (Cheers) and two (Loud Cheers). He added three more of his own selection. In fact, only one of the six who scored on the 'decibel applause measurement' went on to become a Cabinet minister – Roy Hattersley – whereas all three picked by Macleod eventually did so – David Ennals, Geoffrey Howe and Norman St John Stevas.[28]

Political correspondents and other contributors were given 'full freedom', though as Gilmour pointed out 'a good deal of the political writing in the *Spectator* was, to say the least, inconvenient to him'. Watkins found that Macleod 'was sometimes uneasy' about what he wrote. ' "Oh dear," he would occasionally lament on a Wednesday morning, "must you say that about Ted [Heath]? Well if you must, I suppose you must".' It was an article by Watkins on the steel rebellion by Labour backbenchers in February 1965 that led Michael Foot, then editor of the left-wing weekly, *Tribune*, to suggest that Macleod was influencing what his political correspondent wrote. Referring to Watkins's article, Foot had written that:

> The trick is too clever by a quarter. For it surely helps Mr Harold Wilson to be conveniently told in advance how the most skilful of Tory strategists would like restive Labour backbenchers to behave.

Watkins was affronted, Macleod and Gilmour outraged. Watkins was plainly the right man to deliver the most effective riposte, which he duly did a few weeks later:

> Whatever Mr. Foot's or *Tribune*'s practices may be, this column is not inspired by and does not reflect the views of Mr Macleod or indeed of anyone except myself. I write what I like. This may be difficult for Foot to grasp, but it happens to be so.[29]

Gilmour gave his editor as much freedom as Macleod gave his writers, but they shared the same iconoclastic view of the *Spectator*'s contents. A radical spirit like Nicholas Davenport, who happily continued his column on finance, later attested that Macleod had been 'the most charming and considerate of the editors.' Hilary Spurling, who never imagined that she would have any affinity with a Tory politician, was astonished when Macleod declared himself a fan of the televised wrestling on Saturday afternoons. But Macleod wanted to know whether the bouts were fixed, and commissioned Spurling to write an article that would provide the answer – her findings were subsequently published under the heading, 'Does the Kidney Squeeze Hurt?' And it was Macleod who launched Roy Hattersley, one of the Labour intake of 1964, on his prodigious writing career, first commissioning from him an article on Sheffield – 'The Name on the Knife-blade' – which appeared in the series, 'A Place In My Mind'. Hattersley went on to contribute other pieces during Macleod's editorship.[30]

Just as Macleod's first editorial had been devoted to a single, overpowering subject – the assassination of President Kennedy – so he found that when he came to write his final leader 'once more only one subject absorbs me and I write only about Rhodesia'. The Rhodesian crisis dominated politics during the autumn of 1965, and proved damaging politically for the Tories. In the vote on the imposition of an oil embargo against Rhodesia after the Smith regime's Unilateral Declaration of Independence they split three ways: the frontbench (including Macleod) abstained, the right-wing voted against and left-wingers countered by voting with the Government. In his signed leader, Macleod rehearsed the difficult arguments over what could be done about Rhodesia, and in his final 'Spectator's Notebook', Quoodle tried to put a brave face on the Tory three-way split in 'the Black Tuesday division', going as far as to claim that 'the Tory party can only gain from abandoning the pretence of a monolithic approach to the infinitely complex problem of Rhodesia and her rebellion'. It was an unconvincing argument and he sought to score a party political point by suggesting (probably fairly) that if the vote had been on the bombing campaign being waged by the Americans in North Vietnam the Labour Party would have splintered. But if he had been motivated only by a desire to paint the Tory party in the best possible light he would not have taken this argument to its logical conclusion:

If it be true, and I believe it is, that the country is bitterly divided over Rhodesian policy and that the Tory split reflects this faithfully, I must also concede that the Labour party divisions over American policy match opinion in the country more precisely than does the solid support for America offered by the Tory party.

It was a characteristic, startling observation from a man who had only recently returned to the Tory Party's highest counsels.[31]

'Quoodle was a bitch,' Macleod declared, confessing that, 'In my editorial will I have left a request that no witty comments on this undoubted fact should be published.' He declined Nigel Lawson's invitation to continue his weekly column. The *Spectator*'s 1965 Christmas celebrations were combined with a farewell party for Macleod, also attended by Eve. Macleod was presented with a complete set of Edmund Burke's writings in their original handsome leather bindings, specially cleaned and polished and complete with a bookplate designed by Quentin Blake showing a trail of galley proofs lying across the editorial chair. The gift delighted Macleod, who foresaw many long hours browsing through the pages – an optimistic claim, though only because of the pressure on his time, not through any general disinclination to read. As Macleod had revealed during his editorship, when a reader doubted his claim to have indulged in 'a chance re-reading of *Paradise Lost*', by the time he had:

Finished reading Hansard, White Papers, Blue Books, scores of news-papers, journals, pamphlets and reviews, all the letters from my consti-tuents and the *Spectator*'s readers (these have multiplied fourfold during my time as editor), articles and an occasional book, usually because I am going to review it, there is literally no time for literature.

In consequence, 'the dust gathers upon Trollope', but when he occasionally had 'a few precious moments' he tried to read, 'or rather re-read'. His tastes were eclectic. 'The hand that reaches up to my bookshelves may return clutching a James Bond story. Or a book on chess – or *Paradise Lost*.' Or, after 1965, Burke.[32]

The manner of Macleod's departure from the *Spectator*, a couple of weeks after the farewell party, was in marked contrast to his arrival, as his secretary, Joan Baylis, recalled:

On December 30 Iain Macleod walked out of his room and down the stairs to his waiting car: no one was about, for it was a Thursday, the quiet afternoon after the paper had gone to press. To me it seemed strange that the past two years could finish in this oddly subdued way, a kind of anti-climax after the clamour of two years ago. A lion had gone out in the way of the proverbial lamb.[33]

Divided Opposition

It is difficult to appreciate now the extent to which Rhodesia, the subject of Macleod's final *Spectator* editorial, eclipsed everything else during the autumn of 1965. Sir Michael Fraser, Tory Vice-Chairman, reported to Shadow Cabinet on 15 November, that the party's privately commissioned opinion poll research showed that neither the conference nor *Putting Britain Right Ahead* had made any impact on the public. Even more depressing for the Tories, the opinion polls showed that the Government had recovered their lead during the long summer recess. In early December, when Macleod presented his conclusions on the economic outlook, the prospect that it would take time before the Government's policies ran into trouble – prices and unemployment were bound to rise, but not before the second quarter of 1966 – led the Shadow Chancellor to counsel that 'at the moment it points to one political conclusion. There must be the thought in Mr. Wilson's mind that it might be prudent for him to have an election before the Budget, i.e. in late February or March.'[34]

Macleod was under no illusion about the uphill task facing the Tories, although he had scored a personal success a month earlier during the customary debate on the Queen's Speech which opened the 1965–66 par-liamentary session. It was a welcome return to form, complementing his party conference triumph, after the disappointments of his Commons performances as steel spokesman and in the debate on the National Plan in the previous week. His speech is guaranteed a place in the political reference books, since he coined a word that became all too common in the currency of economic commentary as Britain failed persistently over subsequent decades to respond to the manifold cures prescribed by successive Chancellors. 'We now have the worst of both worlds,' Macleod proclaimed on 7 November 1965:

> Not just inflation on the one side or stagnation on the other, but both of them together. We have a sort of 'stagflation' situation and history in modern times is indeed being made.

Macleod reeled off a telling charge sheet against Labour after their first year in office: 'stagflation', with output down by between 1 and $1\frac{1}{2}$ per cent and incomes rising at 8 per cent per annum would push up either imports or prices – the cost of living had already risen 5 points during Labour's first ten months; taxation was up £623 million; a third more days had been lost in strikes; the roads programme and many vital investment programmes in the social services had been cut; all forms of national savings were doing less well; the value of the pound in people's pockets had fallen by a shilling (5p); there had been an intense and prolonged credit squeeze; and Britain had incurred a formidable load of debt. And yet the huge balance of payments deficit inherited by Labour still hung like an albatross round the Tories' neck. In the first part of his speech he offered a detailed defence of the Tory record, recalling Wilson's support for Maudling's reflationary 1963 budget which Labour were now busily denouncing as the cause of all their troubles, and sought to demonstrate that the sterling crisis stemmed not from any Tory legacy but entirely from Labour's maladroit handling of the economy from the moment that Callaghan introduced his first package of economic measures in November 1964.[35]

However, the Tories contrived to make their predicament worse with an ill-timed display of party disunity. The conflict between the two defeated leadership contenders of the previous July, Enoch Powell and Reggie Maudling, on the subject of incomes policy, flared in the New Year of 1966, when Maudling publicly dissociated himself from Powell's argument that incomes should be left to the self-regulating mechanism of the labour market. In Maudling's view, since trade unions existed and would continue to exist, there could be no free market in labour. Neither could labour costs be kept down simply by deflation. He therefore advocated an incomes policy applied to all forms of income, in which restraint by one section would not be exploited by others. But within a week Powell had dismissed as superstition the belief that the unions comprised 'an autonomous force in the economy, capable of obliterating other influences, such as government action, on the level of demand'. 'Trade unionism,' Powell declared, 'though it may be and probably is relevant to economic inefficiency, is irrelevant to inflation and the balance of payments.'[36]

By the end of January, the Tories faced the prospect of an imminent election after the Hull North by-election, at which Labour increased their majority from 1,181 to 5,351, achieving the largest swing to the governing party in any by-election in a marginal seat since May 1924. Heath's immediate priority was to find some formula that would hold together his warring shadow ministers during the campaign, and on 31 January the subject of incomes policy was earmarked for general discussion in Shadow Cabinet in order that 'a concerted policy should be worked out'. It fell to Macleod to chart a path through the political minefield. Reflecting his belief that the best form of defence in politics is attack, Macleod's exposition of 'our attacking line' provided further reassurance for his colleagues – 'the Government's policy was a mess ... the machinery was wrong ... the aim of the policy was wrong ... [and] there was no evidence that the Government would have the resolution to carry out their professed beliefs when it came to the test ...' However, Macleod had to concede that, 'Our constructive line was less straightforward', and was forced to fall back on the vague approach proposed the previous autumn at the time of the publication of *Putting Britain Right Ahead*: 'This was that the whole of our economic policy was, in effect, an "incomes policy". The party 'should not come out against an incomes policy ... and should keep the Prices and Incomes Board.' Maudling and Powell, neither of whom were ready to push their disagreement to the point of splitting the party on the eve of a general election, stated their readiness to accept Macleod's delineation of policy. But Macleod's best efforts to define the Tory position seemed as clear as mud.[37]

Labour's remarkable triumph at Hull North dramatically confirmed Macleod's earlier prediction, based on the state of the economy, that a spring election was Wilson's best bet. After weeks of speculation, it was finally announced on 28 February that parliament would be dissolved on 10 March and polling would take place on 31 March. When Macleod had been interviewed by Anthony King on 21 December, his questioner had found him 'not overly optimistic about the future'. In Macleod's view, the Tories' main trouble was that their themes in *Putting Britain Right Ahead* – modernization, change, competition – were not palatable to a large segment of the electorate. This posed a real public relations problem, prompting Macleod to cite a War Office research study about five years earlier that had indicated that in recruiting, advertising 'adventure' should be played down in favour of 'security'. Macleod thought this, 'deplorable but there it was'.[38]

The two main Tory issues at the next election, almost the only two in Macleod's view, would be the trade unions and taxation. But there were problems with both issues. The unions might be the Tories' best weapon, especially if the London milkmen went on strike at the beginning of the campaign. 'That would finish the Government,' Macleod claimed. Although King's suggestion that Labour could steal Tory clothes in this area was rejected, Macleod felt, as with the party's other main themes, that it was altogether a risky issue since it was impossible to predict 'the way the electoral cat would jump'. Taxation, Macleod judged, would be a good issue for the Tories when the time came, although there was the obvious problem that if they were precise about their tax plans, they could be accused of being irresponsible: however, if they were vague, they were accused of offering 'pie in the sky'.[39]

Events during early 1966 did not make Macleod any more sanguine. Work on drafting the Tory manifesto had begun during the winter, but even as the election loomed there was still no sign of an inspiring, unifying theme for the campaign. This problem was largely Heath's fault, a direct consequence of the approach to policy making that he had adopted a year earlier, when he commissioned a detailed review by a large number of policy groups in the hope that themes would emerge as they presented their proposals. When no such theme was evident, the situation became desperate. On Wednesday 17 February, less than a fortnight before the election was called, Heath chaired an urgent meeting at his Albany flat, off Piccadilly, to discuss the content and style of the manifesto. In the end the urgency of the situation dictated that there should be a brief personal statement by the leader and a short manifesto that consisted solely of an action plan of promises. At the final manifesto meeting at the Albany on Thursday 25 February, attended by only five shadow ministers and four party officials, Macleod expressed his horror at the number of promises that the party were prepared to make – 131 in all. Heath reminded him that all the opinion poll evidence 'goes to show that people think we have run out of ideas', but this comment entirely missed the point. Macleod was unable to do anything about it at that late stage, but he would later quote the 1966 manifesto as an object lesson that it was impossible to convey a large number of detailed, specific promises to the voters without some basic ideas, and the result was that people actually thought the party had no policy.[40]

As an augury for the campaign, Macleod's brilliant invective, delivered in the Commons the day after the election had been announced, flattered to deceive:

For the first 100 days – until Leyton – the Prime Minister was a combination of John Fitzgerald Kennedy and Napoleon. We had all this about decisive action. Then there was the Dunkirk spirit and the reincarnation of Sir Winston Churchill. Then for a time – Heaven help us – over Rhodesia the Prime Minister was Abraham Lincoln, with malice toward none and binding up the country's wounds. He emerged recently as the Duke of Wellington – 'Hard-pounding, gentlemen.' Let us see who can pound the longest. John Fitzgerald Kennedy described himself in a brilliant phrase as an idealist without illusions. I would describe the Prime Minister as an illusionist without ideals.

Yet the campaign was difficult for the Tories. Party morale had sunk low during the winter as Labour chalked up leads in the opinion polls ranging between four and fourteen percentage points. Attempts to blame Labour's mismanagement for the country's economic ills lacked credibility as the pressure on sterling eased. Heath experienced a wretched time as leader, unable to capture the political initiative and seeming ineffective in the Commons and wooden on television.[41]

It was to Macleod that Heath turned to remedy some of the party's communications deficiencies, giving him political control of the election broadcasts. In view of Macleod's skills as a communicator and his professionalism as a television performer it seemed an inspired choice. However, Macleod and Heath had never been close personally, and their working relationship became so strained that Barney Hayhoe, the Research Department official handling television broadcasts, found himself having to act as a go-between for the two men.

Macleod was sceptical of the usefulness of party political broadcasts, believing that it was an achievement if they did not lose votes, and it might be better just to play music for ten minutes. Macleod's fears that Heath would discourage the party's supporters at the start of the campaign by another poor television appearance prompted the Tories to show him in short sequences filmed in different settings, along with ringing tributes from party loyalists, before he delivered a more traditional-style statement to camera. But Macleod's inclination to innovate was constrained by the party's resistance to what they regarded as gimmickry – he had once opened a party political broadcast with shots of Christopher Chataway winning an athletics race. As an adept performer speaking to camera, Macleod acted as anchorman in the next three Tory broadcasts but these were unexceptionable efforts. In the final broadcast, the Tories adhered to the customary format of an address by the leader, with Heath, for once, working closely on his script and managing to appear assured and relaxed. However, the failure of Heath and Macleod to establish even the most basic working relationship affected the party's election broadcasts, which sometimes seemed to bear little relation to the arguments being advanced by the leader.[42]

During the campaign, Macleod contributed a column to the *Daily Mail* and undertook his usual heroic schedule of speaking engagements, including key north-west marginals like Lancaster, to support Humphry Berkeley, and Preston South, in aid of Julian Amery. Yet generally the Tory performance was lacklustre, and was epitomized by the television confrontation between Callaghan and Macleod. Despite being regarded by Labour ministers as one of their most formidable opponents, Macleod seemed below form.

The Tories' campaign seemed particularly ill-fated. Their research showed that their talk of tax cuts appealed only to a small minority of people. The issue of union power surfaced too early in the campaign with allegations of intimidation by union officials in the motor industry and thereafter the press lost interest. As Macleod observed, having begun with a meritocratic message, the emphasis shifted to a more 'tender' vein as a result of the party's own opinion poll findings. Macleod felt that the Tory campaign lacked a 'Paschendaele, or even passion'.

March 1966 was a bad defeat, the Tories' heaviest since Attlee's landslide in 1945. Labour increased its overall majority from 4 to 96. There was some consolation in that the Tories had succeeded in forcing the Government to indulge in lavish forecasts of the economic revival that lay ahead, providing a mass of ammunition to fire back at ministers within a matter of months. Moreover, Macleod remained convinced that union reform was a long term bull-point for the Tories. Nonetheless, a long, hard slog in Opposition stretched ahead.[43]

17

Opposition is for Opposing

In Parliament it should not only be the duty but the pleasure of the Opposition to oppose whenever they reasonably can.

Iain Macleod, the *Spectator*, 26 August 1966.

Differences at the Top

Macleod hated being in opposition. Nonetheless, he was one of the most effective of all Opposition politicians. Yet there is no paradox, for the frustration he felt at not holding the reins of power and making things happen as a minister added an edge to his attacks on the Government and fuelled his invective. Much as he might detest the limitations of serving in Her Majesty's Loyal Opposition, he had the ideal attributes for the role: the most effective political debater of his generation, he could spot an opponent's weakness in a flash, was brutal in his use of tactics, and had a brilliantly savage tongue.[1]

Macleod never doubted the truth of the simple, but often overlooked, proposition that the surest route back to office from the wastelands of the Opposition benches is to oppose the Government. Formulating alternative policies had a part to play, but new policies were not to be put forward until near an election. Seven months after the Tories' heavy defeat in March 1966 Macleod was at pains to remind his party that:

At the first Blackpool conference after our 1945 election disaster there was a sweeping demand from the floor for a policy – as if a policy were a pill to cure the ache of opposition. With luck we will not repeat the same mistake. The policies of March 1966 are still valid. The backroom work on them is far advanced. The further unveiling ceremony can wait. For the time being what is needed is opposition. Just that.

Macleod's message was primarily a warning shot across the bows of Heath, whose propensity for putting forward detailed policies Macleod regarded as counter-productive. However, within a month of the 1966 Tory conference, Heath reconstituted the party's economic policy group.[2]

Depressing as Macleod found the prospect of four or five years of Labour Government, there was at least some consolation for him in opposition. If the Tories had won in March 1966 and Heath had appointed him Chancellor of the Exchequer, Macleod would have entered the Treasury after barely eight months as Shadow Chancellor. He had never dealt with a budget and finance bill in government or opposition, and would have been unable to counter the new Prime Minister's pre-eminence on the economy – certainly not for the first crucial couple of years of a 1966 Heath government. As it was, Heath had been denied the authority as leader that only an election victory and the office of Prime Minister can confer and Macleod had been given time to establish himself in his new portfolio and to prepare for 11 Downing Street.

Macleod was anxious to have as free a hand as possible when he entered Number Eleven. Heath, for his part, was set on his grand strategy of taking Britain into the European Economic Community and implementing his myriad of policies. Macleod had as little regard for Heath's political judgement as Heath had for Macleod's grasp of economics. Towards each other, Macleod and Heath mixed mutual respect with mutual disdain. This, together with their very different characters and approach to politics, was likely to produce a difficult and tense relationship if ever they became neighbours in Downing Street. Macleod could not fathom Heath or relate to the man. It went deeper than their total lack of shared interests. He found Heath pedestrian, lacking in wit, and was baffled that there was nothing to suggest that he had ever had any interest in sex.[3]

The scars of Macleod's battles in the party on Africa and the 1963 leadership crisis never fully healed. The effect intensified a strong inclination to keep himself to himself and to draw the distinction even more sharply between those whom he could trust and those he could not. The then Chief Whip, Willie Whitelaw, found that after he had won the battle to reply to George Brown's ministerial broadcast on the National Plan, he was 'in' with Macleod. But he still felt that Macleod could be a distant figure, even though they would chat happily together and Macleod, with his feel for the mood of the Commons and brilliant tactical mind, was 'extremely kind' to Whitelaw, who was learning the ropes as Chief Whip. As Whitelaw sensed, what mattered to Macleod was that he felt that he could trust him.[4]

Macleod could be short-tempered and ungenerous towards the small band of Powell's free market disciples on the Tory backbenches, but his relationship with Callaghan, the Labour Chancellor and his opposite number, was based on complete trust. Significantly, this mutual respect had been established when Macleod, as Colonial Secretary, was under siege in his own party on Africa, and Callaghan had been a supportive figure on the opposition frontbench. When he again found himself facing Macleod across the despatch box, Callaghan would privately brief Macleod on his assessment of the economy and his thinking, in the same way that he had been briefed regularly by his predecessor, Maudling, before the 1964 election. Macleod's and Callaghan's dealings were no deterrent to Macleod savaging Callaghan's performance as Chancellor, but Macleod never broke any confidences.[5]

After the tensions of the 1966 election campaign, during which Macleod and Heath had barely got on, they gradually managed to develop a working relationship. But it could never be deemed a partnership. Macleod was never one of Heath's confidants, in the way that Carrington, Walker and Whitelaw were. Anxiety about Heath's attitude towards him lingered in Macleod's mind. Following a routine speaking engagement in Bognor, Macleod returned with the usual, stock sentiments expressed by party workers, but made a point of calling Heath to convey these unexceptionable comments personally to his leader.[6]

The insecurities felt by both Macleod and Heath acted as a further bar between them. Macleod, inexperienced on the economy and disinclined to indulge in detailed examination and endless reports on policy, years in advance of an election, was a power in the leadership principally because of his unparalleled success as Tory trumpeter and the scourge of Labour. Heath, unable to inspire and without the slightest inkling how to win Tory affections, asserted his leadership through the techniques that he had learned as a Chief Whip, attending to detail and keeping an iron grip on the Tory machine. While Heath was finding it almost impossible to rally the party faithful as Leader of the Opposition, Macleod would steal the headlines at Tory conferences, year after year. On one occasion, when Macleod received one of his rapturous standing ovations at the party conference, Heath could not resist a sarcastic aside to those around him, saying, 'Well, I'm sure you understand economic policy a lot better now.'[7]

Macleod was equally scornful in private of his leader's ineptitude as a speaker, for instance mocking Heath for delivering a speech in which he identified ten points and then proceeded to plod laboriously through all ten, one by one. As Macleod observed to Watkins, there was no surer way of sending an audience to sleep. He was genuinely puzzled as to why Heath was so lamentable a speech-maker. 'Isn't it astonishing,' he would tell Patrick Jenkin, one of his shadow Treasury team:

> there is a man, an outstanding musician, with a tremendous sense of rhythm and harmony, and yet totally unable to make a speech that anybody can listen to: no feeling for words at all, no feeling for the rhythm of language. And there's me, I can't sing a note. Yet people tell me that I make quite good speeches.

This puzzle is best answered by one of the many appreciative listeners among the younger Tory representatives in the late 1960s whom Macleod delighted with his conference speeches. As a twenty-five-year-old Lambeth borough councillor, first elected in the Tory landslide of April 1968, John Major felt that: 'whatever he [Macleod] said seemed to be said with total conviction, both moral and intellectual.' Having heard a Macleod speech, 'you always felt better than you did before you'd heard it. It was quite an uplifting experience to hear Macleod at his best, either conversationally or on a public platform.'[8]

There was never anything of the economist manqué about Macleod. As William Rees-Mogg, who was a member of the party's main economic policy group when Macleod became Shadow Chancellor, recalls: 'The thing about Iain was that he neither knew much about economics nor pretended to know much about economics. But he had a very clear idea of the political implications of economic decisions, and was very concerned to get them right.' This attribute has been possessed by some of the better Chancellors since the Second World War such as Butler, Jenkins and Healey. There was no reason why Macleod might not have gone on to become one of the more successful tenants of Number Eleven.[9]

A more astringent view of Macleod's economics is held by Enoch Powell, who believes that Macleod was allergic to the subject. 'I used to say to Iain, "You know you ought to take economics seriously",' Powell recalls, but 'it was something he no more wanted to understand than I wanted to understand bridge.' John Biffen, who was one of Powell's strongest disciples in the 1960s, sensed a lack of commitment about Macleod. He felt that Macleod could talk like an economic liberal because he was what the economists term a supply sider, believing in reducing taxes and removing restrictive practices, but there was none of the theological approach that Powell brought to the subject. It was the enunciation of supposedly self-evident truths upon which all economic behaviour could be predicated that Macleod detested. Those who attended the weekly meetings of the Tory backbench finance committee, which Macleod chaired, recall that when Powell became a regular attender and contributor after his enforced return to the backbenches in the spring of 1968, Macleod frequently brushed his interventions aside, saying that this or that theory may be all very well, but they had to deal with the political economy and do what was practical and realistic. Macleod was determined to keep his eye on the political wood, ensuring that even if others lost sight of it for the theoretical trees, he at least would not.[10]

The personal chemistry within the Tory leadership was further complicated by the role of the deputy leader, Maudling. Heath, Macleod and Maudling were all committed to the postwar economic settlement. Although Maudling was convinced that full employment could only be maintained by a more formal incomes policy than the other two thought was possible, the differences between them now seem relatively minor compared with the fundamental disagreements on economic policy that were to divide the party during the 1970s. Nonetheless their contrasting personalities and different approaches to politics created friction. As the newly appointed director of the research department, Brendon Sewill, discovered, Heath was earnest, Maudling relaxed and wanting to pass on or hear the latest gossip, and Macleod more distant, though agreeable to deal with. Heath and Maudling had never got on and, as Whitelaw found, the 1965 leadership contest had been something of a watershed. Thereafter Heath seemed to regard Maudling as too lazy to do anything, and Macleod and Maudling were never as close as they had been. Heath's insistence on detail provided him with some sense of superiority in Shadow Cabinet, whereas neither Maudling nor Macleod felt the need on such occasions to embroil themselves in the minutiae. Maudling possessed one of the quickest brains of his generation on economics and had the confidence to argue any point from first principles. Macleod's approach also differed. As he would tell officials in the research department, 'I'm the barrister. Your job is to give me the facts. I'll present the case.' There was a touch of Lord Derby in Macleod's approach, since it had been Derby who had sought to reassure Disraeli, when the latter confessed his ignorance of financial matters on being appointed Chancellor, by commenting, 'You know as much as Mr Canning did. They give you the figures.'[11]

Maudling, as a former Chancellor and an economics adviser from his days in the research department, still had a locus in economic policy. This was not unreasonable, but his mastery of economics and wealth of experience did not make it easy for either Heath or Macleod when Maudling frequently raised conventional objections to any new proposal and constantly urged delaying decisions till after the next election. Neither Heath nor Macleod possessed Maudling's grasp of economics, and they were necessarily more concerned with the immediate demand of divining a position around which the party could rally that would enable them to score points off the Government. Maudling's involvement was trickiest on the subject of incomes policy, since he was its strongest advocate in the party leadership.[12]

Curiously, in view of the differences of character and politics between Heath and Macleod, Powell felt that Macleod came to act as Heath's adjutant in Shadow Cabinet. Carr, Macleod's close friend, recalls that Macleod 'did create the impression then of not being one of the team,' and remained 'very detached'. Powell 'found it difficult to imagine anyone such as Iain Macleod giving up however bad the hand of cards that he was dealt – giving up the game of being number one.' An explanation came to Powell after Macleod's death:

It's my impression that somewhere after Heath became leader of the party a change came over Iain Macleod and he revised his assessment of what life would be about. It might even have been a premonition of the shortness of his allotted span, because I suspect that sometimes the allotted span casts its shadow forward in a man's life and in retrospect when Iain died it seemed to me to have done in his life.

There is no evidence to substantiate Powell's supposition, either on medical grounds or in terms of Macleod having intimated to anybody that he did not think he had long to live. It was true that Macleod's whole approach to life convinced some of his closest friends that he never expected 'to make old bones', but they did not detect anything different about his attitude in the mid-1960s.

Powell's view may stem from his puzzlement at Macleod's readiness to accept Heath as leader, although he maintains that Macleod's attitude appeared to 'be a much deeper revision of his view of what life would be about.' The difference between the romantic Toryism of Macleod and the technocratic style of Heath was striking, as it was between Macleod's grander, expansive notion of Opposition, and Heath's regarding it as the opportunity to prepare a detailed blueprint for government. Macleod had strong reservations about the detailed commitments into which the party began to enter under Heath's leadership – which explains Carr's sense that Macleod was 'detached' – but unlike Powell he had no wish to challenge Heath. Macleod saw that he would achieve more by trying to work with his leader, or at least not against him, until the next election was settled one way or the other.[13]

In fact, Macleod was far from being a passive rider in the Tory frontbench team. The minutes for the Shadow Cabinet between 1965 and 1970 show that Macleod played an active and often key part in their deliberations, notably on the parliamentary and political tactics of Opposition. Sewill, who took the minute at most meetings, recalls the skill with which Macleod would make his point, succinctly and wittily. The laughter that followed served to punctuate any discussion and made it difficult for others to come back and argue the opposite. His word would often be the last, prompting Heath to sum up, usually more in Macleod's favour than against. Whereas Heath was concerned with preparing the most detailed programme presented at an election by a Tory leader, Maudling with trying to preserve the postwar consensus, and Powell with advancing his *laissez-faire* economics, Macleod made his priority opposing the Labour Government.

Gladiatorial Contest

As Shadow Chancellor, Macleod was summoned by the budget and ensuing finance bill to the gladiatorial arena each spring and summer. Budget day, when the annual process began, saw Macleod embark on his own ritual that would not be completed until the next evening. Tradition decreed that the initial response to the Chancellor's speech was delivered by the Leader of the Opposition, but Macleod had to open the Commons economic debate (which always followed the budget on the following day) and give his televised reply to the Chancellor's budget broadcast. After hearing the budget, Macleod would join the research department team in the early evening at their Old Queen Street offices, and over beer and sandwiches would assess its impact and consider the party's response.

He would then adjourn to White's, accompanied by Barney Hayhoe, who had helped him with his party election broadcasts in March 1966, and continue working with him on the budget broadcasts. They had started discussing their ideas a fortnight or so beforehand, drawing on the pre-budget briefings prepared by Brian Reading, Heath's economics adviser, and the Conservative Research Department. At White's, over a couple of large drinks, Macleod would discuss, fairly discursively, his script for the following night. Although he was far better than other politicians at speaking to camera, he felt that the viewer had to be given something else to look at and as his ideas crystallized he would suggest to Hayhoe the visual aids that might best illustrate his points. Television graphics were primitive in those days and Sewill has an abiding memory of Macleod's broadcasts with people having to operate cardboard devices.

Hayhoe would draft Macleod's television script overnight, ready for typing first thing, when any graphs or diagrams would be prepared. These would be taken to the Commons, where Macleod was working on his speech for the afternoon's debate. When Macleod had checked through the script and made any changes, Hayhoe would go to the studio to ensure that the script was transcribed on to the autocue and that the graphics worked. After his speech, Macleod would leave the Commons to record his broadcast. His professionalism impressed the BBC producers. On one occasion, he willingly swapped ties with Hayhoe, whose tie was thought to be more suitable, although Macleod's disability made this an awkward exercise for him to do quickly. After completing a perfect 'take' he had put his own tie on again when a technical hitch was discovered. It meant another recording but Macleod readily submitted to what was for him the tiresome task of swapping ties again and delivered an even better 'take'. From the outset, Macleod delivered his budget broadcasts straight to camera and honed into a fine art his skill at delivering a brief, punchy message. His arresting voice helped him to capture and then to hold the viewer's attention, while his brown eyes, appearing darker on the screen of a black-and-white set than they actually were, intensified the dramatic effect.[14]

But Macleod regarded the House of Commons as the nation's political cockpit. He relished the contest across the floor of the chamber and excelled at the despatch box. It was in the Commons, Macleod believed, that the great issues of the day were debated and opinion in the country shaped: the arguments that would eventually settle the next election first had to be won in the chamber. It was there that the party's confidence and conviction had to be generated, flowing from the leadership to Tory MPs and through the constituencies to the wider electorate.[15]

It had been in the role of Shadow Chancellor during 1965 that Heath had made his reputation, organizing a highly professional opposition to Labour's first Finance Bill. While Heath handled the key debates, the detailed work on each clause was delegated to his junior frontbench team, each of whom concentrated on a different aspect of the bill. But much as Heath's professionalism was admired, Tory backbenchers complained that he had not sufficiently involved them. Although Macleod broadly followed Heath's example by delegating different aspects of tax legislation to each of his frontbench team, he also involved backbenchers more closely.[16]

Macleod's choice of deputy appears, with hindsight, somewhat surprising. 'Let me have Margaret Thatcher in my team,' he told Heath. His request was scarcely any less surprising at the time. Although she had been promoted to the frontbench as Junior Minister for National Insurance and Pensions in 1961 after only two years in the House, and from 1965 served as junior spokesman on land and housing, Thatcher had had little opportunity to capture the headlines. Jim Prior, one of her contemporaries, later recalled that, 'She was of the Right, but not excessively so.' Nonetheless, she had clearly impressed Macleod. His insistence that she become his second-in-command was her first big break. She did not disappoint him.[17]

During Macleod's first two years as Shadow Chancellor, all stages of a Finance Bill, including the committee stage, were still taken on the floor of the House, and Macleod was unselfish about giving his team opportunities to speak from the frontbench. After one such occasion, in which Thatcher had delivered a highly effective performance, Macleod adjourned to the bar with Angus Maude, his colleague from the early days of the 'One Nation' group, and over a drink confided, 'After listening to Margaret's speech tonight it no longer seems absurd to think that there might one day be a woman Prime Minister.' Seven years after Macleod's death, in July 1977, Thatcher delivered the Iain Macleod memorial lecture as Leader of the Opposition. After she had spoken, Eve Macleod disclosed to the audience of Greater London Young Conservatives her husband's belief that Thatcher would one day lead the party. Thatcher never forgot how much she owed Macleod. Every Christmas since his death she has sent a wreath to his grave.[18]

For Thatcher, as for the other two members of the shadow Treasury team, Patrick Jenkin and Terence Higgins (both elected to the Commons only eighteen months earlier), working with Macleod was a formative experience. He held daily meetings when the Finance Bill was being debated in the Commons, periodically being briefed by the research department, and also receiving specialist advice from accountants and lawyers who were willing to assist. Even years after Thatcher had risen to the top of politics, she could still recall the commitment and excitement that Macleod inspired as they prepared for each day's clause-by-clause debate:

We met every morning, we looked at the days following, and we decided who was in charge of amendments, who was going to move them, what advice we needed. And it was exciting, and you were happy to be totally dedicated to this immediate task.

Whoever was allocated a clause was not only responsible for tabling the amendments but also for conducting the debate and mobilizing backbench support. Sometimes Macleod would take a clause, but would ask one of his juniors, 'Could you wind up the debate?' Thatcher admired Macleod's skill in involving the backbenchers in their meetings 'so that you could draw on a very wide range of experience in the House', from shipbuilding to the financial markets. About thirty or so MPs would be recruited to advise on the various aspects of each finance bill, and Sir Anthony Grant, the opposition whip on finance, recalls the 'tremendous impression' that Macleod made at their first meeting when he told them, 'You're the frontbench, all of you.'[19]

Watching Macleod's management of the Finance Bill had a lasting impact on Thatcher, helping her to develop the highly effective method of briefing herself. While serving as his deputy she saw how he:

worked to get his ideas and to get his decisions. He worked very much by discussing them with a group of people who discussed freely, and then he would gather up the views and draw conclusions from them. And I had the impression that he did it far more that way than by sitting down with a damp towel round his head. And I have a good deal of sympathy with that and maybe I learned a lot from him, being one of the younger people in that group. I did learn that you frequently get the ideas from the interplay of the idea with a personality and not just by reading in a personless atmosphere. And that was one of my very vivid impressions of Iain, this clarity of expression and being able therefore to pick out the wheat from the chaff, as we would say. You have got the basic idea and you eliminated the irrelevant matter.

The similarity in Macleod's approach and that adopted by Thatcher is striking. They both enjoyed arguing a point with somebody and testing the other person's case to destruction.[20]

During the long, all-night sessions on the Finance Bill which used to occupy the Commons three times a week during the summer months until four o'clock in the morning, or even five or six, Macleod would stay and listen till the very end. Callaghan was puzzled by his approach:

It was good that he let his junior frontbenchers get the limelight, but he would sit there for hours, in the corner seat usually occupied by the Chief

Whip, listening to the debate into the early hours. I would say, 'Can't we go home now, Iain?' but he would be determined to stay there all hours and not go home. He seemed to be brooding, while his lieutenants were getting on with the work. He simply wouldn't leave.

Macleod was a hunched figure on the frontbench. Unable to turn round because of the progressive stiffening of his neck and back, he would occasionally prompt one or other of his frontbench team as they addressed the house, 'with wise words of advice out of the corner of his mouth'. He would not tell his team what they should say before they spoke, but he had a perfect sense for the mood of the Commons and would tell them to 'listen to the House'. If they began to lose its attention and MPs started talking, it was no use trying to win them back: better instead to wind up as quickly as possible, unless they were the final speaker in a major debate and had to press on till the ten o'clock vote. Macleod would almost never comment on their speech afterwards, a trait that at least taught them to develop a sense of self-criticism. However, during the Finance Bill's all-night sittings, Macleod recognized that Tory backbenchers had to be given the opportunity to troop through the division lobbies fairly frequently, otherwise they would become restive and start pestering the whips, asking why they were having to stay well past midnight. Jenkin recalls speaking from the frontbench on such occasions and realizing that it was time to finish his remarks when he heard Macleod muttering to him in a low, rasping voice, 'We've got to divide, the party are going mad.'[21]

From the spring of 1968, when the Finance Bill was first sent 'upstairs' to standing committee, Macleod attended as diligently as when the committee stage had been taken on the floor of the House. He was an arresting sight as he headed along the committee corridor, limping as he walked, his shoulders uneven and his upper body rather twisted and his left arm swinging, often deep in discussion with Willie Whitelaw, the Chief Whip. Macleod would be doing almost all the talking as he set out his thinking on tactics on the Finance Bill and his dealings (or lack of them) with the Government, while Whitelaw would be listening and nodding his agreement before finally getting a chance to chip in with his reactions. Macleod's only dispensation – and the only allowance ever made for his disability – was the 'pair' arranged for him by the whips to save him the pain and trouble of having to traipse up and down the stairs to the committee floor for divisions called downstairs in the chamber below.

In committee he would sit in the front row of the benches that run for most of the length of the large room, on the Opposition side facing the windows over the Thames. While his chief lieutenants, Jenkin and Higgins, dealt with the myriad of detail, Macleod would often sit with his briefcase propped open alongside him, taking an opportunity to write pithy notes, commenting on an idea that an MP had put to him, congratulating people on their speeches or offering them support. But he was always alert and would never miss a trick in committee, on occasion orchestrating Tory committee members by passing a note telling them to engineer an artificial row among themselves in order to prevent the next clause being reached until the following day. He would stay for as long as the committee sat, including the all-night sittings, and often, at six o' clock or so in the morning, Jenkin or Higgins would give him a lift back to the Grosvenor House Hotel on Park Lane, where, during the late 1960s, the Lombard Bank provided him with an apartment. If it was not too late, Macleod would say, 'Come back and have a drink', and would unwind and chat about politics.[22]

Although Macleod was keenly partisan, his handling of issues that cut across traditional party political lines illustrates his iconoclastic approach to politics and to Opposition. Callaghan's plan to tax gambling in his May 1966 budget followed the legalization of betting shops and was accepted in principle by the Tories. However, Macleod's clash with the Chancellor over the proposed method of levying the tax led to an episode that had echoes of his raffish past and pointed up his flair for the unconventional. Drawing on his knowledge of betting going back to pre-war days, when memories of an earlier, failed attempt to tax betting were still fresh, he accused Callaghan of being 'sadly innocent' – something that Macleod could certainly not be accused of in this field. The Chancellor, Macleod argued, was 'entirely wrong' to tax 'the cash flow rather than the physical assets', since it would mean that 'the opportunities for evasion are very large indeed'. Callaghan would be repeating the mistake made by Churchill in the 1920s when his turnover tax was evaded by the bookmakers and repealed after three years. But it was Macleod's manner of making his point that was striking and unusual. Sending Callaghan, for 'weekend leisure reading', a copy of Edgar Wallace's popular 1920s thriller, *The Calendar*, Macleod explained that 'the whole plot, the whole story, is about a method of beating the turnover tax as it then existed in this country'. Callaghan enjoyed the read but was not convinced, having been assured by officials at Customs and Excise that this time they would be able to prevent widespread evasion. They were proved right and Macleod wrong. As the gambling tax became a significant source of revenue, he had the grace to admit his mistake.[23]

However, Macleod never felt any need to repent for his opposition to the manner and method of the Government's decimalization of the coinage. The Tories had no objection in principle when the decision to replace £-s-d with a decimal system was announced in Callaghan's mini-budget on the eve of the March 1966 election, but Macleod told the Shadow Cabinet the following January that the question of which system should be adopted 'would affect the country for many years to come, [and] should be lifted out of the usual atmosphere of party politics'. But this non-partisan approach also chimed with his tactical calculation. In their White Paper of the previous November, the Government had opted for the '£-cent-½' system that had been recommended three years earlier by a majority on the Halsbury Committee, appointed to examine decimalization by the Macmillan Government. The principal virtue of this system would be the retention of the pound as the basic unit, but its main drawback was that since the pound was such a large, or 'heavy', basic unit (by far the heaviest by international standards), the smallest unit, the cent, or new penny, would be equivalent to 2.4 old pence. Most banks, consumers' organizations, industry, retailers and the unions preferred the alternative, '10s-cent', system, in which 10 shillings would be the basic unit, with the cent, or new penny, equivalent to 1.2 old pence. Commonwealth countries had decimalized by switching from the £ to 10s as the basic unit, and according to Macleod, it also seemed, on investigation, that the Halsbury Committee had really preferred this '10s-cent' system.[24]

Macleod became a committed 'ten bobber', prefacing his advice to Shadow Cabinet with puckish wit:

'It's always best on these occasions to do what the mob do.'
'But suppose there are two mobs?' suggested Mr Snodgrass.
'Shout with the largest,' replied Mr Pickwick.

Macleod felt strongly that they 'should take action as soon as possible to try and change the Government's mind'. Some of the Shadow Cabinet favoured openly and officially advocating the '10s-cent' system, but Macleod was anxious that the whips should not become involved, otherwise there would be no chance of defeating, or deflecting, a Government that enjoyed a Commons majority approaching three figures. He therefore recommended forestalling the Government's publication of the bill by calling for a debate on the issue, and announcing as soon as possible that the Opposition would allow a free vote and would demand one for the whole House. He also suggested that Heath might consider expressing a personal view in favour of the '10s-cent' system. However, no such debate was forthcoming and by early March, when the Shadow Cabinet next considered the issue, publication of the Government's bill precluded debate on the White Paper. Macleod continued to demand a free vote and remained an unrepentant 'ten bobber'.[25]

Before the decimalization debate was eventually concluded, the unrepentant 'ten bobber' also became the champion of the 'tanner'. The final battle, over the future of the sixpence coin, provoked an extraordinary parliamentary battle during 1969 and 1970. The Government had sought, during 1969, to scrap the sixpence at the end of the change-over period to the new, decimal currency (in February 1971), but they had run into considerable cross-bench opposition. When the legislation reached committee stage, the vote on the sixpence was tied. By convention, the chairman cast his vote for the bill, so the sixpence would be scrapped. But a few moments later, another clause was passed deleting this clause by one vote, so the sixpence was restored. After further toing and froing in the Commons, the Government won and the sixpence was lost. In the Lords, the sixpence was again reinstated, but was eventually lost on report.

By the time that Macleod came to open an Opposition supply day debate on the issue on 19 February 1970, it was becoming clear that the Government would back down. According to Norman Shrapnel in the *Guardian*, Macleod 'treated himself to one of those artfully, placed, purring performances of his – for all the world like a fighting Tom that has been at the cream – congratulating the Government on doing what the Tories had told it to do.' Macleod quipped that it 'can properly be called the SOS – Save Our Sixpence – debate' and would be 'what everyone hopes is the last round in this song of sixpence'. He proposed 'that we should keep the tanner as a 2½p piece, not for all time but for a considerable time ahead'. He therefore urged the Government to reverse their decision and to retain the sixpence after the change-over period to the new, decimal currency. In response, the Chancellor, Roy Jenkins, delivered a holding statement in which he finally conceded that the issue warranted 'further consideration by the Decimal Currency Board', whom he asked to report by Easter.[26]

On 20 April, Jenkins announced the reprieve of the sixpence. For Macleod, the whole episode of decimalization had been a classic example of the Government's 'disregard for parliament' and of 'the gentleman in Whitehall knowing best'. Both were attitudes that he regarded as unforgivable.[27]

The Chickens Come Home, July 1966

Rarely has a Government been blown off course so soon after having won an election landslide as during the summer of 1966. Reviewing the prospects at the Shadow Cabinet meeting on the eve of Callaghan's May 1966 budget, Macleod suspected that Callaghan would compromise, being neither weak nor tough. The atmosphere as the Chancellor delivered his budget is well captured by David Owen, then the newly elected Labour MP for Plymouth Devonport: 'All through the election one had muttered small caveats about the economy, it seemed certain we would have to have a few relatively tough measures . . . Confidently he [Callaghan] produced, like a conjuror, SET, the Selective Employment Tax, to take effect in September and everyone cheered.' An estimated £400 million additional revenue was to be raised, principally through SET, a tax on jobs in the service sector, followed in October by another new tax, on gambling. Some relaxation would come in November with the ending of the import surcharge which had been imposed in the autumn of 1964, and would be partly offset by a scheme for voluntary restraint in investment in the developing countries of the sterling area. 'Only Iain Macleod said it was not deflationary enough,' Owen recalls. 'Only he warned. I breathed a sigh of relief and forgot about everything except for regional variations in SET.'[28]

The proposed SET was attributed to Professor Nicholas Kaldor, then a Treasury adviser, who had argued that the cause of Britain's relatively poor economic performance was a shortage of labour in manufacturing. This theory was undermined by one inconvenient fact – British manufacturing was overmanned. SET operated as a poll tax on everybody in work, levied on the employer – 25s (£1.25p) a week for every man employed, 12s 6d (63p) for each woman or boy, and 8s (40p) for every girl. However, manufacturing firms were able to claim back a premium of 32s 6d (£1.63p) a week for every man employed, 16s 3d (83p) for each woman or boy, and 10s 6d. (53p) for every girl, in effect, a subsidy for wages. Kaldor's brainchild was ripe for ridicule. 'The Labour Party is so obsessed with the attack on the "candy floss society",' Macleod declared:

> that it does not realize that what it is doing is to pay a premium to the manufacturers of pin tables, even in areas of high employment, and to penalize, say, banking and insurance, wherever they are situated, on which virtually all export in one way or another relies.

Moreover, as Macleod bluntly pointed out: 'There is a great deal of labour hoarded in manufacturing industry at present.' Indeed, he would: 'Not be in the least surprised if the amount of labour being hoarded in manufacturing industry was in excess of that being hoarded in the service industries.' Deriding Wilson's pretensions to lead a modernizing Government, Macleod was scathing of the omission of any reference to how SET would apply to disabled workers, whose cause he and his wife, Eve, had long championed.[29]

Callaghan's overall budget misjudgement was soon apparent. The failure to reassure foreign markets was exposed after only a fortnight when a seamen's strike prompted a fresh run on sterling. Although the strike ended on 1 July, publication on the same day of the bill to nationalize steel did little to restore international confidence, and two days later the resignation from the Cabinet of Frank Cousins, former head of the Transport and General Workers' Union and an opponent of incomes policy, threw doubt on the Government's ability to restrain wages. New figures for the reserves and balance of trade triggered a further run on the pound. The bank rate was raised on 14 July, but to little effect. On Wednesday 20 July, Wilson finally unveiled the stiffest deflation since the last devaluation of sterling in 1949, taking £500 million out of the domestic economy and cutting overseas spending by £150 million. Public investment economies, tighter hire purchase restrictions, a surtax surcharge, more building controls and a reduction of the overseas travel allowance to £50 a year (a figure chosen after Callaghan had inspected a sample of travel brochures), were accompanied by a voluntary prices and incomes 'freeze'.[30]

'There are rough times coming,' Macleod warned in the *Spectator* immediately following the July package, 'and probably now they will be rougher
than they need have been.' He recalled Nicholas Davenport's damning
comment, made in the same paper the week before, that Callaghan had '. . .
planned a sacrifice this winter when the British people are due to pass from
a full-employment society to a stagnating under-employed society.' Labour's
economic strategy lay in ruins. The National Plan was dead and buried, its
forecast of 25 per cent more national output by 1970 mere fantasy. Wilson
was forced to concede that unemployment might rise to between 1.5 and 2
per cent by the end of 1967 – the level actually rose to 2.4 per cent in
September 1967. But it was not only the spectre of unemployment that
haunted Macleod. Devaluation was also on his mind, although he took care
to avoid saying anything that might undermine sterling, distancing himself
from the *Spectator*'s calls to reduce the pound's rate against the dollar.
'Perhaps because I am an inhibited politician rather than an independent
editor,' he noted, 'I do not share them.' However, he confessed that he did
'share the dread' recently expressed by Nigel Birch, the acerbic former
Treasury minister, who had spoken of: 'a recurrent nightmare . . . that in
the end we shall have to devalue, but after spending all the proceeds of all
the Government's dollar holdings in America, after spending a large part of
the private investment holdings in America and after contracting still more
astronomical debts.'[31]

July 1966 marked a sea-change in the party political debate. 'The truth
about this parliament,' as Macleod would later declare during one of his
most biting attacks on the Labour Government:

Is that it died three months after the last General Election, when it was
clear that they were elected on a false prospectus. And four years is a
terrible long time to wait for a burial service, while the corpse lies cold in
the lobbies at Westminster.

Macleod exploited this political transformation to the full at that October's
party conference at Blackpool, which was an altogether happier occasion
than their last visit there, three years earlier. Suspecting, tongue-in-cheek,
that his audience 'would judge it discourteous' if he 'did not spare a word
for the architects of our present disaster', Macleod treated the Tories to
waspish comments about the men whom he identified as the culprits. Brown
had been reshuffled to the Foreign Office following the demise of his
National Plan, but although he was 'easiest to attack':

He is also the one I am most reluctant to attack. There is a national society
for not being beastly to George Brown, and I pay my dues like anyone
else! Now that he is Foreign Secretary I only hope – never mind, I only
hope!

As regards the Chancellor – whose name he always pronounced with a hard 'g' – Macleod began by confessing that he:

> could also find some nice things to say without the words sticking in my gullet, about Mr Callaghan. He served, for example, in the Royal Navy throughout the whole of the last war.

A good war record counted for a lot with Macleod. Then, straightaway he delivered the *coup de grâce*:

> But Mr Callaghan suffers from what I hope you will regard as a fatal defect in a Chancellor, he is always wrong, not just sometimes; for Jim Callaghan, the laws of averages have been suspended.

The laughter and applause registered his audience's sheer delight. But his fiercest attack was reserved for the Prime Minister, his waspishness giving way to venom as he read out the last sentences he had used against Wilson in the Commons when he wound up the censure debate on July 27th:

> The charge we bring against the Prime Minister is a simpler and graver one. It is that as long as he sits in this house, on whichever side he sits, we do not feel that we will ever be able to trust him again.

Macleod now added, crushingly, 'To me that was not a peroration, it was a verdict.'[32]

Macleod was to deploy his talent for combining scornful attacks on Labour with his vision of Toryism. But first, he was at pains to reiterate his view of opposition. Sensitive to the pressures that existed for the Tories to issue policy pronouncements, he warned against making 'detailed commitments for the future at this stage in opposition'. As he explained:

> We must not accumulate barnacles as we sail on, because many of the commitments that may sound very popular and easy to make at a conference may well be an embarrassment and may be wholly irrelevant when the time comes for us to take up power again in this country.

This did not prevent Macleod providing an eloquent statement of general principles, focusing on the need for greater competition in the economy, more incentives and trade union reform. But he was not impressed by the economic prescriptions of the international financiers. Criticizing the hapless Chancellor for going 'too far when he claims that overseas bankers are not dictating our policy', Macleod condemned him for having 'lost for us a large measure of economic sovereignty, which always happens when one owes money'. The upshot was that 'we are having to take medicine prescribed for us, if I may say, by people who would never dream of swallowing the same medicine themselves'.[33]

However, Macleod was alert to the dangers of the party becoming intoxicated on the heady brew of policies that would mark a shift to the right compared with those pursued during Macmillan's premiership. As a Tory Radical and a meritocrat, he saw that not enough had been done to change British industry or society during the thirteen years of Tory rule, and indeed part of his frustration over the 1963 leadership crisis, was that it had marked a further missed opportunity to create the drive and policies needed to modernize Britain. But he also saw more clearly than Heath did at this time that a balance had to be struck.

The upshot was that Macleod gave an 'extraordinary performance' that caused the day's 'big stir'. He had, it seemed, chosen 'deliberately to assume for this 30-minute speech the mantle of party leadership', although, having been leader for half-an-hour, he 'was prepared to stand down until this time next year'. As John Dickinson of the London *Evening News* reported from Blackpool:

> Sometimes the little Scotsman cannot help himself and has to let fly. Today was one of those times. Speaking without a prepared script and ranging far and wide of his economic brief, Mr Macleod commended his own personal brand of Tory philosophy as the one the party should adopt in its troubles. And with Mr Heath sitting uneasily at his side he cheerfully lectured the whole Shadow Cabinet in front of the conference on how it should conduct itself in Opposition.[34]

Macleod's call that the party should adhere to the basic tenets of 'One Nation' Toryism was unequivocal:

> Let us remember that we are not all pace-setters, we are not all competitors, and let us remember that change when it comes as it must is often a very cruel thing to an individual or to a township or to a community. So competition needs compassion.

He echoed the sentiments of a representative who had spoken in support of regional development and had paid tribute to the efforts of Tory ministers before 1964. Recalling the card that Lord Woolton used to keep above his desk when he was Minister of Food, which said, 'We not only cope, we care,' Macleod continued:

> That is an old-fashioned sentiment but for me it is the very heart of Tory political faith, and if there is a doubt about us perhaps it is here, because polls, for what they are worth, over many years have shown that the people believed that we can manage economic affairs, that

we can cope better than our opponents, but do they believe that we care as well?

It was a question that would prove the hardest for the Tories to answer during their years in opposition.[35]

18

Means to an End

I think basically over the years this [belief in market forces] is a Whig
rather than a Tory doctrine. Everything has its price. Yes, but that would
mean no regional policy. It would mean a disastrous failure for the
regions, for the development areas, and for Scotland. It is an excellent
policy for the strong, but we are concerned also with the weak.

Iain Macleod, Conservative Conference, Brighton, 9 October 1969.

Sceptical Keynesian

Macleod's approach as Shadow Chancellor was informed by a scepticism
towards economic theory, a loathing of unemployment and a concern to
enter Number Eleven with as much freedom of manoeuvre as possible to
manage the economy. Economics, as far as Macleod was concerned, was a
means to an end – he never lost sight that it offered the means to increase
human happiness. He accepted that the breakthrough in economic management made by the economist, John Maynard Keynes, first implemented in
Britain by Churchill's wartime coalition, enabled governments to establish
business confidence by managing the level of demand in the economy,
thereby preventing an economic slump and mass unemployment. The proof
of this pudding was in the eating. Successive postwar administrations,
Labour and Conservative, had delivered full employment, low inflation and
a growth rate sufficient to generate mass affluence.

As putative Chancellor, Macleod saw his role as being to continue within
this policy framework. 'We are all Keynesians now,' he declared in his
preview of the 1968 Budget. But he was too much of a realist to think that
managing the economy was easy. He simply did not believe that any
economist could provide a panacea, and by the end of the 1960s accepted
that the tools of Keynesian 'demand management' were exceptionally blunt.
But he was even more sceptical of the renewed claims being made for money
supply theory, notably by Milton Friedman and his fellow 'monetarists' at
the University of Chicago, and he never accepted that governments should

abdicate their wider, social responsibilities and allow 'market forces' free rein.

Macleod shared the growing concern in the mid-1960s at the weak performance of the British economy relative to the superior growth rates achieved in western Europe. Whenever a British government sought to boost the rate of growth, the economy 'overheated' as pay and prices began to rise more rapidly and the balance of payments deteriorated, prompting a sterling crisis and forcing the government to deflate. Macleod was as keen as anybody to break out of this vicious circle of 'stop-go', and like almost all businessmen, economists, journalists and politicians at the time he believed that improving Britain's economic performance lay in enabling Keynesian methods of economic management to work more effectively.

In his repeated calls for the modernization of Britain delivered in the columns of the *Spectator* during his editorship, Macleod identified the chief causes of Britain's deep-seated economic ills as an outdated class system, which wasted the talents of its brightest people, and a trade union movement wedded to restrictive practices. His prescription entailed creating a more meritocratic society and removing the dead hand of inefficiency. He believed that government could best help by overhauling an arcane and deficient tax structure in order to increase incentives and encourage savings and capital ownership, and by reforming the unions. It fell to Macleod as Shadow Chancellor to plan the wholesale reconstruction of the tax system, and for the next four years he devoted his efforts behind the scenes to devising the necessary changes.

The trouble in focusing, however correctly, on the importance of longer term reforms was that it left unanswered what a new Tory Government would do about inflation and unemployment before its main reforms began to have any effect – a matter of several years at least, probably longer. Since the voters were regularly identifying inflation and unemployment among the most important problems facing the country, the Tories clearly needed to find some convincing answers.

Powell was then virtually a lone voice in the higher reaches of Tory politics expressing monetarist sympathies, but as defence spokesman he was excluded from the economic policy group and had only the support of about ten to a dozen MPs on the Tory backbenches. Yet the challenge of controlling inflation while maintaining full employment had sparked a fierce debate among Keynesian economists. According to a controversial analysis by Professor Paish, Britain's susceptibility to increased inflation originated because successive governments had run the economy at full capacity, thereby creating not so much full employment as 'over full' employment. This resulted in a severe shortage of labour and strengthened the bargaining power of unions, thereby causing increased pressure for higher wages leading, in turn, to higher prices. The proposed solution was to run the economy at less than full capacity, nearer 95 per cent, entailing an increase in unemployment to an average 2¼–2½ per cent – a notion that reflected the remarkable optimism of the period in the ability of governments to 'fine tune' the economy with great precision. Critics of Paish, notably Frank Kahn, a Cambridge economist, argued vehemently that implementing such a policy would sacrifice 5 per cent of the economy's productive potential and incur a permanent increase in unemployment without any guarantee that inflationary pressures would not return. It requires a huge feat of under-standing, after the shameful levels of unemployment endured during the 1980s and 1990s, to appreciate the real anger aroused by Paish's suggestion that unemployment would increase to 2½ per cent, particularly since this projected increase was well within Beveridge's initial definition of full employment.[1]

Initially, Macleod was interested in Paish's theory. In the spring of 1966, a new parliament, that seemed likely to run its full, five-year term and the relative freedom of Opposition gave Macleod the opportunity to raise the vexed question of the link between inflation and unemployment. Confident that the postwar revolution in economic management had permanently banished mass unemployment, he called for 'a new White Paper on unem-ployment . . . because the old thoughts and fears of the pre-war years are now completely out of date and it would be a good thing if, in modern circumstances, we could see if we could redefine our attitude towards unemployment.' The risk in raising these questions at all was highlighted during a Commons debate that July, when George Brown, then Secretary of State for Economic Affairs, accused the Tories of being bored by the problem of inflation because they knew 'how they could solve it ever so quickly when were they in office. They would have two million people out of work inside three months.' Macleod retorted that this level had been approached only once since the Second World War, during the 1947 coal crisis, which, as he did not need to remind his contemporaries, had occurred under a Labour Government. As Macleod acknowledged: 'The difference in achievement between the two parties in power is statistically negligible, and we know it in our more straightforward moments when talking about unemployment.' The current jobless total stood at a mere 1.1 per cent, yet, as Macleod reminded MPs, the accepted definitions of full employment were higher:

> We know the original Beveridge assumption of 8 per cent as full employ-ment in a free society. With various qualifications, he revised it to 3 per cent. We know what Mr Gaitskell put forward as the target – 3 per cent at the seasonal peak and 2 per cent overall.[2]

Within a week of this bitter exchange between Brown and Macleod, Labour, in effect, implemented Paish's theory. The July 1966 deflationary package signified the Government's acceptance of higher unemployment for the remainder of the 1966–70 parliament. 'I loathe seeing the planning of recession and the planning of unemployment, whoever the Government may be who plan it,' Macleod told the Commons during the confidence debate in the immediate wake of the July measures. But what he hated even more was the Government's 'infirmity of purpose' in failing to bring inflation under control before the 1966 election: 'Inflation hurts the poor, the unorganized and those on fixed incomes. Those who are organized are all right, Jack.' He acknowledged at that October's Tory conference at Blackpool, that: 'You cannot – and we have our share of guilt in this – run the economy without roaring inflation with levels [of unemployment] of 1.1 or 1.3 per cent.' But there was a world of difference between saying this and contemplating an abandonment of the postwar commitment to full employment.[3]

Others, notably Maudling, who like Macleod rejected the road to higher unemployment, were convinced that the only way to solve the conundrum of preventing inflation and maintaining full employment was to adopt some form of control on increases in incomes. Macleod never ruled out an incomes policy. He believed that any government had to have some form of incomes policy, but he was equally certain that the Tories had to oppose Labour's move, imposed as part of the July 1966 deflationary package, from a voluntary prices and incomes policy during 1965 to a six-month statutory freeze on prices and incomes. There was little difference on incomes policy between Macleod and Heath at this stage. It was not the case that Heath was prevented from advocating stronger support for an incomes policy, as Maudling would certainly have preferred, by Macleod's politically motivated opposition to the Government. Both Macleod and Heath wanted to distance themselves from Labour's statutory incomes policy without ruling out entirely some form of incomes policy. During one of the seemingly interminable series of Commons debates of the late 1960s on Labour's prices and incomes controls, Macleod was prevailed upon by Michael Stewart, Minister for Economic Affairs, to acknowledge his disagreement with Enoch Powell's denunciation of incomes policy as dangerous nonsense. 'I disagree with that,' Macleod admitted.[4]

However, the Tory leadership were unable to agree on exactly what should be done. Robert Carr, Shadow Employment Secretary, led the Tories' detailed, clause-by-clause opposition to Labour's later statutory prices and incomes controls, although personally he was closer to Maudling's position. But even though he was one of Macleod's closest friends and political allies, and had served as his junior minister at Labour, he was unsure of Macleod's position. Macleod, he believes, was 'pretty canny' and felt that 'you had to oppose detailed legislation of that [Labour's] kind'. However, opposing statutory pay and prices controls was not a matter of 'saying that you shouldn't try to influence wage settlements'. In Carr's view Macleod thought that 'you should play that card jolly close to your chest. You produce it for taking particular tricks at particular times'.[5]

Macleod's canniness on incomes policy was influenced by his experience as Minister of Labour, where he had witnessed, at first hand, the near anarchy of the trade union movement – despite their good intentions, they couldn't deliver. This difficulty of their delivering weighed with him, as Geoffrey Goodman found whenever they discussed the subject, making him sceptical and believing that at the end of the day a formal incomes policy would not be effective. But Macleod's position was more moderate than that held widely in the parliamentary party. Above all, he was wary of making any detailed commitment, but he was not against discussions with the unions on pay and trying to reach some kind of agreement.[6]

Predictably, in October 1966, at the first Tory conference following the imposition of Labour's pay and prices freeze, demands were made that the party should oppose incomes policy outright. But Macleod was not prepared to commit the party to such an extreme position:

> That this [Labour] incomes policy is not desirable, I think everyone in this hall would unite on; but, in my view, an incomes policy can have a useful, though secondary effect once the Chancellor of the Exchequer has got the level of demand right in the country. You will find, in fact, that all Governments operate a sort of incomes policy. When Mr MacNamara [US Defense Secretary] uses the vast buying power of his Government, acting as a customer, when President Johnson indulges in what is called ear-stroking, this is a form of incomes policy.

At this stage, Macleod regarded incomes policy as a necessary but clearly subordinate element of economic policy. He was more sure-footed attacking Labour on its price freeze, where the Tories agreed, as he showed in the Commons only a fortnight later:

> If the proposals in relation to wages are foolish, the proposal in relation to prices is both perverse and illiterate. It is shooting at the wrong target. It is dealing with the symptom and not with the disease. It is trying to cure the spots and not cure the measles. It is forgetting something that was wisely said recently in the *Wall Street Journal*, 'Price increases cause inflation no more than wet pavements cause rain.'[7]

In the autumn of 1966, as the numbers unemployed began to climb steeply, Heath revived the policy-making exercise on the economy. Previously, the main economic policy group had been chaired by Heath as Shadow Chancellor, and from October 1965 by Macleod, with three sub-groups on taxation, industrial efficiency and the balance of payments. But the main group of about twenty politicians and outside advisers had proved unwieldy and only the sub-group on taxation had made substantial progress. Heath created a new group, restoring himself as chairman, with a core of senior frontbenchers – Maudling, Macleod, Boyle and Lord Harlech – and fewer outsiders and an ambitious agenda.[8]

Macleod was not convinced that these policy meetings of Heath's were much use, although if they had been more purposeful Macleod was unlikely to have been any happier, since he was determined not to let himself be boxed in on policy. His irritation surfaced at December's meeting on the balance of payments, when at the outset he complained that he was not clear on the objective of the discussion or the accompanying paper. Macleod missed the next four meetings at which the discussions ranged over the direct measures available to government to boost the domestic growth rate, including incomes policy, investment grants and labour and regional policies. He did not reappear at the group until budget week in April 1967, by when he had already spoken in the spring budget debate, one of his main speeches on the economy for the year.

During the winter of 1966–67, Macleod became increasingly concerned at the rapid growth in unemployment. He was acutely conscious of the sheer destructiveness of unemployment, but he also saw that it was by far the most effective political weapon with which to cudgel the Government, all the more so since Labour's left-wing were up in arms about it. At the start of December, he warned the Commons that it was not 'the absolute figure of unemployment' that was causing people to worry but 'the trend and the sharpness of the line on the graph'. This insecurity could only militate against solving Britain's problems:

> While there is fear in the country, we are wasting our breath talking about restrictive labour practices; we are wasting our breath talking about demarcation disputes; and we are even wasting our breath talking about a voluntary incomes policy. These things will not happen until fear goes.[9]

Macleod took full opportunity of a televised party political broadcast on 7 December to drive home the attack. 'You know Labour Government works' had been Labour's slogan at the election little more than eight months earlier. 'Does it?' asked Macleod, demanding to know 'How high are these figures going to go?' His condemnation of the Government's record on unemployment was made all the more deadly for having been prefaced by an apparently fair-minded remark. 'I would not dream of accusing my opponents of being callous,' he began, but added, 'I accuse them of incompetence.'[10]

Fighting the Free Marketeers, 1967

The dramatic increase in unemployment by early 1967 served to reinforce Macleod's commitment to the postwar consensus on economic policy, but there were strong pressures pulling the Tory Party in the opposite direction.

The expectation in March of an early statement by the Government on the next step in its prices and incomes policy intensified party divisions and heralded Macleod's most difficult period as Shadow Chancellor.

With the Opposition's approach due to be discussed at a joint meeting of the party's backbench Finance, Labour and Trade and Power Committees on Tuesday 14 March, Macleod advised the Shadow Cabinet on the evening before that they would have to give a definite reaction of some kind. He agreed with Heath that the party's longterm policies for the economy were convincing, but they could not give an answer on what they would do this summer; neither could they replace the present Government's incomes policy. As a result, he felt that although the Opposition did not approve of the Government's policies and had no responsibility for its mess, the Tories could not suggest an immediate return to complete freedom by July.[11]

Macleod had captured the mood of Shadow Cabinet. They felt that it would be neither in the interests of the economy nor in tune with opinion in the country to return immediately to a free-for-all in prices and incomes. The parallel was drawn with 1951 and the end of rationing, when the Tories planned a staged removal of controls. However, Macleod had to report back two days later that he had found very little support from backbenchers for this moderate line. There had been a large attendance at the meeting of the party's backbench committees, and about 30 Tory MPs had spoken, expressing their disillusionment with prices and incomes policy and with the apparent lack of any clear cut distinction between Opposition policy and that of the Government. In the event, the Government's announcement was not forthcoming as early as had been thought and the Tories were spared immediate, public embarrassment.[12]

The Tory dissidents found Macleod not in the least tolerant of their campaign. In fact, he 'was upset and short-tempered about it,' as John Biffen discovered when he dropped Macleod a critical note about his response to Callaghan's 1967 budget. The backdrop was Macleod's growing concern that although unemployment had levelled out at 500,000, the numbers out of work would rise again the following winter (1967–68), and the Keynesian-style policy that this led him to urge on the Government. When John Biffen wrote privately, objecting to Macleod's call for modest reflation, Macleod's reply was terse: 'Why should you assume that anyone who disagrees with you is both a Fabian and a fool? I am neither.' Biffen, in his anger, tore up this note, and sent a second letter only to receive an even more crushing put-down. 'Let me try again,' Macleod wrote, 'and of course in all friendliness', although this was scarcely borne out by the words that followed. 'First, I am allergic to being adjured to abandon Fabianism and to think strategically. I am not old enough yet to be your grandmother but I can suck my own eggs.' Biffen's criticism was dismissed: 'There is the world of difference between calling as I did yesterday for reductions in direct taxation or abandonment of SET premiums and free prescriptions, and "boom" reflation.' Moreover, Macleod maintained that he was not – as had been alleged – simply following the line of the National Institute. If he was wrong, so too were other Tories. 'I – and many others, Higgins, Alison, Howell, et al, have said for months that we thought the Chancellor too optimistic. We may all be Fabians. We may (of course) all be wrong. I doubt it. Ever, Iain.' The upshot was that Biffen, who at university in the 1950s and later in the Bow Group, had seen Macleod as one of the great Tory hopes for the future, felt completely 'turned off'.[13]

Powell's allies on the backbenches continued to agitate on prices and incomes policy, the issue that most troubled the Tory Party. As young ideologues, they were exhilarated at taking on ministers like Brown and Castle in debate and encouraging Labour's own backbench dissidents to speak out. But their tactics further irritated Macleod. In June 1967, during the second reading of Labour's Prices and Incomes Bill, Macleod took Biffen to task for his comment in an article in the *Daily Telegraph* that there had not been an incomes policy in 1957–58. As Macleod argued:

> I agree that an incomes policy means different things to different people, but I should have thought that the beginnings of one was there. There was the price plateau, the three wise men, the guiding light and the rest of it, and this dates back to about 1955.

It was a return to something along the lines of this more informal incomes policy that Macleod preferred.[14]

Heath effectively ruled out all but an informal and minimal version of incomes policy in his major speech on the economy at Carshalton on Saturday 8 July, when he sought to end the factional strife in the party. Assessing press reaction in Shadow Cabinet the following Monday, Macleod went to the heart of the Tory dilemma when he commented that the *Sunday Times* had made a valid point that although the party's:

> Economic policies were wholly credible in the medium term, the question was whether they were credible tomorrow. The fact that we were not going to be the Government tomorrow was, of course, part of the answer to this question. But we had still to convince people of the immediate credibility of our policies and we had somehow to do this without having to spell out all the detail prematurely.[15]

Paradoxically, the tensions in the party were at their worst as the political tide turned strongly in the Tories' favour for the first time since the heyday of 'Supermac', more than seven years earlier. In April 1967, they recorded a sweeping victory in elections for the Greater London Council (GLC), as Labour lost control for the first time since 1934 and saw a majority of 28 (Labour 64 seats, Tories 36) replaced by a 64-seat Tory majority (Tories 82 seats, Labour 18). City councils, many of them former Labour strongholds, fell to the Tories in May – Bradford, Cardiff, Coventry, Leeds, Leicester, Liverpool, Manchester, Newcastle, Nottingham, Southampton, Teesside and Wolverhampton. By August, a clear Tory lead was established in the opinion polls, and in September, the Tories won parliamentary by-elections at Cambridge, with a swing of 8.6 per cent from Labour, and Walthamstow West, with a massive 18.4 per cent swing.[16]

The deep sense of unease among many Tories partly stemmed from an awareness that there was still anything up to three and a half years to go before they might have an opportunity to fight another general election. Macleod appreciated that Heath suffered from being the first Tory Leader of the Opposition not to have served as Prime Minister since Bonar Law in 1911. The trouble, however, went even deeper, as Macleod was acutely, and rather tetchily, aware. There was a general disillusionment among back-benchers and the party faithful who felt that the Conservative Government up to 1964 had pursued increasingly 'pinkish' policies. Wilson's policies were not all that different. They had had enough of 'Butskellism'. After enduring almost three years of hitherto undistinguished opposition, they longed to see the party adopt a distinctive position. But this was not what Macleod wanted at all. He wanted to stand back, let Labour ruin themselves, and return to government with the minimum of commitments.[17]

The party faithful's anger finally erupted at the October 1967 Tory conference at Brighton when the apparent woolliness of Opposition policy towards Labour's introduction of comprehensive schools provoked a sizeable revolt after the speech by Sir Edward Boyle, the Shadow Education Minister. Whereas Boyle had been quite overwhelmed, Macleod's mastery of conference, mingling savage attacks on the Government with rhetoric that reassured the party faithful while resisting the pressures to move the party to the right, was unparalleled. It is not perhaps saying very much to suggest that alongside his speeches those of his colleagues were rendered pedestrian. His efforts might be better compared with an actor's soliloquy or a poet's reading. Indeed, a few of his colleagues had been reminded of his rare talent only a few weeks earlier during a weekend policy discussion at the Conservative college at Swinton, when, at the Sunday morning service in the small chapel, Macleod read the lesson from Corinthians. His reading did not last more than a few minutes, but he put such beauty and passion into it that many years later those who heard it still recalled it quite spontaneously.[18]

At Brighton in 1967, Macleod's compelling voice, his delivery, timing, use of language and choice of phrase were all used to maximum effect. Whereas many Tories appeared defensive, and were half-hearted or leaden-footed, and usually both, in their attacks on Labour there were no half measures from Macleod. The seemingly endless flow of ministerial resignations, sackings and reshuffles was meat and drink to him. The sacking of Douglas Jay that August and the consequent Cabinet changes had given the Department of Economic Affairs – created to effect Labour's modernization of the British economy – its third Secretary of State within thirteen months:

> Secretaries of State come and go. You remember them. We started with George Brown. Happy days. Three per cent mortgages, the declaration of intent, the National Plan. Where have all the flowers gone? Gone to the graveyard, every one.

It was revealing of Macleod's ear for words and his topicality that he chose to quote an anti-Vietnam war song for his punch line. Brown's successor, the uncharismatic Michael Stewart, was dismissed in a phrase: 'Then you remember Michael [pause] – no, of course you do not remember Michael Stewart.'

It was for Wilson that Macleod invariably reserved his most bitter words. Later in this speech he would damn the Prime Minister with the memorable gibe that, 'Doubletalk is Mr Wilson's mother tongue', but here he made play with the Prime Minister's all too transparent concern to secure himself a good press:

> In nominal charge we have the Prime Minister himself, a man whose vision is limited to tomorrow's headlines. He is a man whose favourite phrase is 'government with guts'. We know what that means – his government and our guts.

Callaghan was let off relatively lightly, damned with faint praise:

> Callaghan is much the best of them. He has been, to his credit, steadfast since July 1966. It is only a pity his obstinacy was not expended in a better cause. However, I am determined to pay somebody a compliment of a sort, and I pay it to Mr Callaghan. He is by a long chalk the best of them, although, as Shakespeare said, 'There is small choice in rotten apples.'

An equally withering onslaught was unleashed against Labour's economic measures and record, as he accused them of having 'settled for mediocrity in economic performance because I think they feel at home there'.[19]

'The way lies through less Government intervention, not more,' he declared, offering the rank and file some red meat. 'It lies through the economy of choice and through the pursuit of excellence, rather than the pursuit of equality.' Apart from some pledges on tax reform, and opposition to Labour's creation of the interventionist Industrial Reorganization Corporation, he was careful to avoid specific commitments. But Macleod delivered a peroration that would be recalled a quarter of a century later by Julian Amery, a former ministerial colleague but not a close friend or political ally, as one of the most powerful that he heard at a Tory conference:

Here, members of conference, is the true battleground. Here we fight in Parliament, under Ted Heath's leadership, as you will fight in the constituencies, because twice before, in 1931 and 1951, the theory and practice of state socialism has almost brought this country to its knees. Enough is enough. We can see it coming again, unless we destroy it. We do not seek to destroy socialists; they are unimportant and incompetent men. The fight is against state socialism itself. If we go into that fight with relish – as we will and as you will – the battleground can become the killing ground as well.[20]

These compelling and unrivalled performances from the conference platform greatly contributed to Macleod's clout in the party. He was also adroit at exploiting his conference triumphs. Less than a month after his 1967 *tour de force*, he moved to distance himself from the argument that higher unemployment should be used as a means of curbing inflation. That summer, the economic policy group had considered a draft report for a weekend meeting in late September at Swinton, that accepted the need for higher unemployment. 'Conservative policy,' it suggested, 'must reconcile itself to the need to operate at a safe distance below the capacity ceiling . . .' This implied the need 'to mitigate the social effects of a rather higher level of unemployment than has been normal since the war' and 'to adopt policies which have the effect of raising the capacity ceiling'. But there was still a role for fine tuning: 'With modern methods of economic forecasting and for the management of demand it should not be impossible to keep to steady expansion at a level of about 2 to 2½ per cent unemployment.' The Swinton paper's argument was to reappear in subsequent drafts prepared by the Conservative Research Department for the economic policy group, but it was not formally adopted as official policy.[21]

Macleod's opportunity to attack this approach publicly came when Sir Leslie O'Brien, then Governor of the Bank of England, spoke approvingly of needing a 'larger margin' of unemployment in the economy. The Governor's comments were taken as proof by Macleod that the Government was deliberately pursuing a policy of higher unemployment. 'What we are seeing,' he claimed, 'is a break with the past, because we are seeing for the first time a Government putting into action the theories of Professor Phillips and Professor Paish . . .' They held that 'the economy – perhaps any economy – runs best at about 95 per cent of capacity.' As Macleod added:

This is often crudely translated into a figure of 2¼ per cent unemployment. Its advocates – and they are strong in the Government, and Government Departments – say that when we have become accustomed to that level, growth will be resumed. Its opponents say that when the initial shock has been absorbed inflationary pressures will be renewed and all that will have happened is that we will have sacrificed 5 per cent of productive potential.

Macleod confessed his own interest in the theory 'some years ago'. In fact, he had been more than merely interested in the theory, but now he finally rejected it:

In the ordinary sense of the word it is not a theory at all; it is an observation. This economy has been at 95 per cent so rarely – and then when the economy was going up so fast or down so fast – that we cannot draw valid conclusions. Other countries have managed to work much nearer the ceiling than 5 per cent and why should not we?

Britain had already endured nearly a year of unemployment around 2½ per cent by the autumn of 1967, but Macleod detected 'none of the benefits which are supposed to flow from such a doctrine'. Indeed, unemployment was to rise even higher before the next general election and yet wage inflation was still not quelled.[22]

Devaluation, November 1967

By the summer of 1967, most economists favoured devaluation of the pound from its rate of $2.80, which had been fixed in 1949. Heath was anxious not to have the issue raised at all for fear of stirring new divisions in the party on its economic policy, yet Macleod found himself in an embarrassing and potentially damaging predicament on devaluation. On Thursday 20 July, the party's advisers, and other independent economists, gathered for a seminar on the economy and Tory policy at Church House, Westminster. One of those who attended, Sir Samuel Brittan, has since freely acknowledged his 'gratitude for the courtesy and friendliness' with which Macleod:

Allowed me to put the case for devaluation and floating [exchange] rates to Conservative gatherings in 1967 without making me feel the *odium theologicum* to which one was subject from other quarters in his party.

It is not difficult to guess the principal source of the *odium theologicum*. During the coffee-break, Heath told Brittan that if he must talk rubbish, he should do so somewhere else.[23]

Despite Macleod's more mature approach to intelligent debate, he realized that press reports of the meeting would be exploited by their opponents to suggest that the Conservatives were considering devaluation. But he had an immediate opportunity to disassociate the party from such a potentially damaging position the following Monday when he opened the Commons debate on the Opposition motion of 'no confidence' in the Government. 'I mention, only to reject,' Macleod told MPs, 'the solution of devaluation, because in my view it is no solution at all.' And in an oblique reference to the reports of the previous Thursday's seminar, he argued:

It is idle to pretend that many, and perhaps the majority, of academic economists do not advocate this course. One listens very carefully to what they say, but I do not think that devaluation offers us an easy way, or indeed any way, out of our present difficulties . . . the signals of both interest and good faith alike are set against it. I believe this to be the genuine view of both the Treasury frontbench and the Opposition frontbench.

The effect of this disclaimer was to blunt the edge of the Tory attack. But Macleod was eventually to reap some harvest four months later, when he deployed to great effect Callaghan's own robust rejection of devaluation in the July debate.[24]

In November 1967, the Prime Minister was forced to devalue the pound, having sought to resist it since 1964. On Sunday the 19th, Macleod watched Wilson's televised broadcast at Heath's Albany apartment, along with other shadow ministers and their advisers. This broadcast has entered political folklore as 'the pound in your pocket' speech. In fact, Wilson said: 'It does not mean of course, that the pound here in Britain in your pocket or purse or in your bank has been devalued.' Wilson's purpose, according to his biographer, Ben Pimlott, had been to prevent uninformed people panicking, as they had when the pound was last devalued, in the belief that for every pound of their savings invested in a bank or post office they would only be able to draw 17s. But the folklore version captures the misleading impression that Wilson had created. As Pimlott notes: 'The Prime Minister had persistently argued that devaluation did matter to ordinary people. Now that it had happened, he appeared to be standing on his head, cleverly arguing that it did not.' Macleod spotted Wilson's gaffe the moment that Wilson uttered the words, and was on his feet telling Heath that the Prime Minister had lost all credibility and with it the next election.[25]

On Monday, 20 November, Callaghan made a lengthy statement in the Commons. It was a brave performance, but as Macleod listened he realized what lay behind the Chancellor's words. 'He's going to resign,' Macleod told Peter Walker, alongside him on the frontbench, and urged him to calm down the excitable Tory MPs packed tight on the Opposition benches: 'Tell them all to keep quiet.' When Callaghan concluded his statement, 'a forest of Tories' leapt to their feet to try and catch the Speaker's eye. Convention decreed that the Shadow Chancellor was called first. Macleod rose to the despatch box, his slow and stiff movement adding to the theatre of the moment, silence descended on the chamber. He made no attempt to respond in detail and raise a list of points as Opposition frontbenchers invariably and tediously do following a ministerial statement. Instead the formalities were despatched with utmost brevity. He observed that the Chancellor's 'long statement gives rise to many questions which we shall wish to probe' in the subsequent debate, and briefly echoed his July disclaimer: 'we do not accept either his [Callaghan's] diagnosis or his prescription . . .'[26]

Macleod then moved for the kill. 'I put only one point now to him,' he told the Chancellor, seizing on Callaghan's attempt, as Macleod put it, to 'explain away' the 'utter condemnation' of devaluation that he had made in July. Reminding MPs of Callaghan's assertion only four months earlier that if we devalued 'we should break faith with Governments and private citizens overseas' and that he did 'not want either to devalue or to bring down the standard of life of our own people,' Macleod declared:

> The Chancellor of the Exchequer will know that I am using his own words. He has done all these things. He has broken faith. He has devalued his word. He is planning to bring down the standard of life of our own people. He is an honourable man. Will he resign?

The Opposition benches cheered loud and long. Macleod had previously rejected a suggestion that he should launch a vitriolic attack on Callaghan because of his personal respect for the Chancellor. Yet the effect of his brief, direct charge was devastating. In reply, Callaghan admitted that he had recommended the Cabinet to devalue, adding that it was his 'immediate responsibility to see that the operation is successful'. Callaghan's use of the word 'immediate' was carefully chosen: as Macleod had already realized, the Chancellor would soon resign. Just ten days later, Callaghan, having completed the immediate negotiations with the IMF for standby credit, left Number Eleven and, in a straight switch with Roy Jenkins, moved to the Home Office.[27]

In the perfervid atmosphere following devaluation, the contrast in character and political style between Macleod and Heath was thrown into sharp relief. When the Shadow Cabinet assessed devaluation on 11 December, Macleod 'thought the line being taken by sections of the press, that all should now give full support to the Government, was most dangerous for the Conservative party'. The press had 'followed its usual course', he opined, in his note, circulated prior to the meeting:

> The Tories it is said were too quick to condemn: Mr Wilson deserves understanding and support. In my view he does not. He deserves unrelenting opposition tempered of course with gradual evolution of our own distinctive policies. Mr Wilson's T.V. broadcast, and particularly the sentence that the '£ in your pocket or purse' has not been devalued, damns him for a rogue. And as far as the Press (and I suppose a handful of our own supporters are concerned), perhaps I can recall what I said in

Manchester after the devaluation debate: 'If Mr Wilson's Government embraced voodooism the same leader writers in the same newspapers would say that Mr Heath was wrong to attack the new policy, that recriminations were out of place and that it was the duty of the House of Commons now to make devil worship work.' I do not doubt that on all grounds we were right to attack.[28]

Macleod reported to the Shadow Cabinet that: 'There has been fierce criticism of the "support" line in the [Tory backbench] finance committee, who were in favour of a much stronger attack.' His preference was clearly for putting the emphasis on attack. 'His own line,' he told his colleagues:

Was that we should oppose the Government vigorously and work constantly to get them out; develop and expound our own positive policies with increased energy; and support any Government actions which we thought right and in the national interest.

Others were more cautious. Boyle worried that: 'opinion abroad was keenly watching what politicians of both the main parties in this country said', and 'the less involved people in this country, particularly in the universities, did not like perpetual attack on the Government.' Even the new Party Chairman, Anthony Barber, 'thought it most important that we should not seem to be predicting failure or encouraging any lack of confidence, but should attack the Government for not doing the things we believed to be right'. These concerns weighed with Heath, who concluded that 'we must maintain our responsible position and not try to make party political capital out of the economic situation, while putting forward our views on what we thought should be done.' This latter view was not Macleod's idea of opposition.[29]

The personal rapport that had existed between Macleod and Callaghan was not repeated between Macleod and the new Chancellor, Jenkins. Their relationship never developed beyond the mutual respect they had for one another as politicians. They were protégés of Butler and Gaitskell respectively (Jenkins had initially been counted as a Bevanite), shared the friendship of Ian Gilmour, were indisputably men of the political centre and held liberal views on many non-partisan moral and social issues, including capital punishment. But they never got on.

Of the two Chancellors whom he 'shadowed', Macleod much preferred dealing with Callaghan. His relationship of trust with Callaghan dated from his time as Colonial Secretary, when he often found more support from the Opposition frontbench than the benches behind him. As a result, his relationship with Callaghan was special, and possibly it could never have been as close with any other Labour Chancellor. But it was also a matter of personality and temperament. Whereas Macleod found Callaghan approachable and bluff, he regarded Jenkins as 'vain and arrogant'. Jenkins, for his part, clearly found it difficult to penetrate the shell of Macleod's partisanship and moodiness. Perhaps Callaghan, who is well placed to understand the lack of rapport between the two men, comes closest when he says that Macleod was too 'swashbuckling' for Jenkins.[30]

The Tory romantic and the social democrat shared many views, but they were fundamentally different political animals. Macleod's verdict on the Labour Chancellor was cutting, but also shrewd about a man who, more than a decade later, was to become a founder-member of the Social Democratic Party:

He makes speeches to the House, good speeches, but he has no dialogue with the House. The reason is, of course, that his disdain for his political opponents is only matched by his contempt for his political friends.[31]

Robert Carr, who knew Macleod better than most, never thought that he seemed naturally at home as Shadow Chancellor or that his speeches on the economy were very convincing. Callaghan feels that Macleod lost something of his application as his disability worsened during the 1960s. Although Jenkins was not as good a political debater as Macleod, he capitalized on having the Treasury at his disposal. The new Chancellor soon came to display a good intellectual grasp of his subject and scored some notable triumphs, although his most resounding victory in early November 1969 must be counted as a spectacular Tory own goal. As the trade figures improved, Macleod and Heath inadvisedly followed Barber's lead in persisting with the claim that ministers had falsified the presentation of the statistics, when the Government corrected an earlier underestimate of exports amounting to between £16 million and £20 million a month. Macleod's argument that the presentation of the September returns meant that a misleading figure was flashed to newsdesks was crushed by Jenkins's reference to the first news report after publication, on BBC Radio's *One o' Clock News*, which he thought 'the best of the lot'. The Chancellor was able to conclude, dismissively, 'Really the Rt Hon. Gentleman [Macleod] is making nonsense of it. So much for that little incident.' Macleod, in company with Barber, found himself lampooned by Garland in the *Daily Telegraph* on Guy Fawkes Day as a bedraggled schoolboy who had made the mistake of playing with a Roman Candle firework (Jenkins) that, as he told his mother (Heath) he thought had gone out.[32]

Macleod would have been less than human not to experience some irritation at being worsted in the arena where he had first won his spurs. The approval that Jenkins generally enjoyed in the media also riled Macleod, whose usual, wary scepticism for fashionable opinion mingled with a desire to receive a good press himself. 'Mr Jenkins is the vogue,' he commented caustically in the *Spectator* a fortnight after the Chancellor's first budget in March 1968: 'If he had stood up on budget day and recited the list of trains arriving at Victoria the trendier commentators would have been breathless with adoration.' Like many others at Westminster by the winter of 1967–68, Macleod regarded Jenkins as heir apparent to Wilson. Macleod reckoned privately that there was only a 50–50 chance of the Prime Minister lasting till the following Christmas. If Jenkins could manage the succession peacefully, he thought that Labour's prospects would be transformed. There was, as Macleod observed privately, a strong, Tory 'Wilson must stay' movement. Macleod deftly exploited the speculation when he responded to Jenkins's March 1968 Budget. Paying tribute to 'a lucid elegance about the phraseology which reminded me very much of Mr Harold Macmillan's budget speech in 1956', he twisted the knife by adding that Macmillan 'had time to introduce only one budget before he became Prime Minister'.[33]

Immediately after the 1968 budget, the lack of rapport between Chancellor and Shadow Chancellor contributed to a complete breakdown for six weeks in 'the usual channels' between Government and Opposition whips that lubricate the working of the Commons. Jenkins's first budget was also the first occasion on which the committee stage of an annual finance bill, when government's tax changes are considered clause by clause, was not taken in a committee of the whole House. Instead, it was to be 'sent upstairs' to a standing committee and only a few of the main clauses would be scrutinized on the floor of the House. In addition, the Government imposed a time limit on debate by imposing a 'guillotine'. Macleod laid the blame at Jenkins's door. As he argued, some years there is an agreement on the Finance Bill, and in others there is no agreement:

> But every Chancellor of the Exchequer of all three parties, with the exception of 1931, has always got the Finance Bill without a guillotine . . . that the failure this year is directly due to the petulance, insolence and arrogance of the Chancellor.[34]

The proposal to send most of the Finance Bill upstairs to a standing committee had been mooted the previous year, but Macleod was livid at the Government's high-handedness. He deliberately set out to cause maximum trouble and disrupt Labour's legislative schedule. However, Macleod was nothing if not a realist. His bloody-mindedness had a purpose. As Sir Anthony Grant, then Opposition whip on the Finance Bill, recalls, Macleod was determined to demonstrate through his intransigence that even though the Finance Bill had largely been consigned to a standing committee, the Government of the day would never be able to take the Opposition's compliance for granted and would therefore always have to strike a reasonable agreement about the time allowed for debate.[35]

Towards an Incomes Policy, 1968

In his assessment of the effects of devaluation for the Shadow Cabinet meeting of 11 December 1967, Macleod identified 'the critical wages front' as the first in his list of points that he raised more in the form of questions than as policy proposals. Devaluation would only work if the higher cost of imports was not allowed to boost inflationary pressures. However, if higher prices for imports simply led people to demand, and to receive, higher pay awards, the whole purpose of the exercise would be lost. British exporters would soon lose the competitive edge that devaluation had given them, the balance of trade would deteriorate and Britain would face the prospect of returning to the vicious circle of 'stop-go'. In Macleod's words:

> Do we hold to our line that we are against a statutory policy but that it is the manifest duty of the Government to give a firm lead at the risk of strikes in relation to their own employees and where appropriate those of the nationalized industries? Do we say so?[36]

The need for an answer became more pressing during early 1968. In March, Macleod and Carr, in a joint paper to Shadow Cabinet, urged some softening of the party's opposition to Labour's pay policy:

> While not wishing in any way to weaken the firmness of our policy that a Conservative Government should abolish all statutory powers to interfere with wage settlements, we believe that it would be right, in the present conditions following devaluation, to make some modification in our short-term reactions as an Opposition compared with the line we were taking last summer.

In addition to adopting a case-by-case approach to statutory orders controlling specific pay rises, they recommended not opposing a renewal of the Government's powers to delay any pay rise for up to seven months. However, they advised opposing any reintroduction of the statutory powers to impose a freeze or norm of the kind imposed in 1966. This more emollient line was backed by a majority of the Shadow Cabinet at their discussions on 7 and 13 March.[37]

As the next election approached, Macleod became more convinced that the Tories would be ill-advised to deny themselves any form of incomes policy. It was not only a question of making devaluation work, vital though that was. Before sterling was devalued, Macleod was alarmed at the growth in public spending when the economy was not growing at anything like the ambitious rate projected in the National Plan. As a result, public spending was taking a higher and higher share of national output. A new Chancellor would urgently need to rein back public spending, and this would necessitate a tight grip on public sector pay.[38]

The Conservative policy document, *Make Life Better*, published before the 1968 party conference, affirmed that government had a role in incomes policy. 'Conservatives reject compulsory government control of wages,' the document declared. But in a vital sentence, it added that, 'In key wage negotiations a government may need to exert its influence on the side of lower costs' – a form of words that envisaged the government's role extending beyond the public sector. This formula was immediately tested in conference, during the debate on taxation, when Powellite dissidents moved an amendment calling for the outright rejection of incomes policy. Macleod's rejection of a compulsory incomes policy was unequivocal: 'A compulsory incomes policy is, and always has been, a complete failure. We have fought it at every single stage in the House of Commons.' Commenting that, 'It has been rejected everywhere,' including, as Macleod reminded the Tories, 'even in this hall, by a majority of nearly five to one last week' at the Labour conference, his own rejection could scarcely have been more categoric: 'Conservatives reject compulsory Government control of wages. There it is, and we will have none of it.'[39]

But Macleod also gave his own party some straight talking. Having ruled out a compulsory incomes policy, he came to 'the more important point – or the more debatable point: what, if anything, do we put in its place?' He could 'in theory, possibly accept' the Powellite amendment, because the Tories would not seek to control prices and incomes. But as he explained:

> To do that would be misleading, because we know very well that there is a difference of emphasis between the case they [the movers of the amendment] put forward and the case I wish to put to you, and I do not want to blur the issue in any way before this conference.

And in a key passage, he explained why, during his lifetime, the Tories rejected a 'hands off' approach:

> There are certain facts of life that we cannot talk away. The Government is the largest employer of labour in this country. It is the biggest customer; it is the biggest consumer. It is not conceivable that it can stand aside in these matters. If we were the Government today and were facing a position in which a million people might come out on strike, to the great detriment of our export trade, in a few days' time, would you ask us in those circumstances to do nothing at all?

Acknowledging that the Tories would 'seek to provide' both more competition and 'proper management of the economy', he continued:

But within that policy – whether you call it involvement or a voluntary policy seems to be playing with words – a wages policy has a part to play. Just as every country rejects a compulsory wages policy – and so will we – yet every country, in its own way, brings pressure – and again I quote our own document; 'In key wage negotiations a government may need to exert its influence on the side of lower costs.' You know that to be true. You know that to be the right and responsible attitude. It is the attitude taken by virtually every other Government in the world and you must not deny this weapon to us as well.

Macleod knew that it was politically untenable for the Tories to go into an election defending the possibility of a compulsory incomes policy. They had to oppose it. He was also extremely sceptical of the practicality of any formal incomes policy because of his experience of British trade unions. But he would never rule out the need for an incomes policy of some kind.[40]

Labour's Nemesis, 1969

Barbara Castle's elevation as First Secretary and her appointment to the Department of Employment and Productivity provided Macleod with a tempting political target, particularly since her new ministry was Macleod's old stamping ground. Macleod had warned the previous spring that Castle's actions would be directed against Jenkins's strategy, a view that by the autumn was voiced publicly by the Labour backbencher, Brian Walden. While the Chancellor was concerned that the Government's incomes policy was rigorously adhered to in order to ensure that devaluation would work, the First Secretary was enthusiastically promoting productivity deals that were widely seen as loopholes in official pay curbs. As the Shadow Cabinet learned in November, over the twelve months since devaluation, personal incomes had continued to run ahead of prices, having risen by 8 per cent against the 6 per cent increase in prices. Macleod's criticism that Castle did not know what she was doing prompted the comment that he was displaying a lack of chivalry. But as Macleod responded, the alternative view – that Castle realized what she was doing – was far worse. 'Either the Right Honourable Lady is inside the Trojan Horse and plotting the fall of the city from within the walls,' he argued:

Or she has no idea where Troy is, does not know what the horse is doing there and does not know why she has been locked up inside it. In all chivalry, I appeal to the House to take the kindly view.[41]

As a convert to the cause of trade union reform, Macleod extended his 'warm support' to Castle in her dramatic conversion in early 1969. Following the publication of her White Paper, *In Place of Strife*, in January, she and Wilson were finally persuaded in the spring, principally by the Chancellor, that legislation should be pushed through Parliament before the summer recess. In return, Jenkins was induced to relax the Government's prices and incomes policy. The announcement of the planned union legislation in the April 1969 budget was cheered by the Tories and, as Macleod happily acknowledged, 'by nobody more so than myself'. But though Macleod espoused union reform, he thought that it was unwise for the Opposition to commit themselves to detailed and legalistic proposals of the kind that they had published in their document, *Fair Deal at Work*. Macleod left Carr 'in no doubt that he was not wholly approving' of the activities of his former Parliamentary Secretary at the Ministry of Labour. Macleod would tell friends that his own experience at the ministry had taught him the import-ance of the politics of labour relations and the need, above all, to proceed on reform with the utmost caution.[42]

Labour's much-vaunted plans for union reform lasted less than six months, collapsing ignominiously in June 1969 when Wilson and Castle were forced to back down, defeated by a combination of the resistance of the unions, aided and abetted by Callaghan, and the desertion of almost the entire Cabinet. The 'solemn and binding' deal with the TUC that Wilson conjured from the wreckage was a poor fig leaf. Political disaster quickly turned to farce for the hapless Castle. Unofficial action by eleven women lavatory cleaners had brought an entire factory of Girling's, one of the key suppliers of components to the motor industry, to a standstill. Castle intervened, but her apparent triumph in resolving the dispute was short-lived. Macleod related the denouement with relish from the Opposition despatch box:

> It is fascinating how closely the goddess Nemesis observes and reverses almost any pronouncement by the Treasury and, indeed, all Socialist Ministers. It may be that she takes a particular enthusiasm in doing this to her own sex. It was a stone cold racing certainty that, after that triumphant declaration of the Right Honourable Lady the Secretary of State for Employment and Productivity, that the eleven 'loo' ladies were going back, that they would go back and the rest of the factory would come out. It is a very good epitaph to Socialism. One of the lavatories is working, but the factory has stopped.[43]

Warning of a Monetarist Experiment, 1969

The early summer of 1969 marked Labour's nadir. In May, the month before their final climbdown on union reform, a fresh sterling crisis seemed to confirm that the devaluation eighteen months earlier had not worked. Already, the failure of the Chancellor's deflationary measures during 1968–69 to damp down the domestic economy had led Jenkins to put greater emphasis on monetary policy, an approach favoured by Britain's creditors, the International Monetary Fund. In April, *The Times* had reported, 'IMF will be watching for control of money supply in Budget' and 'Chancellor on road to Chicago', in a reference to the university where Milton Friedman, the leading light of the new American monetarists, was based. At the committee stage of the 1969 Finance Bill, the Labour MP, Robert Sheldon, noted that many MPs were anxious that after the Chancellor's 'doubt and possibly even scepticism' towards monetary policy in early 1968, 'We then saw support for the theory of money supply – then enthusiasm, and now massive commitment.' In the light of subsequent events, notably after 1979 when the Thatcher Government pinned its economic strategy on monetarist theory, Sheldon's talk of 'massive commitment' now seems fantastic. Nonetheless, there was greater emphasis on monetary targets.[44]

The growing doubts about the efficacy of fiscal policy were recognized and shared, to some degree, by the Tory economic policy team. As early as 1966, Macleod and Heath had questioned the effectiveness, ever since Rab Butler's 1955 'pots and pans' budget, of 'small touches on the brake or accelerator'. They were therefore prepared to put 'somewhat more emphasis' on monetary policy, but they would also put greater emphasis than Labour on the control of public spending. There was a presumption that Labour's high spending, high tax policies had created a vicious cycle, so restricting the Chancellor's policy options that he had been forced to rely on monetary policy. Macleod believed that Tory policies would help to free economic policy from this vicious cycle, but he had no great expectation that fiscal policy would remain anything other than a blunt instrument of economic management.[45]

However, Macleod did not accept that governments were thereby absolved from tackling unemployment. His conviction was the exact opposite: inaction in the face of an unquestionable social evil was simply unthinkable. But he was aware in the autumn of 1968 that a general reflation would further undermine any beneficial impact from devaluation, and in November he therefore proposed 'selective regional reflation' in the worst-hit areas such as the North, where unemployment by the autumn of 1968 was 4.2 per cent and male unemployment was 6.2 per cent. He urged: 'the Chancellor to turn his mind to one or two possibilities of labour-intensive works, such as minor works, which are always valuable and have a swift effect in mopping up unemployment.' The following summer, when unemployment in the North had reached 4.7 per cent, the highest in June for over twenty years, Macleod castigated Jenkins for his 'somewhat complacent attitude'.[46]

By the summer of 1969, Macleod feared that the Chancellor was being led further down the monetarist route following the publication, in June, of the Government's new Letter of Intent with the IMF. He was in no doubt that 'the arguments which centre on the money supply' raised 'the most important economic debate and argument since the days of Lord Keynes in the thirties.' Macleod recalled that only ten years earlier, in 1959, the Radcliffe Report had concluded that 'Monetary measures can help, but that is all.' This had been the conventional wisdom, yet in 1969 he perceived 'an utter commitment to this same theory' of monetarism. Although he rejected the policy prescriptions of Labour's left-wing *Tribune* Group, Macleod admitted to sharing 'some of the anxiety' expressed by them and others 'about the unknown territory into which we are venturing'. Acknowledging that the use of the money supply could be expansionary as well as deflationary, he reiterated his conviction that 'there is no easy way out of our problems by the use of money supply doctrines'. Despite Macleod's rhetoric, Jenkins was not, and would never become, a monetarist in the sense of regarding the money supply as the crucial factor in the economy, and it is no more likely that Macleod would have done so. As he warned, 'There is some danger in putting the country's economy largely at the mercy of a thesis that is unproved in practice, however formidably supported in theory . . .'[47]

Of the other radical options which were voiced with added stridency as a result of the May 1969 sterling crisis Macleod was 'fiercely opposed', to import controls. As he pointed out, they were ruled out by the IMF – though like Maudling, he had supported import deposits as a means of improving the balance of trade. He regarded the argument about abandoning a fixed exchange rate and allowing sterling to 'float' on the foreign exchange markets as less clear cut. Jenkins has since disclosed that as Chancellor, he had come to the conclusion by the early summer of 1969 that letting sterling float might be unavoidable unless the trade figures quickly turned round. The idea was also discussed by Tory policy-makers during 1969 in a group on the balance of payments, with Sir Keith Joseph in the chair. Recalling his conversations with Macleod, Joseph found that 'Iain was open-minded about exchange rates'.[48]

In public, Macleod had to tread very warily. In June, he told the Commons that: 'the arguments for a fixed rate are much more attractive than those against apart from the fact that to float would be a unilateral abandonment of many of our undertakings.' But he signalled his open-mindedness when he eschewed further comment on the main issue at stake, explaining that it was: 'dangerous for anybody who has, or even may have, a major responsibility for the economy of the country *to close all the options all the time* [author's emphasis].' His comments on exchange rates suggest that Macleod would have been a pragmatic Chancellor. He appears to have been less inclined than many other politicians to treat the exchange rate as a totem of national virility, and he suggested that: 'The founding fathers of Bretton Woods' [the international economic and monetary system created at the end of the Second World War]:

Never meant us to be so dogmatic, almost as religious, as we have become about exchange rates, and that it would be vastly better if we were prepared to move gently at appropriate stages instead of waiting till forces overwhelmed us.[49]

The force of Macleod's interventionist conviction became apparent when he joined in debate on the exchange rate question with Enoch Powell at the Brighton conference in October 1969. Powell, following his sacking from the Shadow Cabinet eighteen months earlier over his 'River Tiber' speech, had openly preached free market economics and now took up the call to float sterling. Replying directly to Powell's speech, Macleod declared that he was 'not dogmatic on this issue' and recognized 'the force of some of the arguments'. However, he dismissed his former colleague's case, beginning with an echo of his damning comment in the *Spectator* that he was always careful to leave Powell's train before it crashed into the buffers: 'My total admiration for the clarity of Mr Powell's exposition will not, I fear, disguise from you my more or less total disagreement with his conclusions.' Powell had not only criticized Labour but had argued that sterling should have been floated before 1964. Macleod did not let slip this attack on previous Tory administrations: 'Enoch and I came into Parliament together. We were members of these administrations and we accepted their policies: and I am not prepared now to renounce them.'

But the debate had also gone to the root of Macleod's Toryism. There can be no doubting the force of his conviction that it was the duty of government to moderate market forces. Responding to 'the general point that everything has its price', Macleod declared:

> I am a keen believer in market forces, but I do not go as far as this. Indeed, I think basically over the years this is a Whig rather than a Tory doctrine. Everything has its price. Yes, but that would mean no regional policy. It would mean a disastrous failure for the regions, for the development areas, and for Scotland. It is an excellent policy for the strong, but we are concerned also with the weak.

In meeting the argument of a fellow founder of the 'One Nation' Group, Macleod had encapsulated his own vision of 'One Nation' Toryism.[50]

How the Tories proposed to control the cost of living immediately on their return to office, before their longer term policies could take effect, was still unresolved when the Shadow Cabinet gathered for their policy review over the weekend of Friday 30 January to Sunday 1 February at the Selsdon Park Hotel in South Croydon. A paper on the subject had been prepared by Sewill in the Conservative Research Department and was tenth on the agenda, but the discussion on earlier items overran and the issue was only addressed briefly on Sunday morning, when shadow ministers considered a draft manifesto.[51]

The party urgently needed a tougher stance. By the winter of 1969–70, pay inflation was again a serious problem as earnings accelerated in the wake of the relaxation of prices and incomes curbs and the collapse of the Government's alternative policy, their ill-judged initiative on union reform. But the mechanism by which demand management supposedly curbed pay awards was not working – as Maudling noted, the building industry was 'heavily squeezed', but was 'still handing out big pay rise[s]'. In his view, relying on demand management would mean the 'squeeze getting tighter and tighter'. In other words, unemployment would rise, but with little effect on pay. Implicit in Maudling's comments was the need for some form of incomes policy to avoid high inflation on the one hand, or, on the other, high unemployment, or both.

Macleod readily agreed with Maudling, noting that, 'None of the methods once thought to be certain cures', such as unemployment, any longer seemed to work. He also agreed with Heath, and thought that the party's economic policies were 'not politics' (i.e. their proposals were ill-suited to the party debate or an election campaign), and they would also 'take time' to work. In the meantime, Macleod argued, a future Tory government would have to 'rely on arm twisting and stand firm in the public sector'. Recalling his most notable triumph over the unions in a pay dispute in 1958, Macleod believed that the Tories would 'never again find an occasion such as the London bus strike, but there will be an[other] opportunity'.[52]

As the election drew near, Macleod told Gilmour that there would have to be an incomes policy of some sort. He was utterly realistic in his political calculation. He did not doubt that the Opposition had had to oppose the Government's imposition of statutory controls, but neither would he rule out an incomes policy *tout court* on doctrinal grounds. Quite how close his approach came to downright cynicism was to be demonstrated when the Shadow Cabinet finalized the manifesto. Macleod also felt that the Tories had become too non-interventionist generally, and in office they would have to return to policies closer to the postwar economic consensus. The Labour Government had also allowed themselves to be pulled away from the old consensus, firstly through their deflationary policies and latterly at the behest of the IMF. In Macleod's view, Labour had given the game away in the autumn of 1969:

What has happened which is of profound significance is that the commitment of the Labour party to full employment has disappeared. It is no accident that in the Queen's Speech the words are '. . . achieve a more rapid rate of economic growth' and 'safeguard employment'. The words 'full employment' disappeared in the Queen's Speech in 1967 – and it is not surprising.

Macleod was deeply concerned that during the early months of 1970, unemployment was, as Peter Jay wrote in *The Times*, 'unmistakably rising.

The true level is already at a postwar high.' Quoting Jay in the spring 1970 budget debate, Macleod asked, 'We have a strong currency, but at what a price?' He was deeply perturbed at the acceptance by a Labour Government of what was then an historically high level of unemployment, and flatly rejected the right-wing theory 'that higher levels of unemployment pay have taken the sting out of unemployment'.[53]

Macleod was committed to tackling the British economy's deep-seated problems principally by improving the working of the economy, or what economists call the 'supply side', while following a broadly Keynesian approach. As he told the Shadow Cabinet at their Selsdon weekend, 'The object of very major tax reform' of the sort that he was planning, 'would be to make a radical change to the economic climate, changing attitudes to efficiency, savings and productivity'. At the same time, he believed in the need to restore business confidence. In this regard, he was strongly Keynesian, believing in the role of demand management in creating the right conditions for industrial expansion and sustained economic growth. In June 1970, the *Economist* observed that:

> although the Tory drive to cut taxes is very far from being the crude electioneering the Prime Minister claims, it probably would be partly paid for by an attempt to push annual increases in production nearer to the assumed level of annual increases in productive capacity.

In other words, Macleod would have tried to run the economy with less slack, or spare capacity, thereby reducing the historically high level that unemployment had reached by the end of the 1960s. However: 'In a country with the present rate of inflation', as *The Economist* also noted, 'some conservative Conservatives, and not a few liberal economists, would be very wary of this.' However, Jenkins, while rebutting the suggestion that his fiscal rectitude in his last budget cost Labour the election, has since acknowledged that had he remained Chancellor he would have thought it right to do some 'loosening' in the autumn of 1970.[54]

Macleod continued to adhere to the postwar commitment to full employment. He could never countenance the idea that high unemployment was a price worth paying in the battle against inflation. He knew that unemployment offered no cure for Britain's underlying economic weaknesses. Not only would it result in a colossal waste of resources, Macleod saw that the fear of unemployment was not a curative, leading people to work harder, but perpetuated the restrictive practices that hobbled British industry. Above all, he never forgot that those individuals who would be called on to pay the price by sacrificing their own jobs would suffer a bitter, personal tragedy. The motivation for Macleod's Tory radicalism lay in his determination, as a 'One Nation' Tory, to ensure that the preventable social evil of unemployment was, in fact, prevented. As Gilmour recalls, unemployment, like Africa, was an issue that Macleod 'really did mind about . . . he loathed unemployment. I don't think it had occurred to him that unemployment could go as high as it did even in those days.'[55]

19

Preparing for Number Eleven

No party in Opposition has ever done so much as we under Mr Heath have done to prepare for Government. Let us be strictly fair. No government has ever done more to prepare for Opposition than Mr Wilson's present administration.

Iain Macleod, Conservative Conference, Brighton, 9 October 1969.

Tax Reformer

Macleod could justifiably claim that Tory policy work on taxation after 1964 was carried out 'in a more detailed way than has ever been done before by an Opposition, or indeed by a Government': He intended that the fruits of all this detailed work during almost five years as Shadow Chancellor would enable him to become a great, reforming Chancellor. But great reforms are not merely the product of painstaking preparation, important though it is in a field like taxation: they must also be borne of deeper purpose and urgent need. Macleod's political vision was a meritocratic and capital-owning democracy, that he would seek to realize through an extensive reform of Britain's flawed tax structure.[1]

The strength of Macleod's meritocratic ideal was clear from his leading articles during his editorship of the *Spectator*. Like Heath, he was convinced that only reforms based on such values would properly address the urgent need to modernize Britain. The new Tory leadership wanted to see new leadership in industry: managers who were appointed on merit, who were well-rewarded and could build up capital of their own instead of having to pay marginal tax rates higher than in other industrial democracies. However, these aims would bring Macleod into direct conflict with the vested interests of wealth and privilege, who looked to the Tory party to preserve their position.

By 1965, when he became Shadow Chancellor, the tax system was in serious need of overhaul. The standard rate of income tax was 8s 3d (41.25p) in the pound, with additional, punitive taxes on income from savings, so-called 'unearned' income, and on higher earnings. In addition to paying at the standard rate, people earning around £5,000 a year or more were liable for 'surtax', which was collected separately. Those on annual salaries of £15,000 or more were paying surtax at 10s (50p) in the pound, resulting in a tax rate on every extra pound earned of 18s 3d (91.25p) – average annual earnings in 1965 were £1,020 for manual workers and £1,330 for male white collar workers. The system was also archaic, for example having a range of 'earned income reliefs' intended to reduce the effective rate of income tax but which were too complex to be easily understood. And the system was no longer efficient, or 'buoyant', since it failed to yield additional revenue for the Exchequer commensurate with the growth in national income and wealth.

Within two months of his appointment, Macleod signalled his intentions in a fringe meeting at the 1965 Brighton Tory Conference, encapsulating his theme as 'The Pursuit of Excellence'. His starting point was the party's new policy document, *Putting Britain Right Ahead*. As he acknowledged, some people asked whether the party's new approach would be popular, but this was 'not the right question': the Tories had to ensure, through their arguments, and in their appeal to the country, that 'people can understand that the pursuit of excellence is something which the Tory party and this country simply must dedicate itself to'. For Macleod was convinced that:

> Unless we raise this flag again, with all that it means in rewarding excellence, with all its implications for a taxation policy which I fully recognize and accept, then the decline of this country is certain. It won't be dramatic, we are too wealthy for that, we are too strongly based for that. The danger is of a slow decline into the sort of genteel poverty behind lace curtains that so many of us know exists in the different constituencies from which we have come down to Brighton this week. So then we must reward excellence and we must not be afraid of proclaiming it.[2]

Immediate evidence of the risk that Macleod believed the party had to take came before the close of the 1965 conference, when the *Economist*, a paper generally sympathetic to radical Toryism, suggested that 'the poor bleeding heart of the surtax payer is paraded rather a lot. Still, this emphasis is healthier in an expanding economy than the opposite socialist emphasis on any vindictive egalitarianism.' 'Indeed it is,' Macleod retorted in the *Spectator* the following week. 'Surtax payers are people, most of them are pacesetters, many of them are excellent.' But if the Tories were to succeed in 'the pursuit of excellence,' they had to deepen and widen their appeal to people's hearts, not only to their heads. Macleod's answer was to offer people at all levels the opportunity to save from their earnings, building, in

Sir Anthony Eden's phrase, a 'capital owning democracy' in which they had a stake in the success of industry.[3]

Macleod's plans on tax had two objectives: first, to reduce tax on people's earnings; and secondly to simplify the tax system. Just two months after succeeding Heath as Shadow Chancellor, Macleod made clear his priority. 'There are three schools amongst politicians and economists about the level of taxation,' he told the Tory conference at Brighton in October 1965:

> The first holds that the taxpayer is a milch cow of unlimited capacity. I am not of that company. The second school holds that the levels of taxation are onerous but not disastrous. I am not of that company. The third school says that there is a limit, and that we are already beyond it, to the percentage that one can take of the gross national product in public expenditure and to the burden that one can put on personal taxation without a dramatic drop in efficiency and enterprise, and there I take my stand.

Macleod's reference to the burden of *personal* taxation held the key to his reform. As Macleod explained to the Tory party faithful at their 1967 Brighton conference: 'We are not, in fact, in total, the most heavily taxed country in the world, or anything like it. But it is true that we have the heaviest burden of personal direct taxation, and it is also true that we rely too heavily on a few selected items ...' Heath and Macleod recognized that significant reductions in the total amount of taxation could only be achieved at the expense of substantial and politically unacceptable cuts in government spending and cutting back the welfare state as it had developed since the late 1940s. Enoch Powell's claim, made in October 1968, that income tax could be slashed to 4s 3d (21.5p) in the pound with no reduction in the social services was not regarded as realistic.[4]

Macleod worked closely on the detail of his reforms with the Tories' main backroom expert on tax reform, Arthur (later Lord) Cockfield, chairman of Boots until 1967, who had served in the Inland Revenue during the 1940s and, after his departure to private industry, had become a longstanding, unofficial adviser to the Tory party. Cockfield had been given his remit in 1965 to design a theoretically perfect tax system, on the understanding that the politicians would then decide to what extent it was politically feasible. The work proceeded by drawing up different options for reform in 'packages' which were costed and assessed for their political implications. Labour's frequent tax increases, particularly during 1968 and 1969, meant that the process had to be continually revised up to the next election. As a result, although Macleod had not known Cockfield all that well, he became a frequent visitor to the Cockfields' Mayfair home, where much of their work was done. Cockfield found Macleod easy to work with, because he was a man of strong intellectual power and clear and incisive judgement. Although Macleod trusted Cockfield on the nuts and bolts of taxation, Terence Higgins, another member of the policy team, recalls, that Macleod did his homework on the details, understood the minutiae and would weigh in where he saw that they were important.[5]

The thrust of early policy work focused on the highly meritocratic objective of shifting tax benefits from 'owners to earners'. When Macleod became Shadow Chancellor, the policy team that had been set up to redraw the tax system was already considering a radical plan for a dramatic reduction of the top rates of income tax, funded by the introduction of a wealth tax. This proposal was outlined by Cockfield at a private Swinton weekend discussion in the autumn of 1965. According to its advocates on the sub-committee, who included Nigel Lawson, then editor of the *Spectator*, 'if we are really to reduce the top rate of surtax and abolish the discrimination against investment income a wealth tax is in practical political terms the only way we have any hope of doing it'. On this argument, large salaries and more favourable tax treatment for the captains of industry could be justified on the lines that it was part of the new meritocratic ethos of the party to reward work rather than inheritance.[6]

Heath was intrigued by the idea, but Macleod saw that whatever its attractions, it was political dynamite for the party. A wealth tax would risk dividing the party between earners and owners as deeply as the repeal of the Corn Laws by Sir Robert Peel in 1846 had split the party between land owners and trading interests, a disaster that was etched deep on the party's soul as it had denied the Tories office for virtually the whole of the following twenty years. The policy sub-committee were divided and in December 1965, the wealth tax idea was referred up to the main group on future economic policy. Macleod, as the then chairman, endeavoured to find agreement between the two opposing camps. But his efforts were in vain. The majority backed the idea, but a minority were fiercely opposed and could not be persuaded to change their mind. There was no mention of a wealth tax in the 1966 manifesto.[7]

When the newly constituted economic policy group began meeting in late 1966 under Heath's chairmanship, the possibility of proposing a wealth tax was discussed regularly. But the discussions were inconclusive, and when it was mentioned in May 1967, 'Mr Macleod said he thought he himself might be persuaded of its desirability but he was not sure at the moment how far the party as a whole would be prepared to accept it.' In short, nothing would shake his conviction that such a proposal threatened to tear the Tories apart. But a decision had to be made if the Tories were ever to complete their detailed work on tax reform. Cockfield finally forced the issue when he confronted Heath and Macleod and told them that he was not prepared to spend any more time working on a wealth tax unless they were prepared to carry it through. He suspected that they were not. After some hesitation,

Macleod confirmed Cockfield's suspicion, and Heath then also accepted that the reform was a non-runner.[8]

In June 1968, when a revised package of tax reforms was being discussed, several members of the earlier economic policy group pointed out that there was no place for the annual capital, or wealth, tax that had been part of the original plan. According to the official minute:

> Mr Heath said that his considered conclusion, after discussing the matter with Mr Maudling and Mr Macleod, was that the introduction of a wealth tax could not form part of Conservative policy. There were several reasons for this but the simplest and overwhelming reason was that such a policy would be unacceptable to the Conservative Party.

The decision provoked criticism from members of the earlier policy group. In reply, Macleod:

> Had to admit that he had changed his mind. Originally, he had been much attracted by the idea and still felt that ideally, from the point of view of tax simplification, there was much to be said for it; but he had changed his view as to what the impact of such a proposal would be. He thought that the important things on which the Conservative Party ought to be concentrating its attention were earning, owning, saving and learning. A proposal to introduce a wealth tax would distract from these objectives and raise a lot of red herrings about the relative merits of different forms of capital, pictures, land, industrial shares, etc . . .[9]

But the advocates of a wealth tax would not let the matter drop. At their final discussion in July, Sir Keith Joseph still hankered after a wealth tax, since the original plan gave the party a morally defensible package. Although Sir Edward Boyle agreed, he thought that Macleod was probably right on the politics, but he too would favour an investment surcharge as well as other revisions on business taxation. In reply, Macleod reiterated that he was convinced that an annual wealth tax was not politically practicable: 'It was not only the case that there would be very strong opposition to it in the parliamentary party, but everyone he had talked to in the party felt very strongly on the issue of a wealth tax.'[10]

Although Macleod's political judgement was right about the wealth tax, its abandonment signalled a serious defeat for his hopes of truly radical reform since it now became more difficult for him to achieve both a political and an economic balance in his tax package. The rich would be better off than he had intended, and there would be less revenue to redistribute to the less well off than he had hoped. Indeed, at a meeting of the key Steering Committee on policy in April 1968, Macleod had already voiced his worry:

About the problem of redistributing the burden of taxation from the extremes to the middle. If one was going to improve the lot of the poor and reduce taxation on the rich, there must be a group in the middle who were going to be worse off.

As a result, Macleod became more keen, 'to find something to encourage the middle income groups, perhaps linked with home ownership, like the abolition of schedule A and to which we could point.'[11]

Macleod's radicalism was a prisoner of his party's conservatism, but his purpose in reducing personal taxation remained constant. Macleod and his advisers always planned in terms of carefully costed, alternative tax packages, consisting of different options that he could present to the main economic policy group and, as the election approached, to the Steering Committee and the Shadow Cabinet. During 1967, Macleod and his team settled on the main elements of their initial, preferred package. As Macleod later explained to the Shadow Cabinet, the complex system of 'earned income relief':

Had grown enormously in recent years and was now a very substantial disincentive to savings. In speeches he had not gone further than to say that we would restore savings income to its rightful place, but in fact he thought the right course was to abolish the difference between earned and investment income and treat all income in exactly the same way. As soon as this was done, a whole number of possibilities emerged.[12]

Macleod's initial tax package proposed: a single tax on all forms of income, abolishing the differential rates of tax on earnings and income from savings ('unearned' income); income tax to be cut by 1s (5p) to 7s 3d (36.5 p) in the pound; surtax reduced so that nobody paid more than 10s (50p) in the pound tax on their total income, as opposed to a maximum tax of 18s 3d (91.25p) in the pound; reduced levels of corporation tax; and the abolition of Labour's SET, partly financed by a five per cent payroll tax. Macleod also planned to spend £500 million on welfare benefits to protect the position of the poor from the effects of his reforms, principally as a result of the increase in prices following the switch to indirect taxation. The cost of his tax reforms was estimated in 1969 at £1,020 million. Income tax would be cut by £1,240 million, with further reductions of £100 million in estate duty and gifts tax and another £380 million in corporation tax.[13]

Despite his detailed planning, Macleod generally resisted the repeated demands on him to commit himself publicly to specific proposals. However, he was prepared to make a 'special case' on the taxation of married women when the joint income of a married couple reached the surtax level. But one other specific pledge – the outright abolition of SET – made Macleod's calculations much more difficult. This tax, announced by Callaghan in his May 1966 budget, had many faults, but it had broadened the tax base, raising £300 million in 1966–67 and over twice as much by 1970–71. Perhaps nothing could have been done to dissipate the head of steam against SET among the Tory faithful, but Macleod had called for its abolition as enthusiastically as anybody. 'We have no proposals to reform the SET,' Macleod declared at the Brighton Tory conference in the 1967. 'We have no proposals to amend the SET. We will abolish the SET.' Indeed, by the following spring, the Tories' private opinion poll research revealed that 'our policies had not yet got across at all, beyond the fact that we would abolish SET.' Scrapping SET was difficult enough in itself, but it was made even more awkward because the abandonment of the wealth tax proposal meant that Macleod also needed to look to indirect taxation to fund his proposed cuts in income tax. Secondly, the most obvious replacement of SET, a payroll tax, would not levy nearly as much from employers as SET, and so the Tories would have to increase another tax or introduce some new alternative. Macleod's preferred option was the tax on value added (TVA), (or value added tax, VAT). But this was already seen as a possible replacement for purchase tax, which by 1969 yielded £1,075 million. Macleod's task came to resemble the labours of Sisyphus, particularly after the 1967 devaluation, as the Wilson administration introduced one increase after another in indirect taxation. Initially, Callaghan had raised direct taxes on individuals and companies, increasing income tax and introducing capital gains and corporation taxes, and had introduced SET in 1966. Jenkins levied an additional £923 million in his first budget, the biggest single tax rise in peace or war, principally by raising duties and purchase tax. This huge hike in indirect taxes was followed by an additional impost of £250 million in the autumn of 1968 and a further £340 million the next spring. These increases raised serious doubts as to whether indirect taxation could be increased much more.[14]

The genesis of VAT lay in Heath's determination that Britain should enter the European Economic Community. The Common Market countries were already adopting VAT and by the late 1960s it was enshrined in EEC directives. This tax also had some distinct advantages: it covered some items that escaped both SET and purchase tax; it was less likely than SET to be wholly passed on in prices; and it was imposed on imports and rebated or exempted on exports, whereas SET could not be remitted on exports. But if VAT was levied on food, it would hit the poorer harder than the combination of purchase tax and SET – Macleod therefore opted for excluding food. Although it would still be regressive, compared with purchase tax and SET for poor people living alone, it would not be so for poor people living in large families. Some increases in benefits for old people might be needed, but crucially for Macleod, VAT would not undermine any attempt to tackle child poverty.[15]

Macleod took the opportunity of his October 1967 party conference speech at Blackpool to spell out his thinking on indirect taxation more fully. He was still making rash promises on SET, claiming unrealistically that it would 'be abolished as soon as we get into power'. But he also invited the party 'to consider the consequences':

> If we are to have a charge on spending – and I am convinced that that is right – we shall not need purchase tax as well. But the selective employment tax brings in £500 million and purchase tax brings in £900 million, and whatever assumptions you make about growth, savings and public expenditure it would be unrealistic, if we decide that purchase tax is to go, not to consider a replacement.

VAT had been identified as a possible replacement, but presentationally, it was a nightmare. Macleod would confess to Shadow Cabinet the difficulties he found at the annual conference in 'making a serious speech about VAT when he had also to provide some fun and a peroration'. But there was theatricality in his telling the party conference that:

> We have examined 48 different tax packages. We have looked at four different income tax systems and a number of different company tax systems. For each of these different packages we have estimated their effects on the income and expenditure of 28 different representative households, ranging from the single female pensioner to the married couple with the wife earning and a joint income of £4,000 a year. We have looked at each family's expenditure broken down into 22 different headings – coal, meat, dairy products, consumer durables and the rest. We have looked at all the main types of their income. We have processed the whole thing on a computer, using a model of the economy, an input and output model being part of it, in a way that no Chancellor of the Exchequer has ever attempted before. No decisions have ever been supported by such detailed and sophisticated analysis. In all, we are at present analysing no fewer than 50,000 separate results. That gives you some indication of the work which has been going on, the first fruits of which are now beginning to appear and to be presented to this conference.

Cockfield, Macleod's chief adviser on tax reform, could not imagine that anyone else could announce he was going to introduce VAT and receive loud cheers.[16]

Hopes of holding down the rate at which VAT was to be introduced were dealt a blow when Macleod's proposal for a payroll, or employment, tax that was designed to raise £1,755 million (almost as much as VAT) had to be dropped in the face of fierce protests from businessmen and party activists.

He had privately counselled the Steering Committee eighteen months earlier that VAT was 'the crux' of his tax reform, although he had not foreseen quite the extent to which he would come to depend on it. The Tories commissioned Professor Wheatcroft of the London School of Economics, the country's leading authority on VAT, to prepare a draft VAT system for Britain. Even so, considerable preparation in government would be required before the new tax could be launched.[17]

Principal among the further tax changes introduced in the later Labour Government budgets were the aggregation of children's investment income for tax purposes, which disrupted many divorce settlements and the disallowance of loan interest for tax purposes. During policy discussions on the taxation of interest, Macleod rejected the suggestion that interest should be allowed only against income from assets that arose from the loan, and found ready support in Shadow Cabinet for the politically appealing option of allowing loan interest against tax for all family, business and professional purposes. The effect of this commitment, given in the Commons in July 1969, was to renew the subsidy on borrowing for virtually all forms of consumer spending, and ran counter to his emphasis on personal saving as integral to his tax reforms. Nonetheless, encouraging personal saving remained a central aim and Macleod expected that his tax cuts and reforms would, in themselves, lead to an increase in personal saving.[18]

In order to bolster his objective of increased saving, Macleod suggested in discussions on the 1968 draft policy document going further than was proposed and including the idea of a capital-owning democracy. *Make Life Better*, published that autumn, included his plan for a 'voluntary Save-As-You-Earn scheme' (SAYE). He had suggested SAYE before the budget earlier that year, but the scheme captured October's headlines – *The Times* reporting that it was 'particularly designed to attract savings from wage earners who save very little now'. Under the plan, an employee would undertake, through his employer, to save a regular amount weekly for a minimum period – probably three years – and this would be ignored as income for PAYE purposes. Macleod's advisers reckoned that the benefit through reduced taxation, if the employee was on a low rate of tax, could be the equivalent of of an annual rate of interest as high as 14 per cent. This high incentive would require that the scheme be limited to low and medium wage earners.[19]

Although Jenkins included a version of SAYE in his 1969 budget, the Labour Chancellor's scheme was more limited than the Tories had envisaged. Macleod welcomed its introduction, but argued that its scope needed to be extended. One of its weaknesses, in Macleod's view, was the lack of any direct link with equities. He had studied the work of the Wider Share Ownership Council, and in response to the April 1970 budget, proposed that 'the SAYE scheme will be given a considerable boost if [such] an equity element could be introduced'. It was a practical suggestion for advancing the vision of a 'capital-owning democracy'.[20]

The Need for Economies

As the election approached, Macleod became increasingly concerned at the outlook for government spending and came to assume the mantle of an Iron Chancellor, or Iron Shadow Chancellor. Economies were urged by the Tories for several reasons: to restore what they believed as a better balance between the private and public sector and to reduce the total amount of taxation. But Macleod's pressing need was to make room to finance his reform of the tax system.[21]

During policy discussions Macleod would point to a number of expected benefits from his proposed package, but none of them overcame his immediate problem in financing it. Faster economic growth would make his task easier by boosting revenues and reducing spending, but he could not depend on this, particularly in the crucial, first two or three years. Tory backroom advice also suggested that the 'buoyancy' of the reformed tax system was such that in ten years' time it might well yield more revenue than the existing system, but again this did not help in the short or even medium term. Macleod also expected that a switch from consumption to savings would help make room for his tax cuts, but he was more wary in this respect than some of his advisers.[22]

Macleod's task was made all the more difficult by the Chancellor's hefty hike in indirect taxes during 1968 and 1969. These huge increases threatened seriously to restrict Macleod's scope for switching from income tax to taxes on spending. If Macleod relied too heavily on indirect taxation, he would push up prices even more steeply. Jenkins's increases had also raised serious doubts about how much more they could be increased before they became prohibitive. And for the Tories, the alternative of raising additional revenue through extra taxes on capital, property or business would present insurmountable political problems.

Neither were there any obvious new sources of revenue. Although North Sea gas had been landed for the first time in 1967, the great windfall of additional revenue that came with North Sea oil and helped finance tax cuts in the 1980s was still a long way in the future (the first landing of oil did not occur until 1975). Likewise, another great money-spinner for the Exchequer during the 1980s, the large-scale sale of public assets, was not even a gleam in the eye during the late 1960s. Although wholesale denationalization was recommended in a draft report of the policy group on nationalized industries, chaired by Nicholas Ridley, the idea was rejected. Heath believed that ownership was largely an irrelevance to making industry efficient, and was backed by the then Shadow Minister of Power, Margaret Thatcher. Macleod thought that it was 'politically important to denationalize something'. The most obvious candidate was steel, but it was doubtful if buyers could be found immediately. Indeed, so great were the losses being made by the large nationalized industries that it was unlikely that buyers could have been found for any large-scale sale. There was no prospect here of tapping a lucrative source of extra revenue for the Exchequer.[23]

Macleod therefore sought continually to dampen expectations of higher spending. 'There are many ideas, good Tory ideas too, that have not yet found a place in our manifesto,' he warned the Tories at Blackpool in 1968. And, with a neat reference to Labour's introduction of a two-tier system of postal charges, he added, 'they must wait, because we do not intend to promise the people of this country the new Jerusalem by return of post, either first or second class'. A year later, at Brighton, Macleod reiterated that: 'even in a shadow capacity I have often had to say "No" to attractive schemes that were worth their weight in votes. But this is the right course in honour and I think of prudence too.' And, he might have added, it was one of sheer necessity. By the spring of 1969, it was estimated privately that cuts of over £1,000 million in government spending would be required to finance in full Macleod's proposed cuts in income tax and tax reform.[24]

Macleod did not shirk the task of cutting government spending, but the Tory leadership of the 1960s recognized that there was a limit to the extent to which public spending could be cut without lowering the standards of the education, health, and other services. Tory leaders were also aware that there was a limit to the extent to which public sector investment could be cut without a detrimental effect on economic growth. Moreover, Macleod made no pretence that the usual recourse of Opposition politicians seeking economies – eliminating waste in Whitehall – would yield much. As he told MPs, 'There is waste, yes, but it is relatively small. Naturally one concentrates on it to some extent in speeches . . . [But] I have always acknowledged that if we want to make savings, we must make policy changes.'[25]

Macleod's proposed economies were mainly based on the principle of switching from indiscriminate state subsidies and benefits to more selective targeting. 'We must create a climate in which there are fewer subsidies, coupled with lower rates of taxation – this is our aim,' he told the Tories at Blackpool in 1968. At the previous election, the Tories had proposed the reduction of agricultural and housing subsidies. By 1969, it was reckoned that cuts in agriculture and housing would yield £200 million and £100 million respectively, while cutting the regional employment premium would save a further £100 million. A raft of further, comparatively minor economies would yield a further £380 million, including savings and greater efficiency in administration, and what Macleod called the 'paraphernalia of Socialism' – although other items would cause far greater controversy, notably abolishing or cutting minor subsidies (e.g. bus subsidies, school meals and milk); charging for services (e.g. road tolls, museum charges); and reducing spending on goods and services (e.g. royal ordnance factories, universities).[26]

However, on defence the Tories' pledge to reverse Labour's policy of withdrawing British forces from East of Suez would add to spending. Although they claimed that it would cost less than Labour's estimate of £300 million per year, their projected cost of £100 million seemed highly optimistic. Macleod's comment to colleagues fully two years after the initial policy decision that 'no price tag had as yet been applied' to their 'East of Suez policy', and the concern that both he and Maudling continued to express about the cost of maintaining an aircraft carrier East of Suez, suggests that the Tory estimate was probably an underestimate.[27]

Moreover, the costly bulwarks of the welfare state not only emerged unscathed from the Tory policy review, but in some cases had their budgets enhanced. The Shadow Cabinet's agreement to scrap the eleven-plus examination and to raise the school leaving age to sixteen (postponed by Labour as part of their post-devaluation economies), along with other reforms necessitated a further increase in the education budget. In early 1970, Macleod made it clear in the Commons that he had 'always regarded' education 'as a programme which can and must rise more than the average'. Remembering his comment in a speech, ten years earlier, 'that the two blocks of expenditure growing most swiftly in the Tory years were education and overseas aid', he added that, 'They seem to me to be fairly sound priorities', although overseas aid had since suffered 'in a frostier climate'.[28]

The National Health Service would be one of the biggest problems that faced a Tory government – the public were generally satisfied with the NHS but they did not appreciate the enormous expenditure that would be needed to maintain existing standards. Although Macleod agreed that the NHS faced huge problems, he 'came down flatly in favour of continuing broadly with present system'. The logic of the party's position was inescapable: they could not spend more on defence, education, housing (notwithstanding cuts in housing subsidies put at £280 million), and health all at the same time. As an ex-Minister of Health, Macleod 'reluctantly' believed that the percentage of the national output spent on the NHS should be maintained, but not increased. He accepted that this would mean some deterioration in standards, but when it was suggested that fewer doctors and nurses would be employed, Macleod retorted that the problem would be even worse if the country went broke. Before the 1967 Budget, he had suggested setting up a National Lottery to fund the hospital buildings programme, but he did not pursue the idea as a matter of priority. Indeed, he later vigorously opposed Labour's plan for a state lottery, to Jenkins's understandable astonishment.[29]

Targeting Help on Child Poverty

'I have two chief aims,' Macleod declared in April 1967, 'First – to reduce direct taxation. Second – to help poverty in the family.' As part of his general approach of targeting social security benefits more selectively on those in need, he planned to focus on poverty in the family. In a speech made after *Cathy Come Home*, the powerful BBC TV play in 1966 that highlighted the plight of a homeless mother with young children, he argued:

> If you help everybody you help nobody. And the reason we can't help the Cathys of this world is because we're also trying to cope with the problems of the Mary and Jane and Sarah and Tom and Dick and Harry as well. You cannot identify need if the help given be indiscriminate.

Macleod believed that the mood in the party had shifted decisively in his direction.[30]

However, Macleod's aim 'to tackle family poverty especially in large families on a selective basis,' raised a controversial issue – the relationship between the tax and benefits system, and in particular the future of the family income. Tackling child poverty by increasing the family allowance posed a dilemma, because it was a universal benefit and any increase would also be paid to the better-off, the very group who stood to gain most from Macleod's income tax cuts.[31]

Macleod was attracted to a radical proposal being studied by the party's public sector research unit, to cut through the separation between the tax and benefits systems by introducing a single, unified system of 'tax credits', or negative income tax. Such a proposal would eliminate the costly process of collecting taxes and then making separate welfare payments by combining the exercise in a single operation, performed by the Inland Revenue. It could also help overcome the poverty trap, whereby people receiving benefits were discouraged from trying to earn more for themselves, since they were immediately disqualified from various benefits or found themselves liable to tax. Macleod was particularly interested in the plan devised by Barney Hayhoe, in his 1968 CPC pamphlet, *Must the Children Suffer?* Hayhoe proposed a system of negative income tax that would target help on the estimated 250,000 children living in families where parental income was below the level required to qualify for supplementary benefit. By virtually removing family allowances from those over income tax level, there would be a saving of more than £200 million (i.e. after the 1968 budget), and probably another £10 million in administration. But other members of the Steering Committee were concerned at the impact on middle income groups. Macleod saw the point, but suggested that the practical solution was to carry out a complex package exercise, like Butler's in 1952, when so many changes were made that no one could tell exactly whether they were better or worse off. 'The bigger and more complex the exercise the better.' But by the autumn of 1968 Macleod had come to the conclusion that it would be impractical to carry through reform of both the tax and social security system at the same time. Instead, a Conservative Government should concentrate first on their major tax reforms and deal with poverty through the existing system, particularly national assistance. They had, after all, allocated £500 million in government spending to protect the poor from the effects of their initial tax package.[32]

The Tories set up a small study group, chaired by Terence Higgins, one of Macleod's frontbench team, to consider negative income tax. But, as Macleod would observe in the spring of 1970, although everybody seemed to assume that negative income tax was a 'splendid idea', it was proving virtually impossible to devise a workable scheme. Nonetheless, Macleod argued that the absence of 'any relief directly aimed at child poverty' was the 'main omission' from Jenkins's April 1970 budget. In his alternative budget, based on the assumption that, like Jenkins, he also had £170 million to allocate in tax cuts or increased spending, he proposed increasing the family allowance by 10s (50p) with a claw-back recouping the increase from better-off taxpayers, giving a net cost of £30 million. Another £55 million would have enabled him to raise tax allowances, and a further £90 million would have financed 3d cut in the standard rate of income tax, reducing it to 8s (40p).[33]

Macleod's espousal of selectivity, particularly with regard to the family allowance, has since been cited in support of their case by Conservatives, who in the 1980s and 1990s objected to the universality of Child Benefit on the grounds that it is paid to the carer (nearly always the mother) irrespective of his or her income. However, as Gilmour has argued, Child Benefit ought, more accurately, to be renamed 'Child Credit', because when it was introduced in the late 1970s, it was an amalgamation of the family allowance and income tax allowances for children. In this sense, Child Benefit therefore approximates to the integration of tax and benefit sought by Macleod. Moreover he based all his thinking on reform of the welfare state on the assumption of continued full employment.[34]

A Radical Shock for the Shadow Cabinet

As Shadow Chancellor, Macleod had presided, in the words of the *Economist*, over 'a real degree of sophistication in the backroom preparation of Conservative tax projects'. Macleod outlined his tax reforms to the full Shadow Cabinet for the first time at the Selsdon Park Hotel on the morning of Saturday 31 January 1970. The lynch-pin remained the abolition of the distinction between earned and investment income and treating all income the same way. As he told the Shadow Cabinet, removing this distinction:

Opened the way to simplification; it got rid of the psychological disadvantage of a standard rate that was what many people thought that they paid but was in fact greater than what most people in fact paid; it would enable the distinction between income tax and surtax to be abolished; and it would enable one to envisage a smooth progression upwards to whatever final point might be chosen – say, between 14s 0d (70p) and 16s 0d (80p) in the pound. It also enabled one to envisage progress towards self-assessment, which had been adopted in both the United States and Australia, and which enormously reduced the cost of collection.

Macleod's intention was to increase the personal allowance, thereby helping the less well off, so that everybody would pay income tax on a sliding scale that might be 30 per cent on all incomes below about £5,000, before rising to the new 75 per cent top rate.[35]

His package 'would be both enormously expensive and enormously valuable'. Its estimated cost was £1,250 million – 'something between a quarter and a third of the total revenue'. Against this, 'One would expect to have a better growth record from which revenue would benefit through the buoyancy of the tax, and one could expect a better savings record which would reduce the need for taxation'. Even so, such a massive reduction in personal taxation would have to be funded largely by a switch to indirect taxes. However, as Macleod pointed out, the party were also committed to repeal SET and were considering the abolition of purchase tax. Although there was no final commitment to replacing these indirect taxes with some form of VAT, Professor Wheatcroft's study on adopting such a system was almost complete. Macleod had indicated at the Brighton conference the previous October that if VAT was introduced, exemptions would include food and farming inputs, small businesses, broadcasting media, housing and life assurance, and charities. In his presentation to the Shadow Cabinet, he estimated, 'a total target yield for VAT of £2,200 million', and disclosed that although there would probably have to be a number of different rates of VAT, his calculations were based on an overall figure of 15 per cent. He contemplated 'a special low rate for the public services' and thought it might 'be possible to exempt them'.[36]

It was the differing impact of Macleod's proposals on the ordinary voter as against the rich that concerned some of his Shadow Cabinet colleagues and put him in the unusual position of being outflanked on the left. Joseph was concerned that the Shadow Chancellor's figures 'suggested that for the bulk of the population the benefit would be marginal, but the benefit to the large investment incomes would be enormous by comparison'. It was a conclusion that led Joseph to revive the argument for a wealth tax but Whitelaw countered that any idea that the parliamentary party would accept a wealth tax was 'absolute moonshine'. Walker tried to assess the implications for 'the target voter,' and reckoned that higher indirect taxes and the reduction in farm subsidies would add about 30s (£1.50p) to the average housewife's weekly shopping bill. As a result, Walker warned, he 'could see a considerable attack on the lines that a Conservative government would increase the weekly shopping bill and use most of the money to reduce taxation on investment income'. Macleod did not believe that the attack could possibly be as detailed as Walker had suggested unless the party spelled out, quite unnecessarily, all the details of its calculations. Meanwhile, he claimed, 'the party was getting the best of both worlds. The idea had got abroad that the party had an exciting tax policy, but there was some recognition that it could not responsibly give details.'[37]

Although he acknowledged his colleagues' concerns, Macleod was emphatic that the tough decisions could not be shirked: 'If we are going to do anything as dramatic as this, taking one quarter out of the money raised out of income tax, there is a price to pay elsewhere.' He thought that in response 'one could build up something of a counter-argument if one could really get across belief [sic] in saving out of taxed income and the belief that a young man ought to be able to build up some capital for his children'.[38]

Macleod appreciated that his reforms would stand or fall on the figures. During the break for lunch, he checked on the detailed effects of his tax package. Armed with these figures, he began the Saturday afternoon session by assuring the Shadow Cabinet that a reduction of 1s 0d in the standard rate of income tax under the existing tax system would give a man on £2,000 a year (then above national average earnings) relief of £59 on earned income and £81 on investment income; but under his proposed tax package, the relief would be £108 on earned income and £291 on investment income. And he challenged those who feared the political risks by recalling that:

> In 1968 Jenkins in his budget shifted £1,000 million on to indirect taxation with no compensating reliefs at all. Yet this shift had attracted remarkably little political odium, and in his [Macleod's] proposals there were countervailing arguments that public expenditure and direct taxation would be reduced.[39]

Yet whereas all taxpayers would pay less from their income, dividend drawers would pay very much less as a result of ending the distinction between 'earned' and 'unearned income'. Macleod's pruning of state support for industrial investment by £350 million was partly designed to meet this point. As the *Economist* revealed, his advisers argued that it was only reasonable to finance part of the cuts in personal taxes by ending investment grants and other state subsidies to firms from which investors drew their dividends. Tory tax cuts on unearned income would improve the prospects of profitable firms being able to raise funds in a revived private capital market.[40]

Macleod's precise schedule for introducing his reforms would depend on the date of the next election, but in January 1970 he told the Shadow Cabinet that if it was held in October later that year – as he expected – almost everything that he had outlined on personal taxation, with the consequent switch to indirect taxation and economies in public spending, could be included in a budget in the spring of 1971. This extraordinarily demanding timetable was testimony to his confidence in his preliminary work and to his ruthless determination to achieve radical change.[41]

Macleod always placed great emphasis on the detailed work that underpinned his tax package. 'I have never forgotten how SET – that Hungarian goulash – was served up in the last few minutes of a Budget speech,' he told the Tories in 1969, delighting the conference with his passing swipe at its architect, Professor Kaldor. 'If it had been properly thought out and exposed to public debate even for a short time, it would never have survived. Our plans are carefully thought out and we shall invite full comment on them.' But Macleod's notion of consultation was limited, to say the least. When he first announced the Tory plan to adopt VAT, he had declared that the Tories were 'more than ready to listen to advice from all quarters'. Yet Cockfield reckons that he and Macleod received in all only about thirty representations on the new tax before the 1970 election. After they had seen the last of them in his suite at the Grosvenor House Hotel, Macleod closed his folder and commented: 'I have finished my consultations, Arthur.' Cockfield was in no doubt that Macleod meant it. In the event, Anthony Barber, Macleod's successor as Chancellor, received around 1,800 representations before he finally introduced VAT.[42]

But Macleod's radicalism involved high political risks and had alarmed his Shadow Cabinet colleagues at Selsdon. Their fears resurfaced during their general summing up at the end of their policy weekend. Douglas-Home thought that the proposed tax package involved a considerable gamble. Dear food policies had historically been disastrous for the Conservative Party. But he was more concerned at the danger of the tax reforms being represented as feathering the nests of the richest while letting the poor stay where they were. Rather than hold to Macleod's suggested ceiling of a 15s (75p) tax rate, he wondered whether it would be possible to say that those with very large incomes – say £50,000 and above – should perhaps pay up to 19s 0d (95p) in the pound. Such a measure would mitigate the effects of redistribution and help in the presentation of the reforms. Douglas-Home's apprehension rekindled the doubts felt by others, including Barber, Carr and Walker. 'What really worries me,' confessed Barber, 'is that we are doing what has never been done before on this scale.'[43]

Macleod's determination, even obduracy, in his radicalism was clear from his response in the closing minutes of the Selsdon gathering. He was emphatic that the only way that a country could develop its full potential was 'by vastly increasing its trade and production, and that inevitably means dependence on the dynamos within society'. He thought that the policies possessed 'great excitement', which could be mentioned without running into the dangers that had been expressed. In principle, a switch from direct to indirect taxation was popular, as was reducing direct taxation.[44]

On presentation, Macleod was utterly calculating and clear-headed in how much detail, particularly on politically sensitive aspects, should be revealed. All the points that had been raised clearly pointed to publishing only the absolute minimum of detail, and certainly none of the detail talked about at Selsdon. Wilson and Jenkins had already tried to get an attack off the ground on Tory policies on three or four occasions, but the press had not taken it up because they had not had 'enough to bite on'. So long as the manifesto was 'honest about our proposals', he did not share the worry that the Tories would find themselves drawn into a damaging debate on the details. Undoubtedly, Wilson would attack on this front, 'but he had few footholds and provided we gave him none, we could both hold the excitement and give an honourable presentation of what we would do'.[45]

Macleod's room for manoeuvre had been limited ever since he accepted the political impracticality of shifting taxation from 'earners' to 'owners'. He had to rely instead on 'spenders' and economies in the public sector in order to finance his tax package, a dependence that would cause further price rises. However, it is all too easy to overlook the glaring deficiencies of the tax system by the late 1960s. Macleod's meticulous planning and the conviction with which he imbued the task of reform provided the necessary impetus for the improvements made in the early 1970s.

20

A Very Liberal Tory

I have read as widely as I can and thought as deeply as I can on this issue [the death penalty] over many years. My position quite simply is this: I think that capital punishment is an obscenity, and I will have none of it.
Iain Macleod, House of Commons, 15 December 1969.

Liberal First and Foremost

Macleod, as Rhoderick, his youngest brother, recalls, was first and foremost a liberal, whose views did not fit easily into the conventional pattern of party politics. But although he avoided the use of 'Conservative' to describe his own politics, he chose instead to identify, not with the liberal tradition, but with the Tory, or paternalist, romantic tradition, exemplified by Disraeli, and the radical Toryism of Lord Randolph Churchill. Macleod's self-proclaimed Toryism was a rejection of an economic, or *laissez-faire*, liberalism. But his liberal conscience was manifested in his advocacy of compassionate and tolerant politics and in his libertarian attitude on moral issues.[1]

He was not what he once described as a 'vague liberal', meaning somebody who was carried along, unthinkingly, on the tide of progressive opinion. Macleod's liberalism was deep rooted, reflecting the independent-mindedness and strength of character of his parents, whose own formidable personalities were formed on Presbyterian Lewis. He believed in the primacy of the individual conscience, without any of the puritan trappings. This belief created in him a special abhorrence of, in his own phrase, 'the Nanny State', the notion that ministers and their civil servants know what is best for people. It also caused him to be something of a 'free thinker', unusually unwilling in the Conservative Party to defer to authority for its own sake, and instead ready to demand that authority should justify itself on its merits and to advocate a less deferential society. He regarded everybody as being of equal worth, and detested bigotry, snobbery and racial prejudice. On the great, liberal reforms of the 1960s which dealt with criminal justice and moral behaviour, on which there was no party position and MPs voted according to their conscience, Macleod was steadfastly libertarian.

Macleod was unequivocally opposed to the death penalty, taking what he acknowledged to be an 'extreme view':

> I have read as widely as I can and thought as deeply as I can on this issue over many years. My position quite simply is this: I think that capital punishment is an obscenity, and I will have none of it. That has always been my position.[2]

However, the death penalty had been the cause of one of Macleod's most difficult personal decisions as Colonial Secretary. In October 1959, Peter Poole, a Kenyan white settler, was convicted of killing an African during the course of an argument. After a trial by jury, Poole was given the death sentence. He appealed, first to the Court of Appeal for East Africa, then to the Judicial Committee of the Privy Council. He lost both appeals, and on 12 August 1960, the Governor of Kenya confirmed the death sentence. A petition for mercy was submitted to the Queen, and – as was usual in such cases – was referred to Macleod in his capacity as Secretary of State for the Colonies. He declined to advise Her Majesty to intervene, but as a convinced abolitionist he was in mental torment. However, there was no serious dispute about the facts of the case and as far as the great majority of Kenyans was concerned, Macleod was seen to have put justice before race.[3]

Such was Macleod's detestation of the death penalty and his intolerance of injustice, that in February 1961 – in the midst of his battle with other ministers over Northern Rhodesia – he raised in Cabinet the case of Timothy Evans, who had been hanged in 1950 for the murder of his baby daughter, but who many people believed had been innocent. The hapless Evans had been executed several years before it was discovered that his fellow lodger at 10 Rillington Place, John Christie, was a mass murderer. When Christie was hanged in 1953, the Government had sought to allay disquiet over the Evans case by appointing an inquiry, but the conclusion that there had indeed been two murderers lodging in the same small house at the same time struck many people as evidently implausible. The matter was subsequently taken up by liberal campaigners, including Ian Gilmour, Lord Altrincham (later John Grigg) and Ludovic Kennedy – the latter's book, *10 Rillington Place*, was published in early 1961.

Rab Butler, who was Home Secretary when Kennedy's book appeared, referred to it in his Cabinet memorandum of 8 February 1961 when the Government had to consider their response to an Opposition move to try and raise the minimum age for the death penalty from eighteen to twenty-one. But any hope that the same Home Secretary who had blithely stated during the last Commons debate on capital punishment in 1956, that 'no innocent man has been hanged in living memory', might now agree to review the Evans case was soon dashed. Butler advised his colleagues that his conclusion was likely to be that, 'whether Evans was guilty or not, it cannot now be established that he was innocent of the murder of the child'. But when the matter was discussed in Cabinet on Monday 13 February, Macleod disagreed with Butler's view. The Colonial Secretary – who unusually was identified in the generally anonymous Cabinet minute – stated that it was arguable that Evans would not have been convicted of the murder of his child if the court had had before them evidence now available which suggested that his wife had been murdered by Christie. More generally, it seemed possible that Evans would not have been convicted if the court had been aware of the other murders committed by Christie at 10 Rillington Place. However, Butler was unmoved and rejected any idea of a free pardon. The rest of the Cabinet agreed that there was no point in holding an inquiry. It took another five years and a further inquiry before Evans was officially cleared of murder and granted a free pardon on the recommendation of the then Home Secretary, Roy Jenkins.[4]

Immediately after the 1964 election, another Bill to end the death penalty was introduced by the veteran abolitionist, Sydney Silverman. When it received its second reading in December that year, Macleod was to be found in the 'aye' lobby. Although Macleod did not speak during the debate, he gave his 'two main reasons why we should be done with capital punishment' in the *Spectator*, just days before the debate. Echoing – although almost none of his readers could have known – his earlier querying in Cabinet of the terrible injustice suffered by Timothy Evans in the Christie case, he wrote:

> First, because although Home Secretaries in these matters are invariably conscientious and usually humane, they are not infallible. It is surely time now that we admitted that in at least one fairly recent case justice was not done. Timothy Evans's body lies amouldering in the lime innocent at least of the charge for which he was executed. Second, the obscene paraphernalia of capital punishment creates a morbid excitement which is itself evil. Nor do I believe that the argument of the deterrent has any substantial support from the experience of other countries, or even different states within the U.S.[5]

As an abolitionist, Macleod was at odds with the vast majority of people. It was an unhappy predicament for a sincere believer in Lord Randolph Churchill's dictum to 'trust the people', but it explains his conviction that MPs should exercise a special responsibility when they planned to legislate on an issue where there was a great difference of opinion between the views of Parliament and the country. Indeed, before the 1964 election, he had questioned 'the universal assumption that, whichever party wins the general election, in the next parliament the decision [on the future of the death penalty] will be taken after a free vote on a private member's bill.' If ever there was a time to 'trust the people', it was at an election:

> It is often necessary to move in advance of public opinion. It is often right to introduce in later sessions of a parliament bills which may be unpopular and for which there is no specific mandate: this cannot apply to the first bills of a parliament. Should not therefore the parties and individual candidates declare their intentions on this issue? And if the electorate is competent to judge the great issues of peace and war, and in particular to pronounce on the future of the British nuclear deterrent, how can one argue that they should not be allowed to consider the issue of the abolition of capital punishment?[6]

On the eve of the second reading of Silverman's bill, Macleod advocated the abolitionist case but also repeated his qualms at the procedure that was being used to implement this major reform of criminal justice. In reality, he argued, the private member's bill to abolish the death penalty was a Government bill: 'It is in the Queen's Speech, and government time is being found.' Recalling his pre-election comment that 'it would be held out of the Socialist manifesto because they feared (and they were right) that they could not secure a mandate for it', Macleod again voiced his troubled conclusion: 'So we are to legislate behind the backs of the electorate. It may be the only way, but it is hard to find much satisfaction in it.'[7]

When the Home Secretary, Callaghan, sought the Act's renewal at the end of 1969, instead of waiting, as had been agreed, until July 1970, Macleod was concerned not to allow the retentionists to seize an advantage from the Government's mishandling of the issue. Macleod was prepared to sign a motion criticizing the Government for breach of faith, but not one that sought to postpone the decision until after the election. When Lord Dilhorne, the former Lord Chancellor, tabled a motion in the Lords to extend the 1965 Act till 1973, Macleod warned his colleagues that he could not support such a position, since 'a decision had been taken for a review after five years and he felt any extension and stretching into the future was a device designed to improve the case for retention'. As to the substance of the debate, Macleod's position was unchanged. He recalled that during the Swindon by-election, won by the Tories in October, he had been asked, 'What is your party's attitude and what is your own attitude towards capital punishment?' He gave:

> the reply that I always give: 'The Tory Party as such, like the Labour Party, has no views. It has always been to the individual conscience of its members. If you want my own view, I am an abolitionist. I always have been, and I always will be.'[8]

Macleod's convictions were equally clear and consistent on the reform of laws governing a wide range of moral behaviour. His unflinchingly libertarian stance placed him among a tiny number within his party – in the 1960s Macleod supported reforms to the law on homosexuality, abortion, family planning, divorce and matrimonial property. Although these reforms reflected the change in social mores since the 1950s, it is easy to forget that liberalization was by no means a foregone conclusion and that the debates were highly emotive and roused deep passions.

During the 1965–66 session of Parliament, Humphry Berkeley introduced the Sexual Offences Bill, making homosexual acts between consenting male adults in private no longer a criminal offence. When the bill's second reading was announced for Friday 11 February 1965, Macleod cancelled his out of London engagement that he had previously arranged for that day in order to attend the debate and vote for the reform. Although Berkeley's bill received its second reading, it was lost less than three weeks later when Wilson called an election.[9]

Macleod's March 1966 campaign schedule, as Shadow Chancellor and supremo of the party's election broadcasts, was hectic, but he found time to send a spontaneous note of support to Berkeley, who was defending the marginal seat of Lancaster:

My dear Humph,
This written before I sleep – in a sleeper going south from Preston. Just to say there is no one whose success in this goddamn election means more to me than does yours. If there is any message I can send you – I'm quite respectable now! – just tell me. My phone number is Potters Bar 52381. But I'm home really only on Sundays while the circus is on.
Ever,
Iain.

Berkeley took up the offer and asked Macleod to write a letter for publication in the *Lancaster Guardian* saying that no Conservative should abstain from voting for Berkeley because of his bill (Douglas-Home also wrote in Berkeley's support). However, Berkeley reckons that at least a thousand abstained and he lost Lancaster in a swing from Conservative to Labour of 6.1 per cent, well above the national average of 3.5 per cent. After the result was declared, Macleod phoned him to commiserate and also visited his London flat the following Monday, where he spent an hour or so talking about Berkeley's future. Berkeley's bill was taken over by the Labour MP, Leo Abse.[10]

The liberalization of the abortion law and family planning attracted Macleod's strong support. Both measures relaxed the legal restrictions that had previously been imposed on the confidential relationship between patient and doctor. Except in a few circumstances, abortion had been illegal, with the result that many women sought 'backstreet' abortions at consider-able risk to their health. The Abortion Bill introduced by David Steel, the Liberal MP, during the 1966–67 session, placed the prime responsibility on the confidential consultation between patient and doctor (in this case, two doctors), enabling a woman to have an abortion within the first twenty-six weeks of the pregnancy if, in the view of two doctors, continuing with the pregnancy would put her health at serious risk. It was an approach to reform that accorded with Macleod's thinking. Not only was Macleod one of very few Conservatives who voted for Steel's bill on second reading, he also supported it on third reading.

His overriding principle was that people should be able to choose for themselves how to live their lives. Whether or not they were happy with the consequences was their affair. This view extended beyond what are com-monly seen as the traditional areas of moral concern to other aspects of personal life, and at times put him at odds with what was commonly held to be the consensus among liberal, progressive opinion. Macleod parted company from many liberals when they advocated, often for the worthiest of motives, that the state should usurp people's freedom of choice. A classic example was the Labour Government's prohibition, in early 1965, of cigarette advertising on commercial television, 'coupled with a vague threat on future action against other media'. Although it was a cause that many liberals would support, it caused Macleod deep concern. It was not that Macleod supported the smoking lobby. 'Personally I regard the proof of a causal link between heavy cigarette-smoking and the incidence of lung cancer as overwhelming,' he wrote, 'but so is the link between heavy drinking and death on the road. And perhaps between gambling and bankruptcy. Or the presentation of violence and crime itself.' He appreciated that 'The line is a difficult one to draw.' But it was what he regarded as the infringement of personal choice that affronted Macleod:

> This new victory for the Nanny State represents the wrong approach. It is certainly the duty of ministers to make sure that there is full knowledge of the risks thought to be involved in heavy cigarette smoking – and this duty was discharged by Conservative ministers of health and education. If this is done, the decision to smoke or not is for the individual, and it should be left to him'.[11]

Immigration and Race

To the generation who can recall the 1960s, the description of Macleod as a 'liberal Tory' most commonly prompts reference to his liberalism on race and immigration. An unintended consequence of the 1962 Commonwealth Immigrants Act – legislation which Macleod had accepted only with the utmost reluctance – had been to lead hitherto temporary immigrants to become permanent settlers. Moreover, immigration had erupted as an emotive issue during the October 1964 election.

'The speed with which both Government and Opposition have moved to the right on immigration is remarkable,' Macleod was lamenting by early 1965. 'The movement has been towards Sir Cyril Osborne,' the Conservative MP who had long campaigned for immigration controls and who had criticized the 1962 Act as weak and ineffective. Even Christopher Chataway, one of the minority of Tory MPs who had opposed the 1962 Act, was persuaded that 'some restriction – and probably some further restriction' was necessary, while Lord Brockway, the veteran campaigner for racial equality, had conceded that 'for the sake of racial goodwill I would be prepared to limit immigration'.[12]

Although Macleod had only been restored to the Conservative frontbench a couple of months earlier it was a tough speech on immigration by his party leader, Sir Alec Douglas-Home, in February 1965 that provoked him to deliver a barbed corrective to this rightward shift in opinion. Pointedly echoing his 'brotherhood of man' speech and emphasizing the contribution made by immigrants in running the health service, Macleod tartly commented in the *Spectator* that:

Perhaps it is time to remind ourselves, lest we forget, that we have gained a great deal from the work of the immigrant community: that many of our hospital wards could not keep open if we kept coloured nurses away; that we are still brothers one to another. But that is where we came in, and it is unpopular now to mention it.

Macleod sought to counter the growing clamour for tougher action by maintaining that the 1962 Act, which he accepted so reluctantly, had 'on the whole worked well'. There had been 'no repetition of the sorry scenes at Nottingham and Notting Hill'. And although he was prepared to recognize 'the danger of a flood of unskilled workers', he believed that the existing legislation was adequate, referring to the voucher scheme that had been put into effect before the 1964 election in order to prevent the entry of unskilled Commonwealth workers.[13]

Nonetheless the number of single, male immigrants from New Commonwealth countries was drastically cut by the Labour Government in their White Paper on immigration in August 1965. The number permitted entry each year as voucher-holders was slashed from 20,800 to 7,500 each year, of whom about 5,000 were expected to be doctors or similarly qualified men. In effect, Labour ministers were preventing the entry of virtually any male immigrants to urban working class areas. But it was another aspect of the White Paper that confirmed Macleod's worst fears at the rightward shift in opinion on immigration. In a reversal of the principle expressed by all parties that everybody in the country must be treated as equal, the Government announced that they would seek powers to repatriate Commonwealth citizens if the Home Secretary 'considers the public interest to require it'.[14]

Macleod set out his arguments against the White Paper in an editorial in the *Spectator* which also carried, as one of its main articles in the same issue a defence of the White Paper by the young Labour MP for Birmingham Sparkbrook, Roy Hattersley, who argued that it 'was a genuine, if badly presented, essay in integration'. Macleod was sensitive to the fact that he had criticized Hattersley's argument in the course of his leader, and sought out Hattersley before publication to forewarn him. Macleod was unapologetic, but it was a considerate gesture that his contributor appreciated, and they found some amusement in the paradox that a Tory representing suburban Enfield was criticizing a toughening of the Government's curbs on immigration whereas a young Labour MP representing inner city Birmingham with many immigrant constituents was defending it.[15]

Macleod was perturbed that ministers had inadvertently introduced 'racial discrimination to the British statue book'. His editorial on the subject appeared a couple of weeks after the White Paper, immediately following the bloody race riot in Los Angeles. In case there was any doubt of the relevance of the death and destruction on the far west of the United States, Macleod cited an horrific incident in Wolverhampton, where 150 whites had marched on a black household, chanting 'Let's get the niggers!' Judged against these events, the White Paper was held to be doubly wrong: it would strengthen the position of militant leaders among the immigrant community and give 'tacit approval to the idea that coloured immigrants are unwelcome second-class citizens'.[16]

There can be no doubting Macleod's genuine detestation of any form of racial discrimination, yet he parted company from many like-minded people on the question of legislating against it. When Labour fulfilled their election pledge and published their proposed bill against racial discrimination in April 1965, Macleod feared a piece not so much of legislation as of 'political skywriting'. While he respected the ideals of those like Brockway who had campaigned for legislation for years, he argued that:

> Those who (like myself) resisted such a bill care no less for racial harmony: we thought legislation undesirable and impossible to draft. The bill proves us right. It does not attack landladies who turn coloured people away. Clubs can go on with their open or private prohibitions ... Employers and trade unions alike can go on with their objections to coloured labour. The bill touches none of these matters, because the Government realizes that it cannot, That, at least, is sense.[17]

In his principled objections, he went to the heart of the liberal dilemma. 'For the first time,' he warned, 'the concept of colour will be introduced into the body of our statute law.' Specifically, 'the new offence of racial hatred is difficult to construe' and he was alarmed that the legislation envisaged an erosion of freedom of expression. He argued:

For the real danger of this well-intentioned bill is that it will prove to be a threat to free speech. Free speech is not only for the major political parties. It is (within law that already makes comment likely to provoke disorder an offence) also for the League of Empire Loyalists and for Colin Jordan.

Macleod's resolution of the dilemma was unequivocal:

I hate all forms of discrimination, but legislation does not change people's hearts. This is a process of education, of knowledge, and the gradual movement towards the brotherhood of men in all countries.[18]

The controversy that, along with devaluation, dominated domestic politics from the autumn of 1967 until the spring of 1968 centred on the Kenyan Asians. It is important to understand their position in the light of the 1962 Commonwealth Immigrants Act and subsequent legislation concerning minority rights in Kenya. Kenya's Asians, who numbered between 150,000 and 200,000, were people of Indian origin whose parents or grandparents had been brought to East Africa as 'coolie' labour by the British. They were relatively well-off by African standards, since a disproportionate number ran businesses and shops, or worked in the professions, and were resented in some sections of majority African opinion, not least because few of them had actively campaigned for Kenyan independence. Under the 1962 Commonwealth Immigrants Act citizens of the United Kingdom and Colonies who did not belong to territories still dependent were exempt from the new controls. As Kenya was still a dependent territory, this exemption applied to white settlers of British descent and Kenyan Asians alike, who qualified as United Kingdom passport holders with a right of entry to Britain.

When Kenya became independent in December 1963, the British Government included minority safeguards in the Kenyan constitution, including the right to retain British citizenship. This provision was primarily designed to give Kenya's whites the security to stay and help make a success of the country, knowing that they could come to Britain if things went badly. But the Kenyatta Government pursued their commitment to Africanization and ruled that dual citizenship would no longer be allowed. The whites and Asians were given two years to decide whether to opt for British or Kenyan citizenship. Many thousands of Asians retained their citizenship of the United Kingdom and Colonies, thereby maintaining their rights as United Kingdom passport holders, but there was no reliable estimate of their number until the political storm was already raging in Britain.

The crisis was triggered in 1967 when the Kenyan Government passed a law that required all non-Kenyan citizens to apply for work permits: only people who were considered essential to the economy would be allowed to stay. This raised the prospect of many thousands of Kenyan Asians seeking entry to Britain. The crisis might have been averted had the Wilson Government acted decisively. If ministers had reiterated the British pledge to UK passport holders, Kenyan Asian fears that they should leave quickly in order to avoid being shut out of Britain as a result of tighter controls would have been allayed. In view of Macleod's later intervention in the row, he and some other senior Tories (including at least two former ministers at the Colonial Office) would have reiterated their support for upholding Britain's commitment. In that event, the rush that ensued might well have been forestalled and the crisis that it triggered probably averted.[19]

In Opposition, the Conservatives had called for tougher immigration controls, but neither Heath nor Hogg seemed to have their heart in the policy and the initiative was now seized by Duncan Sandys and Enoch Powell. The close attention that Sandys paid to the Kenyan Asians from the summer of 1967 was significant because he had negotiated Kenyan independence as Commonwealth and Colonial Secretary between July 1962 and October 1964. Many representatives at the 1967 Brighton Conservative conference cheered when he proclaimed that the aim of party policy should be to preserve the British character of Britain. On the first day of the 1967 Tory conference in Brighton, speaking at Deal in Kent, Powell urged tougher controls and specifically referred to the Kenyan Asians. He argued that their exemption from the 1962 Act had been unintended, describing it as 'an unforeseen loophole in legislation' and saying that it was 'monstrous' that it 'should be able to add another quarter of a million or so . . . without any control or limit whatever.' His claim that the exemption of Kenyan Asians from the 1962 Act was a 'loophole' was rejected by Jenkins during his last Commons speech as Home Secretary the following month.[20]

By the autumn, the press were carrying reports of charter flights filled by Kenyan Asians hurrying to London. The crisis finally came to a head in February 1968. Sandys, interviewed by the *Sunday Telegraph* on 4 February about the commitment made to people in Kenya who had retained British citizenship, claimed that 'it was certainly never intended to provide a privileged backdoor entry into the UK.' The following Friday in Walsall, Powell made an emotive speech repeating his familiar demands for tough restrictions. Official estimates indicated that there were 167,000 Asian UK passport holders exempt from the 1962 Act in Kenya alone, 63,000 in other African countries and 140,000 in Malaysia and Singapore. A year later, after the brouhaha had subsided, the Home Office admitted that they had grossly overestimated the numbers and that the Asians in the Far East had no intention of coming to Britain. But this was not being said in February.[21]

Macleod was outraged at Sandys's comments and disturbed by Powell's speech. He and Hogg voiced their disquiet over Powell's tone at Shadow

Cabinet on Monday 12 February. Powell sought to defend himself, but was curtailed by an intervention from Health. As regards the immediate crisis of the Kenyan Asians, the Shadow Cabinet were divided between those, like Macleod, who felt that the party 'could certainly not in any way go back on this undertaking' and others who thought that since the circumstances were now very different, further curbs of some kind had to be introduced.[22]

Macleod saw that if he was to maintain his principled support for the right of entry by the Kenyan Asians and remain on the frontbench, he should act before the Shadow Cabinet next considered the crisis. There was every likelihood that at their meeting on Wednesday 21 February the demand for some restriction on Kenyan Asians would be adopted as party policy. Indeed, Macleod may well have got wind that the Cabinet were reviewing their position on Tuesday 20th. But he faced a dilemma. On the one hand, if he spoke out publicly before Wednesday's Shadow Cabinet, he would be accused of seeking to pre-empt the party's position. On the other hand, if he deferred till after the meeting and then spoke out, he risked an act of gross disloyalty. But another option was afforded Macleod by his knowledge of the weekly printing schedule of the *Spectator*. Taking as his pretext Sandys's intention of introducing a private member's bill, Macleod sent 'an open letter' to his former Cabinet colleague for publication in the paper at the end of that week. 'I would have preferred to say nothing on this delicate problem,' he wrote, but added, that 'that is no longer possible for me and silence would be taken as consent to your views'.[23]

The ruse of setting out his position in the *Spectator* meant that he was not breaking party policy when he wrote his letter, since the paper went to press before Wednesday's Shadow Cabinet meeting. But by committing himself in print before any change in party policy he would be in a strong position later to argue that he was duty bound to oppose any control that the Government might impose on Kenyan Asian immigration, whatever line the Shadow Cabinet adopted. With the right-wing clamour reaching a crescendo, the last thing that Health wanted was to lose Macleod. In different circumstances, another leader might have argued that he should not have committed himself in print precipitately, but Macleod was fortunate in his choice of opponent (Sandys) and nobody reading his letter could doubt his conviction that a matter of principle was at stake. Nonetheless, it was an astute ploy that would enable Macleod, if the eventuality arose, to have his cake (stay in the Shadow Cabinet) and eat it (dissent from the party line).

This eventuality arose almost immediately. At their meeting on 21 February, the Shadow Cabinet agreed a statement urging that, in the event of a failure to find a solution through talks with the Kenyan Government, the Government 'should seek a solution to this national and Commonwealth problem by phasing the entry of these immigrants, in the light of the social conditions existing in Britain'. The following day, Thursday 22nd, the Cabinet concluded their discussion and Callaghan, Jenkins's replacement at the Home Office, told the Commons that the Government would introduce emergency legislation to extend the 1962 Act to cover United Kingdom passport holders not connected by birth or descent with the United Kingdom. This provision would remove from Kenyan and other Asians who were exempt from the 1962 Act their right of entry to Britain. Hogg gave the Opposition's general assent. However, in view of the argument that ensued, it should be noted that during his statement, Callaghan also admitted that a form of undertaking existed.[24]

On the same afternoon that the Home Secretary announced the emergency legislation, journalists and MPs were busily perusing Macleod's dissenting testament in the *Spectator*. 'The true question,' he told Sandys in his open letter, 'must be whether such a bill as you propose would break an understanding given freely by this country and her Conservative government. More specifically did you give your word? Did I?' In a crushing riposte to Sandy's denial of an intention to provide 'a privileged backdoor entry into the UK,' Macleod wrote:

> Leaving aside the emotive words that is exactly what was proposed: special entry in certain circumstances which have now arisen. We did it. We meant to do it. And in any event we had no other choice.

Briefly tracing the history, Macleod recalled that his decision as Colonial Secretary in 1961 to move Kenyatta from his desolate confinement nearer to Nairobi and 'ultimately to freedom and full participation in his country's affairs, was greeted with great hostility.' He continued:

> There was much loose talk, some of it irresponsible, but some of it arising out of genuine anxiety, that we were creating a new Congo in Kenya. And so the strictest safeguards for *all minorities* were demanded and gladly given [author's emphasis].

Macleod then turned to the argument that lay at the heart of his opponents' case. In their view, the commitment to UK passport holders could not be allowed to stand because it was clearly at odds with what ministers had intended in the 1962 Commonwealth Immigrants Act. However, referring to the Kenyan Independence Bill that Sandys had presented to the Commons in late 1963, Macleod recalled that:

> The constitution on which it was founded was detailed and exact. The provisions for citizenship and for renunciation were clear. The earlier Act [the 1962 Commonwealth Immigration Act] must, of course, have been in your mind. Your Under-Secretary said in the house after explaining the bill: 'There is thus no question of anyone becoming stateless as a result of the bill's provisions.'

As Macleod reminded Sandys, 'The only pressure in the House was for you to widen not restrict the protection given to minorities and you responded.'

Moreover, two further bills were passed in 1964, both concerned with the question of citizenship of the UK and colonies. The minister introducing the first bill, that became the British Nationality Act and was designed to facilitate the resumption and renunciation of British citizenship, stated that: 'It was the independence of Kenya and Tanganyika that brought the problem to mind.' The second bill provided 'for the acquisition of citizenship of the UK and colonies by certain classes of people who would otherwise be stateless'. As Macleod wrote, 'How can one argue now that we did not know?'

There was, of course, no great political row in Britain over the right of entry by white UK passport holders. Sandys certainly did not want to stop them, and Macleod turned this aspect of his adversary's argument on its head to reveal its racialist connotation. 'No doubt,' Macleod acknowledged:

The interests of the Europeans were first in our minds, but it would be outrageous to deny to Kenyan Europeans anything less than unrestricted entry. On what grounds, then, other than that of colour, can one deny similar rights to the other minorities many of whom are third or fourth generation Kenyans?

Moreover, Britain could not take away UK citizenship from the 120,000 or so Kenyan Asians whom Macleod reckoned did not acquire Kenyan citizenship 'without leaving them as stateless persons and quite apart from our obligations we would be offending against international law'.

In practice, Macleod believed: 'Nothing like all these people will come and they are in the main prosperous and hardworking.' He was exceptional among Tory politicians in not only perceiving but also in being prepared to argue the case publicly that: 'Their exodus is being speeded by the fear that we will break our word on which they have relied.' Moreover, Macleod was prepared to recognize the concern that had been expressed about the increased number of immigrants entering the country and offered a *quid pro quo*. 'Last year,' he noted,

More than 61,000 Commonwealth citizens were admitted under the Commonwealth Immigrants Act, including nearly 53,000 dependants. We have no such legal obligation here and if need be, although I would dislike it, that flow could be checked or even stopped while we try to achieve with a Kenya a reasonably phased Africanization.

Macleod was 'sure that we can do this', warning that if it was not done, 'it will not only be the work permits of Asians which will be at risk'. His call to 'trust Kenya and President Kenyatta as we [he and Sandys] both did once before', was unlikely to win Macleod many friends in the prevailing climate of opinion.

In his final appeal to Sandys, Macleod argued forcefully that:

We cannot ignore the past nor the pledges we gave. In what we did for the minority communities we were supported by all political parties and by the press. Indeed, those who were strongest for the safeguards are exactly those who now would have us recant. It is, of course, true that no one said in terms to the Asian community 'we are providing for you a privileged backdoor entry, etc'. But your Kenyan constitution is devastatingly clear. So is Hansard. So are all the statutes. And so, therefore, is my position. I gave my word. I meant to give it. I wish to keep it.

In suggesting that 'the problems of colour and race are too explosive' to be 'hammered into shape on the anvil of parliamentary debate', Macleod expressed his belief that 'a bi-partisan approach to this difficult and complicated problem' was still possible. By the time his open letter was published, a bi-partisan view had, indeed, emerged, but it was Sandys who was able to claim that he was acting in a 'bi-partisan spirit'. [25]

On the eve of the emergency bill's second reading on Tuesday 27 February, the Shadow Cabinet agreed, despite certain specific concerns, to vote with the Government. Macleod made it clear that he would have to vote against. Boyle and Carr only voted in favour on the understanding that the Opposition would not vote against the new Race Relations Bill that the Government had promised during the 1967–68 session. The new Commonwealth Immigrants Bill passed through all its stages in Commons in three days. Not only Macleod but also every other former Colonial Office minister in both houses, except Sandys, opposed it. The fourteen Conservative rebels in the Commons were drawn from all wings of the party, ranging from Michael Heseltine, a liberal on such matters, to senior backbenchers like Sir Cyril Black, Sir Douglas Glover and Lieutenant-Commander Maydon, who by no stretch of the imagination could be regarded as liberals. Thirty-five Labour MPs and the Liberals also voted against, as did eighty peers in the Lords. The 1968 Commonwealth Immigrants Act became law on 1 March, eight days after Callaghan's announcement.[26]

Yet Macleod's stand was vindicated. Soon afterwards, the new controls on Kenyan Asians were nullified when Callaghan admitted that because those with British citizenship had no right of entry to anywhere else, Britain would admit them if they were expelled from Kenya and had nowhere else to go. In July 1968, agreement was reached with India to admit Kenyan Asians. The following autumn came the Government's admission that their estimates of the numbers likely to enter Britain had been exaggerated, as Macleod had had the courage to suggest at the height of the storm.[27]

Final Rift with Enoch

February's storm was the prelude to April's hurricane. The warning signals were raised again in the Tory party before Easter, when the Government finally published their new bill on race relations, extending the law in various ways and covering discrimination in employment and housing. The Shadow Cabinet faced a tactical minefield, since there was every risk of an embarrassing party split in the vote on second reading. They were deeply divided, but had little time for further backbench consultation since the Commons was about to rise for the Easter recess and the debate would be held the day after its return. If they were to table a motion for the debate, they had to act straight away. They finally agreed to move a reasoned amendment to the bill. It had to be drafted at once, and Maudling, as Deputy Leader, was given the task of heading a small sub-committee to find a form of words that might preserve party unity. The sub-committee included some of those who felt strongest on the issue — Boyle and Carr, whose support for the bill restricting Kenyan Asian immigration had been conditional on the Opposition not opposing the Race Relations Bill, and Powell, who had been delivering increasingly stern warnings on the dangers resulting from mass immigration. A final decision about the vote on second reading would be taken later. Boyle, Carr and Joseph made it clear that they would decide their positions when they had considered the terms of the reasoned amendment.[28]

The Shadow Cabinet would not consider the matter again until their next meeting, immediately after the Easter recess, on Monday 22 April, the eve of the second reading debate. In the meantime, Powell had a longstanding party speaking engagement in Birmingham on Saturday 20th, in which he returned to the theme of the fears of 'ordinary English people' in urban areas where immigration from the New Commonwealth had concentrated. Speaking of their 'sense of being a persecuted minority', Powell said that he would 'allow just one of those hundreds of people to speak for me'. He then quoted a letter he had received from a woman in Northumberland relating the experience of an elderly white woman in his own constituency. 'She is becoming afraid to go out,' Powell's correspondent wrote, 'Windows are broken. She finds excreta pushed through the letterbox'.[29]

According to Powell's biographer, Cosgrave, it was 'his most explosive anecdote so far, the use of which alone would probably have been enough to ensure his dismissal from the Shadow Cabinet'. Powell went on to argue that the concentration of immigrants in certain areas enabled them to remain separate from the host community, creating a dangerous and divisive situation that the Race Relations Bill would exacerbate. In his famous (and often misquoted) conclusion, Powell declared that as he looked ahead: 'I am filled with foreboding. Like the Roman, I seem to see, "The River Tiber foaming with much blood".'[30]

Powell's Shadow Cabinet colleagues were furious. His participation in drafting the reasoned amendment should have made him fully aware of the sensitivities in the party on this issue. For his part, Powell, when he left the Shadow Cabinet discussions was apparently convinced that what he was going to say in Birmingham ten days later was in line with party policy. Yet in February, his Walsall speech on the same subject had caused Hogg, the Shadow Home Secretary and the party's chief spokesman on immigration and race relations, and also Macleod, to voice their distress in Shadow Cabinet at the tone of what he had said. Immediately they heard of Powell's comments, Macleod and other shadow ministers urgently conferred with Whitelaw and Heath by telephone. Whitelaw was in no doubt following his conversations with Macleod, Hogg, Boyle and Carr that 'the whole shooting match' would quit. But Whitelaw found that Heath was more affronted than anybody. Heath dismissed Powell from the Shadow Cabinet that evening for the 'racialist' tone of his speech.[31]

Two months earlier Macleod had been allowed to remain in the Shadow Cabinet, despite voting against the Opposition on the Kenyan Asians, but now Powell was sacked for the tone of his comments. This contradiction has several explanations. Firstly, Macleod was able to justify his act of rebellion on the principle that he could not be expected to break a pledge that he was convinced had been given and for which he had had ministerial responsibility. The politics also worked to Macleod's advantage. His handling was exceptionally adept and his revolt could be reconciled more easily than Powell's speech with the liberal sympathies of Heath, Hogg, and, indeed, the majority of the Shadow Cabinet. More importantly, there was a feeling in the Shadow Cabinet that this speech of Powell's was the last straw. Powell's exposition of *laissez-faire* economics had caused difficulties for the party, and Heath took a less tolerant view than Douglas-Home had. Powell had spoken intemperately on an issue on which shadow ministers had struggled collectively to find a finely balanced formulation that would preserve party unity in a vote that was due only three days after his speech. In Hogg's telling phrase, Powell had been 'flicking ash' in a room full of gunpowder.[32]

The headlines focused on Powell and the reactions to his dismissal, but on Monday 22 April *The Times* published a letter from Macleod in which he sought to protect the position of many of his supporters on the left of the party who were unlikely to vote for the Opposition's reasoned amendment on the second reading of the Race Relations Bill. Indeed, the line being taken by the leadership had caused one of Macleod's closest supporters, Humphry Berkeley, the former MP for Lancaster, to resign from the party. 'I can at least agree with you,' wrote Macleod, commenting on *The Times*'s support for the bill, 'that the departure of Mr Humphry Berkeley is a real loss to the Conservative party. I believe he will return.' Macleod explained his support for the reasoned amendment, but hoped that members would make up their own minds which way to vote 'without pressure or reproach'. More than twenty Conservatives abstained, including Boyle on the frontbench. On third reading, later in the summer, the party faced an even more difficult choice since there was no opportunity to move a reasoned amendment at the final stage of the Commons' deliberations. Moreover, as Hogg told the Shadow Cabinet, during the committee stage the party had started to meet in separate groups outside the committee room. Macleod sought to protect the left, resisting pressure for the party to vote against the bill.[33]

Macleod was deeply shaken by Powell's speech and its impact, creating an unbridgeable gulf between the two men that time never healed. 'Enoch's gone mad and hates the blacks,' he told young Tory friends. 'Iain never forgave him [Powell],' recalls Patrick Jenkin. He was deeply shaken by the unpleasantness and, in some cases, sheer viciousness, of the flood of mail that poured in defending what Powell had said. 'You lift the stones,' he commented, '[but] you have no idea of how nasty some of the things underneath them are.'[34]

The intensity of Macleod's anger was evident to everybody who knew him. Shortly after Powell's speech, Colin Harding, Macleod's close friend from Cambridge in the 1930s, happened to be spending an evening playing cards at the Portland Club, where he had arranged to stay overnight. When he went to collect the keys to his usual room, he found that it was already booked by a 'Mr Macleod'. The Portland had a reciprocal booking arrangement with White's, and Harding realized that it must be his friend. Ordering a couple of brandies, he went to chide Macleod for having taken 'his room'. As they chatted over their nightcap, Powell's speech was mentioned and Harding said that he thought many people would agree with Powell. Macleod was furious and they argued long and hard into the night over three more brandies each. Yet Macleod's wit had not deserted him, even on this subject. Soon afterwards, Harding received a letter from Macleod addressed to 'Colin Harding, FRS'. When they next met, Harding asked what Macleod meant by 'FRS'. 'Filthy, Racialist Swine,' Macleod quipped, and whenever he wrote to Harding thereafter he always added 'FRS'.[35]

According to Powell, Macleod cut any contact with him: 'his dealings with me,' Powell recalls, were 'those of one's dealings with a pariah. There was nothing in it for him to be in any way associated with me.' Powell maintains that Macleod: 'knew what I said was not motivated by what is crudely called racialism, but he behaved as if he did not so know.' However, Macleod was clearly appalled at the apparent disregard in Powell's April 1968 'River Tiber' speech for the effect of his powerful language on a subject where passions can be easily excited and prejudices quickly inflamed. There is some evidence that Macleod sought a rapprochement at the October 1968 Conservative conference at Blackpool. 'Mr Macleod, whom many representatives have seen in close and friendly conversation with Mr Enoch Powell in the hotel rooms,' reported the *Daily Telegraph* in the course of covering Macleod's speech. Powell has no such re-collection.[36]

Had self-interest been his main concern, Macleod would never have acted as he did a year later when his close friend, Nigel Fisher, Conservative MP for Surbiton, was faced with the threat of deselection by a group of local right-wingers, whom Wilson dubbed 'the skinheads of Surbiton'. Their plan was to replace the arch-liberal Fisher with a candidate who shared Powell's views on immigration. The story broke in a front-page story in *The Times* on Saturday, 25 October. Macleod contrived to get a letter to the paper that appeared at the top of the correspondence columns on the Monday morning expressing his agreement with Fisher on immigration and defending an MP's right to take his own line. At the same time Macleod wrote to Fisher:

> My dear Nigel,
> As you will see I have written to *The Times*. I have also written to Willy [Whitelaw] and said that if you go I go. And so I will.
> Ever,
> Iain.

When Fisher received this letter, he immediately telephoned Macleod to thank him and say that his gesture was out of the question: he was Shadow Chancellor and could not possibly quit. Macleod simply replied, 'You must know me well enough by now to know that I never write things I do not mean,' and then rang off.[37]

What must not be forgotten or lightly cast aside is that taking a liberal stand on immigration and race relations was immensely difficult in the Tory Party, particularly in the wake of Powell's 'River Tiber' speech. In August 1968, the *Guardian* reported Macleod telling an international conference of business and professional women in London that:

> The greatest human value for him [Macleod] would be to recognize the truth of Shylock's plea for Jews to be the same as Gentiles – 'if you prick us, shall we not bleed . . . if you wrong us shall we not revenge?' The torment of race and colour would lead to an explosion if we did not recognize that differences were only superficial. The state to aim for was colour blindness.

A calculating politician would never have been as uncompromising as Macleod in his public statements and his support for Fisher. It was this courage and quixotic loyalty of Macleod's that inspired many people of all political persuasions and made a lasting impression on a younger generation of Tories. As one of this latter group, John Major, observes:

Macleod's support then, publicly on issues it was not always popular to go public upon, was total. Not many politicians would have done that. That's the sort of thing that inspired the affection that people had, and still have, for him.[38]

Crisis at Christmas

There was nothing false or forced about Macleod's rapport with young people. He did not patronize them either by pretending that he agreed with everything they said or by discounting their opinions. It never occurred to him that he should treat them with less respect than anybody else. Spending time with them and including them among his friends was unexceptional to Macleod.

In an age when there was still a surprising degree of deference and when there was anguished debate about the 'generation gap', Macleod's approach was like a gale of fresh air that blew away the awkwardness and distance that often impaired contact between young and old. John Major recalls an occasion when Macleod was due to address about sixty to seventy Young Conservatives. It was 'a small, unthreatening audience for a senior politician', but Major noticed that as Macleod sat at the platform table waiting to speak, 'you could see his hands held together under the table, and they were shaking as though with nerves'. In Major's view:

Perhaps part of his communication with small groups and young people particularly, was that even for them, where there was no threat to him at all, where he could have recited the telephone book and they would have loved it, he still had the time, and the care, and the interest to be concerned and worried, and perhaps a bit nervous, about what he was going to say.[39]

The most enduring, tangible legacy of Macleod's rapport with young people has become one of the country's main charitable organizations. While Macleod was editor of the *Spectator*, he received a letter from William Shearman, a young Tory activist, who had formed the East London Conservative Association (ELCA), asking if he would give it his support and speak at meetings. Shearman had joined the Young Conservatives in East London after National Service, but depressed at the moribund state of the party and their irrelevance in an area dominated by Labour set up ELCA to show that the Tories could make an impact. Inspired by Macleod's qualities as a speaker, Shearman identified with his 'One Nation' radical Toryism and forthright opposition to racial prejudice. His initiative in setting up ELCA, with its emphasis on playing a role in the community, epitomized Macleod's belief in turning Tory idealism into practical action.[40]

Macleod's response was wholly enthusiastic. He was soon addressing his first public meeting in Stepney and during the latter half of the 1960s would visit the East End to speak for the association, canvass tower blocks and socialize with the young Tory activists who joined ELCA. 'Here's £20, get the drinks in, Bill,' Macleod would say to Shearman at the start of the evening, and after his speech would stay talking till the early hours. Sometimes he and Shearman would spend an evening chatting in one of the Conservative clubs in his Enfield constituency. Their difference in age and position simply did not matter and their friendship meant a great deal to Macleod.[41]

It was through Shearman's meeting Catholic voluntary workers in the East End that Macleod learned of the appalling plight of the homeless. Many of them in those days were older, single men, who had slipped through the state welfare system and were often sleeping rough. Some had become alcoholics, including crude spirit, or 'meths', drinkers, who gathered on bombsites and in parks. In the New Year's Day issue of the *Spectator* in 1965, 'Quoodle' quoted a graphic passage from *Non-Citizens of Britain*, a report by the Simon Community and the Homeless in Britain Fund, on the shocking state of meths drinkers in Stepney and urged readers to offer help or send a cheque to the Fund.[42]

In the early autumn of 1967, Shearman and his colleagues discussed with the Macleods what they could do to tackle these problems. It was quickly realized that anything they did would be more effective if it was removed from party politics. A simple concept emerged of organizing a one-off initiative when all parties should bury their differences and work together with the relevant charities to raise funds for the homeless. The most appropriate time would be Christmas. As various titles for the project were tossed around, Eve suggested 'Crisis at Christmas'.

With the Christmas of 1967 only a couple of months away, Macleod began drumming up support. He became a co-sponsor, donating £100 to the float for expenses, along with Reg Prentice, then Labour MP for East Ham North and Minister for Overseas Development. Among Macleod's other fund-raising efforts was a speech to the Young Conservatives' annual Christmas ball. Shearman's close acquaintance, Nick Beacock, a young curate, became chairman of 'Crisis at Christmas' and they set up headquarters at the vicarage of St Barnabas, Little Ilford, where he was then serving. Beacock and Shearman recruited people of their own age from across the political spectrum, and worked tirelessly for six weeks to organize and publicize the appeal. The Shadow Chancellor would visit the vicarage and was kindly and unassuming in his help and support. His dry wit was treasured. Calling the BBC to persuade them to report 'Crisis at Christmas', he was eventually put through to a producer. Their conversation began with the producer asking pompously:

'Who am I speaking to?'
'Iain Macleod.'
'Oh God!'
'No, just a humble politician.'[43]

The centrepiece of the 1967 appeal was a rally and candlelit vigil in Hyde Park on Sunday 17 December. During the day, four sponsored walks from Redhill, St Albans, Upminster and Windsor, together with a fifth walk from Cable Street in the East End (designed specifically to draw attention to homelessness), converged on the park. There, from the back of a lorry, Macleod and other speakers, including Dr Horace King, Speaker of the House of Commons, Dr David Owen, then a Labour MP, the Bishop of London and the Revd Donald (later Lord) Soper, addressed a gathering of over a thousand people. Owen was enormously impressed by Macleod's involvement. 'It was strangely disconcerting,' Owen has recalled, 'to discover this degree of commitment and concern in a Conservative, who was no closet egalitarian.' Afterwards, with Eve driving and Iain in the passenger seat, the Macleods somehow crammed seven people in their car to give them a lift, a spectacle that alarmed passers-by whom they asked for directions.[44]

Four days later, Macleod intervened, exceptionally for a senior front-bencher, in one of the Christmas adjournment debates in the Commons. W.S. Hilton, the MP for Bethnal Green, who had secured a debate on crude spirit ('meths') drinkers, estimated that there were about two hundred addicts in his constituency. Providing a graphic account of the problems they caused local people, Hilton argued that voluntary agencies had made the problem worse and urged that meths drinkers should be given compulsory treatment. Macleod recognized the anger felt in the community but, speaking with the authority of a former Minister of Health, rejected Hilton's approach. Referring to the 'united appeal' that he and Prentice had sponsored the previous Sunday, he argued that the problem was wider and also included ex-prisoners, alcoholics, the mentally disturbed and drug addicts.

Macleod reckoned that the numbers involved were far higher than official estimates of 13,000 homeless single persons and 1,000 sleeping rough. Voluntary bodies could help tackle the problem, along with the Government and local authorities. He commended the Simon Community, who offered 'friendship and shelter' and the possibility that those they helped might haul themselves 'out of the misery of Skid Row into which they have sunk'. But he acknowledged the special problem of meths drinkers, accepted that more needed to be done and called for further research into their problems.[45]

The 1967 Crisis at Christmas appeal raised £7,000, which was distributed to six charities working with homeless people. The following year's appeal was a disappointment and other politicians might have retreated gracefully – as Shadow Chancellor with an election drawing near Macleod would have had the perfect pretext had he done so. Instead, his and Eve's commitment was as strong as ever. By now Beacock and Shearman were regular visitors to the Macleods' home, where they would have dinner and Macleod used to chat with them till the small hours about all manner of things. He now encouraged them to feel that they could do better in 1969 and 'really give it a go'. As a result they developed the idea of a 'reverse pilgrimage' from Canterbury to London.

Christmas 1969 proved a turning point. The pilgrimage attracted enormous media interest. Television news bulletins on Sunday 14 December showed Archbishop Ramsay and Macleod leading the start of the pilgrimage as it left the cathedral close in Canterbury, heading into the nearby streets. At the final rally in Westminster Central Methodist Hall, Macleod contrasted the romantic aspect of the pilgrimage with the grim reality of life for the homeless. Crisis at Christmas never looked back. The one-off appeals were firmly established as an annual event. In the early 1970s it registered as a charity, with Eve becoming one of the trustees, and in 1972 launched its 'Open Christmas', providing food, shelter, bedding and clothing for the homeless. Macleod never imagined that homelessness and poverty would reach such horrifying levels. Without his early inspiration, Crisis at Christmas might never have happened, or might only be remembered as a distant, one-off event. Instead, it was there to respond as homelessness inexorably increased. Crisis now operates all the year round. Since its inaugural appeal in 1967, it has given £10 million to over 600 day centres, hostels and resettlement schemes in every part of the UK. In 1992 alone it raised over £2 million, and 1,200 people volunteered to help run its Open Christmas. In Macleod, 'Crisis at Christmas' found not only one indefatigable champion but two, for Eve was equally committed. Crisis is a tribute to their shared social concern.[46]

His Own Man

More than most Tories Macleod defied neat categorization, even in a party in which any reliable taxonomy of factions is exceptionally difficult. Macleod's politics reflected his independent-mindedness. Macleod would decide his position by intense ratiocination, in which first principles would be addressed and the practicalities and politics weighed. This solitary, mental process invariably produced cogent and concise reasoning, whatever the subject. It also produced a distinctive Toryism. Even when his views accorded with the party's position, he never appeared to be simply toeing the line but had consciously decided that he agreed with it.

The future of Southern Rhodesia was the single issue that polarized the Conservative Party for more than fifteen years until, in 1980, the Thatcher Government became the unlikely midwife of an independent Zimbabwe led by Robert Mugabe, the Marxist and former guerilla leader. At the end of 1965, 31 Tory MPs voted with the Government in favour of an oil embargo.

Among them were some of Macleod's closest political friends, including Nigel Fisher, Humphry Berkeley and Christopher Chataway, Terence Higgins and, from 1966, whenever the embargo came up for renewal, Nick Scott. Many of this group came to assume the nearest thing to a left-wing caucus in the Conservative Party. They naturally looked to Macleod as one of their leaders. Yet he took a different line.

On 11 November 1965 the Smith regime in Salisbury declared unilateral independence (UDI). On Monday 15th, Heath told his Shadow Cabinet that they should allow the Government's bill, which made provision for sanctions, to be passed, and should not go into lengthy discussion of the details. Macleod countered that the Opposition should not get involved in supporting the Government on sanctions. The aim of a peaceful outcome, Macleod believed, could best be achieved by making life for the Rhodesians moderately uncomfortable and very boring, in the hope that in time, through some mediator, relations could be restored. Also, the Tories should not rule out the idea that Smith might continue to hold power in Rhodesia and that they might have to deal with him and his Government again.[47]

The row over sanctions raged the following evening at the Tory backbench Finance Committee, where, as Shadow Chancellor, Macleod was formally elected chairman for the 1965–66 session. A group of younger backbenchers reportedly met right-wing opponents of sanctions with a demand for a more thoroughgoing support for the Government. Macleod avoided committing himself, but suggested that it would be a wise course not to close doors against Smith. His *Spectator* editorial at the end of the week in parts read like an admonitory letter to the Tory left. 'It is frequently said,' he asserted:

> That there is a striking contrast between how Britain has been prepared to act in previous colonial situations and how she is acting now in Rhodesia. But those situations were very different. In Kenya, Nyasaland and Cyprus, Britain was in a meaningful sense the governing power. Her repressive and security actions flowed naturally from this power. Her policy changed when this power was eroded and the game no longer seemed worth the effort. That Britain has no such power in Rhodesia is shown quite clearly by the fact that had Mr Smith been prepared to stick to the 1961 Constitution without titular independence, Mr Wilson openly stated that Britain would have done absolutely nothing about it.

In words that would have a particular resonance on the Tory left, Macleod encapsulated the underlying assumption of his step-by-step approach:

> Dealing with the Rhodesian situation is not a matter of having your heart in the right place. It is a matter for the head. Its solution, as always,

requires calm and patience and, above all, doing nothing of which the likely consequences have not been most carefully calculated in advance.

The Tory left were, in the words of Fisher, one of their number, 'distressed and disturbed' and wanted to hear Macleod's arguments against sanctions. Fisher therefore invited him to his house on the evening of Wednesday 8 December to meet privately between twenty and twenty-five friends and admirers of Macleod's. Nonetheless, 'it was a painful evening'. Macleod dealt 'patiently' with every point, but most of those present were unconvinced.[48]

As Macleod feared, events rapidly took over after UDI. On Tuesday 14 December, he led for the Opposition in a debate on two orders that, in effect, froze the assets of the Reserve Bank of Rhodesia. He did not divide the Commons, but his hope that 'we shall get through the whole of this Rhodesia crisis without a division' was shortlived. Three days later, the Government imposed an oil embargo. The Conservative leadership tried to hold the party together but the right wing regarded the embargo as a penal sanction and, at the end of the debate on 21 December, insisted on dividing the House. As a result, 50 right-wing Tories trooped through the 'Noes' lobby and 31 left-wingers made their way through the 'Ayes' lobby with the Government, while the frontbench abstained.[49]

'Of course the Tory Party is divided on this great issue,' Macleod wrote at the end of a sorry week for the Tories, 'so is the country.' It was a lame mitigating plea. Macleod did not believe that oil sanctions would work and also saw in them something more sinister: 'Our Commonwealth policy is being run not by the Cabinet,' he claimed:

But by the UN and the OAU [Organization of African Unity]. It has been a sorry story of retreat, from the first imposition of sanctions (judged in themselves to be sufficient and effective), to the Security Council resolution, to the more stringent measures, to the dispatch of the Javelins to Zambia, to the seizure of Rhodesia's gold and sterling assets, to oil sanctions.

Protesting that, 'A Commonwealth force is the next demand, and in due course war,' Macleod declared that, 'Force never was, and is not now, the answer. For this proposition Mr Heath is entitled to demand the support both of the Monday Club and of PEST.'[50]

Macleod continued to believe, as he told the Shadow Cabinet in 1968, that they should be prepared to go a long way to achieve a settlement, even though this might involve agreeing terms that cut across earlier commitments. He was reluctant to pursue tougher policies which would cut Rhodesia adrift because of the grave consequences, particularly in southern Africa. Shortly before the 1970 election, following Smith's proclamation that

Rhodesia was a republic, the Shadow Cabinet again took stock of their policy. It was agreed that the Tories were bound to say that they would talk to Smith's government on returning to power. But if there was no agreement or settlement, the Tories would have to consider their position on sanctions and the problems of dealing with the UN and other African states. Macleod accepted this general line, but thought that it would help if they said that they owed one more try, not least to the four and a half million Africans in Rhodesia: it was an exercise to get the right answer for all the people of Rhodesia.[51]

The differences between Macleod and the Tory left revealed a faultline that ran through liberal Tory thinking on southern Africa. The scheduled tour by South Africa's cricketers to England during the 1970 season was bound to revive the row over sporting links, but feelings were running high months before the Springboks were due to arrive. Since their last visit, the MCC had cancelled their 1968–69 winter tour to the Republic because the South Africans made it clear that they would not play against Basil D'Oliveira, the Cape Coloured cricketer. Anti-apartheid campaigners in Britain had also become more militant, and there were threats of disruption. Some Tory left-wingers felt that the tour should be called off, notably Nick Scott, a key figure in the left-wing Tory caucus, who shared Macleod's near fanatical devotion to the game.[52]

From the moment the subject was first raised in Shadow Cabinet in December 1969, Macleod took a leading role in arguing that it was of the utmost importance that the tour should go on and that the minority who were violent should not prevent the majority who wished to watch the game from doing so. The following spring, when Wilson defended the right of people to demonstrate against the South African cricket tour, Macleod was anxious that the Tories should take up the matter since he felt that while the vast majority of people detested apartheid they also wanted to see these matches played. Yet the Tory broadside that Macleod had encouraged almost immediately raised anxieties in Shadow Cabinet that it might prove counter-productive. In an unexpected reversal of their usual roles, it was Douglas-Home who specifically raised the bad effect that he thought the controversy might have for the party with young voters who tended to be very anti-apartheid and, in the words of the official minute, 'pro-colour'. The Party Chairman, Anthony Barber, also stressed that if the party continued to attack Wilson so vigorously they might give some people the wrong impression that they were complacent about apartheid. Macleod would not be assuaged on the issue. As Heath and Maudling sought a unifying position for the party, Macleod continued to press his independent-minded line in Shadow Cabinet. The threat by African countries to boycott the Commonwealth Games if the tour went ahead provoked a particularly fiery outburst, in which he condemned the threat as 'blackmail' and, in the case of Kenya, hypocritical, since racialism was clearly practised there.

Macleod was also too astute a politician not to be aware of the likely benefit of his position to the Tories as the party of law and order. During the final, pre-election meetings of the Steering Committee, Macleod stressed the importance for the 'women's vote' of law and order. In the event, the 1970 South African cricket tour was finally called off at the eleventh hour.[53]

The Tories were committed to the controversial policy of resuming arms sales to South Africa which had been banned by the Government in 1964. A number of Labour Cabinet Ministers had subsequently wanted the ban relaxed, but they were out-manoeuvred in Cabinet in 1968. When the controversy over arms sales flared after Macleod's death, there was some debate over his stance, because Tory opponents of the policy included some of his closest friends and supporters. Yet he generally took a different line from them on southern Africa and, as a letter to *The Times* from his wife in the autumn of 1970 made clear, the issue of arms sales was no exception. The rift between Macleod and some of his closest political allies had no effect on their friendship. A poignant incident symbolized the position. In May 1970, Humphry Berkeley, having rejoined the party the previous September, explained in the *Guardian* that he would vote Labour at the forthcoming election because of the Conservative Party's intention to sell arms to South Africa, their support for the South African cricket tour and their commitment to a further round of talks with the Smith regime. Berkeley has recalled that when he spoke with Macleod on the telephone: 'Iain spoke to me more in sorrow than in anger.' Macleod had publicly welcomed Berkeley's return to the party, but they both realized that the break was now final. 'We each said that our personal friendship would not be altered but to my sorrow this was the last time we ever spoke to each other.'[54]

The question arises whether Macleod, since leaving the Colonial Office, had generally become less radical on Africa. As Shadow Chancellor, he would have had some justification in paying less attention to the continent's affairs and accepting the policies proposed by Heath and the Shadow Foreign Secretary, Douglas-Home. However, Macleod argued in Shadow Cabinet against the party leadership's quiescence towards the Government's stance on the Nigerian civil war between the Federal Government and secessionist Ibos in the eastern region (Biafra). The Ibos had reacted to the massacre of their people in tribal violence during 1966 by declaring Biafra independent in May 1967. After two years of fighting, there was still no end in sight. It seemed from the reports emanating from Biafra that General Gowon's Federal forces were relying on mass starvation of the Ibos to do their job for them, while there was a suspicion that the Biafran leader, General Ojukwu, was seeking to exploit the alleged suffering in order to win international support.

In the summer of 1969, Macleod and several others in the Shadow Cabinet voiced their grave concern at what was happening in Biafra. Douglas-Home had argued that there was not very much new that could be said about the Nigerian situation, apart from the limited proposal that Britain and the US could escort planes with supplies into Biafra and might police the distribution of food. However, Macleod countered that Biafra was a separate country in African terms and would remain so. In his view, the moral issues were overwhelming, and the Tories should go further than Douglas-Home suggested and say that if an arrangement on mercy flights could not be reached, Britain would stop supplying arms to the Federal Government.[55]

By the autumn, the Biafrans' plight was growing worse. At Shadow Cabinet in November, Macleod demanded a review of party policy. The Biafran war had lasted for over two years and he argued that the Tories had fulfilled their obligation as an Opposition to give the Government the benefit of the doubt. They should say that they could no longer support the Government if ministers were not prepared to go to the UN and to take positive action on flying in aid to Biafra. In a full discussion two days later, Douglas-Home, having reconsidered the party's position, felt that the Government should be pressed on some points, but that cutting off the supply of arms unilaterally would be taken as a rebuff for the Federal Government and would damage our reputation with them. Macleod was unimpressed. He did not think that this line would do more than tide the Opposition over the next debate in the Commons.[56]

Macleod's success in securing a review of policy was confirmed when Lord Carrington, Leader of the Party in the Lords, undertook a fact-finding mission to Nigeria. However, Carrington found political deadlock and military incompetence. He felt that there was little part that Britain could play. The Nigerians were determined that it was their own war. He could only advise waiting to see what would be the result of the next fighting period. Deeply worried by Carrington's findings, Macleod reasserted his view that 'One Nigeria was a myth'. The Opposition were in a very serious situation where both they and the Government 'kept hoping that something would happen before the next debate, and nothing ever did'. He felt that 'it was both morally and politically wrong to do nothing'. He wanted it made clear that Britain would join an international embargo, and if Russia wanted to veto it, let her. If the Government did not restrict the supply of arms, the Opposition would no longer support them. The Shadow Cabinet were deeply divided, leaving Heath no option but to suggest discussing the matter again in the New Year.[57]

In January 1970 the civil war finally ended. The Nigerian Federation survived. Macleod was proved wrong on the main point at issue in the civil war. But more importantly, he had forced the party leadership to confront the humanitarian and moral aspects. By force of character and through bloody-minded determination, he had ushered into the Shadow Cabinet's presence the sense of outrage felt by people of all political persuasions, and particularly the young, at the suffering in Biafra.

Peers and People

Macleod was sceptical of the proposals for constitutional reform put forward during the later 1960s. He saw the priority in modernizing Britain as a matter of economic reform and changing social attitudes, and though he supported Tory policy work on making the machinery of government more efficient, he was disinclined to embark on further upheavals.

When the Labour Government rather gingerly put in train their plans after the 1966 election for reforming the House of Lords, Macleod evinced little enthusiasm – notwithstanding his meritocratic ideals. Macleod was appointed, in his capacity as a former Leader of the Commons, one of the four Tory representatives (the others being Maudling, Lord Carrington and Lord Jellicoe) on an all-party conference on the subject. However, Macleod was doubtful of the whole exercise. On 18 December 1967, when the Shadow Cabinet discussed the conference's likely proposals, he made clear his strong reservations. The main proposal was to create a two-tier second chamber, consisting of voting and non-voting members. All first generation peers would be voting members for life, and the rest of the intended two hundred and forty voting members would be nominated by either the Government or the Opposition. The Government party would be guaranteed a majority over other parties but not over the whole house.[58]

In Macleod's view, the proposals created a danger of 'fossilization'. If there was a Labour Government and an upper chamber with a voting strength of 240, there would be 105 Labour voting peers, 80 Conservatives, 15 Liberals and 40 crossbenchers. But on a change to a Conservative Government, the Tory strength would have to be brought up from 80 to 130 to give them a majority over the other parties. Fifty new peers would have to be created for life, building into the proposals a lack of responsiveness to the shifting opinion of the country. Macleod also saw great difficulties in the role allotted to the crossbenchers, and, as the official minute notes, 'thought it odd that the greatest constitutional issues between the two Houses of Parliament would be settled by a rather motley selection of political independents.' Macleod 'regretted deeply that the present discredited Prime Minister and Government should have the responsibility for reforming the Lords', and had prefaced his views by stressing that it would be wrong if a radical change in the composition of either house was made during the lifetime of a parliament.[59]

The conference's proposals, published in January 1968 as a House of Lords paper, provoked fierce debate within the Shadow Cabinet. Carrington favoured declaring the party's support for the scheme, as did Douglas-Home, who felt that it would be no mean achievement if a Labour Government were prepared to underwrite an upper chamber that retained definite powers and in which there was still an hereditary element. When the Government finally approved the main points of the conference's report in March, most of the Shadow Cabinet favoured accepting the proposals, with Macleod's proviso that they should not come into force until after the next general election.[60]

The Government finally produced their White Paper in the autumn of 1968. In the two-day Commons debate in November 1968, Maudling opened for the Opposition on the first day and Macleod on the second. Macleod discharged his duty as a member of the inter-party conference to support the main proposals but barely disguised his scepticism. Admitting that he had started 'with more doubts about reform than any other member' of the conference, Macleod noted a press report that the Home Secretary, Callaghan, 'was not very enthusiastic' about the proposals and added, 'I am sure that exactly the same comment could be, and will be, made about my speech today.' Macleod, however, strongly opposed the Government's plan to bring in the reforms before the next election. He did not dispute that there were precedents for diminishing the powers of the Lords during the lifetime of a parliament, but argued that:

It would be utterly wrong for the Prime Minister in the declining months of this parliament to seek to exercise unprecedented powers of patronage by nomination on the basis of a general election held in March, 1966.

In the end Macleod voted for the White Paper, but 'made it clear that if, at a later stage, the Government are not more flexible on timing,' he would 'oppose the Bill, if one is produced, with all my strength'.[61]

The Government's bill, published the following January, provided for the reforms to come into effect at the start of the session following its enactment, i.e. the newly constituted Lords would begin work in the autumn of 1969, and the remaining (1969–70) session of the present parliament would be treated as a separate parliament. Macleod sought an early discussion in Shadow Cabinet, arguing that the provision for treating the 1969–70 session as a separate parliament was extraordinary. Whatever loyalty he and Maudling owed as members of the inter-party committee had been discharged and he proposed that the Opposition should table a reasoned amendment about the date of implementation. However, he received little support from the other three Tories who had served on the all-party conference.[62]

In the event, the bill never reached the statute book. Despite their mutually contradictory positions, the bill's backbench opponents, notably Foot and Powell, mounted a brilliant and relentless campaign of obstructionism. On 17 April 1969, after two months of painfully slow progress in committee, Wilson announced its abandonment. Macleod had said during his speech on the White Paper five months earlier that if the House 'rejects our work, I shall regret it, but I shall accept it'. By the following spring, the Government's mishandling of the reform left him little cause for regret. As Powell recalls of Macleod, 'he knew a dog's breakfast when he saw one'.[63]

Macleod had been a consistent supporter of British membership of the European Economic Community since his participation in the Cabinet's historic decision in July 1961 to apply for entry. But he was acutely aware that Heath's single-minded determination to achieve British entry exposed his party to huge political risks in the face of deep public suspicion of the EEC. Wilson would not hesitate to exploit the position if Heath was allowed to put the Tories out on a limb. Heath's cold-shouldering of the sizeable minority of Tory anti-marketeers would not make them disappear, and Macleod was anxious to find some formula that would help hold the party together. On 12 March 1970, when the Steering Committee considered the third draft of the manifesto, Macleod argued that a simple, short sentence should be inserted on negotiations with the EEC saying that there was a price that the Tories would not pay. The party's pro-European line, subject to this proviso, had been very effective during the Bridgwater by-election, where polling was being held that day.[64]

Macleod's anxieties on the European issue intensified during the spring, and were echoed elsewhere in the party. When the advisory committee on policy, comprising representatives from the voluntary side of the party, discussed a fourth draft of the manifesto on 6 May 1970, the feeling was expressed that people were not being consulted, whether on capital punishment or Europe. It was feared that Wilson's past lack of enthusiasm for Europe would give him an advantage, in that people thought he would be less likely than Heath to take Britain into the Common Market if the price were too high. One representative suggested that the party should seriously consider promising that parliament would only decide on British entry after a referendum had been held. Barney Hayhoe, who was attending the meeting as a member of the research department, felt that the idea of a referendum had some political merits. There was a precedent in that Stanley Baldwin had proposed a referendum (on tariff reform), although one was never held. If the party were to put forward the idea, they would have a political advantage and defuse the Common Market issue at the election.[65]

Hayhoe's intervention reveals Macleod's own thinking. As Hayhoe recalls, he wrote a paper 'with some encouragement from Macleod' that was intended for the Shadow Cabinet. Hayhoe acknowledged that the party disapproved of referendums, but raised the question what they should say if announcing a referendum on British entry into the EEC would win them the election. The paper never reached Shadow Cabinet, but the idea of a referendum was one of the options considered at the Steering Committee's meeting on 13 May. Just how strongly Macleod was arguing behind the scenes for a referendum is recalled by Jim Prior, then Heath's Parliamentary Private Secretary:

Before the 1970 election campaign, Iain Macleod was very keen that we should commit ourselves to a referendum on British entry to the EEC.

He thought this would remove much of the opposition within the party and would make it impossible for Wilson to come out in favour of one, a trick he was convinced Wilson would play unless we moved first. It took at least two meetings with Ted and Alec to shake Iain off this point.

In Hayhoe's recollection:

Douglas-Home was against it [a referendum], and the idea was sunk, but Macleod had been prepared at least to countenance the idea, and think it through.

In the absence of a referendum, only a free vote in the Commons would help to meet Macleod's concern that the Tories should give some reassurance that they would not take Britain into the EEC, regardless of the terms. He was determined that this should be the party's position.[66]

21

The Cruellest Blow

Whom the gods love dies young
> Greek epigram, cited by Reggie Maudling with regard to Iain Macleod.

Unlikely Father of 'Selsdon Man'

Macleod expected that Wilson would call the election in October 1970 rather than risk soldiering on for the full five-year term until the spring of 1971. By the early autumn of 1969 the gap between the two parties in the opinion polls had narrowed to single figures after virtually eighteen months when the Tories had enjoyed a double-figure lead. When the Tories met at Brighton for their annual conference, the mood was described by the seasoned political observer, Ronald Butt, as 'if we win', rather than 'when we win'.[1]

Macleod was right that the 1969 Conservative conference was to be the last before the election, although he could not know that it was also to be his last. His main purpose was to rally the troops when they were experiencing their first doubts of victory at the very worst moment. From the outset, he signalled his intention that Wilson and the Government's record were the main targets. Within moments of beginning his speech, he launched a damning indictment of Wilson itemizing his broken promises and declaring:

> There have been three Socialist Prime Ministers of this country – Mr Ramsey MacDonald, Lord Attlee and Wilson – and each of them has devalued the pound. The story of the Wilson Government has been a story of deceit, deflation, devaluation and debt – and that is what we are going to ram home in every constituency throughout the country.

Macleod's dramatic delivery roused the conference to thunderous cheers. As the applause subsided, he added, 'But before I leave him' – a phrase that excited renewed anticipation:

There is one phrase to which I wish to refer, or rather one charge, repeated over and over again: the charge that the Tory Party, because we oppose him politically, is unpatriotic. Sir, we are used to robust politics in this country, and we do not shrink from them. To some, this sort of accusation may not matter, but it does to me. And I reply that when a man, even if he be Prime Minister, not in the heat of an angry debate, but as part of a carefully scripted, carefully calculated smear, accuses a party that represents half the country of being unpatriotic, then that man has stepped down into the gutters of public life [pause] – and there, where better, we can leave him.

The venom of Macleod's attack prompted a reaction in the body of the hall of part shock, part pleasure, that somebody on the platform had dared to express a grievance felt deeply by many Tory workers, and had articulated it so bluntly. His punchline, timed to perfection, released loud cheers and prolonged applause.[2]

A few months later, Macleod was to play a key part in creating the myth of 'Selsdon Man', Wilson's clever name for the allegedly reactionary policies adopted by Heath and the Shadow Cabinet during their weekend at the Selsdon Park Hotel at the end of January, 1970. The origin of this myth owes much to the circumstances surrounding Heath's off-the-record press briefing on Saturday lunchtime. Heath had concluded the Shadow Cabinet's morning discussion of taxation by agreeing with Macleod's view that on the whole the less said about their proposed tax reforms the better, but he had forgotten all about meeting the press before luncheon until Fraser told him that the lobby correspondents had arrived. There was hurried, not to say desperate, discussion of what he might say. As Heath tried to gather his thoughts Macleod quipped, 'It's quite easy, Ted. Just tell them we believe in law and order, that always goes down well.' The official note merely refers to Heath 'considering whether to say that the party would put greater emphasis on law and order, mentioning strengthening and organization of the police'. In fact, Heath took up Macleod's suggestion, hook, line and sinker. The result sparked headlines in the Sunday and Monday newspapers that suggested a startling shift to the right.[3]

Wilson believed that Heath had made a serious misjudgement, and mocked the coming of 'Selsdon Man'. However, the Prime Minister's reaction benefited the Tories as much as his attack hindered them, since in the crucial months before the election it helped Heath overcome a deep concern among party workers that their leader had not done enough to distinguish the Tory Opposition from the Labour Government. Moreover, the press coverage of the Selsdon weekend had highlighted an issue on which the Tories enjoyed a clear lead over Labour.[4]

'Selsdon Man' is the stuff of political legend. Endowed with an ideological fervour that never gripped the Selsdon Park conferees, its memory has been perpetuated by right-wing Conservatives in the self-styled Selsdon Group. 'Selsdon' now conveys the antithesis of the Toryism espoused by Macleod. But Macleod was concerned at the level of public disquiet about law and order, as he had made clear only seven weeks before the Selsdon weekend, during a discussion of the key inner group of shadow ministers and their advisers. As the official minute notes, 'Macleod thought law and order could be a big issue at the next general election,' adding that 'he had been struck by the number of ordinary people who were getting angry at the sight of scroungers on national assistance and of demonstrators punching policemen.' It seems, then, that Macleod was both genuine and cynical – he was concerned about law and order, and, at the same time, saw it as a good way of dealing with the press and of appealing to the public.[5]

There is no contradiction between Macleod's stance, on the one hand, on law and order and, on the other, his liberal convictions and social compassion. Put simply, he was not a soft touch. He did not believe in turning a blind eye to those who defrauded the welfare state, thereby depriving the needy of help, or tolerating violent, as opposed to peaceful, protest. He realized that many ordinary people were concerned about these issues and believed that the Tories were more in touch with their anxieties than were Labour, and could also provide practical remedies. But he did admit to doubts about how the law and order issue could best be handled. As he commented during further discussion in the Steering Committee in the spring of 1970, the Tories 'had to watch the danger of appearing gimmicky on the issue and of looking like old Tory ladies wanting hanging and flogging'.[6]

Macleod's approach shows a politician focusing on the democratic competition for votes, and although his professionalism caused him to display apparent cynicism at times, it would be wrong to characterize him as a cynic. Watkins, his former political correspondent on the *Spectator*, does not believe that he was a cynical politician. When Macleod was deploring the Tory Party's 'growing opposition to comprehensive schools', Watkins asked him why he felt so strongly. Macleod replied:

More parents have children who fail the 11-plus than pass it. It is a matter of simple arithmetic. There are lots of votes to be got from comprehensives, although even the Labour party doesn't seem to realize it properly.

'Oddly,' as Watkins has recalled, he did not think that Macleod:

Was being wholly sincere: not so much in his support for comprehensive education, which was honest enough, as in the reason he provided for that support ... the romantic ... was playing at being the political realist, cynic even.[7]

Yet the most striking instance of Macleod's realism-cum-cynicism occurred on the question of prices and incomes policy, which had troubled the
Tories all through their Opposition years. Whereas some Shadow Ministers
argued that the Conservatives should not rule out a compulsory prices and
incomes policy completely in the manifesto, Macleod's instincts were strongly opposed to any such commitment appearing. Macleod's attitude during
the Shadow Cabinet's discussion on the manifesto has been characterized as
follows:

> Either we've got to say we're going to have an incomes policy, or say we're
> not going to have an incomes policy. It would be crazy to say we're going
> to have one, so we must say we're not going to have one. And if the time
> comes when events make us change our view, OK we'll have to change
> our view.

In keeping with Macleod's argument, the 1970 Tory manifesto promised
that, 'Labour's compulsory wage control was a failure and we will not repeat
it'. The imposition of statutory prices and incomes controls less than two
years after the election was to be the Heath Government's biggest U-turn.[8]

In the spring of 1970, Macleod began preparing for a bloody battle. With
television playing an increasingly important role in campaigns, in early April
he fired an early warning shot across the bows of his *bête noire*, the BBC.
He had been irritated by their coverage of the Bridgwater by-election,
claiming that it was virtually impossible to tell that the Conservatives had
won, and attacked the left-wing bias in its current affairs programmes.
Macleod's criticism was too outspoken for the party managers, and he found
little comfort in Barber's promise to look into the party's system for
monitoring television. As Sir Robin Day has since revealed, he telephoned
Macleod privately, in the hope of persuading him to appear in the BBC
programme, *24 Hours*:

> Macleod's response was crushing. He had already declared publicly that
> the political programmes of the BBC were 'of such sustained hostility to
> the Conservative Party that it is a net loss to appear.' He said the same
> to me only more acidly.

Recalling that Macleod had 'a bell-like orator's voice which sounded magnificent on the platform,' Sir Robin discovered that, 'Even on the telephone
it rang out as if he were in the pulpit, uttering a fearsome imprecation'.[9]

April's English and Welsh county council election results confirmed the
Tory lead in the opinion polls, indicating a swing of 9–10 per cent from
Labour since the 1966 general election, sufficient to give the Tories a
substantial majority in the Commons. However, glimmers of a Labour
revival were evident in London, where they won back 16 seats on the Greater

London Council, performing exceptionally well in inner London. Jenkins's spring budget signalled a further improvement in the Government's fortunes, and on 22 April, the *Daily Express* published a Harris poll that put Labour ahead for the first time in any opinion poll since March 1967. An October, or even a June election looked distinct possibilities. Much would depend on the municipal elections during early May.

By Friday 9th, Wilson was reportedly 'purring like a Persian cat'. The municipal election results indicated an overall Labour majority of 50 in the Commons. A June election was now on the cards. When Gallup put Labour ahead of the Tories by seven points Macleod was plunged into deep despair by Wilson's seemingly miraculous political renaissance.[10]

The pre-election tension boiled over during Prime Minister's Questions when Macleod's inability to contain his hatred for Wilson reflected the Opposition's intense disappointment and frustration. His outburst was triggered when Wilson replied to a question about children's road safety by drawing a clear comparison between the Tory and Labour years, claiming that if road casualties had continued to rise at their 1960–64 rate there would have been an increase of about 8 or 9 per cent during 1964–69. 'The Prime Minister need not bring that into politics,' interjected Macleod angrily. 'Right Honourable Gentlemen opposite have brought a lot of people's deaths into their propaganda,' retorted Wilson. At this, the official record notes demurely in square brackets, 'Interruption'. In fact, Macleod had yelled 'Swine!' across the despatch box. The Speaker responded to Labour protests by saying that if Macleod had used the word, he should withdraw. Macleod acknowledged that he had done so and withdrew, but he also defended his action and placed on the record that he 'thought it unforgiveable to bring children's deaths into a political argument and to make capital out of it'. Boyle, who witnessed the angry exchange, judged that Macleod's defence 'earned him the sympathy of the greater part of the House'.[11]

The election was formally announced on Monday 18 May for exactly a month's time – Thursday 18 June. Macleod hurriedly planned his campaign from his office at the Commons, above Star Chamber Court. When Jenkin, his frontbench lieutenant, went to discuss their plans, he found that Macleod was 'extremely grim'. Macleod did not believe the opinion polls, but he thought that they showed the trend. 'You'll be all right, you're young enough, you'll come back next time,' he told Jenkin. 'But for us older ones, this is the end.'[12]

Before the campaign proper began, Macleod and Eve took advantage of the spring bank holiday for a short break on the Costa Brava at S'Agaro. While he was away, the Government finally advised the cricket authorities that they should cancel the South Africa cricket tour, a decision that Macleod condemned as 'contemptible, miserable weakness, a surrender to the mob'. Over the previous months, this issue had divided him and some of his closest friends and he now wrote to one of them, Nick Scott: 'I am so sad that on a subject that combines cricket and race we take different views . . . For you I have the highest hopes for the future. For myself I sniff the breeze like an old war horse and I love it.'[13]

The 'old war horse' relished the fray. He had also told Jenkin: 'We'll go out and have a bloody good fight, but I am worried about Ted.' Macleod was 'distressed about Ted Heath's pessimism and Central Office's gloom and went to see Heath before leaving for his first campaign meeting in Potters Bar on 28 May. His message to Heath had been to reiterate the argument he had pressed during the final meetings of the Steering Committee on 11 and 13 May, that the women's vote would be crucial because they had benefited less than men from increases in wages and were more sensitive to the issues of prices and law and order. 'Go on the box,' Macleod now told Heath, 'and appeal to the women voters, they'll be the ones who'll decide this election.' As Macleod told Colin Turner, 'I'm the only person he'll listen to.'[14]

Last Break with the Isles

On the first full day of the campaign, Monday 1 June, Macleod made an immediate impact, although not in the way that Heath would have wished. At the end of the previous week, prominent politicians in all three parties had faced a barrage of questions about British entry into the EEC, and had ruled out a referendum on constitutional grounds. Speaking in his constituency, Macleod had also ruled out a referendum, but his comment that he and all other MPs would take the views of their constituents into account prompted a questioner to ask: 'In other words, you are committed to a free vote of the House?' 'That's inevitable,' Macleod replied, 'I don't think there's any question about that.'[15]

But there was a very big question about it, as Macleod well knew. In response to similar questioning, Heath and Wilson had both ruled out a free vote on the issue in the Commons. There the matter might have rested, except that a correspondent from *The Times*, Leonard Beaton, had attended Macleod's early constituency meetings in order to write a profile of him. When the profile duly appeared on 1 June, journalists attending Heath's first morning press conference seized on this evident contradiction between the Tory leader and Macleod. Heath sought unconvincingly to argue that there was really no difference, but during the campaign, seemed to soften his position. Less than eighteen months later, Conservative MPs were allowed a free vote on the terms for British entry.[16]

Macleod was the key figure, apart from Heath, in the Tory campaign, not only because he was Shadow Chancellor and the economy is the main battlefield of modern elections, but also because he was a formidable campaigner. Indeed, Beaton in his profile wrote of Macleod's ability to deliver 'a speech such as few men in public life now put on; ordered and economical to the intelligent and brilliantly rousing to the faithful'. Macleod began his national campaigning on Monday 1 June in East London, speaking in Hornchurch that evening. But his electioneering was immediately disrupted. That night, Macleod's elderly mother died at her home in Carleton Road, Skipton. Only a couple of months earlier, the family had gathered at the Devonshire Arms, Bolton Abbey, a few miles to the east, in Wharfedale, to celebrate her ninetieth birthday. On hearing the news, Macleod immediately cancelled his campaign commitments for the rest of the week in order to arrange her funeral and grieve for her.[17]

Macleod was devoted to his mother and her death deeply affected him. Replying to a letter of sympathy, Macleod wrote to Nigel Fisher's wife: 'It is so desolate to be no one's child.' Rhoderick, his youngest brother, believes that 'his mother personified for him [Iain] all the strings of his island inheritance. Her death was a breaking of the link.' 'Lab' Macleod, who had returned to live in Skipton in November 1968, had been the centre of the family. Macleod loved to tease her and, by the same token, she never quite accepted that her sons' age or position should deter her from her mother's duties. Rhoderick was staying with her on one occasion when he and Iain attended the Old Fettesians' dinner at the Commons. Both men were, by this time, former ministers (Rhoderick in Kenya), but as Rhoderick left, his mother checked that he had a clean handkerchief and added, for good measure: 'Do see that Iain has a clean handkerchief and that he doesn't drink too much!' Lab Macleod was a great character, whose comments entertained the family. On one occasion, after she had settled in London, she met a woman and assumed, from her accent, that she was Scottish. The woman explained that she was from Ulster, and after they had parted Lab Macleod was heard to comment: 'Damn fool woman, doesn't know where she comes from.' Eve had arranged her ninetieth birthday party, including a piper to play after dinner, but when Mrs Macleod heard the first skirl of the pipes she commented: 'Damn fool girl, doesn't know there are no pipes on the Island (Lewis), only on the mainland.'[18]

Lab Macleod's funeral was held in Yorkshire on Friday 5th. She was cremated and her ashes buried in her husband's grave, near to that of her daughter, Rhodabel (who had died in 1962) in the village churchyard of Gargrave, in Airedale, a few miles upstream from Skipton. As the vicar, Revd Kenneth Cook, stood with Macleod and his brother 'in the sunshine of this summer churchyard', he noticed that 'Iain, in one of his characteristic abstractions, gazed for a time intently down this lovely dale of ours, along the crest of Sharphaw, to where the tip of his native Skipton shows, backed up by Rombald's Moor'.[19]

Macleod's deeply felt reaction to his mother's death showed the emotional core of his personality. At the same time this episode revealed how little he was understood. While he was in Yorkshire grieving for his mother, a cold insensitivity to his feelings was evident among some party workers at

Conservative Central Office, who resented that Macleod should take a week off from the campaign. Others at the heart of the Conservative campaign were deeply angered by such crass and heartless talk. In fact, Macleod missed only four days, and his return to the hustings was out of the question before his mother's funeral on the Friday. But behind the backroom mutterings also lurked the fear of impending defeat and a suspicion that Macleod might be distancing himself from a doomed leader.[20]

Macleod made an immediate impact on his return to the campaign. On Sunday 7th, he attended the 90-minute Shadow Cabinet election strategy meeting at Heath's Albany apartment, where it was decided that the Tories should continue to concentrate on exposing what they held to be the weakness of the economic structure on which the balance of payments surplus was based. On the evening of Monday 8 June, Macleod appeared in his first party election television broadcast of the campaign (it was the Tories' third), which was devoted exclusively to the state of the economy. Macleod's robust attack on Labour delighted Tory activists. Conservative Central Office were soon on the phone, pleading with Macleod to appear in the next broadcast, just three days later.[21]

Macleod and Eve based themselves at the Devonshire Arms, Bolton Abbey, where they had spent their honeymoon and only recently celebrated Lab Macleod's ninetieth birthday. It was well placed for their forays to the key marginal seats in Lancashire and Yorkshire, before they headed north to Scotland. Eve drove them everywhere in her automatic car – very fast and very safe – as she had done at previous elections. They were accompanied by Gerry Wade, Chairman of the Greater London Young Conservatives, who served as Macleod's personal assistant.

Wade was immediately struck by Macleod's leisurely approach to campaigning. His day would start by reading the papers, and he would then draft any articles that had to be written together with a new section for his main evening speech responding to the topical issues of the campaign, for pre-release to the press. He would then show Eve and Wade what he had written. On the road, requests from Conservative Central Office for immediate press statements were dealt with as efficiently as Macleod dispatched his articles and press releases during the morning. Macleod could always be relied on to respond in time for the news deadlines. Wade, who had never seen him campaigning before, was struck at how little he enjoyed meeting people and indulging in small talk. The Macleods always packed sandwiches to avoid having to waste valuable time eating meals with candidates and local associations, but Macleod was usually anxious to escape as fast as was decently possible. At the end of his public meetings, he would look to Wade to ensure that he was not trapped for too long – on one particularly awkward occasion Macleod told Wade out of the corner of his mouth 'Get me out of here!' After Macleod had spoken for an unimpressive candidate, he commented as they drove away, 'lobby fodder!'[22]

Yet Macleod's performance on the hustings was truly professional. 'Seasoned observers of the General Election game smiled approvingly,' reported *The Times* in its election round-up, when he returned to the fray by touring Yorkshire constituencies on Monday 8th. What a 'miserable, wet, complacent bunch' the Government were, Macleod declared at Keighley, savaging Wilson as not only wicked but frivolous, living in his own 'Walter Mitty world' where promises and pledges were forgotten and only today's headlines remembered. As the report observed: 'Mr Macleod really does this kind of thing rather well.' Not only would Macleod refine his speech according to the latest twist in the campaign, he would play to different audiences. His accent would be varied subtly, so that if he was speaking in Yorkshire he would add a slight touch of his home accent, whereas when he visited Scotland he slightly accentuated his Scottish phrases and pronunciation. Likewise, he had a fine appreciation of which aspects of his speech would elicit the strongest response from different audiences, and would even vary his punch-lines depending on the area. He would also use his disability for emphasis, sometimes swivelling his whole body round as he stressed a point. At the end of every day, Macleod would throw all his papers away – letters, notes, papers, nothing at all would be kept.[23]

At first, he refused all pleas from Conservative Central Office for him to appear in the fourth party election broadcast on Thursday 11th, saying that he would not disrupt his schedule. He even refused when a Leeds studio was booked for him. In the end, Central Office offered to send a film crew to his hotel. As soon as this had been arranged, Macleod sat down without any fuss and drafted his script. He was clear-headed about what he wanted to say, and made no fuss about preparing it. This penultimate Tory broadcast of the campaign took up the theme that Macleod had repeatedly urged on Heath by appealing directly for the housewives' vote. The first part of the programme featured a film of Sylvia, a young housewife from Wandsworth, who had appeared in a vox-pop clip in an earlier broadcast. She told how she found it difficult to make ends meet as she went about her daily chores and did the shopping. Although she thought her husband would vote Labour, she would vote Conservative. Macleod's talk to camera followed immediately. Declaring straight away that she was right, he asked viewers whether they could afford the 'ten bob' pound (he had claimed during the campaign that under Labour the 1964 pound would be worth only ten shillings by 1974) and a frozen wage packet. Socialism meant high prices and taxes. He urged voters to throw Labour out. 'They just don't care,' he declaimed.[24]

Yet at the end of the second week, the opinion polls went from bad to worse for the Tories. The next evening, Friday 12th, less than a week before polling, the Tories heard that the latest NOP survey, due to be published on Saturday morning, put Labour 12 points ahead. When Macleod heard, he took the trouble, just before midnight, to phone Barney Hayhoe, who was standing for the Tories in Heston and Isleworth. He warned that a very bad poll was about to appear, but that Hayhoe should not worry too much because he had heard that another better poll was due out. Gallup's poll published on Sunday 14th gave Labour a 2½ point lead.

There are conflicting versions of Macleod's views of the likely outcome of the election. Immediately before his brief holiday in late May, he had thought the Tories would lose. On his return, dining with the Rothermeres, he predicted that the Tories would return to office with a majority of 31 or 32 seats, and Eve recalls that Macleod expected the Tories to triumph. After touring the Lancashire and Yorkshire marginals he told Nigel Fisher that the Tories would win, and a week before polling day predicted a 35-seat Tory majority. Walker, who was confident from his canvass returns that the Tories would win, spoke 'eight or nine times' with Macleod on the telephone during the campaign and found that he agreed. When they spoke on the final weekend, Macleod 'was very positive', and told him, 'I'm absolutely certain we're going to win it, there's a marvellous mood and spirit, I couldn't care less about these polls.' Sir Keith Joseph also recalled that, 'Macleod was very confident that we would win and he said so all the way through'.[25]

However, others suggest that Macleod had doubts. As Whitelaw has commented: 'Iain was an incredibly good gambler, he was saying that but I don't think he really believed it. I think he thought it was the only possible way of getting a good result and I think he was right.' Wade, who spent the campaign with Macleod and discussed all the polls with him is clear that Macleod thought the Conservatives would lose. 'For all his public talk about not taking any notice of the polls', Wade recalls: 'He had a little book in his jacket breast pocket which he would produce whenever he was looking at an opinion poll and from which he could see exactly who would lose their seats on the basis of the share of the votes'. This was scarcely the behaviour of a man confident of victory. As Macleod calculated which members of the parliamentary party would be defeated, he might say: 'Oh dear, that means that Nick Scott will lose.' The prospect of defeat did not seem outwardly to depress him. Instead, he was quite matter of fact about it.[26]

These pocket-book calculations of Macleod's again raise the question of whether he was considering his prospects of the leadership if the Tories lost. Defeat would certainly have meant the end for Heath and a leadership contest in which the composition of the electoral college of Tory MPs in the new parliament would determine the outcome. At one point during their frequent talks, Wade asked Macleod if he would still be interested in trying for the leadership. 'Of course,' Macleod replied quite simply, as though Wade had been silly to doubt it. It is hard to imagine any senior politician not giving at least a passing thought to the possibility of his becoming leader of his party, but Wade's impression remains that Macleod's overriding wish was to become Chancellor of the Exchequer. He was not old, having celebrated his fifty-sixth birthday in November 1969, and he might have contemplated an active political career stretching well into his sixties. At the election after next, assuming that it was held in October 1974 or 1975, he would have been almost 61 or 62, still younger than Macmillan had been at the start of his six-year premiership. Yet because of his ill-health and because he wanted to make some money before he retired, Macleod had decided to leave the Commons after completing his reform of the tax system, which he believed would take two or three budgets.[27]

Powell's role towards the end of the campaign provoked a strong reaction from Macleod. Powell's interventions had attracted considerable attention following an outspoken attack by Tony Benn on him on 3 June. Powell had called in his election address for a halt to immigration. On Thursday 11th, he attacked those in power for misleading the public on immigration. On Saturday 13th, the day of the NOP poll giving Labour a 12-point lead, he attacked the 'enemy within', by which he meant the small minority who were infiltrating and brainwashing decent people into accepting the collapse of law and order. Macleod told Nigel Fisher that he was furious with Powell over his disloyalty to the party and its leader, and commented to Wade that 'we might lose this campaign, but we shall do so with honour.' Macleod was consulted about how to handle Powell and counselled that it was wise to avoid any public response, since it would only exacerbate the problem and make the party look even more divided. Heath's statement on Sunday 14th stopped short of widening the breach with Powell, and stressed the Shadow Cabinet's commitment 'never to use words or support actions which exploit or intensify divisions in our society'.[28]

Suddenly, at the start of the final week of the campaign, everything seemed to go well for the Tories. On Monday 15th, the publication of May's trade figures, after nine months of good returns, showed a £31 million deficit. Speaking in Wellingborough that night, Macleod seized on this as proof of what the Tories had argued all along: the economy was in a much worse state than Labour had ever let on. Attending the London press conference the next morning, Macleod derided Wilson's attempt to recover from the embarrassment of the trade figures by quoting an economic forecast from the Paris-based international organization, the OECD. When Macleod spoke in Enfield that night, he claimed that there was some mystery about the existence of the OECD report – he had tried to find out more, but neither the Treasury nor the Board of Trade knew of it. At his final constituency meeting on Wednesday 17th, he seized on the announcement of a fall in industrial production to conclude on the theme that he had developed during the campaign. Describing the output figures as: 'alarming when taken in conjunction with the recent trade figures', Macleod declared, 'We now have the volume of exports static, the volume of imports rising and production stagnant'.[29]

On polling day, he felt ill and stayed at home in bed while Eve went round the constituency committee rooms. But he was able to get up that evening and, after the polls had closed at 10pm, went to his own count. While he was waiting for his own declaration, he listened to the first results coming through on a transistor radio and realized almost immediately after 11pm, when the first result was declared and David Howell increased his majority at Guildford, that the Tories would win. Macleod's majority in Enfield West increased to 11,962. Immediately after the declaration, Macleod headed across London for Dulwich, to join Diana, his daughter, who had spent the campaign working in the local, marginal seats, for a memorable election night party. Early the next morning, still jubilant at the Tory victory, he telephoned Barney Hayhoe and congratulated him on his having been elected to the Commons for the first time.[30]

Spoils of Victory

Wilson conceded defeat at midday on Friday 19 June, although it was not until 2.15pm that the Conservatives won their 316th seat and with it an overall majority (they finally won 330 seats and an overall majority of 30). At 6.50pm the Queen, having spent the afternoon at Royal Ascot, asked Heath to form a government. Macleod was one of the first ministers to be appointed the next morning, Saturday 20th, calling on Heath in Downing Street at 11.00am. The Prime Minister asked him to become Chancellor of the Exchequer. It was the prize he wanted, and he was delighted to hear that his longstanding personal friends and political allies, Maudling and Carr, were to be appointed Home Secretary and Employment Secretary respectively.

Macleod emerged from Number Ten buoyed up at the prospect of realizing his last political ambition and establishing as great a reputation as a reformer at the Treasury as he had achieved at the Colonial Office ten years earlier. As David Wood of *The Times* noted: 'Mr Macleod clearly welcomes the challenge after the spell in the wilderness that is so little in tune with his temperament.' However, Macleod was already ill and the failure of his health would ultimately deny him his opportunity to test his mettle in one of the great offices of state.[31]

The Chancellor's private office, run by the principal private secretary, Bill (later Sir William) Ryrie, and numbering about twenty in all, had reported for work on the Saturday morning to await official confirmation that Macleod had been appointed and in case he wanted to go straight to his Great George Street office. But Macleod had other plans. He headed for the home of Diana, his daughter, and David Heimann, her husband, in Upper Brook Street, Mayfair, where Sir Douglas Allen (later Lord Croham), the Permanent Secretary at the Treasury, visited him. The two men had already met. When a General Election appeared imminent, Macleod had privately invited Allen to dinner. Allen had been immediately struck by his 'very clear, active and able mind' and never doubted that Macleod would not be able 'to get his way with the Cabinet and the Prime Minister'.[32]

Allen now offered the new Chancellor his congratulations and went through the formalities of handing over his official brief, prepared by the mandarins during the campaign, and telling him his private secretary's and driver's names and telephone numbers. As they chatted, Macleod mentioned that he was not feeling well and thought he had food poisoning, but hoped he would feel all right over the weekend. When Macleod telephoned his private office, Ryrie was immediately impressed by his style. After Ryrie had congratulated him and mentioned that the private office were at their desks, Macleod said: 'Yes, I hear you've got the staff in. Well, tell them all to go home, and come and have lunch with me tomorrow.'[33]

Macleod planned to spend the rest of Saturday at Lord's, where the first cricket Test was being played between England and a Rest of the World XI, a series arranged at short notice in place of the cancelled South African tour. Among those with Macleod in the hospitality box were Diana and David Heimann, Nigel Fisher, Nick Scott and Gerry Wade. When Macleod appeared on the balcony, the crowd cheered spontaneously. But Macleod seemed more hunched with pain than usual and had to leave the ground early. That evening he telephoned Walker to congratulate him on being appointed to the Cabinet. He also hoped that Scott would become a minister, but warned him that Heath was committed to reducing the number of ministers. When it later became clear that Scott had not been appointed, Macleod asked him to serve as his Parliamentary Private Secretary, promising that after a year he would see that he was made a minister.[34]

During Ryrie's visit to the White Cottage for Sunday luncheon, Macleod declared his intention to work at the Treasury only from ten o'clock till five in the afternoon, and not to take papers home or go to any cocktail parties in the evening. Ryrie tentatively expressed the opinion that the enormous burdens on a modern Chancellor might make this impossible, but Macleod was very firm about his proposed hours. Macleod's resolve to impose such a strict time limit on his work, and the self-denying ordinance on drinks' parties for somebody who had always enjoyed the good life, suggests more than the wise precaution of preventing civil servants from dominating their minister's life, and indicates an awareness of the frailty of his health.[35]

Macleod was cock-a-hoop when he entered the Treasury on the morning of Monday 22nd. Civil servants recall him smiling and greeting them cheerily. Everybody who spoke with the new Chancellor remembers his sheer elation. When the Treasury's new ministers – Maurice Macmillan, Chief Secretary, Patrick Jenkin, Financial Secretary, and Terence Higgins, Economic Secretary – first entered Macleod's office, he rose to greet them declaring: 'Isn't it absolutely marvellous, here we are.' Jenkin recalls Macleod's 'joy at being back in office, and his joy at being in the Treasury and feeling he'd really now got his hands on the levers and that we'd got a lot of work to do.' Walker, too, remembers attending his first Cabinet on Tuesday 23rd and Macleod greeting him inside Number 10, saying 'this is the right place to be' and expressing his own delight at being Chancellor. Rees-Mogg, editor of *The Times*, spoke with Macleod on the telephone, and recalls that: 'he was full of the joy of having become Chancellor and the opportunities that existed, and very confident, and there was not the least suggestion that he was other than on the top of his form'.[36]

For their part, Treasury officials were buoyed by Macleod's presence. They were ready to respond to his lead. Contrary to the popular misconception that Whitehall mandarins like a weak minister, they are in fact happiest when their minister is a powerful figure in his or her own right, who can command the Commons, carry the Cabinet with him or her and win the Prime Minister's backing. Nobody in the Treasury harboured any doubts about Macleod's not fitting the bill on each count. On his first day, Macleod had a longer discussion with Sir Douglas Allen. He told him that his presumed food poisoning had not cleared up over the weekend, and he still felt ill, but he gave Allen a precise list of specific points for immediate action. Allen organized a short series of meetings for the Chancellor with senior officials, although Macleod was caught up for much of the week in the frantic round of ceremony, familiarization and public relations that occupies the first week of new Cabinet ministers.[37]

Macleod began as he had said he intended to carry on. His lunches were frugal, consisting of a sandwich and a banana, eaten in his room at the Treasury. He did venture out for at least one lunch as Chancellor, when he was a guest of the *Financial Times*. As he had planned, he left his office by the late afternoon. However, this is easier to achieve in the first few weeks, when ministers are mainly commissioning new work and seeking more information from their officials, than later when the weight of reaching decisions and facing new problems inevitably begins to increase. Whether he could have maintained his extraordinary regime is extremely doubtful, but Macleod was probably the only modern Chancellor with even a chance of doing so. He made it clear from the outset that he expected his ministers and officials to comply with his working habits.

His private secretaries were astonished at the speed at which Macleod worked. Peter (later Sir Peter) Middleton recalls that he was the quickest reader he had ever seen. Indeed, Middleton found Macleod's reading the 'most amazing thing about him', because he appeared to 'read books while you watched him', and had actually taken in what he had read. Jenkin, who was having to learn the ropes in his first ministerial appointment, recalls that: 'if you were going to comment on anything that was going on you had to do it overnight. If you left it till the next day you were too late. It had all been done. The decisions had all gone out.'[38]

Unlike some incoming ministers after a change of government, Macleod had no suspicion of his officials because they had been working for a Labour Government for almost six years. Allen 'formed the impression that this would be a productive and constructive relationship'. Macleod regarded his role as Minister in its traditional sense. Ryrie recalls that the new Chancellor assumed that:

> The Minister was somebody who received well-considered advice, dealing with all the technicalities, and so on, and who mastered it quickly and decided. He either received it orally or in writing, but his business was not to spend a long time mulling it over, and discussing it, but to take decisions.

In this respect, there was a marked similarity with his immediate predecessor, Roy Jenkins, who, like Macleod, was not an economist but was a respected politician and good administrator. Both men would expect the Civil Service to provide the technical work on which they would pronounce, although Jenkins was more apt to discuss matters intellectually. Macleod preferred small meetings to larger ones and dispatched the business 'very efficiently'. His officials found him easy to get on with, incisive, quick and shrewd.[39]

Now that Macleod had his hands on the wheel, how did he set about steering the economy? Treasury officials of the period now talk of it as one in which the 'Butskellism' of the 1950s had been replaced by 'Macleod-Jenkinsism'. The main difference between the new Tory Chancellor and his Labour predecessor was the former's emphasis on reducing direct taxation and removing the power of the state. Fiscal policy remained the main instrument for managing the economy, and Macleod intended to announce a package of measures in the autumn, in advance of his first budget in the spring of 1971.[40]

When Macleod entered the Treasury in June 1970, unemployment was high by the standards of the 1950s and 1960s, output was depressed and yet inflationary pressures were at their strongest since 1951. According to Croham, the new Chancellor

> thought that as long as you had a reasonable balance in fiscal policy, which you achieved to a large extent by keeping down public expenditure, and that you got the economy moving, you would deal with inflation in that way. None of the Government at that point really believed in trying to deal with inflation by interest rates. We were beginning to move into trying to react in a way with what you would call monetary policy, but it had not got very far by 1970.

Terence Higgins, the Treasury Minister responsible for monetary policy until April 1972, recalls that the Tories saw this as an aspect of policy that was important and was related to fiscal policy, but it was not regarded as the only, crucial instrument of economic management.[41]

Macleod delivered only one speech in the Commons as Chancellor, when he spoke during the traditional debate on the loyal address on Tuesday 7 July. It was a disappointing performance – he was in great pain – but he confirmed his commitment to demand management primarily by means of fiscal policy, while also maintaining that the levels of both public spending and taxation were too high. Noting the similarity with the economic situation several years earlier that he had christened 'stagflation', he felt that the conflicting evidence that confronted him as Chancellor meant that 'it would be premature at the moment to take action to stimulate demand'. However, he gave a clear hint of his plans for some reflation when he referred to the talk on an autumn package, and insisted that a chancellor must be free: 'to take such action as may seem necessary at the appropriate time, and clearly it is more likely, unless the indicators change, that one will wish to stimulate demand rather than restrain it.' In stark contrast to the notion of a monetarist framework of the kind introduced after 1979, Macleod believed that, 'demand management, which includes the management of monetary policy, is not a matter for one day in a year [i.e. budget day] but for continuous operation'.[42]

But in his first fortnight in office, Croham found that Macleod 'was much more interested in getting us moving on the various changes he wanted made, starting to see who would do it, how it would be presented, what the timetable was and so on'. These changes primarily concerned reductions in public spending, designed to facilitate tax reductions, and the abolition of bodies like the Prices and Incomes Board and the Industrial Reorganization Corporation, and the slimming down of others. The Conservatives were committed against a statutory incomes policy, but they sought to keep track of what was happening to pay settlements through a Cabinet committee chaired by Maudling. Macleod's officials found that the new Chancellor did not appear to have any theology, or preconceived ideas, on incomes policy or monetarism, but in his Commons speech he reiterated his declaration as Shadow Chancellor that the Government had a duty to set an example and use their influence 'firmly and openly on the side of non-inflationary [pay] settlements' in the public sector. Macleod left no room for any doubt about his resolve as Chancellor.[43]

Macleod also claimed that the outlook on prices was more serious than anybody had realized. As he warned MPs, 'We find ourselves faced with a situation in which yearly price increases are either already in prospect or known to be coming forward over a large part of the nationalized industries field.' And he continued:

We said before the election that we should scrutinize very closely all proposed price increases in the public sector and that these increases would be allowed only where there was a proved case for them. We intend to carry out that promise. It is most important for the economy in general that we should take a firm grip on prices in the public sector because of the contribution that a break in the wage–price spiral can make towards the stability of the economy as a whole.

Ruling out a 'price freeze' in the public sector, Macleod declared that the Government found it 'hard to accept' that there was 'not considerable scope for absorbing high costs by increasing efficiency rather than by the easier course of simply passing on higher costs through higher charges'.[44]

Where Macleod probably differed from most other Chancellors was in his enormous interest in the tax system and its reform. His enthusiasm and detailed knowledge were welcome to officials. Cockfield, who had undertaken much of the detailed work in Opposition, was away from London, but on his return some days later found a letter from Macleod waiting for him, that started, 'Where on earth are you, would you please come round to the Treasury immediately?'[45]

The economies that Macleod immediately began to seek throughout Whitehall were, as he told the Commons on 7 July, 'the essential prerequisite to our plans for lower levels of taxation and higher levels of savings'. The targets for economies were identified in a composite list derived from the proposed cuts listed by the research department in 1969, a similar list compiled from government estimates by Patrick Jenkin and Terence Higgins shortly before the election, and the Treasury's list drawn up by officials during the campaign in case the Tories won. However, the launch of the cost-cutting exercise in Whitehall within days of the election caused consternation at the Conservative Research Department, because they heard that ministers were planning only to announce spending cuts in the autumn without any countervailing reduction in taxation. Their deep anxiety prompted a 'fraught' session on the terrace of the House of Commons with Terence Higgins, who was able to give them some reassurance. Patrick Jenkin had wanted to send a copy of the Treasury's brief on the economy to the Research Department, and hear their views, but the civil servants to whom he suggested this recoiled in horror and immediately reported his intention to the Chancellor. Macleod summoned Jenkin and lectured him on the sanctity of Treasury confidentiality.[46]

The public spending review during the summer of 1970 confirmed the Treasury view that it is easier to bring public expenditure under control at the start of a new administration than later in its life. Ministers seemed almost desperate to make a good impression by volunteering economies in their programmes. The most notable exception was the new Secretary of State for Education, Margaret Thatcher. Macleod was concerned that education spending should not be cut across the board, and instead preferred to scrap one of his particular *bêtes-noires*, the proposed Open University (the creation of Harold Wilson and Jennie Lee), which had yet to admit any students. The Treasury gave Thatcher the option of either scrapping the Open University or introducing a series of other cuts, including the abolition of free school milk and the imposition of charges on libraries and museums, expecting that Thatcher would do Macleod's bidding by axing the Open University. To their great astonishment she fought to save it and instead cut her other programmes.[47]

The details of the spending review were handled by the Chief Secretary, Maurice Macmillan, who soon found himself having to run the entire department. The Macleods had moved into Number Eleven on Monday 29 June, the day that the new parliament assembled before the official state opening later that week. They held a family dinner there that evening to celebrate his appointment as Chancellor. At the end of the dinner, Macleod paid tribute to Eve for all her help, and gave Torquil the bible on which he had sworn allegiance and Diana his scroll of office as Chancellor.

On the morning of Tuesday 7 July, worsening pain caused Macleod to consult a doctor, who thought that he might need an operation for appendicitis. But Macleod insisted that he would first attend to his duties at the Commons. His officials recall that he was in tremendous pain when he came into his office beforehand. At the Commons, he managed to answer Treasury questions and deliver his speech. He liked his speeches to flow, but on this occasion he was expected to deliver an appraisal of the economy and had to base much of his script on detailed drafts by officials, which he had rewritten. This was the only occasion on which he read almost his entire speech from a prepared script, and he regarded it as the worst speech that he ever made. Soon afterwards he returned to Number Eleven, where a further examination confirmed that an immediate operation was necessary. Eve telephoned Ryrie to tell him the news and that night drove her husband to St George's Hospital, Hyde Park Corner.[48]

Struck Down

Macleod was suffering not from appendicitis but from a benign, abdominal condition, a pelvic diverticulum, which had ruptured by the time that he entered hospital. His operation was a success, and he began recuperating. His daughter, Diana, had undergone a serious back operation at University College Hospital at about the same time, and Eve spent her time travelling from one to the other. Soon after his operation, he was visited by Reggie Bennett, his friend and former PPS, who was surprised to discover Macleod sitting up reading the *Evening Standard*. Macleod said that he had woken up about an hour earlier and had asked a nurse to get him the evening paper. 'What would you want with an evening paper?' she had asked. 'I want to know how I'm getting on,' Macleod had replied.[49]

Macleod appeared to be making a satisfactory recovery. He was soon reading books at his usual prodigious rate. Nigel Fisher and his wife visited him on Sunday 12 July. They thought he looked tired, but he told them that, 'the enforced rest had done him good and that he could hardly wait to get down to serious work in the department.' Macleod then outlined to Fisher his future plans and hopes for tax reform. The Fishers were also struck that the only photograph beside his bed was a large one of Gary Sobers, the great Barbadian cricket all-rounder, who was captaining the Rest of the World team that summer. During the 1960s in his speeches on 'the pursuit of excellence' Macleod used to cite as a clearly identifiable example, the sight of Sobers on a cricket field.[50]

Although he was still in hospital on Saturday 18 July, Macleod insisted that the annual Enfield cricket match that he used to organize and which was scheduled for that day, should go ahead. On Sunday 19th, he was well enough to return to Number Eleven, where his cousin, Catherine Ross, had arrived a few days earlier to help Eve while she was caring for both her husband and her daughter. Macleod stayed in bed for the rest of the day reading Cabinet and departmental papers. The next day, Monday 20th, several people visited him, including Patrick Jenkin, Bill Ryrie and Nick Scott. He remained in bed, was weak and feeling low, and clearly would not be able to attend Cabinet on Tuesday 21st as he had hoped. His officials had assumed that on his return to Number Eleven he would be able to cope with more paperwork, but Eve advised Ryrie that he was still not well enough, as Ryrie immediately realized when he saw the Chancellor. Macleod was depressed by the news from Jenkin that, in his absence, his publicly declared intention of breaking the wage–price spiral by holding down nationalized industry prices had already been cast aside and approval given to increase electricity prices. 'It's all slipping away,' was his gloomy reaction. Macleod was also depressed at his own progress, and Jenkin tried to encourage him by telling him that he would soon be back.[51]

Macleod did get up that evening to have dinner at Number Eleven with his doctor, Matthew Forster. After Forster had left, Macleod chatted on the telephone with a friend about a visit to Australia, New Zealand and Singapore that they were planning for the autumn. He then put on his dressing gown and walked across the hall to the small television room to watch a report on the Commonwealth Games from Edinburgh, where he had spent his schooldays. On the way back to bed at about 10.30pm he was suddenly taken ill with heart trouble. Catherine Ross ran to help him and he was able to get to bed. Eve immediately telephoned St George's, as she had been told to do if there was any problem, but there was a delay before a doctor reached Downing Street, and Macleod suffered a severe heart attack.

Macleod died at 11.35pm on Monday 20 July. Within half an hour Heath and Whitelaw visited Eve and were a great comfort. Dr Forster, the family's doctor, also returned quickly to Downing Street and was an immense help.

Ryrie and Higgins handled matters in Downing Street and helped prepare the announcement of the Chancellor's death, which was finally released at about 2.30am. Such was the shock at Macleod's death that many people can recollect what they were doing when they first heard about it. Enoch Powell received an anonymous telephone call at about 3am, when a stranger's voice said that he wished to express his condolences at the loss of his friend, the Chancellor of the Exchequer. Jenkin, who had not heard the phone ringing during the night, was deeply upset when he switched on the radio for the early morning bulletin and heard what had happened. John Major, who was staying with his future wife and mother-in-law at their home, was stunned when he picked up the morning paper and saw the headline. Nick Beacock, who had done so much to organize 'Crisis at Christmas' in its early years, had been invited by Macleod to tea at Number Eleven that afternoon but saw the news when he opened his morning newspaper on the underground.[52]

The suddenness of Macleod's death at the age of 56, when he had been recovering from his operation, fuelled speculation. His death certificate gives the cause of death as 'coronary infarct', in plain language, a heart attack. After surgery, even when the operation itself has been a success, there is a risk that a clot of blood from the wound can circulate to the heart and cause death. This appears to have happened in Macleod's case. Also listed as subsidiary causes on the death certificate are 'ankylosing spondylitis' and 'chronic renal failure'. The former subsidiary illness had given Macleod virtually constant pain for twenty years and prevented him exercising. Macleod's kidney problem was later described by one of his doctors as having been longstanding. Dr Forster, who certified his death, and the surgeons at St George's, subsequently confirmed in writing that there was no evidence that he had cancer.[53]

Macleod had become increasingly aware that he had to take care of his health. However, even his closest colleagues and friends, who had sensed that he had seemed less ebullient over the preceding months and looked particularly tired after the election, found his death a complete shock. Eve considers that his mother's death, only seven weeks earlier, had come as a terrible blow to him, and it was only when his operation forced him to stop that the full sense of his loss suddenly hit him.[54]

Macleod's funeral was held on Friday 24 July in the village church of Gargrave. His body had lain overnight in a chapel of rest in Skipton, only a quarter of mile from his birthplace, Clifford House. On the afternoon of the service, the bells of Skipton parish church were rung half-muffled from 2pm to 3pm. Diana, his daughter, still in pain from her recent back operation, was flown to Leeds by RAF aeroplane and driven to Gargrave by ambulance. Although a wheelchair was available at the church, she insisted on walking up the aisle and helping to support her mother. Over 300 people had gathered in the rain outside, and inside, the packed congregation included many ministerial and parliamentary colleagues.

The simple service was conducted by the vicar, Revd Kenneth Cook, with the assistance of the Bishop of Bradford and the support of the Archdeacon of Craven. The lesson was read by the Prime Minister. As the local *Craven Herald* observed: 'Perhaps the simplicity and the genuine grief manifested by all present, irrespective of rank and status, were the most enduring memories of a beautiful service which lasted just 25 minutes.' Macleod was buried close to his parents and sister, near the spot where he had recently stood, lost in his own thoughts, as he gazed down Airedale towards Skipton. The epitaph inscribed on the cross above his grave is by Chesterton, one of his favourite poets, and was selected by Diana, his daughter:

> The men that worked for England
> They have their graves at home.[55]

22

The Loss and the Legacy

I cannot help feeling that a man who always held all the bridge scores in his head, who seemed to know all the numbers, and played *vingt et un* so successfully would have been useful.

Lord Butler on Iain Macleod's likely capabilities as Chancellor of the Exchequer, *The Art of Memory*, 1982.

A Fatal Blow to the Heath Government

Macleod's death, only a month after embarking on his last, great, political challenge, was a tragedy. The sense of what might have been is still keenly felt by people of all political persuasions, and twenty years after his death his name has become a talisman for Conservatives seeking to distance themselves from the Thatcher years. Why is it that his name, as opposed to those of his Tory contemporaries, has come to have special resonance? Among Macleod's contemporaries, Nye Bevan, Hugh Gaitskell and John F. Kennedy now stir the same kind of poignant memories as Macleod and their names have assumed a similar talismanic status. Even so, early death alone does not fully explain Macleod's aura any more than it does Bevan's, Gaitskell's and Kennedy's. All four were distinguished by outstanding political triumphs, but whether in defeat or victory they were men of personality who could make the pulse race: courageous and inspirational, they excited admiration and hatred with equal passion. Macleod is the only modern Tory who qualifies for inclusion in this select band.

But would things have been any different if Macleod had lived even a few more years? Speculating about the impact that one individual might have had is bound to risk exaggerating his or her importance. Nonetheless, it is surely beyond dispute that Macleod was, apart from Heath, the most important minister to the success or failure of the 1970 Conservative administration. Had he lived, the history of the Heath Government would almost certainly have been different, even if, as he said he intended, he had retired to the Lords after three years as Chancellor. It follows that the Tory

Party and Britain would very probably have taken a different course during the 1970s and 1980s.

When Macleod died, Harold Macmillan lamented that he had been the last Tory orator. This loss of the most effective political communicator of his generation – in the Commons, on the conference platform and on television – would have been damaging at any time, but it came when the Tories could ill afford it. In Carr's opinion: 'We lost our trumpeter, which in Ted's [Heath's] Government was our greatest need.' Overnight, the Cabinet visibly shifted to the right and its political stature diminished. Not since the days of Neville Chamberlain's Government over thirty years earlier, during the eighteen months between Eden's resignation and Churchill's appointment in September 1939, had the Tory frontbench in the Commons appeared so lacking in star quality.[1]

Perhaps Macleod's going would have been less wounding to the Tories if they had been elected on a Baldwinesque platform of 'Safety First'. Instead, the Heath Government were committed to a programme of reform, paramount of which was the contentious overhaul of the law on trade unions, coupled with a fresh attempt to achieve the historic objective of taking Britain into the European Common Market. Justifying these ambitious plans and other sweeping institutional changes would have posed an immense challenge to a Cabinet full of Macleods. Although, as Chancellor, Macleod would have been burdened with the daunting tasks of managing the economy and recasting the tax system, nonetheless his flair, his firepower in debate and the touch of magic he brought to politics were sorely missed as Heath and his ministers wearied the country with unmemorable speeches and wooden performances.

Yet it was not only the loss of Macleod's presentational skill, important though it was, that damaged the Heath Government. With Macleod's death, the Cabinet lost the only political heavyweight, with the backing of a major department of state, who was capable of standing up to the Prime Minister and whom Heath respected as an equal. Indeed, Heath recognized as much in his reaction to Macleod's death: besides being deeply moved at the personal tragedy, he was devastated at the impact on his Government. Of the other senior ministers, Douglas-Home at the Foreign Office concentrated on foreign affairs and in any case had no clout on his economy or domestic policy; Hogg had returned to the Lords as a Life Peer (Hailsham of St Marylebone) on his appointment as Lord Chancellor and was, to all intents and purposes, removed from the political fray; and Maudling, the Home Secretary, preferred a quiet life and in 1972 had to resign over the inquiry into the Poulson affair. As for the rest, they were Heath's placemen, in no position to challenge a leader whose authority had been boosted by having won the 1970 election against all expectations.[2]

Most important of all, Macleod had offered an alternative pole to Heath, around whom other opinions could gather. But the immediate removal of this alternative pole from the Cabinet, in the view of a former senior civil servant 'totally destabilized the Tory Government and made it for a long time virtually a one-man band'. Macleod had relished playing his part at the Cabinet table, possessing the qualities of imagination, independence of mind and political judgement, that contribute to good Cabinet government. Carr is convinced that Macleod's ability to understand people and to know instinctively what was possible politically would have made him a very powerful influence in the Cabinet. Without Macleod, Cabinet debate was stultified.[3]

Heath came to rely increasingly on a small number of ministers and on the advice of senior officials, notably Sir William, later Lord, Armstrong, Head of the Civil Service. It is inconceivable that Macleod, who was a politician to his fingertips with, in Whitelaw's view, 'a very good feel for what was happening in Parliament and the feel of the chamber itself', would have allowed Heath to become so detached from the Commons, the party and the world beyond Whitehall. That contribution in itself would have been a major step towards avoiding the political catastrophe that engulfed the Government during the winter of 1973–74.[4]

As regards Macleod's likely performance as Chancellor, his Cabinet colleagues never felt that he had come to terms with economics and finance as Shadow Chancellor in the same way that he had mastered other subjects. Certainly, his only speech as Chancellor was below par, but he was ill and should never have delivered it. Its contents were cautious and non-committal, but this reflected a sensible prudence early in his chancellorship rather than proving that he had instantly become a creature of his officials. If Macleod had lived and had served anything like a reasonable term at Number Eleven, the changes in economic policy between 1970 and 1974 would, in all probability, have been less angular than was the case. As an expert at tacking in politics, he would surely have shown greater skill in steering the Tories away from their *laissez-faire* rhetoric to the more centrist position on economic policy that he believed was necessary in office. As shrewd a judge of fellow politicians as Rab Butler had a point when he spoke of his own wish to have Macleod as his Chancellor, had he been asked to form a government: 'How he would have got on I do not know, but I cannot help feeling that a man who always held all the bridge scores in his head, who seemed to know all the numbers, and played *vingt et un* so successfully would have been useful.'[5]

Almost from the word 'go', Macleod's loss created a fundamental imbalance at the heart of government economic policy-making. Barber, his replacement, was a political lightweight. Heath had never served in the Treasury and distrusted the department. His doubts were reinforced during the early months of Government when, after Macleod's death, senior officials presented their economic forecast to Heath at Number Ten and failed to predict the weakness of the dollar and, as a corollary, the strength of the pound – sterling and other currencies were eventually revalued against the dollar in a general realignment at the end of 1971. Whereas Macleod might have tempered, if not entirely allayed, Heath's deep distrust of the Treasury, Barber simply lacked the clout of his predecessor and was quite unable to do so. Barber knew that, in the last resort, the Prime Minister could always call his bluff: even if Barber were to resign it would have little impact. Macleod had been in a different league. He would have been able to bring his political judgement to bear on his officials' advice, and Heath would have been less inclined to take a jaundiced view of opinions emanating from Great George Street. Macleod was nobody's poodle. If he had been convinced of the correctness of the Treasury's analysis, he would not have allowed Heath to brush it aside (as later happened) without an almighty fight.[6]

Moreover, Macleod had entered Number Eleven already deeply concerned at the level of unemployment and privately convinced that the Tories had become too non-interventionist in Opposition. It is virtually certain that in his autumn 1970 economic package he would have given a stronger stimulus to the economy than Barber, whose measures were broadly neutral in their overall effect on demand. He was also less likely than Barber to have underestimated what needed to be done in the spring 1971 budget to boost growth and create jobs. In short, Macleod would very probably have taken stronger action sooner, to prevent the steep climb in unemployment that appeared to take ministers completely by surprise. As a result, the political pressure on the Government would not have been as intense during the winter of 1971–72, when the numbers unemployed reached the one million mark.

Since Macleod was likely to have acted more decisively sooner, there would have been less likelihood of the over-reaction by Heath in the spring of 1972. As it was, Treasury ministers and their officials found themselves powerless to stem the tide of extra state spending. The experience is still etched on their memories. Ministers recall returning to the Treasury in despair as their efforts to exert some kind of control on spending were rejected by Number Ten. It is inconceivable that Heath would have been able (or would have dared try) systematically to marginalize the Treasury had Macleod been Chancellor.[7]

Although Macleod, like Heath, was an interventionist, a Keynesian and a modernizer, his feet were too firmly rooted on the ground to pin his hopes on some grandiose plan while brushing inconvenient political and economic realities under the carpet. He did not distrust the Treasury, but even if he had been persuaded to reject their advice on the 1972 budget when they warned of the risks of massive reflation, his sensitivity to other points of view suggests that the warning signals from the Bank of England and the IMF would have been detected sooner and treated more seriously.

Had Macleod kept to his original intention, he would have left the

Government some time during 1973, after he had seen through his reform of the tax system. Barber sought loyally to implement Macleod's detailed programme, but again the politics went badly awry. Whereas Macleod was clear and decisive about what he would have done, Barber had neither the knowledge nor the background and, as a result, was at the mercy of his officials. Macleod's plan had been to implement the whole of the reform of income tax so that it would come into effect in April 1972, but after his death the Inland Revenue made strong representations that this timetable was impractical. Barber therefore agreed that although most of the reform of income tax should come into force in 1972, the reforms that mainly affected top earners should not take effect until April 1973. The Chancellor was warned of the political danger in dividing the package by Arthur, later Lord, Cockfield, who had worked with Macleod in Opposition and whom Macleod had appointed as his adviser on the tax reforms, but Barber would not overrule his officials.[8]

As a result, the vast majority of taxpayers received their tax reliefs in 1972, but the top earners' reliefs were postponed until 1973. Politically this was disastrous. The Shadow Chancellor, Denis Healey, astutely claimed that £300 million had been 'given away' to the rich. Cockfield is convinced that Macleod would never have had any truck with dividing the reform of income tax over two years. Moreover, it was later admitted privately that the official advice had been mistaken and that the Inland Revenue could have coped if the income tax reforms had been introduced in one fell swoop, as Macleod had envisaged.[9]

Had Macleod decided to continue as Chancellor, his former Cabinet colleagues and senior advisers believe that he would have made the crucial difference between defeat and triumph in the battle over Stage Three of the Government's statutory prices and incomes policy. Above all, Macleod's exceptional bargaining skills would have helped prevent the Government from boxing themselves in. The basic objective of Stage Three was to avoid a clash with the miners by ensuring that the National Coal Board were able to offer and negotiate a pay deal that was acceptable in the coalfields. This is what Heath and William Armstrong thought they had achieved following a private talk in the garden of Number Ten with Joe Gormley, the miners' leader, when they took up his suggestion of allowing special payments for 'unsocial hours'. But they failed to appreciate that Gormley intended that this loophole should apply only to the miners and not to all shift workers. They also put too much faith in Gormley, who failed to carry his union executive with him. A shrewd negotiator like Macleod would have been less likely to have misinterpreted a specific solution to a specific problem and to have misjudged his opposite number's ability to deliver.[10]

The second key passage occurred in early January 1974 as the miners' dispute escalated into a confrontation with the Government. At the regular monthly meeting of the NEDC, the TUC made an unprecedented offer that if the Government allowed a deal between the Coal Board and the miners as a 'special case', this would not be used by other unions in their own pay negotiations. Barber rejected the offer out of hand, and was subsequently supported by Heath and other ministers, who were deeply sceptical of the TUC's suggestion.[11]

Macleod was unlikely to have looked a gift horse in the mouth. Had he been presiding as Chancellor at the NEDC meeting when the TUC made their offer he would have been more likely, at the very least, to keep open the Government's options. Heath's biographer, Campbell, suggests that Heath regarded a deal of this kind with the TUC as too cynical. This would not have been a primary concern for Macleod, faced with the urgent need to find a politically acceptable settlement. Again, Macleod's standing *vis-à-vis* Heath is important. He had sufficient weight to negotiate a deal without feeling, as Barber did, that he always had to refer back to Heath. Perhaps Carr comes closest to the likely outcome in suspecting that Macleod might have 'squeezed the odd trick or two out of a rather unfortunate looking lot of cards'.[12]

This conclusion points to the final irony. Maybe Macleod was destined never to be Tory leader. Had he lived and continued in the Cabinet, he would have been an immensely strong candidate to succeed Heath following the latter's demise after the two election defeats of 1974. Macleod would have been only sixty-one that autumn. His wealth of experience, depth of political wisdom and inner steel would have attracted wide support and easily seen off any other candidates who might still have put their names forward. Would Macleod have challenged Heath in the first ballot, as Thatcher did, while Whitelaw declined out of loyalty to his leader? Macleod was no shrinking violet, but whether he had stood in the first or second round, Whitelaw and the other leftish Tories would not have stood against him. It is a moot point whether Thatcher would have stood against Macleod. After all, she had stood, and was eventually elected, primarily to remove Heath, not as the champion of nineteenth-century liberalism. Yet Macleod's presence in the Cabinet would almost certainly have prevented some of the mistakes made by the Heath Government. He might well have averted the final showdown with the miners in February 1974. But by helping Heath to survive as Prime Minister, Macleod would have scuppered his own, last chance of ever becoming Tory leader.

Macleod's Toryism and Modern Conservatives

Although Macleod was destined never to become Tory leader, there is little doubt that he would have made a difference to the Conservative Party and to Britain had he lived longer (he would have celebrated his seventieth birthday in November 1983). If there was one person whose political skills might have prevented the downfall of the Heath Government and the demise of 'One Nation' Toryism as the party's dominant set of values, it was Macleod. Even if he had been unable to prevent the débâcle of 1974, it is unimaginable that he would have remained silent while the adherents of nineteenth-century liberalism began to storm the commanding heights of the Conservative Party during the latter half of the 1970s. Macleod, more than any other politician of his generation, embodied 'One Nation' Toryism. He passionately believed that neither *laissez-faire* economic theory nor narrow-minded prejudice had any role as guiding principles of the modern Conservative Party.

Although he was a 'One Nation' Tory, he was not complacently so. He had the capacity to become the key, pivotal figure in the Conservative Party, guiding it from the Toryism of Macmillan and Butler to a new, liberal Toryism more consonant with the economic, social and political changes that had had a profound impact on the country during the decades after the Second World War. Macleod was committed to the ideals that had inspired the postwar settlement, but at the same time he welcomed many of the changes that undermined the old pillars of class-dominated industrial relations and two-party loyalties in late-1940s and 1950s Britain.

Macleod's advocacy of a more liberal, less class-ridden society chimed with the times during the late-1950s and 1960s. But the social changes that he identified and, in the main, supported, also meant that governments could no longer rely so readily on the old bonds of class, party loyalty and deference (whether to company bosses, union leaders or privileged grandees) to deliver the necessary consent. Macleod appeared capable of offering the more imaginative form of Conservative leadership required to govern a rapidly changing society with success. He was acutely sensitive of the need continually to work at winning people's support and building a consensus for any new policy or reform.

Macleod's whole approach to politics and government assumed that the existence of one nation in Britain, forged in the shared experience of war and shaped in the postwar commitment to full employment, a mixed economy and the welfare state, had to be sustained and renewed as society evolved. This did not mean casting in bronze every institution and mechanism of the 1945 settlement, but instead meant that any reform necessitated by economic or social change should adhere to the overriding objective of maintaining one nation. Shortly after Macleod's death, Gilmour observed of his Toryism that:

> If the country was one nation, this was not an inevitable development. The one nation had to be preserved and constantly re-created. The Tory Party had to devote its energies to that task and not fall back into contemplating past glories.

Macleod's insight that the existence of one nation is not inevitable is the crucial, defining difference between Macleod's Toryism and the *laissez-faire* thinking that dominated the Conservative Party from the mid-1970s. While favouring market forces, Macleod always realized that if allowed to go unchecked they would be deeply corrosive of social cohesion and inimical to one nation.[13]

Both his Scottishness and his Yorkshire background were integral to his sense of identity and gave him an affinity with people outside the ranks of the English upper-middle class and the home counties. Unlike almost all his contemporaries at the top of the Conservative hierarchy, Macleod knew in his blood what it was like to be ruled by the English, and by a narrowly-drawn group of Englishmen at that. Unlike Macmillan, who was also distinguished by his non-English ancestry (albeit Highlander as opposed to Islander), Macleod was first generation emigrant. His parents had been born and brought up on Lewis during the land disturbances of the late nineteenth century. Macleod's crofter, Gaelic and northern origins set him apart as an outsider while giving him a perspective on politics that was the opposite to that of most senior Conservatives. His distinctive outlook has virtually vanished from the higher reaches of the Conservative Party, which have become even more English in the years since his death.

But what was it that had made Macleod a Tory in the first place? According to Enoch Powell, his former close colleague and fellow member in 1950 of the original 'One Nation' group:

> It's a strain in the Conservative Party – and one recognizes belonging to it and the others who belong to it – a strain of those who can't help it, who have not arrived at Conservatism by a process of ratiocination, still less on economic grounds.

This is a vital observation, coming as it does from one of the earliest exponents among postwar Conservatives of *laissez-faire* economics and monetarism, but who never regarded adherence to these theories as the true test of Tory faith. Macleod was a liberal with a small 'l' for whom socialism never held any attraction. But his father's vocation as a doctor and his mother's commitment to voluntary work, bred in him a conviction that community and social concerns were important in their own right, and that economic policy should be as much their servant as their master. He was also shrewd enough to see that his island romanticism and his rural, market-town, middle-class background enabled him to take the high Tory road to power as a Conservative politician, as opposed to the urban-based, Chamberlainite Liberal route. At the same time, Macleod's Hebridean parents and Yorkshire upbringing imbued in him a practical, hard-headedness that is invariably held to be lacking in the caricature image of liberal-minded and left-inclined Tories (latterly dubbed 'wets'). Macleod was almost obsessively practical as a policy-maker and as a minister, in which-ever department he was running and at the Cabinet table. It is difficult to envisage Macleod approving a policy that was as flawed and politically catastrophic as the Thatcher Government's poll tax.[14]

For Macleod, 'One Nation' Toryism entailed more than the electoral imperative of widening the Conservative Party's appeal, vital though this objective was after the legacy of the 1930s and the Tory débâcle of 1945. 'One Nation' represented a much deeper conviction, born of his background and forged in the crucible of wartime military service, that had been uniquely unifying. In this sense, he was in the tradition of Eden and Macmillan from an earlier Tory generation: his wartime experience marked his political outlook as indelibly as the trenches marked theirs. He was not sentimental, in the fashion of Macmillan, about working people and trade unions, but he shared the political hallmark of many of his generation who had endured both slump and war – the core belief that strong government, mobilized by political will, can tackle any problem.

Macleod's interventionism, born of his belief that government had an essential role in managing a mixed economy and providing protection against the vagaries of market forces, placed him in the Tory paternalist tradition. But it was the reformist Disraeli who appealed to Macleod. His paternalism did not extend to a traditionalist, unquestioning acceptance of authority, class distinction or the *status quo*. On the contrary, Macleod was a democrat and a meritocrat. The readiness with which Lord Randolph Churchill's cry to 'Trust the people', sprang to his lips reflected more than his ear for a good slogan, and revealed his natural cast of mind. At the same time, he was a vehement opponent of egalitarianism and unashamedly championed 'the pursuit of excellence'. He extolled equality of opportunity and frankly acknowledged the resulting inequality of outcome. After his death, this lack of apology for inequality came to be associated with Lady Thatcher, while John Major, an avowed admirer of Macleod, indulged in vague talk of a 'classless society' when he really had in mind a meritocracy.

Macleod was a liberal, but not in a way that many people would regard as conventional or predictable. The equality of every individual's dignity and worth as a human being was a deeply held conviction. He did not possess a trace of class prejudice or racialism. But unlike many progressive liberals who shared his views, he abhorred the 'Nanny State'. During the 1960s, when many people were concerned to appear 'trendy', he was never bothered whether or not this supposed accolade was bestowed upon him. His animus against the BBC, and his championing of commercial television in the 1950s and 'pirate' off-shore radio stations in the 1960s, suggests a populist streak, but his convictions were sincere.

By the standards of his time, Macleod's liberalism made him a radical Tory and, on many moral issues, a libertarian. There was no contradiction between his hard-headed realism and his liberal views: to his mind, enlightened self-interest decreed compassionate, liberal Toryism. His independent-mindedness made his politics highly distinctive, and on occasion put him at odds with his usual allies on the Tory left. He could never be described as an establishment Tory, and he was vigorously opposed to the so-called radicalism that developed on the right of the party. He was neither a Powellite, nor a prototype Thatcherite.

In contrast to Macleod and also Powell, Thatcherites evince no understanding of 'One Nation'. Indeed, they dismiss such idealism among the Conservative leadership prior to 1975 as a factor in Britain's postwar malaise and hold that its continued influence would frustrate any attempted revival. In contrast to Macleod, they assume that a market-oriented Britain, red in aggressive tooth and competitive claw, can also be a law-abiding and peaceable society, akin to the Grantham of the 1930s. Macleod fought throughout his career against the notion that *laissez-faire*, nineteenth-century economics offered a sensible guide for government or society in the second half of the twentieth century.

Macleod's commitment to full employment always remained his political lode-star. Unemployment, or 'Idleness', had been identified by Beveridge in his historic report of November 1942 as one of the five giants that had to be slain (the other giants were Disease, Ignorance, Squalor and Want). It seemed during Macleod's political career that joblessness had been successfully vanquished, but during the 1970s it returned as a scourge. Its tolerance during the 1980s and 1990s marks the biggest, single contrast between Macleod's Toryism and modern Conservatism. Indeed, by the 1990s few Conservatives seemed to realize how far their party had been drawn away during the previous decade from the 'One Nation' Toryism. Macleod had appreciated that the trail of economic and social destruction wrought by joblessness demands that its conquest should remain a priority.

But are the politics of unemployment in the 1980s and 1990s so different from the 1950s and 1960s that Macleod's views are merely of historic interest and have no longer-term relevance? Whereas Macleod and his contemporaries had assumed that it would be political suicide for the Conservatives to adopt policies that led to high unemployment, the Thatcher Government succeeded in presiding over record levels of postwar joblessness while inflicting massive defeats on the Labour Party in the general elections of 1983 and 1987. Whatever the political explanation for these Conservative landslides, it appeared that high unemployment no longer carried a prohibitively high political cost for the Conservatives.

This political sea-change, which differentiates the 1950s and 1960s so starkly from the 1980s, does not render obsolete Macleod's belief that government has a primary duty to prevent mass unemployment. After all, the Conservative Party had achieved remarkable success between the two world wars, holding office, either alone or in coalition, for eighteen of the twenty-one years. Yet the inter-war period scarcely ranks as the most glorious in Conservative history and in 1945 the party reaped a bitter harvest for the mass unemployment that had scarred those years. Macleod and other postwar Tories had to fight tirelessly to overcome the Conservatives' image as the party of high unemployment.

As in the 1930s, the absence of 'One Nation' policies during the 1980s brought short-term political advantage. While the country was becoming more polarized during the Thatcher years, the most deprived third of the population (the poor, the unemployed and those living in economically depressed areas) chalked up bigger Labour majorities in Labour's urban strongholds, while a sufficient number among the comfortable two-thirds (those with jobs, mortgages on their own homes and often living in better-off areas) returned the Conservatives to office at successive elections. Whatever the eventual political consequences for the Conservatives of becoming a more narrowly-based regional and sectional party, the damaging social effects of this polarization are longterm and will be felt for decades to come. To imagine that Macleod's Toryism could have easily accommodated the two nation politics of the 1980s would be to misunderstand fundamentally the man and his vision of a truly national Conservative Party.

But might Macleod have been forced to accept the inevitability of high unemployment by the sheer force of events? After all, the resurgence of joblessness has not been a uniquely British phenomenon. Unemployment increased throughout the western industrial world after the halcyon days of the 1960s. Macleod's political career coincided almost precisely with the postwar *belle epoque* of cheap energy and rapidly rising living standards. At the time of his death, the inflationary financing of the Vietnam war was beginning to make ripples in the world's economic order and a few years later the explosion of oil prices ushered in more testing times. Under these pressures, economic priorities changed.

It would be idle to imagine that any British politician in the second half of the twentieth century could single-handedly stem the tide of events. Nonetheless, Macleod's passionate conviction that unemployment was an avoidable social problem and not some act of God (or 'iron hand' of the market) was sorely missed. He was capable of providing a powerful antidote to the all-too-willing and insidious acceptance by many economists and politicians of the supposed inevitability of large-scale, longterm, mass unemployment. More than a decade of deflationary policies brought only limited success in the fight to eradicate inflation, while the sheer scale of unemployment has been appalling. But there was a failure of leadership throughout western democracies to create and mobilize the political will needed to tackle unemployment. This paralysis is reminiscent of the 1920s and 1930s, although it is worse since the lessons of Keynes, having been learned, were discarded. Macleod was unlikely to have been quite so Bourbon-like in his approach to economic policy. He also realized that in a modern economy, government had to have some form of incomes policy and he remained an advocate of regional policy.

Macleod held that social policy was nothing less than a prime duty of the state, along with defence and managing the economy, whereas Thatcherites, despite their protestations, give every impression that they would love to be rid of the welfare state. However, there is scope for debate about the working of the welfare state, and Macleod, with Powell, was an early proselytizer of 'selectivity', i.e. targeting benefits and services on those in need, as opposed to a system of 'universality', in which benefits and services are provided irrespective of a person's means. But when Macleod first argued for more selectivity, the welfare state was still based predominantly on universality. It is equally clear from his subsequent contributions to policy discussions that he never favoured pursuing selectivity to extremes and replacing the social security system by a modern-day Poor Law. Moreover, Macleod always discussed any reform of the welfare state on the assumption that the government would maintain full employment as an overriding priority.

However, his call for greater selectivity in the social services risked exacerbating the 'poverty trap', since the introduction of more means-tested benefits and services is bound to create some disincentive (however marginal) for the unemployed to take a job. Macleod saw the problem. The need to overcome the 'poverty trap' was one of the reasons that, as Shadow Chancellor, he advocated a 'tax credit' system, whereby the tax and benefit systems would be merged. Macleod possessed the necessary political will to have ensured that this ambitious reform would not have become yet another victim of bureaucratic inertia. The proposal for a tax credit system surfaced as a Green Paper after Macleod's death, but any plans for taking it further fell with the Heath Government in 1974. The prospect of any such fundamental reform has become more distant since 1979, while the 'poverty trap' has worsened.

There is no mistaking Macleod's radicalism. He believed emphatically that a dynamic, wealth creating economy could only be created by rewarding the 'dynamos' in society. To this end, as Shadow Chancellor, he planned a sweeping reform of taxation fundamentally different from the concentration on cutting income tax that predominated after 1979. Macleod instituted the shift in the burden of taxation from direct to indirect taxation, but in paving the way for the introduction of VAT, he was at great pains to ensure that the worse-off would be fully protected, principally by exempting, or 'zero rating' many necessities. Macleod also wanted to realize Eden's vision of a 'capital-owning democracy', in which many more people, not just the rich, would have the ability and inclination to build up capital. He believed that the creation of a 'capital owning democracy' would break down the class divisions that permeated British industry and society, and would provide people with independent means. But he was not a rabid de-nationalizer.

Mention of Macleod's name by Conservative ministers suddenly became politically correct after Lady Thatcher's fall from the premiership in 1990. John Major's Government were even heralded as heirs to Macleod's Toryism, and the suggestion was made that Britain was at last seeing 'Macleod in power'. This theory was later disproved, not least because of the Major Government's lack of political competence. The clue to Macleod's competence lay in the comment of a permanent secretary during the Macmillan administration, who confessed his surprise that so many ministers appeared not to have developed a set of attitudes that they could apply to whatever issue might come before them. By contrast, Macleod had a clear set of political beliefs and, as a result, had no need to spend hours pondering his response to every issue that came before him. Whereas the beliefs of many politicians have little pattern and at times appear to resemble an ill-assorted pile of bricks, Macleod's thinking reflected a coherent structure of ideas. He knew his own mind, realized what he was about, and could despatch the day-to-day business while focusing on his main priorities.[15]

However, in one, important sense, Major's Government could justifiably claim to be Macleod's political heirs. By the standards of many Conservatives, Major took a generally liberal stance on social issues, notably on race – Brixton man was not 'Essex man', the aggressively right-wing, upwardly mobile voter, epitomized by Lord Tebbit. Indeed, the liberalism of the post-Thatcher generation of Conservatives, many of whom became politically active in their teens and twenties when Macleod was at his most influential, is Macleod's most enduring legacy. Butler, Heath and other contemporaries of Macleod also showed immense courage in preventing the Conservative Party completely abandoning any pretence at liberalism during the 1950s and 1960s, when there were pressures on the leadership to pursue illiberal and intolerant policies on law and order, immigration, race and other social questions. But Macleod became the main inspiration and torch-bearer for liberal Toryism.

Although Macleod never resigned, he took the fight to the Conservative right wing as Colonial Secretary, and he made public his readiness to quit the party in the late 1960s rather than have them kow-tow to right-wing activists. Macleod's unflinching liberalism earned him the obloquy of the right-wing, but this became a badge of honour. The liberal line was held.[16]

With Macleod's death, the poverty-stricken people of the Third World, and of Africa in particular, lost one of their most eloquent and forceful trumpeters in the West. He would have applauded the Thatcher Government's historic achievement in 1979–80, when the diplomatic skills of Lord Carrington, Lord Gilmour and Lord Soames enabled them to negotiate independence for Zimbabwe (formerly Southern Rhodesia) and preside over a democratic transfer of power to the former guerilla leader, Robert Mugabe. But Macleod's vision went much wider, extending to the ideal of 'One World', as he made clear at the 1960 Tory conference. Macleod's concept of 'One World' did not represent some woolly notion of a single world government, but instead sought to harness the idealism that existed in the West, particularly among the young, to the enormous challenge of alleviating poverty and meeting people's needs in the developing and less developed countries. Macleod urged the case for increased spending on overseas aid on humanitarian grounds and for reasons of enlightened self-interest.

Macleod was a formidable politician. His greatest strength has been best captured by Lord Fraser of Kilmorack (formerly Sir Michael Fraser), who knew him from their schooldays at Fettes, during the 1930s at Cambridge and in London, and subsequently at the Conservative Research Department and in the higher echelons of the Conservative Party. As Fraser explained in a BBC radio broadcast five days after Macleod's death:

> [But] I have always believed that the greatest quality that a leading politician can have, is an elusive but important one, which I would define as 'constructive imagination' – the capacity to have a vision of what you think should happen and then the practical ability and force of character to make its realization possible. Iain certainly had constructive imagination.[17]

In no other instance was this quality of 'constructive imagination' better illustrated than during Macleod's two years as Colonial Secretary. At heart he was a romantic and was inspired by the growing African aspiration for self-rule, but he immediately grasped the realities of Britain's dwindling capacity as a world power. When he applied all his practical ability and force of character to achieving his objectives, he was hated by old-style Tory romantics, while many of his fellow Conservatives doubted the haste with which he expedited British withdrawal and African majority rule. Macleod knew that whatever the political cost to himself, any other course risked disaster. His foresight and decisiveness made him the man for the hour. His historic achievement is that he speeded African independence and extricated Britain from its African Empire, while averting the very real danger of a massive loss in blood and treasure.

Macleod was a paradox: romantic, but hard-headed; a politician to his fingertips, but statesmanlike on Africa. Acerbic, ambitious, courageous and passionate, he realized, probably more than any other postwar Tory, that a prime task of political leadership is to provide inspiration. People needed to have their sights lifted above sectional interests and beyond the immediate present if his ideals of 'One Nation' and 'One World' were to have any substance. Macleod had a rare ability to inspire through the imagery and power of his words and by appealing to people's better nature. There is little better that can be said of a democratic politician. Like a meteorite, Macleod blazed briefly, lighting up the political skies and dazzling his audience. His demise left a gaping crater in the Conservative Party. And always there will remain the question of 'what might have been?'

Notes

CPA refers to files in the Conservative Party Archive at the Bodleian Library, Oxford. PRO refers to files at the Public Record Office, Kew. Details of the books referred to by author and date of publication are provided in the Bibliography.

CHAPTER 1: TIR-AN-OG

1. Conservative Conference, Brighton, 11 October 1961, Official Record. Scottish Conservatives have their own annual conference, traditionally held in early May.
2. Fisher, 1973, p. 309; interview with Sir Duncan Watson.
3. Transcript of speech at Thomas De La Rue & Co. Ltd., annual dinner, 13 June 1957; Rhoderick Macleod, 1976, pp. iii, 9.
4. Iain's younger brother, Rhoderick, subsequently completed a comprehensive genealogical history of his family and their forebears – Rhoderick Macleod, 1976, pp. iii, 9, 19, 23–4; Smout, 1972, p.40.
5. J.D. Mackie, 1978, p. 345; interview with Rhoderick Macleod.
6. Information from the Mary Erskine School, Edinburgh (Edinburgh Ladies' College was one of the Edinburgh Merchant Company Schools and merged with the Mary Erskine School); interviews with Rhoderick Macleod, Eve Macleod.
7. Interview with Rhoderick Macleod.
8. Interviews with Rhoderick Macleod, Mrs Eileen Weston (née Waugh).
9. Interviews with Rhoderick Macleod, Ellis Butchart.
10. Photograph of Dr Norman Macleod, North Yorkshire County Library, Skipton; interviews with Rhoderick Macleod, Ellis Butchart, Cedric Robinson, Mrs Fisher (Skipton), Mrs Eileen Weston (née Waugh).
11. Interview with Mrs Eileen Weston (née Waugh); Fisher, 1973, p.27.
12. Rhoderick Macleod, 1976, p. 36; interviews with Rhoderick Macleod, Torquil Macleod (brother), Ellis Butchart, Cedric Robinson.
13. Rhoderick Macleod, 1976, p. 40; interviews with Rhoderick Macleod, Torquil Macleod (brother), Cedric Robinson, Mrs Eileen Weston (née Waugh), Ellis Butchart.
14. Rhoderick Macleod, 1976, p. 40; interviews with Rhoderick Macleod, Torquil Macleod (brother).
15. Interviews with Rhoderick Macleod, Torquil Macleod (brother), Torquil Macleod (son), Eve Macleod.
16. Fisher, 1973, p. 56 – Macleod assumed that his father voted for him in 1945; interviews with Torquil Macleod (brother); Torquil Macleod (son); Rhoderick Macleod, 1976, p. 41.
17. Interviews with Torquil Macleod (brother), Rhoderick Macleod, Diana Heimann (daughter).
18. Rhoderick Macleod, 1976, p. 40; interviews with Rhoderick Macleod, Torquil Macleod (brother).

19. Interviews with Torquil Macleod (brother), Rhoderick Macleod.
20. Interviews with Rhoderick Macleod, Cedric Robinson, Torquil Macleod (brother).
21. Interviews with Torquil Macleod (brother), Rhoderick Macleod, Cedric Robinson; Fisher, 1973, p. 31.
22. Spencer, 1979, pp. 17–19; telephone interview with G.E. Dickson; Fisher, 1973, pp. 31–32.
23. Spencer, 1979, pp. 17–19; letter from R. Gerald Cooper, telephone interview with G.E. Dickson; Fisher, 1973, pp. 31–32.
24. Interview with Dick Cole-Hamilton, Keeper of the Register, Fettes College; letter from Dr. W.D. Arthur.
25. Telephone interview with G.E. Dickson; Harvey, 1971, p. 18; letters from R. Gerald Cooper, Dr W.D. Arthur, Gordon Barr and Ronald Turnbull.
26. Letter from Ronald Turnbull; Harvey, 1971, p. 22; letters from Dr W.D. Arthur, Rollo Campbell.
27. Letters from R. Gerald Cooper, Gordon Barr; telephone interview with G.E. Dickson.
28. Letter from W.D. Arthur; telephone interview with G.E. Dickson; letter from Ronald Turnbull; *The Fettesian*, 1929–30, 1930–31, 1931–32.
29. Telephone interview with G.E. Dickson; *The Fettesian*, 1930–31.
30. Letters from Ronald Turnbull, Rollo Campbell.
31. Fettes College records; letter from James Anson.
32. Interview with Dick Cole-Hamilton, Keeper of the Register, Fettes College; *The Fettesian*, 1931–32, 1956–57.
33. Rhoderick Macleod, 1976, p. 40; Scaliscro Lodge was to become a small hotel; Selby, 1980, pp. 146–48; interviews with Rhoderick Macleod, Torquil Macleod (brother).
34. Interviews with Rhoderick Macleod, Torquil Macleod (brother); MacGregor, 1933a, p. 23.
35. Interview with Rhoderick Macleod; MacGregor, 1933a, pp. 26–27; Fisher, 1973, p. 29–30; interview with Torquil Macleod (brother).
36. MacGregor, 1964, pp. 24–25.
37. MacGregor, 1933a, pp. 23–27; Fisher, 1973, p. 30.
38. MacGregor, 1933a, pp. 55–69; 'Siol Torquil' is Gaelic for 'the seed of Torquil,' and refers to the Macleods, who are the descendants of Torquil, second son of Liotr, or Leod (born c. 1200), and grandson of Olaf the Black, King of Man and the Isles.
39. Interview with Torquil Macleod (son).

CHAPTER 2: 'TEMPERED BY WAR'

1. Anne Neary, Archivist, Gonville and Caius College; letters from Dr W.D. Arthur, James Anson and Ronald Turnbull.
2. Quoted in Fisher, 1973, p. 37.
3. The *Spectator*, 8 August 1965; interview with Lord Fraser of Kilmorack (Michael Fraser); Michael Fraser, *The Week in Westminster*, BBC Radio Four, 25 July 1970; interview with Colin Harding; Fisher, 1973, p. 36.
4. Fisher, 1973, pp. 37–38; interviews with Torquil Macleod (brother), Rhoderick Macleod and Diana Heimann (daughter).
5. Interview with Colin Harding.
6. Interview with Colin Harding; *The Times*, 17 November 1934 and 18 February 1935.
7. Interview with Colin Harding.
8. Interview with Colin Harding.
9. Biographical History of Gonville and Caius, Volume V; interviews with Torquil Macleod (brother), Rhoderick Macleod.
10. Interview with Sir Arthur Norman.
11. Interviews with Colin Harding, Sir Arthur Norman, Rhoderick Macleod, Torquil Macleod (brother).

12. Interviews with Colin Harding, Sir Arthur Norman.
13. Interviews with Colin Harding, Sir Arthur Norman.
14. Interviews with Colin Harding, Torquil Macleod (brother), Lord Fraser of Kilmorack.
15. Interview with Colin Harding; Daniels, 1982, pp. 184–85.
16. Interviews with Rixi Markus, Colin Harding.
17. Interviews with Rixi Markus, Colin Harding.
18. Interviews with Colin Harding, Lord Fraser of Kilmorack, Torquil Macleod (brother).
19. Interview with Colin Harding.
20. Interview with Eve Macleod.
21. Interview with Eve Macleod; Fisher, 1973, p. 43.
22. Interviews with Eve Macleod, Torquil Macleod (brother), Lord Fraser of Kilmorack.
23. Barclay, 1953, pp. 196, 205; Brereton and Savory, 1993, pp. 287–88.
24. Interview with Eve Macleod; Brereton and Savory, 1993, pp. 288–89. Fisher, 1973, p.45.
25. Interview with Eve Macleod; Fisher, 1973, p. 43.
26. Rhoderick Macleod, 1976, p. 40; interview with Eve Macleod.
27. Interview with Eve Macleod.
28. Interviews with Sir Alan Dawtry; Lord Fraser of Kilmorack.
29. Interview with Sir Alan Dawtry.
30. Interview with Sir Alan Dawtry; Fisher, 1973, pp. 47–48.
31. Fisher, 1973, pp. 48–50.
32. Interviews with Eve Macleod, Torquil Macleod (brother).
33. Interviews with Torquil Macleod (brother), Eve Macleod; Macleod's interview was broadcast during April 1970, and is quoted in Fisher, 1973, p. 50.
34. 'One Man's D-Day,' *Spectator*, 5 June 1964.
35. Fisher, 1973, p. 51; 'One Man's D-Day,' *Spectator*, 5 June 1964.
36. 'One Man's D-Day,' *Spectator*, 5 June 1964.
37. 'Spectator's Notebook,' *Spectator*, 5 June 1964.
38. 'One Man's D-Day,' *Spectator*, 5 June 1964.
39. 'One Man's D-Day,' *Spectator*, 5 June 1964.
40. Fisher, 1973, pp. 53–54; Macleod was interviewed for the Nuffield election studies series, 21 December 1965.

CHAPTER 3: POLITICAL APPRENTICE

1. Maudling, 1978, p. 36; interview with Enoch Powell.
2. Douglas Jay's phrase comes from his 1937 book, *The Socialist Case*. He was, in fact, arguing that socialists should accept that people *do* know what is best for themselves, and was specifically referring only to the *exceptions* where 'the gentlemen in Whitehall know best. . .' Education, health and nutrition were his exceptions. However, the general point remains, since Macleod never accepted that there were any exceptions.
3. Interviews with Eve Macleod, Torquil Macleod (brother), Rhoderick Macleod; Fisher, 1973, p. 55.
4. Election Address of Major Iain Macleod, National Government candidate for the Western Isles Division of Inverness and Ross and Cromarty, General Election, 1945.
5. Ibid.
6. Ibid; for a full exposition of the war-time mood of 'never again', see Peter Hennessy, 1992.
7. Interview with Eve Macleod; Fisher, 1973, pp. 55–56; interview with David Clarke.
8. Rhoderick Macleod, 1976, pp. 37, 40–41; interviews with Torquil Macleod (brother), Rhoderick Macleod.
9. Iain Macleod to Diana Macleod, 8 October 1945.
10. 'Spectator's Notebook,' *Spectator*, 20 August 1965.
11. 'A Christmas Tale,' *Spectator*, 25 December 1964.

12. Letter, Eleanor Yorke to Ethne Bannister (Rhodabel's daughter), 21 July 1970; Ramsden, 1980, pp. 102–05; interview with David Clarke.
13. Interview with David Clarke; 'Macleod Remembered,' by David Clarke, *Swinton Journal*, summer edition, 1973, pp. 36–38; private information; interview with Enoch Powell.
14. Maudling, 1978, p. 36; interview with Lord Fraser of Kilmorack.
15. Private information; Maudling, 1978, p. 43.
16. *Spectator*, 16 July 1965; interviews with Eve Macleod, Diana Heimann (daughter); Cosgrave, 1989, p. 123; interview with Enoch Powell.
17. Interview with Enoch Powell.
18. CPA, CRD 2/53/5,6,7,55; interviews with David Clarke, Enoch Powell, Lord Fraser of Kilmorack.
19. Interviews with David Clarke, Lord Colyton, Lord Fraser of Kilmorack.
20. Private information; in July 1954, Hopkinson, then Minister of State at the Colonial Office, committed a serious gaffe when he told MPs that Cyprus would never become independent.
21. Interviews with David Clarke, Lord Colyton; CPA, CRD 2/53/55.
22. Iain Macleod to his parents, 30 October 1946.
23. CPA, Iain Macleod, Letter Books, 1946–50.
24. Interviews with David Clarke, Lord Fraser of Kilmorack.
25. Iain Macleod to his parents, 30 October 1946; interview with Lord Carr of Hadley.
26. CPA, Iain Macleod, Letter Books, 1946–50.
27. Interview with Lord Fraser of Kilmorack; Maudling, 1978, p. 43; CPA, CRD 2/53/5.
28. Interview with David Clarke; CPA, CRD 2/53/5.
29 Interview with David Clarke; Butler, 1982a, p. 146, quoted in Howard, 1987, p. 157.
30. CPA, Iain Macleod, Letter Books, 1946–50.
31. CPA, Iain Macleod, Letter Books, 1946–50.
32. Interview with David Clarke; CPA, Iain Macleod, Letter Books, 1946–50; Ramsden, 1980, p. 133.
33. CPA, Iain Macleod, Letter Books, 1946–50.

CHAPTER 4: 'ONE NATION' TORY

1. Election Address of Iain Macleod, Conservative candidate for Enfield West, General Election, February 1950.
2. Interview with Rixi Markus; Fisher, 1973, p. 66.
3. *Enfield Gazette*, 7 June 1946; interviews with Colin Turner, Lady Hayhoe; Tebbit, 1988, pp. 11–12.
4. Interviews with Colin Turner, Lady Hayhoe.
5. Interview with Colin Turner; *Enfield Gazette*, 7 June 1946.
6. Interviews with Colin Turner, Lord Carr.
7. Interview with Colin Turner.
8. Letter, Macleod to his parents, 30 October 1946; interviews with Eve Macleod, Lord and Lady Hayhoe, Colin Turner.
9. Interviews with Lord and Lady Hayhoe, Colin Turner.
10. Interviews with Colin Turner, John Lennox, Alan Whitaker, Lord and Lady Hayhoe, Diana Heimann (daughter).
11. Interviews with Lord and Lady Hayhoe, Colin Turner.
12. Interview with Colin Turner; private information; interview with Eve Macleod.
13. Lord Jay told me the story about Cripps's insistence on holding the election early in 1950 during research for a Channel Four television series on post-war Britain.
14. *This Is The Road*, Conservative 1950 election manifesto; quoted in *One Nation*, 1950.
15. Election Address of Iain Macleod, Conservative candidate for Enfield West, General Election, February 1950.

16. Ibid.
17. Interviews with Enoch Powell, Lord Orr-Ewing.
18. *Hansard*, 14 March 1950, cols. 960–64; *Spectator*, 27 November 1964.
19. *Hansard*, 14 March 1950, cols. 960–61.
20. *Hansard*, 14 March 1950, cols. 961–62.
21. *Hansard*, 14 March 1950, cols. 963.
22. Ibid.
23. *Spectator*, 27 November 1964; interview with William Shepherd.
24. Interviews with Lord Orr-Ewing, Lord Amery, Lord Carr, William Shepherd.
25. Interviews with Lord Alport, Enoch Powell; Campbell, 1993, pp. 76–77.
26. Interviews with Lord Alport, Sir Gilbert Longden, Enoch Powell.
27. Interviews with Lord Alport, Sir Gilbert Longden; Fisher, 1973, p. 76.
28. Macleod and Maude (eds.), 1950, passim p.7; 'One Nation' minutes, 1951–54; private information.
29. Macleod and Maude (eds.), 1950, passim p. 84.
30. Macleod and Maude (eds.), 1950, pp. 17–56; during the 1950 Conservative conference, Lord Woolton, the Party Chairman, indicated that the platform would accept demands from the floor that the party should adopt the target of building 300,000 homes a year. But the target only became party policy when Churchill endorsed it during his speech to the party rally, that immediately followed the conference.
31. Macleod and Maude (eds.), 1950, pp. 56–57.
32. Macleod and Maude (eds.), 1950, pp. 72–78.
33. Macleod and Maude (eds.), 1950, pp. 91–93.
34. 'One Nation' group minutes, 1951–52; interviews with Lord Alport; Sir Gilbert Longden.
35. Harvey, 1971, p. 73; 'One Nation' group minutes, 1951–52; interview with Sir Gilbert Longden; CPA, CRD 2/27/9.
36. Webster, 1988, p. 181.
37. Webster, 1988, p. 180; Cosgrave, 1989, p. 119; Macleod and Powell, 1952, preface; interview with Enoch Powell.
38. Macleod and Powell, 1952; *The Times*, 17 January 1952; Cosgrave, 1989, pp. 118–19; interviews with founder members of the 'One Nation' group.
39. Macleod and Powell, 1952, pp. 34–35.
40. Macleod and Powell, 1952, pp. 29–35; Powell was solely responsible for the changes in the second, revised edition of their pamphlet that was published in June 1954.
41. Macleod to McGibbon, Programme Director, Alexandra Palace, 4 April 1950, BBC Archives, Caversham; Macleod, 1952; *The Times*, 9 April 1952; Cosgrave, 1989, p. 487; interview with Lord Deedes.
42. Interview with Humphry Berkeley.
43. Interview with Rixi Markus.
44. Brittan, 1971, p. 189; Papers of R.A. Butler, E11/7; Campbell, 1973, pp. 79–80.

CHAPTER 5: THE DOCTOR'S SON

1. Webster, 1988, p. 185.
2. Minutes of 'One Nation' group, 1951–52; CPA, CRD 2/30/H, minutes of the Conservative backbench health and social security committee, 1951–52.
3. Webster, 1988, p. 188–92; minutes of 'One Nation' group, 1951–52; CPA, CRD 2/30/H, minutes of the Conservative backbench health and social security committee, 1951–52.
4. Crookshank Papers, cited in Webster, 1988, p. 193; minutes of 'One Nation' group, 1951–52.
5. *Hansard*, 27 March 1952, cols. 841–74.
6. *Hansard*, 27 March 1952, cols. 877–86; interview with Enoch Powell.
7. *Hansard*, 27 March 1952, cols. 886–88.

8. *Hansard*, 27 March 1952, col. 889; Fisher, 1973, p. 82.
9. Fisher, 1973, p. 82.
10. *Hansard*, 27 March 1952, cols. 889–91.
11. *Hansard*, 27 March 1952, cols. 892–94.
12. *Hansard*, 27 March 1952, cols. 894–95.
13. Fisher, 1973, p. 84; *Hansard*, 27 March 1952, cols. 961–67.
14. Interview with Michael Foot; Foot, 1973, pp. 360–61; interviews with Lord Carr, Sir Reginald Bennett, Lord Boyd-Carpenter, Lord Deedes, Lord Alport, Sir Gilbert Longden, Lord Orr-Ewing; *Hansard*, 27 March 1952, col. 961.
15. *Hansard*, 23 April 1952, cols. 419–686; Macleod to Crookshank, MH 80/60, cited in Webster, 1988, pp. 194–95.
16. Interview with Eve Macleod; Fisher, 1973, pp. 85–86.
17. Henry Hopkinson had been the first of the 1950 intake to become a minister; Heath had been appointed as a Government whip; *Manchester Guardian*, 8 May 1952, *Sunday Times*, 11 May, 1952.
18. *Manchester Guardian, The Times, Daily Telegraph*, 8 May 1952.
19. Minutes of 'One Nation' group, 8 May 1952 – following Heath's appointment as a Government whip, the group had resolved on 15 November 1951 that no member of the Government could remain a member of the group (Maudling and Vaughan-Morgan had joined the group following Heath's departure); interview with Enoch Powell.
20. Macleod was later to describe the removal of any financial barrier to visiting the doctor as 'one of the most welcome results of the NHS,' leader in the *Spectator*, 24 July 1964; Webster, 1988, p. 196.
21. Webster, 1988, pp. 193–96.
22. Webster, 1988, p. 238–45.
23. Seldon, 1981, p. 265–66; Dame Enid Russell-Smith, quoted in Webster, 1988, p. 202.
24. CPA, CRD, 2/30/H, minutes of the Conservative backbench health and social security committee, 10 June 1952; Fisher, 1973, p. 87; Macleod, 17 June 1952, quoted in Webster, 1988, p. 393; *The Times*, 29 September 1952.
25. PRO, CAB, CC (52) 63rd meeting, 26 June 1952; *Hansard*, House of Lords, 26 March 1952, cols. 982–92.
26. Interviews with Eve Macleod, Torquil Macleod (son), Diana Heimann (daughter); Fisher, 1973, pp. 91–92.
27. Interview with Enoch Powell; Cosgrave, 1989, p. 125; *Spectator*, 16 July 1965.
28. Interviews with Eve Macleod, Diana Heimann (daughter); Fisher, 1973, pp. 87, 91–92; private information.
29. Membership records, White's Club; interviews with Sir Reginald Bennett, Lord Amery, Lord Hayhoe.
30. Interviews with Sir Reginald Bennett, Lord Amery, Lord Gilmour; *Listener*, 30 July 1970.
31. Interview with Michael Foot; Fisher, pp. 105–06; Saracens Rugby Football Club.
32. PRO, T.SS 5/13/02A, DHSS 94501/9/1, Macleod to Butler, 14 January 1953, cited in Webster, 1988, p. 204.
33. PRO, T.SS 5/13/02A; CAB 129/59, C (53) 30 and 58, 28 January, 11 February 1953; CAB 128/26, CC (53) 6th meeting, 3 February 1953, CC (53) 11th meeting, 12 February 1953; T.SS 5/13/02A, Butler to Thorneycroft, 17 February 1953, Thorneycroft to Butler, 18 February, cited in Webster, 1988, p. 204.
34. PRO, T.SS 5/13/02A, cited in Webster, 1988, pp. 204–05; *Hansard*, 1 April 1953, cols. 1228–35.
35. PRO, T.SS 5/13/02A, T.227/185, Mitchell to Clarke (citing Macleod letter to Butler, 28 October 1953), 14 November 1953, cited in Webster, 1988, p. 205.
36. CPA, CRD 2/30/H, minutes of the Conservative backbench health and social security committee, 1951–52; PRO, T.SS 5/332/01B, Stuart to Macleod, 22 January 1953, Macleod to Stuart, c. 30 January 1953, cited in Webster, 1988, p. 211; PRO, CAB 128/26, CC (53) 6th and 8th Conclusions, 3 and 10 February 1953; PREM 11, Macleod memoradum, CC (53) 240, 16 July 1954.

37. PRO, DHSS 94501/9/2A, Guillebaud Committee (53) 1st meeting, 13 May 1953, cited in Webster, 1988, p. 206.
38. PRO, T.SS 267/02B, cited in Webster, 1988, p. 206.
39. PRO, CAB 129/32, C (52) 190, 11 June 1952; CAB 128/25, CC (52) 63rd meeting, 26 June 1952; CAB 124/1189, Salisbury to Macleod, 8 June 1953; CAB 134/913, HA(53)50, 20 May 1953; CAB 134/192, HA(53) 12th meeting, 21 May 1953, cited in Webster, 1988, pp. 228–31.
40. PRO, PREM 11, Macleod memorandum, CC (53) 240, 16 July 1954; CAB, CC (54) 51st Conclusions, 20 July 1954.
41. PRO, T.SS 267/02A, Macleod to Butler, 26 April 1954, cited in Webster, 1988, pp. 216–17; *Daily Telegraph*, 9 February 1955.
42. PRO, EA(54) 25th meeting, 25 November 1954, T.SS 267/02A, T.HOP 223/443/01; CAB 129/69, CC (54) 348, 16 November 1954, CAB 128/27, CC (54) 80th meeting, 29 November 1954; T.SS 267/02A-B, Macleod/Brooke correspondence, 8 December 1954 – 4 February 1955, cited in Webster, 1988, p. 217
43. PRO, T.SS 66/226/02A, Stuart to Butler, 17 September 1955, Macleod to Butler, 19 September 1955, cited in Webster, 1988, pp. 217–19; *Hansard*, 31 October 1955, cols 642–44.
44. Conservative Conference, Margate, 9 October 1953, Official Record, pp. 90–91.
45. PRO, T.SS 267/02A, Macleod to Butler, 26 April 1954, cited in Webster, 1988, pp. 334–40; Seldon, 1981, p. 269.
46. *The Times*, 31 October 1952; Fisher, 1973, p. 93.
47. Conservative Conference, Margate, 9 October 1953, Official Record, pp. 90–91.
48. Seldon, 1981, pp. 268–69; Fisher, 1973, pp. 100–01.
49. Seldon, 1981, p. 269; Fisher, 1973, pp. 96–97.
50. Webster, 1988, pp. 380–86.
51. CPA, CRD 2/30/H, Conservative backbench health and social security committee minutes, 13 May 1953; Webster, 1988, pp. 372–73.
52. Fisher, p. 99; Seldon, 1981, p. 266.
53. *The Times*, 13 February 1954; Webster, 1988, pp. 232–34.
54. PRO, MH55/1011, Macleod to Boyd-Carpenter, 29 January 1954, cited in Webster, 1988, p. 234 – the 'prime mover' was Dr Horace Joules, medical superintendent of the Central Middlesex Hospital, and a member of the Cancer and Medical SACs.
55. *The Times*, 13 February 1954; *Spectator*, 24 July 1964.
56. PRO, DHSS 94192/2/7, DHSS 94151/2/2H, cited in Webster, 1988, p. 234; Conservative Conference, Blackpool, 9 October 1954, Official Record, pp. 108–09.
57. Leathard, 1980, p. 87; interview with Lady Monckton, cited in Leathard, 1980, pp. 93–94; the phrase 'a conspiracy of silence' was used by Lord Simon of Wythenshawe, letter to *The Times*, 29 October 1955.
58. Leathard, 1980, p. 87; interview with Lady Monckton, cited in Leathard, 1980, pp. 93–94.
59. FPA archives.
60. FPA 25th annual report, 1955–56, p. 5; FPA executive committee minutes, 8 December 1955; Leathard, 1980, pp. 93–94, 99.
61. PRO, PREM 11/1438.
62. PRO, PREM 11/1438; *The Times*, 1 December 1955, 6 December 1955; CPA, CRD 2/30/H, Conservative backbench health and social security committee minutes, joint meeting with home affairs committee, 5 December 1955.
63. Report of the Guillebaud Committee, 1956; Webster, 1988, pp. 207–09; CPA, CRD 2/30/H, Conservative backbench health and social security committee minutes, 22 February 1956.
64. PRO, PREM 11/1492, Macleod to Eden, 22 November 1955; HP(55) 16th meeting, minute 9, 25 November 1955.
65. Interview with Michael Foot.

CHAPTER 6: RISING STAR

1. Interview with Lord Rees-Mogg; CPA, CCO 150/2/3/2/2/I; Fisher, 1973, pp. 96–97.
2. CPA, CCO 150/2/3/2/2/I, 10th meeting, 22 December 1953.
3. CPA, CCO 150/2/3/2/2/I-III; *Hansard*, 17 April 1957, col. 1954.
4. CPA, CCO 150/2/3/2/2/I, 26th and 27th meetings, 13 October & 8 November 1954.
5. CPA, CCO 150/2/3/2/2/III; CRD 2/30/H, 21 November 1954, note by Charles Bellairs.
6. CPA, CCO 150/2/3/2/2/III.
7. CPA, CCO 150/2/3/2/2/III; *United for Peace and Progress.*
8. CPA, CCO 150/2/3/2/2/III; CRD 2/53/5; Ramsden, 1981, p. 176.
9. CPA, CRD, 2/53/5; *United for Peace and Progress*; *The Times*, 18 May 1955.
10. Interview with Eve Macleod; Fairlie, cited in Fisher, 1973, p. 108; Monckton Papers, Box 5, ff. 208–09, 213.
11. Campbell, 1993, pp. 89, 91; Rhodes James, 1986, p. 424; Eden, 1960, p. 318.
12. Interview with Sir Reginald Bennett.
13. Interviews with and notes from former Ministry of Labour officials; interview with Sir Reginald Bennett.
14. Interviews with and notes from former Ministry of Labour officials; interview with Diana Heimann (daughter).
15. Private information.
16. Interviews with Lord Carr of Hadley, Dame Mary Smieton; notes from Ministry of Labour officials.
17. Cairncross, 1993, pp. 106–07; Goodman, 1984, pp. 114–22.
18. Goodman, 1984, pp. 122–24.
19. PRO, PREM 11/1883, Macleod to Eden, 27 February 1956.
20. Goodman, 1984, pp. 122–24; Middlemas, 1986, p. 263; Monckton Papers, Box 6, 10–11; PRO, PREM 11/1883, Macleod to Eden, 27 February 1956.
21. PRO, PREM 11/1883; Goodman, 1984, pp. 124–28; *The Times*, 4 June 1956.
22. PRO, PREM 11/1402, Macleod to Eden, 4 June 1956.
23. Goodman, 1984, pp. 128–29.
24. PRO, PREM 11/1405, CP(56) 113, 4 May 1956; CAB CM(56) 34th & 35th Conclusions, 8 & 10 May 1956.
25. *The Times*, 10 May, 5 & 22 June 1956.
26. *Hansard*, 28 June 1956, cols. 704–10; Jones, 1986, pp. 145–47; Conservative Conference, Llandudno, 12 October 1956, Official Record, p. 83.
27. *The Times*, 11, 18, 24 & 27 July 1956; Goodman, 1984, pp. 129–32; Conservative Conference, Llandudno, 12 October 1956, Official Record, p. 83.
28. Goodman, 1984, pp. 133–36.
29. Middlemas, 1986, pp. 278–79; Conservative Conference, Llandudno, 12 October 1956, Official Record, p. 83.
30. Conservative Conference, Llandudno, 12 October 1956, Official Record, p. 84–89; PRO, PREM 11/2110, Macleod to Macmillan, 9 August 1957 – Cousins's inability to restrain his members in the Covent Garden strike during the summer of 1957 confirmed Macleod in his doubts about secret ballots.
31. Macleod defended the Government's policy in a review for the *New York Herald Tribune* in the spring of 1964 of Professor Herman Finer's book, *Dulles over Suez: the Theory and Practice of his Diplomacy* – cited in Fisher, 1973, pp. 114–15; in the course of his rejoinder to a letter from David Astor in the *Spectator*, 3 July 1964, Macleod declared, 'Of course I didn't oppose Suez.'
32. Hennessy and Laity, 'Suez – What the papers Say,' in *Contemporary Record*, Spring 1987; PRO, PREM 11/1152, Eden to Sandys, 22 August, Sandys to Eden, 23 August 1956.
33. PRO, PREM 11/1152, Brook to Eden, 25 August 1956; CAB 128/30, CM(56) 24th Conclusions, 21 March 1956.

34. PRO, CAB 128/30, CM(56) 24th Conclusions, 21 March 1956; PREM 11/1098.
35. PRO, PREM 11/1172, Macleod to Eden, 14 August 1956; *The Times*, 7 September 1956.
36. PRO, PREM 11/1172, Bishop to Eden, 17 August 1956 CAB 128/30, CM(56) 64th Conclusions, 11 September 1956.
37. Dooley, 1989, pp. 499–500; PRO, PREM 11/1152, Lennox-Boyd to Eden, Home to Eden, 24 August 1956; Brook to Eden, 25 August 1956.
38. Kyle, 1991, pp. 200–331; Carlton, winter 1992, review in *Contemporary Record*, pp. 593–95; Dooley, 1989, pp. 508–11.
39. PRO, CAB 128/30, CM(56) 71st Conclusions, 18 October; 72nd Conclusions, 23 October 1956, Confidential Annex (with very limited circulation).
40. PRO, CAB 128/30, CM(56) 73rd Conclusions, 24 October; 74th Conclusions, 25 October 1956.
41. Dooley, 1989, pp. 512–14; Kyle, 1989, pp. 334–35.
42. PRO, CAB 128/30, CM(56) 75th Conclusions; Kyle, 1989, pp. 356–57; interview with the Earl of Selkirk.
43. Dooley, 1989, pp. 514–15; Kyle, 1989, p. 428; PRO, CAB 128/30, CM(56) 78th Conclusions, 2 November 1956.
44. PRO, CAB 128/30, CM(56) 79th Conclusions, 4 November 1956; Kyle, 1991, p. 442; Rhodes James, 1986, pp. 566–67.
45. Churchill, 1959, p. 287; Fisher, 1973, pp. 116–17; interviews with Lord Carr, Lord Rees-Mogg; private information.
46. Interviews with Lord Rees-Mogg, David Astor.
47. PRO, PREM 11/1127, Astor to Macleod, 14 November 1956.
48. Interview with David Astor; PRO, PREM 11/1127, Bishop to Eden, 15 November 1956.
49. PRO, CAB 128/30, CM(56) 85th Conclusions, 20 November 1956.
50. Shepherd, 1991, pp. 145–48.
51. Interview with David Astor; Blake, 1985, p. 279; Lord Beloff, 'The Crisis and its Consequences for the British Conservative Party,' in Louis and Owen, 1989, p. 333.

CHAPTER 7: 'POLITICAL GENIUS'

1. Wigham, 1982, p. 114; Goodman, 1984, pp. 138–39; PRO, PREM 11/2513, Macleod to Eden, 7 January 1957.
2. PRO, PREM 11/2513, Macleod to Eden, 7 January 1957; Goodman, 1984, pp. 138–39.
3. PRO, PREM 11/3125, Macleod to Macmillan, 11 March 1957; PREM 11/3125, Macleod to Macmillan, 4 June 1956.
4. PRO, PREM 11/3125, Macleod to Macmillan, 11 March 1957.
5. PRO, PREM 11/3125, Macleod to Macmillan, 11 March 1957; CC (57) 19th Conclusions, 14 March 1957.
6. PRO, PREM 11/3125, Macleod to Macmillan, 19 March 1957.
7. Ibid.
8. Ibid.
9. PRO, PREM 11/3125, Macmillan to Butler, Butler to Macmillan, Macleod to Macmillan, 22 March 1957; PREM 11/2513, Macleod to Macmillan, 27 March 1957; Wigham, 1981, pp. 115–16.
10. PRO, PREM 11/3125, Macleod to Macmillan, 25 & 27 March 1957; Wigham, 1981, pp. 115–16.
11. Fisher, 1973, p. 113.
12. PRO, PREM 11/3125, Macleod to Macmillan, 24 & 27 April 1957.
13. Wigham, 1982, p. 116; Fisher, 1973, pp. 113–14.
14. PRO, PREM 11/3125, Macmillan to Macleod, 8 April 1957.
15. PRO, PREM 11/3125, Macleod to Macmillan, 11 April 1957.
16. Ibid.
17. Interview with Geoffrey Goodman; notes from Ministry of Labour officials.

18. Interview with Geoffrey Goodman; notes from Ministry of Labour officials.
19. PRO, PREM 11/2878, PREM 11/3125, Macleod to Macmillan, 27 April 1957.
20. PRO, PREM 11/2878, PREM 11/3125, Macleod to Macmillan, 27 April 1957; Brittan, 1970, p. 210.
21. Conservative Conference, Brighton, Official Record, 11 October 1957; notes from Ministry of Labour officials.
22. Middlemas, 1986, p. 308; notes from Ministry of Labour officials.
23. PRO, CAB 134/1327, Social Services Committee; Lowe, 1989, pp. 505–15.
24. PRO, CAB 128/30, CC (56) 71st Conclusions, CC (57) 1st Conclusions; Lowe, 1989, pp. 515–17.
25. PRO, PREM 11/1935; Fisher, 1973, pp. 113–14; *Hansard*, 17 April 1957, cols. 1952–54.
26. Lowe, 1989, pp. 518–20; Brittan, 1970, pp. 207–19.
27. Notes from Ministry of Labour officials; interview with Enoch Powell; PRO, PREM 11/2306; Lowe, 1989, pp. 517–26; Boyd-Carpenter, 1980, pp. 137–39.
28. Lowe, 1989, pp. 517–26; Boyd-Carpenter, 1980, p. 139.
29. PRO, CAB, CC (58) 3rd Conclusions, 5 January 1958; Macmillan, 1971, p. 368.
30. Powell, Thorneycroft, quoted in Horne, 1989, pp. 76–77; Lowe, 1989, pp. 519–20.
31. Interview with Geoffrey Goodman.
32. Goodman, 1984, pp. 164–67.
33. PRO, PREM 11/2513, Macleod to Butler, 20 January 1958, Ministers' meeting, 21 January 1958, Butler to Macmillan, 24 January 1958; CAB 129/91, C(58) 15, 21/1/58; C(58) 17, 23/1/58; C(58) 20, 23/1/58; CAB 128/32, CC (58) 8th, 9th, 10th Conclusions, 22, 24/1/58.
34. PRO, CAB 128/32, CC (58) 9th & 10th Conclusions, 24/1/58; Wigham, 1982, pp. 118–19; Fisher, 1973, p. 125; PREM 11/2513, Butler to Macmillan, 24 January 1958.
35. Interviews with, and notes from, former Ministry of Labour officials; Goodman, 1984, pp. 167–68.
36. PRO, PREM 11/2513, Macleod to Macmillan, 4 February 1958; Goodman, 1984, pp. 170–72.
37. Goodman, 1984, pp. 174–76; Wigham, 1982, p. 120.
38. PRO, PREM 11/2513, Macleod to Macmillan, 10/5/58, Cabinet paper by Macleod, 10/5/58; Macleod to Macmillan, 12/5/58; Goodman, 1984, pp. 174–76; Wigham, 1982, p. 120.
39. *New Statesman*, 26 April 1958.
40. *Hansard*, 8 May 1958, cols. 1422–52; interview with Sir Reginald Bennett; Fisher, 1973, pp. 127–28.
41. *Hansard*, 8 May 1958, cols. 1452–53; interview with Sir Reginald Bennett; *Daily Telegraph*, *Guardian*, 9 May 1958.
42. Goodman, 1984, pp. 184–85; PRO, PREM 11/2512, Macleod to Macmillan, 22 May 1958, Macleod meets TUC, 22 May 1958.
43. PRO, PREM 11/2512, Macleod to Macmillan, 22 May 1958; Goodman, 1984, pp. 184–85.
44. PRO, PREM 11/2512, Macleod to Macmillan, 6 June 1958; Goodman, 1984, pp. 184–85; PRO, PREM 11/2512, Macleod to Macmillan, 22 May 1958.
45. Goodman, 1984, pp. 189–91; PRO, PREM 11/2512, Macleod to Macmillan, 23 June 1958.
46. Notes from Ministry of Labour officials.
47. CPA, CRD 2/53/24, 26.
48. CPA, CRD 2/53/28, PSG, 1st & 2nd, 15 February & 15 March 1957.
49. CPA, CRD 2/53/24, Macleod to Macmillan, 10 July 1957; CPA, CRD 2/53/28, PSG, 9th, 15 July 1957.
50. CPA, CRD 2/53/24, Macleod to Macmillan, 10 July 1957.
51. CPA, CRD 2/53/30, SC, 1st, 23 December 1957; interview with Lord Fraser of Kilmorack.
52. Macleod to Powell, 19 February 1959, Powell to Macleod, 27 February 1959.
53. CPA, CRD 2/53/30, Macleod to Macmillan, 10 July 1957; Brittan, 1970, pp. 224–26; Cairncross, 1993, pp. 110–11.
54. Conservative Conference, 8 October 1958, Official Record, p. 57; Cairncross, 1993, p. 111.
55. *The Times*, 19 March 1959; *Hansard*, 18 March 1959, cols. 433–46.

56. Brittan, 1970, pp. 24–26; Cairncross, 1993, p. 111–12.
57. CPA, CRD 2/53/30, SC, 4th, 20 March 1958, verbatim note.
58. CPA, CRD 2/53/31, SC, 6th, 23 July 1958.
59. CPA, CRD 2/53/31, SC/6, Trade Union Legislation, note by Macleod, 24 September 1958.
60. CPA, CRD 2/53/31, SC/6, Trade Union Legislation, note by Macleod, 24 September 1958; SC 7th, 5 November 1958.
61. CPA, CRD 2/53/34, SC, 10 July 1959.
62. CPA, CRD 2/53/31, SC/59, Liberty Under the Law, note by Macleod, 1 September 1959.
63. *The Next Five Years*, Conservative Central Office, 1959.
64. *The Times*, 21 & 30 September 1959; Butler and Rose, 1960, pp. 61–2, 87–8.
65. *New Statesman*, 26 April 1958.

CHAPTER 8: STATESMAN

1. Macleod interviewed by W.P. Kirkman, 29 December 1967.
2. Macleod interviewed by W.P. Kirkman, 29 December 1967.
3. Private information.
4. Members of the 'One Nation' group were unable to agree a common approach on foreign and colonial policy. From 1954, the founding members were split over the handling of Suez.
5. Kahler, 1984, p. 316.
6. Interview with Lord Amery.
7. Interview with David Astor.
8. Macleod interviewed by W.P. Kirkman, 29 December 1967; interview with Rhoderick Macleod; Lapping, 1985, p. 436.
9. PRO, PREM 11/2583, Macleod to Macmillan, 25 May 1959; D.J. Morgan, 1980, pp. 96–115.
10. PRO, PREM 11/2583, Macleod to Macmillan, 25 May 1959; in the mid-1970s, Stirling was one of a number of former military commanders whose apprehensions at the state of Britain led them to consider mobilizing private militias.
11. Interview with Sir Michael Blundell; Blundell, 1967, p. 255.
12. PRO, PREM 11/2583, Macleod to Macmillan, 25 May 1959; Macleod interviewed by W.P. Kirkman, 29 December 1967.
13. PRO, PREM 11/2583; CPA, CRD, 2/53, SC/45, 23 June 1959.
14. PRO, Cabinet meeting, 11 June 1959; Macleod interviewed by W.P. Kirkman, 29 December 1967.
15. Interview with Lord Alport; Macleod interviewed by W.P. Kirkman, 29 December 1967.
16. Horne, 1989, p. 183.
17. Interview with Lord Carr.
18. Horne, 1989, p. 185.
19. Interview with Lord Alport.
20. Horne, 1989, pp. 183–84.
21. Macleod interviewed by W.P. Kirkman, 29 December 1967; interview with Lord Rees-Mogg, who recalled the late Peter Goldman's comment.
22. Macleod interviewed by W.P. Kirkman, 29 December 1967.
23. Macleod interviewed by W.P. Kirkman, 29 December 1967; *Spectator*, quoted in Fisher, 1973, p. 142.
24. Macleod interviewed by W.P. Kirkman, 29 December 1967.
25. Interviews with Sir Leslie Monson, 'Max' Webber, Sir Duncan Watson.
26. Interview with Sir Hilton Poynton. The responsibilities of the colonial administration included defence, health, education, veterinary services, and so on. Another burden on Poynton was the review of the future of the Colonial Office being conducted by the Commons Select Committee on the Estimates during much of Macleod's time as Colonial Secretary.
27. Interview with Sir Duncan Watson.

28. Macleod interviewed by W.P. Kirkman, 29 December 1967.
29. Fisher, 1973, p. 149.
30. Macleod interviewed by W.P. Kirkman, 29 December 1967; Fisher, 1973, p. 150.
31. Interview with Sir Leslie Monson.
32. Interviews with Sir Leslie Monson, Sir Duncan Watson.
33. Interview with Lord Perth.
34. Interview with Sir Leslie Monson.
35. Interview with Colin Legum.
36. Interview with Lord Amery.
37. Interview with Lady Antonia Fraser.
38. Macleod interviewed by W.P. Kirkman, 29 December 1967; the quote comes from Chesterton's 'The Rolling English Road.'
39. Macleod interviewed by W.P. Kirkman, 29 December 1967.
40. Interviews with Sir Hilton Poynton, Sir Leslie Monson, Max Webber.
41. PRO, CAB 134/1558, CPC (59) 5th meeting, 5 November 1959; CAB 128, CC (59) 57th meeting, 10 November 1959.
42. Macleod interviewed by W.P. Kirkman, 29 December 1967.
43. PRO, CAB 134/1558, CPC (59) 6th meeting, 20 November 1959.
44. PRO, CAB 134/1558, CPC (59) 7th meeting, 23 November 1959; CAB 128 CC (59) 60th meeting, 26 November 1959.
45. PRO, PREM 11/2586, Macleod to Macmillan, 29 December 1959, Macmillan to Macleod, 30 December 1959; PRO, PREM 11/2888, record of conversation, 19 December 1959; Sir David Hunt, *Sunday Telegraph*, 4 February 1990.
46. Macleod interviewed by W.P. Kirkman, 29 December 1967; PRO, PREM 11/2586, Macleod to Macmillan, 29 December 1959.
47. PRO, PREM 11/2586, Macleod to Macmillan, 29 December 1959.
48. PRO, CAB 128/34, 18 February 1960.
49. PRO, PREM 11/2586, Macleod to Macmillan, 29 December 1959.
50. Macleod interviewed by W.P. Kirkman, 29 December 1967; PRO, PREM 11/3031, Macleod to Macmillan, 16 February 1960.
51. PRO, PREM 11/3030, Macleod to Butler, 15 January 1960.
52. Macleod interviewed by W.P. Kirkman, 29 December 1967.
53. PRO, PREM 11/3030, Macleod to Butler, Butler to Macleod 15 January 1960.
54. Macleod interviewed by W.P. Kirkman, 29 December 1967; PRO, PREM 11/3030, Sir Norman Brook to F. Bishop, 18 January 1960.
55. PRO, PREM 11/3030, Macleod to Macmillan, 21 January 1960, de Zulueta to Bligh, 20 January 1960, de Zulueta to Butler, 26 January 1960.
56. Macleod interviewed by W.P. Kirkman, 29 December 1967.
57. Macleod interviewed by W.P. Kirkman, 29 December 1967; PRO, PREM 11/2586, Macleod to Macmillan, 27 January 1960.
58. Macleod interviewed by W.P. Kirkman, 29 December 1967.
59. *The Times*, 1 February 1960.
60. PRO, PREM 11/3030, Macleod to Macmillan, 1 February 1960.
61. PRO, PREM 11/3030, Butler to Macleod, Macleod to Macmillan, 1 February 1960, Macmillan to Macleod, February 1960.
62. PRO, PREM 11/3030, Macleod to Macmillan, 8 February 1960.
63. PRO, CO 822/2025, Blundell to Macleod, 2 February 1960; Macleod interviewed by W.P. Kirkman, 29 December 1967; interview with Sir Michael Blundell; Blundell, 1967, p. 271.
64. Blundell, 1967, pp. 270–76.
65. Mboya, 1963, p. 117.
66. Blundell, 1967, p. 271; Macleod interviewed by W.P. Kirkman, 29 December 1967.
67. Blundell, 1967, pp. 272.
68. PRO, PREM 11/3030, Macleod to Macmillan, 8 February 1960.

69. Macleod interviewed by W.P. Kirkman, 29 December 1967.
70. PRO, PREM 11/3030, Macleod to Macmillan, 8 February 1960.
71. PRO, CAB 128/34, CC (60) 9th meeting, 12 February 1960; PRO, PREM 11/2882, Macleod to Butler, 15 January 1960, Butler to Macleod, 19 January 1960; PRO, PREM 11/3030, Butler to Blundell, 12 February 1960.
72. PRO, PREM 11/3030, Sir Norman Brook to Macmillan, 15 February 1960, citing CPC (60)3.
73. Mboya, 1963, p. 116; Macleod interviewed by W.P. Kirkman, 29 December 1967.
74. PRO, CAB 128/34, CC (60) 9th meeting, 12 February 1960; PRO, PREM 11/3030, Macleod to Macmillan, 20 February 1960.
75. PRO, PREM 11/3031, Macleod to Macmillan, 16 & 17 February 1960; Macmillan, note for the record, 17 February 1960.
76. PRO, PREM 11/3030, Macleod to Macmillan, 20 February 1960. PRO, PREM 11/3031, de Zulueta to Pearson, 25 February 1960; *The Times*, 22 February 1960.
77. *The Times*, 22 February 1960.
78. PRO, PREM 11/3030, Macmillan to Macleod, 21 February 1960.
79. Macleod interviewed by W.P. Kirkman, 29 December 1967.
80. Quoted in Lapping, 1985, p. 437; Blundell, 1967, pp. 270–76; interview with Sir Michael Blundell.

CHAPTER 9: AFRICAN OMELETTE

1. Macleod interviewed by W.P. Kirkman, 29 December 1967.
2. Macleod interviewed by W.P. Kirkman, 29 December 1967; Lapping, 1985, pp. 462–75; PRO, PREM 11/3075, Macleod to Macmillan, 3 December 1959.
3. PRO, PREM 11/3075, Macleod to Macmillan, 3 December 1959.
4. PRO, PREM 11/2784, Sir Norman Brook to Macmillan, 15 October 1959, Bligh to Macmillan, 16 October 1959 – Bligh noted, 'Lord Home is always saying that the effect of Africa on people who have never been there before is very marked. I expect therefore that he and his chaps [sic] would want to qualify many of Mr Trend's views.' Macmillan, 22 October 1959 – suggested sending the report to Home and Macleod.
5. Macleod interviewed by W.P. Kirkman, 29 December 1967.
6. PRO, PREM 11/3075, Macleod to Macmillan, 3 December 1959; Macleod interviewed by W.P. Kirkman, 29 December 1967.
7. PRO, PREM 11/3075, Macmillan on Trend's report, 28 December 1959. Macleod interviewed by W.P. Kirkman, 29 December 1967; PRO, PREM 11/3075, Macleod to Macmillan, 3 December 1959.
8. PRO, PREM 11/2586, Macleod to Macmillan, 29 December 1959.
9. PRO, PREM 11/3075, Macleod to Macmillan, 3 December 1959.
10. PRO, PREM 11/3075, Note for the record, 1 January 1960.
11. PRO, CAB 128/34, CC (60) 1st, 4 January 1960; PRO, PREM 11/3075, Macleod to Macmillan, Macleod to Armitage, 4 January 1960.
12. PRO, PREM 11/3075, Acting High Commissioner (AHC), Salisbury, to Home, Welensky to Home, AHC, Salisbury to CRO, 7 January 1960; Macleod, Leeds, 7 January 1960; Macleod and Home to Macmillan, 15 January 1960.
13. PRO, PREM 11/3075, Macleod to Macmillan, 17 January 1960, Armitage to Macleod, 18 January 1960, Macleod to Macmillan, 20 January 1960.
14. PRO, PREM 11/3075, Macleod to Macmillan, 24 January 1960.
15. PRO, PREM 11/3075, Macmillan to Macleod, 27 January 1960.
16. PRO, PREM 11/3075, Macleod and Home to Macmillan, 28 January 1960, Macmillan to Macleod, 29 January 1960.
17. PRO, PREM 11/3075, Macmillan to Macleod, 27 January 1960, Macmillan to Home, 12 February 1960.

18. PRO, PREM 11/3075, Macleod to Macmillan, 4 January 1960, Macmillan to Macleod, 29 January 1960.
19. PRO, PREM 11/3075, CRO, Salisbury, to Cape Town, 3 February 1960, Governor-General to Home, 4 February 1960.
20. PRO, PREM 11/3075, CRO to Pretoria, 3 February 1960, CRO to Cape Town, 4 February 1960, Macleod and Home to Macmillan, 4 February 1960.
21. PRO, CAB 128/34, CC (60) 6th, 9 February 1960.
22. PRO, PREM 11/3075, Home to Macmillan, 9 February 1960.
23. PRO, PREM 11/3075, Sir Norman Brook to Macmillan, 10 February 1960.
24. PRO, PREM 11/3075, Macleod to Armitage, 15 February 1960 (two telegrams).
25. PRO, CAB 128/34, CC (60) 10th, 18 February 1960, CC (60) 27, 16 February 1960.
26. PRO, CAB 128/34, CC (60) 9th, 16 February, and 10th, 18 February 1960.
27. PRO, PREM 11/3076, Home to Macmillan, 20 & 21 February 1960.
28. PRO, CAB 128/34, CC (60) 11th, 22 February 1960.
29. PRO, PREM 11/3076, Home to Macmillan, 22 & 23 February 1960.
30. PRO, CAB 128/34, CC (60) 12th, 23 February 1960.
31. PRO, PREM 11/3076, Watson to Macleod, 23 February 1960.
32. PRO, CAB 128/34, CC (60) 12th, 23 February 1960.
33. Macleod interviewed by W.P. Kirkman, 29 December 1967; PREM 11/3076, Home to Macmillan, 20 & 21 February 1960.
34. Macleod interviewed by W.P. Kirkman, 29 December 1967.
35. PRO, PREM 11/3076, Home to Macmillan, 25 February 1960; CAB 128/34, CC (60) 13th, 25 February 1960.
36. PRO, PREM 11/3076, Macleod to Home, 25 February 1960; Macleod to Macmillan, 26 February 1960.
37. Wood, 1983, p. 765, citing Loft to Macleod, 26 February 1960, Macleod to Welensky, 3 March 1960; PRO, PREM 11/3076, Macleod to Macmillan, 2 March, Jones note of meeting with Banda, 10 March 1960.
38. Macleod interviewed by W.P. Kirkman, 29 December 1967; PRO, PREM 11/3076, Macleod to Macmillan, 31 March 1960.
39. Macleod interviewed by W.P. Kirkman, 29 December 1967; PRO, PREM 11/3076, Macleod to Macmillan, 3 April 1960.
40. Macleod interviewed by W.P. Kirkman, 29 December 1967.
41. PRO, PREM 11/3076, Macleod to Macmillan, 3 April 1960.
42. PRO, PREM 11/3076, Macleod to Macmillan, 3 April 1960; Macleod interviewed by W.P. Kirkman, 29 December 1967.
43. Macleod interviewed by W.P. Kirkman, 29 December 1967.
44. PRO, PREM 11/3076, Macleod to Macmillan, 3 April 1960.
45. Macleod interviewed by W.P. Kirkman, 29 December 1967.
46. Interview with Sir Leslie Monson.
47. Interviews with Diana Heimann, Sir Roy Welensky.
48. PRO, PREM 11/3076, Macleod to Macmillan, 31 March 1960.
49. PRO, PREM 11/3076, Macleod to Macmillan, 31 March 1960, 3 April 1960.
50. PRO, PREM 11/3240, Macleod to Macmillan, 31 May 1960.
51. PRO, PREM 11/3240, Macleod to Macmillan, 31 May 1960; Macleod to Welensky, 30 May 1960.
52. PRO, PREM 11/3076, Macleod to Welensky, 30 May 1960.
53. PRO, PREM 11/3077, Bligh to Macmillan, 1 July 1960.
54. *The Times*, 5 August 1960; Macleod interviewed by W.P. Kirkman, 29 December 1967.
55. PRO, PREM 11/3077, Macleod to Macmillan, 1, 2 & 3 August 1960.
56. PRO, PREM 11/3077, Macleod to Macmillan, 1, 2, 3 & 6 August 1960.
57. PRO, PREM 11/3077, Macmillan to Macleod, 6 August 1960.
58. PRO, PREM 11/3077, Macleod to Welensky, 2 August 1960; Macleod interviewed by W.P. Kirkman, 29 December 1967.

59. PRO, PREM 11/3078, Macleod to Macmillan, 11 August 1960; Wood, 1983, p. 807.
60. PRO, PREM 11/3078, Macleod to Macmillan, 15 September 1960.
61. PRO, PREM 11/3078, note, 16 September 1960; PREM 11/3078–79, October 1960.
62. PRO, CAB 128/34, CC (60) 57th, 8 November 1960 – Welensky eventually backed down over making public the correspondence; PREM 11/3076, Bligh note, 11 October 1960.
63. Conservative Conference, Scarborough, Official Record, 12 October 1960.
64. PRO, PREM 11/3078, Macleod to Macmillan, 4 October 1960.
65. Conservative Conference, Scarborough, Official Record, 12 October 1960.
66. PRO, PREM 11/3080, Dalhousie to Sandys, 11 November 1960.
67. PRO, PREM 11/3080, Macleod to Sandys, 15 November 1960.
68. PRO, PREM 11/3080, Wyndham note, Macleod and Macmillan, 13 November 1960.
69. Horne, 1989, pp. 208–11; Wood, 1983, 848–56; Lapping, 1985, pp. 487–88.
70. Horne, 1989, pp. 208–11; Wood, 1983, 848–56.
71. Macleod interviewed by W.P. Kirkman, 29 December 1967.
72. Wood, 1983, p. 857.

CHAPTER 10: 'THE BROTHERHOOD OF MAN'

1. PRO, CPC(61) 1, 3 January 1961.
2. Macleod interviewed by W.P. Kirkman, 29 December 1967; PRO, CPC(61) 1, 3 January 1961.
3. Macleod interviewed by W.P. Kirkman, 29 December 1967.
4. Macleod interviewed by W.P. Kirkman, 29 December 1967.
5. Macleod interviewed by W.P. Kirkman, 29 December 1967; interview with Sir Reginald Bennett.
6. *Financial Times*, 10 January 1961; *Daily Express*, 13 January 1961; Wood, 1983, pp. 862–63.
7. PRO, PREM 11/3485, Admiralty House meeting, Macleod to Hone 23 January 1961.
8. PRO, PREM 11/3485, Macmillan to Sandys 25 & 27 January 1961.
9. Macleod interviewed by W.P. Kirkman, 29 December 1967; Wood, 1983, p. 868.
10. Macmillan, 1973, pp. 309–10.
11. Macleod interviewed by W.P. Kirkman, 29 December 1967; Wood, 1983, p. 868.
12. Macleod interviewed by W.P. Kirkman, 29 December 1967; PRO, PREM 11/3487.
13. *The Times*, 10 February 1961; CPA, CRD, Commonwealth Affairs Committee, 9 February 1961; Wood, 1983, p. 873; Macleod interviewed by W.P. Kirkman, 29 December 1967; *The Times*, 13 February 1961.
14. Wood, 1983, pp. 871–72.
15. PRO, CAB 134/1364, A.F. (M) (61) 2nd, 14 February 1961; Wood, 1983, pp. 879–80.
16. PRO, PREM 11/3487, note of meeting, Macmillan and Macleod, 17 February 1961.
17. *The Times*, 20 February 1961.
18. PRO, CAB CC (61) 8th Conclusions, 20 February 1961; *The Times*, 22 February 1961.
19. Wood, 1983, pp. 890–91; PREM 11/3488, Hone to Macleod, 23 February 1961.
20. CPA, CRD, CAC, 23 February 1961; PRO, PREM 11/3488, Macleod to Macmillan, 23 February 1961; note of meeting, 23 February 1961, Macmillan to Macleod, 26 February 1961.
21. PRO, PREM 11/3488, Acting High Commissioner to Sandys, 28 February 1961; Wood, 1983, p. 896.
22. House of Lords *Hansard*, 7 March 1961, cols. 306–07.
23. House of Lords *Hansard*, 7 March 1961, cols. 307, 307–15, 312, 360–61.
24. House of Lords *Hansard*, 8 March 1961, cols. 363, 486–508.
25. Interviews with Lady Antonia Fraser, the Earl of Perth.
26. PRO, PREM 11/3488, Macleod to Macmillan, 10 March 1961.
27. PRO, PREM 11/3489, Macleod to Macmillan, 16 March 1961.
28. PRO, PREM 11/3495, Knox Cunningham to Macmillan, Patrick Wall to Macmillan, Redmayne to Macmillan, 17 March 1961.

29. PRO, PREM 11/3495, Macleod to Redmayne, 20 March 1961.
30. PRO, PREM 11/3489, Macleod to Macmillan, 17 March 1961.
31. PRO, PREM 11/3489, Macleod to Hone, 24 March 1961; Macmillan to Trend, 30 March 1961; Trend to Macmillan, 7 April 1961.
32. PRO, PREM 11/3495, Macleod to Macmillan, 10 May, 23 May 1961.
33. PRO, PREM 11/3491, Macleod to Sandys, 26 May 1961; Macleod to Macmillan, 7 June 1961.
34. PRO, PREM 11/3495, Macleod to Macmillan, 4 June 1961, Macmillan to Macleod, 5 June 1961, Macleod to Macmillan, 7 June 1961; Horne, 1989, p. 394.
35. PRO, CAB, CC (61) 33rd, 19 June 1961.
36. PRO, CAB, CC (61) 34th, 20 June 1961; Wood, 1983, pp. 932–35.
37. Macleod interviewed by W.P. Kirkman, 29 December 1967; Macmillan, 1973, p. 316.
38. *Hansard*, 25 July 1961, col. 264.
39. Macleod interviewed by W.P. Kirkman, 29 December 1967.
40. Macleod interviewed by W.P. Kirkman, 29 December 1967.
41. PRO, PREM 11/3240, Macleod to Macmillan, 31 May 1960.
42. PRO, PREM 11/3183, Nyerere to Macmillan, 27 February 1961, Turnbull to Macleod, 6 March 1961; Macleod interviewed by W.P. Kirkman, 29 December 1967.
43. Macleod interviewed by W.P. Kirkman, 29 December 1967; Morgan, 1980, p. 147
44. Morgan, 1980, pp. 147–49, citing CO, WIS, 64/175/03, 1957–59, Home to Lennox-Boyd, 31 July 1959, Amery minute, 6 August 1959; note by A.R. Thomas, former Assistant Secretary, West Indies Section, Colonial Office.
45. Morgan, 1980, pp. 148–57, citing CO, DP (60)4, note of 6 January 1960.
46. PRO, PREM 11/3240, Macleod to Macmillan, 31 May 1960; note by A.R. Thomas.
47. Macleod interviewed by W.P. Kirkman, 29 December 1967; *Daily Gleaner*, 6 June 1960, *Trinidad Guardian*, 17 June 1960, *Evening Standard*, 21 June 1960; note by A.R. Thomas.
48. Morgan, 1980, pp. 166–68.
49. Note by A.R. Thomas.
50. Note by A.R. Thomas; Morgan, 1980, pp. 169–70, citing CO, WIS, 897/6/01, 1960–62, items 2,4; WIS, 897/20/03, 1960–62, items E/47, E/51.
51. Macleod interviewed by W.P. Kirkman, 29 December 1967; note by A.R. Thomas.
52. Note by A.R. Thomas; Morgan, 1980, pp. 169–70, citing C, WIS, 897/20/03, 1960–62, item 44, note of 6 July 1960 from Secretary of State's oral account of that day.
53. PRO, CPC (61) 1, 3 January 1961; Macleod interviewed by W.P. Kirkman, 29 December 1967.
54. Morgan, 1980, p. 172; Macleod interviewed by W.P. Kirkman, 29 December 1967.
55. PRO, CAB, C(61) 142, 26 September 1961; CAB, CC 52(61) 4, 28 September 1961; Morgan, 1980, pp. 174–75.
56. Macleod interviewed by W.P. Kirkman, 29 December 1967.
57. Macleod interviewed by W.P. Kirkman, 29 December 1967.
58. Macleod interviewed by W.P. Kirkman, 29 December 1967.
59. Macleod interviewed by W.P. Kirkman, 29 December 1967.
60. Macleod interviewed by W.P. Kirkman, 29 December 1967; PRO, PREM 11/3240, Macleod to Macmillan, 31 May 1960; CAB, CPC (60) 26, memorandum by Macleod, 16 December 1960, CC 2(61), 24 January 1961.
61. Macleod interviewed by W.P. Kirkman, 29 December 1967; PRO, PREM 11/2586, Macleod to Macmillan, 29 December 1959, PREM 11/3240, Macleod to Macmillan, 25 May 1960, PREM 11/3240, Macleod to Macmillan, 31 May 1960.
62. Papers on Macleod's visit to Aden and the Protectorates, 3–6 April 1961, Rhodes House; Lapping, 1985, pp. 283–310.
63. PRO, PREM 11/3240, Macleod to Macmillan, 31 May 1960.
64. Macleod interviewed by W.P. Kirkman, 29 December 1967; Listowel, 1968, pp. 384–86.

65. Macleod interviewed by W.P. Kirkman, 29 December 1967; Listowel, 1968, pp. 387.
66. PRO, PREM 11/3240, Macleod to Macmillan, 31 May 1960; Macleod interviewed by W.P. Kirkman, 29 December 1967.
67. Macleod interviewed by W.P. Kirkman, 29 December 1967.
68. Lapping, 1985, pp. 437–38.
69. Macleod interviewed by W.P. Kirkman, 29 December 1967; PRO, PREM 11/3240, Macleod to Macmillan, 31 May 1960.
70. Macleod interviewed by W.P. Kirkman, 29 December 1967; PRO, PREM 11/2586, Macleod to Macmillan, 29 December 1959; private information.
71. Lapping, 1985, pp. 438–39; Macleod interviewed by W.P. Kirkman, 29 December 1967.
72. Macleod interviewed by W.P. Kirkman, 29 December 1967; Lapping, 1985, pp. 439–42; Hargreaves, 1988, pp. 193–96; Maudling, 1978, pp. 92–95.
73. PRO, PREM 11/3240, Macleod to Macmillan, 31 May 1960; Macleod interviewed by W.P. Kirkman, 29 December 1967.
74. Macleod interviewed by W.P. Kirkman, 29 December 1967.
75. Macleod interviewed by W.P. Kirkman, 29 December 1967.
76. Macleod interviewed by W.P. Kirkman, 29 December 1967.
77. PRO, PREM 11/3493, Macleod to Trend, 10 August 1961.
78. PRO, PREM 11/3493, Hone to Macleod, 24 July 1961, Hone to Macleod, 15 July 1961, Alport to Commonwealth Relations Office, 16 July 1961, Macleod to Hone, 17 July 1961.
79. PRO, PREM 11/3493, Macleod to Macmillan, 9 August 1961.
80. PRO, PREM 11/3493, Hone to Macleod, 5 August 1961, Macleod to Hone, 6 August 1961, Hone to Macleod, 7 & 8 August 1961, Hone to Macleod, 9 August 1961.
81. PRO, PREM 11/3493, Macleod to Macmillan, 9 August 1961, Macleod to Trend, 10 August 1961.
82. PRO, PREM 11/3493, Hone to Secretary of State, Perth to Hone, 18 August 1961.
83. PRO, PREM 11/3493, de Zulueta to Macmillan, 25 August 1961, Macmillan to Bligh, 28 August 1961.
84. PRO, PREM 11/3493, Perth to Macmillan, Bligh to Macmillan, Macmillan to Bligh, 29 August 1961, Bligh to Macmillan, 1 September 1961.
85. PRO, PREM 11/3493, Bligh, note for the record, 5 September 1961.
86. PRO, PREM 11/3493, Bligh to Macmillan, 5 September 1961, Bligh note, 6 September 1961, Hone to Macleod, 7 September 1961, Macleod to Sandys, 8 September 1961, Bligh to Macmillan, Bligh note, 11 September 1961.
87. PRO, PREM 11/3493, Macleod to Macmillan, 12 September 1961.
88. PRO, PREM 11/3493, Macleod to Hone, 13 September 1961, Alport to Sandys, 14 September 1961, Hone to Macleod, 21 September 1961; PREM 11/3494, Macleod to Perth, 21 September 1961; PREM 11/3494, Macmillan to Bligh, 22 September 1961; Macleod to Perth, 21 September 1961, Bligh to Macmillan, Macmillan to Bligh, 27 September 1961, Bligh to Howard-Drake, 28 September 1961.
89. Macmillan, 1973, p. 318.
90. Macleod interviewed by W.P. Kirkman, 29 December 1967.
91. Conservative Conference, Brighton, 11 October 1961, Official Record, pp. 24–25.
92. *The Times*, 12 October 1961; interview with Lady Antonia Fraser.
93. William Roger Louis, *Times Literary Supplement*, 10–16 February 1989, p. 146.
94. 'Trouble in Africa,' *Spectator*, 31 January 1964.
95. 'One World,' address by Iain Macleod to the Conservative Political Centre, 13 October 1960, Scarborough.
96. Ibid.
97. The description of Macleod as probably the greatest Colonial Secretary since Joseph Chamberlain and perhaps the greatest ever, is Alan Watkins's, *Sunday Telegraph*, 26 July 1970.

CHAPTER 11: DEFEATS, DRIFT AND SCANDAL

1. *Daily Mail, Daily Express, Daily Mirror, Daily Herald, The Times, Economist, New Statesman,* October 1961.
2. Howard, 1987, p. 285; Horne, 1989, p. 255.
3. Macmillan to Macleod, Lady Antonia Fraser's diary, quoted in Fisher, 1973, pp. 201–02; Butler, 1982b, p. 105; Horne, 1989, p. 255.
4. Butler, 1982b, p. 106; *The Times,* 10 October 1961.
5. Howard, 1987, p. 286, footnote; Thorpe, 1989, p. 330.
6. Thorpe, 1989, p. 330; Lady Antonia Fraser's diary, quoted in Fisher, 1973, p. 199.
7. Fisher, 1973, pp. 199–200.
8. Interview with David Clarke.
9. Interviews with Lady Thatcher, Viscount Whitelaw.
10. Howard, 1987, p. 285; Butler, 1982b, p. 106.
11. Butler, 1987, pp. 69–70; Fisher, 1973, pp. 203.
12. Macleod interviewed by Kenneth Harris, *Observer,* 26 November 1961 (Harold Nicolson's comments had appeared in the paper on 12 November 1961).
13. Macleod interviewed by Kenneth Harris, *Observer,* 26 November 1961: *The Times,* 14 October 1961.
14. CPA, CCO 20/31/1, Macleod to Macmillan, 26 October 1961; CCO 20/31/1, Macmillan to Macleod, 29 October 1961; CRD 2/52/9, CC/14, Chairman's Committee, sixth meeting, 17 July 1962; CPA, CRD 2/52/9, Chairman's Committee, CC/1, first meeting, 4 December 1961.
15. Peter Goldman, interviewed for the Nuffield election study series, 14 January 1964; interview with Lord Rees-Mogg.
16. CPA, CCO 20/2/4, letter from Macleod, 13 November 1961; minute by James Douglas, 29 November 1961; CCO 20/1/9, Selwyn Lloyd to Macleod, 5 December 1961; Macleod to Selwyn Lloyd, 11 December 1961; Selwyn Lloyd to Macleod, 16 December 1961.
17. Interview with John Biffen.
18. Interview with Sir Harry Boyne; *New Statesman,* 12 October 1962.
19. Hailsham, 1990, p. 351; interview with Michael Foot.
20. *Hansard,* 7 November 1961, col. 927; Castle, 1993, p. 214; paraphrased in Fisher, 1973, pp. 206.
21. PRO, CAB 134/1469, Commonwealth Migrants Committee, 1961; PREM 11/2920, 3238. *Hansard,* 31 October 1961, col. 28.
22. *Hansard,* 7 November 1961, col. 926; note of meeting of 1922 Committee, 17 November 1961, Butler Papers, H 96.
23. *Spectator,* 14 May 1965.
24. *The Times,* 4 November 1961.
25. Fisher, 1973, p. 207.
26. *Time and Tide,* quoted in Fisher, 1973, pp. 208.
27. *The Times,* 26 January 1962.
28. *Spectator,* 28 August 1964.
29. Macleod, 1961, p. 13.
30. Fisher, 1973, p. 212.
31. PRO, PREM11/3228, Norman Brook to Macmillan, 4 July 1961, 14 July 1961 with memorandum to Macleod.
32. PRO, PREM11/3228, Norman Brook to Macmillan, 4 July 1961; PRO, PREM11/3228, Norman Brook, note for the record, meeting with Lord Avon, 18 October 1961.
33. PRO, PREM11/3228, Norman Brook, note for the record, meeting with Lord Avon, 18 October 1961; Norman Brook to Macmillan, 19 October 1961; Robertson (Cabinet Office) to Harold Evans, Number 10, 19 October 1961; Tim Bligh to Norman Brook 20 October 1961; Evans note for the record, 23 October 1961.

34. Watkins, 1982, p. 100; interview with Michael Foot.
35. CPA, CRD 2/52/9, Chairman's Committee, second meeting, 12 February 1962; CCO 20/8/5, Macleod to Macmillan, 27 April 1962; CRD 2/52/9, Chairman's Committee, third meeting, 19 March 1962.
36. CPA, CRD 2/52/9, Chairman's Committee, third meeting, 19 March 1962.
37. CPA, CRD 2/52/9, Chairman's Committee, third meeting, 19 March 1962; CCO 20/8/5, Macleod to Macmillan, 21 March 1962; cited in Fisher, 1973, p. 214.
38. Butler Papers, H 96, note on meeting of 1922 Committee, 22 March 1962.
39. PRO, PREM11/3911.
40. CPA, CCO 20/8/5, Macleod to Macmillan, 2 April 1962.
41. Brittan, 1971, pp. 258–59 and 264–65.
42. Brittan, 1971, pp. 265–66; *The Spectator*, 'Quoodle', 11 December 1964.
43. CPA, CCO 20/8/5, Macmillan to Butler, 25 April 1962; Macleod to Macmillan, 27 April 1962 – an observation that Macleod developed into a well-known aphorism to the effect that budgets that were well received were unpopular a few months later, whereas budgets that were badly received later became more popular.
44. CPA, CCO 20/8/5, Macleod to Macmillan, 27 April 1962.
45. PRO, PREM11/3765, Butler to Macmillan, 2 May 1962; PRO, PREM11/3765, note by Norman Brook of Cabinet discussion, 3 May 1962.
46. PRO, PREM11/3765, verbatim transcript of Macmillan's opening remarks to the Cabinet, 28 May 1962.
47. Interview with Lord Fraser of Kilmorack; Thorpe, 1989, p. 275.
48. These proposals were the 'guiding light' for pay rises; a National Incomes Commission; the protection of consumers against price rises; and a Consumers' Council. Horne, 1989, p. 340; Thorpe, 1989, p. 338; CPA, CCO 20/8/5, Macleod to Macmillan, 21 June 1962.
49. CPA, CCO 20/8/5, Macleod to Macmillan, 11 July 1962; CCO 20/8/5, Tim Bligh, private secretary to the Prime Minister, to Macleod, 11 July 1962.
50. CPA, CCO 20/8/5, Macleod to Macmillan, 11 July 1962; *Daily Mail*, 12 July 1962.
51. Horne, 1989, p. 342.
52. Horne, 1989, p. 344; Macmillan had seen Mills on Thursday 12th; Michael Foot, *Daily Herald*, 8 October 1962.
53. Michael Foot, *Daily Herald*, 8 October 1962.
54. CPA, CCO 20/8/5, Macleod to Macmillan, 18 July 1962; *Sunday Express*, 22 July 1962; Fisher, 1973, pp. 221–22.
55. The Horniblow Report, cited in CPA, CCO files, Aldington to Macleod, 1 August 1962; CPA, CCO 20/8/5, Macleod to Macmillan, 24 September, 1962.
56. CPA, CCO 120/4/1, Macleod to Selwyn Lloyd, 28 September, 1962. Conservative Conference, Llandudno, Official Record, 12 October 1962, p. 126.
57. The Selwyn Lloyd Report was published on 6 June 1963, the day after John Profumo had resigned; Selwyn Lloyd was assisted by Ferdinand Mount and Diana Leishman, Thorpe, 1989, p. 365; The Selwyn Lloyd Report 1963, Conservative Central Office.
58. CPA, CRD 2/52/7, Fraser to Macleod, 12 February 1962; CPA, CRD 2/52/9, Chairman's Committee, third meeting, 19 March 1962; these ministries were split in 1988 to form the Department of Health and the Department of Social Security.
59. CPA, CRD 2/52/9, Chairman's Committee, third meeting, 19 March 1962.
60. CPA, CCO 20/31/1, Rodgers to Redmayne, 21 March 1962; the phrase about shooting Santa Claus was Michael Fraser's. Fraser also wrote warning Macleod of the political risks in talking about reform of the welfare state, CRD 2/52/7, Fraser to Macleod, 12 February 1962.
61. CPA, CCO 20/31/1, Macmillan to Macleod, 25 May 1962; CCO 20/31/1, Macleod to Macmillan, 6 June 1962; CCO 20/31/1, Macmillan to Macleod, 7 June 1962; CRD 2/52/9.
62. Chairman's Committee, sixth meeting, 17 July 1962.

63. Michael Foot, *Daily Herald*, 8 October 1962.
64. The average male manual weekly wage was £15/18s; Conservative Conference, Llandudno, Official Record, 12 October 1962, p. 126; CPA, CCO 20/8/5, Macleod to Macmillan, 24 September 1962.
65. Conservative Conference, Llandudno, Official Record, 12 October 1962, p. 126.
66. CPA, CCO 20/8/5, Macleod to Macmillan, 24 September 1962.
67. CPA, CCO 20/8/5, Macleod to Macmillan, 24 September 1962; *Enfield Gazette*, April 1962, quoted in Fisher, 1973, p. 222; PRO, PREM11/3765, note by Norman Brook of Cabinet discussion, 3 May 1962; cited in Fisher, 1973, p. 223.
68. CPA, CCO 20/8/5, Macleod to Macmillan, 24 September 1962; Anthony Howard's column, *New Statesman*, 12 October 1962.
69. *New Statesman*, 12 October 1962.
70. PRO, PREM11/3668, Macmillan to Bevins, 10 December 1962. The BBC's Director-General sent an apology.
71. Interview with Lord Gilmour; CPA, CCO 20/8/5, Macleod to Macmillan, 27 November 1962, citing Gilmour's report on the Norfolk by-election.
72. CPA, CCO 20/8/5, Macleod to Macmillan, 27 November 1962.
73. CPA, CCO 20/8/5, Macleod to Macmillan, 27 November 1962.
74. West Point, 5 December 1962; Horne, 1989, p. 449.
75. CPA, CCO 20/8/6, Macleod to Macmillan, 25 January 1963.
76. CPA, CCO 20/8/6, Macleod to Macmillan, 25 January 1963.
77. Interview with Enoch Powell; CPA, CCO 20/8/6, Macleod to Macmillan, 25 January 1963: interviewed by D.E. Butler and Anthony King, 17 December 1963.
78. Fisher, 1973, pp. 201–02.
79. Ian Gilmour, *London Review of Books*, 27 July 1989.
80. Interview with William Shepherd; quoted in Knightley and Kennedy, 1987, p. 146.
81. Interview with Diana Heimann (Macleod's daughter); PRO, CAB, CC (63) 37th Conclusions, 12 June 1963; C (63)99, 12 June 1963. Macmillan prepared the note because the Lord Chancellor, Dilhorne, who had conducted an inquiry into the Profumo affair, had been unable to discuss the matter with Macleod owing to the latter's absence in America. Curiously, the references to Ivanov's intentions are deleted in the redraft of the note, dated two days after the subject had been raised in Cabinet. It would appear that Ivanov's message was that the Soviet leader, Krushchev, would accept a summit conference in London in order to break the deadlock over Cuba.
82. Private information; interview with Lord Orr-Ewing.
83. Quoted in Knightley and Kennedy, 1987, p. 128; as Macleod later stated, *Hansard*, 17 June 1963.
84. Knightley and Kennedy, 1987, p. 146.
85. Rawlinson, 1989, pp. 94–5.
86. Howard, 1987, p. 298, quoting BBC Radio profile, 29 January 1978.
87. PRO, CAB, CC (63) 37th Conclusions, 12 June 1963.
88. *Hansard*, 17 June 1963, col. 166.
89. Private information.
90. Prior, 1986, p. 28.
91. Interviews with Lord Aldington, Charles Longbottom.
92. *Hansard*, 17 June 1963, col. 167.
93. Private information.
94. Grace Wyndham Goldie, BBC Head of Talks, memorandum to Controller of Programmes, quoted in Wyndham Goldie, 1977, p. 248–49; *Gallery*, BBC Television, 13 June 1963.
95. Horne, 1989, p. 479; PRO, CAB, CC (63) 37th Conclusions, 12 June 1963 and CC (63) 38th Conclusions.
96. PRO, CAB, CC (63) 38th Conclusions, 13 June 1963; *Hansard*, 17 June 1963, col. 167.

97. Private information; predictably, this incident is not mentioned in the official papers released at the Public Record Office in January 1994 under the 30-year rule.
98. PRO, CAB, CC (63) 39th Conclusions, 20 June 1963 and 40th Conclusions, 21 June 1963; Macleod is quoted in Howard and West, 1965, p. 51.
99. Cmnd 2152, para 170; Howard, 1990, p. 253.
100. CPA, CRD 2/52/9, Chairman's Committee, seventh and eighth meetings, 26 November 1962 and 4 February 1963; Butler Papers, H 104, SC/63/9, 17 July 1963; H 104, SC/63/13.
101. Conservative Conference, Blackpool, Official Record, 12 October 1963, pp. 47–48; *The Times*, 11 October 1963; CPA, CCO 20/1/11, Macleod to Boyle, 10 July 1963.

CHAPTER 12: THE TORY LEADERSHIP: BEDLAM AT BLACKPOOL

1. Randolph Churchill, in his book on the struggle for the Tory leadership, refers to Macleod and his colleagues who sought to block Home's succession as 'the Caballeros' – see R. Churchill, 1964, p. 136.
2. *Spectator*, 17 January 1964.
3. Ibid.
4. Walters, 1989, pp. 110–11; Hailsham, 1990, p. 349; *Spectator*, 17 January 1964; Lord Aldington had resigned as deputy chairman in the spring of 1963; Walters, 1989, pp. 111–12.
5. *Daily Telegraph*, 20 June 1963; Bogdanor, 'The Conservative Leadership, 1902–90,' citing Goodhart, 1973, p. 191, and the Butler Papers, Box G. 40; Sawston, Cambridgeshire, 6 July 1963; *Panorama*, BBC TV, 8 July 1963; Macleod's speech was delivered at Rusper, Sussex.
6. Hailsham, 1990, p. 333; R. Churchill, 1964, pp. 84–85.
7. R. Churchill, 1964, p. 86; *New Statesman*, 14 December 1962, quoted in R. Churchill, 1964, pp. 91–92.
8. *Hansard*, 28 March 1963, cols. 1548–53; *Hansard*, 27 June 1963; R. Churchill, 1964, pp. 88.
9. Hailsham, 1990, p. 349.
10. Interview with Lord Rees-Mogg.
11. Interview with Lord Rees-Mogg; Hailsham, 1990, pp. 354–55.
12. Interview with Lord Amery; Horne, 1989, pp. 536–37.
13. Horne, 1989, p. 537; *Spectator*, 17 January 1964; Hailsham, 1990, p. 350.
14. Horne, 1989, pp. 537–39; interview with Lord Amery, Howard, 1987, p. 309.
15. Horne, 1989, p. 541; Douglas-Home, 1976, p.180; Young, 1970, pp. 162–63; *Spectator*, 17 January 1964.
16. *The Times*, 9 October 1963; interview with Dr Reginald Bennett; Fisher, 1973, p. 234.
17. Iain Macleod, 'The Riddle of Randolph,' in Halle, 1971, p. 205.
18. Interview with Lord Deedes; *The Times*, 9 October 1963.
19. Horne, 1989, p. 544; Howard, 1987, p. 311.
20. Interview with Lord Hayhoe; *Spectator*, 17 January 1964; Butler, 1982b, p. 110.
21. Interview with Diana Heimann (daughter); Fisher, 1973, pp. 242–43.
22. Fisher, 1973, p. 238; interviews with Lord Amery, Eve Macleod, Sir Reginald Bennett, Alan Watkins.
23. Interview with Julian Amery.
24. Horne, 1989, p. 545; R. Churchill, 1964, p. 103; Home, 1976, quoted in Horne, 1989, pp. 544–45; R. Churchill, 1964, p. 103.
25. Howard, 1987, p. 310; quoted in Howard, 1987, p. 310; interview with Lord Boyd-Carpenter.
26. Interviews with Sir Harry Boyne, Elizabeth Sturges-Jones.

27. Interviews with Dr Reginald Bennett, Lord Carr, Lord Hayhoe, Lord Rees-Mogg; Walters, 1989, p. 127.
28. Howard, 1987, pp. 311, 313.
29. Conservative Conference, Blackpool, 10 October 1963, Official Record, p. 46.
30. Quoted in R. Churchill, 1964, p. 107; *The Times*, 11 October 1963.
31. Interview with Alan Watkins.
32. Hailsham, 1990, p. 352; R. Churchill, 1964, p. 109.
33. Interviews with Viscount Whitelaw, Lord Jenkin of Roding, Lord Hayhoe; R. Churchill, 1964, p. 109.
34. Interview with Lord Jenkin of Roding.
35. Interview with Lord Rees-Mogg.
36. Interviews with Lord Boyd-Carpenter, Enoch Powell, Viscount Whitelaw, Prior, 1986, pp. 32–33.
37. Prior, 1986, p. 33; interview with Sir Reginald Bennett; letter from Dr Bennett to *The Times*, 18 March 1980; *Spectator*, 17 January 1964.
38. Hailsham, 1990, p. 351; interviews with Sir Gilbert Longden, Lord Carr.
39. Interview with Sir Reginald Bennett; *Sunday Express*, 4 October 1973, quoted in Maudling, 1978, p. 127.
40. *Sunday Express*, 4 October 1973, quoted in Maudling, 1978, p. 127; interviews with Lord Hayhoe, Sir Harry Boyne.
41. *The Times*, 10 March 1980; interview with Sir Harry Boyne.
42. Butler, 1982b, p. 96; Butler, 1982b, p. 110.
43. *Spectator*, 17 January 1964.
44. Butler, 1987, p. 79; interview with Enoch Powell.
45. Fisher, 1973, p. 238.

CHAPTER 13: THE TORY LEADERSHIP: 'THE MAGIC CIRCLE'

1. Interview with Lord Gilmour; also, see Walters, 1989, pp. 130–31, for an account of the Hailsham camp's lobbying for support.
2. Interviews with Lord Carr, Sir Reginald Bennett; Howard, 1987, p. 316.
3. Horne, 1989, p. 555; R. Churchill, 1964, p. 126.
4. Fisher, 1973, pp. 236–37; Fisher, 1973, p. 237; Horne, 1989, p. 555; CPA, File, 'Letters regarding October 1963 leadership crisis,' minute from first secretary to the Prime Minister about the customary processes of consultation in relation to the leadership of the Party, dated 15 October 1963 (Macmillan's minute, 'Leadership of the Party' is attached).
5. R. Churchill, 1964, p. 128.
6. *Spectator*, 17 January 1964; Boyle's comments of 4 February 1964 were noted as background for the Nuffield general election series.
7. *Spectator*, 17 January 1964.
8. *Spectator*, 17 January 1964.
9. Bogdanor, in his article, 'The Conservative Leadership, 1902–90', cites the letter from Professor A. W. Bradley in *The Times*, 16 January 1987, reporting a talk by Sir Knox Cunningham, Macmillan's PPS at the time, in which it was said that three questions were asked of MPs; Redmayne was interviewed by Dr Norman Hunt for BBC Radio's Third Programme, and extracts published in the *Listener*, 19 December 1963; Macleod's typescript – his reference to the number of whips was cut from the published version; R. Churchill, 1964, p. 133; Horne, 1989, p. 555; *Observer*, 19 January 1964.
10. Interviews with Viscount Whitelaw, Sir Reginald Bennett, Lord Walker: *The Times*, 5 January 1987.

11. The letter was signed by former whips Batsford, Chichester-Clark, Hamilton, Hill, Pearson and Pym: *The Times*, 7 January 1987; *Listener*, 19 December 1963.
12. *Spectator*, 17 January 1964; R. Churchill, 1964, pp. 84–85; *Spectator*, 17 January 1964; Horne, 1989, footnotes, p. 687.
13. *Spectator*, 17 January 1964.
14. *Spectator*, 13 October 1973, 17 January 1964.
15. Confirmed to the author by a member of Macmillan's Number Ten staff; Horne, 1989, pp. 559–62; Horne, 1989, footnotes, p. 688; *Spectator*, 17 January 1964.
16. Horne, 1989, pp. 561–62, and footnotes, p. 687; Horne, 1989, pp. 561–62.
17. *London Review of Books*, 27 July 1989; interview with Enoch Powell; Horne, 1989, p. 561; interview with Eve Macleod.
18. Boyle's comments of 4 February 1964 were noted as background for the Nuffield general election series; see also John Grigg, *Spectator*, 24 April 1982; *London Review of Books*, 27 July 1989.
19. *Spectator*, 17 January 1964.
20. Howard, 1987, p. 317; *Spectator*, 17 January 1964; Howard, 1987, pp. 316–17.
21. *Spectator*, 17 January 1964; interview with Lord Rees-Mogg.
22. Interview with Sir Harry Boyne.
23. *Spectator*, 17 January 1964.
24. *Spectator*, 17 January 1964.
25. Walters, 1989, p. 132; Butler, 1987, p. 81; *Spectator*, 17 January 1964; Cosgrave, 1989, p. 187; interview with Lord Rees-Mogg.
26. Horne, 1989, p. 563; Walters, 1989, p.; Butler, 1987, p. 80; Maudling, 1978, p. 129; *Spectator*, 17 January 1964; interview with Sir Harry Boyne.
27. *Spectator*, 17 January 1964; interview with Lord Aldington; Junor, 1990, p. 133; Walters, 1989, p.135; according to Professor R.T. McKenzie, whose comments of 4 February 1964 were noted as background for the Nuffield general election series.
28. *Spectator*, 17 January 1964.
29. R. Churchill, 1964, p. 137.
30. Howard, 1987, pp. 319–20; *Spectator*, 13 October 1973; Butler, 1987, p. 81.
31. *Spectator*, 17 January 1964; Hailsham, 1990, p. 356.
32. Butler, 1987, p. 81; *Spectator*, 17 January 1964; Junor, 1990, p. 134.
33. Boyle's comments of 4 February 1964 were noted as background for the Nuffield general election series; Thorpe, 1989, p. 379; Walters, 1989, p. 137.
34. Interviews with Viscount Whitelaw, Alan Watkins; *Spectator*, 17 January 1964.
35. *Reputations*, BBC TV, presented by Anthony Howard, 13 July 1983; Powell quoted Macleod; *The Day before Yesterday*, Thames Television, October 1970.
36. Butler used this phrase during his speech as a guest of parliamentary journalists who belong to the Guinea Club at a lunch on his retirement in 1965 (private information).
37. Home, 1976, p. 185; interviews with Viscount Whitelaw, John Biffen.
38. *Spectator*, 17 January 1964; interviews with Sir Reginald Bennett, Lord Rees-Mogg.
39. Among those who warned Macleod were John Boyd-Carpenter and Patrick Jenkin; interview with Lord Carr.
40. *Spectator*, 17 January 1964; interview with Lord Gilmour.
41. Interviews with Sir Reginald Bennett, Alan Watkins, Lord Gilmour, Lord Hayhoe.
42. Interview with J.W.M. Thompson.
43. Horne, 1989, p. 582.

CHAPTER 14: EDITOR

1 George Younger, a grandson of a former Tory Party Chairman and the son of an hereditary peer (Viscount Leckie), was rewarded by being adopted as the Tory candidate for Ayr in time

for the next general election, and which he represented until his retirement from active politics in 1992; interview with J.W.M. Thompson.

2. Interview with Lord Gilmour.
3. Interview with J.W.M. Thompson; John Freeman served as British High Commissioner to India from 1965 to 1968; *Spectator*, 13 December 1963, p. 785.
4. Interviews with Lord Gilmour, Enoch Powell.
5. Macleod, background interview with Butler and King for the Nuffield general election series, 17 December 1963; Fisher, 1973, p. 244; Thompson, *Spectator*, 25 July 1970; interview with Lord Walker.
6. Interview with Sir Harry Boyne.
7. Fisher, 1973, p. 244.
8. Interview with Lord Aldington.
9. Interview with Lord Gilmour; memoir by Joan Baylis.
10. Interview with Lord Gilmour.
11. *Daily Telegraph*, 2 November 1963; interview with Lord Gilmour; memoir by Joan Baylis; *Spectator*, 15 November 1963; the exchange of letters was reproduced in the *Daily Telegraph*, 2 November 1963.
12. *Daily Telegraph*, 2 November 1963.
13. *Daily Telegraph*, 2 November 1963; *Observer*, 3 November 1963; memoir by Joan Baylis; *Daily Telegraph*, 2 November 1963.
14. *Daily Telegraph*, 4 November 1963;
15. Memoir written by Joan Baylis; *Spectator*, 8 November 1963; 15 November 1963.
16. *Daily Telegraph*, 8 November 1963, *Spectator*, 13 December 1963.
17. Interview with Malcolm Rutherford.
18. Watkins, 1982, p. 104.
19. Memoir by Joan Baylis.
20. Interview with J.W.M. Thompson; memoir by Joan Baylis.
21. Interview with J.W.M. Thompson; memoir by Joan Baylis.
22. Interviews with Lord Gilmour, Malcolm Rutherford; memoir by Joan Baylis;
23. Interviews with Malcolm Rutherford, J.W.M. Thompson.
24. Interview with J.W.M. Thompson.
25. Interview with Malcolm Rutherford; *Spectator*, 10 January 1964.
26. Interview with Malcolm Rutherford; *Spectator*, 6 December 1963; *Spectator*, 4 December 1964, 11 December 1964.
27. Interview with J.W.M. Thompson; memoir by Joan Baylis; Gilmour, *Listener*, 30 July 1970.
28. Memoir by Joan Baylis; Watkins, 1982, p. 105; interview with Lord Gilmour.
29. Watkins, 1982, pp. 106–08.
30. Watkins, 1982, p. 101; interview with Elizabeth Sturges-Jones.
31. Interview with J.W.M. Thompson; Thompson, *Spectator*, 25 July 1970;
32. Interview with J.W.M. Thompson; Thompson, *Spectator*, 25 July 1970. interviews with Alan Watkins, Malcolm Rutherford.
33. J.W.M. Thompson, *Spectator*, 25 July 1970.
34. Interviews with Sir Alan Dawtry, Roy Hattersley.
35. Interview with J.W.M. Thompson; Watkins, 1982, p. 101.
36. Interviews with Michael and Ethne Bannister.
37. Interview with Lord Hayhoe.
38. *Spectator*, 6 December 1963.
39. Index of unsigned article written for the *Spectator*. Unfortunately this index was discontinued in early 1965; interviews with J.W.M. Thompson, Alan Watkins.
40. *Spectator*, 13 December 1963, 4 December 1964.
41. Gilmour, *Listener*, 30 July 1970; interviews with J.W.M. Thompson, Alan Watkins.
42. *Spectator*, 4 December 1964, 24 January 1964. Reporting Lord Beaverbrook's eighty-fifth

birthday party, in May 1964, Quoodle wrote of 'the touching scene when Tom Driberg, Michael Foot, Hugh Cudlipp, Sir Hugh Carlton Greene and other well-known left-wing propagandists rose with the company to sing "Land of Hope and Glory" to the press baron' (*Spectator*, 29 May 1964). Macleod had thus bracketed the BBC's then Director-General with two Labour MPs and the owner of Labour's main supporter in Fleet Street. Greene's letter of complaint the following week was published but summarily dismissed; *Spectator*, 10 January 1964.

43. *Spectator*, 15 May 1964.
44. Watkins, 1982, p. 109; King, 1972, p. 312; private information; *Spectator*, 27 March 1964, 20 December 1963.
45. Goldie, 1977, pp. 243–45, reveals Macleod's advocacy of televising parliament during a dinner at Broadcasting House on Monday, 22 October 1962; *Spectator*, 13 December 1963.
46. *Spectator*, 13 December 1963, 10 January 1964, 17 January 1964, 24 January 1964, *Sunday Mirror*, 12 January 1964.
47. *Spectator*, 20 December 1963, 27 December 1963.
48. Interviewed by David Butler, 9 July 1964; *The Times*, 17 January 1964; broadcast on BBC Radio Third Programme, 25 October 1963.
49. Gilmour, *Listener*, 30 July 1970; interview with Lord Gilmour; *Daily Mirror*, *Daily Mail*, *Daily Express*, *Evening Standard*, 17 January 1964; memoir by Joan Baylis.
50. *Spectator*, 17 January 1964.
51. *The Times*, 17 January 1964, 18 January 1964; interview with Lord Gilmour.
52. *The Times*, 6 November 1963; interviews with Lord Gilmour, J.W.M. Thompson.
53. Butler papers, G43, Macleod to Butler, 15 January 1964; Howard, 1987, p. 331; Butler, 1982, p. 96. *The Times*, 17 January 1964.
54. *Observer*, 'Pendennis' column, 19 January 1964; Gilmour, *Listener*, 30 July 1970; *Spectator*, 17 January 1964.
55. Gilmour, *Listener*, 30 July 1970; Macleod's typescript was kindly made available to the author by Lord Hayhoe; *Spectator*, 17 January 1964; Anthony Howard, *Listener*, 9 October 1980;
56. Macleod's typescript; *Spectator*, 17 January 1964.
57. *The Times*, 17 January 1964, *Spectator*, 24 January 1964.
58. Interview with Sir Peter Tapsell; *The Times*, 18 January 1964; *Spectator*, 24 January 1964; *Sunday Times*, 26 January 1964.
59. Interviewed by David Butler, 13 February 1964; *The Times*, 29 January 1964; Fisher, 1973, p.253.
60. Note of meeting, Nuffield College, 22 January 1964; *The Times*, 18 January 1964; *Daily Express*, 18 January 1964; interviewed by David Butler, 18 February 1964; *The Times*, 18 January 1964.
61. *The Times*, 18 and 21 January 1964; interviewed by David Butler, 22 January 1964; *The Times*, 20 January 1964; *The Times*, 25 January 1964.
62. Interviewed by David Butler, 13 February 1964; *Spectator*, 24 January 1964.
63. Berkeley, 1972, p. 96; interview with Sir Peter Tapsell; *The Times*, 18 January 1964; Gilmour, *Listener*, 30 July 1970; private information; Berkeley, interviewed for '*Reputations*,' BBC Television, and quoted in Howard, *Listener*, 9 October 1980.
64. Interview with Viscount Whitelaw.
65. *Sunday Telegraph*, 26 January 1964; *The Times*, 25 January 1964.
66. Interview with Malcolm Rutherford; J.W.M. Thompson, *Spectator*, 25 July 1970.
67. Gallup political index, in Butler and Sloman, 1980, p. 238; *Sunday Express*, 19 January 1964; *Sunday Times*, 26 January 1964; *The Times*, 25 January 1964.
68. *Sunday Express*, 19 January 1964; interviewed by David Butler, 22 January 1964.

CHAPTER 15: POISONED CHALICE

1. Interviewed by Butler and King, 17 December 1963, 2 July 1964.
2. *Spectator*, 17 January 1964; *Spectator*, October 1990, quoted in Shepherd, 1991, p. 159; interviewed by Butler and King, 17 December 1963.

3. Interviewed by Butler and King, 2 July 1964.
4. *Sunday Times*, 26 January 1964; *Spectator*, 31 January 1964; 7 February 1964; 14 February 1964.
5. *Spectator*, 28 February 1964.
6. *Spectator*, 28 February 1964; *The Times*, 15 May 1964;
7. *Spectator*, 24 April 1964.
8. *Spectator*, 24 April 1964, 24 July 1964.
9. *Spectator*, 12 June 1964. *Spectator*, 24 July 1964, 24 April 1964.
10. David Watt, Political Commentary, *Spectator*, 21 January 1964; *Spectator*, 13 March 1964.
11. *Spectator*, 4 September 1964.
12. Interviewed by Butler and King, 2 July 1964, and later for Nuffield Study of 1966 election.
13. Hinchingbrooke, having succeeded to a peerage, had subsequently disclaimed his title; Quoodle's reflections on Tory forgiveness appeared in *Spectator*, 21 February 1964.
14. Interviewed by Butler and King, 2 July 1964.
15. *The Times*, 5 October 1964; interviewed by Butler and King, 17 December 1963.
16. *Spectator*, 25 September 1964.
17. *Spectator*, 17 April 1964.
18. *Spectator*, 9 October 1964.
19. *The Times*, 18 September 1964; *Spectator*, 2 October 1964; *Economist*, 19 September 1964.
20. *Spectator*, 2 October 1964.
21. *Spectator*, 9 October 1964; quoted in *Spectator*, 9 October 1964.
22. *Spectator*, 2 October 1964, 16 October 1964.
23. *The Times*, 15 October 1964; interview with Lady Hayhoe.
24. *Spectator*, 9 October 1964; Butler and King, 1965, p. 289; Butler and King, 1965, p. 289.
25. *Spectator*, 23 October 1964, quoting Enoch Powell in *Sunday Telegraph*.
26. *Spectator*, 6 November 1964.
27. Butler and King, 1965, p. 289; interviewed by Butler and King, 1 June 1965.
28. John Grigg, *Spectator*, 24 April 1982; Pressure for Economic and Social Toryism (PEST), 'Will the Tories Lose?' January 1965, cited in Butler and King, 1965, pp. 297–99; PEST was a forerunner of the Tory Reform Group.
29. Hailsham, 1990, p. 358; Butler, 1982b, p. 110; interviews with Lord Rees-Mogg, Viscount Whitelaw.
30. Interviewed by Butler and King, 1 June 1965.
31. Interview with Enoch Powell.
32. Berkeley, 1972, p. 96.
33. *Spectator*, 23 October 1964.
34. *Spectator*, 16 October 1964.
35. *Spectator*, 23 October 1964.
36. *Spectator*, 6 November 1964.
37. *The Times*, 10 November 1964.
38. *Spectator*, 13 November 1964; *The Times*, 10 November 1964; Crossman, 1975, p. 50, 9 November 1964.
39. Crossman, 1975, p. 27, 22 October 1964; Fisher, 1973, p. 260; interview with Lord Gilmour; Crossman, 1975, p. 62, 18 November 1964; CPA, LCC (65) 2.
40. CPA, LCC (64) 4th, 11 November 1964; Fisher, 1973, p. 260.
41. CPA, LCC (64) 7th, 2 December 1964.
42. CPA, LCC (64) 7th, 2 December 1964.
43. CPA, LCC (65) 16th, 3 February 1965; Macleod to Humphry Berkeley, 10 December 1964; CRD 3/22/10–11, Macleod to Douglas-Home, 14 December 1964; LCC (65) 4.
44. *The Times*, 6 January 1965; Macleod to Humphry Berkeley, 2 January 1965; Shepherd, 1991, p. 163, private information; Sir Peter Emery, interviewed for Shepherd, 1991.
45. *Spectator*, 5 March 1965.
46. CPA, CRD 3/22/10–11, Macleod to Douglas-Home, 14 December 1964.

47. *Spectator*, 5 March 1965.
48. Interview with Sir Anthony Grant.
49. Berkeley, 1972, p. 97.
50. Interviews with David Rogers, David Howell, Sir William van Straubenzee, Lord Walker.
51. CPA, CCO, 20/47/1; interview with Nick Scott.
52. Interviews with David Rogers, David Howell, Nick Scott.
53. *The Times*, 5 January 1965, 25 January 1965.
54. *The Times*, 9 January 1965; *Crossbow*, January – March 1965; *The Times*, 18 January 1965.
55. *The Times*, 18 January 1965.
56. *The Times*, 18 January 1965. *Crossbow*, January – March 1965.
57. *The Times*, 15 February 1965.
58. CPA, LCC (65) 13th, 1 February 1965.
59. *Spectator*, 19 March 1965; interviewed by Butler and King, 1 June 1965.
60. *Spectator*, 26 March 1965; CPA, LCC (65) 38th, 31 March 1965; *The Times*, 3 April 1965.
61 Berkeley to Macleod, 31 March 1965. *Spectator*, 12 March 1965.
62. *The Times*, 3 April 1965; interview with Lord Hayhoe; *The Times*, 30 March 1965; *Spectator*, 9 April 1965.
63. *The Times*, 2 April 1965.
64. CPA, LCC (65) 45th, 28 April 1965.
65. CPA, LCC (65) 30; LCC (65) 29;
66. *The Times*, 1 May 1965; CPA, LCC (65) 47th, 5 May 1965; LCC (65) 31.
67. *Hansard*, 6 May 1965, cols. 1600–03; *The Times*, 7 May 1965; Watkins, in *Spectator*, 14 May 1965; CPA, LCC (64) 48th, 10 May 1965; LCC (64) 49th, 12 May 1965.
68. *Spectator*, 28 May 1965; Crossman, 1975, p. 210, 11 May 1965.
69. *The Times*, 25 June 1965.

CHAPTER 16: FROM LOST LEADER TO PRODIGAL SON

1. CPA, LCC (65) 59th, 5 July 1965; LCC (65) 60th, 7 July 1965.
2. Prior, 1986, p. 7; *Sunday Times*, 18 July 1965.
3. Thorpe, 1989, p. 393; Berkeley, 1972, p. 98; *Spectator*, 1 August 1970.
4. Thorpe, 1989, p. 394; Prior, 1986, p. 36; *The Times*, 21 July 1965; Berkeley, 1972, pp. 97–8;
5. Interview with Enoch Powell; *Spectator*, 16 July 1965.
6. *The Times*, 23 July 1965.
7. Interviews with Viscount Whitelaw, Lord Jenkin of Roding.
8. Interview with Lord Walker.
9. Interviews with Lord Gilmour; Lord Rees-Mogg; *Spectator*, 30 July 1965.
10. Interview with Lord Gilmour.
11. Maudling, 1978, p. 136; interviews with Alan Watkins, Viscount Whitelaw; Lord Walker, who organized Heath's campaign, overestimated Maudling's support by six votes; Watkins, 1982, p. 108.
12. Watkins, *Spectator*, 30 July 1965.
13. *Spectator*, 30 July 1965; interviewed by Butler and King, 1 June 1965.
14. *Spectator*, 30 July 1965.
15. F.T. Blackaby, 1978.
16. Interviews with David Howell, Lord Walker; Fisher, 1973, p. 263.
17. Interview with Viscount Whitelaw; Whitelaw, 1989, p. 57.
18. *The Times*, 17 September 1965, 18 September 1965.
19. CPA, LCC (65) 71, 27 October 1965; *Spectator*, 17 September 1965; *Hansard*, 3 November 1965, cols. 1067, 1074–75; *The Times*, 4 November 1965.
20. CPA, LCC (65) 65th, 15 September 1965; LCC (65) 43; *Spectator*, 8 October 1965.
21. *The Times*, 7 October 1965; *Spectator*, 8 October 1965.

22. *Spectator,* 17 September 1965, 8 October 1965; CPA, LCC (65) 66th, 23 September 1965; LCC (65) 43.
23. Interview with Brendon Sewill.
24. Conservative Party Conference, 14 October 1965, Official record, p. 77.
25. Conservative Party Conference, 14 October 1965, Official record, pp. 77–78; *Economist,* 22 October 1965.
26. *The Times,* 12 October 1965.
27. *Spectator,* 25 July 1965; Watkins, 1982, p. 109.
28. *Spectator,* 13 August 1965, 27 November 1964; Hattersley and Ennals entered the Cabinet in 1976, Howe and St John Stevas in 1979.
29. Gilmour, *Listener,* 30 July 1970; Watkins, 1982, p. 106; *Spectator,* 2 April 1965.
30. Davenport, 1974, p. 192; conversation with Hilary Spurling; *Spectator,* 7 and 21 May 1965, 18 June 1965, 20 August 1965, 1 October 1965, 17 December 1965.
31. *Spectator,* 31 December 1965.
32. Memoir by Joan Baylis, p. 207; *Spectator,* 2 April 1965.
33. Memoir by Joan Baylis, p. 207.
34. CPA, LCC (65) 77th, 15 November 1965; LCC (65) 69; LCC (65) 83rd, 6 December 1965; LCC (65) 66
35. *Hansard,* 7 November 1965, col. 1165, 3 November 1965, col. 1167
36. *The Times,* 5 January 1966, 13 January 1966; *Spectator,* 14 January 1966; Butler and King, 1966, p. 20.
37. Butler and King, 1966, p. 22; CPA, LCC (66) 91st, 31 January 1966.
38. Interviewed by Anthony King, 21 December 1965.
39. Interviewed by Anthony King, 21 December 1965; CPA, LCC (65) 65, 30 November 1965.
40. Ramsden, 1980, p. 252; CPA, CRD files, 1966 Election Manifesto, 3rd and 4th Drafts and Correspondence.
41. *Hansard,* 1 March 1966, col. 1225; interviewed by Anthony King, 21 December 1965.
42. Interview with Lord Hayhoe; Butler and King, 1966, p. 138.
43. Interviewed by David Butler and Anthony King, 10 May 1966.

CHAPTER 17: OPPOSITION IS FOR OPPOSING

1. Interview with John Biffen.
2. 'Political Commentary,' in the *Spectator,* 26 August 1966; Ramsden, 1980, p. 252.
3. Interview with Lord Rees-Mogg; private information.
4. Interview with Viscount Whitelaw.
5. Interviews with John Biffen, Lord Callaghan.
6. Interview with David Rogers.
7. Cosgrave, 1989, p. 226; interview with Lord Rees-Mogg.
8. Interviews with Alan Watkins, Lord Jenkin of Roding, John Major.
9. Interviews with Malcolm Rutherford, Lord Rees-Mogg.
10. Interviews with Enoch Powell, John Biffen, Brendon Sewill, Sir Anthony Grant, Lord Rees-Mogg.
11. Interviews with Brendon Sewill, Viscount Whitelaw; Blake, 1966, p. 311 (Canning had been chancellor in 1827).
12. Butler and Pinto-Duschinsky, 1971, p. 74; Ramsden, 1980, pp. 255–56.
13. Interviews with Lord Carr, Enoch Powell.
14. Interview with Lord Hayhoe.
15. Interview with Viscount Whitelaw.
16. Interview with Sir Anthony Grant, Conservative MPs from the 1959 intake.
17. Interview with Lord Hayhoe; Prior, 1986, p. 53.
18. Maude was interviewed by Michael Cockerell, BBC TV *Panorama,* 14 May 1979; interview with Eve Macleod; private information.

19. Interviews with Lord Jenkin of Roding, Lady Thatcher, Sir Anthony Grant.
20. Interview with Lady Thatcher.
21. Interviews with Lord Callaghan, Lord Jenkin of Roding, Terence Higgins.
22. Macleod had moved from the flat previously provided by the Lombard Bank in Park Street, St. James's.
23. *Hansard*, 4 May 1966, col. 1646; interview with Lord Callaghan; Callaghan, 1987, p. 193.
24. CPA, LCC (67)147th, 16 January 1967.
25. CPA, LCC (67) 119, for LCC (67)147th, 16 January 1967; LCC (67)147th, 16 January 1967; LCC (67)148th, 18 January 1967.
26. *Guardian*, 20 February 1970; *Hansard*, 19 February 1970, cols. 606–26.
27. CPA, LCC (69) 325th, 29 October 1969.
28. CPA, LCC (66) 103rd, 2 May 1966; Owen, 1991, p. 95; Cairncross, 1992, p. 158; *Hansard*, 4 May 1966, col. 1653.
29. *Hansard*, 4 May 1966, cols. 1648–54.
30. Pimlott, 1992, pp. 422–24; Owen, 1991, p. 7.
31. *Spectator*, 22 July 1966.
32. Conservative Conference, Brighton, 14 October 1966, Official Record, p. 96.
33. Conservative Conference, Brighton, 14 October 1966.
34. *London Evening News*, 14 October 1966.
35. Conservative Conference, Brighton, 14 October 1966, Official Record, p. 98.

CHAPTER 18: MEANS TO AN END

1. Interview with John Biffen; CPA, CRD Box 9, EPG, File 6, Correspondence, 22 June 1966; CPA, EPG/66/4, 4 November 1966; Paish, F.W., 1962, *Studies in an Inflationary Economy: The United Kingdom, 1948–61*.
2. *Hansard*, 7 November, 1967, col. 858; *Hansard*, 18 April 1966, cols. 1644–45; *Hansard*, 14 July 1966, col. 1752, cols. 1841–42.
3. *Hansard*, 27 July 1966, col. 1842; *Hansard*, 27 July 1966, col. 1836; Conservative Conference, Blackpool, 14 October 1966, Official Record, p. 97.
4. Interview with David Howell; *Contemporary Record*, vol. 3, no. 3, February 1990, pp. 36–38, report of symposium organized by Institute of Contemporary British History on Conservative Party policy making, 1966–70; *Hansard*, 20 October 1966.
5. Interview with Lord Carr.
6. Interview with Geoffrey Goodman.
7. Conservative Conference, Blackpool, 14 October 1966, Official Record, p. 97; *Hansard*, 25 October 1966, col. 866.
8. CPA, EPG/66/14, 2nd, 24 November 1966.
9. CPA, EPG/66/23, 4th; EPG/66/25, 5th; EPG/66/26, 6th; EPG/66/28, 7th; EPG/66/18, 3rd, 22 December, 1966.
10. Conservative Party Political Broadcast, 7 December 1966.
11. CPA, LCC (67) 162nd, 13 March 1967.
12. CPA, LCC (67) 162nd, 13 March 1967; CPA, LCC (67) 163rd, 15 March 1967.
13. Interview with John Biffen; *Financial Times*, 6 April 1967; *Hansard*, 12 April cols. 1214–16; Macleod to Biffen, 6 and 7 June 1967; interview with John Biffen.
14. Interview with John Biffen; *Hansard*, 13 June 1967, cols. 423–9.
15. CPA, LCC (67)183rd, 10 July 1967.
16. All the three polls, Gallup, NOP and ORC, showed a Tory lead for the first time in August 1967. The Tories would retain this lead for over two and a half years, until May 1970.
17. CPA, LCC (67)185th, 17 July 1967; Conservative Conference, Brighton, 19 October 1967, Official Record, p. 82; Interviewed by D.E. Butler and Austin Mitchell, 28 February 1968; interview with John Biffen.

18. Butler and Pinto-Duschinsky, 1971, p. 75. Boyle quit politics a couple of years later: Thatcher, who had joined the shadow cabinet in 1967, replaced him as shadow education minister; Interviews with Lord Fraser of Kilmorack, Terence Higgins, David Clarke.

19. Conservative Conference, Brighton, 19 October 1967, Official Record, p. 82.

20. Conservative Conference, Brighton, 19 October 1967, Official Record, p. 82; interview with Lord Amery.

21. CPA, Report for discussion at Swinton in September 1967, quoted in note by Brendon Sewill, January 1968; EPG/66/130, Conservative Economic Policy, General Review, 6 June 1969; Memorandum on the Swinton Weekend, September 1967, by James Douglas, Conservative Research Department.

22. Speech by Sir Leslie O'Brien, Rio de Janiero, autumn 1967; *Hansard*, 7 November 1967, cols. 858–59.

23. Butler and Pinto-Duschinsky, 1971, p. 75; Brittan, 1969, p. 267; interview with Sir Samuel Brittan.

24. 'Divided views on sterling put to Tory seminar', *Financial Times*, 21 July 1967; see also *Daily Telegraph* of the same date; *Hansard*, 24 July 1967, col. 68.

25. Jenkins, 1991, pp. 213–14; Butler and Sloman, 1980, p. 254; Pimlott, 1992, pp. 483–84; interview with Lord Swaythling (David Montagu).

26. Interviews with Lord Walker, Sir Anthony Grant; *Hansard*, 20 November 1967, col. 939.

27. *Hansard*, 24 July 1967, cols. 100–2; *Hansard*, 20 November 1967, col. 939; interview with Lord Hayhoe.

28. CPA, LCC (67)203rd, 11 December 1967; LCC (67)164, 7 December 1967.

29. CPA, LCC (67)164, for LCC (67)203rd, 11 December 1967.

30. Speaking in Exeter, *Daily Telegraph*, 23 November 1968; see Jenkins's chapter on Macleod, in Jenkins, 1993; interview with Lord Callaghan.

31. *Hansard*, 25 November 1968, col.149.

32. Interviewed by D.E. Butler and Austin Mitchell, 28 February 1968; interviews with Lord Carr, Lord Callaghan; Jenkins, 1991, p. 229; *Hansard*, 3 November 1969, cols. 659–62, 672–88; *Hansard*, 25 November 1968, col. 149; *Daily Telegraph*, 5 November 1969.

33. *Spectator*, 5 April 1968; interviewed by D.E. Butler and Austin Mitchell, 28 February 1968; *Hansard*, 20 March 1968, col. 430.

34. *Hansard*, 16 May 1968, cols. 1414–15.

35. Interviews with Sir Anthony Grant; Lord Jenkin of Roding; Sir Anthony Grant.

36. CPA, LCC (67)164, for CPA, LCC (67)203rd, 11 December 1967.

37. CPA, LCC (68) 174, 4 March 1968; LCC (68) 222nd, 7 March 1968; LCC (68) 222nd, 7 March 1968 and 224th, 13 March 1968.

38. Cairncross, 1992, pp. 170–1; CPA, LCC (67)234th, 29 April 1968.

39. Interviewed by D.E. Butler and Austin Mitchell, 28 February 1968; CPA, SC/68/2, 1st Meeting, 15 February 1968; CPA, SC/68/7, 4th Meeting of SC, 30 April 1968; CPA, SC/68/10, 5th Meeting of SC, 11 June 1968; C/68/12, 6th Meeting of SC, 17 July 1968; *Make Life Better*, Conservative Central Office, 7 October 1968; Conservative Conference, Blackpool, 10 October 1968, Official Record, p. 62.

40. Conservative Conference, Blackpool, 10 October 1968, Official Record, p. 62.

41. The speech by Walden during the 1968 Finance Bill, was cited by Macleod, *Hansard*, November 1968, cols. 146–47; CPA, LCC (68)268th, 25 November 1968.

42. *Hansard*, 16 April 1969, cols. 1163–64; CPA, LCC (67) 245th, 24 July 1968; interviews with Lord Carr, Colin Turner.

43. *Hansard*, 25 June 1969, col. 1543;

44. *The Times*, 4 May 1969, 17 April 1969, 18 May 1969, cited by Macleod, *Hansard*, 25 June 1969, col. 1537; *Hansard*, Official Report, Standing Committee F, 11 June 1969, col. 2.

45. CPA, SC, Paper on Economic Policy, 29 April 1969; EPG/66/14, 2nd Meeting, 24 November 1966; SC, Paper on Economic Policy, 29 April 1969; *Hansard*, 25 June 1969, col. 1546.

46. *Hansard*, 5 November 1968, cols. 703–4; *Hansard*, 25 June 1969, col. 1544.

47. *Hansard*, 25 June 1969, cols. 1536–46.
48. *Hansard*, 25 June 1969, col. 1540; Jenkins, 1991, p. 277; Report on symposium on Conservative Party policy making, *Contemporary Record*, vol. 3, no. 3, February 1990.
49. *Hansard*, 25 June 1969, cols. 1540–41; *Hansard*, 25 June 1969, col. 1541; *Hansard*, 25 June 1969, cols. 1541–42.
50. Conservative Conference, Brighton, 9 October 1969, Official Record, p. 69.
51. Interview with Brendon Sewill; CPA, CRD Papers, Box 12, Selsdon Weekend, 1 February 1970, verbatim note.
52. CPA, CRD Papers, Box 12, Selsdon Weekend, 1 February 1970.
53. Interview with Lord Gilmour; see also *Dictionary of National Biography*; *Hansard*, November 1969; *Hansard*, 15 April 1970, cols. 1393–94.
54. CPA, CRD Papers, Box 12, Selsdon Weekend, 1 February 1970; *Economist*, June 1970, p. 79; CRD Papers, Box 9, Maudling to Macleod, 13 March 1970; Jenkins, 1991, p. 292.
55. Interview with Lord Gilmour.

CHAPTER 19: PREPARING FOR NUMBER ELEVEN

1. Butler and Pinto-Duschinsky, 1971, p. 83, quoting an article in *The Banker*, April 1967.
2. Extract from Macleod's speech at a 'fringe' meeting, long-playing gramophone recording of Macleod's speeches.
3. *Economist*, 22 October 1965; *Spectator*, 15 October 1965; as Macleod promised in his conference speech the day after addressing the 'fringe' meeting – see Conservative Conference, Official Record, Brighton, 14 October 1965, p. 78.
4. Conservative Conference, Official Record, Brighton, 14 October 1965, p. 77; Macleod wrote in an article entitled, 'Taxation: Planning for Office,' in the *Banker* in April 1969, that: 'In order to achieve a vital economy, taxation must be cut. But let us be clear what this does and does not mean. It does not mean that by international standards, the proportion of income taken in the UK is above average. On the contrary, if anything, it is below average. It does mean that we tax the wrong things in the wrong way.' Yet by the time that this article appeared, in 1969, Macleod *was* arguing that the *total* amount of tax was too great and had to be cut. Commenting on this article, Butler and Pinto-Duschinsky note that it was probably written earlier and they were assured by 'senior Conservatives' that it represented Macleod's views earlier in the 1966–70 parliament. They add that 'Nearer the election there was a shift in emphasis . . .' Butler and Pinto-Duschinsky, 1971, p. 72.
5. Interviews with Lord Cockfield, Terence Higgins.
6. Ramsden, 1980, p. 245.
7. Interviews with Lord Swaythling (David Montagu), Lord Rees-Mogg.
8. Ramsden, 1980, p. 245; interview with Lord Cockfield.
9. CPA, EPG/66/87, 25th meeting, 13 June 1968: preliminary consideration of tax package, papers EPG/66/104 & 107.
10. CPA, EPG/66/93, 26th meeting, 27 June 1968: preliminary consideration of tax package, papers EPG/66/104 & 107.
11. Interview with Lord Cockfield; CPA, SC/68/5, 3rd meeting, 3 April 1968; discussion of major policy decisions required, paper SC/68/3; EPG papers, Maudling to Macleod, 3 July 1968; SC/68/5, 3rd meeting, 3 April 1968; discussion of major policy decisions required, paper SC/68/3.
12. Conservative Conference, Official Record, Brighton, 19 October 1967, p. 80; CPA, Box 12, Economy, Selsdon Weekend, 3rd session, 31 January 1970.
13. CPA, EPG/66/130, paper by Brian Reading, Tax Policies and Public Expenditure, 29 April 1969. It was estimated that replacing the existing forms of indirect taxation would yield an extra £800 million in revenue (the new taxes would levy an estimated total of £3,705 million, as against

£2,905 million from the taxes that they would replace); Conservative Conference, Official Record, Brighton, 19 October 1967, p. 80.

14. Conservative Conference, Official Record, Brighton, 19 October 1967, p. 80; CPA, LCC (68)234th – 29 April 1968; EPG/66/93, 26th meeting, 26 June 1968: preliminary consideration of tax package, papers EPG/66/104 & 107; *Hansard*, 25 June 1969, col. 1546; EPG papers, Maudling to Macleod, 3 July 1968.
15. Interview with Lord Cockfield.
16. CPA, SC/68/2, 1st meeting, 15 February 1968; SC/68/4, 2nd meeting, 18 March 1968; LCC (67)164, for LCC (67)293rd, 11 December 1967; SC/68/5, 3rd meeting, 3 April 1968; discussion of taxation policy, major policy decisions required, paper SC/68/3; SC/68/7, 4th meeting, 30 April 1968; discussion of first draft of policy document; *Make Life Better*, 7 October 1968. Conservative Conference, Official Record, Brighton, 19 October 1967, p. 80; CPA, LCC (69)321st, 13 October 1969, discussion on party conference; EPG/66/108, 28th meeting, 26 July 1968; papers EPG/66/104 & 107; interview with Lord Cockfield.
17. CPA, EPG/66/110, 29th meeting, 25 October 1968; EPG/66/114, final draft dated 16 January 1969; EPG/66/130, Tax Policies and Public Expenditure, 29 April 1969; CRD, EPG Correspondence, Macleod to Heath, 19 May 1969; *Hansard*, 20 May 1969, col. 336; EPG/66/130, Tax Policies and Public Expenditure, 29 April 1969; Conservative Conference, Official Record, Brighton, 9 October 1969, p. 69.
18. CPA, LCC (69)314th, 7 July 1969 (see also Macleod's speech, standing committee F, 1969 Finance Bill, cols. 441–44); *Hansard*, 18 July 1969, col. 1163; interview with Lord Cockfield.
19 EPG/66/108, 28th meeting, 26 July 1968: preliminary consideration of tax package, papers EPG/66/104 & 107; SC/70/1, 3rd meeting, 12 March 1970, discussion of third draft manifesto; SC/68/5, 4th meeting, 30 April 1968; discussion of first draft of policy document; *The Times*, 7 October 1968.
20. *Hansard*, 16 April 1969, cols. 1164–65; CPA, Box 12, Economy, Selsdon Weekend, 3rd session, 31 January 1970; *Hansard*, 15 April 1970, col. 1398.
21 CPA, LCC (67)164 for LCC (67)203rd, 11 December 1967; CPA, LCC (68)207th, discussion on Commons debate on government spending.
22. CPA, EPG/66/108, 28th meeting, 26 July 1968: preliminary consideration of tax package, papers EPG/66/104 & 107; speaking during the committee stage of the 1970 finance bill, Macleod cited an article by Brian Reading and David Lomax in the *Westminster Bank Review*, *Hansard*, 12 May 1970, col. 1123.
23. CPA, EPG/66/70, 19th meeting, 8 February 1968: discussion of report by policy group on nationalised industries, LCC (68)197.
24. CPA, EPG/66/105a, 19 July 1968 – note by Brian Reading, attached to paper EPG/66/105, in which he suggests that devaluation and the additional foreign debt incurred by the Labour Government will require, until the mid-1970s, a higher level of taxation than would otherwise have been necessary; Conservative Conference, Official Record, Blackpool, 10 October 1968, p. 63; Conservative Conference, Official Record, Brighton, 9 October 1969, p. 70; CPA, EPG/66/130 Tax Policies and Public Expenditure, 29 April 1969.
25. CPA, EPG/66/105a, 19 July 1968 – note by Brian Reading, attached to paper EPG/66/105, in which he indicated that with the exception of defence and possibly housing, demands on the main categories of public expenditure would be higher in the next decade than in the last. *Hansard*, 25 November 1968, col. 144; CPA, SC/70/10, 3rd meeting, 12 March 1970; discussion on third draft manifesto, paper SC/70/3.
26. CPA, EPG/66/130 Tax Policies and Public Expenditure, 29 April 1969; *Hansard*, 16 April 1969, col. 1166.
27. CPA, EPG/66/75, 21st meeting, 7 March 1968: the policy group on defence had not reported by this stage; CPA, CRD Papers, Box 12, Selsdon Weekend, 6th session, 1 February 1970; CPA, LCC (70)351st, 2 March 1970.

28. *Hansard*, 21 January 1970, col. 546; *Hansard*, 21 January 1970, col. 547; CPA, SC/70/10, 3rd meeting, 12 March 1970; discussion on third draft manifesto, paper SC/70/3.

29. CPA, EPG/66/130 Tax Policies and Public Expenditure, 29 April 1969; CRD Papers, Box 12, Selsdon Weekend, 1 February 1970; Macleod's 1967 Budget preview, *Financial Times*, 6 April 1967.

30. *Financial Times*, 6 April 1967.

31. CPA, EPG/66/130 Tax Policies and Public Expenditure, 29 April 1969.

32. CPA, SC/70/10, 3rd meeting, 12 March 1970; discussion on pledges to pensioners, paper SC/70/9; CRD Papers, Box 12, Selsdon Weekend, 1 February 1970; Macleod's Budget preview, 6 April 1967.

33. CPA, CRD Papers, Box 12, Selsdon Weekend, 1 February 1970; *Hansard*, 15 April 1970, col. 1400; *Hansard*, 15 April 1970, cols. 1399–1400.

34. Tebbit, 1988, p. 74; the real nature of Child Benefit is explained by Gilmour, 1992, p. 131, footnote.

35. *Economist*, 13 June 1970, p. 79; CPA, CRD Papers, Box 12 Economy, Selsdon Weekend, 3rd session, 31 January 1970.

36. CPA, CRD Papers, Box 12 Economy, Selsdon Weekend, 3rd session, 31 January 1970; VAT was increased to 15 per cent by Lord Howe in the first budget of the Thatcher Government in June 1979; CPA, CRD Papers, Box 12 Economy, Selsdon Weekend, 3rd session, 31 January 1970, verbatim note.

37. CPA, CRD Papers, Box 12 Economy, Selsdon Weekend, 3rd session, 31 January 1970.

38. Ibid.

39. Ibid.

40. *Economist*, 13 June 1970, p. 79.

41. CPA, CRD Papers, Box 12 Economy, Selsdon Weekend, 3rd session, 31 January 1970.

42. Conservative Conference, Official Record, Brighton, 9 October 1969, p. 70; Conservative Conference, Official Record, Brighton, 9 October 1968, p. 64; interview with Lord Cockfield.

43. CPA, CRD Papers, Box 12 Economy, Selsdon Weekend, 8th session, 1 February 1970.

44. CPA, CRD Papers, Box 12 Economy, Selsdon Weekend, 8th session, 1 February 1970.

45. CPA, CRD Papers, Box 12 Economy, Selsdon Weekend, 8th session, 1 February 1970; discussion on draft manifesto, paper SP/70/1, and on legislative programme, SP/70/11.

CHAPTER 20: A VERY LIBERAL TORY

1. Interview with Rhoderick Macleod.

2. *Hansard*, 15 December 1969, col. 1045

3. Interview with Torquil Macleod (son).

4. PRO, CAB 129/104, C(61) 20, 8 February 1961, CAB 128/35, CC (61) 6th Conclusions, 13 February 1961.

5. *Spectator*, 11 December 1964.

6. *Spectator*, 26 June 1964.

7. 'Spectator's Notebook,' the *Spectator*, 11 December 1964; *Spectator*, 1 January 1965, 12 March 1965.

8. CPA, LCC (65)58th, 30 June 1965; LCC (69)332nd, 24 November 1969; LCC (69)337th, 10 December 1969, *Hansard*, 15 December 1969, cols. 1045–47.

9. Interview with Humphry Berkeley.

10. Personal letter, Macleod to Berkeley, 15 March 1966; Butler and King, 1966, statistical appendix by Michael Steed; Berkeley, 1972, p. 99.

11. Macleod's comments were made before the introduction of breathalyser tests and the compulsory wearing of seat belts; *Spectator*, 12 February 1965.

12. *Spectator*, 12 February 1965, 1 January 1965.

13. Enoch Powell served as Minister of Health for more than three years between 1960 and 1963; *Spectator*, 12 February 1965.

14. *Spectator*, 1 January 1965; Lapping, 1970, p. 111–12.
15. *Spectator*, 20 August 1965; interview with Roy Hattersley.
16. *Spectator*, 20 August 1965.
17. *Spectator*, 16 April 1965.
18. *Spectator*, 16 April 1965; speech in Redhill, Surrey, reported in *The Times*, 10 April 1965.
19. CPA, LCC (67)171st, 1 May 1967 and LCC (67)141.
20. Deakin, 1970, p. 125; CPA, LCC (67)169th, 24 April 1967: speech by Powell, Deal, 18 October 1967, quoted in Cosgrave, 1989, pp. 240–1; *Hansard*, 15 November 1967, cols. 453–73.
21. Quoted in CPA, LCC (68)169; Cosgrave, 1989, p. 242; Deakin, 1970, pp. 132–33.
22. CPA, LCC (68)213th, 12 February 1968.
23. *Spectator*, 23 February 1968.
24. CPA, LCC (68)216th, 21 February 1968. The statement is quoted in the Conservative Campaign Guide, 1974, p. 421; Deakin, 1970, p. 131; *Hansard*, 22 February 1968, col. 662.
25. *Spectator*, 23 February 1968, 1 March 1968.
26. CPA, LCC (68)216th, 26 February 1968; Fisher, 1973, p. 297.
27. Lapping, 1970, p. 122.
28. CPA, LCC (68)231st, 10 April 1968; *The Times*, 11 and 12 April 1968.
29. Powell, Birmingham, 20th April 1968, quoted in Cosgrave, 1989, pp. 246–50.
30. Cosgrave, 1989, p. 248; Lapping, 1970, pp. 123–24; Powell, Birmingham, 20th April 1968, quoted in Cosgrave, 1989, pp. 246–50.
31. Cosgrave, 1989, p. 245; interview with Viscount Whitelaw; *The Times*, 22nd April 1968.
32. *Hansard*, 23 April 1968, col. 75; interview with Lord Carr.
33. *The Times*, 22nd April 1968; CPA, LCC (68)244th, 19 June 1968.
34. Interviews with 1960s Young Conservatives; interview with Lord Jenkin of Roding.
35. Interview with Colin Harding.
36. Interview with Enoch Powell; *Daily Telegraph*, 11 October 1968; Tebbit, 1988, p. 74;
37. *The Times*, 27 October 1969; this personal letter from Macleod to Fisher is reproduced in Fisher, 1973, facing p. 257.
38. *Guardian*, 21 August 1968; interview with John Major.
39. Interview with John Major.
40. Telephone interview with William Shearman.
41. As Eve Macleod made clear when she wrote to William Shearman after her husband's death.
42. *Spectator*, 1 January 1965.
43. Telephone interview with William Shearman; interview with Nick Beacock.
44. Owen, 1991, pp. 97–98; interview with Nick Beacock.
45. *Hansard*, 21 December 1967, cols. 1553–64.
46. Telephone interview with William Shearman; interview with Nick Beacock; information provided by Crisis.
47. CPA, LCC (65)75th, 15 November 1965.
48. *The Times*, 17 November 1965; *Spectator*, 19 and 26 November 1965; Fisher, 1973, p. 275.
49. *Hansard*, 14 December 1965; 21 December 1965.
50. The Monday Club, formed in reaction to Harold Macmillan's 'Winds of Change' speech, was on the right of the party, and PEST (Pressure for Economic and Social Toryism) was on the left; *Spectator*, 24 December 1965.
51. CPA, LCC (68)242nd, 12 June 1968; LCC (70)352nd, 4 March 1970.
52. Interviews with Nick Scott, Lord Hayhoe.
53. CPA, LCC (69)337th, 10 December 1969; LCC (70)363rd, 15 April 1970; CPA, LCC (70)364th, 27 April 1970; 369th, 13 May 1970; SC/70/15, fifth meeting, 11 May 1970.
54. Butler and Pinto-Duschinsky, 1971, pp. 28–33. This incident acted as the catalyst of George Brown's resignation in March 1968 over the conduct of Government business; interview with Eve Macleod; Berkeley, 1972, p. 100.
55. CPA, LCC (69)339th, 18 December 1969; 289th, 10 March 1969; 313th, 2 July 1969.

56. CPA, LCC (69)332nd, 24 November 1969. Sir Alec Douglas-Home was absent; CPA, LCC (69)333rd, 26 November 1969.
57. CPA, LCC (69)334th, 1 December 1969; 339th, 18 December 1969.
58. CPA, LCC (67)205th, 18 December 1967.
59. CPA, LCC (67)205th, 18 December 1967.
60. CPA, LCC (68)208th, 22 January 1968; LCC (68)211th, 31 January 1968; LCC (68)221st, 6 March 1968; LCC (68)229th, 1 April 1968; LCC (68)230th, 3 April 1968; LCC (68)235th, 1 May 1968.
61. *Hansard*, 20 November 1968, cols. 1331–34.
62. CPA, LCC (69)275th, 20 January 1969.
63. *Hansard*, 20 November 1968, col. 1327; interview with Enoch Powell.
64. Interviewed by D.E.Butler and Austin Mitchell, 28 February 1968; CPA, SC/70/10, third meeting, 12 March 1970, manifesto – spring 1970, third draft, SC/70/7; the Bridgwater by-election, won by Tom King for the Conservatives, was the first occasion on which 18-year-olds were able to vote in a parliamentary election in the United Kingdom.
65 CPA, ACP(70)109th, 6 May 1970, fourth draft of manifesto.
66. Interview with Lord Hayhoe; CPA, SC/70/19, sixth meeting, 13 May 1970; SC/70/14, paper on 'The General Election Campaign,' by Michael Fraser, 11 May 1970; Prior, 1986, p. 85.

CHAPTER 21: THE CRUELLEST BLOW

1. CPA, LCC (69)325th, 29 October 1969; *The Times*, 9 October 1970.
2. Conservative Conference, Brighton, 9 October 1969, Official Record, p. 68.
3. Interview with Lord Walker; CPA, CRD Papers, Box 12, Selsdon Weekend, third session, 31 January 1970.
4. Various conversations with Lord Prior.
5. CPA, SC/69/6, second meeting, 12 December 1969, SC/69/3, Draft manifesto – spring 1970; CPA, SC/69/6, second meeting, 12 December 1969, SC/69/5, Publication of Policy during 1970.
6. CPA, SC/70/19, sixth meeting, 13 May 1970.
7. Watkins, 1982, p. 110.
8. CPA, SC/70/10, third meeting, 12 March 1970; interview with Lord Walker.
9. CPA, LCC (70)357th, 8 April 1970; Day, 1989, p. 225.
10. Butler and Pinto-Duschinsky, 1971, pp. 133–35.
11. *Hansard*, 14 May 1970, cols. 1119–20; Sir Edward Boyle, in Fisher, 1973, p. 19.
12. Interview with Lord Jenkin of Roding; *Hansard*, 20 May 1970, cols. 53–55.
13. Quoted in Fisher, 1973, p. 304.
14. Fisher, 1973, p. 303; CPA, SC/70/15, 11 May 1970, SC/70/19, 13 May 1970; interview with Colin Turner.
15. *The Times*, 1 June 1970.
16. On 28 October 1971, the Commons voted by 356 votes to 244 in favour of British entry; 69 Labour MPs voted in favour and 39 Conservatives against; 20 Labour MPs and two Conservatives abstained. Labour MPs were whipped to vote against.
17. *The Times*, 1 June 1970.
18. Fisher, 1973, p. 29; interviews with Rhoderick Macleod, Eve Macleod; Fisher, 1973, p. 29.
19. Interview with Rhoderick Macleod; *Craven Herald*, 31 July 1970, quoting Rev. Cook who recalled the incident during his address at Macleod's funeral service, seven weeks later.
20. Private information.
21. *The Times*, 8 June 1970; Butler and Pinto-Duschinsky, 1971, p. 223.
22. Interviews with Gerry Wade; Elizabeth Sturges-Jones.
23. *The Times*, 9 June 1970; interview with Gerry Wade.
24. Interview with Gerry Wade; Butler and Pinto-Duschinsky, 1971, pp. 223–23.

25. Fisher, 1973, p. 303; interview with Eve Macleod; Fisher, 1973, pp. 303–04; this latter prediction was made at a press conference in Glasgow the day after the poll giving Labour a huge lead. Whatever Macleod's private thoughts, he could scarcely have done anything other than predict a Conservative triumph; interview with Lord Walker; *Contemporary Record*, vol. 3, number 3, February 1990, symposium on Conservative Policy making, 1964–70.
26. Interviews with Viscount Whitelaw, Gerry Wade.
27. Interviews with Gerry Wade; Eve Macleod; Fisher 1973 p. 307.
28. Quoted in Butler and Pinto-Duschinsky, 1971, pp. 160–63; interview with Gerry Wade; Prior, 1986, pp. 59–60; Fisher, 1973, p. 304;
29. *The Times*, 17 and 18 June 1970.
30. Interviews with Gerry Wade, Eve Macleod, Diana Heimann (daughter), Lord Hayhoe; Fisher, 1973, pp. 304–05.
31. *The Times*, 22 June 1970.
32. Interview with Lord Croham.
33. Interviews with Lord Croham, Sir William Ryrie.
34. Interviews with Nick Scott, Gerry Wade; Fisher, 1973, p. 305.
35. Interview with Sir William Ryrie.
36. Interviews with Lord Jenkin of Roding, Lord Walker, Lord Rees-Mogg.
37. Interview with Lord Croham.
38. Interviews with Sir Peter Middleton, Lord Jenkin of Roding.
39. Interviews with Lord Croham, Sir William Ryrie, Sir Peter Middleton.
40. Interview with Lord Croham.
41. Interview with Lord Croham; Macleod was not in favour of using high interest rates to squeeze inflation out of the system.
42. *Hansard*, 7 July 1970, cols. 507–10.
43. *Hansard*, 7 July 1970, col. 505.
44. *Hansard*, 7 July 1970, cols. 510–11.
45. Interview with Lord Cockfield.
46. *Hansard*, 7 July 1970, cols. 510; interviews with Brendon Sewill; Lord Jenkin of Roding; Sir Peter Middleton.
47. Interviews with Lord Jenkin of Roding; Terence Higgins; Thatcher won her battle with Macleod's successor, Barber, to keep the Open University.
48. Fisher, 1973, p. 314; interview with Eve Macleod; St George's Hospital has since been closed and, after extensive renovation, has become the Lanesborough Hotel.
49. Interviews with Eve Macleod, Sir Reginald Bennett.
50. Interviews with Eve Macleod, Sir Peter Middleton; Fisher, 1973, p. 306.
51. Interviews with Eve Macleod, Sir William Ryrie, Lord Jenkin of Roding; Fisher, 1973, p. 307.
52. Interviews with Enoch Powell, Lord Jenkin of Roding, John Major, Nick Beacock.
53. Letters to Eve Macleod.
54. Interview with Eve Macleod.
55. *Craven Herald*, 31 July 1970.

CHAPTER 22: THE LOSS AND THE LEGACY

1. Interview with Lord Carr.
2. Interview with Lord Aldington.
3. Private information; interview with Lord Carr; Prior, 1986, p. 66.
4. Interview with Viscount Whitelaw.
5. Butler, 1982b, p. 110.
6. Interviews with senior officials and members of the Cabinet during the 1970–74 Heath Government.
7. Private information; see also Campbell, 1993, p. 446.

8. Private information.
9. Interview with Lord Cockfield; private information.
10. Prior, 1986, pp. 87–88; Campbell, 1993, pp. 562–63.
11. Prior, 1986, p. 92; Campbell, 1993, pp. 580–81.
12. Campbell, 1993 interview with Lord Carr.
13. Gilmour, *The Listener*, 30 July 1970; Patrick Middleton provides a perceptive analysis of Thatcher's attitude towards social issues in, 'For "Victorian" read "Georgian:" Mrs Thatcher Corrected,' in *Encounter*, July/August 1986.
14. Interviews with Enoch Powell, John Biffen.
15. 'Bagehot', *Economist*, 15 December 1990; interview with David Clarke.
16. Interview with John Major.
17. Lord Fraser of Kilmorack, *The Week At Westminster*, BBC Radio Four, 25 July 1970.

Select Bibliography

PRIMARY SOURCES:

Conservative Party Archives, 1945–70, Bodleian Library, Oxford.

Government Papers, 1952–63, Public Record Office, Kew

Interview recorded with Iain Macleod by W.P. Kirkman for the Oxford Colonial Records Project, on Macleod's period as Colonial Secretary, 1959–61, recorded at the White Cottage, Enfield, 29 December 1967, Rhodes House, Oxford.

R.A. Butler Papers, Trinity College, Cambridge.

Joan Baylis, autobiographical memoir, unpublished.

Interviews recorded for *Reputations*, profile of Iain Macleod, BBC Television,1981.

Interviews recorded for *End of Empire*, Granada TV series for Channel Four, 1985, Rhodes House, Oxford.

ARTICLES AND BOOKS BY IAIN MACLEOD:

1950, *One Nation*, London, Conservative Political Centre (Macleod was joint editor with Angus Maude, and co-author with other members of the 'One Nation' group).

1952, *The Social Services: Needs and Means*, London, Conservative Political Centre (Macleod was co-author with Enoch Powell).

1952, *Bridge Is An Easy Game*, London, Frederick Muller.

1960, *One World*, London, Conservative Political Centre.

1961, *Neville Chamberlain*, London, Frederick Muller.

1963–70, Various articles published in the *Spectator*, *The Times*, and *Financial Times*.

1965, 'Britain's Future Policy in Africa', in *Weekend Telegraph*, 12 March.

NEWSPAPERS AND MAGAZINES:

Daily Express, London; *Daily Mail*, London; *Daily Mirror*, London; *Daily Gleaner*, Kingston, Jamaica; *Daily Herald*, London; *Daily Telegraph*, London; *Economist*, London; *Evening Standard*, London; *The Fettesian*, Vols. 1927–32, and Vol. XCII, No.3, 'Centenary Year', Summer 1970, Fettes College, Edinburgh; *Financial Times*, London; *Manchester Guardian*, London; *Listener*, London; *London Review of Books*, London; *New Statesman*, London; *Rhodesia Herald*, Salisbury; *St Ninian's School Magazine*, No. 29, vol. VII, Summer Term 1923, Moffat, Dumfriesshire; *Spectator*, London; *Sunday Times*, London; *The Times*, London; *Trinidad Guardian*, Port-of-Spain, Trinidad.

SECONDARY SOURCES:

B.W.E. Alford, 1988, *British Economic Performance, 1945–1975*, London, Macmillan.

Lord Alport, 1965, *The Sudden Assignment: Central Africa 1961–63*, London, Hodder and Stoughton.

Brigadier C.N. Barclay, (ed.), 1953, *The History of the Duke of Wellington's Regiment 1919–52*, London, William Clowes and Sons.

John Baylis, 1984, *Anglo-American Defence Relations, 1939–1984; The Special Relationship*, London, Macmillan.

Humphry Berkeley, 1972, *Crossing the Floor*, London, George Allen and Unwin.

F.T. Blackaby (ed.), 1978, *British Economic Policy, 1960–74*, Cambridge, Cambridge University Press.

Robert Blake, 1966, *Disraeli*, London, Eyre and Spottiswoode.

Robert Blake, 1977, *A History of Rhodesia*, London, Eyre Methuen.

Robert Blake, 1985, *The Conservative Party from Peel to Thatcher*, London, Fontana.

Sir Michael Blundell, 1964 *So Rough A Wind: the Kenya Memoirs of Sir Michael Blundell*, London, Weidenfeld and Nicolson.

Christopher Booker, 1992, *The Neophiliacs: The Revolution in English Life in the Fifties and Sixties*, London, Pimlico.

John Boyd-Carpenter, 1980, *Way of Life*, London, Sidgwick and Jackson.

J.M. Brereton and A.C.S. Savory, 1993, *The History of the Duke of Wellington's Regiment (West Riding) 1702–1992*, Halifax, The Duke of Wellington's Regiment (West Riding).

Samuel Brittan, 1968, *Left or Right: the Bogus Dilemma*, London, Secker and Warburg;

Samuel Brittan, 1971, *Steering the Economy*, London, Penguin.

Peter Browning, 1986, *The Treasury and Economic Planning, 1964–85*, London, Longman.

David Butler, 1952, *The British General Election of 1951*; 1956, *The British General election of 1955; 1960 (with Richard Rose), The British General Election of 1959*; 1965 (with Anthony King), *The British General Election of 1964*; 1966 (with Anthony King), *The British General Election of 1966*; 1971 (with Michael Pinto-Duschinsky), *The British General election of 1970*, London, Macmillan.

Lord Butler, 1982a, *The Art of the Possible: the Memoirs of the Late Lord Butler*, London, Hamish Hamilton.

Lord Butler, 1982b, *The Art of Memory: Friends in Perspective*, London, Hodder and Stoughton.

Mollie Butler, 1987, *August and Rab: A Memoir*, London, Weidenfeld and Nicolson,

James Callaghan, 1987, *Time and Chance*, London, Collins.

John Campbell, 1993, *Edward Heath*, Jonathan Cape, London.

David Carlton, 1981, *Anthony Eden: A Biography*, London, Allen Lane; 1988, *Britain and the Suez Crisis*, Oxford, Basil Blackwell

Lord Carrington, 1988, *Reflect on Things Past*, London, Collins.

Barbara Castle, 1984, *The Castle Diaries, 1964–70*, London, Weidenfeld and Nicolson.

Barbara Castle, 1993, *Fighting All the Way*, London, Macmillan.

Patrick Cosgrave, 1989, *The Lives of Enoch Powell*, London, The Bodley Head.

Richard Crossman, 1975, *The Diaries of a Cabinet Minister, 1964–66*, London, Hamish Hamilton and Jonathan Cape.

David Daniels, 1981, *The Golden Age of Contract Bridge*, New York, Stein and Day.

John Darwin, 1984, 'British Decolonization since 1945: A Pattern or a Puzzle?', in *Journal of Imperial and Commonwealth History*, London, No. 2, London, special issue, Perspectives on Imperialism and Decolonization.

John Darwin, 1988, *Britain and Decolonisation: The Retreat from Empire in the Post-war World*, London, Macmillan.

John Darwin, 1991, *The End of the British Empire: the Historical Debate* Oxford, Macmillan.

Nicholas Davenport, 1974, *Memoirs of a City Radical*, London, Weidenfeld and Nicolson.

Sir Robin Day, 1989, *Grand Inquisitor*, London, Weidenfeld and Nicolson.

D.W. Dean, 'Conservative Governments and the restriction of Commonwealth immigration in the 1950s: the problems of constraint', in the *Historical Journal*, vol. 35, no. 1., (1992), pp. 171–94.

William Croft Dickinson, 1961, *Scotland from the Earliest Times to 1603*, London, Thomas Nelson.

Howard J. Dooley, 1989, 'Great Britain's "Last Battle" in the Middle East: Notes on Cabinet Planning during the Suez Crisis of 1956' in *The International History Review*, Vol. XI, No. 3, pp. 486–517, London.

Sir Alec Douglas-Home, 1976, *The Way the Wind Blows*, Constable, London.

Peter Duignan and L.H. Gann, 1984, *The United States and Africa*, Cambridge, Cambridge University Press.

J.K. Ellwood, 1982, *Life In Old Skipton: A Photographic Recollection*, Clapham, via Lancaster, Dalesman Publishing.

D.K. Fieldhouse, 1986, *Black Africa 1945–80: Economic Decolonization and Arrested Development*, London, Allen & Unwin.

Nigel Fisher, 1973, *Iain Macleod*, London, André Deutsch.

Nigel Fisher, 1977, *The Tory Leaders*, London, Weidenfeld and Nicolson.

Michael Foot, 1973, *Aneurin Bevan*, vol. II, 1945–60, London, Davis Poynter.

David Frost, 1993, *An Autobiography*, London, Harper Collins.

Andrew Gamble, 1974, *The Conservative Nation*, London, Routledge and Kegan Paul.

Prosser Gifford and William Roger Louis, (eds.), 1982, *The Transfer of Power in Africa: Decolonization, 1940–60*, Yale, Yale University Press.

Ian Gilmour, 1977, *Inside Right: A Study of Conservatism*, London, Hutchinson.

Ian Gilmour, 1992, *Dancing With Dogma: Britain Under Thatcherism*, London, Simon and Schuster.

David Goldsworthy, 1971, *Colonial Issues in British Politics, 1945–61*, Oxford.

David Goldsworthy, 1990, 'Keeping Change Within Bounds: Aspects of Colonial Policy during the Churchill and Eden Government, 1951–57', in *Journal of Imperial and Commonwealth History*, London, Vol. 18, No. 1, pp. 81–108.

Philip Goodhart, with Ursula Branston, 1973, *The 1922*, London, Macmillan.

Geoffrey Goodman, 1984, *The Awkward Warrior: Frank Cousins, His Life and Times* (second revised edition), Nottingham, Spokesman.

Lord Hailsham, 1990, *A Sparrow's Flight*, London, Collins.

Kay Halle (ed), 1971, *Randolph Churchill: The Young Unpretender*, London, Heinemann.

John D. Hargreaves, 1988, *Decolonization in Africa*, London, Longman.

Ian Harvey, 1971, *To Fall Like Lucifer*, London, Sidgwick and Jackson.

Denis Healey, 1989, *The Time of My Life*, London, Michael Joseph.

Peter Hennessy, 1992, *Never Again: Britain 1945–51*, London, Jonathan Cape.

Peter Hennessy and Anthony Seldon (eds.), 1987, *Ruling Performance: British Governments from Attlee to Thatcher*, Oxford, Basil Blackwell.

Robert Hewison, 1981, *In Anger: Culture in the Cold War, 1945–60*, London, Weidenfeld and Nicolson.

Robert Hewison, 1986, *Too Much: Art and Society in the Sixties, 1960–75*, London, Methuen.

R.F. Holland, 1984, 'The Imperial Factor in British Strategies from Attlee to Macmillan, 1945–63', in, *Journal of Imperial and Commonwealth History*, No. 2, London, special issue, Perspectives on Imperialism and Decolonization.

Alistair Horne, 1988, *Macmillan*, Vol. I (1894–1956); and 1989, Vol. II (1957–1986), London, Macmillan.

Anthony Howard, 1987, *RAB: The Life of R.A. Butler*, London, Jonathan Cape.

Anthony Howard, 1990, *Crossman: The Pursuit of Power*, London, Jonathan Cape.

Anthony Howard and Richard West, *The Making of the Prime Minister*, 1965, London, Jonathan Cape.

Sir David Hunt, 1975, *On the Spot: An Ambassador Remembers*, London, Peter Davies.

George Hutchinson, 1980, *The Last Edwardian at No. 10: An Impression of Harold Macmillan*, London, Quartet Books.

Douglas Jay, 1980, *Change and Fortune: A Political Record*, London, Hutchinson.

Roy Jenkins, 1991, *A Life at the Centre*, London, Macmillan.

Roy Jenkins, 1993, *Portraits and Miniatures*, London, Macmillan.

Jack Jones, 1986, *Union Man*, London, Collins.

Sir John Junor, 1990, *Memoirs: Listening for a Midnight Tram*, London, Chapmans.

Miles Kahler, 1984, *Decolonization in Britain and France: The Domestic Consequences of International Relations, Domestic Sources of Foreign Policy*, Princeton, Princeton University Press.

Cecil King, 1972, *The Cecil King Diary, 1965–70*, and 1975, *The Cecil King Diary, 1970–74*, London, Jonathan Cape.

Phillip Knightley and Caroline Kennedy, 1987, *An Affair of State: The Profumo Case and the Framing of Stephen Ward*, London, Jonathan Cape.

Keith Kyle, 1991, *Suez*, London, Weidenfeld and Nicolson.

Brian Lapping, 1970, *The Labour Government 1964–70*, London, Penguin.

Brian Lapping, 1985, *End of Empire*, London, Granada / Channel Four.

Nigel Lawson, 1992, *The View From Number 11*, London, Bantam Press.

Audrey Leathard, 1980, *The Fight for Family Planning*, London, Macmillan.

J.M. Lee, 1967, *Colonial Development and Good Government: A Study of Ideas Expressed by the British Official Classes in Planning Decolonization, 1939–64*, Oxford, Clarendon Press.

Judith Listowel, 1965, *The Making of Tanganyika*, London, Chatto and Windus.

William Roger Louis, 1985, 'American anti-colonialism and the dissolution of the British Empire', in *International Affairs*, Vol. 61, pp. 395–420, London.

William Roger Louis, 1989, 'Taxing Transfers of Power', in *The Times Literary Supplement*, London, 10–16 February, p. 146.

William Roger Louis and Roger Owen, 1989, *Suez 1956: The Crisis and its Consequences*, Oxford, Clarendon Press.

Rodney Lowe, 1989, 'Resignation at the Treasury: the Social Services Committee and the Failure to Reform the Welfare State, 1955–57, in *Journal of Social Policy*, vol. 18, no. 4, pp. 505–26, London.

Rodney Lowe, 1993, *The Welfare State in Britain since 1945*, London, Macmillan.

Donald MacDougall, 1987, *Don and Mandarin: Memoirs of an Economist*, London, John Murray.

Alasdair Alpin MacGregor, 1933a, *The Haunted Isles, or Life in the Hebrides*, London, Maclehose.

Alasdair Alpin MacGregor, 1933b, *Searching the Hebrides with a Camera*, London, George G. Harrap.

Alasdair Alpin MacGregor, 1964, *The Golden Lamp*, London, Michael Joseph.

Alasdair Alpin MacGregor, 1967, *The Enchanted Isles*, London, Michael Joseph.

J.D. Mackie, 1978, *A History of Scotland* (Second edition, revised and edited by Bruce Lenman and Geoffrey Parker), London, Allen Lane

Rhoderick Alexander Macleod, 1976, *Notes on the Ancestry of Rhoderick Alexander Macleod*, Ardnamurchan, published privately.

Harold Macmillan, 1969, *Tides of Fortune, 1945–55*.

Harold Macmillan, 1971, *Riding the Storm, 1956–59*.

Harold Macmillan, 1972, *Pointing the Way, 1959–61*.

Harold Macmillan, 1973, *At the End of the Day, 1961–63*, London, Macmillan.

Richard D. Mahoney, 1983, *JFK: Ordeal in Africa*, Oxford, Oxford University Press.

Rixi Markus, 1988, *A Vulnerable Game: the Memoirs of Rixi Markus*, London, Collins.

Reginald Maudling, 1978, *Memoirs*, London, Sidgwick and Jackson.

Tom Mboya, 1963, *Freedom and After*, London, Deutsch.

Keith Middlemas, 1986, *Power, Competition and the State: Volume One, Britain in Search of Balance*, London, Macmillan.

Austen Morgan, 1992, *Harold Wilson*, London, Pluto Press.

David J. Morgan, 1980, *The Official History of Colonial Development, Vol 5, Guidance Towards Self-Government in British Colonies, 1941–71*, London, Macmillan.

Kenneth O. Morgan, 1990, *The People's Peace: British History 1945–89*, Oxford, Oxford University Press.

Frank O'Gorman, 1986, *British Conservatism: Conservative Thought from Burke to Thatcher*, Harlow, Longman.

David Owen, 1991, *Time To Declare*, London, Michael Joseph.

Dame Margery Perham, 1970, *Colonial Sequences, 1949–69*, London, Methuen.

Ben Pimlott, 1992, *Harold Wilson*, London, Harper Collins.

A.N. Porter and A.J. Stockwell, 1987, *British Imperial Policy, 1938–64*, Vol. I, 1938–51, and, 1989, Vol II, 1951–64; London, Macmillan.

Jim Prior, 1986, *A Balance of Power*, London, Hamish Hamilton.

John Ramsden, 1980, *The Making of Conservative Party Policy: the Conservative Research Department Since 1929*, London, Longman.

Guy Ramsey, 1955, *Aces All*, London, Museum Press.

Peter Rawlinson, 1989, *A Price Too High*, London, Weidenfeld and Nicolson.

Robert Rhodes James, 1986, *Anthony Eden*, London, Weidenfeld and Nicolson.

Paul B. Rich, 1986, *Race and Empire in British Politics*, Cambridge, Cambridge University Press.

David Scott, 1981, *Ambassador in Black and White: Thirty Years of Changing Africa*, London, Weidenfeld and Nicolson.

W. Scott Lucas, 1991, *Divided We Stand: Britain, the U.S. and the Suez Crisis*, London, John Curtis / Hodder and Stoughton.

Bettina Selby, 1989, *The Fragile Islands*, Edinburgh, Richard Drew Publishing.

Anthony Seldon, 1981, *Churchill's Indian Summer: The Conservative Government, 1951–55*, London, Hodder and Stoughton.

Robert Shepherd, 1991, *The Power Brokers: the Tory Party and its Leaders*, London, Hutchinson.

Philip Short, 1974, *Banda*, London, Routledge & Kegan Paul.

Tony Smith, 1981, *The Pattern of Imperialism*, Cambridge, Cambridge University Press.

T.C. Smout, 1972, *A History of the Scottish People, 1560–1830*, Fontana/ Collins, p. 40.

Peter Spencer, 1979, *St Ninian's: A Centenary History of a Scottish Prep. School*, Moffat.

Norman Tebbit, 1988, *Upwardly Mobile*, London, Weidenfeld and Nicolson.

Francis Thompson, 1988, *The Western Isles*, London, B.T. Batsford.

D.R. Thorpe, 1980, *The Uncrowned Prime Ministers*, London, Darkhorse Publishing.

D.R. Thorpe, 1989, *Selwyn Lloyd*, London, Jonathan Cape.

Dennis Walters, 1989, *Not Always With the Pack*, London, Constable.

Alan Watkins, 1982, *Brief Lives*, London, Hamish Hamilton.

Charles Webster, 1988, *The Health Services Since the War: Volume One, Problems of Health Care: The National Health Service Before 1957*, London, HMSO.

Sir Roy Welensky, 1964, *Welensky's 4000 Days; The Life and Death of the Federation of Rhodesia and Nyasaland*, London, Collins.

William Whitelaw, 1989, *The Whitelaw Memoirs*, London, Aurum.

J.R.T. Wood, 1983, *The Welensky Papers*, Durban, Graham Publishing.

Kenneth Young, 1970, *Sir Alec Douglas-Home*, London, Dent.

INDEX